Joseph Landon

Principles & Practice of Teaching & Class Management

Joseph Landon

Principles & Practice of Teaching & Class Management

ISBN/EAN: 9783337003692

Printed in Europe, USA, Canada, Australia, Japan

Cover: Foto ©Paul-Georg Meister /pixelio.de

More available books at **www.hansebooks.com**

THE PRINCIPLES AND PRACTICE OF TEACHING

AND CLASS MANAGEMENT

BY

JOSEPH LANDON, F.G.S.

VICE-PRINCIPAL AND LATE MASTER OF METHOD IN THE SALTLEY
TRAINING COLLEGE; AUTHOR OF 'SCHOOL MANAGEMENT'
IN THE EDUCATION LIBRARY.

SECOND EDITION

LONDON
ALFRED M. HOLDEN
23 PATERNOSTER ROW E.C.
1895

"The earnest living interest of the teacher in the subjects and objects of his work will not fail to be reflected in the minds of his pupils, and to be more fruitful in results than the most philosophical methods in the hands of the formal and half-hearted precisian."—PROFESSOR S. S. LAURIE.

Printed by T. and A. CONSTABLE, Printers to Her Majesty,
at the Edinburgh University Press.

PREFACE

THE following pages are the outcome of nearly a quarter of a century's experience as lecturer on School Management in a Training College, and of still longer experience as a teacher, as well as of a considerable amount of reading, and of numerous observations and experiments in teaching carried out at various times and in various ways.

The book is intended to meet the wants of students in Training Colleges, of teachers generally, and of any who are interested in the practical work of education. The attempt has been made to present in a direct and intelligible way the broader outlines and essential characteristics of the teacher's work; more especially the theory of oral teaching, the preparation of lessons, the use of the teaching devices, class management, and the various methods of carrying on instruction in those branches of knowledge which are commonly taught in schools.

The subject is treated from the *art* side rather than from the *scientific*, so that it may be of as thoroughly practical and useful a character as possible; but the underlying *science of education* has been carefully kept in mind, and it is believed that the teacher will have nothing to unlearn in the further prosecution of his studies for the purpose of associating his practice more fully with the laws which govern the development of the child's mind and the modes of mental action.

The views expressed are sometimes out of harmony with current opinion, and still more frequently opposed to common practice; but it is hoped that they will be found neither intolerant nor unreasonable. They have not been adopted lightly, and in some cases are the result of an attempt to find a scientific foundation for practical rules and requirements. It has been my endeavour not to avoid any difficulty, and I have made an honest effort to place some disputed points on a rational basis.

I have tried throughout to make the subject suggestive, and, while laying stress upon principles and essentials, to leave room for that originality of treatment by the teacher himself, and for that elasticity and expansiveness in practice, which characterise all good method. Mere unintelligent *imitation* of the detailed plans of others is not what is required in school work, and should not be the aim of any true teacher.

One never knows how much one owes to one's friends and teachers, be they men or books. I am deeply indebted to both; but to acknowledge every point in detail would have been as impossible to me as it would have been wearisome to the reader.

It is with a lively sense of gratitude that I offer my thanks to those kind friends who have aided me in the revision of the proof sheets, and by their wise advice have enabled me to remove many defects. One, to whom I owe much for useful suggestions and friendly criticism, has passed away before the work was completed.

Some apology is due for the delay which has occurred in the issue of the book. The leisure at my command has not been great; the task proved to be a much heavier one than I anticipated; and during the progress of the work I found that many points had to be carefully re-examined if they were to be left in a state which would be at all satisfactory to me.

J. L.

SALTLEY, *January* 4, 1894.

CONTENTS.

CHAPTER I.

EDUCATION—THE TEACHER—METHOD—STUDY.

	PAGE
Various views of education,	1
The *Science* and the *Art* of education,	2
Qualifications of the teacher,	2
Method in education,	5
General laws of method,	6
Limits of special methods,	8
The advantages of a good method,	10
Suggestions respecting study,	12

CHAPTER II.

GENERAL VIEW OF ORAL TEACHING.

What is meant by teaching,	25
Order of development of the child's faculties,	26
Qualities of good teaching,	27
Influence of the personal element in teaching,	29
Too much done by the teacher,	31
Temptation to indulge in mere talk,	33
Want of background,	33
Speed in teaching,	34
Summary of the more important characteristics of good teaching,	35

CHAPTER III.

WHAT IS MEANT BY A LESSON—TYPICAL METHODS OF PROCEDURE IN TEACHING.

General characteristics of a lesson from an art point of view, 36

	PAGE
Defects—looseness, etc.,	39
Purpose in teaching,	39
The form in which the information should be presented,	39
Typical Methods of procedure,	40
(1) The Conversational method,	42
(2) Empirical methods,	44
(3) The Developing method,	45
(4) The Comparative method,	45
(5) Inductive and Deductive methods—Analysis and Synthesis,	47
Tabular view of the logical methods,	50
The natural order in teaching,	50

CHAPTER IV.

Notes of Lessons.

Varieties of Lessons,	52
(1) Instructive or information lessons,	52
(2) Training lessons,	52
(3) Drill lessons,	54
(4) Review lessons,	54
Need for preparation of lessons,	54
What is meant by 'notes of lessons,'	56
The teacher must prepare his own notes,	57
Two types of lessons,	58
Preparation of the subject matter,	58
(1) Acquisition,	58
(2) Selection,	59
(3) Arrangement and connection,	61
(4) Grouping,	62
Preparation of the method,	62
'Outlines' of lessons,	65
Series of related lessons,	68
Specimen notes of a lesson on *Straight Shots*,	70
Specimen notes of a lesson on the *Comparison and Contrast of the Butterfly and the Beetle*,	73

CHAPTER V.

The Teaching and Criticism of a Lesson.

Illustration from landscape photography,	77

Attention to small things, ... 77
The facing of difficulties, ... 78
Long introductions, ... 79
The part the child is called upon to play, . . . 79
The over-teaching of a point, ... 80
Practial hints respecting the teaching of a lesson, . . 81
Criticism lessons, ... 82
The nature of criticism, ... 82
Clumsy teaching and ignorant teaching, . . . 86
Common faults in teaching, ... 87
Types of faulty lessons, ... 89

CHAPTER VI.

THE TEACHING DEVICES.

Influence of fashion in teaching, ... 91
No one device applicable in all cases, ... 92

I. QUESTIONS.

Questioning, an old device, ... 92
Conditions of skilful questioning, ... 93
Good questioning, ... 96
Kinds of Questions, ... 97
   (1) Testing questions, ... 97
   (2) Training questions, ... 99
      Socratic questioning, ... 101
Comparison of testing and training questions, . . 102
Chief purposes for which questions may be employed, . 102
Forms and qualities of questions—Modes of use, . . 103
The qualities and treatment of answers, . . . 118
Simultaneous answering, ... 128
Common mistakes in dealing with answers, . . . 129

II. ELLIPSES.

Definition and function of ellipses, ... 131
Advantages of ellipses, ... 132
Suggestions and cautions as to their use, . . . 133
Defects in their employment, . . . 134

III. ILLUSTRATIONS.

	PAGE
The office of illustrations,	135
Advantages of their use,	136
Illustrations which appeal to the senses,	137
Oral illustrations by comparison or analogy,	142
Suggestions as to the use of illustrations,	144
Illustrations on the black-board,	150

IV. LECTURE.

Nature of lecture as a teaching device,	151
Suitability to the age and power of the pupils,	152
Influence of a definite purpose,	154
Simplicity and directness of statement,	155
Connection of ideas,	155
Deliberation and emphasis,	156
Vividness and interest,	157
Explanation,	158
Common errors in explaining,	159

V. FIXING DEVICES.

Repetition,	162
Recapitulation,	163
Black-board heads or summaries,	163
Review,	164

CHAPTER VII.

CLASS MANAGEMENT.

Influences conditioning class management,	166

I. CLASS MANAGEMENT AS DETERMINED BY ORGANISATION.

General conditions as directly affecting the scholars,	166
(1) The room,	167
(2) The lighting,	168
(3) The warming and ventilation,	169
(4) Change of posture and place,	170
Furniture as affecting school work,	171
(1) The galleries,	171

CONTENTS xi

	PAGE
(2) The desks,	173
Proper arrangement of scholars and work,	175
(1) Classification,	175
(2) Proper officering of the classes,	177
(3) Arrangement of time and subjects,	178
The bearing of apparatus and books.	180

II. CLASS MANAGEMENT FROM THE DISCIPLINARY SIDE.

Nature and difficulty of the work,	185
General disciplinary qualifications of the teacher,	186
Disciplinary training and class control,	188
(1) Order,	188
(2) The exercise of authority,	191
(3) The exercise of tact,	193
(4) Obedience and uniformity of pressure,	195
(5) Class movements, etc.,	197
(6) Reproof and punishment,	198
Summary of important points respecting class discipline,	205

III. CLASS MANAGEMENT FROM THE SIDE OF TEACHING.

General treatment of children during teaching,	208
(1) Employment,	208
(2) Praise and encouragement,	210
(3) Treatment of forward children,	210
(4) Corrections during teaching,	211
(5) Some points concerning the teacher,	212
The securing of interest and attention,	213

CHAPTER VIII.

THE TEACHING OF THE PRIMARY, FUNDAMENTAL, OR INSTRUMENTAL SUBJECTS OF SCHOOL INSTRUCTION.

I. READING.

Common causes of the defective teaching of reading,	220
Importance of correct and successful teaching of the subject,	221
General principles and considerations,	223
Methods of associating sound and symbol,	231
(1) The Alphabetic or Name method,	232

	PAGE
(2) The Phonic method,	233
(3) The Phonetic or Phonotypic method,	234
(4) The 'Look and Say' method,	236
(5) The Syllabic method,	237
(6) The Phono-Analytic method,	238
(7) Word-building plans,	238
Tabular view of the so-called reading methods,	239
Nature and elements of good reading,	240
(1) Pronunciation, enunciation, and articulation,	241
(2) Accent, emphasis, and stress,	243
(3) Tone, pitch, and intensity,	244
(4) Pace and fluency,	245
(5) Pauses and phrasing,	246
(6) Modulation, intelligence, and expression,	247
Position of class and teacher,	249
Explanations in the reading lesson,	250
Correction of errors,	252
The teacher's model reading,	253
The use of simultaneous utterance,	254
Spelling in the reading lesson,	255
Word saying and style,	256
Miscellaneous suggestions,	256
Various modes of teaching the Alphabet,	257
Lessons introductory to reading,	260
First series of reading lessons without the Alphabet,	261
Second series—Incidental mode of teaching the Alphabet,	262
Jacotot's reading method,	264
The primer stage,	265
Easy narrative stage,	268
Lower intellectual stage,	272
Higher intellectual or literary stage,	275

II. SPELLING AND DICTATION.

Uniformity of spelling a matter of modern growth,	278
Principles and considerations,	279
The learning of spelling through reading,	281
Transcription as a means of teaching spelling,	283
Mode of conducting dictation,	284
Formal lessons in spelling,	291

CONTENTS xiii

PAGE

Spelling Rules, ... 293
Miscellaneous list of difficult words, ... 297
Incidental aids to spelling, ... 298

III. WRITING.

The kind of writing required, ... 299
General considerations in teaching writing, . . . 300
The so-called writing methods, ... 306
   (1) Copying plans, ... 306
        Jacotot's method, ... 308
        Sentence method, ... 308
   (2) The tracing plan, ... 309
   (3) Constructive plans, ... 310
        Pestalozzi's method, ... 310
        Mulhaüser's method, ... 311

Method of teaching writing, ... 313
   (1) Introductory lessons, . . . 313
   (2) Pencil writing, ... 314
   (3) Early lessons in writing with the pen, . . 315
   (4) The withdrawal of mechanical aids, . 317
   (5) Introduction of the capital letters, . . 317
   (6) Small hand, ... 318
   (7) The passage from exact imitation to freedom, . 319

IV. ARITHMETIC.

Scope and object of arithmetical teaching, . . . 320
General considerations respecting the conduct of the work, . 325
   (1) The relation of mental to written arithmetic, . 325
   (2) Explanatory work, ... 326
   (3) Conduct of practice work, nature of examples, etc., 329
   (4) Good habits of calculation, ... 332
   (5) The learning of tables, ... 333
   (6) Shortened processes, approximations, etc., . 334
   (7) Books, etc., ... 335
Nature of the teaching in the early stages, . . . 336
   (1) First ideas of number, ... 336
   (2) Realisation of simple abstract numbers, . . 337
   (3) First notions of oral addition and subtraction, . 338

(4) Representation of numbers by written symbols,	338
(5) Principles of the decimal notation,	339
(6) Gradual withdrawal of objective demonstration,	339
(7) **Grube's method,**	340

The teaching of the rules, ... 344
    (1) Notation and numeration, . . . 345
    (2) Addition, ... 347
    (3) Methods of working subtraction, . . . 348
    (4) Multiplication, ... 351
    (5) Division, ... 353
    (6) The compound rules, ... 355
    (7) Vulgar fractions, ... 356
    (8) Decimals, ... 360
    (9) The 'unity method' and proportion, . . 362
    (10) Higher rules, ... 364

V. DRAWING.

Instrumental value of drawing, ... 366
Training of hand and eye, ... 368
General nature of the work, ... 369
Early exercises, ... 370

CHAPTER IX.

The Teaching of The Secondary or so-called Class Subjects.

I. GEOGRAPHY.

Recent attention to the subject, ... 372
Nature and order of the instruction, . . . 372
Suggestions respecting the method of teaching geography, . 377
    (1) Elements of geographical description, . . 377
    (2) Relative position—meaning of a map, . . 379
    (3) The Mother Country, ... 382
    (4) The earth as a whole—land and water, etc., . 386
    (5) The British Empire, ... 388
    (6) Detailed geography of particular countries, etc., . 390
    (7) Geography through reading books, . . 392

II. HISTORY.

	PAGE
A difficult subject to teach,	393
General considerations,	393
(1) What history should do for the child,	393
(2) Influence of the teacher's qualifications,	394
(3) Guiding principles,	395
(4) Scope of the teaching—where to begin,	396
(5) Common mistakes,	397
Three stages of historical teaching,	398
(1) Picture and Story stage,	398
(2) Outline teaching—information stage,	399
(3) Epoch teaching—more distinctly intellectual stage,	401
Suggestions respecting the method of teaching history,	402
(1) The ordinary course of lesson procedure,	402
(2) The use of the comparative method,	403
(3) The emotional element—moral teaching,	404
(4) The use of a text-book,	405
(5) Supplementary reading, etc.,	405
(6) Teaching of history through reading books,	406

III. ENGLISH.

Neglect of the subject,	407
General considerations,	407
(1) Scope and object of the teaching,	408
(2) Relation of grammar to language,	409
(3) The grammatical element in English,	410
(4) Value of grammar as a school study,	411
(5) Age at which formal grammar should be begun,	412
The teaching of English Grammar,	412
(1) General principles and outline of the method,	412
(2) Earliest teaching—introductory work,	416
(3) The Sentence—Subject and Predicate,	416
(4) Easy Analysis—the Parts of Speech,	417
(5) Detailed grammar—formal analysis and parsing,	419
(6) Auxiliary exercises—derivation, word-building, etc.,	421
(7) The place of historical grammar,	423
(8) The use of a text-book,	423

	PAGE
English Composition,	424
(1) Qualities to be aimed at in composition,	424
(2) Means to be employed in teaching composition,	426
(3) The nature of the exercises,	428
English Literature,	433
(1) Educative value,	433
(2) Object and nature of the teaching,	433
(3) Early teaching of literature,	434
(4) More advanced teaching of literature,	434
(5) Treatment of works chosen,	435
(6) The question of criticism,	435

IV. ELEMENTARY SCIENCE.

Claims to a place in the school curriculum,	436
The aim and purpose of the work,	436
The general nature of the teaching,	438
Early instruction,	440
The teaching of individual subjects,	441
(1) Botany,	441
(2) Elementary Physics,	442
Value of the study of science,	443
Conclusion,	443
INDEX,	445

TEACHING AND CLASS MANAGEMENT.

CHAPTER I.

EDUCATION—THE TEACHER—METHOD—STUDY.

EDUCATION has been so much talked about in these days, that, as in the case of some other terms in common use, we are in danger of forgetting what it really should mean. Interpreted by its use in one direction it would seem to stand for little more than educational machinery—the provision of rooms, appliances, teachers, and so forth; from another side all it is apparently intended to express is the power on the part of children at school to reproduce a number of facts, and exhibit a certain mechanical skill in such instrumental branches as reading, writing, and arithmetic.

To the teacher education should mean neither of these things; it is *not mere knowledge, and its processes are not mechanical.* The giving of information is the *means*, not the end; the all-important thing, so far as the child is concerned, being *how* the knowledge is given and received.

The teacher, of all persons, should never forget that **true education means growth, development**—the acquisition of mental and moral strength; and that to secure this the faculties of the child must be exercised in an intelligent and rational manner. Knowledge crammed into the mind, in such a way that it is not assimilated, is not power, but so much almost useless lumber.

<small>It is possible for a man to be a kind of walking encyclopædia and yet not be educated in any true or right sense. The exercise of the memory is important; but when it is the *only* faculty used, some of the most important sides of the mind are left dormant. If children are treated in this way in school, and they happen to grow</small>

up intelligent, their real education has been gained elsewhere, and it has been gained in spite of the school, not by means of it.

The great difficulty is that while every teacher claims to *know* these things, the temptations to forget them in practice are so great, that it is to be feared that education in its true sense is making very little if any progress whatever. Nor is this to be wondered at so long as it is possible to gain credit by merely external and easily tested results and the present nineteenth-century craze continues for estimating everything by statistics.

The child's future welfare must be the first and great consideration in any true system of education, and not merely the passing of this or that examination. To *know* what is right and needed is not all; we must turn our knowledge into a living faith that issues in action and controls our practice.

From the teacher's standpoint the **theory of education** includes everything which it is important for him to know bearing upon the **training, informing,** and **developing of the child.** This knowledge has two sides :—

(1) The **Art of Education,** which gives us all necessary **rules** and directions **how** the work is to be performed; that is, it is a **description of all the best methods** of teaching and of conducting every part of school work.

(2) The **Science of Education,** which gives us the foundation truths upon which the art of education must rest. It furnishes us with the **laws** which should govern our methods, and tells us **why** we should teach or train a child in a particular way. It concerns itself with the growth of the child's mind, and its modes of action; it throws light upon the question as to what may be expected from a child at a certain age and what may not; in short it **renders the art side of our work intelligent** by interpreting our practice for us, and enabling us to judge of the correctness of our methods of procedure.

Both sides of educational theory are important, but the **art side,** at least in its main outlines, should be **mastered first,** as being much the easier and the one more directly bearing upon practice; the **science of education** may be profitably *brought in to test the correctness of our work at every point, and to enable us to make with success original departures in our teaching.*

THE TEACHER.—It is sometimes urged that the teacher, like the poet, is *born, not made.* There is a sense, of course, in which this is true; but too frequently it wears the look of an apology for ignorance. It does not mean that the teacher is not helped to an immense extent by theoretical information as to the best means of doing his work; but only that *knowledge of the theory of education alone, no matter how complete, can never make a teacher.* Practice and experience, in teaching, as in every other art, are essential things. Experience truly is a good teacher, but as has been said, her school fees are apt to be very heavy. To neglect the theory of educational work because teaching is a practical matter is a fatal mistake, and the effects are not confined to the teacher, but are sure to act prejudicially on the methods he adopts, and so will be reflected upon the children under his charge.

Neglect of the art of education simply means that the teacher must at best blunder his way into success, laboriously correct his errors by the failure or the mischief produced, and slowly discover things for himself which others have discovered before him. It is to throw away all the advantages which the accumulated results of the wisdom, invention, and experience of those who have gone before should give us; and such a doctrine, if generally adopted, would effectually prevent any further progress in the development of educational processes. From the waste of time and energy, and from the disheartenment and disappointments necessarily attendant upon such a course, we may save ourselves if we will. Why should we thread the thorny path of error, or traverse the dreary swamps of failure, when a safer, pleasanter, and shorter path has been pointed out to us by those who have travelled the road before us?

While, however, it is highly important that the teacher should know theoretically *how* his work may best be performed, many other **qualifications besides knowledge** are necessary for success in school work.

Some men, from their cold unsympathetic nature, impatient disposition, or dull heavy manner, are naturally unfitted to be teachers; others again fail from being almost entirely wanting in any natural power of controlling children; while still others make school work a burden to themselves and their scholars because teaching is to them no more than an unpleasant necessity—merely a weary and toilsome mode of earning a living. There are comparatively few, however, who cannot by painstaking care and patient work learn to become sensible and useful teachers. *The world's work is not done by its men of genius.*

The **chief qualities** which every teacher who desires to be successful should do his utmost to cultivate, are the following :—

(1) **Earnestness and uprightness** of personal character. "*No bad man can be a good teacher.*"
(2) A real and living **interest** in teaching.
(3) A liking for little children, and ready **sympathy** with them.
(4) **Cheerfulness**, brightness, and ease of manner.
(5) Keen **observation** and an ever vigilant **watchfulness**.
(6) The **power to govern** without being demonstrative, stiff, or magisterial.
(7) Ready-wittedness, **tact**, and decision in cases of difficulty.

The **teacher's work is of a threefold character.**—He has in the *first place* to **organise his school**, including the consideration and settlement of such matters as the *arrangement* of the furniture and fittings so as to serve their purpose in the most efficient way, the *classification* of the children, the best provision and distribution of the *teaching staff*, the order and duration of the lessons, etc., as shown in a well constructed *time-table*, the most useful *apparatus and books*, and lastly the *registration*.

He has *secondly* to **govern his children** in such a way as not only to *keep order* and *administer punishments* judiciously, but also to *train them to right action*—to put them in the best possible state for receiving instruction, and cultivate in them habits of prompt and ready obedience, love of right, and the faithful performance of duties. In a word, the teacher must be a *good disciplinarian*.

He has *thirdly* to **teach** in a manner which, while it secures examination results, also *cultivates and develops the faculties* of the children; trains them in the intelligent use of the rudimentary arts of reading, writing, and arithmetic, and furnishes them with that *elementary knowledge* which is to serve as food for mental and moral growth in the present, and as a foundation and starting-point for further acquisitions. In brief, the teacher has to *provide the means, arouse the interest, and point out the way whereby the child may continue his education for himself in the future.*

For the teacher to do these things successfully needs all the resources of which he is master, and an intimate knowledge of the most rational and trustworthy methods by which they can be accomplished.

METHOD.—By **method** (Gr. *methodos*, a proceeding in regular order; from *meta*, after, and *hodos*, a way), in a general sense, is meant the *path or way followed to arrive at a certain result*. It is such a clear realisation and arrangement of things, thoughts, and proceedings as will enable us to do what we wish *without confusion, in a successful manner, and with the least loss of time and effort*.

Used in connection with education the word 'method' stands for the **pre-arranged course of procedure adopted to secure success in teaching and training**; it comprehends the employment of all the *devices and plans* to be made use of in imparting information, and it prescribes the *means whereby the development of the child is to be secured*. It is a **series of principles, rules, and instructions respecting school work**, by the adoption of which the teacher can make the best use, in his treatment of his scholars, of such knowledge, skill, and judgment as he possesses.

Method is not simply pre-consideration, or order, or regularity, or arrangement, or progress; though it involves and includes more or less of all these ideas, and covers all those considerations and expedients which secure a **regular and consistent advance** from a distinct starting-point towards a clearly realised end or required result. The absolutely essential things are a **perfectly clear aim** and **some natural and right means of reaching it**. The teacher must ask himself, **What** are you going to do? **Why** are you going to do it? **How** are you going to do it?

It may be that the means adopted have for their end the development of the faculties, the conveying of information, or even the testing of that which has been previously mastered; or, further, method may refer to the external arrangements and conditions under which the work is to be performed, and so deal with matters of organisation and discipline.

Method is entirely **opposed to leaving things to settle themselves by chance**, to that happy-go-lucky style of procedure in which no thought is taken, in the hope that things will somehow or other come out right in the end, and matters are neglected till the teacher is driven by the spur of the moment to give them consideration. "Teaching involves too many delicate and important questions to be left to the improvised and hap-hazard solutions which the pressure of necessity may from time to time force from the teacher as he proceeds." Upon his method the success of his work is almost entirely dependent.

It must not be supposed however that method is creative; it is simply a **measure of provision and guidance**, securing that the treatment and teaching of the child are such as will foster the growth of such powers as he possesses, and strengthen them by suitable exercise in right thinking and right action. *Method is an external thing, growth an internal one.*

Carlyle's notion of method as the "**union of like to like**," is worth bearing in mind, inasmuch as it brings out into distinctness the natural **interdependence**, the **sequence**, and **connection** of the various parts, which should characterise the work, and without which it is not what it should be.

The principles to be followed in school work which are of very general application, and should govern the structure and development of a lesson, together with the various instructions relating to the correct use of the teaching devices, we commonly speak of as **General Method**. These principles, though they may vary in phase and degree, and may have stronger applications in this or that direction, are **invariable in spirit**, and **should govern all our teaching**. It is for the teacher to employ them wisely, to judge correctly as to where their application will be most advantageous, and to recognise how they are to be interpreted to meet the needs of any part of the work which is in hand. To be properly effective no part of his work can proceed counter to them, they form the foundation of the most distinctly fixed portion of the theory of teaching, and serve as guide-posts to point out the way and to warn him where he is likely to fall into error.

The consideration of teaching in its general aspect, the characteristics and forms of lessons, and the use to be made of questions, illustrations, and other teaching devices, will be treated of hereafter; but some of the more important **GENERAL LAWS OF METHOD** may here be usefully summarised as follows :—

    (1) **We must proceed in accordance with nature;** hence our teaching and training must conform to the laws of the child's growth, and the modes in which the mind acts. The *order of mental development is to be kept in mind.* Education may begin from the cradle, but not book-learning.

    (2) **Methods must be exactly suited to the needs of the pupils,**

their capacity, knowledge, and stage of development. Simplicity and force of language are important. We must *educate as well as instruct.*

(3) The **child's first impressions**, being the most powerful, **should be the correct ones.** *He should have nothing to unlearn as he progresses.*

(4) The **cultivation of the general intelligence** in children should form the **foundation of any special training.** *All the faculties must receive proportionate attention.*

(5) The **senses should be largely exercised** in the case of little children. It is better to appeal to both eye and ear than to either alone. Handwork may usefully be associated with mental exercise.

(6) **Teaching must be as far as possible rational, not merely formal or mechanical.** It should appeal to the judgment as well as to the memory.

(7) **The individuality of the child must never be lost sight of.** Such power as he possesses is to be respected. He should be encouraged to self-effort at all points; it is the educator's business to clear the path to knowledge. *It is better for the child to discover than to be told.*

(8) **Education is not imparted by words but by clearly realised ideas and things.** We must be careful not to let the mere symbols of knowledge (words) stand for knowledge itself. Knowledge and language must grow together but must not be confused.

(9) The child should **begin to learn what is nearest** to him. He should proceed from the near, the actual, and the practical, to the remote, the abstract, and the ideal.

(10) We must proceed from **known to unknown, simple to complex, examples to rules, facts to laws.** The most elementary and familiar points are to be presented first, and each dwelt upon until it is fully grasped by the child. Exactness and definiteness characterise all true learning. *Consciousness of complete mastery stimulates the pupil and inspires him with confidence and interest.*

(11) Progress must be carefully made **step by step.** One thing at a time. The natural sequence and connection of the items

of knowledge must be clearly brought out. *There must be development of a line of thought.*

(12) **Knowledge should be so presented as to be stimulating to both teacher and taught.** Dulness in the teaching can only end in failure. Exercises must not be made so difficult as to discourage.

(13) **Interest in study is one of the first things which a teacher should endeavour to excite** in the children. Learning mainly depends upon interest.

(14) **Reasoning for children should be direct,** the conclusion being arrived at last. *"Therefore" is a better word for a child than "because."*

(15) **Confidence and the fullest sympathy between teacher and taught are essential to any true education.** The teacher must have a heart.

(16) Without **constant repetition and review** much will be lost. One of Jacotot's favourite maxims was "Repeat without ceasing"; and Comenius calls repetition "the father and mother of memory."

(17) **Activity and curiosity are natural characteristics of childhood.** When things have been learned they should as far as possible be put into practice. *Knowing and doing should proceed together.*

(18) **Change and recreation are necessities.** We must not overfatigue the faculties. *Learning is to be made as pleasant as possible,* but it is too serious to be turned into a game.

(19) **Idleness is the parent of a whole family of evils.** A good method will provide for the *full employment of every child.*

(20) "**Learners should not do with their instructor what they can do by themselves,** that they may have time to do with him what they cannot do by themselves."—(*Marcel.*)

The **applications** of the general principles to the teaching of set subjects in such a way as to make out distinct methods of action— that is, the particular plans and processes to be used in securing the acquisition of this or that branch of knowledge, or in arriving at any particular educative result—are usually denominated **Special Methods.** Thus we speak of the methods of teaching reading, writing, arithmetic, geography, grammar, and other subjects; the methods of organising a school, and so forth.

These **special methods are variable in their elements and limited in their application.** They will differ according to—

(1) The object aimed at, whether knowledge, training, etc.
(2) The subject and nature of the study.
(3) The stage of advancement and age of the children.
(4) The skill, knowledge, and predilections of the teacher.
(5) The attendant circumstances—as number to be taught, apparatus, physical conditions, etc.
(6) The conditions and needs of the school.

Here invention, knowledge, and acuteness of judgment have full play; every teacher has the widest liberty to arrange for himself the details of any particular plan, in the way which seems to him to be most reasonable and to promise the greatest measure of success. An original device, especially in the hands of its originator, is often a powerful weapon. We want to **avoid the error of allowing our teaching practice to crystallise**—to become merely an imitative art.

The field of discovery is open, and it would be greatly to the advantage of educational work if skilled and experienced teachers, with full knowledge of what has hitherto been accomplished, would direct their attention to further experiments and discoveries in method, so as to add to the general stock of our resources. To the young teacher such work is scarcely possible, neither his knowledge nor experience would be sufficient for the purpose, and the first thing he has to do is to make himself thoroughly acquainted with the successful methods which have been framed by others and have obtained the sanction of general recognition. This, however, need never make him a mere thoughtless imitator, or render his work unintelligent and mechanical. His **observation and judgment may be exercised at every step**, and many a detail may be modified to suit his own case, according as he finds such change advisable, or his power greater in this or that direction.

There is **no one method of teaching any given subject**, and the only questions should be, Is the method a right one? and if so, Is it the best possible under the circumstances? The rules and directions of method are not rigidly fixed things, but are open to modification at every point where any improvement of process is possible.

In every walk of life we find the **value of an orderly and systematic conduct of affairs**; with a distinct plan or regular scheme of work we can do more, and do it with greater economy of effort, than without one, and the same is true of teaching and of every department of school work.

The **need of a knowledge of method and of a methodical habit** meets the teacher at the very outset of his work; and at no point in his career can he manage to do without both. Method is valuable at the beginning of a teacher's career, it is valuable throughout it. Nor is it necessary, as is sometimes supposed, only to the poorly qualified or unskilful teacher; it is just this knowledge, and the power to use it, which makes the skilled teacher what he is. The more a man learns about teaching the greater, not the less, attention will he give to method. Method is essential to the highest genius, whether it be in teaching or in other matters; and the wonderful results arrived at by clever men are largely due to the excellence of the method employed. "If I have any advantage over other men," says Descartes, "I owe it to my method."

Want of method is at the bottom of many a case of failure in teaching. It is impossible to do the work of development, training, and instruction, without very carefully considering the means and the way of accomplishing these things. The fact that it may happen once and again that some valuable result is obtained without any attention having been given to the mode of securing it, is no argument against that regular and habitual attention to method, without which the work as a whole is certain to be of the most imperfect character. *Drawing a bow at a venture is not good practice for the teacher.*

Briefly we may say some of the **advantages of a good method** are:—

(1) It **economises the time** both of teacher and taught.

(2) It secures a **maximum of result** with a **minimum of effort.**

(3) Not only is **labour saved**, but what is more important, the mischief arising from wrongly directed effort and the **harmful effects of worry are minimised.**

(4) It **prevents weariness and overstrain** on the part of the children.

(5) It **tends to thoroughness**, and assists in securing attention by making the work interesting.

(6) It **helps to banish spasmodic effort, and inspires the teacher with the confidence necessary for good work.** He feels he is prepared to do his best, and, though he may not accomplish all he could wish, he at least avoids the more dangerous pitfalls which surround the careless and unwary teacher at all times.

(7) It **prevents as far as possible the disheartenment attendant upon failure.**

(8) It **leaves the teacher's mind free** to make the best use of any opportunities that may arise in the course of his work.

There are those who preach the doctrine that nothing is needed for success but hard work; they would have us believe that teaching is mainly a matter of drill, and that time spent in devising new methods is wasted. There can scarcely be a more harmful delusion. Every one will grant that work—earnest, painstaking, thorough work—is needed; and few will deny that the steady and persistent drill of facts has a place, and a useful one, in school work; but *work is very far from being all that is necessary, and drill must never be allowed to usurp the place of intelligence.* The "pegging-away system," as its advocates are sometimes pleased to call it, almost always means shirking the mental activity and intellectual effort necessary for skilled teaching; and the putting of mere steadily continued physical exertion in the place of rational and thoughtful work. This **treadmill theory of education**, as it ought to be called, *leads to much wearisome, uninteresting, and unnecessary labour* on the part of both teacher and children, and tends to lower them to the level of machines; it *robs the teaching of all intellectual stimulus*, stamps out all the pleasure of learning, and reduces it to a never-ending and unintelligent grind of tasks.

The believers in such a theory pride themselves on being eminently practical, while they plod on from day to day in the same groove of dull routine, and succeed only in making the minds of their pupils storehouses for dead lumber. Is it to be wondered at that the children under such conditions are listless and worn, and suffer from over-pressure; and that the teachers find life "flat, stale, and unprofitable," look upon teaching as a wearisome and monotonous business, and leave their day's work jaded and spiritless? *With a system like this surely the joy of life is gone for all concerned.*

It has been said, "**He who shortens the road to knowledge lengthens life**"; and in the ordinary work of educating the young we can only hope to accomplish this by clearly recognising and mastering, both theoretically and practically, those principles and plans which most conduce to the result required. **The fact that the teacher is energetic and industrious does not absolve him from the obligation to employ the best methods** which his knowledge, his skill, and the conditions under which the work is to be performed, will allow him to devise. It is a **duty** he owes **to himself**, that he may not waste his time and strength; it is a duty he owes **to his scholars**, that they may not receive stones when they ask for bread; it is a duty he owes **to the parents**, that he may faithfully carry out the important responsibility with which he has been intrusted.

Those who talk grandly about the teacher's inspiration, and declare that to fetter him with a method, is to make his teaching artificial and mechanical, fail to realise what true method is. Such ideas may be all very seductive, and we come to know intimately the result of their application in practice; they will assuredly not be so when we do.

The remark is as old as Cicero, that "**by teaching we learn.**" The value to the teacher of the discipline of teaching and of the antecedent study of the best method of presentation, is very great; they lead to a thoroughness of realisation and completeness of grasp, a clearness of vision and rapidity of assimilation, scarcely to be gained so fully in any other way. **The teacher who deems his work worthy of his best intellectual efforts, will find his intelligence brightened and his knowledge broadened and deepened, and will discover that, in attempting to do good to others, he is himself proportionally benefited.** During his teaching, in many and many an instance, he will find it brought home to him, that he only partially understood what he previously thought he knew thoroughly; and he will be thankful for the deeper insight and completer understanding which the necessity of making his points clear to others has given him. **Nothing tends more to render our ideas definite and exact than correct teaching.** Professor Hart says, "We fix a thing in our minds by communicating it to another; we make it plain to ourselves by the very effort to give it explanation, or, to state the thing more paradoxically, we learn a thing by telling it to somebody, we keep it by giving it away." How true this is every one who has tried to teach intelligently knows full well; nor is the moral gain from the conscientious performance of duty and from the continual conquest of difficulty to be lost sight of. Truly, "*it is more blessed to give than to receive.*"

HOW TO STUDY. If the teacher would be successful in his work of informing and training others, he must learn to be a successful student himself. The value of good intellectual habits, the necessity for getting exact knowledge of that which he has to teach, and the importance of a careful mastery of the theoretical portion of his work, can scarcely be too strongly urged upon the young teacher. **Teaching and study act and react upon each other in the most beneficial way. To have learned a thing well is the first step towards teaching it well.** The teacher's own habits of thought and modes of working will be sure to be reflected more or less in his pupils. If he is clear-headed, exact, and thoughtful himself, and has fully mastered the meaning and bearing of what he teaches, this is certain to tell upon the children in his presentment of facts; while if he has only hazy and uncertain notions of things, no clear understanding of them will be possible to those under him, and they will learn to rest satisfied with half-formed ideas. *When the teacher is a successful learner himself he is in sympathy with the efforts of his scholars, he is not inclined to pass over difficulties to avoid the trouble of removing them, and he is able to realise readily at what exact point the difficulty occurs.* A **teacher should never cease to be a student of something or other** throughout his career, otherwise his mind will grow stagnant, his methods will become fixed and mechanical, he will lose sight of the learner's point of view, and he will be certain to find his skill decreasing.

The insistence however upon the necessity for correct study is one thing; the difficulty which meets the young student at the beginning of his career—how to study—is quite another. It is not merely right views as to the importance of what is to be done, but aid in doing it which he needs; and help in this direction is far too often neglected. He has generally to grope his way as best he can, failing to make the most of his opportunities, and losing thereby much valuable time and energy which ought to be employed to better purpose. In such a case, too, he can scarcely help falling into **bad intellectual habits**, which are a bar to his progress, and have to be laboriously corrected before he can arrive in practice at those right methods of intellectual acquisition so necessary to success.

The following **suggestions**, it is hoped, will not merely prove helpful to the student-teacher himself, but will point out to him **how he may aid his pupils also in learning** in what way they may employ their time, power, and opportunities to the best advantage. *Judicious help of this kind given to children may be made in a high degree useful.* Not only may they be **trained to habits of application, attention, discrimination, and exactness**; but they may be taught how to study so as to secure the ready employment of what they have learned. Such training may also be made the means of interesting them in useful and **wholesome reading**, so as to raise them above the taste for that sensational fiction, often of a demoralising kind, in which the ordinary schoolboy is apt to indulge if left to himself.

(1) **Do not attempt too wide a range of studies**; otherwise you will dissipate your energy over so large an area as to do nothing well. This is not meant to unduly restrict studies, or to apply to matters taken up for recreation or amusement, but to point out that **more should not be attempted than can be properly done**. Ask your-

self definitely what you want to get out of your studies. See that those which are necessary or useful as a preparation for life, those which are most valuable for present purposes and will best serve as a foundation for future work, receive attention first.

Do not take up a subject of study lightly, but when you have taken it up, do not abandon it, unless there is some good cause for so doing. Knowing your own limitation of power and opportunity, learn to say no to any subject which may strike your fancy for the moment, but which would certainly lead you off from more important things. Unless you do this you are in danger of falling into *one of the most serious mistakes a student can make*, that of *beginning a number of things, and then, when the first novelty has worn off, dropping them one by one for others with new attractions*; so that, of many studies taken up, scarcely any are carried forward to a stage where the student can be said to really know anything about them, even of an elementary character.

This **beginning many things and completing nothing**, this frittering away of time and strength in glancing from one thing to another, is a habit easily fallen into, but it is one of the worst which the student can acquire, and tends to intellectual ruin.

Such a course not only wastes time, and prevents any work worthy of the name being done, but it often beguiles the student into the belief that he knows something of a subject because he has looked into it, and leads to that **sham knowledge**, that mere superficiality, which is so common. A smattering of this kind, which is worse than valueless, must not however be confused with **elementary knowledge**. The latter, so long as it is real and exact, is not to be despised, no matter how small its amount; **the distinguishing mark of the smatterer is his vagueness and uncertainty**.

The student should be precisely **acquainted with the limits of his own knowledge**, and endeavour to get some adequate idea of the extent of his subject. To put it paradoxically, **he should know exactly what he knows, and what he does not know**; otherwise he is apt to see the few things he has learned out of all proper relationship and proportion to the rest, and to over-estimate the amount of his possessions. Socrates said, "A knowledge of our ignorance is the first step towards true knowledge." It is impossible to know everything even of a single subject, the difficult and important thing is to know exactly *what is fundamental*, that it may receive attention first.

(2) **Learn to study intelligently.** That knowledge which is gained

in an intelligent manner by right methods is most valuable as knowledge, apart from the importance of the mental discipline involved in acquiring it; it is most easily remembered, most ready for use; it is more exact, real, and lasting, than knowledge gained by merely artificial means. Mere **rote learning** of book words has a distinct value in some directions; but it must be kept in its place, and must not be applied to subjects in which fulness and clearness of understanding is the great thing. Our knowledge should not grow by mere aggregation of facts—by mere mechanical addition of one thing to another. There must be **organic growth**, one thing leading the mind naturally on to the next in a definite order, so that the whole may be firmly connected.

Bear in mind that **strength comes from self-effort**; strive to conquer unaided any difficulty that may present itself; one such victory is of more value than a great deal of help. "To remember what we have read," says Noah Porter, "we must make it our own, we must think with the author, rethinking his thoughts, following his facts, assenting to or rejecting his reasonings, and entering into the very spirit of his emotions and purposes."

The eye must not be allowed to glance over the sentences without the mind taking in their meaning. Do not be in a hurry. Allow yourself time to clearly apprehend and think over what you read. There must be no bolting of intellectual food, or mental indigestion is sure to follow.

Hurried study is faulty study. Turn the points over in your mind till you know them from all sides. Close the book and attempt to recall what you have read, and do not leave it till you are able to do this.

Locke says, "It is not enough to cram ourselves with a great load of collections, unless we chew them over again they will not give us strength and nourishment."

The **same method of study will not answer for all subjects**; each subject has its own peculiarities of fact and structure, which must be allowed for in learning. That **mode of study** is best which leads to the readiest and most rational acquisition of the facts, the fullest and most intelligent understanding of them, and the firmest holding of them in the memory; and which packs them away in the mind in such a manner as to give the maximum power of using them on the instant whenever they are required. **Strive to get at the ideas**, to grasp them clearly and firmly, and to comprehend them as fully as possible. *Too many students get up a book instead of studying a subject.* Take care your knowledge is not a mere matter of words; when it is so, it is the worst kind of cram. Such study is sure to show itself in teaching in want of interest, lifeless presentment, faulty explanations, weak and unsuitable illustrations, and dull routine. If the **book words** of that which you are studying are at all unfamiliar, **look up their meaning** in the dictionary (which should always be at hand); think how the ideas might best be re-presented so as to be more easily understood by others. **Accuracy of idea and precision of statement should go together.** **Vagueness is a fatal enemy to memory.** As Professor Huxley has pointed out, the next best thing to being right is to be completely and wholesomely wrong.

A clear distinction again should always be kept in mind between facts and theories. Truth is unchangeable in its nature, though the form in which it may be presented to the mind may be varied. The facts remain; the theory which is intended to give them coherence and combined meaning is sure to change as time goes on. From its very nature theory involves growth; it is but an attempt to relate all known facts in a certain group; and with fuller knowledge and fresh discoveries is pretty sure to come the necessity for modification of our working hypothesis, and it may be the substitution for it of one more in accordance with the new truths. *A good theory is of the very greatest assistance;* but this explanation, fixed upon the facts by human ingenuity, well founded though it may be, must not be confused with the truths of observation and experience upon which it is built.

(3) **Do your utmost to make out the relative importance of the facts** you have to get up. Sift the information, and endeavour to discriminate between essential and unessential things. **Many a student wastes his time by beginning** on the outside of a subject, learning a few details here and there; go to the heart of the matter at once; try to find out the main line of thought, the fundamental ideas, and work outwards from these. We have not yet fully appreciated the wisdom of Jacotot's maxim, "*Learn something accurately, and refer the rest to that.*" Properly understood, few wiser sentences for the student have ever been penned.

In studying a book for the first time do not attempt to remember everything it contains at once, **seek out a series of key facts** which will form a framework of the subject as it were, and fasten the mind upon these till they are known. The rest will fall naturally into their place. The more fundamental, the more far-reaching, the more suggestive a fact is, and the greater the number of its connections, the more valuable it is. To know what to select for present mastery, and what to leave for a second or third reading, or it may be to leave out altogether, needs judgment; but it is one of the secrets of successful study, and is deserving of much care and attention.

It must not be forgotten too that **facts have different relative value according to the subject in hand or the connection in which they occur.** A point may have little or no value in one connection, which in another may be of the utmost importance. The utter want of recognition of the relative subordination in the different items of knowledge, is one of the commonest faults of undirected study. All that the book contains is got up as though it were all of equal importance. A useful help to fixing the relative value and position of facts is to classify and arrange them in a brief **topical analysis.** Such a judicious grouping in natural order has many uses. It should be short and clear, and suggest the details, not state them.

Few young students have any real appreciation of the **perspective of facts**, but it is a matter which should receive careful consideration. The most essential things must be got clearly in mind first; then those which are related to them, but of less intrinsic importance; and lastly, merely illustrative or explanatory matter, and facts which, while of little value in themselves, are useful in giving completeness of conception and realisation of the whole. These groups should be stored away in the mind in such a manner that when wanted, the first to suggest themselves are those of most value. Facts which change from time to time are generally best learned as wanted.

(4) **Note any correlation or interdependence of facts, and link one thing with another.** There must be continuity of thought if the various items are to hold together. Fix the mind on any existing natural affinity, any relation of cause and effect, any logical sequence of ideas, any striking contrast. This is to make use of those **laws of association** or suggestion which play so important a part in the holding and reproduction of facts by the memory. *Any relation which the mind can easily and firmly grasp is useful.*

In tracing out an argument—and many arguments are stated in a very involved way—try to make out the steps in order; note these in the shortest possible form as they occur, and endeavour to see how they are connected, and whether they justify the conclusion.

(5) **Where possible study from things rather than from words.**— Good books are of the greatest value, and are often our only means of obtaining information, but, no matter how excellent, they must

not be allowed to exclude other important means of study, where such exist, and so prevent our getting that **first-hand knowledge of things** which is of such vital moment. *To know a thing from actual experience of it is a very different matter from knowing what has been said about it.* **Put as many of your questions as possible to nature herself;** knowledge obtained in this way is much more real and lasting than that obtained merely from books.

Hence the great value, in all the physical and natural sciences especially, of **experiments, observations, field-work,** and so forth. The reality of geographical knowledge which has been obtained by travel is clear to every one; as is also the fact that we know much more certainly about an object from having seen it and handled it, than we can do from having heard it described or merely from having read about it.

(6) **Work systematically; have set times for study and a programme of work.** Without systematic effort little is to be done of value. To have a definite and well-considered scheme of study is a great gain. It saves a large amount of time; and where a number of subjects have to be studied it prevents undue attention being given to those things which the student likes best, to the neglect and detriment of others which may even be more important.

Whatever may be said in the case of advanced students for that **stratification of studies** in which one subject is begun and finished before another is taken up; it seems clear, that, for young students, the **simultaneous plan** of carrying on a series of studies side by side, is to be certainly preferred. The power of long-continued effort at one thing, necessary in the former plan, is only to be gained as a matter of training and experience.

A too elaborate plan is to be avoided. Be cautious in commencing a course of reading; and, having a distinct purpose in view, carefully arrange the method you intend to follow so as to make it suit your own powers, wants, and circumstances. Decide how much you ought to be able to get through in a given time, say a month, three months, or what not; portion out your work and time accordingly, and do your utmost to cover the ground in the allotted period. **Desultory aimless reading in matters requiring study is to be carefully shunned.** It gets the mind into the bad habit of shirking continuous work and steady consecutive thinking; so that the power to grasp the scope and meaning of a difficult book during reading is not acquired.

The **distribution of the available time** among the different subjects should not be settled without thought and care; but when the teacher has come to a decision upon the matter, the carrying out of the scheme should not be interfered with unless for some really weighty reason. The mind is often only too ready to accept some plausible excuse for neglecting the duty of the moment unless the will steps in to prevent it.

Waste no time in thinking about beginning; **have a care of the minutes**, and settle down at once. During the period set apart the mind should be kept firmly to its work; **study should be a steady and regular application, not a series of spasmodic efforts.** There should be no haste, and no confusion, no mixing of play and work; one thing should be attended to at a time, and that patiently carried out to the best of the student's ability.

The **length of the period** to be given to continuous study will depend upon the power of the individual student and the opportunities he has for such work. The younger the student and the intenser the work, the shorter the period which should be allowed and the longer the times of rest. Study should not be so long continued as to induce overfatigue, nor so short as to prevent that continuity of effort to which the student has to train himself.

Many students are restless; they **work by small jerks**, reading a few minutes at one subject, and then throwing it on one side for another. They thus spend their time and opportunities without result; they seem to be continually employed, but are without anything to show for their labour at the end. Any such tendency the student should do his utmost to correct.

(7) **Cultivate as sedulously as possible the power of keeping the attention concentrated on what you are about.** Be a "whole man for one thing at a time;" do not allow the mind to go wool-gathering, or to sink into the state we call day-dreaming. Attention is an absolutely necessary condition of learning. It grows rapidly with suitable exercise, and its cultivation must be carried on until the power to fix the mind's working intensely upon one thing for a considerable period becomes a habit. No more valuable intellectual habit can be formed, none which has greater influence upon success in life.

The difference between clever men and ordinary men is often mainly a difference in the **power of directing and controlling the mind through the attention.** *Newton* declared he owed his discoveries more to patient attention than to anything else; and *Charles Dickens* spoke of attention as "the grand secret of success, the quality most valuable to a man." The temptation is often strong to allow the mind to follow its own course unrestrained, and to flit from point to point in a desultory way. This must be strongly withstood, and the mental gaze kept fixed upon the limited area before it to the exclusion of everything else.

(8) **Endeavour to interest yourself thoroughly in what you are studying.** Learn to love knowledge for its own sake. Attack what you have to do courageously. Do not allow the mind to slip into that "indifferentism" which is so common nowadays; it is not easy to throw off, and when once it has become a habit it is a serious evil. **Studies which give us no pleasure will scarcely be taken up with that earnestness which distinguishes all good work;** and things which are of no interest are not likely to be remembered. Acquisition and the power of recollection are proportional to the interest excited : set the mind in a glow and it works rapidly and surely, and retains strongly that which it takes in. **Every new subject has its initial difficulties,** one of the most formidable being simply the **strangeness of the ideas,** or it may be of the terminology. The mind seems out of its element for a time, but a little earnest application soon puts another face upon the work ; and it is often a matter of astonishment to us that the subject should ever have been such a source of trouble. **New information always takes time to soak into the mind.** It is sure however to do so at length ; and if at first progress seems to be painfully slow the student should not be discouraged.

It is remarkable how interesting even a hard dry subject may, and often does become, if we attack it boldly and master thoroughly the first steps. Though the knowledge itself may not at first give us much pleasure, this comes to us from the **conquest of difficulty and the consciousness of progress.** In this way we are encouraged to further effort. If, however, we take up the matter in a half-hearted way and allow ourselves to dwell upon its difficulty and unpleasantness, the mind works feebly, soon tires, and disgust at our failure is pretty sure to follow.

(9) **A good text-book is essential, but it must be chosen with discrimination and used with judgment.** Carlyle has said that "the true university of these days is a collection of books ;" and certainly the student is much more dependent upon his books for knowledge than upon his teacher. Method, guidance, help in difficulty, he may obtain from the latter ; but for the facts which are to become his mental stores he has to look, mainly at least, to his books. **An assemblage of good books is indeed a valuable possession, if we have come to know them and to look upon them as friends** ; but it is

better to know a few books thoroughly than to have a merely nodding acquaintance with a great many. Further, a large number of books may to the young student become a source of bewilderment rather than of help. In commencing any subject it is of much consequence that he should select a suitable book, **not necessarily the best book** in the abstract, but the *best for him*—the book that will give him in the clearest and most intelligent form just what he needs.

In the present profusion of text-books, it is a difficult matter to know exactly what is best; and not unfrequently the student, in his endeavour to discover a royal road to what he wants, falls into the error of trying one book after another, *casting each aside in turn and mastering none*. At least he may save himself from this harmful blunder.

It is a great mistake to use too large a book at first. It prevents that mastery of the broad principles and the general outline of fundamental facts which should form the basis of reading in any particular subject. In a large treatise the multiplicity of details is so great that the student not only finds the difficulty of discovering their relative importance greatly increased, but he is **discouraged by having so many things thrust upon him at once**, and by the very slow progress he is able to make. Books for reference he may have in plenty, but **his reading in any subject should be based upon one book**. This should be kept to, and read again and again until thoroughly mastered, and he has come to know his way about it so completely that he can find anything it contains on the instant. When the first book has been thus got up, the various points may be strengthened and extended, and new ones added, by further reference or the **study of a larger book**. In going through the latter the student will find that much of it he already knows; and he should **direct his attention strongly to the new matter, noting carefully its relation to and connection with what he already knows**. Proceeding in this way he will soon find that new facts become fewer and fewer as his knowledge extends, and that his reading consequently becomes more rapid.

Beyond the ordinary text-book stage in learning a subject, a **list of references to places where further information upon this or that point may be found** is very valuable. Such an **index of what has been read**, forming a *condensed key to knowledge*, every student should construct for himself. It must be as simple and brief as possible, so that what is wanted may be found with ease and rapidity; any over-elaboration will only make the work burdensome and tend to decrease its usefulness. **The next best thing to knowledge is to know exactly where to find it.**

Unless for some special purpose, it is not well, as a rule, to burden the mind with matter only occasionally wanted; in most cases a reference is all that is needed. The mind is limited in capacity, and secondary matters are very apt to crowd out more important ones. **Keep the mind with cleared decks ready for action.**

(10) **Review your work frequently.** Not to forget the knowledge we have gained is as important as to acquire new, and to secure that such loss does not take place, systematic review is essential. To omit it is a mistake, the full seriousness of which the student may not at once realise; it is really one of the greatest he can make, and is pretty sure to lead to that uncertainty and inexactness of information which it is so important to avoid.

Things which have cost us much time and trouble to learn it is the height of folly to let go because we may not need them at the moment. A small amount of energy properly employed will prevent them from getting rusty. To relearn them when forgotten means much additional toil, the necessity for which might easily have been prevented. (See author's *School Management*, pp. 75-79.) **To apply our knowledge practically in any direction tends to fix** it, whether it be by teaching, writing, or conversation. Frequently however such opportunities of employing his acquisitions do not occur to the student, and then it is his business to arrange for fixed times of review.

A well arranged scheme of review—
   (1) Keeps the **mind in touch** with the main lines of the subject.
   (2) Secures the **freshness and exactness** of knowledge gained.
   (3) Shows us what has been **imperfectly learned**, and affords opportunity for remedying the defect.
   (4) Strengthens the **recollection**, and accustoms the mind to readily recover and give up its stores.
   (5) Saves **waste of energy**, and the formation of a **bad mental habit**.
   (6) Leads to **complete assimilation** of the material learned.

Review does not mean restudying the subject, but going rapidly over the outlines and noting their suggestive connections. Additions may be left for further reading, but any broken link in that which has been acquired should be repaired at once. In carrying out the work the analyses previously mentioned may be made useful. Frequently it is best to review a subject by writing—the student jotting down in the briefest possible way, at least the main points. **Writing is a great aid to the memory.** In this connection also another very valuable means of review may be mentioned—**examination**, either written or oral. *A skilfully set examination paper is a very great help*, and may often be employed where *viva-voce* work is impossible.

(11) **Do not neglect recreative reading or other sources of intellectual relaxation.** To give all one's available time to severer studies is a great mistake from any point of view. A bow kept always bent loses its elasticity. The amassing of knowledge is not everything; and even if it were, the mind will do more, in a given time, if allowed proper periods of change and recreation, than when kept always on the strain. Change of occupation indeed, in which a different set of faculties is brought into play, is in itself restful. Language is a relief to mathematics, literature to science. What is urged here, however, is that **special times ought to be set apart for purely recreative reading, the first essential of which must be its power of giving pleasure.** It should be to the mind what fresh air and exercise are to the body. So long as it is thoroughly enjoyed anything may be read which is wholesome and well written, whether novels, poetry, biography, travels, or what not.

Music again affords an exquisite relief from book-study, and the same may be said of many pastimes and amusements. A good reliable hobby is often a very great gain to a hard-working student, and may be made to conduce largely to mental health. Absolute lack of occupation is often very far from being rest; too frequently the mind simply goes on pondering over its work though the ordinary surroundings of study may be absent. What is wanted is something which will take the mind completely away from its previous employment.

Recreative reading however must not be taken up as a task, or the performance of it be looked upon as a duty. The mind should come to it spontaneously, and revel in it with the delight of a schoolboy let loose from lessons. All the same, reading for pure diversion **need not be aimless**; it may be made to **serve important purposes of culture**, while it can scarcely fail to broaden our views, and prevent that one-sided development of our nature, which leaves us with little power to enjoy, and ends in making life dreary and uninteresting.

(12) **Look to exercise and physical surroundings.** See that your study is carried on under the best physical conditions that can be

arranged for. Look to proper light, fresh air, and the avoidance of harmful bodily postures. Discomfort of any kind is certainly opposed to vigorous study; while too much ease on the other hand is apt to lead to mental sluggishness.

Do not study too long at once. Physical exercise is *necessary*, if the mental powers are to be kept in the best working order. So long as the mind acts with freshness and ease it may be allowed to proceed; but if we find that it moves slowly, and extra trouble is needed to keep the attention fixed, it is far better to break off and take a walk, or some other recreation, than to go plodding on until complete fatigue ensues. To continue to force the mind in this way is likely to lead to injurious results, and may end in that nervous prostration from which recovery is so slow and troublesome. Judicious exercise is, from a study point of view, a saving and not a waste of time. **Violent exercise to the limit of bodily weariness is not what is wanted.** With a tired body little mental work is possible. *Violence and lethargy succeed each other naturally.* Useful exercise as a change from study should recruit energy, not exhaust it.

CHAPTER II.

GENERAL VIEW OF ORAL TEACHING.

WHAT IS MEANT BY TEACHING.—Teaching is too commonly regarded as having an independent existence apart from learning, as though to have secured a theoretically correct mode of placing knowledge before the pupil were all that ought to be required. But there is much **more in teaching than mere method of presentment** of knowledge, no matter how perfect theoretically that presentment may be. We may compel a child to listen to a very excellent discourse, we may employ all the skill at our command, and exhaust all the devices of which we are master, but if he learns nothing there is no true teaching.

For the **external phase called Teaching, to be real and useful there must be the internal phase called Learning** ; there must be the objective or outward influence of the teacher's mind on that of the pupil, and the subjective or inward effort of the learner's own mind. The two are but different aspects of what is essentially one process. Thus **true teaching involves work on the part of both teacher and taught,** and not of either singly. It includes not only the intellectual influence of offering knowledge in the most suitable form, but further, the moral one of inducing the child to take in what is presented, in such a way that he may be benefited thereby. Briefly, we may say, that *to teach is to provide the materials and to put the child under the most wholesome influences for growth in knowledge, mental strength, and moral power.*

The teacher must know his children. It is not to be expected that he can train and instruct his pupils satisfactorily if he is ignorant of their nature and peculiarities. Such knowledge in fact **lies at the base of all true success in education.** To be ignorant of what a child may be expected to do and what not, of how his mind acts, and how his feelings may be stirred, of how he may be interested and how he may be spurred on to effort without the application of external force, is, for the teacher, a very heavy drawback in his work, and may lead to very serious mischief being done. He who would successfully and intelligently teach little children must **know something of the laws which govern mental and physical growth**, of the order in which the different phases of the mind's action commonly called faculties show themselves, which of these may be most usefully appealed to at a certain age, and how far they may be employed without harm or strain. He must be able to recognise the **intellectual value of the various exercises** through which he puts the child, and be able to use them in a way which will conduce to the child's future good.

Much useful information respecting these things may be **learned from books**; but for such knowledge to be of real practical value to the teacher, he must **grow into it by experience** day by day. He must *learn to observe the effect of the methods he employs*, to note carefully where he fails, and where he succeeds, and endeavour to learn the cause in each case. In preventing him in many instances from blindly falling into error, in directing him as to what to look for, in interpreting his observations and giving certainty to his conclusions, his book-knowledge will be of the greatest service.

The **order of the development of the child's powers** may be roughly indicated as follows :—

(i) *In the earlier years of a child's life* **the senses** *should be constantly appealed to*, so that a large stock of ideas may be formed directly from sensations. Teaching should be given mainly by means of objects, experiments, pictures, etc. As far as possible the child should be allowed to *handle and examine things for himself*, the teacher directing his observation and interpreting his experience for him. Upon the excellence of this sense-training will depend, to a considerable extent, the clearness with which he will be able afterwards to realise ideas through the agency of words.

(ii) A little later in time the **memory** may be usefully cultivated, and, as the **holding power of memory is probably greatest somewhere about the age of ten**, any facts which the child will need always to remember in the same form may profitably be learned, as far as practicable, during this second period. With this employment of the memory may also come exercise in the simpler phases of the **imagination**.

(iii) The third period is marked by the power to follow **easy processes of thought**; the **judgment** and the **reasoning power** being gradually strengthened by suitable training until the force of a logical argument can be appreciated, and the child becomes able to think connectedly and continuously for himself.

Not only however does the teacher need to know the child generally, as one of a group, he needs to **know him as an individual**—his power and his weakness, his peculiarities and temper, and his present standpoint with respect to knowledge. In teaching it is well to **take**

nothing for granted in the case of children, and to proceed only on such knowledge as we have proved them to possess. Nevertheless we must be on our guard. *It is often astonishing how much they know when we have taken the trouble to discover and bring it to the surface.* Having been learned in the child's own way it exists in different terms, as it were, from those to which we are accustomed, and without the greatest care we may easily overlook it. This is a loss to the child and to the teaching.

To learn to recognise readily and surely when a child knows, and how far he knows, is doubtless a difficult matter, but the teacher should be keenly alive to its importance. He has to find the least common denominator, so to speak, of his own ideas and those of the child; and, when he has succeeded in doing this, he will often discover that his method of procedure needs to be radically changed. **After all, the child himself is the most valuable of all method books.**

To estimate accurately the **child's peculiarities of moral character** is frequently even more difficult than to come to know him intellectually: but it is a not less weighty matter even from a teaching point of view. Nowhere is he more himself, nowhere less fettered by his surroundings, than in the playground. A teacher, who takes no interest in his children when at play, fails to learn many a point as to their true nature, and throws away many an opportunity of doing good.

Teaching must be pleasant so as to secure interest and attention; it must follow the path of least resistance. How to quicken the intelligence of children, so as to arouse in them an eagerness to listen, and to attract their attention in such a way that their minds work and their feelings vibrate in sympathy with the teacher, is often a very hard problem to solve. Unless, however, a solution is found, little real good can be done in the way of teaching, and the difficulties of management and control are certain to be largely increased. A **necessary condition of success is to secure the happiness of children,** while under instruction. The lesson should be made as interesting as possible with respect to information, and the teacher must add to this interest by all the little devices of manner at his disposal. **Dulness is an unpardonable fault in teaching.** A monotonous delivery and lifeless nonchalant manner will often ruin what might otherwise have been carried through successfully. **Cheerfulness, vivacity, and enthusiasm are contagious,** and are often powerful aids in attracting children. There must be life, "go," movement in the work—movement controlled and directed by a distinct purpose.

Teaching may be very correct, and at the same time very uninteresting: and, if it is so, the continuity, at least, of the subject-matter will be lost; for every break in attention means a break in the connection and sequence of the various parts of the lesson, and much of its meaning and value goes.

Under suitable circumstances, the teacher need not fear to be amusing, but he should never act ludicrously or talk absurdly. *There is all the difference between children laughing at the teacher and laughing with him.* A joke in its place will often refresh the class, arouse flagging attention, and may even enforce the remembrance of some point; but **the dignity of knowledge should not be lost sight of**—it is too serious a matter to be burlesqued, or turned into a farce.

It is a **great mistake to be stiff and pompous with children**. They will work all the better for an occasional laugh; but **any pleasantry should be well under the teacher's control**, and should not distract them from the lesson. It becomes harmful when they are always on the look-out for something funny to turn up—for the teacher to say or do some comical thing. He also should try to **avoid being unconsciously humorous**; as when a very short teacher, standing on tiptoe against his blackboard, said in all earnestness to his class, "The elephant is fifteen feet high, and fancy an elephant three times as big as I am."

In good teaching the facts are vivified and transformed in such a way, that they may be learned in a pleasant easy natural manner. There is **no unnecessary formality**, no putting knowledge into a strait-waistcoat of our own manufacture, **no parrot-like repetition** of the facts in the words in which they were learned. If a teacher talks like a book, and doles out so much in a given time, he is sure to fail in all the higher aspects of his work. The artificiality and want of anything like freedom or freshness in his presentation, will effectually kill out all interest. The **brimstone and treacle method** of dosing all the scholars alike, and compelling every one to swallow the same amount of knowledge in the same form, is not teaching, but shows grievous ignorance of educational needs.

Even under the best conditions, the teacher will frequently find it necessary to put forth all his power, in order to secure continuous interest and attention, and will often have to lend his aid with motives of various kinds. Rest, however, until he has secured the full co-operation of the children, he should not. He should **see** that the **inattentive ones have something to do,** allow no slovenly or slouching attitudes or lolling about; and if he finds he is boring his pupils, and they are staring in some other direction, or occupied with their own thoughts, he should strain every nerve to bring back their minds to the subject in hand. What he is saying may be very good, it may have cost him much time and labour to prepare, and may even be skilfully put, but it is **all of no use unless attention is secured.**

Some teachers seem to be very dull in detecting what is amiss, and are always ready to put down any defect to the badness of the children. It may be that the physical conditions under which the child is working are at fault; otherwise, *the sensible teacher looks to himself.*

Much variety is necessary in teaching children—especially little ones. Watch your opportunities, and return to an important point over and over again, if necessary, with an illustration, an anecdote, a few minutes of questioning, or a change of style, in between. **Learn to detect by a child's looks, by his eyes, whether he is following you or not.** Many a child will behave well, and will sit with motionless limbs and gaze fixed on the teacher, without taking in a single idea. Such children must be amused, interested, and *set to work somehow*; and perhaps scarcely any two teachers would effect this in exactly the same way. Every one must depend upon his own powers and invention, and be able to take in swiftly all the circumstances that can be made to tell towards a solution of the difficulty.

The influence of the personal element in teaching is very great, and especially so with children. No amount of knowledge will make up for the want of this. Generally speaking, it is not so much the subject which attracts them as the teacher's power over them—the **stimulus of his ability, manner, and sympathy.** Children are wonderfully acute in reading character, and seem to feel instinctively when the teacher is in sympathy with them; they expand under his influence, and this subtle play of spirit upon spirit brings out all that is best in both. Where such a relationship does not exist, the teaching is barren of all the higher and finer results of educative training. From some teachers children will learn almost anything with ease; while with others even the simplest things are apt to become difficulties.

It is a great thing to be able to *teach* little children; to have the power to attract them to knowledge by speaking to them in a manner which at once enlists them on our side, to be able to get into their hearts, to understand their ways, and *to recognise how important often to them are things which appear to us of small moment.* To accomplish this successfully is a pretty sure index of a happy loving disposition, and of much freshness of mind. It is just this subtle sympathy exciting kindly feeling and mutual interest, this **power to be child-like without being childish**, this elasticity of nature, which puts us as it were into electric communication with our children, and makes what we say not only heard but heeded and felt.

Canon Farrar quotes a very beautiful **story from the Talmud**, which tells how "once in a great drought the greatest Rabbis prayed and wept for rain, and the rain came not. And at last a common-looking person got up and prayed to Him who causeth the wind to blow and the rain to descend, and instantly the heavens began to cover themselves with clouds, and the rain began to fall. 'Who art thou,' they cried, 'whose prayers have alone prevailed?' And he answered, '*I am a teacher of little children.*'"

A good teacher will do his utmost to keep his nature fresh and cheerful and pliant, and endeavour to prevent as far as possible the labour and trouble and worry of life from deadening his sympathies. The man or woman who has forgotten what it is to be a child, who cares nothing for children, and cannot enter, when fit occasion offers, into their little enthusiasms with pleasure, has allowed one of the best sides of our nature to become petrified. The world has darkened to such a one, and much simple and true happiness has vanished.

The work of almost every skilled teacher bears the impress of his own individuality. His knowledge, mental habits, and the peculiarity of his own powers, lead him to teach on definite lines, and mark off his work from that of others. His pupils soon come to be aware of this, they recognise instinctively how he is likely to regard a thing; they are used to his mode of expression, and follow his line of thought much more easily than they would that of a stranger. **Originality of method** is a good thing, but it is not to be gained by a restless shifting from one plan to another. The amount of real originality in teaching, possible to most men, is small; and such peculiarity as exists results generally more from **differences of manner** than from essentially different ways of presenting things. Long practice in teaching is pretty sure to beget some amount of **bias** in favour of special modes of procedure, and frequently develops some trick of hand or voice or gesture, some employment of pet phrases, distinctive of the teacher. These are not things to be desired, but they serve to give character to the work; and so long as the teacher is perfectly natural—is himself —so long as they are kept within proper bounds, and not allowed to become so prominent as to distract attention from other things, they can do no harm. *We do not want teachers all of one pattern*, no matter how good the pattern may be. Not unfrequently however these peculiarities are not the teacher's own, but are merely learned from others ; they are then to be strongly deprecated.

Unfortunately **weak imitators always pick up these mere externals,** and copy the mannerisms peculiar to the individual as though they were essentials not accidentals ; while of the deeper meaning and spirit of the work they catch nothing. A young teacher is especially liable to fall into this external imitation. What is wanted for him is to see many good models, not one only.

If the teacher is to succeed he must be in earnest, he must cultivate his own powers and believe strongly in his work himself. There must be no perfunctoriness. It is not an uncommon thing for a teacher to work in such a hesitating or careless way that he seems only to half believe himself in what he is saying. *Indifference in the teacher is sure to beget the like in the children.* Let them see that you feel the importance of the instruction you are giving, but do not count much on their being influenced by the value of knowledge to themselves. They are creatures of the present, and realise very little any needs of their future life. It would not be natural or well for them to do so. **A child should be a child** ; it is the *teacher's* business to have in mind what the pupil is being trained for.

<small>Reliance must be placed upon the force of the impression made, the guidance given, the good habits formed, and what is really useful will come up for employment all in good time. One cannot sow and reap on the same day. The teacher must trust to his own insight as to what is best to be done, and he will soon learn, if he is in earnest, how to direct his teaching into the best channel, and what course to take in order to reach the end he has in view.</small>

There is often too much done by the teacher in teaching. That he should go through a series of mental gymnastics himself is not teaching. *Good teaching does not do all for the pupil* ; it does not allow him to remain a mere passive listener, but prescribes earnest effort on his own part ; it endeavours to overcome his mental inertia, it stimulates and arouses anxiety to learn, it aids him in every possible way good for him, but it leaves him to do alone all the work he is capable of. Suitable employment must be found for every individual in the class, not merely for the willing few. **Children must be made to face diffi-**

culties for themselves, and the more they do this the more real and permanent will be their learning.

Easy come, easy go. Nothing for nothing is a law in education, as in other matters. **The teacher must work** *with* **the pupil, not** *for* **him.** Take his hand, beguile the tediousness of the way, allow proper rest, and do not hurry or overstrain him; but *see that he walks*, do not carry him.

A clever teacher guides the child's thought from point to point; an unskilful one is ever reining up his pupils to make them imitate his own mode of working. If children are to learn, so that what is gained may remain as a mental possession, they must be **allowed to think for themselves, and say things in their own way.** Except in the case of some law, or definition, or some such thing, where the *form* is important, the teacher's *words* are best not remembered, so long as the ideas are clearly grasped. The great test that a child has been *taught* is his power to re-express in his own way what he has learned, and from his own point of view.

Teachers too frequently do not keep touch with their class. They become absorbed in what they are saying, not in how it is being received. When a teacher has not mastered his subject-matter thoroughly before the lesson begins, he has to do the thinking, which should have been done previously, while the teaching is going on. Under such circumstances any child is allowed to answer questions, and the **quick ones get the benefit while the dull ones are neglected;** and though any general lapse of attention may be noticed, individual instances of inattention commonly escape remark. The teacher does not hold the children by his eye, he is really to a great extent looking inward, and neglects to see that they have their full share of work.

The mind of a good teacher is ever on the alert. He is able to look ahead and be working towards a point, though the pupils may be quite unconscious as to where they are going. **Attention is directed only to one step at a time,** but each is mastered in turn, until at last the children are surprised to find themselves safe over a difficulty and all clear. **The object to be reached must be all along present to the teacher's mind:** but just as it is not every good stroke which is direct, so many a point may be taught, and its meaning made clear, by being referred to here and there in connection with other things as the teaching progresses, which it would be scarcely possible to teach with equal efficiency by a single direct statement, no matter how forcible or exact this may be.

Nor is it always the formal lesson which has the most powerful influence for good. *Many of the deepest and most lasting impressions we make upon children, both we and they may be unconscious of as direct efforts*—some chance word gone home, some kind look, some forgiving smile, and the influence may be the turning point of a life.

In teaching there is often a temptation to indulge in mere talk; there is too much beating about the bush without ever starting the hare. Lesson-giving sometimes reminds one of the riding of horses round a circus: there is a good deal of show but no real progress. The children may be interested, but that is not enough—they have to learn. There must be no attempt to astonish them by pouring out a stream of words, "full of sound and fury, signifying nothing." It is not a sign of learning, but oftener of ignorance, to use big high-sounding words; and further, it is a constant bad example to the children. **The words used in teaching should be the simplest which will express the ideas well**—those which have the fullest meaning for the individuals to whom they are addressed. Care must be taken, however, that, in endeavouring to use familiar speech, the teacher does not slip into either vulgarity or slang. The hurry consequent upon attempting too much for the time at disposal is a frequent source of obscurity. **It is very easy even for a good teacher to say too much**, instead of having a little patience. A child's difficulty is oftener with the ideas than with the words; one might almost say, *look carefully to the ideas and the words will take care of themselves.*

An inexperienced teacher is very apt to be wordy and roundabout from **insufficient preparation.** He has not decided upon what he will say, or thought how he is to approach a point, consequently he begins stammeringly, starts afresh, tries another and another mode of expression, and ends by getting into a tangle of words and bemuddling both himself and his scholars. **A teacher should be especially careful to settle how he will begin a lesson.** A good opening well managed gives confidence, and this brings out the teacher's power, so that he is able to continue without trouble.

But not only is there a danger of using too many words; there is an opposite one of using too few, of **robbing teaching of its proper background.** Without necessary explanations, illustrations, and subsidiary matters, important points are not brought out into relief; there are no contrasts, no lights and shades, and a lesson sinks into a mere series of bald statements, reiterated until the wording of them is known. Crisp hard facts seem to be what are wanted for examination purposes, and these only are given. **Result-grinding is a deadly enemy to true teaching**; it is as soulless and as uninteresting as a never-ending round of five-finger exercises. The view is a pernicious one, that, to use Professor Harrison's words, "whatever does not mean success in examinations is not education."

Speed in Teaching should depend commonly upon the amount of difficulty experienced by the pupils in mastering what is given. Thus it may be said to be governed by the ability of the children, the extent of their familiarity with other parts of the subject, the simplicity of what is offered, and the amount of graduation. If the subject is one well within their comprehension, one which appeals largely to their previous knowledge and experience, or if the information has been broken up into a series of short steps following each other without a break in thought, the teacher may proceed with comparative rapidity. **A lesson should rarely or never be taught at the same speed throughout.** A complex idea should have much more time given to it than a simple one; it should be approached gradually, the minds of the children being prepared to receive it, and it should be sufficiently illustrated to make it clear before it is left. The **fatigue of the class**, again, should be taken into account; if the children are wearied, the teacher should go much more slowly, and state the points with extra clearness and force.

Variation in the speed of teaching may also be made to serve a further double purpose—to **give emphasis to the main points** by stating them very deliberately, and to **bring out the perspective of the facts** by going more rapidly over the less important points, over merely illustrative matter and information brought in to give completeness of realisation of the central ideas, but which it is scarcely to be hoped will be remembered apart from them.

Many teachers go too fast—not so much talk too quickly, as cover too wide a range of ideas in a given time. They fail to recognise the capability of a child's mind, and judge his power of apprehension by their own. The **changes are too rapid**, and confuse a child rather than instruct him. No time is given for proper apprehension; the crowd of things rapidly pressed upon his attention one after another leaves his mind in a state of daze. It is like looking at figure after figure in a kaleidoscope quickly turned, or like viewing a series of landscapes from an express train. It is necessary to be on one's guard against the feeling that what is perfectly clear to us, must, when we have explained it, be equally clear to others.

We may sum up **the more important characteristics of good teaching** as follows :—

(1) It is **simple** and **graduated** in form, and shows a steady development of the subject with which it deals.

(2) It shows a **definite purpose** and direction, and **secures mental discipline** as well as information.

(3) It shows a **definite line of thought**, gives **ideas before reasoning**, and does not leave what is learned a jumble of more or less important fragments.

(4) It **concentrates, vivifies**, and **enforces** the facts ; and forms a foundation for further knowledge.

(5) It **follows the path of least resistance**, and allows no accumulation of difficulties.

(6) As far as it goes it substitutes **clear, exact**, and **complete** notions for those which are confused, indefinite, and partial.

(7) It **distributes the work** between teacher and taught, the excellence of the teaching being in proportion to the learning.

(8) It encourages **self-effort**, and trains the scholars to **good habits of thought and work.**

(9) It secures **attention**, and is given in an **intelligent, pleasant, and natural manner.**

(10) It is **helpful, persuasive, suggestive, stimulating**—the best ideas embodied in the best way.

(11) It **excites a love of what is true in knowledge and noble in conduct.**

(12) It is **stamped by the individuality of the teacher**, and is the outcome of careful and thoughtful preparation.

CHAPTER III.

WHAT IS MEANT BY A LESSON—TYPICAL METHODS OF PROCEDURE IN TEACHING.

LESSON CHARACTERISTICS.—If we examine with sufficient care and insight any worthy product of art—whether it be a cleverly painted picture, a beautiful piece of music, a fine poem, or a skilfully constructed novel—we shall find its production has been governed by certain principles, acted upon consciously or unconsciously by the artist. Hence every true **work of art** is characterised by special features, which in their general form and spirit are the same for any art, though the material acted upon, the design developed, the particular end aimed at, will vary with the circumstances of the case.

So **teaching is governed by general principles** just as any other art is, and a thoughtfully perfected lesson will have its laws of structure, its principles of composition, and will be marked by distinctive features which separate it off in the clearest manner from a mere inartistic statement of facts.

> The strange thing is that **teaching is about the only art which is supposed not to need earnest study and constant and painstaking practice** to learn efficiently. There are still many, it is to be feared, who see nothing in teaching beyond simply telling children what they have to learn, and who look upon knowledge of a subject as the only necessary condition for teaching it. No amount of earnestness or exertion will enable a person, who has not learned by laborious effort how to do so, to paint a picture, or play a musical instrument. Why should it be expected that teaching alone will come by intuition? And the matter becomes stranger still when we consider the immense importance of the issues at stake; and take into account the terrible waste of time and effort and the mischief done to young minds as a result of bad teaching.

The **general characteristics of a lesson from an art point of view** may be stated to be—

(1) **A distinct form.**—The lesson has clearly marked parts; it is not a mere collection of unconnected facts but **an orderly development**, the information being systematised and bound together on a definite

plan. Some clearly worked out design there must be, but this is quite a distinct thing from having an artificial stereotyped form for all lessons. The beginning, middle, and end, must be recognisable in the treatment of the subject-matter, not merely by sequence in time. Every fact must be necessary to the view taken, must have a distinct place in the scheme, and there must be a reason for that place. The form of a well-constructed lesson will be as evident as that of a logical argument.

(2) **Unity of idea.**—The lesson is governed by a clearly realised aim, and shows **a central line or axis of progressive thought and fact,** round which all the other ideas group themselves naturally in proper relationship of interdependence and relative importance. The facts are coherent, and are, as it were, made to face all one way in order to bring out strongly the general effect, and give completeness of view as far as the work extends. There is no muddling up of several views of the same subject; the lesson tells its own story distinctly, and is so arranged that not only has every point a meaning in itself, but a meaning also as a part of a larger whole.

(3) **Harmony of effect.**—Everything is in keeping with the general design—in agreement with the style, tone, and substance of the teaching. There are no antagonistic or discordant elements, but **each part aids in the realisation of the rest.** The mode of presentment is consistent throughout, and is suited to that which has to be taught. There is no grotesque treatment of grave matters, no overweighting of trivial ones. The facts are put forward in as striking, forcible, and picturesque a manner as possible, but are kept strictly within the limits of truth.

(4) **Proportion and Symmetry.**—Each part is treated proportionately to its importance, and stands out accordingly. The mind grasps readily the outline of the knowledge presented; no point is allowed to obtrude itself unduly, and illustrative matter is kept in its proper place. There is no purposeless digression into irrelevant matters, no over-development of one portion of the lesson, and hasty scampering over another. The facts are arranged symmetrically, and grouped into divisions, which, as nearly as can be naturally secured, balance one another. Thus the pauses for recapitulation and summing up occur at about equal intervals of time.

(5) **Variety in detail.**—While it is important that the central line

of thought should be distinctly marked, there must be plenty of variety in the subject-matter and in the mode of treatment to prevent dulness in the teaching, and consequent weariness on the part of the pupils. Sufficient diversity in detail there must be in any work of art if it is to engage attention ; and children are especially influenced by the varied nature of the facts brought before them, and by versatility in the manner of presentment. There must be **no sameness, no monotony** ; one teaching device may be made to afford relief to another, illustrations may be drawn from different sources, facts may be approached in a diversity of ways, and even repetition may often usefully be conducted in a changed form.

(6) **Originality.**—No one cares much for mere copies. It is a source of pleasure to have a thing put for us in an original way. The new view is attractive, and we like to be able to recognise the action of the artist's own mind. So with teaching : mere imitation of some one else's plan is pretty sure to be wanting in any strong elements of success. A properly contrived lesson will exhibit originality of thought and invention. of **power to lift the subject out of the region of dull commonplace.** The teacher will by the freshness of his treatment, the novelty of his arrangement and illustrations, and the aptness of his language, invest it with quite new interest.

(7) **Perfection of Workmanship.**—The lesson will be marked by thoroughness. Each point will be taught with skill and ease as far as is necessary, and will be arrived at in the shortest way. There will be no over-elaboration, no attracting of attention to the means whereby the results are reached, no waste of effort, and the whole will be accomplished without the work being felt burdensome by either teacher or taught.

We may perhaps usefully but very briefly sum up these points thus : A skilfully perfected lesson, of a type intended to train as well as instruct, will be distinguished by having a **definite form,** in which there is a reason for the order and grouping of every part ; it will be dominated by some **leading thought** around which the other ideas cling naturally ; there will be **sufficient variety** both of subject-matter and treatment to interest the children and give them completeness of conception ; the facts will all be so arranged as to **harmonise** with one another, and fit into the scheme in a way which will produce a **proportionate** and **symmetrical** whole ; and lastly, there will be ample evidence that the lesson has passed through the crucible of the teacher's mind, in such a way as to refine the information at disposal, and get rid of the dross of unsuitable or irrelevant matter, while at the same time those portions are distinctly brought out which it is most important for the pupil to learn.

One of the commonest defects of a lesson is looseness—a want of logical coherence and clearness of plan, arising almost always from a want of thoughtful preparation, comparatively rarely from want of knowledge. There is a lack of true meaning in such a lesson ; just as a heap of coloured tiles necessary for some beautiful design may suggest little or nothing when distributed into small heaps, or even when arranged in groups according to colour, and have only a true and full significance when the pattern is worked out.

The teacher should be perfectly clear as to what his lesson is intended to do—what benefit it will confer upon the children. He must settle with himself whether its **object** is to convey entirely new information, or to sum up and formulate what they already know in a scattered and uncertain way ; and he will decide how best to carry out the work so that it may sharpen their intelligence, strengthen their moral tone, and promote a love of reading and study. In any case a **distinct purpose** must run through his work, and he must treat his subject in such a manner that the children may get a definite meaning and value out of it.

He who would teach well must learn to **look at knowledge in the right way**, to recognise that it is not an unconnected and disorderly array of individual items, without relationship or organisation, but that **each truth is only a part or aspect of some larger truth**, that each group of facts is but a portion of some still greater whole, and has a distinct place in the great system of human knowledge, just as everything in nature has its place in the system of the universe. Many a great discovery is nothing but the result of looking at a group of truths in a new way, and puzzling out their combined meaning.

The more rational and natural is the teacher's **scheme of arrangement** of his lesson—the more freely and spontaneously one fact seems to arise out of another and the relationship of the various points is made clear—the more easily will the purport of the whole be made out and each particular item fall into its place, and the greater will be the impetus and assistance given to further acquisition and discovery.

The ordinary **book form of information** is rarely the most suitable one for teaching; too little attention is paid to the orderly development and connection of the ideas, the steps are not sufficiently marked, and the presentation is too abrupt, and generally in too condensed a form, for the facts to find ready entrance and lodgment in a child's mind. **It is the province of a good lesson to substitute a simple, orderly, and easily grasped statement of knowledge for one which is more difficult and complex.** The points have to be transformed, rearranged, and fully illustrated. Between the teacher and the child there is a great difference in intellectual power, and this must be allowed for. The subject has to be presented from the **teaching point of view**; and unless it has been fully comprehended by the teacher, he will scarcely be able to translate it into the particular form the circumstances may require.

TYPICAL METHODS OF PROCEDURE.—Perhaps almost the first question the teacher asks himself respecting a lesson is **what method** he shall adopt in teaching it—in what way ideas are to be evolved out of the material at disposal, and where the new ideas are to lead him. Now this will depend to a very large extent upon that which he has to accomplish by means of the lesson; and the fundamental question is *what are the results it is desirable to produce.* In settling this point it must be borne in mind, that, in any teaching of an intelligent kind, strength and discipline, suppleness of intellectual fibre, and increased power to progress, are to be developed side by side with the growth of knowledge; that **training and instruction should run hand in hand and support and assist each other.** To forget the value of knowledge for its own sake is a mistake; but to fail to recognise that together with knowledge there must be advance in the power to use it—that its acquisition is to be made the means of intellectual and moral culture—is an equally serious error.

Much **sound judgment** is necessary in making up one's mind exactly how a lesson of the highest kind should be taught. To know how and when to modify practice without abandoning principle, to be able to make out how far a method will carry us and where it is likely to fall short, to decide what it may be expected to do for us and our pupils and what it will certainly fail to achieve, to discover how it may be strengthened wherever necessary, and what may be done to supplement it so as to make it adequately cover the needs of the case, will often tax the ability even of the most skilful teacher. To accomplish all this to good purpose needs **earnest thought**, and a **patient carefulness** that is not above taking any trouble necessary to secure complete success. Truly, to rise to the highest perfection in his work, the teacher needs to have that **genius which is the outcome of "an infinite capacity for taking pains."** He must not only take off his hat to wisdom, he must make her intimate acquaintance and seek to secure from her such aid as is granted to a constant and loving friend.

No two teachers' knowledge, habits, experience of life, and power of interpretation will be of exactly similar character; no two will see a thing in quite the same way; hence each will need to make out for himself a plan of attack which will bring out in the fullest degree such possibilities of success as exist in his own case.

To attempt to stretch all lessons on the same Procrustean bed is to allow method to make us a slave to a preconceived idea—to forget that it is a *means* of learning and discipline, and not an end in itself. There must be no method for method's sake; our plans must be elastic, and allow us all proper freedom of action. To adhere rigidly and mechanically to some set course of action is to drift into a **dead formalism** utterly contrary to the spirit of true method. Knowledge is many-sided, and there is no mode of unfolding it to the pupil which, even in its general aspect, is of universal application. So far as the teaching is concerned, ordinary oral lessons will be, in all but the broadest outlines of method, as variable as the nature of facts to be dealt with; and even the same lesson under different conditions will often need to be approached and treated in a totally different manner.

Now although in the details of the work every lesson has thus its own peculiarities of treatment and device, yet there are certain broad **types of method**, the *principle* of one or other of which is very commonly adopted in the teaching of a series of lessons which admit of being presented in the same general way. Hence we frequently hear the method of a lesson characterised as conversational, empirical, inductive, deductive, developing, analytic, synthetic, comparative; or indicated by other names less commonly current. Though he will often employ the processes denoted, the ordinary teacher needs to trouble himself but little about the terms so far as the *practice* of his art is concerned; nevertheless, as they are in pretty general use, and their meaning should be understood by every intelligent educator, a few words of explanation about them may not be out of place.

These so-called methods, however, must not be looked upon as in all cases distinct and mutually exclusive types of treatment, but rather as indicating views of the teaching process from different standpoints. For instance, a lesson, as we shall see, may easily be developing, inductive, and analytic at the same time; and what name shall be applied to its method will depend upon how we elect to look at it.

(1) **The Conversational method.**—This is so called because the teaching takes the form of conversation, the lesson being divested of its usual formality, and becoming simply a pleasant chat about things. The teacher plays the part of a sympathetic friend, and endeavours to make the children feel quite at home. He talks in a free and easy way, suggests this or that, and supplies necessary information; but he does this with an **absence of any evident desire to instruct,** so that the children forget that they are being taught, and do not feel learning to be drudgery. They are encouraged to talk without constraint, to state what they know, and to ask any questions they please; while at the same time the teacher directs their thoughts and attention, puts frequent questions to them, and really guides the work at all points.

The **spontaneousness, simplicity, unconventionality,** and **pleasantness** of the method render it especially suitable for employment with little children. With older pupils it forms a very agreeable change from the ordinary routine teaching of the school; and more or less it may often be advantageously introduced into object lessons, and others of a similar character. Some skill and judgment, however, are needed to carry it out with effect.

Many good examples of the "conversational method" may be found in books, especially in some of the best story-books for children; but we must be on our guard against that *sham conversational plan* to be found in the ordinary "question-and-answer books." In these there is no true dialogue; all the brightness, freedom, and naturalness of conversation are absent; and the information is presented in an entirely artificial and often pompous way, which is as unlike the skilful guidance of the child to think and discover for himself as anything can well be. To call the method in such a case "Socratic," as some writers of these books do, is an absurdity which is only equalled by the ignorance displayed in such a statement.

The well-known chapter on "Eyes and no Eyes" in *Evenings at Home* is a capital instance of the spirit and way in which teaching by conversation should be carried out; and in the following admirable dialogue from the Rev. Edward Thring's *Theory and Practice of Teaching* the method is seen at its best.

Master.—Did you ever hear of Fortunatus's purse?
Boys (two or three).—Oh yes, it always had money in it.
M.—Would you like to have one?
B.—I should just think so, rather.
M.—Why don't you get one?
B.—Oh, it's only a Fairy-story; don't I wish I could!
M.—What! you don't mean to say you don't believe it?
B.—Of course not. Who believes in Fairy-stories?
M.—I do: really, now don't you know where the purse hangs?
B. (quite puzzled).—No.
M.—Fairy purses hang on the Fairy-tree, to be sure; I have one.
B. (incredulous).—You don't say so?
M.—But I do (pulling out a shilling); that came from it.
B. (very much taken aback).—Are you serious?
M.—Quite serious. Where did this shilling come from?
B.—Oh, it's yours.
M.—No doubt. I did not steal it, I hope, but how did it become mine?
B.—Oh, I suppose you were paid for keeping school.
M.—Well, why don't you keep school? You told me you would like some money.
B.—I can't.
M.—Why not?
B.—I don't know enough.
M.—Oh! but what has that to do with it?
B.—Of course you must have knowledge to keep a school.
M.—Indeed!! Do you mean to tell me that my knowledge turned into money?
B.—Yes.
M.—What!? This shilling part of a Greek verb?
B. (laughing).—I suppose so.
M.—What are you, pray, doing here?
B.—Oh! we come to learn.
M.—Not to get knowledge? surely?
B.—Of course we do, though.
M.—You don't mean to say you are climbing the tree of knowledge?
B. (twinkling somewhat).—Well! I suppose so.
M.—To go back: Where does the Fairy-tree grow?
B. (promptly).—In Fairy-land, to be sure.

M.—You forget. I said I had climbed it.
B. (dubiously).—No, I don't. Is it the tree of knowledge?
M.—Where did my shilling come from?
B.—From the knowledge you have.
M.—But where does the Fairy-purse hang?
B.—You told me on the Fairy-tree.
M.—But the shilling came from the Fairy-purse.
B.—O-o-h-h!!
M.—And *you* agreed that the Fairy-purse hangs on the Fairy-tree. Now, what is the Fairy-tree?
B.—It is the tree of knowledge.
M.—And *you* told me that the Fairy-tree *of course* grew—in?
B.—O-o-h-h! Fairy-land.
M.—And Fairy-land is?
B. (many broad grins).—School.

The **method has advantages beyond mere learning**. The child will have to take his place as a unit in society, and it is important for him to be able to talk properly, as well as to listen. The plan should generate a love of knowing, and should train the child to communicate information to others with ease and correctness. "Conversation," says Bacon, "makes a ready man." Some caution is needed, however, on the part of the teacher, to prevent random wandering from the subject, rashness of statement, or conceited forwardness of manner.

(2) **Empirical Methods.**—An empirical method is one based entirely on practical experience, one which has been found to answer by actual work and is adopted merely as a convenient "rule of thumb," without any effort being made to know why it succeeds, or to discover the limits of its application. Such methods, though based upon no scientific knowledge, may be correct enough when properly applied, and in given circumstances may answer well; but, as their **underlying principles are not understood** by those who employ them, they tend to become mechanical, and are often used in unsuitable cases. The great defect of methods employed in a non-intelligent way lies in the fact that they **fail to meet the requirements of successful intellectual training**, from the absence of the discrimination necessary for making the numerous small modifications which are sure to be needed in teaching.

The necessity in these days for rapidly educating our children, that they may get all the good possible in the short space of their school life, renders it incumbent on the teacher to employ those methods which will best fulfil the requirements of the case. The process of "trial and error," of blundering into knowledge by trying plan after plan till one is found to succeed, and then following it blindly, has had its day. The science of education however is yet to a great extent in its infancy, and we are by no means so sure of our ground as to entitle us to condemn all methods not founded on scientific laws. In fact, empirical methods are often deserving of careful investigation, and may guide the teacher to the discovery of new and useful educational principles.

(3) **The Developing Method.**—By this is commonly meant a method in which the essential feature is the direct exercise of the child's faculties, with a distinct purpose, and in such a way that they may be naturally developed. The **nature and powers of the child are carefully taken into account at every stage**, and the teaching adjusted accordingly; mental action is aroused, the senses are largely appealed to, new truths are made to grow out of old ones, and, as far as possible, the pupils are led to discover facts for themselves, the teacher acting the part of guide and interpreter. The method is based upon psychological principles, as opposed to merely empirical processes.

In a somewhat narrower sense the term "developing" is sometimes applied to any method of teaching conducted in accordance with recognised principles, and for the most part carried on inductively, so that the lesson *grows* naturally outwards, and at every step affords training as well as information.

The "developing method" was the outcome of the reaction, started by such men as Pestalozzi, against the artificial methods and narrow aims of the time; and was in the first instance elaborated into a scheme and applied to the teaching processes in Germany, mainly by Herbart and his followers. It is essentially the same method that is called by some French writers the "**Genetic Method.**"

(4) **The Comparative Method.**—This is rather a subsidiary method to be employed in conjunction with others, where any gain will result from its use, than one sufficiently complete and far-reaching in its application to be continuously employed. The distinguishing feature of the method, as its name implies, is the placing of one thing or series of facts alongside another, and the examining of the two in close connection. Its meaning should be widened to cover **contrast** or the noting of differences, as well as actual **comparison** or the discovery of points of agreement.

The examination of two things side by side greatly strengthens the impressions made by the details of each. Their mere contiguity is suggestive; and at the same time the keen observation and careful discrimination necessary to make out their resemblances and divergencies, are of the greatest assistance in rendering the facts definite and exact, and are in themselves a training of a highly useful kind. This will perhaps be more fully recognised, when it is remembered that the discrimination of differences and the detection of similarities have been given as two of the three fundamentally distinct properties of intellectual action.

Where it can be judiciously employed the comparative method is of the greatest value, and it **deserves to be far more extensively used** than at present it appears to be. The process is almost always an interesting one to children, exciting their curiosity and keeping them active, if they are led, as they should be, to discover the points for themselves. In such subjects as history, geography, and natural science, the method is frequently useful; and wherever facts have to be taught inductively it naturally plays an important part. To compare objects with strongly marked similarities is a gain both in teaching and knowledge. (See lesson on *Comparison and Contrast of the Butterfly and the Beetle*, p. 73, where a list of lessons will also be found.)

The following example, taken from Professor Meiklejohn's *New Geography on the Comparative Method*, well illustrates how a skilful employment of comparison and contrast gives point and force to two series of facts, and assists the mind in grasping and remembering them, with a success which it would be difficult to secure without bringing the two statements into juxtaposition.

The Alps and the Himalayas.

(i) **Comparisons :—**

1. Both are highest in the middle.
2. Both have the form of a semicircle.
3. Both have their long slope to the north; their short and steep slope to the warmer regions of the south.
4. Both have numerous Alpine lakes.

(ii) **Contrasts :—**

ALPS.	HIMALAYAS.
1. West group of Alps higher than east.	1. West of Himalayas lower than east.
2. Points of semicircle to the south.	2. Points of semicircle to the north.
3. Southern slope goes down rapidly.	3. Descends by four terraces.
4. The passes are numerous and easily crossed.	4. Few, very high, very difficult and dangerous.
5. The Alps send waters both north and south.	5. The Himalayas only to the south.
6. The Alps are everywhere open to winds and sea influences.	6. The Himalayas contain shut-in valleys, great deserts, and vast solitudes.

(5) **Inductive and Deductive Methods—Analysis and Synthesis.**

In **induction** we first examine a large number of particular cases, or separate facts, and from the consideration of these pass to some general truth respecting them. Thus our method is inductive if we perform a series of experiments, and from a careful scrutiny of the results arrive at a natural law governing the individual phenomena; or if we observe closely a succession of objects, and thereby make out some common characteristic of a group which we can state as a test of classification, or as a definition. So again, we employ the same method, when, by sifting and carefully investigating a large number of cases, in which a certain effect is produced, we seek to discover the essential condition, or *cause*, as it is called, of such results. If we trace our knowledge back to its ultimate sources, we shall find that the greater part of it, at least, is due to inductive inquiry, whereby "the materials of knowledge are brought to the mind and analysed.'

In the **deductive process**, on the other hand, we move downwards from general truths to particulars or individual items of knowledge. Thus, we employ this method when we start with axioms, or admitted truths, and from these by pure reasoning we pass to further truths, and so on, it may be, to individual facts. So, when we take some scientific law and apply it to explain existing phenomena; or again when we begin with a study of causes, and from these endeavour to show that certain effects follow naturally as consequences.

We make use of the **inductive method of teaching** whenever we place before children a number of facts, experiences, or objects, and direct their attention carefully to the points we wish them to observe; then endeavour to lead them to draw their own conclusions, or to discover the underlying principle or general truth for themselves, and finally to put the result into as simple and exact a form as possible, so that it may be readily remembered. The ideas are given first; the statement of them in words comes afterwards. **Deductive teaching** begins in the opposite way; it passes from the word-statement to the ideas; it secures first the learning of the definition, or law, or rule, then carefully explains its meaning, and lastly illustrates it fully by appeal to facts.

Thus, in **teaching how to recognise a part of speech** in Grammar, the deductive method would begin with the definition; and then endeavour to make the meaning and application of it clear to the children. On the inductive plan the children would be first led to examine a group of words so as to make out their use or function, and finally they would with the teacher's help frame a satisfactory definition.

So in the **teaching of an arithmetical rule** inductively a series of easy examples would be taken in order, and fully explained; the wording of the rule, based on the previous teaching and experience, being the last step. Taught deductively, the statement of the rule would be given first, and then explained and illustrated till known.

Roughly speaking, the one method, as applied in teaching, seeks to lead a child to the understanding of a fact, and then to accept it because he sees it to be true ; the other presents the fact to the child as a truth, and then seeks to support it by simplifying and explaining it until its meaning and application are grasped.

In **Elementary Science** it is better to employ experiments, and assist the child by questions and suggestions till he is able to discover what the experiments show, than to simply state the fact first and then illustrate it.

If however the inductive method is adopted, and the lesson is based on experiments, the points should be really demonstrated. It will not do to make a pretence of appealing to experience, and then to fail in the experiments, or to manage them in such a bungling way as to show nothing, so that after all the children have to depend merely upon the teacher's word. There should be one thing or the other; not the confusion of the two methods.

To employ the **inductive method** well needs considerable skill and careful preparation. It is a slow method, and does not lend itself readily to the rapid teaching of certain results required for examination; but it **affords an exceedingly valuable training,** and that of a kind which is needed in the *education* of children. It cannot always be followed, but there is no doubt that in the great majority of cases it is a more suitable method in elementary teaching than the deductive one. The common rule that **definitions should come at the end of a lesson,** not at the beginning, is a practically useful one. Children may be taught to use their senses, to observe and compare so as to find out a common element in objects presented, before they are capable of reasoning in the ordinary sense ; and in fact they should have a considerable experience of *things* before the latter is attempted. Hence **deductive teaching cannot be used with success so early as simple teaching of an inductive character.**

We not unfrequently meet with the term **method of discovery** or **method of investigation,** and what is almost always implied is the method of induction, that being the method by which by far the greater part of all knowledge is acquired *in the first instance.*

On the other hand the deductive method is spoken of as the **method of instruction** by

TYPICAL METHODS OF PROCEDURE 49

which is meant the **method of scientific exposition**, *not* the method to be adopted in the teaching of the young.

The deductive method of arguing from principles or causes is also called the **à priori method**; while the inductive method of proceeding from effects to causes, and so on, is called the **à posteriori method**.

Probably no two words used respecting teaching have given students of the art so much trouble, and have led to so much confusion, as the terms **analysis** and **synthesis**. As Professor Bain points out, we should be better without them, but as we have them in common use it becomes necessary to get some adequate idea of their meaning.

The confusion arises in a twofold manner; from the use of the terms in a loose popular way as well as in a philosophical sense, and from the fact that the same process may be regarded logically as analysis or synthesis according to the standpoint from which we view it.[1]

Generally speaking **the two methods of analysis and synthesis correspond closely to those of induction and deduction**, and it will be well for the teacher to fix this point firmly in mind. **Analysis** is really taking to pieces, either actually or mentally. We employ this process when we examine a thing closely in order to make out its natural parts, or to consider its various qualities separately. In *induction* we do this in the case of a number of things to discover some common element, or characteristic; and again, similarly, we analyse a series of phenomena or effects that we may be able to make out some fixed relation or constant condition common to all—that is, some general law or cause. **Synthesis** is the opposite of analysis—the putting together again or building up of what has previously been taken to pieces. In this method we begin with simple things or ideas (the word "simple" being used in the sense of single, or not further separable, but *not necessarily in the sense of being easy to understand*) and combine these simple notions into more complex ones.

Thus "in **Euclid** we begin with certain simple notions of points, straight lines, angles, right angles, circles, etc. Putting together three straight lines we make a triangle; joining to this the notion of a right angle, we form the notion of a right-

---

[1] The student who has read a little logic will easily see that this must be so, inasmuch as **analysis in extension is synthesis in intension**, and *vice versâ*; the *extension* (breadth of application, or number of *things* to which the term applies) being decreased as the *intension* (depth or number of *qualities* implied by the term) is increased. (See Jevons' *Elementary Lessons in Logic*.)

D

angled triangle. Joining four other equal lines at right angles to each other we gain the idea of a square, and if we then conceive such a square to be formed upon each of the sides of a right-angled triangle, and reason from the necessary qualities of these figures, we discover that the two squares upon the sides containing the right angle must together be exactly equal to the square upon the third side, as shown in the 47th Proposition of Euclid's first book. **This is a perfect instance of the synthetic process.**"—(*Jevons*.)

The following brief statement of the **general relationship of these logical methods** will be found sufficiently accurate for all purposes connected with the teacher's work.

(1) **Inductive Method** (facts to laws, effects to causes, properties to definitions).

= **Analysis** (breaking up into particulars to find that which is general).

= **A posteriori Method** (inferring from consequences what the general truth or cause is).

= (In the main) **Method of discovery**, or method of investigation.

(2) **Deductive Method** (axioms, laws, definitions, causes, etc., to particular truths or effects).

= **Synthesis** (consideration of general truths side by side in order to pass to truths of a more particular character).

= **A priori Method** (inferring effects or consequences from causes or laws).

= (In the main) **Method of Scientific exposition**, or method of instruction.

Properly speaking, neither of these processes should be viewed as a *complete* method, analysis being naturally followed by and associated with synthesis. The former prepares the way for and makes plain the truths which the latter takes up and applies; and hence it is that, if we examine closely the conditions of any complete teaching work, we shall find that **both processes need to be employed, synthesis succeeding analysis**, sometimes in the same lesson, more generally in succeeding lessons of a series.

The **natural order in teaching** is analysis, so as to separate unessential things and simplify what is left, and then synthesis, so as to reconstruct, from the children's standpoint, these simplified parts into a whole. It has often been said that the teacher should do the analysis and the children the synthesis; and this in some cases is no doubt true, but the rule is far too sweeping for general application.

In many lessons, especially in such subjects as elementary science, it is much better for the children to do the analysis for themselves, as far as they are able, the teacher guiding the work, directing observation, and giving all necessary help in difficulties. When some principle has been thus thoroughly taught, it may be used synthetically in succeeding lessons to explain phenomena similar to those examined in the first instance.

As a rule, the analytical method properly carried out may be employed—as already noted in the case of induction—at an earlier stage of the child's development than the synthetical one. **In elementary teaching synthesis alone does not afford sufficient training of a kind suited to children**, and in numerous instances is far too difficult a process to be employed with success. The child is unable to reason in the way required, the process is less interesting to him than the analytical one, and the closeness of attention necessary cannot be secured. There are however, it is not to be denied, many lessons where the reasoning is of a quite elementary character, and where consequently the synthetical mode of treatment is distinctly useful. Further, in many such cases, the analytical process would prove so slow and tedious, that the necessary progress would not be made, and the difficulty of keeping up the interest would be greatly increased: in fact, the gain would certainly not be commensurate with the trouble involved. A good deal of judgment is not unfrequently needed in deciding which method it is better to employ, the teacher having to be guided by whether the children best know the *parts* or the *whole*. For the *beginner* in teaching, it is doubtless better to **hold fast to the principle "known to unknown,"** than to trouble himself at all as to whether his lesson shall be taught analytically or synthetically.

Taking into account all the various types of method we have discussed, it may be said, that **teaching methods are almost always very properly mixed methods**, this or that typical mode of treatment being employed just where it is calculated to do the work in the best way; and hence help may be drawn from many of these methods even in a single lesson. **Good teaching fixes as well as presents**, and is a standing example to the pupils as to how a subject may best be viewed so as to get out of it the fullest meaning, and how this meaning may be most clearly expressed in language and fixed in the mind.

CHAPTER IV.

NOTES OF LESSONS.

VARIETIES OF LESSONS.—We have hitherto spoken almost entirely of lessons of a high type, in which the gaining of knowledge by the child and his training and development should go hand in hand. These however do not cover all the necessities of school work, as at present conducted, when examinations have largely to be taken into account. Nor is it every subject of instruction which lends itself equally to treatment from such a point of view.

We may usefully distinguish the following varieties of lessons, the province and function of each of which should be clearly recognised by the teacher :—

(1) **Instruction or Information Lessons.**—In these the **thing of great importance is the knowledge** to be conveyed. They should be taught in an intelligent manner and elements of training should not be forgotten. The necessity for securing that the facts are clearly understood and firmly fixed in the memory will govern the form and method of the lesson ; but so long as learning is made certain, in an expeditious and thorough way, everything which can be done through such learning for the cultivation of the intelligence should receive attention. The **information should be made real** to the children, not merely crammed, as it so often is ; and the lessons should never be degraded to the level of a mere drill of facts. To the information type will belong most lessons in geography, history, and grammar, much of elementary science when taught as a *subject*, explanations in reading, the teaching of rules in arithmetic, and other lessons of a similar character.

(2) **Training Lessons.**—In these, mental discipline—the **cultivation of the intelligence**, and the provision of suitable exercise for the faculties, so that they may be properly strengthened—is the primary object ; while the pursuit of knowledge for its own sake, though still

necessary and important, drops into the second place in consideration. Here the needs of the child's development will be the special concern of the teacher, and will govern the methods employed.

Object Lessons should have training for their definite purpose, and this should be the case even when the term is used in a wide sense to include "occupation lessons" for infants and lessons in elementary science—whether the latter are taught in a connected series or not, so long as they form part of an *object-lesson course.* Teachers who test the value of such lessons solely by the amount of information pigeonholed, complain that there is no room for them, and urge that fuller information in the elementary subjects is of more value. This is a lamentable mistake, which it is strange to see teachers making. Object-lessons are not, and **never should be looked upon as, an "extra subject" to be learned from the examination side** ; and to treat them as though they were—so that the child's energies are bent upon learning strings of facts—is to defeat the purpose for which they should be given. Properly used, they may to some extent furnish a corrective to the mechanical methods fostered by too close attention to examination requirements in the ordinary subjects. The **increased power and intelligence gained** by the children—the training of observation and attention, the quickening of interest and curiosity, the relief afforded, and the increased pleasure imparted to the work —should tell upon the teaching of the other subjects in every direction. To take the lowest view, object lessons should "pay" indirectly by their influence, even though they may not do so directly to any large degree by the information conveyed.

Too frequently the **object lessons** given in school are completely dissociated from each other. They are selected without any attempt to establish a bond of union between them, and without regard to similarity of subject, to the further application of any principle taught, or to the help which one lesson may be made to afford in the mastery of others. It is much better, as far as possible, to arrange them in short series, each of which shall contain related lessons, so that each lesson of the series may be clearly joined to, and in many cases grounded upon, the preceding one.

The method of training is slow, but it is sure, and it is very much to be doubted whether, in the end, as much *information* would not be gained in a given time as by the supposed quicker methods at present in vogue of teaching facts. Of course much will depend upon the teacher, but it is surely worth the trial.

(3) **Drill Lessons.**—These have a distinct use in school work, and if properly employed, and kept in their place, may be made of much service. To fix a series of facts with certainty in the memory of a child requires much reiteration—often in fact more than can well be spared in ordinary teaching—and this the drill lessons should supply. They include such things as the repetition of tables, dates, names, summaries, and classifications; together with writing, reading, and arithmetic practice, and other work of a similar kind. They must not be confused with ordinary lessons, and **should never be allowed to take the place of intelligent teaching.** They should follow it, where they are necessary at all, and fix thoroughly those points which have been previously explained and taught.

Thus, for instance, what is known as "map-drill"—the learning of names and positions on a map by repetition—is useful if taken after the ordinary geography lesson, to secure the holding of the facts taught; but it is baneful when used alone as a method of teaching what in such a case would be called geography. The present tendency is for far too large a portion of school work to take this drill character.

(4) **Review Lessons.**—These are definite lessons, mainly of a recapitulatory and examinatory kind, which should be given at fixed times to review and sum up the teaching of a previous series of lessons. Skilfully employed such review lessons are **of great value in keeping information fresh and ready for use,** in giving a general grasp of the subject, and in enabling the pupils to look over a **wider** expanse so as to make out the relationship of the points they have learned. Without some systematic arrangement for review of previous work, much valuable knowledge is sure to be lost, or at least to sink into that no-man's-land of memory from which it is so difficult to recall it. The value and necessity of review lessons are not yet sufficiently appreciated; were such lessons more frequently employed, mere drill lessons would be less necessary.

NOTES OF LESSONS. Need for preparation of lessons.—Of this it is perhaps not necessary to say much. Every one who has ever attempted to really *teach* a difficult lesson, must have felt not only the importance of preparing the work, but the necessity for it. Unprepared lessons, even with skilled teachers, are very apt to be, and with unskilled teachers are certain to be, wanting in definiteness and point, loose in construction and arrangement, shallow as to the treatment of the subject-matter, and lacking in suitability, thoroughness, and impressiveness. If the teacher trusts to evolving everything just as it is wanted out of the "depths of his inner consciousness," his work is pretty sure to be random, unequal, and disjointed; and he is not likely to do justice to his subject, his scholars, or himself. Proper preparation should secure that he **fully understands what he is about**, and should limit his efforts within the bounds of what may reasonably be expected to be accomplished by deciding definitely what is to be taken and what left out.

In the very best steam-engine it is not possible to get more than a comparatively small proportion of the heat power actually changed into work; the rest goes to waste. Similarly **a teacher will be certain not to get all that is theoretically possible out of his teaching**, and this must be allowed for. In many lessons *very much of the teaching runs to waste* from defective handling, and passes off into the limbo of non-productive effort. To prevent as far as may be this **spending of strength without effect**, all lessons (except where some known method can be applied with but slight modification—as in reading, writing, etc.) should receive preparation to such a degree as is necessary to secure the greatest practicable efficiency. **The amount of preparation will of course vary with the knowledge, experience, and skill of the teacher**—with his power of being able at once to throw himself mentally into the position of the learner, to look at things from the latter's point of view, and to recognise at a glance exactly what is wanted, what is the nature of any difficulty, and what is best to be done. In the case of most teachers **such power is only to be gained by persistent exercise**, and at first much thought and steady consideration are necessary. To carefully prepare a lesson, and to put the work down on paper in the best form which can be devised, is one of the most valuable means of securing the training required; and has a disciplinary value apart from teaching. To the young teacher such work is especially important; but the "notes" must be something beyond a few stray hints, or an ill-digested assemblage of facts, if they are to do good.

What is meant by Notes of Lessons.—Notes of lessons are not a means of displaying the teacher's knowledge, or of showing how skilfully he can make a digest or analysis; they are not simply storehouses of facts, or illustrations, questions, and explanations; they are not simply notes on or about the information required. They are a short statement of the **best form in which the teacher can develop the ideas of his lesson**, so that the whole may be **orderly, consistent**, and **complete**, as far as it goes; as well as of the best means he can employ for bringing the ideas clearly before the children, and securing that they shall be both understood and retained. "Notes" are his plan of battle settled distinctly before he begins, so that there may be **no failure, no hurry**, and **no confusion** when he actually sets about the accomplishment of his purpose. And just as a general pre-arranges all the details of a fight, so far as is possible, and ponders over the disposition of his forces and the contingencies likely to arise in the struggle; so the teacher looks to all the possibilities of his work, and endeavours to realise and prepare for any difficulties which may present themselves in the lesson. To put the matter in another way: "notes" should be to the lesson what the artist's careful design, or sketch in colour, is to the finished picture—a sketch containing all the essentials, but not burdened with the many small details which will come out in the work itself.

Briefly, we may define "notes" as **a draft of the lesson put upon paper, with all the important points, whether of matter or method, clearly marked.** They should convey to another person a distinct idea of the teacher's power of arranging his subject-matter, and of his skill in presentation—of what the lesson would be like in all its main features. They should show not only what information is to be communicated, and how it is to be conveyed from the mind of the teacher to the minds of the scholars, but also to what extent the intelligence of the latter will be exercised and what permanent benefit they are likely to derive from the lesson.

Preparation must leave the teacher free.—As instrumental in securing right knowledge, clear views, and pre-consideration of the teaching, "notes" are of much importance; but they should not be prepared in excessive detail, and must not be followed slavishly. From the main lines of the work, as laid down, it is unwise to depart; but **there should be no mere recitation of the notes**, nor should the teacher have them so much in mind as to be constantly thinking of them rather than of his work. Known they should be, but they **must not constrain the teaching.** The teacher should cultivate the power to think in front of his class, and to seize upon everything which may be used to advantage; and at the same time keep himself sufficiently free to be able to adopt any change for the better which may suggest itself during the teaching. Often, when the mind is thoroughly imbued with the interest of the actual work, the teacher will see a better mode of developing a point, or of overcoming a difficulty, than the one which occurred to him during preparation. To secure the freedom and interest necessary, however, he must have confidence; and this will depend to a considerable extent upon the fact that he has always the prepared methods to fall back upon. The teaching will often rise above the "notes"; it should never fall below them.

The teacher must prepare his own "**notes**."—As *models*, to show on paper how the work of preparing a lesson may be carried out, "**notes**" **by others**, if carefully drawn up, may be made of much use; but the teacher is warned, as he values any vividness and reality in his teaching, and any increase in his power of dealing with a lesson, that *such "notes" must not be used to teach from*. If his work is to meet successfully the special needs of the children under his care, and make use of such powers as he possesses, the lesson must be the **outcome of his own thought.**

His notes upon a subject may be inferior in the abstract to those drawn up by another person, but practically to him they are of much greater value; and he will find his own sling and stone far more serviceable and trustworthy than the untried weapons, even of most elaborate pattern and perfection of finish, supplied by others. The **great fault of the vast majority of so-called "notes of lessons" found in books is** that they are merely summaries of facts, arranged in a way suited to cramming them for an examination, but not so presented as to be in a good form for teaching. Nor are they, even from this point of view, usually sufficiently full, as sources of information, to give a teacher ignorant of a subject the understanding of it necessary for teaching purposes. The artificiality of treatment, and the conventionality both of arrangement and headings, which are so lamentably common in "notes" drawn up by young teachers for inspection, seem to be largely traceable to this source.

In considering how the preparation of lessons may be most usefully made, it is convenient to view them as separable into the two following types :—

(1) **Lessons intended to impart skill in doing something, or knowledge of an applied kind.**—In these—as reading, writing, arithmetic, drawing, much of grammar work, etc.—*the method is the important thing*, and, as a rule, will alone need consideration. In writing out the notes, it will be entered on the paper in clearly arranged steps, showing what the children will do at every stage of the work.

(2) **Lessons in which knowledge is viewed as information or facts to be learned.**—In these both *the arrangement of the subject-matter and the method of presenting it are important.* They will be entered on the notes in separate columns, and will run side by side. Of this kind are object-lessons, and lessons in geography, history, science, the information part of grammar, etc.

> It is impossible to lay down any hard and fast rule that all lessons in a certain subject should be prepared according to one or other of the types just mentioned. The teacher must use his common sense as to which form his notes should take. Thus, for instance, the description of the teaching of an arithmetical rule would be entered on the notes as method only, and it would be absurd to enter the sums used for illustration in a separate column *as subject-matter*, for the remembrance of them as facts is not of the least importance. But, on the other hand, notes of a lesson intended to teach the meaning of a group of arithmetical terms should be divided into matter and method, as here there are distinct facts to be fixed in the mind.

I. PREPARATION OF THE SUBJECT-MATTER OF A LESSON. It is not sufficient to have knowledge of the subject to be taught. The teacher needs to settle definitely the limits of the lesson he intends to give, and to put the information in the best form for the children to learn. Proper preparation of the facts involves several processes which it will be well to consider separately. These are :—

(1) **Acquisition.** — The teacher will generally know a certain number of facts about the subject he intends to treat, but lying, it may be, scattered in his mind in a broadcast sort of way. These he will need to **collect** and **sift**; and then to **supply any deficiencies** by reading, by observation, or in whatever way **may be necessary, so that his subject will be mastered with** sufficient thoroughness for him to go before his class with confidence. **He must possess wider knowledge than just the amount to be given to the children,** that he may have something to fall back upon in case of difficulty, and be able to see in their proper relationship and relative importance the points which he teaches. He has to analyse his facts, and to look all round

them till he knows them from every side, and in any guise of words.

Imperfect knowledge in the teacher and wrong learning on the part of the children generally go together. He who has not mastered his subject is unable to take advantage of many points that turn up in the teaching, because he does not know where they lead to ; while the explanations given are almost sure to be defective, and wanting in clearness even as far as they go. **It is impossible to explain properly what one but half understands one's-self,** and any adequate treatment of the facts so as to afford the necessary training of the intelligence is out of the question.

> A large proportion of the failures in teaching are due to defective knowing, especially in the case of young teachers. They have book words but no sufficient realisation of the corresponding ideas; they rest content with delusive half-truths, and consequently are obscure in their statements and easily upset by a difficult question.
>
> Not unfrequently, too, they are very ambitious, and choose the most difficult subjects. They take what they consider the necessary facts from some summary in a book, and fail to realise how much skill and knowledge are required to handle such subjects well, because they have never taken the trouble to really understand them. In such cases the teaching is certain to be shallow, even where correct ; and it will often be marked by such inaccuracy of information, fallacy of reasoning, and rashness of statement, as to make it worse than useless to the children.

(2) **Selection.**—So long as the teacher has complete control over his knowledge, and can *keep it in the background till wanted*, he cannot know too much about his subject. It is impossible, however, to teach everything, about even the simplest topic, in a single lesson. Hence the teacher is at once confronted by the consideration of the **amount of information** to be given. This will depend upon the following **conditions** : the *time* at his disposal, the *capacity of the children*, the *difficulty or strangeness of the subject*, and his own *skill*.

> To settle just the amount of matter which can be properly treated in a lesson of fixed length requires judgment and experience ; but it is a matter to which attention should always be given. The difference between essential points and merely illustrative material must be kept in mind. It is a mistake to overcrowd a lesson, but it is better to have too much information than too little.

Having settled the amount of information which should be taken, the teacher has to decide *which facts are to be selected.* The **selection will be governed by several considerations** :—

(a) The **aim** or purpose of the lesson, which will guide him as to the suitability and importance of the facts.

(b) The **particular view** of the subject taken, so that there may be *no crossing and re-crossing of several lines of thought in the lesson*, and the facts may be cemented into a *coherent and compact scheme*, in which there is nothing irrelevant or accidental, and in which nothing essential is omitted.

(c) The **range of the lesson**, which should be sufficiently narrow to *leave the outlines distinct*, and to prevent the necessity for bridging over spaces between widely separated facts.

(d) The **difficulty** of the individual points, so that nothing may be taken hopelessly beyond the grasp of the children.

In attempting to make a lesson simple, care must be taken not to leave out essential parts of the subject-matter. **Difficulties are not conquered by omitting them.** There must be a skeleton of hard fact to support the lesson, but at the same time the latter should never be a mere collection of dry bones.

To one group of children a lesson may be admirable, which, taught in exactly the same way to another of different age and advancement, would be a failure. **The average child in a class should be thought of,** though some harder things may be reserved for the quicker ones and some things taken sufficiently simple to be within the power of even the dullest.

A point may be connected with the subject, may be simple enough, and worth knowing; but, if it does not find a definite place in the scheme of the lesson, it should be sunk until some future occasion. The "**Art of leaving out**" is a very useful one to the teacher.

Some good lessons do not travel beyond matters with which the children have some previous acquaintance, but which they know for the most part in a hazy, partial, and disconnected way. The work here is to explain, illustrate, arrange, and formulate the information so that it may serve the purposes of training, and become real and useful knowledge. **A clever teacher will make the most commonplace subject interesting;** in fact, when treated in a fresh and original way, such subjects are often the most interesting to children.

In selecting the facts for teaching, the teacher should not think only of the lesson in hand; but, especially when some **scientific principle** is involved, should have in mind the **possibilities of its future development** in other directions. He should treat the facts in such a way that they may be suggestive, may have **hook-attachments,** as it were, to which other ideas may be linked and by means of which it may be possible to extend the principle taught into a chain of lessons. The importance of this will be illustrated further on.

(3) **Arrangement and connection.**—Of course the arrangement of the information will be **more or less controlled by the method adopted** in teaching it; but the method must not be imposed upon the lesson without considering carefully in what order the facts can be most readily and surely learned by the children. Practically the two things work together. The **order adopted should be the most natural one** which the circumstances of the teaching allow, so that each fact may have its nearest relatives for neighbours, and there may be a gradual passage from the **familiar to the unfamiliar.** The lesson must be so developed that every fact has a proper place; that there is a graduation in difficulty, and the whole has a clear meaning, as well as the items of which it is made up. The arrangement will, as far as possible, bring out the **true subordination of the ideas**; there will be **no breaks in the sequence** of the facts, and they will be firmly connected like atoms in chemical combination, not merely placed side by side like the particles in a mechanical mixture. The first relationship is a natural one, the second merely artificial. "We merely reverse the ignorance of savages," says Richter, "who sowed gunpowder instead of making it, when we attempt to compound what can only be developed."

<small>The **value of classifying the ideas** and of logical development in a lesson is very great; but it is somewhat apt to be forgotten in teaching. In many lessons, as taught, the facts have no settled places; and there is often such an absence of structure that the teacher might almost as well have begun with one section of the lesson as with another. Fact is simply added to fact. There is a sequence in time, but no sequence in thought, and no completeness.</small>

One of the greatest difficulties which the teacher usually experiences in arranging his lesson is **where and how to begin.** He must not go too far back, otherwise time which should be given to the lesson will be taken up with introductory matter. The initial steps are important; the information given must take its proper place in the child's mind, and there must be **firm ground to start from.** It very rarely happens, however, but that the pupil has some previous knowledge to which the new ideas may be attached, or which at least may be made to form stepping-stones from the old to the new. A teacher who knows his children will generally be able to judge pretty readily what ideas they are likely to possess which he can make use of. A little **preliminary questioning**, when he comes to the teaching, will bring these to light, freshen them up, and put the pupils into the right groove for proceeding. The **first steps should be easy ones** for them to take. The lesson, once started, will follow the lines already laid down, **each succeeding part growing out of that which has gone before** and the line of thought which runs through the work remaining unbroken.

(4) **Grouping.**—Having selected and arranged his facts in order, the teacher has lastly to group them into **suitable divisions** for teaching. It would not be wise as a matter of method, even if children could stand the strain on their attention, to continue the presentation of facts throughout the lesson without a pause. The **breaks at the end of divisions are a change**, and consequently restful, but they also serve other important purposes. They afford the teacher useful **opportunities for testing** the success of his work, and teaching over again any point shown not to have been properly understood; of **bringing up the laggards**, so that they may not be hopelessly left behind; of **impressing important points**, by recapitulatory questioning; and of **summing up** the teaching in a compact epitome, which should contain the key facts, and be entered on the notes as blackboard heads. The **number of divisions** should not be so great as to unduly break up the teaching, nor so small as to afford insufficient opportunities for recapitulation. So far as the subject-matter will allow, the **groups should be fairly balanced as to length**, and should end at convenient points, so as to be as natural as possible.

_{In entering the matter upon the *notes* it is well to put it in **analytical form**, so that the sequence of the points may be readily made out. The facts should be stated briefly, so as to suggest rather than include the details, but given at sufficient length to show exactly what points are to be dealt with. Each division should have a **short descriptive heading**. Such headings are of assistance to the mind in retaining the order of the groups, and act as **sign-posts** to any one who has to look over the notes.}

II. PREPARATION OF THE METHOD OF THE LESSON.—Having prepared the subject-matter of the lesson, the next thing is to think out the best way of presenting it to the children, that it may be fully understood, and all important things fixed in the memory, while at the same time it is so handled as to be educative. Here it will be well to bear in mind the various points in method which have already been treated from the general standpoint, and need not be repeated.

The **mode of treatment** should be as **fresh** and **vivid** as possible, but at the same time **simple** and **direct**. The teacher will not seek to invent some grand scheme, which will look well on paper, but will try to get to the heart of the matter at once, with as little elaboration of accessories as will secure the result aimed at. Novelty of method is desirable in itself; and the increased power of handling a subject, which comes from trying as many effective ways of work as possible, is a gain both to teacher and taught. The limits, however, of what is practically useful must not be overstepped.

In order effectively to prepare his method, the **teacher should rehearse the lesson in his own mind**, and think exactly as though his class were before him. This will lead him to consider how the facts are likely to strike the children, and how they may be most successfully treated. If a point is one which the children are to discover or reason out for themselves, special care should be given to the preparation, and a **line of questioning** (not a list of questions) devised whereby it may be reached. To carry preparation into such minute matters as settling what questions are to be asked is a waste of time, and to adhere to such questions is a pretty sure way of rendering the lesson artificial. In ordinary cases the actual questions should be left to the needs of the moment, so that each may grow naturally out of the preceding answers; and, even when some difficult point is to be reached by questioning, the most that can be usefully done is to think over a *possible* series of questions which follow the line it is intended to take. For a teacher, especially an inexperienced one, to have such a series in his mind as *suggestions* may be of great assistance, and will often prevent him from wandering. The questions themselves however are pretty sure to be greatly modified, and may be quite changed, when the point comes to be taught. Where a fact needs **illustration**, the best which the teacher can think of should be provided; where **lecture** is the means to be employed, attention should be directed to attractive statement, and the easiest and readiest way of making the children grasp any explanation given. In fact *some means* which may be used for securing the necessary learning, should be definitely settled, so that when the teacher comes to his work he may *know exactly what to do at every stage*.

The **preparation should not be overdone.** The main thing from the practical side is to discover what difficulties are likely to arise, and to be ready with a plan for overcoming them. To do this the ground has to be carefully surveyed, obstructions removed, and bridges built; so that such assistance may be given as will best serve the interests of the pupils, encourage them to effort, and at the same time leave them free to perform their share of the work in their own way. Not unfrequently when a teacher, in preparing a lesson, comes to a **difficulty,** instead of bracing himself to overcome it, he shirks the necessary thought, and satisfies himself with the reflection, that some solution or other will occur to him when the time comes for facing it practically. It *may* do so, but it is a very unsafe and unsatisfactory way of proceeding. If a difficulty cannot be solved when the whole mind may be bent upon it, and there is plenty of time to take in all its bearings, it is scarcely likely to be successfully met when attention is required in many directions, and the difficulties of thinking are very greatly increased. **Happy inspirations** do come, and are by all means to be made use of; but they should not be trusted to, and the teacher should have a plan in reserve in case no better plan offers.

The method notes will be entered on the right-hand side of the paper, and will indicate the plan to be followed with sufficient fulness to leave no doubt as to the main line of the teaching; but the teacher will not on paper go through the work in detail; that is the business of the lesson. Teaching and preparation are not the same thing, though closely allied. In some lessons the **matter** will need most attention; in some the **method,** and this can be easily arranged for on the notes by having the columns of different width to suit the case.

When the teacher has worked out a division, he will recapitulate, and sum up the teaching in a neat and expressive **summary** or **black-board head.** This may be written on the paper under both columns, and will serve to further mark the limits of that section of the teaching.

In the above instructions, so far as entering his lesson on paper is concerned, it has been assumed that his notes are for inspection. For private use, while the preparation should be in essentials the same, **a short condensed outline** will be sufficient; only so much being put down as will serve to show the order of the facts and the method adopted for unfolding them to the children.

The mere mechanical process of writing down some information from a book, and making a few notes on the method—and many notes of lessons are nothing more—is practically a waste of time. The thoughtful adaptation of the work to the needs of the children and to the teacher's own powers is much harder to secure. The one thing it is difficult to get young teachers to do is to forecast and *think*; and without this the rest is mere lifeless formality.

The **work of preparation** has been fully described in order that its nature may be understood; but the teacher is again cautioned that he must not let it so dominate his teaching as to make it stiff and stilted. It is a means, a help, and useful so far as it secures what is best for the children, but no further. As previously indicated, the notes upon the way in which the lesson is to be taught should be a series of useful suggestions, to be employed where nothing better occurs to the teacher when he actually comes to present his points, and should not be looked upon as rigidly fixed instructions to be followed in all circumstances. The method must be elastic enough to leave the teacher entire freedom of action, and so to allow of that ease and variety and play of thought which are so essential to good teaching. To follow with scrupulous exactness all the details of a prepared scheme—to teach solely from memory—is to take all the life and stimulus out of the teaching.

Specimens of **full notes of lessons** are given at the end of the present chapter, and others will be found in connection with the discussion of the methods of teaching the various subjects of school-instruction.

Where notes have not to be shown for inspection, the written preparation of a lesson may be carried out in a much shorter time than when such is the case, as all that will then be necessary is for the teacher to think carefully over his work in the manner described above, and, so far as writing is concerned, to map out briefly in an informal way the course to be pursued in order to fix it in his own mind. The digest or "**outlines**" of the work so prepared will be chiefly concerned with the subject-matter, and will show at a glance the general arrangement of the ideas, and suggest the line of development to be followed. As regards method, only hints of a general nature need be incorporated, and even these are better omitted unless distinctly helpful. Any essential points, however—as striking illustrations, a particularly happy mode of overcoming a difficulty, or a valuable original device—should be noted, but these need not be stated in a separate column.

The "notes" or "outlines" of all the more important lessons he prepares should be preserved by the teacher, so that he may be able to reproduce them at any future time without again going over the full labour of preparation. Such slight modifications as are necessitated by any alteration of circumstances may easily be made. These records must **not be so full as to make the work burdensome**, or they are sure to be abandoned. They should show the line of thought taken in a lesson, but details should be omitted, and the statement should be the briefest that will enable the teacher to recover what he wants. Such outlines will also be a useful assistance in reviewing a course of lessons, the importance of which has been already pointed out.

The following rough sketches will illustrate the **nature of the "outlines"** of lessons that have been prepared, which it is suggested should be entered in the teacher's note-book.

A BELL—*Standard 2.*

1. Show hand-bell—sound—what is bell doing that it was not doing before? Prove that it is *moving* by touching with strip of paper or suspended pith ball (see), then with a metal point (hear).
2. Nature of the movement—trembling—rim moves very quickly in and out—said to *vibrate* (teach the word).
3. Bell will not sound if hand be laid upon it—why? Show that nothing must touch the bell while sounding.
4. Of what made? Question from children that it must be made of some substance that will vibrate readily. Why not of wood? of lead? Would glass do? It would vibrate, but easily broken.
5. Would steel do? Strike short suspended steel bar. Why not use steel? Not so good—more trouble to make—hence cost more money.
6. Why bell-metal used? Vibrates readily and so gives good sound—easily cast.
7. Clapper—how hung? Must get out of way of vibrating rim after the blow—why?
8. Where is bell held when sounded? Where does bell vibrate least? Test by touching with hard point or suspended pith ball. Question from children where the handle should be placed.

THE EAGLE—*Standard 3.*

1. Describe mode of life of large bird of prey, emphasising the necessity for seeking, seizing, carrying, and tearing the animals upon which it feeds. From this work out the structural characteristics of such a bird, making constant use of blackboard.
2. Bird must be able to see its prey from a long distance—hence **strong sight**.
3. Must have the power to seize and hold its prey readily—hence **sharp hooked claws and great power of grip**.
4. Often has to go long distances to seek prey, and when found has to carry it away—hence **long and powerful wings**.
5. Describe method of tearing its food—hence **beak of peculiar hooked shape and strong neck and legs**.

6. Will have many enemies, and must therefore live where it cannot easily be got at—hence position of eyrie among rocks, etc.
7. Show picture of eagle, and question from children that it possesses all the characteristics described above and lives in inaccessible places.

THE TOP—*Standard* 4.

1. Top shown—try to balance on peg or spike—falls—why?
2. Suppose when just about to fall a side pull given to it—then before it can fall in new direction another side pull is given, and so on. Effect of pulls properly timed and proportioned.
3. Spin top—question as to why it does not fall—falling prevented by turning.
4. Nature of top's motion—central line or axis of least motion—all parts except this move out of their place, but return periodically to same position.
5. Different speeds of different parts of surface (mark various points with chalk)—quickest movement farthest from axis.
6. How spinning would be retarded by applying anything to moving surface—question as to where greatest amount of rubbing or friction would take place for each turn of top. Apply point of pin to spinning top at various points, and note effects.
7. Why top stops spinning—(a) friction of the air, (b) friction of the spike.
8. Why top "wabbles" more and more before falling—tendency to fall gradually overcoming pull from spinning.
9. The heavier the top for the same size the longer it will spin. Why?
10. Conditions of good spinning.
    (a) Regular winding of string so as to run off easily without tangling.
    (b) Sufficient and steady pull of string.
    (c) Rubbing surface of spike as small as possible.
    (d) Hard surface to spin on, so that spike cannot bore into surface and increase friction.
    (e) Sufficient weight to overcome friction of the air.

☞ A lesson such as the above may be made of much service as introductory to lessons on the "motions of the earth," "twilight," "the varying rates of movement of different parts of the earth," "cyclones, "the precession of the equinoxes," etc., though of course it is not suggested that all these lessons should be taught to Standard IV.

Reference has been made to the **importance of connecting lessons in series**, especially where some scientific principle is involved. Not only are lessons thus taught more likely to be remembered from the fact that each to a certain extent reviews previous work and impresses the principle or essential points which have been taught, but further, more ground can be covered in a given time, inasmuch as the teacher can at once start from what he knows the children to have learned, and hence does not need to take up time with otherwise necessary preliminary work. The plan has also the great advantage of giving the children a **connected body of knowledge** instead of a collection of fragments. Each teacher should thus arrange his lessons in connected series for himself, so as to suit his own circumstances, his knowledge, and the needs of the children. The following will sufficiently illustrate what is meant by a **series of related lessons** :—

(I.)

1. Physical properties of water.
2. Why water seeks its own level.
3. What becomes of a shower of rain.
4. Springs.
5. Artesian wells.
6. Sea waves.
7. Solid, liquid, and gaseous states of water.
8. The changes that take place from ice to steam.
9. Convection.
10. Clouds and rain.
11. Mist and fog.
12. Snow and hail.
13. Snow-fields and avalanches.
14. Glaciers.
15. Icebergs.

(II.)

1. The pressure of liquids.
2. A fountain.
3. The pressure of air.
4. The sucker.
5. The pump.
6. The diving-bell.
7. The air-pump.
8. The water-barometer.
9. The mercury-barometer.
10. The use of the barometer in foretelling the weather.
11. The aneroid barometer.
12. Variations in air pressure as we ascend above the sea-level.
13. The use of the barometer for measuring heights.

(III.)

1. The pump.
2. The syringe.
3. The force-pump.
4. The fire-engine.
5. The hydraulic "jack."
6. The Bramah press.
7. The cause of motion in the steam-engine.

(IV.)

1. Why a kite flies.
2. The windmill.
3. Cause of movement in a sailing vessel.
4. Effects of "high" winds.
5. Whirlwinds.
6. How a bird flies.

(V.)

1. Gravitation.
2. The fall of bodies to the earth.
3. Weight.
4. The pendulum.
5. Jets and globules.
6. Floating bodies (buoyancy).
7. Why the earth moves round the sun.
8. The motions of the planets.

(VI.)

1. Nature of light.
2. Shadows.
3. A looking-glass.
4. Why a stick appears bent in the water.
5. A lens.
6. The telescope.
7. Prismatic dispersion.
8. Achromatism.
9. The spectroscope.
10. What the sunlight tells us.

70   TEACHING AND CLASS MANAGEMENT

(*Specimen of Notes of a Lesson drawn up for inspection.*)

NOTES OF A LESSON ON

STRAIGHT SHOTS.

Time 45 m.   Stand. VII.

MATTER.	METHOD.

I. Effects of spin upon a moving ball.

1. When the hand partially immersed in water is moved rapidly forward the water rises in a heap in front and a hollow space is left behind.

2. Hand twisted rapidly to right or left during forward movement—water on one side carried towards heap or *place of greatest pressure*—water on other side moves backwards towards hollow or *place of least pressure*.

3. So with a spinning-ball driven through water, if front of ball spins to right *increased* pressure is on left and *decreased* pressure on right.

4. This difference of pressure causes ball to be deflected to that side towards which the front of the ball spins.

5. Similar effects produced with spinning ball or round bullet moving rapidly through air—distribution of pressures—ball turns in a curve to that side towards which the spinning carries the forward half.

Have a large vessel of water in front of class so that every child can see. Move the hand several times in way described. Direct children's observation, and question them as to what they see.

Twist the hand while moving it forward, and again make children note effects. Illustrate further by twist given to cricket ball and its effects.

Explain how air exerts pressure upon a bullet which is moving rapidly forward and spinning to right or left at the same time.

Draw various diagrams on B. Bd. illustrating direction of pressures, etc., under different circumstances.

Recapitulate so as to bring out clearly the principle involved, and sum up the teaching for B. B. Hd. ; or better still for entry into "Note books" with which so advanced a class should be provided.

B. B. Hd. or Summary.—*If a spinning ball be moving swiftly through air its course will bend to that side towards which the ball spins.*

II. How spin is communicated to a round bullet, and its effects.

1. Effect produced by rolling a ball down a straight groove and allowing it to touch only one side—spins to right or left according to the side it touches.

2. Case of gun-barrel—impossibility of making spherical bullet fit perfectly all round—"windage"—how bullet is

Show experiments with a glass marble in a groove of semi-circular section—question results from the children.

Draw diagrams on B. Bd. to shew how bullet from a gun would wander from the straight path, and how it was possible made to spin by gases from exploded powder in escaping forcing it against one side of the barrel or the other—wandering of the bullet according to the spin.

3. Robins's experiments in making a gun, very slightly bent near the muzzle, shoot round a corner. Bullet wandered in *opposite* direction to that in which barrel was bent.

4. Uncertainty and inaccuracy of smooth-bore guns with round bullets owing to the spinning set up.

for Robins's bullet to go round a corner. Question from the children that the bending compelled the ball to touch a particular side, and hence to spin in a certain direction.

Note that in every case illustrated the bullet moved to that side towards which it was made to spin.

Question as to importance of stopping this spinning if a gun is to shoot straight.

Recapitulate and sum up.

B. B. Hd. or **Summary.**—*A round bullet shot from a gun is almost certain to spin, and consequently will wander more or less from the mark it is intended to hit.*

III. Early attempts to stop the spinning of the bullet.

1. Importance of having the bullet as accurately spherical as possible, and of just the size to fit the barrel. No complete remedy to be found in this direction.

2. An early plan tried by the French was to cast the head of a wire tack in the bullet, so that the projecting wire (about an inch long), prevented the bullet from turning round in the barrel, and helped to keep it straight after leaving.

3. A bullet made in this way, and as perfectly round as possible, gave *four times the accuracy* of an ordinary ball.

4. The defects were :—
   (a) Much increased wear and tear of barrel.
   (b) Waste of explosive force not stopped.
   (c) More or less spinning was often set up after the ball had left the barrel.

Question children as to the gain from having the bullet (1) properly shaped, (2) to fit accurately. Note and explain the imperfection of these remedies.

Show bullet with a wire nail cast in it, or illustrate on B. Bd. and get children to state advantage of such a form.

Explain how the wire acting as a tail would help to keep the bullet straight.

Question as to how the tack would injure the barrel, and bring out clearly in what directions improvements were necessary.

Examine upon the facts of the division, and lead up to the following summary.

B. B. Hd. or **Summary.**—*A French plan for stopping the spinning, which led to much improved results in shooting, was to cast a wire tack into the bullet.*

IV. Introduction of cylindrical bullets, and of the "rifling" of the barrel.

1. Three things to be prevented :—
   (a) Spinning being set up in the barrel.
   (b) Loss of force through escape of exploded powder.
   (c) Spinning after leaving the barrel.

2. To prevent spinning being set up by the action of the barrel, cylindrical bullets with conical or rounded ends were introduced.

3. To stop the escape of the exploded powder, and consequent loss of force, the bullets were made hollow at the back with a small plug to close the mouth of the opening. When the powder exploded, the pressure on the plug caused the back of the bullet to open, and so fit the barrel exactly. There was the further advantage that the front half of the bullet was the heavier.

4. To stop the spinning to right or left *after leaving the gun,* spiral grooves called "rifling" were cut in the barrel, so as to make the bullet rotate round an axis coincident with the line of flight—that is, to give it a "boring" or "corkscrew-like" motion.

5. When the powder exploded, the soft rim of lead round the hollow of the bullet was driven into the grooves or "rifling," and this compelled the ball to follow their course.

Obtain from the class a statement of each of the things to be remedied, and question upon them until they are perfectly clear and the answers can be given readily.

Try then, by directing the attention of the children to one point at a time, and giving a hint here and there, to get them to suggest any means of remedying the defects.

Show cylindrical bullet and allow children to examine it. Remove plug and explain its action by diagram on B. Bd. Allow children to look down a rifled barrel—note grooves, the twist given to them, etc.—number of grooves different in different cases.

Explain the screw motion of the bullet, showing by diagram how the lead would be driven into the grooves of the barrel.

Question briskly and thoroughly on the facts of the division so as to fix them clearly in the children's minds, and then sum up.

Note.—The lesson will close with a rapid examination upon the whole of what has been taught.

B. B. Hd. or Summary.—*The spinning from rolling of the bullet in the barrel was stopped by lengthening the bullet into a cylinder with a rounded end in front.*

The waste of powder force was done away with by having a hollow with a plug at the back of the bullet.

The spinning to right or left after leaving the muzzle was almost entirely prevented by the introduction of "rifling," which compelled the bullet to rotate round its longer axis.

☞ The trajectory, elevation, and use of "sights" should be dealt with in another lesson, which might be called "**Long Shots.**"

(*Specimen of Notes of a Lesson drawn up for inspection.*)

NOTES OF A LESSON ON THE

COMPARISON AND CONTRAST OF THE BUTTERFLY AND THE BEETLE.

Time 45 m.   Stand. IV.

MATTER.	METHOD.
I. The Body. 1. Both butterfly and beetle are *insects*—so called because body is cut into or clearly divided. Three distinct parts— (*a*) Head. (*b*) Thorax or chest. (*c*) Abdomen or belly. 2. Body of **butterfly** long and slender —covered with soft hairs and minute feathers, making a kind of "down." 3. Body of **beetle** broader and thicker — often short — covered with hard horny case in plates like armour.	Prepare specimens of several kinds of butterflies and beetles on slips of cork, also large drawing of a "type" of both insects. Show butterfly, direct attention to its body, and question from children all they can see respecting this. Mark parts distinctly, and show on diagram. Put enlarged sketch on B. Bd. of any part of body children fail to make out clearly. Treat the beetle in a similar way. Then put beetle and butterfly alongside each other, and question first as to the similar parts in both, and afterwards as to the points of difference, adding any necessary explanations. Sum up by recapitulatory examination, and get children as far as possible to frame statement for B. Bd.

B. B. Hd.—*The body of an insect is made up of Head, Thorax, and Abdomen. The butterfly's body is long and slender, and covered with soft down; the beetle's body is broader and shorter, and covered with horny plates.*

II. The Wings. 1. The **butterfly** has four true wings. These are :— (*a*) Covered with "down," generally beautifully coloured, veined, opaque. (*b*) Nearly as broad as long, generally rounded, sometimes angular.	Show butterfly, and use diagram. Obtain the facts from the observation of the children by questioning. Note position of wings, and that both sides are coloured. Show specimen set with wings closed. Show beetle with wing-cases closed. Draw from children's

(c) Drawn up over the back when not in use.

2. The **beetle** has two true wings, and two wing-cases (elytra).

The *true wings* are :—
(a) Veined, transparent (like goldbeater's skin), often slightly tinted brown.
(b) Longer than they are broad, have rounded ends, and are never angular.
(c) Neatly folded up out of sight under the wing-cases when not in use.

The *wing-cases* are :—
(a) Hard, horny, opaque, and shining ; mostly dark, but sometimes brightly coloured (as in "diamond" and "burying" beetles, etc.).
(b) Rounded at hinder margin, and come to a point at end of line of junction.
(c) Close-fitting when shut down, thus protecting the delicate wings during burrowing, etc.

experience that beetles fly. Where are the wings ? Open wing-cases of newly caught specimen with penknife, and spread out the true wings (or show specimen with wings set out as in flight). Note how tightly wing-cases fit, and the way in which wings are folded beneath. Show large paper model of wing to illustrate manner of folding. Question from the children all they can see respecting, first, the true wings, then the wing-cases, guiding the attention of the pupils where necessary. Show several specimens with brightly coloured wing-cases. Lay separated wing and wing-case side by side on the page of a book—print seen through the one, not through the other.

Put side by side butterfly and beetle with wings spread, and let children examine them again in connection. Elicit points of likeness first, then points of difference. Sum up so as to arrive at B. B. Hd.

B. B. Hd.—*The butterfly has four soft bright-coloured wings ; the beetle has two thin transparent wings, which, except in flight, are folded closely beneath two horny shining wing-cases.*

II'. The Head and its Appendages.

1. In the case of the **butterfly** :—
(a) The head is small and round—varies little in different species.
(b) The jaws, each of which is lengthened out into a half-tube, are joined to form a kind of trunk by means of which the juices of flowers are sucked.
(c) The feelers (or antennæ) are

Show large drawing of butterfly's head (or sketch on B. Bd.), and compare with several mounted specimens. Place some beetles and butterflies together, and compare the shapes of the head, emphasising by sketch on B. Bd. any special difference noted.

Explain, with help of diagram on B. Bd., the way in which the jaws of the butterfly are elongated. Use specimens and

long and slender, and end in knobs.
(d) The eyes are large and prominent.

2. In the case of the **beetle** :—
(a) The head is irregular in shape, and varies much in size in different species.
(b) The biting-jaws (or mandibles) are large, in some cases (as "stag-beetle") very large. There is a second pair of jaws for chewing food.
(c) The feelers vary very much—some taper to a point, some are thicker at the ends—some short, some very long. (One of the long-horned beetles has antennæ over 3 inches long.)
(d) Eyes usually small.

B. Bd. to make clear the difference between the biting and the chewing jaws of the beetle. Exhibit "stag-beetle," and compare large biting jaws with those of some common species.

Place butterfly and beetle together, and question as to differences in the feelers; if necessary make difference clear by use of B. Bd. Show specimens of long-horned beetle to illustrate length of feelers in some species. Show position of the eye in both insects, and give a word of explanation as to structure of the eye itself.

Question thoroughly upon what the children have observed; then briefly run over the chief points again so as to get the children to sum them up in a convenient form for the B. Bd.

B. B. Hd.—*The heads of the butterfly and the beetle differ in shape; and the beetle has two pairs of jaws for biting and chewing, while the butterfly has only a trunk or tube for sucking.*
The butterfly's feelers are slender and end in knobs; the feelers of beetles vary very much in shape, and some are very short, others very long.

IV. The Legs.

1. In the **butterfly** :—
(a) There are six legs arranged in three pairs fixed near each other on the thorax.
(b) They are long and slender.
(c) Each leg consists of three larger parts, corresponding to thigh, lower leg, and foot, together with some smaller joints.

2. In the **beetle** :—
(a) Legs are arranged in the same way as in butterfly, but sometimes the pairs are farther apart.

Sketch large diagram of leg of insect on B. Bd.—show children that there are three larger parts, and question from them what these correspond to.

Exhibit specimens of both insects mounted with under side uppermost; let children examine these, and make clear any difficulty by drawings on B. Bd.

Question as to points of resemblance and of difference till these are known, and sum up in B. B. Hd.

(b) They vary in length, but are generally thicker and more angular than those of the butterfly—often have spines or hairs on them.

(c) Divided into the same larger parts as in butterfly—foot furnished with hooks.

Note.—The B. B. Hds. should be read in connection several times by the whole class. They should then be cleaned off (or the board be turned), and the lesson should close by a brisk examination, in order to bring out distinctly the main points learned.

B. B. Hd.—*Both insects have six legs, each divided into three larger parts—a thigh, lower leg, and foot.*

The butterfly's legs are long and slender, those of the beetle are usually thicker and shorter.

☞ The above lesson is worked out rather more completely, and is in many instances expressed more fully, than would be needful in practice. This has been done in order to make it as intelligible as possible, and to illustrate clearly not only the mode of preparation but also the COMPARATIVE METHOD of treatment. The lesson, again, would probably be found too long to teach thoroughly with an ordinary class in the time stated; in actual work, however, it could easily be taken in two shorter lessons; and as an illustration of the mode of drawing up a lesson it seems preferable to give the whole at one view rather than to break it up into two parts. In preparing such a set of "notes" for inspection it would also be well to insert simple pen-and-ink sketches (which cannot be given here) of the B. Bd. illustrations.

The lesson might be followed by another, dealing in a similar way with the mode of life, food, and times of flight of the two insects; and this again by a third, comparing the various transformations of the two insects, from the egg through the larva and chrysalis states to the perfect insect.

The following are a few examples of lessons that may usefully be taught by the **comparative method** :—

1. The daisy and the dandelion.
2. Cotton and flax.
3. Barley and wheat.
4. The potato and the artichoke.
5. The leek and the onion.
6. Peas and beans.
7. Dates and plums.
8. Arrowroot and tapioca.
9. An egg and a seed.
10. The bee and the wasp.
11. The lion and the tiger.
12. The hand and the foot.
13. Hair and feathers.
14. Wings and fins.
15. Hunger and thirst.
16. Hearing and seeing.
17. Sugar and salt.
18. Water and oil.
19. Gas flame and candle flame.
20. Wood and iron.
21. Clay and slate.
22. Peat and coal.
23. Glass and horn.
24. Paper and parchment.
25. Pen and pencil.
26. Writing and printing.
27. Travelling by stage-coach and by railway.
28. The horse and the camel.
29. River and canal.
30. The earth and the moon.
31. A meteor and a comet.

CHAPTER V.

THE TEACHING AND CRITICISM OF A LESSON.

THE TEACHING OF A LESSON.—To make clear the nature of the work to be done at various stages in the teaching of a lesson, we may draw an **illustration from landscape photography.** The photographer has to choose his subject, and study how to secure that point of view which will give the most satisfactory picture; to adjust and focus his lens so that the image may be as sharp as possible; to prepare his plate, and expose it in the right light, and for exactly the proper length of time; to bring out the view by "developing" it, and finally to fix it so that it will not fade. Similarly the teacher has to make choice of his subject, and determine in what way it may be looked at so as to bring out all that is most valuable for the children to acquire; their attention has to be focussed by the interest of the first steps, and their minds sensitised that the coming instruction may produce its proper effect; the information has to be so presented as to be luminous, and while sufficient time is taken over the process to secure distinctness, the darkening, which results from the "over-exposure" of saying too much, is avoided; the subject having been taken in by the children is brought to light again by judicious questioning, and rendered permanent by examination, summarising, and review.

Much of the success of a lesson often depends upon attention to small things. The skilled teacher knows the value of this. He tries his experiments over so as to be certain of their success; he makes sure his models will work at the critical moment; he has all the objects needed just ready to hand, and arranged as they will be required in the lesson. He attends to his own tone, gestures, and place before the class. He looks to the comfort of his children, and secures that every one can see the black-board easily. In fact, throughout his work **his mind is keenly alive at all points**—seizing on points of vantage, strengthening this and testing that, adopting any improvement that suggests itself, and making use of every lucky chance, finding a way out of every dilemma, overcoming every accident, ready with a remedy for every defect. He must have confidence in his own power of invention, that he may be able to gauge how far it will be wise to follow up any hint which may occur to him, and may cultivate that readiness of resource which makes the best of whatever happens. It is easy to say, "Do not be upset by an accident," but it is not so easy to put the rule into practice. Patience, however, and the constant **facing of difficulties courageously** will soon give the teacher confidence. He must not be discouraged at finding that things do not turn out exactly as he supposed they would, nor must disheartenment be allowed to creep over the class. Vexation at the failure of some carefully prepared scheme the teacher may not always be able to avoid, but it must not be allowed to show itself, and another plan must be cheerfully tried till the end is gained.

In teaching a lesson, difficulties of many kinds are liable to turn up which even the most thoughtful teacher cannot always provide for. These he must learn by experience how to meet, and exercise all his tact that the teaching may be retarded as little as possible. In case he finds that he cannot, even by the most skilful handling and judicious curtailment of matter of secondary importance, get through all he intended, it is far better to teach thoroughly as far as he goes, and finish the subject in a second lesson, than spoil the whole by dashing over the later portions of the work, regardless as to whether the children are following or not. To complete a lesson within the allotted time is important; but such **completeness may be purchased much too dearly**, especially where training is the more weighty matter. It is not the lesson but the children that should be the first consideration; if they gain nothing the lesson is useless.

Sometimes the difficulty of completing a lesson is one of the teacher's own making, and arises in many cases from his being led away by the interest of some point into a **digression** which would have been better omitted. To avoid this altogether, even when one has had considerable experience, is not so easy as it appears on paper. When, however, the teacher finds that he has been unconsciously led off the main lines of the lesson, he should rapidly work his way back;

not stop suddenly and go off at right angles. By such a break in thought the difficulty is much increased; the children lose touch of the teaching, and take some little time to find out where they are.

With young teachers a **common cause of slow progress in the lesson** is the blundering or clumsy way in which the facts are stated, so that correction after correction has to be applied before the children lay hold of the information properly. Unfortunately this is generally credited to the stupidity of the pupils, instead of to its right source in the teacher himself.

Much time again is very often wasted over **long introductions**, very commonly employed merely to bring out the title of the lesson. These are a harmful misdirection of energy, and serve no useful purpose whatever; for **the subject is generally best left for the children to discover as the lesson progresses**. Such introductions must, however, be carefully distinguished from the initiatory steps which are to connect the child's previous knowledge with what is to follow. These really form the commencement of the work, and lead into the lesson proper. Any teaching of a merely introductory kind must be brief, but if given at all it should be sufficiently full to be understood, and interesting enough to secure attention. Sometimes a teacher begins so abruptly that the first items of information seem to be flung at the children. This is a mistake.

It is important in teaching a lesson to realise how a child views what is being said, how far it is in accordance with his habits of thought, and to what extent the effort necessary to take it in is readily possible to him. **Once saying a thing is rarely sufficient with children.** *Mentioning a fact is not teaching it.* Strange ideas especially need much reiteration, and often presentation in a variety of ways, before the teacher can ensure their being grasped. Frequently too, in the same class, there is considerable **difference of apprehension** between the most advanced and the most backward children, between the brightest and the dullest. In such a case the safe thing is to steer a middle course, and adapt the teaching to neither exclusively. The clever children have to be thought of as well as the dunces, and a skilful teacher will *keep all employed*, by making the one set help the other. **Every child should, as far as he is able, contribute his share to the lesson**, and should be encouraged to independent action. To go simply with the brightest intellects, is to leave the majority hopelessly behind. But, on the other hand, to allow the teaching to sink to the level merely of the weakest members of the class, is to make it wearisomely slow for the quicker ones, and so to fail to stimulate any. It is often a good thing for a dull child to have to put out all his strength, and if he is anxiously trying to keep up, and asks a question, or strives to express something in his own way, the teacher should have the patience to listen to what he says; not snub him for his want of brains and pass on, as is too frequently done. To give him every encouragement consistent with the welfare of the rest is right; but to take up a large amount of time, trying again and again to make him understand something while the others remain idle, is to forget what class teaching should really be. Common sense here, as everywhere in teaching, is the safe guide. **What is theoretically best for the individual is not always possible**; the thing is to do the best which the circumstances of the case admit.

Throughout the teaching such knowledge as the children are found to possess is to be made use of; that which is **hazy** must be made clear, what is **defective** supplemented, what is **false** supplanted; and this must be done in a way which will weld firmly together the old knowledge and the new. In dealing with what children know, **care must be taken not to overteach a point.** The teacher has decided, say, to present it in a certain way, but finds when he comes to it, that it is already known, or that the children find much less difficulty in taking it in than he supposed. He nevertheless goes on, teaching it exactly according to his preconceived plan. This is to make a wrong use of preparation, and shows a great want of intelligence. Directly the children know a thing the teacher should leave it, and pass on to the next; he should hit the right nail on the head, but not go on pounding away till the wood is all battered, and the nail hidden from sight.

<small>A lesson to children is not like a long and difficult lecture to adults; the amount of information needed is comparatively small, and should certainly be so well known as not to necessitate any such crutches as having notes in hand before the class. **The less effort is needed to remember the lesson the better.** To be continually referring to a paper of points, in order to see what is to come next, is pretty certain to destroy any ease of treatment or freedom of thought, and consequently to make the teaching heavy. *The children again are scarcely likely to feel the necessity for learning what they see the teacher himself does not know*, or to have that confidence in his superior knowledge and power which is such an important element of **intellectual sympathy** between teacher and taught, and goes so far towards making a lesson successful.</small>

The general characteristics of good teaching have already been dealt with in Chap. II. and we may usefully close this section of the work with the following **PRACTICAL HINTS**, which will form a summary of the more important points that should be borne in mind in the **teaching of a lesson**. Their substance should be so well known as to have a constant influence on the work, without the necessity for their being consciously called to mind by the teacher.

(1) Distinguish clearly in teaching between the **means** and the **end**. Let your **aim** be ever present to your mind throughout the lesson.

(2) Remember **teaching is the cause, learning the effect**. *Presentation is a great matter, but reception is a still greater.*

(3) Avoid too wide a **range**, and keep to the view you take. Look to the **sequence** and **connection** of your work, and do not wander from the subject. Cultivate the art of knowing when to stop and what *not* to say.

(4) Distinguish carefully between **important** and **unimportant** facts. Connect your information as much as possible with a few leading truths.

(5) Strive earnestly to secure **sympathy** and **attention** from your class. Use every means to make the work **enjoyable** for the children. *Dulness is a deadly fault.*

(6) Remember the child's love of **change** and **action**; keep the lesson "going," and endeavour to take every one with you. In class teaching every child must receive **individual attention**.

(7) Make sure that the children grasp what you say. **Try to lead them to think**; do not rest content with loading the memory.

(8) Allow time for information to soak in. See that progress is being made, but **do not hurry**; much good work is spoiled by being scampered over.

(9) Let your teaching be **varied**, not only to keep up interest and give completeness of conception, but that by some means or other you may reach every child's mind.

(10) Whenever you can do so, *without round-about teaching*, **question** the facts from the children, **group**, and **summarise** them.

(11) Be careful to provide for **recapitulation** and **review** in your work, and for such **rest** and **change of method** as will prevent any weariness or strain from too prolonged effort.

(12) Keep the machinery of the lesson out of sight as much as possible. Bear in mind "*the great art is to conceal art.*"

A commonplace book should be kept by every teacher who wishes to study his art thoroughly. In this should be recorded the **results of experiments** in teaching ; **important mistakes** and their causes ; any **unusually effective method** or arrangement which may be devised ; any **invention in the way of apparatus** ; **useful sources of information** on particular points ; **references** to any specially excellent explanation, illustration, or definition ; etc. As a rule, teachers note remarkable **blunders** for the amusement they afford ; but such blunders have a much higher value than this, and are often of assistance in unravelling pecul'arities of mental working in the case of children. The mind, however, should not be studied only by means of its aberrations ; and it is equally important to record the **brilliant things children frequently say, peculiarities of thought and view, variations in the power of different faculties** at different ages, and at the same age in different individuals—in fact anything which will serve to assist the teacher in *getting below the surface of his work*, and in understanding its nature more thoroughly.

THE CRITICISM OF A LESSON.—Criticism lessons if properly carried out are a very valuable means of improvement for young teachers, and the **gain is by no means confined to the lesson-giver** : indeed, in many cases, the critic is as much benefited by his own criticism and that of others, as the lesson-giver himself. Such lessons should be to those engaged pretty much what clinical lectures are to the young doctor. They should be a **joint investigation for the purpose of correcting and explaining errors in practice**, and of discovering the most perfect mode of giving the lesson under the conditions imposed by the circumstances, and should thus serve to show how theoretical knowledge may best be employed in guiding and elucidating actual teaching. Many points of method and details of work may be brought into notice and illustrated in this way, which it is scarcely possible to make real, or even to treat at all, in a text-book or an ordinary lecture. **Bad teaching frequently arises from ignorance of the possibilities of better things.**

If he perform his work aright the critic is compelled to give attention to details, and he is led to discriminate correctly between that which is right and wrong in teaching, useful and valueless, skilful and clumsy. Such criticism, if deserving of the name at all, is not mechanical, and is not to be learned by a blind following of rules however well framed these may be.

In **true criticism**, the keen exercise of the observation in seeing correctly all that there is to be seen, the earnest effort and attention necessary to fathom a lesson to the bottom, and understand another teacher's work, the quickening of the insight and the strengthening of the power to make out the relationship and importance of the various points, the cultivation of the judgment in at once arriving at a decision, and the deepening of knowledge which comes from recognising how far any plan which has been devised actually serves its purpose when applied in practice, form a training second only in importance to teaching itself, and tell advantageously in every department of mental work, not in this direction alone.

The ability to interpret work in this way, is not only useful, but is also in itself a source of pleasure—the pleasure of the discoverer. The power however is not to be gained without considerable knowledge and much patient exercise.

To secure the advantages, the critic must work as well as the teacher. **The mere listless and perfunctory jotting down of a few superficial points is a waste of time**, and should be classed with other forms of idleness. It is easy to catch the mere externals of criticism, to quote the cant phrases and commonplaces, and to indulge in a peddling talk about unimportant details. This is just what the weak critic is apt to do; he overestimates the importance of such things as he is able to make out with little or no trouble, and not unfrequently attempts to cover up his ignorance and uncertainty by force of assertion and a show of decision.

In many instances, the critic contents himself with doing little more than reporting what took place, when he ought to be occupied in sifting his observations and judging of results, or in arranging in his own mind the suggestions he intends to offer, as to how the teaching might have been improved.

Often too the unity and design which lie beneath the surface of the teaching are lost sight of while the critic is stopping to examine fragments of the lesson with more minuteness than is desirable. Each point in the work must be viewed in connection with the rest, and attention must be given to the mutual bearing of the various parts, not to each as an isolated fact.

It is a common remark that to become a good critic of teaching one must learn to become a good teacher; and although this is not *necessarily* true from the practical side, inasmuch as some defect of manner may prevent one who is thoroughly acquainted with the nature and requirements of teaching from realising his own ideal in practice, yet the two things usually go together. In fact, to criticise a lesson well the critic needs such a thorough acquaintance with the work as is rarely if ever gained except by actual teaching, added to a sound knowledge of the principles and methods of school work. From merely personal bias criticism should be as free as possible, and should be directed mainly to the consideration of (1) the correctness and value of the subject matter, and (2) the power and skill displayed in unfolding it to the children.

It is the critic's business to put himself into harmony with the work, and to mentally adjust himself to the teacher's conditions. He has to interpret as well as to appraise—to see deeply, to expound clearly, and to judge justly and intelligently. Sympathy with the work is essential. Good criticism is not intolerant, and is never simply either praise or blame; it is broader, deeper, and more helpful than opinion alone, no matter how correct. It is an intense illumination of the inner and finer qualities of the work, a full recognition of its spirit and purpose, and an accurate display of its meaning and value.

All really excellent criticism, whether of art or literature, is of this character; and not unfrequently an able critic will make evident to us far more in the work of an artist or an author than either probably saw or fully understood himself. It is not every excellence which is there of set purpose. **Genius works by intense sympathy, which gives an almost instinctive power and enables its possessor to bring out what is essentially right, often without any very clear recognition as to why it is so.** Ruskin revealed more in Turner's painting than any one had ever seen before, and the great Shakespearean critics have shown us many wonderful things in the poet's work of which he himself was in all probability quite unconscious. **It is characteristic of the finest work, that it will stand almost endless analysis and interpretation:** every one finds in it something which vibrates in sympathy with his own nature, and every examination reveals some new beauty, some delicacy of touch, some fresh phase of thought, some new meaning that before was hidden, while **indifferent art is exhausted at the first scrutiny.**

Lesson Criticism of a right kind takes a high standard, and sets forth in what respects the work comes up to or falls short of this standard, both in plan and treatment. It brings out the conditions of successful practice into clear light, and **bases all its more important judgments upon the laws of educative development.** It endeavours to discover and emphasise the principles by which the teacher has actually been guided, and does not, to the neglect of these, seek to lay down others by which the lesson *might have been controlled.* It estimates the extent to which the lesson served its purpose, the value of the method employed, and the suitability of the facts and the mode of treatment to the needs of the case; it shows to what degree interest was excited, and how far the work was judiciously distributed and each child stimulated to mental effort. It does not scruple to mark errors and failures clearly and decidedly, but at the same time it shows generous appreciation of successes; it **assists the teacher to understand his strength and his weakness more distinctly than he otherwise would**; and while it indicates where he went wrong, and directs his attention to what may be improved, it goes further and suggests the means whereby defects may be remedied and difficulties more successfully overcome.

It is a common tendency of lesson criticism to degenerate into mere **carping or fault-finding**, far too much being made of personal peculiarities, and of comparatively unimportant mistakes, or even of slips of which the teacher is himself quite conscious; while the weightier matters connected with logical arrangement, correctness of method, and skilfulness of handling are frequently neglected. **Far more stress also than they are entitled to is often laid upon merely individual preferences**: success is success, and should be judged on its merits, not upon how far it accords with our own predilections. It is easier to praise than to blame justly.

It is only rarely that in practice criticism is expressed in an unkind way: when it is so, it will generally be found that **a cavalier manner and a self-righteous spirit go together**. Mischievous or useless criticism is not so much that of unreasonable disagreement as of baseless remark. The critic, from want of observation, has no material to go upon, and indulges in sweeping generalities, without instances in proof of the positions advanced—mere talk without any real conviction at the back of it.

A thorough discussion of work in a kindly spirit is at all times helpful, and the young or inexperienced teacher need not be discouraged to find that even his best efforts in teaching are marred by many flaws. He is blameworthy only in so far as he has not done his best; and he **should not view criticism in the light of censure**. No one is above criticism. No matter how skilful and experienced a teacher may be, directly he feels his work is faultless, he may be quite sure that conceit is blinding him to his own imperfections. In fact **every true teacher will be his own sternest censor**; he knows best how far he has fallen short of what he intended, and, though many defects may have escaped him which are easily detected by others, he is often able to see, even more clearly than they, how many possibilities he has been unable to realise.

This **self-criticism** is most important if the teacher would progress in skill; and it should be applied to all the more difficult essays in teaching, which he is called upon to make. A few minutes spent now and again at a leisure time, in thinking over his failures and successes, and in endeavouring to make out their cause, may do much towards that continuous improvement which, as a teacher, he should ardently desire.

A clear distinction should always be made in criticism between "clumsy teaching" and "ignorant teaching." A lesson may be taught very awkwardly and defectively and yet show that the teacher has clear and correct views as to what teaching should be, or at least that he is trying anxiously to learn. He is not above taking pains, and fails for the most part, if not entirely, from lack of practical experience in the work. This time will cure. What is needed by way of criticism in such a case is mostly encouragement and suggestive hints as to how his methods may be still further improved and applied with greater certainty and success, or how they may be modified to suit altered conditions. On the other hand, a lesson may be given with much greater show of skill, and a certain confident ease of manner, and yet reveal the fact that the teacher is ignorant of almost all essential principles of teaching. *He blunders without knowing it, and fails because he has never taken the trouble to learn*; his knowledge is insufficient even to show him that better work is possible. A lesson by a teacher of this kind is very apt to deceive a shallow or unobservant critic; but experience shows that many cases of this kind are amongst the most hopeless. The teacher is so puffed up with ideas of his own cleverness that he does not open his mind to the advice of others, while he is too careless and superficial to think and discover for himself. Ordinary suggestive criticism remains unheeded, and little or nothing of this kind can be given usefully in such a case, until the teacher is convicted of error and convinced of the radical worthlessness of his mode of procedure.

The lessons of the so-called "clever amateur" are often of this description; and in many instances the favourable criticism extended to such work is apt to foster the idea that teaching is a kind of gift—the possession of the fortunate few—and not a thing to be learned by patient and persevering effort. It is true that it is learned with much greater ease by some than by others, but learned it must be even in the case of the cleverest.

Cases do sometimes arise in which, though the critic may be quite conscious that something is amiss with a lesson, it is **difficult to say exactly what that something is.** The selection of the information is

suitable, the arrangement is passable, the methods seem skilfully
employed, the teacher is earnest and good-humoured, and yet, though
technically correct in all essential particulars, the lesson is not a
success. Here and there such instances may be explained by physical
circumstances—the children are fatigued in body or in mind, or
atmospheric conditions may be against them; but this explanation
is by no means always applicable. There still remain cases in
which there is, from some subtle cause, a **lack of understanding**,
difficult to characterise, between teacher and class, some **unnoticed
discontinuities of thought** which the children have been unable to
bridge for themselves, or, it may be, some **moral influence** at work that
has prevented them from putting out their energies, and in spite of
all the teacher's efforts his work fails to produce its proper effect.
Such cases need the keenest observation and the most cautious and
careful analysis to unravel.

<small>The story is told that **Sir Joshua Reynolds** was once taken by a friend to see a picture.
The great painter was anxious to give a favourable verdict, and examined the picture
with much care. "Capital Composition; correct drawing; the colour and tone
excellent; but—but—it wants—it wants *That*," said he, snapping his fingers. It was
not easy to put its defects into words, but wanting "that," excellent though it might
be in technical matters, the picture was a failure. So it may be said the lessons we
have just been considering want "that."</small>

The qualities of a good lesson may easily be gathered from the
principles and characteristics previously given; and from these the
critic or the teacher will readily be able to construct a scheme of tests
of excellence for himself. The following *résumé*, however, of some of
the **COMMON FAULTS IN TEACHING** will perhaps prove of advantage
as presenting at one view many of the points to which the critic's
attention should be directed, and as an additional warning to the
young teacher to avoid at least the grosser of the defects mentioned.
Many other faults will be clear from a consideration of the right
modes of employing the teaching devices and of errors in their use.

(1) **Absence of any definite plan**—no clear idea of what the lesson
should accomplish. No logical sequence and connection
of the parts; so far as the lesson shows, the facts might
have been taken in any order.

(2) **Attempting too much** and consequent hurry and want of
thoroughness. Lesson too wide in scope.

(3) **Long and useless introductions**—sometimes very elaborate—often used, as already noted, merely to arrive at the title of the lesson.

(4) **Defective knowledge of the subject**, and failure to realise its actual difficulties. The teacher talks in book phraseology, and has the semblance of knowledge (words), and not knowledge itself (ideas). Faulty reasoning on the facts given.

(5) **Lack of appreciation of the really important points**, hence absence of emphasis and perspective, all the facts being taught with equal force and fulness.

(6) **Too much drill and too little educative work.** Parade of the method or plan of the lesson before the children.

(7) **Clumsy presentation**—repeated restatement by the teacher before the ideas are clearly worded, from his having no adequate notion of what he is going to say. Language too difficult—teacher and children thinking on two different planes.

(8) **Lesson not stimulating**—subject-matter and style of teaching unsuited to the children—work slow, dull, and mechanical, even when correct in method. Children wearied by too long continuance at one thing. Want of brightness and vivacity in the teacher.

(9) **Too much done by the teacher** while the children are not allowed their proper share of the work—injudicious help given in the conquest of difficulties.

(10) **Unreasonable digressions**, sometimes from the teacher being led away by a question or a statement from the children, occasionally from fulness of knowledge.

(11) **Introduction of too many ideas at once**—facts not mastered one at a time. Children bewildered by having to attend to too many things together, sometimes by the teacher going back without warning to teach a point which was merely alluded to in connection with several others.

(12) **Waste of time in purposeless questioning**, sometimes from ignorance or want of insight, sometimes merely to kill time. Aim of questioning forgotten. Defective dealing with answers. Ignorant treatment of children's questions.

(13) **Abuse of lecturing.** Mere talk, adopted from idleness or unskilfulness, not true lecture. Lecture too continuous—saying too much—pointless and round-about explanations —wordiness—twaddle. The art of saying nothing in many words is not teaching.

(14) **The teaching of things by word-statements which children should learn directly through their senses** (observation, touch, etc.). Experiments performed without any guidance being given to the observation of the children. Founding of a lesson on experiments, failing to perform them, and then expecting children to accept a statement of the results merely on the teacher's word. Confusion of illustrations with things illustrated.

(15) **No proper means taken to fix the points taught**—defective recapitulation—bad summing-up, or absence of it altogether.

(16) **Artificiality or imperfection of disciplinary measures.** Mechanical corrections (of boys in back row, etc.) given by the teacher to fill up time while he seeks his next point. Teacher noisy, fussy, and bustling.

Mr. Oakeley, Her Majesty's Inspector of Training Colleges, gives in his Report for 1887 the following instructive and interesting summary of some **types of "faulty lessons" and common errors in teaching** as sufficiently frequent, in the lessons taught before him, to deserve notice.

(1) "The **echo lesson**, consisting of statements and questions, *e.g.*, 'Liverpool is the second port in England, what is Liverpool?'

(2) The **lecture lesson**, which very soon exhausts the children's power of attention, and they listen no more.

(3) The **lesson with superfluous introduction**, the latter being either direct but far too long, or indirect by 'eliciting' the subject by a devious and tedious route.

(4) The **desultory lesson**, a number of disconnected and independent points being introduced.

(5) The **discursive lesson**, where the subject is left in order (for instance) to give an unnecessary derivation, flying off in the tangent instead of circling round the central point.

(6) The **lesson where the wrong person is taught,** it being delivered at the inspector.

(7) The **disproportionate lesson,** where a want of due relation magnifies the unimportant and glosses over the essential.

(8) The **disregard of the previous knowledge of the class,** either by a long explanation of what the children know very well, or an assumption of greater knowledge than they possess ; this error is often noticed in lessons on arithmetic.

(9) The **indefinite questioning,** where many answers might be admitted, but the teacher will only accept the particular one which he has in his head, *e.g.,* ' in what is iron found ? ' the answer 'ironstone' was rejected as wrong, and the boy much disconcerted thereby.

(10) The **question that admits of but one obvious answer, for which, however, praise is given,** as in a lesson on 'sound,' after making a noise on some instrument which might have been heard in the street, the teacher praised a boy for saying he had heard it.

(11) The **illicit use of the word elicit,** for which many young teachers have a sort of fetich worship, thus some have sought to 'elicit' the height of a mountain or length of a river of which the children have never heard."

CHAPTER VI.

THE TEACHING DEVICES.

In teaching, as in other matters, a considerable influence has always been exerted by what is called fashion. The view entertained as to what education should be, the tendency of the age, the operation of new ideas and discoveries, the increasing recognition of the rights of children, the success of some eminent worker in a special direction, and many another influence now perhaps scarcely recognisable, have largely affected the way in which the work of teaching has been carried out. Ideals have been given up, and methods have been tried and abandoned, while others have taken their places, though perhaps to be in turn discarded. Change for better or worse has always been going on, and with this great advantage, at least, that stagnation has been prevented.

In no part of the teacher's work probably has the influence of fashion been more clearly discernible than in the **importance attached at different times to the various devices** used in imparting instruction and to the mode of their employment. At one time teaching has been little else than lecture, at another questions have been thought the only important thing; now 'picturing out,' now concrete illustrations, now ellipses, have been the order of the day. Some influence or other has operated to bring this or that method into prominent use, until almost exclusive attention has been devoted to it as the one characteristic of excellence; then reaction has set in and the pendulum has swung in the opposite direction, so that, from excessive employment and over-estimation of its importance, the device has sunk into unmerited neglect. We have passed through a long transition period, in which our views as to the nature of the work to be done have become clearer, and methods more intelligently understood and more skilfully employed in practice; but it cannot be too distinctly recognised that **we are yet a long way off anything of the nature of finality in matters of teaching.**

What is best in method for the teacher now may be very far from perfect in any absolute sense; the main thing for him is to learn to employ in the most skilful and advantageous way *all* the devices at his command, to extend his possibilities as far as he is able, and not to decry or cast aside any device which, though only in special circumstances, will enable him to reach his point in a thoroughly satisfactory way. **Usually it will be found that those who disparage a device most, are those who cannot employ it effectively.** It is foolish to abuse the use of a chisel because it cannot be made to do the work of a plane.

Even where of several satisfactory ways of doing a thing one is superior to the others the latter should not be neglected. They are valuable for the sake of giving variety to the teaching, and afford relief from the monotony of always accomplishing the same purpose in the same way. Further, it should not be forgotten that **different minds are to be reached in very different ways**, and that a mode of treating a point which may be quite successful with some pupils may be ineffectual in the case of others. A wise teacher will bear this in mind and adapt his method accordingly.

The teaching devices are, so to speak, the teacher's tools; and he should be so apt in their use as to be able to employ any one of them just where his knowledge and judgment suggest it will prove most serviceable, so as to enable him to teach quickly, intelligently, and thoroughly. **No one device, be it questioning or what not, is applicable to all cases**, even in the same lesson, and certainly not to all the various lessons which in the course of his instruction the teacher is called upon to give. His intellectual habits and greater skill and experience in certain directions will often predispose him towards the employment, in a greatly preponderating degree, of some special device; but this should not make him exclusive or lead him to become fanciful and eccentric.

I. QUESTIONS.

Questioning is perhaps the most valuable of all the teaching devices, and in one way or another it has been employed from quite early times. It was used, to the exclusion of other methods, by Socrates; and with him it was an instrument of discipline, as well as a means of unfolding information to the mind. Its value in restricting thought to one topic at a time doubtless led to its adoption in the preparation of those who were to be admitted into the early church; and, after the Reformation, to the employment of "catechisms" and "question and answer books." The distinct recognition, however, of questioning as a device of great value in education, and one especially suited to the needs of school teaching, seems to have been the outcome of the impetus given to the development of new methods by such men as Pestalozzi, and does not date further back than the beginning of the present century; while its common adoption in practice, and its employment in a deliberate and dexterous way, may be said, at least in England, to be the growth of the last fifty years.

To question a class may seem, to one ignorant of teaching, a very simple thing to do, but it is not so easy as it looks. **To question and to question efficiently are two very different things**; and so much is involved in the latter that it is really one of the most difficult matters the teacher has to learn. **Few things mark off more clearly the able teacher than really felicitous questioning**; and in many cases the character and success of the work are determined by it. It must not be supposed, however, that any one can become an expert questioner by merely reading about how it is to be done; here, certainly, "all is but lip-wisdom that wants experience." No device should be more persistently and patiently practised; it should not be taken up in a mechanical half-hearted way, and the teacher should not rest content until he can question easily and skilfully in any direction needed.

The skilful employment of questioning depends upon—

(1) **Accurate and full knowledge on the part of the teacher**, so that he may know exactly what to ask for, without having to pause or put several questions where one would do, and may see readily how best to bring out the relative bearing and importance of the various facts.

Want of knowledge is not so common as want of thoroughness. The teacher often knows his facts from one side, but thinks only in the words he has been accustomed to, and finds great difficulty in turning his points round and round so that the children may arrive at clear and full ideas.

(2) **Power to analyse rapidly any subject which needs to be broken up**, and to simplify difficulties by directing attention only to as much at a time as the children are able to grasp.

Want of analytical power is a frequent failing in inexperienced teachers, arising generally from want of practice, coupled with defective observation, and the habit of accepting things without any appreciation of the difference between a general truth and the particulars upon which it is founded, or by which it may be illustrated.

(3) **Knowledge of those under instruction**, their needs, power, and previous acquirements; as well as of the way in which their minds may be best made to work in storing and in giving out information.

The more thoroughly the teacher knows those under his charge, the more judiciously directed and the more exactly suited to the needs of the case the questioning will be, the more easily will he detect the exact nature of any difficulty which the answering shows to exist, and the more effective will be his mode of overcoming it.

(4) **Experience in the use of the device**, so as to be able to question with ease, variety, and certainty, and to recognise intuitively when to stop.

It is astonishing how few young teachers question well, or realise the importance of putting out all their energies to improve in this very essential part of their work. **Purposeless questioning is one of the commonest of faults.**

(5) **Mental quicksightedness and good judgment**, which enable the teacher to rise above a mere mechanical following of rules.

Tact is necessary at all points in deciding what to do and what to leave undone; as well as readiness of resource in seizing upon points of vantage, in "adapting the means to varying and unforeseen circumstances," and in making the most profitable use of whatever may be given by the children in the way of answers.

(6) **Brightness of manner**, and such **strong sympathy with children** that they feel the stimulus and enter into their share of the work with eagerness.

Many a teacher's work is marred by hesitancy and heaviness of manner. Few things damp the natural vivacity of children more effectually: to keep them active and full of ardour is half the battle, and this is especially true in the employment of questioning.

(7) **Power of expression and readiness of speech** so as to exactly suit the questions to those under instruction, and to vary the form of a question on the instant if necessary.

Ease in framing questions in a simple, brief, and direct way tells powerfully towards success in teaching, but it **demands much quickness of appreciation and skill in the use of words.** Teachers frequently fail in these particulars, and the questions are consequently clumsily-worded or round-about, and the exercise becomes slow and uninteresting.

The frequent use of questions is absolutely indispensable in the teaching of the young, and no one who has learned to question well, and has realised the value of the process, will ever be likely to give it up. The fault, in the case of many teachers, is that they do not use questioning nearly enough. At the same time, it must not be forgotten that questioning is not, as some would have us believe, the only device to be used in teaching, and is not to be used on all occasions and for all purposes. We do not cut bread with a razor, or prune trees with a sword, useful as the razor or the sword may be in its own particular way.

Valuable as it is, **questioning cannot cover the whole work of teaching**, and the attempt should not be made to stretch its province in this way. It is **the natural complement of lecture and illustration**, and should not usurp their province; though it may always in teaching be used advantageously in connection with them. In order that the teacher may learn to recognise where questions may be judiciously employed, he must attend carefully to the results of his efforts, as the necessary insight is mainly the outcome of experience.

Many teachers use questioning as though it were an end in itself, and fail to see that it is **easy to over-question to such an extent as to retard the teaching**, and smother up the point to be learned in a cloud of answers. This purposeless questioning has done much to bring the device into disrepute. Directly the object is gained, the teacher should pass on. Anything beyond what is necessary for clear understanding and firm grasp only bewilders the children, and darkens what it should illuminate. Not unfrequently, too, in teaching, a large amount of **time is wasted in endeavouring to question from children ordinary matters of fact**, which they can only learn by being told directly. To question again and again in the hope that the point may be guessed, or arrived at by a process of exhaustion, is to misunderstand completely the use of questioning, and is not only stupid but blameworthy.

<small>The **objections sometimes urged against the use of questions**—that they are a round-about and tedious mode of teaching, that they encourage a habit of rash speculation and guessing, that they discourage children by presenting too many difficulties, and so on—are scarcely worth consideration. They arise usually from a misconception of the real nature of questioning, and apply only to its wrong employment or abuse. The fact that such defects are common, is no argument for the abandonment of the device, but points distinctly to the necessity for learning to question properly.</small>

Questioning properly conducted is neither tedious nor confusing to children. As a matter of fact, they are always pleased to tell what they know; they like to be active, and to have their share in the work recognised. To answer questions is much more engaging work to them than to sit as passive listeners, and they are frequently more keenly alive, and more deeply interested, during questioning than in any other part of the work. As Richter says, " the questions of the teacher find more open ears than his answers." It is the teacher's fault if children feel answering to be a bore or are bewildered by a multiplicity of points of view.

Good questioning is an intellectual exercise valuable to teacher and pupils alike, securing to the latter mental activity and clearness of comprehension, and keeping them constantly in contact with the work. It breaks down the formality of merely didactic teaching, gives a pleasant conversational tone to the lesson by allowing the children their share of the talking, and further, it affords them a valuable training in readiness of thought and speech. In fact, **questioning may be made one of the most powerful instruments at the teacher's disposal,** and this not only from the educative side, but also from the disciplinary point of view. Effectively used it should spur the indolent, stimulate the sluggish, challenge the inattentive, restrain the forward, control the rash, expose the careless, encourage the timid, and help the dull; and at the same time it should fully employ the more intelligent members of the class in such a way as to make available the knowledge of individuals for the benefit of all.

Nevertheless **questioning is not a quick method** albeit a sure one: even where legitimately employed it will usually take more time to question a fact from a child than to tell it to him directly. This has led some teachers, especially in America, to prefer a more direct mode of proceeding. But the longer way round is often the shorter way home. In the one case the child is made to think consecutively, and express his thoughts clearly, and thus his mind is exercised in a way highly conducive to thoroughness; while in the other case he has only to listen, and *this children do very imperfectly*. Even where the teacher's statements are repeated again and again, the pupils are very apt to pick up the words only, and to fail to acquire any real knowledge of the underlying truths.

I. KINDS OF QUESTIONS AND THE PURPOSES FOR WHICH THEY MAY BE USED.—It is quite common, in the treatment of questions from the theoretical standpoint, to find a more or less minute classification of them given, in which certain names are applied to the various groups according to the slightly different objects with which they are employed. Thus at different times, though by no single writer, questions used in particular ways have been called preliminary, tentative, testing, assaying, recapitulatory, examinatory, experimental, catechetical, educative, Socratic, illustrative, instructive, etc. Some of these terms are of course but different names for the same thing; but any such elaborate scheme as is here referred to is of no practical value, in fact it is apt to confuse rather than assist the teacher, and tends to cloud over the essential features which mark the two great and distinct classes, viz. *Testing Questions* and *Training Questions*. These differ in their nature, their aim, and their modes of use; and for the ordinary purposes of teaching it is helpful, and it is sufficient, to consider all questions as belonging to one or other of these groups.

(1) **Testing Questions.** The distinguishing mark of testing questions is that they **seek to secure from the child the re-expression of something he is supposed to have learned**—either during the lesson, or previously—in order that he may know it more securely by having again to direct his attention to it, and in many cases by being made to state it in his own words. They **demand for the most part an effort of memory** in supplying the desiderated ideas; and though the answers may necessitate clear understanding and some exercise of judgment, yet such questions **turn the child's thoughts in a backward direction**, and set him seeking for what is wanted among facts he has already acquired. It must not be supposed that questions of this kind do not require thought in order to answer them well, but they do not involve the discovery of anything new to the child. They should represent the ideas in the most natural order, and as far as possible cement them together in such a way as to form a coherent body of information; so that the recollection of them may be aided by the influence of that "*association*" which acts so powerfully in the case of memory.

Nothing tells the teacher so much about his work, or may be made more helpful in pointing out where his practice needs amendment, than a judicious use of questions. They test the *quality* of the teaching, by showing him how far the facts given have been well learned, and in what manner they are arranged in the child's mind; and they further afford the teacher actual **proof of** the *amount* of information which has been gained.

Testing questions, then, ask directly for facts, and bring them to light again for various reasons and purposes. The chief of these are the following :—

(a) *At the opening of a Lesson* they **enlighten the teacher as to what knowledge the children possess**, either of a related or similar kind, which may be made the groundwork of the teaching; and show him not only how much it will be wise to attempt, but also where best to begin. They **help the children to discriminate between what they know and what they do not know**, and by thus defining the limits of the known enable them to make the passage to the unknown with greater certainty and success. Skilfully used such preliminary questions **turn the minds of the scholars into the right groove**, as it were, prepare them for what the teacher is going to say, and set them fairly on their course. They **open up a subject** by showing in what direction learning is to take place, **arouse a desire for knowledge** by exciting interest and curiosity, and **stimulate the children** by affording a glimpse of possibilities.

(b) *During the teaching* testing questions are in a high degree **useful in directing the thought and effort of the children**, and in banishing any haziness of conception or inaccuracy of apprehension; while at the same time they form the **most serviceable and trustworthy means which the teacher has at his disposal of discovering how far he has been understood**, and the cause of any failure which may become apparent. He is thus able to determine readily where his work has been too difficult, too vague, or too hurried; and is led to see in what direction increased caution is necessary, what gaps leading to error have to be stopped, what weak places need strengthening, or where further explanation or illustration is required. Such questioning also affords him **opportunities of putting misconceptions right** ; and offers him a safe guide, not only as to whether the lesson is level with the child's comprehension, but also as to the speed with which the teaching should be given.

Frequently, *before an explanation* is given, a few questions are valuable to prepare the children's minds for what is coming, to **narrow the mental view** to the single difficulty in hand, to **remove obstacles** to understanding, and to enable the teacher to make out the best mode of approach. Unless the children are thus led to appreciate the nature of the difficulty, and to feel their want, the explanation is apt to be unheeded. "Food proffered where there is no appetite is nauseating; information proffered prematurely is worse than wasted."

(c) *At the end of divisions and at the close of the lesson* questioning may be employed with great advantage for the purpose of **fixing the facts taught,** of **making good the connection between them,** and. of **giving emphasis to the most important points** in such a way as to put the whole into proper perspective. It is astonishing how little of a lesson children remember, even when well taught, and how fragmentary and unsatisfactory their information soon becomes, unless it is tested and impressed again and again by rapid, searching, and vigorous questioning in the way of recapitulation or review. In many cases they fail to grasp the facts even at the time, and the **systematic employment of testing questions** at stated periods in the lesson affords the best means of supplying deficiencies and of correcting errors. It is never safe to assume that children know what they are supposed to have learned until it has been proved by questioning.

The practice of frequently testing knowledge by questioning is valuable both from the point of view of learning and that of discipline. If the child knows he will be required to give back what has been presented to him he is much more likely to listen attentively than where such exercise is omitted. To be of use, however, testing questions must be sufficiently searching to determine how far the child has understood and remembered what has been taught, and must not be confined to asking merely for a. few points which even inattentive children can give.

(2) **Training Questions.**—The chief characteristic of training questions is that they seek to **lead the child to discover new facts for himself by guiding him through easy processes of thought or reasoning.** That which is known is used as material out of which, by suitable treatment, fresh ideas may be developed. The old information is brought to light that new may be evolved out of it, the one leading up to and into the other. Training questions thus **involve a seeking**

forward, not backward. They may be said to put information *into* the mind, and this in such a way as to call out into active exercise such powers as the child possesses. It is therefore easy to see why such questions have been termed **educative** or **instructive**. They are also **illustrative**, inasmuch as they throw light on what is known, and this in a manner calculated to bring out all it implies and show its bearings in relation to other matters. It is also clear that they cannot be used in all cases, but only where an extension of the child's knowledge, or power, can be secured by his own efforts, without direct communication from the teacher.

In the *earliest stage*, before the child can be properly said to be able to reason, training questions should be **mainly directed to the eliciting of relationships** between the facts which are brought before him, these involving for the most part only such matters as can be observed, or interdependence of the simplest kind as cause and effect.

In the *later stages* of a child's school career the great use of training questions is to **present easy steps of analysis until a general conclusion can be reached**; or to elicit inference after inference in a way which will lead to the appreciation of logical connection, and exercise the pupil in continuous thinking. A most valuable training of the intelligence is thus secured; and all investment in intellectual activity will pay a dividend. Nothing encourages a child more than to show him how much he can accomplish for himself, if he puts out his strength in the right way. The conquest of difficulty invigorates him; and what he thus learns has a fuller meaning for him, and is much more permanent, than what he is simply told.

The comparative neglect into which training questioning has fallen is doubtless to be traced to the craving for putting everything into a cut-and-dried form, so that it may be just ready for easy quotation during examination. It is urged, and correctly so far, that training questioning is not an *easy and expeditious* means of storing information; but it is deplorable that this latter should be made almost the only end of education. "The time spent in questioning with a view to train cannot be spent in carting in knowledge with a view to turn it out again on demand."

The success with which training questions are employed will depend largely on the teacher's skill in suggesting lines of search, and in keeping the inquiry within proper limits. He has to stimulate the children to make the necessary effort, and to give help judiciously where a difficulty presents itself too great for them to overcome unaided. **He must be perfectly clear as to what he wishes to arrive at,** and must put his questions in such a way as to lead in the right direction. The most consummate adroitness is sometimes necessary in order to carry out these points efficiently.

SOCRATIC QUESTIONING.—Training questioning and Socratic questioning are often spoken of as though the two terms were in all respects synonymous; and specimens of Socratic dialogue are frequently given, as though by imitation of these a correct method would be arrived at for use with children. But anything like a careful examination of the dialogues given by Plato and Xenophon will surely reveal how completely unlike, in most cases, the method is to proper training questioning *for children*. Commonly the teacher is not even warned that there are **two very distinct phases of the Socratic method—the ironical one, and the developing one.** True, the *principle* of the latter is a correct one in ordinary teaching, aiming as it does at giving birth to mental activity and discovery by the pupil himself; but even here **it is the principle itself which is of value, not the way in which Socrates employed it,** and the teacher who fashioned his teaching upon the model of Socrates' ordinary method of procedure would almost inevitably go wrong.

Socrates had not the spirit of a teacher of little children, and judging from his practice as we know it he would certainly in that capacity have been a failure He usually *drove* his hearers to the conclusion he wanted; it is the business of the teacher of children to *guide and lead*, and they require much more help and direct explanation, interspersed with the questions, than the ordinary Socratic dialogue would give.

Socrates was in almost all cases dealing with adults, and often well-trained and acute adults, so that in many instances he directed his questioning to convict them of ignorance, or to confound them by leading them into difficulties. His method was frequently subtle and artful; and he was not above leading his interlocutor astray in order to entrap him and jeer at his confusion. Now surely all this is wrong in dealing with children. Except in the rare case of a rash and conceited pupil, we do not want to disconcert them by convincing them how ignorant they are, and how valueless is what they know; but rather by our questioning to make clear to them how far they know accurately, and show them what they need. **With children employment of ridicule at all needs careful management, and it should form no regular part of a method of teaching.**

Apart even from the objectionable features mentioned, **the Socratic method, if carried out in detail, is too negative in character, and gives far too little information, to be suitable for common use in schools.** Employed, however, in a kindly way, for a special purpose, and with discrimination by a skilled teacher, the method may be used occasionally with good effect. The dialogue previously quoted from Mr. Thring is an admirable instance of this. Perhaps the most useful point for the teacher to remember about the Socratic dialogue is its *sequence and connection*—the cross examination to bring out the truth without any break in thought.

It will perhaps assist the clear appreciation of the **characteristics** of **testing and training questions** if we map out their chief points of contrast as follows :—

Testing Questions.	Training Questions.
1. Appeal mainly to **memory** and **understanding**.	1. Appeal chiefly to **reasoning** and the conceptive faculty.
2. Turn attention **backwards** upon the known.	2. Direct attention **forwards** to the unknown.
3. Travel over ground already surveyed for the purpose of testing the quality and quantity of the work. **Discover what the pupil has found out.**	3. Carry thought into new regions so as to lead to further acquisition of knowledge. **Find out what the pupil can discover.**
4. **Fix acquired truths** by bringing them again to light, and are thus said to question information *out of* the child's mind.	4. Develop new truths out of what is already known, and are thus said to question information *into* the child's mind.
5. Call upon the child to **pause** and examine what he has acquired.	5. Call upon the child to **progress** by means of what he has acquired.
6. Demand answers depending upon **accurate knowledge** and readiness in finding and expressing it.	6. Demand answers depending upon **insight** and the power of the children to think connectedly.
7. May be employed in connection with all subjects.	7. Are limited in application mainly to matters which can be reasoned out.
8. **Enlighten the teacher** as to the nature of his success and the value of his method.	8. **Enlighten the children** as to the bearing and development of what they know.

To sum up, we may say that the CHIEF PURPOSES FOR WHICH QUESTIONS MAY BE PROFITABLY EMPLOYED in teaching are the following :—

(1) **To carry on the lesson and develop the information** by appealing to the children's reason, previous experience, or present observation. The questioning should give point and meaning to what is already known, and open up a view of the details which probably has not before attracted attention.

(2) **To test the clearness and accuracy of information** supposed to have been gained, either from previous work, or as a result of the teaching given in the lesson, and so to enable the teacher to adapt his procedure exactly to the requirements of the case.

(3) **To train the children** by guiding them through easy processes of observation, thought, or conception; as well as to afford them a

useful exercise in rapidity of apprehension, and in ready expression of their ideas with neatness, exactness, and force.

(4) **To stimulate the children** to use to the utmost such power as they possess ; **to awaken curiosity** as to coming knowledge, so that they may have a desire to know more ; and to **increase interest** in the work by calling upon them to take their proper share in it.

(5) **To focus the attention and intellectual effort upon one point at a time,** and so help the children by directing the mental gaze and excluding the consideration of everything but the matter in hand.

(6) **To fix the ideas which have been presented** to the child by causing them to be again brought into conscious existence in varied form and definite order—through the agency of repetition, recapitulation, or review—a sufficient number of times to secure permanency.

(7) **To bring out the perspective of facts** by dwelling most forcibly upon the more essential matters, and to assist the children in realising the logical connection and relationship of the ideas.

(8) **Occasionally to vary the method of teaching,** and prevent the deadening effect of sameness of treatment ; or possibly to inspirit a flagging class, and give brightness, pleasantness, and "go" to the lesson.

II. FORMS AND QUALITIES OF QUESTIONS, WITH SUGGESTIONS AS TO THEIR USE.—Questions, as applied to children in teaching, should, as we have seen, turn the mind's energy in one direction, and thus, by narrowing the range of effort, put the pupil in the best position for performing his part in the lesson. They should guide him in his search for new facts, and exact of him in a reasonable way the reproduction of that which he has learned. Hence questions should be—

(1) *Pointed and direct.*—A very common defect in questions is their want of definiteness as to what is required. They should **ask exactly for what is needed,** and nothing but that. Thus, as far as possible, a question should **admit of only one answer,** and though the teacher may not always be able to reach this standard it should be aimed at. Vagueness or ambiguity in the questions is a great enemy to anything like clear and exact thought on the part of the child. When it is possible for him to give several answers, each of which is

a correct reply to the question, he is apt to be confused by the possibilities open to him; and, feeling that the teacher only wants one reply, he either hazards a guess, or lets the opportunity pass in trying to decide what answer to give.

All such questions as "What is the river Severn like?" "What sort of story is the one you have been reading?" "What do they do in quarries?" "What should you say Gibraltar is made of?" "What do we eat to keep us alive?" are to be carefully avoided. They simply diffuse instead of concentrating the child's attention, and serve no useful purpose whatever.

Nor must the questions be allowed to wander from the subject, as they are very apt to do unless the teacher has his lesson well in hand, and frames his inquiries to elicit just what he wants. **Irrelevant questioning is oftener the result of indolence than of lack of skill.** Something more is required in teaching than the loose and indirect form of questioning commonly employed in ordinary conversation, although there should be the same freedom and ease. If the teacher asks questions without knowing where he is going, he will soon find both himself and his children adrift, and no real progress being made.

Every question should be of value as a real part of the teaching, and have some distinct bearing and influence on the lesson. Sometimes a number of questions are asked without order, and in an aimless drifting sort of way, merely to occupy time, or because the teacher feels that some questions ought to be asked. They begin anywhere and lead nowhere. The utter worthlessness of such questioning has been already referred to.

(2) *Clear as to meaning and simply worded.*—If the child is to grasp the bearing of a question readily, it must be **unequivocal in meaning**, and sufficiently simple both in thought and language. The **ideas must be well within the child's comprehension**; and so long as clearness is secured, **the shorter the question the better.** In no part of his work is it more worth the teacher's while to be economical of words; and those used must be such as the child is accustomed to, so that whether the answer is forthcoming or not there is no doubt in his mind as to what is asked. There must be **no useless verbiage in the way of introductory phrases,** no round-about and consequently lengthy statements, and no unnecessary elaboration of idea. It is impossible to get children to think properly when their energies are consumed in endeavouring to unravel the complexity of the question,

or to discover its import. **The proper choice of words in asking a question is a point deserving of much attention.** Several short questions are better than one long one ; and if the teacher finds that he has in his question taken too great a step at once, or has employed words too difficult for the children to understand—as he may easily do, especially in using technical terms—it is better for him to break up his question into easier ones, or to put it in another form, than to fill in the answer himself and pass on.-

All such round-about ways of beginning a question as " Now, my good children . . ." "I shall be glad if you can tell me . . . ," " Now, if you try I am sure you will be able to say . . . ," etc., are to be avoided, not only as a waste of time, but as tending to confuse the child by taking his attention from the point of the question.

Those who are unaccustomed to talk to children often find great difficulty in framing suitable and simple questions, and sometimes fall into ludicrous mistakes. No *teacher* would ever think of asking such a question as the following : " Will you be good enough to tell me, if you happen to remember from what you have been told or from what you have read, under what circumstances mercury placed in a long tube, closed at the upper end, rises or falls?" Such a question errs in many ways.

A question may be clear as to meaning, and yet framed in such a clumsy or slipshod way as to be objectionable, especially so when addressed to children. A faulty form, of very frequent occurrence in teaching, is one in which what should be a statement, or an ellipsis, is changed into a question by the addition of some word or phrase that ought in most cases to have come first. The words usually employed for this purpose are *what, when, where, how,* and the like.

For instance : " Falstaff was a very what?" " The man we spoke of went where ? " " Botany is the science of what ? " " He ascended which of the two mountains ? "

Another rather common error is for the teacher, either from carelessness or from not having thought out his lesson properly, to begin a question and then to alter the wording, it may be several times : *e.g.* " What is the function of —— what purpose do the leaves serve, of what use are they to the plant?" If a question has been begun wrongly, it is better to abandon it altogether than to patch and alter it until the children are confused.

Sometimes again the mistake is made of welding into one two questions which ought to have been put separately, so that the children are in doubt as to which to answer first, and hence some say one thing some another.

"What part of speech is the word *sailed*, which word does it tell us something about?" "Who won the battle of Hastings, was it really fought at Hastings?" "Where does the river Thames rise, has it more than one source?" are instances, the climax of absurdity being reached in such forms as—"Who dragged whom round the walls of what city, and why?"

(3) *Sufficiently difficult to necessitate effort.*—Questions which may be answered without any exercise of mind are not only valueless, but give rise to bad habits, and are apt to delude both the teacher and the children as to the amount learned. At the best they give undue prominence to those who are merely smart and quick, and consequently discourage the thoughtful; while they are **almost certain to lead to rash guessing, carelessness, inattention, and superficiality.** There are various types of these objectionable questions.

In some cases the worthlessness of the question arises from the fact that it asks for information which has been given as a statement the moment before: as, "The Black Forest contains a great many fir-trees. What does the Black Forest contain?" It is very easy for a teacher to get into a habit of using these "**echo questions**," as they have been termed.

Another type of questions, which should be very rarely if ever employed in teaching, are those called "**leading questions.**" These merely ask for the assent of the pupil to something said by the teacher, or in some way or other suggest what is required.

The clue to the answer may be conveyed to the pupil by the **form** of the question, by the **emphasis** laid, consciously or unconsciously, upon some particular word or phrase, by **inflection of the voice**, or, it may be, by some significant **gesture**, or the **expression** of the face. It is astonishing how quick children are in catching any suggestion from one they know, however unintentional it may be, and hence they may appear to answer well when questioned in this way while they really know little or nothing of the subject about which they are being asked. Apart even from any suggestion whatever, or fault in the questioning, they will answer a teacher to whom they are accustomed much more readily than when interrogated by a person whose manner and mode of questioning are quite strange to them.

Such questions as—"Bricks are made of clay, are they not?" "Plants *grow*, what is the difference between a plant and a stone?" "Is not Snowdon a high mountain?" "Does the Ganges enter the ocean by one mouth or by *many channels*?" demand nothing from the child but a little attention.

The following example of the "**method of stupefying mind**" by this wrong questioning is given by Mr. D. P. Page.

"*Charles*, (*Reads.*) A man being asked how many sheep he had, said that he had them in two pastures; in one pasture he had eight; that three-fourths of these were just one-third of what he had in the other. How many were there in the other?

"*Teacher.* Well, Charles, you must first get one-fourth of eight, must you not?
"*Charles.* Yes, sir.
"*Teacher.* Well, one-fourth of eight is two, isn't it?
"*Charles.* Yes, sir; one-fourth of eight is two.
"*Teacher.* Well, then, three-fourths will be three times two, won't it?
"*Charles.* Yes, sir.
"*Teacher.* Well, three times two are six, eh?
"*Charles.* Yes, sir.
"*Teacher.* Very well, (a pause). Now the book says that this six is just one-third of what he had in the other pasture, don't it?
"*Charles.* Yes, sir.
"*Teacher.* Then if six is one-third, three-thirds will be three times six, won't it?
"*Charles.* Yes, sir.
"*Teacher.* And three times six are eighteen, ain't it?
"*Charles.* Yes, sir.
"*Teacher.* Then he had eighteen sheep in the other pasture, had he?
"*Charles.* Yes, sir."

It is customary to condemn the use in teaching of all **questions which require only yes! or no! for answer**; but this general condemnation is too sweeping. Much depends upon whether the question calls for a decision between two alternatives, or does not; the real point is, not whether the answer is "yes" or "no" but whether the question appeals to the child in a useful manner. If, as is commonly the case, questions of this kind are put in such a way that there is practically no doubt as to the nature of the reply expected, and even the most thoughtless can answer them, then by all means they should be avoided by the teacher. Many cases, however, arise in teaching, where a question may only demand "yes" or "no" but to decide correctly which of the two necessitates an exercise of judgment, and it may be a difficult one, on the part of the pupil. There seems to be no reason why such questions should not be used, if judiciously employed, and if guessing is discouraged by frequently following up the reply with other questions respecting the grounds upon which the answer is based.

Sometimes a difficult question of the "yes or no" form is used merely to start an inquiry, or to direct attention to and excite an interest in the next point to be considered. The confirmation of either of the possible replies is deferred for the time, and the matter decided by eliciting the facts which justify the one conclusion rather than the other, or by an appeal to experiment, or possibly by the association of both these plans. For instance, the teacher may have been explaining about the pressure of the air in all directions, and asks, "If I fill a glass full of water, place a card over the mouth of the glass and turn it upside down, will the water run out?" He listens to the expressions of opinion but does not definitely accept either one view or the other, and then proceeds to question those who take either side as to why they believe themselves to be correct. The children being now thoroughly interested in the result, and fully prepared for the experiment, the teacher performs it and settles the point. In this way the experiment is much more clearly understood and remembered than if the result had been merely foretold by the teacher. The thoughtful members of the class are rewarded by the satisfaction of being right, and the rash or careless are taught a useful lesson as to the necessity for cautious judgment, while both are stimulated to further effort.

When children have been taught certain facts, and the teacher needs to **gather up the ideas rapidly in order to pass to some further truth**, the occasional use of "yes or no" questions, mixed with others of easy form, is often justifiable as an expeditious method of marshalling his points in order that their bearing may be made out. It is not *thought*, so much as *rapid review*, which is here wanted. Ordinary questioning would be too slow, while the plan just mentioned is often to be preferred to direct address as giving more variety and brightness to the work.

_{Something might also be said for the occasional use of questions demanding "yes" or "no" with infants, where much encouragement is often necessary to get answers given at all, and those must be of the simplest possible character.}

Allied to the forms discussed above are the **questions which contain their own answers**, and simply offer a choice between two things, as—"Is iron a hard or a soft metal?" "Is this green or blue?" "Is the sun a hot or a cold body?" As a rule, questions of this kind should certainly be shunned; for, apart from the fact that they involve no intellectual effort, **no form of question is so likely to lead to guessing.** Even if nothing in the question, or in the mode of putting it, suggests what is wanted, the child knows he will be able to give the correct answer at a second try, at most, and therefore makes a shot at it.

It is often amusing to watch a class questioned in this way. The moment the teacher has pronounced one of the possible replies wrong, out go the hands of those on the watch for such a chance ; and, though they may know absolutely nothing about the subject, they plume themselves on having answered the question. Where such a method of questioning is common many of the children will make no effort themselves, and watch again and again for the second opportunity.

(4) *Such as not to demand answers of greater length or hardness than children can be expected to give.*—It is not at all uncommon to find teachers, who know little of children and are unable to look at things from their point of view, asking questions which are far beyond the powers of those interrogated, and at times even such as would tax the powers of a trained mind to answer correctly. The difficulty to the pupil may arise from a variety of causes.

In some instances the question includes so much as completely to bewilder the child, even when the details are within his knowledge, and he would be able to give them correctly if asked for one at a time. He is unable to frame properly so long a statement as is required ; he finds great difficulty even in discovering where to begin, and being unable to think continuously without help he is pretty certain to give a very incomplete reply, or to flounder his way through a sentence or two and break down.

"How is a glacier formed?" "Why does a stick appear bent in water?" "What becomes of a shower of rain?" "What occurred when Cæsar came to Britain?" "What were the circumstances in which William the Conqueror met his death?" are examples of this kind of question.

Sometimes the mistake is made of **asking for information which the children cannot reasonably be expected to give.** In many cases of this kind the facts asked for are such as it is the purpose of the lesson to teach ; and, although they have not been touched upon in any way by the teacher, he puts the questions in the hope of their being answered from previous knowledge. He is misled by taking his own past experience for that of the children, and fails to see that what may have been for a long time perfectly familiar to him, or brought under his notice almost daily, may, from the different character of their surroundings, be quite unknown to them. Not only are such questions useless, but, if at all frequent, **the failure to answer them tends to relax effort and to discourage the children,** while the long pauses which are likely to occur take all the spirit out of the lesson.

<small>It is easy to fall into the error described in the case of **terms not generally current,** but common enough in certain districts. The following actually occurred. A teacher was giving a lesson on the *Manufacture of a Tea-cup and Saucer,* and after describing the various materials and the way in which they are ground and mixed, he said, "Now what is the white liquid made of all these things called?" As no hand was raised he proceeded, "Well, surely some of you can tell me that; what is the liquid called? Come, do think." Perhaps, in the district from which the teacher came, most boys would have been able to give the reply, but no amount of thought would have enabled those in front of him to do so.</small>

Another rather common case of demanding too much from the pupil is asking questions which call upon him to give a definition, when nothing in the lesson has led up to it. It may seem an easy thing to answer such questions as "What is an animal?" "What is salt?" "What is a plant?" and so on. No doubt the child knows the things when he sees them, but to give an adequate answer in cases like these is a matter of considerable difficulty. He has not only to settle upon the necessary distinguishing characteristics, but also to find the words whereby to express them in a neat and correct form; and this he ought not to be expected to do until he has been prepared for it by the foregoing teaching. Even then it is generally better to direct attention to each point in turn by a *series* of questions, and to work up to the complete statement as the final step. When a child is asked point blank for a definition he has not been taught, all he generally does is to give some obvious quality and omit the rest, or to mention an instance or an illustration. For example, a child asked "What is sin?" is pretty certain to give some such reply as "stealing," "using bad language," "telling a lie," "being cruel," etc.

If, when the teacher is about to ask for a definition, he would think what answer he himself would give, the question would probably be at once changed in form, or broken up into several; and, at least, he would be saved from looking upon the children as stupid on account of their faulty replies. Even where the definition is correctly approached, very unnecessary anxiety is often shown to set forth simple things in a cut-and-dried formula, when really all that the child needs is clear ideas.

The story is told that a gentleman once asked a class, "What is a window?" and, after rejecting such answers as, "A hole in the wall to let in the light," complained of the want of intelligence shown by the children. On being requested to give the reply he expected, he hesitated, and then said: "A window is an aperture. . . . Everybody knows what a window is." Exactly, but it is not every one who can express such knowledge properly in words.

In dealing with young children the mistake is sometimes made of asking questions which demand that a process of reasoning shall be gone through before the answer can be arrived at. Until the child's mind has been sufficiently developed it is impossible for him to give such a reply as is needed. He has first to be taught how to reason by placing before him two familiar things, directing attention to each in turn, then taking them in connection, and finally establishing a relation between them. Questions are here of the greatest use, but they must be of the simplest description; and even when these early exercises can be managed with some success, a conclusion should be reached through a *series* of questions, not demanded as a single effort until the child can reason readily for himself.

Some teachers are very fond of **asking a simple question requiring a decision, and then following it up with—Why?** This is in many cases a more difficult exercise than is commonly recognised, and needs to be used with a good deal of discrimination. It may often be profitably employed in the case of elder children; but it should be borne in mind that to give reasons for a conclusion is generally more difficult than to arrive at a correct inference, and that consequently the question *Why?* should be sparingly used with little ones. A child will often, by a kind of instinctive judgment, arrive at the right answer, when he is quite unable to go back and state the grounds upon which he has based his reply.

Occasional questions beyond the power of the majority of the children may be used with advantage, in order to give the brighter members of the class a chance of putting out their strength, and to prevent them from growing listless and inattentive. Care must be exercised, however, not to take up too much time with the answers to such questions.

Sometimes, too, **a hard question at the close of a lesson may be left for the children to ponder over** and try to find out the answer for themselves. The point may easily be taken up again when the next lesson of the kind is given.

(5) *Varied in form and difficulty.*—The teacher should be careful not to cast all his questions in the same mould or even to confine them to certain set patterns. Children soon become accustomed to a particular form of questioning, and this leads them to answer to a certain extent mechanically; while the work under such circumstances is liable to grow tedious and uninteresting from the want of relief. Besides, to frame all questions according to a few fixed models, no matter how correct these may be, shows such poverty of resource and want of skill in the use of language as seriously to detract from the value of the teaching.

The words used in putting a question upon a fact should not, as a rule, be those which have been used in teaching it.

Want of variety in the questioning is pretty certain to lead to a similar defect in the answering, and the pupil loses the benefit which comes from repeatedly having to express his knowledge in some new way. Even when the same fact has to be asked for several times during the course of a lesson—as occurs again and again in practice—it is a mistake to use the same words on each occasion; for when the child recognises that the question has been previously put he turns his mind back to find the answer he gave before, whereas a new setting of the question would have led to an independent effort to find the right idea.

When, again, a **prepared passage from a book** has to be examined upon, and the remembrance of the ideas or contained facts is alone important, **the words of the text should be avoided in framing the questions,** and as far as possible, the child should also be induced to express the answers in his own way. Unless this is done the teacher cannot be certain that the child *knows*; he may give the correct answer so far as *words* are concerned, but have no corresponding *ideas*.

The wise teacher will vary the form and wording of his questions as much as possible; and if at first he finds himself unable to accomplish all he could wish in this matter, a little earnest practice will soon remove most of the difficulty. More teachers fail in this and in other respects from not knowing what to aim at, or from not taking sufficient pains to learn, than from any **lack of ability.**

In employing questions for securing the repetition of some important point, it is often necessary to transform a question again

and again that the matter may be looked at from all sides, although, really, the information involved is the same in each case.

<small>Thus, supposing the children to have been taught that the atmospheric pressure under ordinary conditions is about 15 lbs. per square inch, the fact may be fixed directly by having the statement repeated several times, or better, by questioning somewhat as follows: "What is the amount of the pressure of the atmosphere on a square inch?" "Of what did we say 15 lbs. was a measure?" "If I take a square inch of the surface of this table what is the weight of the air upon it?" "What does 15 lbs. per square inch represent with respect to the atmosphere?"</small>

With very young children this repeated asking for information in a changed form is often most valuable; the reiteration not only deepens the impression made, and so strengthens remembrance, but helps to secure that the pupils understand the fact brought forward, by giving them time to completely realise what it means.

<small>The following is a very simple instance: "What was the name of Abraham's son?" "Who was Isaac's father?" "What relation was Isaac to Abraham?" "What relation was Abraham to Isaac?"</small>

In class-teaching it is not possible to make every question suitable for every child, as though he alone had to be considered; but, in any continuous use of questions, they should be so **varied in difficulty** that, while the larger number of them ought certainly to afford useful exercise for the average members of the class, others are calculated more particularly to meet the needs of the duller or of the brighter children.

As to whether the questioning is to be considered difficult or not will depend upon the circumstances. It is a relative matter, not an absolute one. The **chief considerations to be kept in mind in estimating the difficulty of questions** are the following :—

(a) The experience, knowledge, and power of apprehension of the children.
(b) The mode in which the questions are worded.
(c) The nature of the mental exercise involved in giving the answers—*e.g.* observation, recollection, judgment, reasoning.
(d) The extent to which it is assumed that the child can express his thoughts fluently in suitable language.
(e) The strangeness or otherwise of the subject, and of the terms employed in connection with it.

(*f*) The way in which the questions are connected in series, the difficulty of thinking being lessened where each question leads the mind in the direction of the next.

(*g*) The state of the class—that is, whether the children are fresh to their work, or tired owing to previous exercises, physical conditions, or any other cause.

(6) *Connected in series.*—The value of connecting information and of associating ideas of a like kind—of packing them away as it were in the right place in the mind—has been touched upon already. **To systematise knowledge in this way for the child, and link together individual items of information so that they have a combined meaning, is a matter of the most vital importance in teaching,** and to secure its accomplishment no device may be more beneficially and successfully employed than questioning.

It is not difficult, therefore, to see how much depends upon the **proper sequence and connection of the questions,** and to recognise that, in putting them, care should be always taken to keep to some distinct line of thought. Each question should be based upon, or at least related to, the preceding answer, so that not only may the child be assisted in associating properly the various points brought before him, but, by having his attention turned in a definite direction, he may the more readily pass from what he has already acquired to that which he has yet to learn.

Rambling or disjointed questioning prevents continuous thinking on the part of the child, and often leaves him confounded, not because the question is beyond his power or knowledge, if it had been properly led up to, but on account of the broken and zigzag course pursued by the teacher.

Some teachers have a most unfortunate method of trying to avoid a pause, if the next point does not occur to them, or they are at a loss for a word. This is to ask a question abruptly about something dealt with earlier in the lesson, so that, while the children are expecting to go forward, they are suddenly called upon to turn their attention to some matter completely dissociated from that under consideration.

Examination questions are naturally more discursive than those used during the teaching; but even here there should be a definite order in which the points are again brought under the notice of the child, and the questions must be kept within the area covered by the previous teaching.

The steps from one question to another must be such as the children can take; and it is necessary for the teacher to be on the watch at all points that he may make sure he is being intelligently followed. Unless he is cautious in this respect the connection between the ideas is likely to exist only in his own mind, and while the questions may appear to him to be consecutive and fitly framed to develop the lesson, the pupils, unable to take such long leaps, may be in a state of perplexity so far as any relationship between the various facts is concerned. In such circumstances the teacher is very liable to credit to the stupidity of the children, rather than to the imperfection of his own questioning, their failure to grasp what is being taught.

(7) *Put in an engaging way.*—The success with which questioning is conducted so as to be made attractive to children depends very much upon the way in which the questions are asked. Few influences are more stimulative to children than a cheerful, appreciative, and sympathetic manner on the part of the teacher; and this is especially the case in questioning. The exercise should be, **as far as possible, like a pleasant animated conversation**, and entirely free from the stiff formalism which sometimes characterises it. Vivacity and pleasantness put the pupils on good terms with their work, arouse in them a desire to do their best, and prevent their flagging or becoming wearied of answering so soon as they otherwise would.

Any means which will give zest and animation to the questioning, and banish drowsiness and indisposition to effort, is worth consideration; but at the same time the teacher must not put on a melodramatic air and *act* his part. · The more perfectly easy and natural he is the better. Some teachers make the mistake of being **fussy and bustling**, which is tiresome and disconcerting; others of being **stilted and magisterial**, which is chilling and depressing; a few of being **too exacting**, and correcting mistakes in a harsh snappish way, which renders the children afraid to answer, and eventually silences them.

Questions should be asked in a brisk spirited way, without hesitation, but at the same time without hurry. If clearly given, they should not be repeated again and again, as is often done, in the teacher's anxiety to obtain answers quickly. This repetition of the question, frequently with the added behest to think, defeats its own purpose, and so far from assisting the child, simply embarrasses him.

To put the questions in a slow, dull, or drawling way, as though the teacher himself found the work tedious, and, it may be, with long pauses while he considers what he shall ask next, naturally damps out interest in answering, and rapidly leads to weariness and inattention.

The tone of voice should be bright and encouraging, and the words should be given with sufficient deliberation and force for every child to hear with ease. When very considerable effort is necessary to catch the words of the question, this is so much energy withdrawn from the answering.

(8) *Well distributed over both the lesson and the class.*—The employment of questioning is no exception to the rule that a method should not be used so exclusively and persistently as to weary the children by the monotony of the exercise; but, this being kept in mind, questions may with advantage be introduced at any point, and into any subject where they can be made to accomplish effectively and quickly what is required. Questioning should be so woven into the teaching that, while continually employed as an auxiliary to other devices, its more deliberate and specific use as a distinct method should be judiciously distributed over the lesson.

It is sometimes said that nothing should be told to a child which it is possible for him, with the aid of questioning, to discover. This is an over-statement of the case which is calculated to do more harm than good, and to destroy that faith in the value of the device properly employed which every teacher should have. Where the discovery cannot be made without unreasonable difficulty, or an extravagant expenditure of time, questioning should be abandoned for some method less exacting and more direct. The point for consideration is not whether the information can be arrived at by the greatest exercise of ingenuity, and after a large number of attempts, but whether questioning is the best means, all things considered, for fixing the facts with certainty and intelligence in the minds of the children.

The best **general way of asking a question** is to address the whole class, on the understanding that all who can answer are to hold up one hand, and then to select one or more pupils to give the reply. Much good judgment may be shown in the way this selection is made. If the question is an easy one, it may well be answered by the less able members of the class; but if it is fairly difficult it is, *as a rule*, better to allow some child to answer who may reasonably be expected to do so correctly. Those, however, who show any sign of inattention should be frequently challenged, and in some cases called upon to repeat the question. The main thing is to keep the lesson "going," and to secure that every child shall be on the alert by giving him his due share in the work. Each one should feel that he is liable to be called upon at any moment, and that directly he begins to gaze about, or in any way to show that he is not properly attending to what is being said, he is almost certain to be chosen by the teacher to give an answer. The stolid look and the dull eye soon betray to the watchful teacher when the child is not learning.

The greater ease and quickness with which answers may be obtained from the brighter children is a great temptation to the teacher to overlook the duller and more ignorant ones during questioning. He should bear this carefully in mind, in order that the latter may receive their full share of attention; but, in his anxiety to do the best that is possible for such children, he must not fall into the opposite error of directing to them a greater proportion of the questions than is their due, and so of neglecting the needs of those who are able to move more rapidly. Very occasionally, and in special circumstances, it is a good plan, for the sake of variety, to go round the class with a series of questions, calling upon each boy in turn to answer one; this plan, however, should not be generally adopted.

If properly treated children are easily interested, and soon become inquisitive about any subject which is made attractive to them. When quite at their ease, and in sympathy with the teacher, it is therefore perfectly natural for them to ask questions; so much so that a child has been called "an animated interrogation point." This **questioning of the teacher by the children**, if kept within proper limits, is a thing to be distinctly encouraged, especially with little ones; and if managed at all skilfully will not only banish all idea of lesson drudgery from the minds of the children, but also afford the teacher just the opportunities he wants for putting his own questions in return. In fact, in many cases, by a series of well-directed questions the child may be made, greatly to his satisfaction, to find the answer to his own question. Any honest seeking for further information, or statement of a real difficulty, should be listened to patiently, and answered in the most fitting way which the teacher's knowledge and the circumstances allow. A little management on his part will soon ensure that the questions asked are kept within the limits of the subject in hand, and are not put merely for the sake of asking. Any inquiry which is useful in itself but which has no direct bearing on the lesson may, if more than a word or two are required, be easily answered at some more suitable opportunity.

Sometimes it is useful, as a relief from routine work, to allow children to question one another. One boy stands up and the others ask him any question they please on the lesson, or the subject selected, the teacher indicating the order in which this is to be done. Directly the one questioned fails to reply correctly, the questioner, after giving the right answer, takes his place, until he in turn is deposed, and so on. Children in such circumstances often display great acuteness and ingenuity in framing questions, and the exercise affords a useful training in smartness and readiness of reply; while at the same time it encourages confidence and independence of view. It almost always excites the keenest interest, and the children are generally refreshed by it; the questioning, however, is naturally of too desultory a character to be employed otherwise than as a relaxation.

III. THE QUALITIES AND TREATMENT OF ANSWERS.—If the child is to gain all the benefit which should result from his being questioned correctly it is **quite as important for the teacher to attend to the answers given as to the mode of questioning.** This is not always recognised, at least in practice, the teacher apparently feeling that if the question has been properly put the faultiness of the replies is entirely due to the children. **The nature, however, of the answering will be pretty much what the teacher makes it**; and not only will it be impossible often for him to frame his questions in the most suitable way unless the answers are properly considered, but neglect on his part in this matter will tell most prejudicially upon the intellectual habits and training of the children. If on the other hand they see that no carelessness is ever passed over, and that the teacher will not rest content with anything less than the best they can give, they naturally soon learn to answer, at least passably, in the way required. **Questioning and answering act and react upon one another,** and neither is likely to be what it should be when the teacher is content with a low standard in the other.

(1) *Qualities of good answering.* The chief things to be aimed at in good answering are, first, **readiness in finding the right ideas**, and, second, **aptness in putting them into the best form of words** whereby they may be made clear to others. In very many cases it is evident that the child knows what is asked of him, but is unable, from the limited nature of his vocabulary and his defective experience in the use of words, to state exactly what he means. To answer a question well in all respects is often far from an easy matter; and it is not to be expected, even with the most careful handling, that all the answers of children can be made to come up to a theoretically satisfactory standard. Much, nevertheless, may be done in this respect if the teacher is alive to what should be required, and gives in a kindly and judicious manner such help as is needed.

The way in which the teacher deals with the answers given will, if he adopts the right course, soon make evident to the children what they should aim at, and will encourage them to take pains in stating properly what they know.

Good answers should be :—

(a) **Exact as far as they go**—showing that the pupil recognises the point of the question, and endeavours to give clearly and precisely what he believes to be wanted. Truth and error are often strangely mixed in the answers of children, but if there is no doubt as to which is which, such replies are easily dealt with. The greater difficulty, however, is the haziness of conception, and consequent vagueness of answering, which results from half-formed ideas and leaves it uncertain to what extent the child is right or wrong in what he says. This indefiniteness the teacher should do his best to banish.

(b) **Complete.** The answer should be expressed with sufficient fulness to be intelligible to the class, and should give all that the question asks, but nothing else. Unless the teacher is heedful in this matter, the child, either from indolence or carelessness, will in many cases merely hint at the reply instead of stating it, flinging in a word or two and leaving the rest to be imagined. It may be evident that his knowledge is not at fault; that is not enough, he must be made to state what he has to say with as much completeness as he is capable of.

Partial answers, if correct as far as they go and properly expressed, have frequently to be accepted; and in such cases the missing information should be supplied by other pupils until the complete statement is arrived at. But, generally speaking, when this has been done, the pupil first called upon should be made to give the full reply.

It is **sometimes urged that all answers should be sentences**, single words or short phrases not being allowed. In answering questions *in writing* this no doubt should be adhered to, but whether it is wise to insist upon it *in teaching* will depend almost entirely upon the nature of the questions. There are, of course, many cases—more particularly with elder children, and where thought is appealed to rather than memory—in which nothing short of a complete reply should be accepted; but to compel children always to give answers so expressed as to be intelligible without the question, especially where the object is merely to test the remembrance of certain facts, would destroy the spirit of the exercise and render it slow, formal, and tedious. Good as the discipline referred to may be in the abstract, practical needs here often outweigh theoretical considerations, and no hard and fast rule should be adhered to in the matter. After all it is really a question of good judgment on the part of the teacher.

(*c*) **Correctly, concisely, and simply expressed.** When answering is properly managed it is not only a training in exactness of thought, but also affords valuable exercise in the use of language; and further, gives children confidence and ease in putting their thoughts before others. What is required should be stated directly, in grammatically correct form, and in such a way that the substance of the reply may be readily grasped by all the members of the class. **Clearness of meaning and neatness of expression are features in answering which it is worth while to take a great deal of trouble to secure.** And this not so much from the increased excellence of the answer—though that is an important thing in itself—as from the thought and judgment which the qualities just mentioned involve before the reply can be fully given.

Of course when testing questions are used more especially for the purpose of recapitulation, the answers should be known, and, as they usually demand only few words, rapidity of reply in most cases may be reasonably expected; but, in answering more difficult questions, if the child is to be thoughtful, and consider how best he may put into words what he has to say, he must not be hurried or distracted by his surroundings. **Hurry lies at the root of many defects in learning; and to it the blunders and badly expressed replies of children are due in a far larger measure than is commonly realised.** It is one of the defects of class questioning that the competitive element—useful as it is in other ways—tends to encourage hasty answering. The pupil, naturally eager not to be behind his neighbours, does not give himself time to be certain and exact; and consequently his answers, even when within his knowledge and power, are very apt to be rambling and clumsy, if not unintelligible.

For the teacher to pause long enough before accepting a reply to give time for thought is useful; but this only partially meets the case, for the child, constrained by seeing other hands go up, puts out his own the moment anything like an answer occurs to him; and no matter how much time is given after this, his attention is fixed upon the teacher, and he does not reconsider or try to amend his first rough draft of a reply. Something may also be effected in the way of cure by commending deserving answers from the more steady and cautious children, and by refusing to accept ill-considered and badly-worded replies. These the answerers may well be compelled to re-express, whenever it can be done without unduly delaying the teaching.

Simplicity of wording is a thing to be distinctly encouraged. Sometimes from love of display, a pupil will use big words or pretentious phrases, which, in all likelihood, he very imperfectly understands. Such attempts should meet with no favour from the teacher, and occasionally it may be well to point out how much better the answer would have been if given in a simpler form.

Children have to take in information through the teacher's words; they should be encouraged to give it back again in their own. **The re-expression of information in their own terms is the best test of understanding,** and often throws light upon the way in which they most naturally regard things. Except where the word-form is important—as in a quotation, definition, or the statement of a scientific law—the child should feel, from the way in which the teacher accepts the answers, that originality of wording is looked upon by him as an additional excellence to correctness of idea.

(*d*) **Prompt.** The rapidity with which answers should be accepted, as we have just seen, will depend upon the nature of the questions. So long as the replies are satisfactory, the more promptly they are given the better. **Smartness and interest generally go together and stimulate the child to further effort.** The welfare of the class as a whole, however, must not be sacrificed to the quickness of a few. **Reasonable time must be given for the children to collect their ideas and put them in order;** but, this being granted, there must be no sluggishness or loitering in giving the answer, no bungling hesitation and hazarding of guesses, and no looking to one another for some suggestion to put them on the right track.

In answering upon what has been previously given in the lesson **the readiness with which the learners answer is generally an indication as to how far the teaching has been grasped with success.**

(*e*) **Distinctly given**—in the natural tone of voice and with sufficient deliberation and clearness to be heard without effort by all concerned. The teacher has to avoid, on the one hand, letting the answers be shouted out to the annoyance of neighbouring classes and the general increase of noise ; and, on the other, allowing the children to give their replies in such an indistinct and mumbling way that only a word here and there can be caught.

(2) *Qualities of bad answering.* In addition to the several faulty modes of answering already incidentally referred to, there are others of even more pronounced character to which the teacher's attention should be directed.

(*a*) One of the commonest as well as one of the most harmful types of bad answering is **guessing.** In most of such cases the child makes no real effort to think or discover the correct reply, but heedlessly hazards an answer, or it may be several one after another, on the mere chance of being right. **The evil of allowing children to fall into the way of thus gambling with words is a very serious one** ; and the practice should be discouraged at all points in any reasonable way that may offer itself. No understanding accompanies the guess even when correct ; and frequently the replies given are so senseless as to show that the child is not even conscious of the import of what he is saying. This is "disrespectful to the teacher and a nuisance to the class."

In some instances the defect of the answer may be shown by a further question, in others the absurdity of the reply should be distinctly exposed, while any gross case should be met by a direct reprimand. A little wholesome ridicule also, if wisely applied, will prove frequently of considerable service.

The teacher who shuts his eyes to guessing is really helping to foster habits of carelessness and rash statement altogether opposed to true educational influences. Not only does the child in such circumstances lose the good which the questioning should secure to him, but the bad effects of the practice are manifested in many ways, and extend beyond the period of school life.

(b) Closely allied to guessing is that **reckless dashing style of answering** where the child simply jumps at a conclusion, or blurts out probably the first idea that enters his head, without taking the trouble to settle how far the answer is correct. Oftentimes if the teacher pauses and puts the question again, in a way which shows that it must not be trifled with, the answerer is able quite readily to correct his own statement. Such answers are stupid blameworthy blunders, not *mistakes* of any kind ; and they should not be allowed to go by without reproof. " Real mistakes," says Mr. Thring, " are one thing. Sham mistakes are another. And the learners ought to have the distinction sharply and strongly cut across their minds. A boy ought to be made to see always that what he *can* do he *shall* do. . . . It is not the knowledge of the miserable tense or case, that is the question, but the slackness of mind that is so deadly, the trained activity that is at stake." The teacher must look to himself as well as to the children, for **vague questioning is sometimes at the bottom of the fault** ; and in any case he has himself to blame if such answers are at all common in his class, at least for any length of time.

(c) Another frequent form of bad answering is what Mr. Thring calls the "**no answer plague**," in which the reply given is not what is asked for, but some other piece of information generally allied to it.

Thus it is asked, "What is the height of Snowdon?" and the reply is "It is the highest mountain in England and Wales"; or, "When was the battle of Bannockburn fought?" and the forthcoming answer is "It was fought between the English and the Scotch." "Who was the Duke of Wellington?" "He fought the battle of Waterloo."

In the great majority of instances, where answers of this kind are given, they are due to culpable carelessness which takes one of the following forms—imperfect listening to the question so that only part of it is heard, inattention to what the question really asks, and heedlessness or indolence in framing the answer.

In other cases the child, not knowing the information wanted, is eager to show that he knows something else, and volunteers this instead. It is scarcely necessary to say that replies of this kind should be strongly discouraged. Such lapses, however, are by no means confined to children, or to answering in class ; examination papers would often supply abundant and sometimes glaring examples.

The variety of ways in which what is given may be wide of the question is almost endless. It is not possible here to do more than refer to one or two further instances.

It often happens, for example, that children will go all round a question without touching the real point at issue ; or give replies which, while dealing with the subject-matter required, present it in a form that is no direct reply to what is asked. In the latter case the wrong part of speech, as nouns for verbs and *vice versâ*, or the wrong phrase, is substituted for the one really needed to meet the question exactly. The following examples will make this clear :—

"What is meant by alms?" "To give money to the poor." "What is a sentence?" "Putting words together to make sense." "What is meant by exports?" "To send goods out of the country."

The looseness of attention, inexactness of thought, and lack of effort involved in such **intellectual sauntering** are serious drawbacks to any real training being given. Children need bracing up in such circumstances, and the correction of the error should be unmistakable. In particular cases it may be advisable to point out in what respect the answers are wrong, and to explain clearly what is needed by way of correct reply. Anyway the child must be led to understand clearly that he must keep exactly to the point, and that nothing short of a direct answer to the question will be accepted.

(*d*) **Sometimes a pupil is very anxious to display what he knows** in the hope of pleasing the teacher by the amount of his information, and, not content with giving what is asked for, goes on to state other matters beyond what the question requires. He should be stopped at once when he begins to do this ; but not snubbed into silence, as is sometimes done. A judicious teacher will have no difficulty in dealing with such a case. One way is to call upon the child to repeat the question, so as to direct his attention to just what is needed, and then make him give this without any addition. He will soon learn that volunteered information is not what the teacher wants. Where the fault remains unchecked it will grow, and a good deal of time may be wasted, apart from other considerations.

Some children again are very fond of giving **speculative answers**. They are aware that the teacher is working up to some point, and, eager to show that they know what he is aiming at, they endeavour to anticipate him by giving the final conclusion instead of, or in addition to, the fact required at the moment. Such answers are often very troublesome, and sometimes spoil an important step in the teaching by bringing it forward prematurely. They are very apt to disconcert a young teacher; and it is not always easy for one more experienced to deal with them satisfactorily. The particular treatment will depend much upon the attendant circumstances of the case. The child, however, should be made to see distinctly that to gain the teacher's approbation he must confine himself to the question, and be taught to keep his discoveries to himself until the proper time comes, when they will receive that recognition which is denied to them so long as they are given out of place.

(*e*) **Foolish or ridiculous answers** are sometimes purposely indulged in. They are of course bad as answers; but the lesson may be dry and uninteresting, and the children glad of any relief. It is not necessary to treat an occasional attempt at a joke as a breach of discipline; in fact it would be very unwise to do so, and, if at all quick-witted, the teacher may easily keep in order any offender, inclined to overstep reasonable bounds, by turning the laugh upon him. The main thing is to keep the matter entirely under control, and to prevent its delaying the teaching: it will then do no harm.

Where however foolish answers are given with the deliberate intention of disconcerting the teacher, or turning the lesson into a farce, they should at once be taken seriously in hand. The best way is to look upon them as gross rudeness and treat them accordingly.

(3) *Modes of receiving and of dealing with answers.* The way in which answers are accepted and treated has an important bearing on the success of the teaching. **No child should be allowed to escape contributing something to the lesson**, and this to the best of his ability. The exercise should be so conducted, that, while errors in

fact, or faultily-worded replies, are not allowed to escape correction, the spirit of the treatment is such that every one is stimulated to let no opportunity pass without trying to give what is wanted. **Effort is the great thing needed, and this is not to be secured without encouragement.** Harshness, impatience, and want of sympathy in dealing with answers, soon discourage children to such an extent that they remain silent, even when they know, either from fear of drawing down the teacher's scorn upon them, should they make a mistake, or because they feel that their best attempts meet with no recognition from him.

(a) **Answers which are specially good and show that the point asked has been carefully thought out should be commended.** In some cases a word of encouragement should be given, even when the answer is not all that could be wished, if it appears that the child has intelligently grappled with the question, and done his utmost to give a satisfactory reply. Where the answers, though correct, are not marked by any special excellence, and no word of commendation is advisable, they should be **accepted in a pleasant appreciative way**, which will be in itself an encouragement to the child. A word of caution too is necessary. It is easy for the teacher to fall into the **habit of constantly following an answer by some stereotyped phrase of approval**, as "quite right," "exactly," "very good," "just so," "good boy," etc. This is to be avoided.

(b) **Answers which are wholly wrong should be decidedly and clearly rejected.** This should never be done snappishly or sarcastically, so as to destroy the spontaneity of the answering, but such mistakes should not be passed over in a way that will leave the child in doubt as to their true nature. **Honest mistakes are better than silent uncertainty.**

It is not necessary that the rejection should always be given the moment the answer is received. Cases frequently arise where the child may be led by a further question to find out his error for himself; or the correction may be given by others. In the end, however, it should be clear to him where he was wrong. It is often a good plan, when a correct answer has at length been obtained with the aid of other members of the class, to call upon one or other of those who answered wrongly to give the right reply over again; or it may be to put it in their own words.

(c) **Many answers are a mixture of truth and error,** and it would be a waste of time to pause in all instances and extract the grain from the accompanying chaff; but sometimes this may be done with distinct advantage both to the individual and the class.

Much depends upon the extent to which the answer is correct. In some instances it is sufficient for the teacher to point out what is right and leave the rest; in others the answer may be passed over altogether. Cases often occur, however, where a bad answer shows that the child has the right idea in his mind but has blundered in putting it, and here he may usefully be made to amend or complete his reply, others being called in to assist where he is at a loss.

Faulty answers may be frequently turned to good account by a skilful teacher; and **a good deal may sometimes be learned by getting to the bottom of a child's difficulty.** But, on the other hand, if this is improperly managed, the children are very apt to lose the thread of the lesson, and to have their attention entirely misdirected by too much talk, and that possibly wide of the subject in hand. Discretion and judgment are necessary in this matter at every point, and the teacher must walk warily if he would avoid the many pitfalls which beset his path.

(d) **A bold, forward or conceited manner in answering should be reproved or repressed by coldly passing over the individual who exhibits it.** Children should not be encouraged merely to outdo their neighbours; and a pupil who turns round with a glow of triumph to some one who failed to answer should have his power taxed to the limit of failure.

Anxiety to answer is in itself deserving of recognition, but it must not be allowed to lead to indiscriminate calling out of replies. If this is permitted the class soon falls into disorder, and with bad discipline good answering is impossible. A boy who jumps up or comes out of his place in order to press his answer upon the teacher should, for that very reason, not be allowed to give the reply.

(e) **If the answers again and again are not forthcoming, or show a general lack of understanding, the teacher should at once exert himself to find out the cause, and look carefully to his own side of the work.** The probability is that the fault is to be traced to his own want of clearness, defective explanation, or imperfect illustration in presenting the facts; or the weakness may arise from the mode of questioning.

In either case the matter should be set right, either by going over again with greater care that part of the teaching, or by amending the style of questioning. Sometimes, however, the cause of such a failure lies with the children themselves—arising from inertness, inattention, or weariness; or again it may be due to bad physical conditions, such as unwholesome atmosphere, excess of heat or cold, or too long a continuance in one position.

(4) *Simultaneous Answering.* This is an attractive mode of receiving replies, and in certain circumstances may be used with advantage; but both insight and caution are necessary to employ it properly, and it may easily become not only a useless but a harmful exercise.

Its **advantages** are that it engages every one at the same time, it is stimulating to a dull class, it is a rapid method, its force is impressive, it gives confidence to the shy and timid, it imparts animation to the work, and it is a relief and refreshment after severer exercises.

Its chief **defects** may be said to be that it makes a show of work, and is apt to delude both the teacher and taught as to the amount learned; it smothers individual effort and fosters a bad habit of relying upon others; it is noisy, and if badly managed may interfere with the work of neighbouring classes, or develop a sing-song tone that is very objectionable; while, inasmuch as the answers need to be simple and obvious, so that every child may have a chance and use the same words, it affords little or no training of any kind, and leads to superficiality and the glib quoting of phrases without any real understanding.

As a means of rapid repetition or recapitulation to fix certain truths in the minds of the pupils, simultaneous answering is distinctly useful, if properly employed; but as a means of testing information, or of teaching new truths, it is comparatively worthless. In the case of little children, where pleasantness and continuous occupation of an easy kind are the things needed rather than steady thought, and where a training in smartness and attention is more important than the learning of facts, simultaneous answering should be frequently made use of; with older children it should be employed much more rarely. Where the exercise is used as a means of relief or change it should be dropped directly the end aimed at has been reached.

No style of answering demands such unceasing vigilance and care-

ful listening on the part of the teacher; lacking these he may be completely deceived. Children are exceedingly quick in picking up answers from a few leaders, and will often chime in mechanically without even listening to the question. This is a mischievous habit and needs frequent correction, but it is by no means impossible for the teacher to overcome it; rather the fault is to be laid to his charge if it is at all common.

Children should be in no doubt when a simultaneous answer is required, some direction, or understood signal—as a wave of the hand—being employed by the teacher to give the required intimation. The noise also of the exercise should be kept down as much as possible. The children should speak, not whisper, and speak loud enough to be heard distinctly; but they should never be allowed to bawl out the answers in a high pitched artificial tone, as is very often the case.

(5) *Some common mistakes made by the teacher with respect to answering.* The general mode of treating answers has been already described, and all that remains to be done here is to note briefly a few common cases where caution is necessary to prevent the teacher from falling into error.

(a) It not unfrequently happens that in asking a question the teacher has in his mind some particular form of answer. Unless he attends carefully to the *substance* of the replies, rather than the words, he may easily make the mistake of **refusing good answers** because they differ in statement from what he is expecting. So long as the answer is direct, and is expressed with reasonable correctness, it is far better to accept the child's own words, than to insist upon some more perfect form which the teacher himself may be able to give. We want children to think; and, if they do this naturally, they are in many cases pretty certain to see things in a somewhat different light from that in which the teacher regards them. Sometimes the answers given are much more rational and accurate than the one the teacher is trying to obtain.

A teacher once asked—"Why do the little birds build their nests?" and after refusing several really intelligent replies, expressed surprise that no one could give the one he wanted, which was—"Because it is their instinct so to do." This was a blunder in several ways.

(b) **Unless, again, the teacher is observant he is very liable to select**

I

the same children to answer again and again—usually either those just in front of him, or those who are most forward and demonstrative. In either case a considerable number of children have no attention paid to them and remain in comparative idleness. **Over-answering by the few means mental torpor on the part of the many.** When a child finds that he is rarely or never noticed by the teacher he naturally grows careless, and inattention soon follows. Nor does the mischief end here; for in such a case those timid and retiring children, who need to be continually encouraged and brought to the front, are entirely neglected.

(c) Another error arises mainly from the **impatience of the teacher.** In his anxiety to obtain answers promptly the question is repeated again and again while the children should be thinking. They are distracted rather than aided by such repetition; and in many instances the teacher cuts the matter short by answering the question himself and passing on. This scrambling through a lesson is not teaching; and it may be laid down as a safe general rule, that **except in rare cases the teacher should not answer his own questions.** Sometimes, again, when an answer is not at once forthcoming, the teacher gives the beginning of what is wanted, and the children's minds being now turned from finding the reply for themselves, they either guess wildly or remain silent, so that word after word is added by the teacher until the answer is completed, or so nearly that all gain arising from the question is entirely lost.

(d) **Not only should the teacher avoid prompting the children himself, he should be particularly careful that where a question is specially directed to individuals the children do not prompt one another.** When this is done in an underhand way it should be treated as dishonesty; but even where this is not the case it is a harmful practice. We want to train them to self-reliance, and this will certainly not be done unless they are made to depend upon themselves. Until a child has made the best effort he is capable of, or the teacher has passed him over, the others should remain silent, but ready to give what he has failed in.

(e) **Some teachers readily contract a habit of repeating mechanically almost every answer given.** This should not be done. The fault may perhaps arise from the attempt to gain time while the next question is thought of; but where the teacher feels it difficult to frame questions quickly it is better to pause than to fall into this useless and clumsy practice. If it is due to the belief that unless the facts are impressed they will rapidly fade from the children's minds, this is the wrong method to adopt—except in very special instances.—to secure the object aimed at. Any really necessary repetition should be given by the pupils themselves.

(*f*) **Wasting time over answers is another frequent error.** This tends not only to destroy the interest of the teaching but to break the connection of one point with another. It is quite possible to be over-particular in receiving replies. To stickle too much over small points in the vain endeavour to make all answers perfect, and to discuss every possible difficulty and defect, while the more important matters of the lesson are at a standstill, is to confuse children by the multiplicity of the corrections, and to mistake the real nature of what class-teaching should be.

II. ELLIPSES.

By an **ellipsis** in teaching is meant the omission of one or more words at the end of a statement, on the understanding that these missing words are to be supplied by the children. That ellipses may fulfil their object in the best way, they must not be mere chance statements made in the course of the teaching, but **must be specially framed** to admit of just that being supplied which the teacher wishes to obtain from the children.

The **function of ellipses is to a large extent that of easy questions**, but they are sufficiently distinct in form, and have sufficient advantages of their own, to render them worthy of consideration as a separate device.

We owe the introduction of ellipses into common use to David Stow, who made them a part of his system of training. He considered that their employment *along with questions* formed a more efficient instrument for developing the faculties than questions alone. However this may be, at least one thing is certain, that, employed in the right way and with proper restrictions, ellipses may be made of considerable service in teaching.

The greater the number of the devices which the teacher can employ readily and effectively, that is, the greater the number of ways he has at his command of doing with skill and certainty what is required of him, the easier will be his work to himself and the more helpful and satisfactory to his pupils. It is therefore unwise for him to neglect the use of ellipses, as is frequently done, because at the present time they appear to be somewhat out of favour.

I. ADVANTAGES OF ELLIPSES.—(1) As before mentioned the child's difficulties in answering a question are twofold—the finding of the right idea, and the expression of this in suitable language when found. Now **ellipses are purposely framed to remove, as far as needful, one of these difficulties by giving the framework of the reply**, so that the mind is left free to exert its power on the discovery of the thought or fact required.

(2) **They are less formal, and affect the pupils less like a direct challenge, than questions.** The teacher seems to the children to take his part more as one of themselves than as one intent upon giving them definite instruction, while his work is brought into such direct contact with theirs that the result appears as a joint effort. Hence **ellipses tend to give confidence and encouragement to little children**, who are apt to be shy and timorous when anything is demanded from them in a formal way.

(3) There is a gain too in the **briskness and animation of the exercise.** The ellipses are filled in rapidly and the lesson kept moving; and if they are skilfully put the interest of the children is excited, and consequently their attention arrested. Further, **activity and cheerfulness are secured**; and, after all, these are two very important things in the case of young children, even if but little information is given.

(4) Nor must the advantage of using ellipses as **a change and relief from severer questioning** be overlooked. To continue any one device, no matter how valuable, for too long a time is simply to weary the children; and after more difficult work a short series of ellipses will be found to refresh and brighten the class.

(5) They are **useful also in running quickly over a series of points again** to bring the latter distinctly before the children's minds before proceeding to some further point, so that the connection may be clear; and in summing up or rapid review they may frequently be made to serve a similar purpose.

(6) To some extent the employment of ellipses affords **a simple and useful training in language.** The complete statements accustom the child to correct forms, and serve the purpose pretty much of a series of model answers to more direct and difficult questions which might have been asked. In fact in some cases it is useful, after an ellipsis has been filled in, to put a question demanding the complete state-

ment for answer. By filling in ellipses, too, the child learns the correct use of the words supplied, and so improves his vocabulary.

II. SUGGESTIONS AND CAUTIONS AS TO THE USE OF ELLIPSES.—
(1) The considerations given above lead distinctly to the conclusion that **ellipses may be suitably and wisely resorted to as a common device in the teaching of young children**; but that the higher we go in the school the less frequent should be their employment, until **in the upper classes their use should be confined to special cases, or cease altogether.**

With infant classes they form a stirring and encouraging exercise; but, since, as a rule, they demand but little thought, anything like frequent employment with elder classes would lead to a waste of time and eventually to a disinclination to the strenuous and continuous effort to which it is important to accustom older scholars. Much will, however, depend upon the good judgment and skill of the teacher, and it would be unwise to lay down any hard and fast rule as to how far the use of ellipses should extend.

(2) **In no case should the teacher rely solely upon the use of ellipses.** If these are employed exclusively, the children soon learn to fill them in mechanically, and a superficiality of attention is engendered which looks only for the word without proper grasp of the underlying idea. Stow insists very strongly on the constant admixture of questions and ellipses in differing proportions according to the age of the class. Used in connection they assist and support each other.

Stow says: "Questioning is simply developing or leading out. It is not training until the child's ideas are not merely *led out* by questioning, but *led on* by ellipses and questions combined. ... There must uniformly be an analysis, *based on simple and familiar illustrations*, and conducted by questions and ellipses mixed, which must be within the extent of the knowledge and experience of the children present."

(3) **Ellipses, like questions, may be used for the purpose both of testing and of training.** In the first case, they must not be given in a haphazard way, but should be expressly framed to elicit what the children have *learned*; for, if they require points upon which no previous teaching has been given, they will not be filled in with the requisite certainty. In the second case, they must be sufficiently easy for each step to be readily followed, so that the children are assisted in reasoning in a very simple way for themselves.

Many of the suggestions already given with reference to the

employment of questions apply with equal force to the use of ellipses. They **must not be too easy**; the word or words left for the pupils to fill in should necessitate the finding of an idea, and must be sufficiently important to ensure a certain amount of effort. Care should also be taken to avoid the **common fault of suggesting too much**. In no case should merely half a word be required, so that only the final syllable, perhaps, remains to be given. The **difficulty of what is to be supplied will depend upon the class**: with the younger children it should be a single and fairly obvious word; with more advanced scholars it may be a more difficult word or phrase.

Vagueness is another fault to be avoided. This is pretty certain to lead to guessing of a useless and harmful kind. If ellipses are so framed that a number of different words may be filled in, and yet make sense of the statement, the definite and uniform answer which the teacher wants is not forthcoming. Some say one thing and some another, and confusion results.

(4) The usefulness of ellipses depends in a great measure on their being **filled in simultaneously**; hence, except in very special cases, they should be addressed to the class as a whole, and the reply should be given by all. **Smartness and movement are essential.** If an ellipsis is not filled in, it is rarely of use to put it over again in the same form; as a rule it is better to go back a step and approach the point again in another way.

Ellipses are subject to the same defects, and liable to the same abuses, as questions to which simultaneous answers are expected. Where they are not well employed they **lead to much unnecessary noise** and may readily become absolutely worthless. The ease with which they may be used is seductive but delusive, for their skilful employment is much more difficult than it seems; and the show of work made is very apt to deceive the teacher as to the reality of what is done. Unless he is vigilant in looking out for those who do not reply, and listens carefully for imperfect responses, a considerable proportion of the pupils may be mentally idle, and either not take the trouble to answer at all, or trust to their neighbours to give them the cue to the right word. The evil effects of the bad habits thus formed it is unnecessary to dwell upon; but the teacher should be fully alive to the fact that **ellipses need quite as much care and judgment to use properly as any other teaching device.**

III. ILLUSTRATIONS.

An illustration is something already known, or easily apprehended through the senses,. which is made use of to assist the mind in its efforts to comprehend something which is unknown. Thus, in illustrating an idea, we, for the moment, substitute in its place either some concrete embodiment of it, or some closely related idea which the pupil has already acquired ; so that through the consideration of this he may be enabled to pass to and grasp, as fully and clearly as is necessary, the notion which we wish to convey. He has to realise the unfamiliar by means of the familiar, to apprehend the former of these as it were in terms of the latter, until finally *the new* is assimilated and in its turn becomes *the old*. The stranger the idea presented, that is, the less it is related to such results as are already stored in the mind, the greater is the difficulty experienced in conceiving it clearly through the medium of words. Many ideas are so unrelated, or so remotely correlated, that they can only be properly grasped when the presentation is made directly through the senses ; and hence, in such a case, the illustration takes the form of some object, picture, experiment, etc.

Our fundamental ideas are gained through the action of the senses, and we associate with them certain symbols, or words, by means of which we are able to recall them before the mind. By thus bringing these ideas into consciousness, and combining or modifying them in various ways, we are enabled to arrive at other related ideas—to form generalisations, abstractions, and so on. Thus new ideas are acquired (1) *directly*, through impressions conveyed to the mind by means of the senses ; and (2) *indirectly*, by combination, comparison, or modification of ideas with which the mind is already familiar.

It would be impossible, by any description or appeal to other experiences, to give any adequate notion of certain flavours or odours, or of such sensations as those produced by an electric shock. But we could give a person familiar with the elements which go to make up landscape, a very fairly satisfactory idea of some scene we have witnessed.

The employment of illustrations is in exact accordance with the **fundamental principles**, that, in teaching we should (1) appeal to the senses as much as possible, (2) pass to the unknown by the help of the known, and (3) approach what is complex through that which is simple and related. It is to this they owe their power and usefulness.

An illustration, as its name implies, should light up or illuminate so as to **make bright and clear**, that which is to be presented to the mind. An illustration which does not do this is not only useless, but may easily become harmful; inasmuch as the pupil fails to see the necessary connection between the ideas, his attention is turned in a wrong direction, and no effort is induced to pass beyond the illustration itself. Bad illustrations "rather shadow the light than shed light."

I. ADVANTAGES OF ILLUSTRATIONS.—The chief advantages of illustrations as a teaching device may be briefly summed up as follows:—

(1) They offer a most **useful and efficient means of overcoming and clearing up difficulties of apprehension.** They give definiteness to the child's ideas, and enable him to grasp intelligently many things which it would be almost impossible for him to comprehend fully by any amount of mere telling or explanation.

(2) They are a **great aid in simplifying and in giving vividness to explanations.** They thus render the teaching more exact and thorough than it would otherwise be. The understanding of such matters as abstract ideas, technical terms, and scientific laws is very largely dependent upon the use made of illustrative cases within the child's comprehension.

How dependent the child is upon instances in such cases, and how difficult it is for him to express the nature of any abstraction independently of them, is shown by the fact that when he is asked for the meaning of some abstract term, which has been explained to him, he almost invariably gives illustrative examples.

(3) They are **stimulative and excite interest and curiosity in things which without their aid would often be dry and unattractive.** They thus not only **strengthen attention**, but **give force and picturesqueness and consequently impressiveness to the teaching.** An increased glow of pleasantness is imparted to learning, and the lesson is prevented from becoming dry and wearisome.

That children take the greatest pleasure in examining into things is within the observation of every one, pictures especially being an unfailing source of delight to them. This tendency turned in the right direction may be made helpful in many ways.

(4) Illustrations have not only an *illuminating* power but a *fixing* power also. They **strengthen the retention and assist the recollection of facts** by the additional clearness of comprehension, by the interest and attention aroused, and by the linking or association of one thing with another.

A striking illustration, particularly if it be some object or phenomenon, produces not only a fuller but a more lasting impression than any description alone, and may often be made to suggest that which it was used to illustrate when the latter would otherwise have passed beyond recall.

(5) Correct illustrations may be made a most **valuable means of cultivating the observing powers**, and of training the senses generally to greater acuteness of perception, and correctness and rapidity of action. Observation and experiment underlie all real progress in the so-called natural and physical sciences, as they also certainly do all successful understanding of or attainment in them.

What is sometimes called the **intuitive or inductive method** is really to a great degree a constant appeal to things and phenomena, so that the knowledge of the pupil is his own discovery and the outcome of actual experience of the facts. The importance of this **first-hand knowledge** is very great.

(6) Properly used illustrations **assist in the formation of good intellectual habits**, not only by accustoming the pupil to exactness of acquisition and patient investigation, but also by the constant demand made upon him for careful discrimination and close attention in the various comparisons and parallels brought under his notice. With a teacher who handles his illustrations with skill, the pupil soon comes to learn how easily he may go wrong, unless he exercises caution in interpreting what he sees, and care and deliberation in arriving at any conclusion respecting results.

II. KINDS OF ILLUSTRATIONS.—We have seen, from the nature of the mode in which we arrive at new ideas, that illustrations must be essentially of two kinds: (1) those which act directly through the senses, and (2) those which influence the mind through the medium of related ideas expressed in words.

(1) *Illustrations appealing to the senses.* (*Natural, concrete, or objective illustrations.*)

(a) **Objects.** The absurdity of teaching an object-lesson without the object, or some representation of it—a thing by no means unknown—has been already pointed out. Wherever the knowledge of some object plays an important part in a lesson, an illustration is essential. Every school should possess a **store of objects for teaching purposes**, and these need be neither rare nor costly. What is wanted is **not a collection of curiosities**, but a well-arranged series of common objects which are likely to be of frequent use as illustrations in ordinary teaching, or to which reference is likely to be made in reading-books. Many will form fitting subjects for independent lessons. As Mr. Thring well says: "Common things have the priceless advantage of being common, of being there. And as soon as common things have the spark, the fuse (of questioning) thrown in amongst them, there is no limit to the possible effect. All the world with its startling contrasts and secrets becomes one great lesson-book."

A teacher who is on the outlook will have no difficulty in collecting, with the help of the children, a supply of such things as will be useful; and with a few purchases of individual things here and there he may easily put together a valuable collection. The objects sold in cabinets or boxes are often much too small for teaching purposes, and are not always well selected.

The objects should be as varied as possible, and in the case of natural substances should be **well selected typical specimens,** not anything that comes to hand. Every object should have a fixed place in the case or cabinet, and should be properly labelled and numbered; so that by means of a catalogue it may be found at once, if its place is not remembered.

The collection should include such things as the following :—

1. A series of **dried plants** mounted and named.
2. The more important **rock-forming minerals**; such as quartz, mica, felspar, etc.
3. The **commoner types of rocks,** both igneous and sedimentary. These should be broken with a hammer to about the same size, and classified and arranged in a natural order.
4. The **metals in ordinary use,** with specimens of their ores.
5. **Vegetable and animal products** in the raw state and in various stages of manufacture—especially such things as cotton, flax, hemp, wool, silk, leather, horn, cereals, woods, etc.

Many **school museums** are simply collections of odds and ends, without classification or arrangement. Mere curiosities are, as a rule, best kept by themselves, and should be open to the children's daily inspection. Many things, however—such as coins, medals, casts, relics, old weapons, the weapons, implements, etc. of savage nations, in fact anything which will illustrate the manners and customs of the past or of different nations—may be turned to good service, especially in history and geography lessons. Collections of such things as shells, insects, and fossils, also have their uses.

Children should be encouraged to make collections of natural objects for themselves. Not only will this provide them with an interesting amusement and healthful recreation, but it will **bring them into direct contact with nature herself.** They will then be induced to observe ôn their own account, and will learn many important truths in a way they are not likely to forget; while the curiosity aroused will frequently lead them to seek for further information from books or friends.

The **want of observation** displayed by many grown-up people and their ignorance of ordinary natural phenomena and objects which are brought before them almost daily are striking facts, and show how much the school has yet to do before it can be said to educate, as it should do, those brought within its walls.

(b) **Pictures and Diagrams.** Where it is impossible to make use of the object, or to obtain a model of it, the teacher must fall back upon some pictorial representation of it. One or the other however ought certainly to be employed. **Pictures are intelligible to children long before they are able to form ideas with any success from a word description,** no matter how careful this may be.

The **essential characteristics in a picture or diagram for class teaching are boldness, clearness, and truthfulness as far as the representation goes.** Those points should be brought out most strongly which it is useful for children to observe, rather than merely artistic effects. The latter are not to be despised, so long as the necessary qualities are secured; but minute detail is a drawback, and high finish is not necessary. Inaccurate representation of facts, bad drawing, and false or coarse colouring, are much commoner defects than they should be.

Both **pictures and diagrams** which contain a number of different things on the same sheet are to be avoided in the teaching of children. Only one thing should be presented at once, otherwise the attention is sure to be distracted; and without the greatest care the teacher will find that there is so much haziness as to what is actually illustrated that most of the value of the illustration is lost.

Every school should possess a **series of good coloured prints of animals** of the most striking types, as well as of those of common occurrence or economic importance. The collection of dried plants may be supplemented in the same way. There should also be a **collection of diagrams** of such things as the mechanical powers, machinery, common scientific instruments, plant dissections, the human body, the solar system, the tides, the seasons, the structure of the earth's crust, volcanoes, coral reefs, etc. A geological section or two of the district, and a generalised one across England, will also be found useful. Many of these may be easily constructed by the teacher himself.

It will also be found desirable to collect in a folio any **coloured prints, photographs, or engravings** likely to be of service; particularly those illustrating the scenery of foreign countries, natural phenomena, or historical events.

<small>A few may be bought, others may be taken from the larger illustrated periodicals, others again obtained as gifts, etc. It is astonishing how much may be done in this direction if the teacher is inclined to take a little trouble.</small>

Diagrams are often of much more use in teaching than pictures, and will be frequently found a valuable supplement even to objects themselves. The great advantage of diagrams is that they bring out essential points, and sink unimportant details or attendant facts unrelated to the matter in hand. There is less for the children to look at, and hence less chance of producing a merely vague impression.

(c) **Maps.** A sufficient supply of these should be provided both for the purpose of illustrating the direct geographical teaching, and for pointing out the position or relations of any place of which mention is made in other lessons. The maps should be **clear in outline, with the physical features boldly marked** so as to strike the eye, and they should not be overcrowded with either details or names. In addition to the ordinary maps, one of England and another of Europe, outlined in white on a "slated" surface to be written on with chalk, or, it may be, filled in with further detail as the teaching requires, will be found useful where time has to be economised or the teacher is but an indifferent draughtsman.

(d) **Models.** These are frequently of the greatest service in the illustration of such things as machinery, scientific instruments, mechanical processes, geometric forms, the meaning of geographical terms, the movement of the heavenly bodies, and so on. The most useful models are not those that are bought, but those that are made by the teacher. He knows exactly what he wants, and may, in most cases, easily make what is required, by the exercise of a little trouble and ingenuity, out of such simple materials as paper, cardboard, wood, and clay. If the models will take to pieces, so that the parts may be examined separately and then put together before the class, so much the better.

(e) **Experiments.**—In teaching science a carefully arranged series of experiments is often an absolute necessity if the teaching is to be real. Each point should be illustrated in succession, and appeal made to the child's observation and judgment, as far as his power in these directions will permit. Mere telling is beside the mark; **what the child wants is direct contact with the truths he has to learn,** and a science-lesson which can be based upon experiments should never be allowed to degenerate into a mere cram of facts.

One often hears the complaint, as an excuse for neglect or bad teaching, that the teacher has not the necessary apparatus. In nine cases out of ten, however, all that is wanted might easily be put together out of the common things within almost everybody's reach, with the expenditure of a few pence. It is a mistake to suppose that expensive apparatus is necessary or always works the best. **Even really good scientific investigation has again and again been conducted with the simplest of materials.** Very much may be done with ordinary glasses, pickle-jars, and Florence oil-flasks, with the addition of some glass tubing, india-rubber tubing, and a few corks, if the teacher has learnt how to manipulate these things, as every teacher should do.

In addition to being inexpensive, the **home manufacture of apparatus** has the further advantages, that it affords the teacher a very useful training and encourages children to experiment for themselves by showing how much may be done with a very little.

A few shillings spent upon materials may, in the hands of a skilful teacher, be made to do more than as many pounds spent upon more elaborate apparatus; and few managers would object to the outlay of a small sum now and again in this way, where many would object to the purchase of a collection of more or less costly things.

Every school should possess a spirit-lamp (or better, a Bunsen burner where there is gas), some test-tubes of different sizes, some chemicals for common experiments, a pair of bar magnets and a horse-shoe magnet, a mariner's compass (this is easily made), a glass prism, and a few similar things. Of course, wherever the school can afford it, many instruments which the teacher could not make (such as an air-pump) may be added with very great advantage.

(f) **Sketches on the Black-board.**—These are such a ready and often effectual means of illustrating a lesson, and may be used in so many instances where any other mode of illustration is not feasible, that **the black-board should be present in every lesson,** and the teacher should constantly practise its use until he can put down upon it rapidly anything he needs. **Its effective employment is by no means difficult to learn,** even where the teacher is an indifferent draughtsman.

The **advantages** of this mode of illustration are manifold. It is **always available** where any difficulty turns up in the course of the work, and in many cases it is the best mode of illustration which can be used. **Exact adjustment to requirements can be secured throughout,** just that being presented by itself to which attention needs to be directed at the moment. In this way **thought is concentrated on the point in question,** and the children are greatly assisted in distinguishing it from other things likely to be confused with it. The sketch may be drawn of sufficient size for every one to see distinctly, and as the teaching progresses the **drawing may be filled in bit by bit,** or any part of it may be further represented on an enlarged scale. If an illustration fails it may be **modified or extended,** or another may be substituted for it with the greatest ease. The black-board may also be made to **supplement the use of printed diagrams** by the teacher's sketching any important part separately, or representing it from some other point of view.

Coloured chalks, which may now be purchased very cheaply, are frequently a great help in giving clearness to black-board diagrams—the different colours being used for those things which it is important the pupils should clearly distinguish from one another.

Occasionally, where a somewhat more complex or more than commonly accurate drawing is required, and it is not worth while to prepare it on paper, it may be sketched on the black-board previous to the lesson and turned away from the children till wanted. As a rule, however, **black-board illustrations should be drawn in the presence of the class during the progress of the lesson.** When employed in this way they are more effective as an aid to the understanding, while the sight of the diagram growing under the teacher's hand is an attractive one to children and stimulates both attention and curiosity.

(2) *Illustrations presented in words.* (*Oral illustrations by comparison or analogy.*)

Words represent ideas, and these if known may fittingly be used to illustrate other *ideas* ; but they should not be used to illustrate *things* except where the difficulties of employing any other mode of illustration are too great to be overcome. In numerous cases where an intermediate step by way of illustration is necessary, in order that new knowledge may be gained and linked on to that which is already possessed, concrete illustrations are not possible. Stored ideas or known facts should then be brought before the mind in such a way as to bridge the gap in thought between ideas which have been acquired and kindred facts which have to be apprehended, but which from their strangeness or complexity are difficult to grasp. The child's mind is thus led into the right channel of thought, as it were, and **the difficulties of realisation are lessened through the comparison of qualities or truths, already familiar in the illustrative instance or example, with other qualities or truths demanding severer effort.**

The effectiveness of oral illustration depends upon the number and importance of the points of similarity or analogy existing between the illustration and that which is illustrated. The element of comparison really underlies the whole process, the child being assisted, as far as necessary, in noting such points of resemblance as are of use in the effort to realise the less well known by the better known. Hence, in teaching, it is necessary that the **illustrations should be sufficiently well within the children's knowledge or experience to be conceived readily and fully,** so that the relationship of the points brought forward may be easily discerned by them.

Since, however, the discrimination of differences, as well as the detection of similarity, is a most important element in the process of learning to know, **it is frequently of service to bring out any strong points of contrast** as well as of resemblance or analogy. That this is useful in illustration, and does throw light upon the matter in many cases, is clear from the fact that we are often assisted in defining the limits of a thing, and learning exactly what it *is*, by seeing distinctly what it *is not*.

In ordinary teaching the oral illustrations employed are mainly of two varieties :—

(a) **The presentation of some known particular example or instance to assist the realisation of some other less known case having strong points of similarity.**

Thus we use this mode of illustration when we compare such things as the cat and the tiger, a small stream and a river, treacle and melted glass, the sliding of snow on a roof and an avalanche, the vibration of a string and that of the vocal chords, the action of an oar in water and that of the webbed foot of a waterfowl, and so on.

(b) **The illustration of some general truth or abstraction by the examination of one or more individual instances or exemplifications.**

Thus we make clear a definition by appeal to a number of examples; we illustrate such abstract conceptions as valour or magnanimity by the recital of some marked instance of brave or magnanimous action; we assist the realisation of some general law by recalling to mind individual experiences, for example the absorption of heat when a solid changes into a liquid by drawing attention to the cold experienced during a thaw.

There is however **a third variety of oral illustration**, the usefulness of which in particular cases is rarely recognised in teaching, though not unfrequently employed by writers and speakers. Thus it may happen that two things, *neither of which can be said to be at all fully known*, may, by being studied side by side, be made to light up each other, force and clearness being given in this way to the conception of both. This is especially so in the case of **parallels in history, language, or literature.** Here, through the help of comparison and contrast each truth becomes more fully comprehended by being considered side by side with some other drawn from a different connection.

Thus we can illustrate many modern grammatical usages by comparison with historical forms; and every one knows how much light is thrown upon the exact meaning of a word by referring back to its root, and to any changes of signification which the word has undergone. It is not here the illustration of the unknown by the known, but of the partially or imperfectly known by that which is previously unknown, but which may be without difficulty understood. The same may be said with respect to literary forms, manners, customs, government, etc.

Similes are really brief illustrations used not so much for the sake of assisting understanding as of giving force and picturesqueness to the ideas, and of increasing interest by presenting some striking parallel. In similes the illustration and the thing illustrated are noted as separate though analogous ideas; in **metaphors** these ideas have become condensed and fused into one in such a way that the symbol of the illustration is used for both. The two ideas are for the time being treated as identical, and the relationship or parallel is left to be supplied by inference or by the action of the imagination.

III. SUGGESTIONS AS TO THE USE OF ILLUSTRATIONS.—In using illustrations the teacher has to guard against (1) **indistinctness or incomplete apprehension** from diffusion of the attention over too wide an area, or from the illustration being carelessly or hastily slurred over, so that the children fail to obtain any clear notion of what is presented; and (2) **confusion or misapprehension** from want of proper discrimination, or, from the falseness or inaccuracy of the analogy, so that in place of the correct idea only a distorted or completely mistaken conception of it is gained.

If the child has a great many things thrust upon his notice at once he is pretty certain to grasp none of them satisfactorily, all the impression left being an indistinct blur. **Many teachers make their illustrations far too elaborate.** Where there are too many details to attend to, the children—being unable to take in such a variety of impressions at once—fail to separate what is essential from what is subordinate or unnecessary, and hence become so perplexed that the illustration fails to make clear to them that which it was intended to illumine.

The simpler the illustrations the better, so long as they are effectual. They are a means to an end, and, if displayed as if they had a value of their own, there is great danger that the point will be lost, and the thing illustrated sink out of sight in the illustration.

This is markedly the case where illustrations have a "strong individual interest," and are therefore likely to attract attention merely to themselves. It is astonishing how little even many grown-up people, let alone children, will often see in an experiment except its prettiness or some point connected with the way in which it is performed. What is to be illustrated—what the experiment means—is lost sight of, and is only to be exposed to view by a running fire of well-directed questions.

The temptation to talk too much about an illustration, to let it pass beyond reasonable bounds because it happens to be interesting, has constantly to be withstood. This is particularly so with illustrative anecdotes. In some cases, too, the teacher is apt to forget the **great difference between illustration and digression**, and to allow himself to be drawn off from the line of his lesson to talk about other matters suggested by the illustration. That which has to be illustrated must be kept throughout distinctly present to the teacher's mind, and must also be clear to the children, or the illustration will fail to produce its proper effect.

Sympathy, considerable knowledge of children, and some experience, are necessary to enable the teacher to judge correctly when an illustration is required, how far it is required, and just where the help may most efficiently be given. In preparing his lesson he will of course provide illustrations in all obvious cases of need, so that the best obtainable may be presented and the effort of thinking before the class reduced as much as possible. Many cases however will arise where the teacher needs to be sufficiently ready in the use of the device to hit upon a suitable illustration on the spur of the moment, or make use of anything that may be to hand.

K

Some teachers experience a good deal of difficulty in doing this; others again are naturally inventive and ready in resource, and thus are seldom at a loss to supply what is wanted. The power, however, is not difficult to cultivate, if once the teacher recognises its importance, and accustoms himself to be on the outlook for analogies between things.

With children it is better to have too many illustrations than too few, so long as these are properly employed. In all cases the illustration must be so related to that which is illustrated that the analogy is not only a real one, but also a useful one, and such as can be readily apprehended. **Accidental relationships are valueless.** A child is simply confused if an illustration is inapposite; while purely fanciful or strained analogies, if used in teaching, do harm in blunting the child's perception of resemblances that are natural and essential in character. In most cases the closer the parallel the better; though, as a rule, it is **only one or two strong and important points of resemblance that need to be insisted upon.** These should be brought out distinctly, but in no case should an illustration be pushed too far.

Illustrations, too, should, as far as practicable, be such as are likely to **add to the pleasantness of the lesson** and excite the children's curiosity. They may be correct and simple, and yet so devoid of interest or attractiveness that it is difficult to keep the children's attention sufficiently fixed to ensure that the object aimed at is secured. **A good illustration is suggestive**; the main points are kept perfectly distinct, but they are handled in such a way that other ideas may be readily attached to them. It is a mistake for the teacher to attempt to give an exhaustive explanation of an illustration. Something may well be left to the imagination of the child.

In employing illustrations **the child must not be allowed to be merely a passive recipient,** or to rest content with quoting statements made by the teacher. He has to be guided as to what is to be made out, and assisted as far as necessary, but **he must see for himself. What the teacher thinks about the matter is to be subordinated to what the pupil can be made to think.** Thus in using concrete illustrations—whether pictures, diagrams, or what not—much depends upon the skill of the teacher in introducing them in such a way, that the children may have clearly in mind what they are to see, and consequently may be prepared, the moment the presentation is made, to turn their attention to that which it is important for them to observe. In order, however, that they may master the relationships which the illustration brings before them, **sufficient time must be given** for them to realise what is wanted, and they must neither be hurried nor worried.

A considerable amount of judgment is often necessary in introducing illustrations, so that they may be **presented in the nick of time**, when the children have been led to feel their difficulty, and appreciate the help. **The element of surprise also is often useful in illustrations.** Hence such things as pictures, models, etc., which are likely to attract attention, should be kept out of sight till required.

It is a common fault with young teachers to have some important illustration so much in mind that they are over anxious to introduce it, and are thus led to bring it in without properly leading up to it, or, as often happens, before its connection with the lesson can be made apparent. As a consequence the children are unprepared for it, and fail to understand what it was intended to illustrate. It is not an unknown thing also for teachers to introduce illustrations simply because it is felt that some ought to be used, and not because they have any direct bearing on the teaching. Such illustrations are not only useless but a waste of time.

Something must be allowed for individual peculiarities and difference of experience in the pupils themselves. One child may be benefited by an illustration which another fails to understand. Some are ready in detecting relationships of one kind, some of another; and frequently the resultant effects of an illustration upon the various members of the class are much more widely different than from the nature of the case would be supposed. In using illustrations, therefore, **the work should be thoroughly tested at every step by questions**; so that the points may be properly fixed, and those pupils who have difficulties may have a chance of being helped as far as the teaching will allow. It follows also that **the illustrations in a lesson should never be all of one type.** In fact the more varied the illustrations the better, the impressions obtained through one sense being supplemented and rendered more accurate by those received through another. Nor must the **value of contrast**, as well as of comparison, be forgotten. The former is frequently useful in stopping gaps leading to error; for, as Professor Bain points out, "contrast is an ever ready resource, and shortens the labour by excluding at once the notions liable to be confounded with what is meant."

The younger the child the more will illustrations be needed, inasmuch as the range of sense experience, and the consequent stock of ideas to which attachment may be made, is less. In the initial stage of education the teacher is particularly concerned with providing for the child a large number of exercises of the perceptive faculty. These have a double value, for not only do they render the teaching clear but they afford the pupil a useful training in how to observe. The teacher's success, both in the first steps and later on, will be largely dependent upon adequate sense training and the ideas so obtained. Unless this is attended to, it can scarcely be possible that the conceptions of the child will be accurate in character or readily arrived at. Hence **in the case of young children the illustrations used should be, as far as possible, concrete**—something for them to see or handle. "What we know as children," says Dr. Abbott, "is for the most part what we can see."

"In all branches susceptible of it, the exercises, the result of study, should be presented to the eye as the best organ of communication with the mind. Whatever is acquired through this medium is better retained than when entering through any other. It may be said, *the eye remembers*. It is more *attentive* than the ear. Its objects are not confused. It takes in a single and perfect image of what is placed before it, and transfers the picture to the mind. Hence all illustrations in our teaching, which can possibly be addressed to this organ, should be so applied." —(*Dunn.*)

Although, however, concrete illustrations should be most commonly employed in early years, they are of course of great value throughout the child's school career, and in many cases the teacher will find that such illustrations are the only ones that are of any real service. The great difficulty attending their use lies in the fact that it is often by no means easy to get children to see just what is necessary. The teacher should keep in mind that as a rule they observe very inaccurately, and that, without the greatest care, many of them are pretty certain to recognise little or no connection between what they see and what he is intending to impress upon them. **Observation of the kind needed is looking, and not mere seeing**; there must be action of the mind as well as of the eye. **Only that is really seen to which the attention is directed.** Hence careful management of illustrations, with reference both to their introduction and to the constant direction and testing necessary during their presentation, is essential to success.

The truth of the remark that "**the eye sees only that which it brings the power of seeing**" must be apparent to every one. Not only does individual peculiarity and taste give a colour to what is seen, but each mind, with its own peculiar interests and powers, observes those things most clearly to which it has been accustomed to turn its attention. How strikingly different would be the accounts given, say, by a savage, an agriculturalist, a naturalist, a geologist, and an artist, of some district each had travelled over, even if all had passed along the self-same track.

The difficulties of children in properly observing what is brought before them are often greatly increased by the nature of the things presented. Objects of insufficient size to be seen at all clearly, especially if enclosed in small bottles, as is often the case with cabinet specimens, are quite useless as illustrations when held in the teacher's hand before the class; and the same may be said of small woodcuts in books, which one sometimes sees used in the same way. Only the most imperfect examination can be made in such a case, even under favourable circumstances; and there is often added the difficulty with respect to discipline which arises from the children crowding confusedly round the teacher, in the endeavour to see what he is doing or what he has got.

Where small objects—such as grain, spices, coffee-berries, small plants, flowers, etc.—are needed for purposes of illustration, and a plentiful supply can be secured, one or more, according to the nature of the object, should be served out to every boy; or, what will answer almost as well in many cases, to the middle boy of every three, so that his neighbours on each hand can look over. Either way is better than passing the objects round the class for each boy to view in turn; for on this plan only a cursory examination is possible, and even then time is wasted, while the child loses the great and important advantage of having the object in hand during the time the teacher is talking about it, so as to be able on the instant to verify the facts pointed out. Where only a specimen or two can be procured, the best way out of the difficulty is for the teacher to shew the object, and then rely for illustration purposes on a large diagram or picture of it. In any case the aid of the black-board may usefully be called in.

Where objects have to be represented together, as in a picture or diagram, or parts drawn on an enlarged scale, **comparative size should receive very careful attention.** Children frequently get the most distorted notions of size from seeing things, widely different in this respect, drawn as though they were of the same magnitude, or even in grossly reversed proportions. **The actual size of the objects represented should always be pointed out,** and fixed by further illustration; as should also the scale of any enlargement. Microscopic sections are especially difficult to deal with in the case of children, and demand the greatest care.

Illustrations on the black-board should be drawn in bold, clear lines, and should be as accurate as rapid manipulation will allow. There is no time for elaboration or finish, nor are these necessary; as a matter of fact they often detract from the usefulness of drawing as an illustration. **The teacher should be careful also to place his board so that the drawings may be distinctly seen by all**; and the remark applies equally to such things as pictures, diagrams, and maps. Neglect of this precaution is of quite common occurrence with unobservant teachers, the usefulness of the illustration to many of the children being thus completely marred.

It is a good plan, where it can be managed, to **allow the children to take a share in the presentation of the illustrations**; to select individuals from the class to help in the distribution and manipulation of the things used, or to assist, as far as they are able, in the performance of experiments. Where any boy has learned to conduct an experiment successfully himself it will afford him great pleasure to be allowed to perform it for the teacher before the class.

Experiments are seldom as easy as they appear to be when read about, and if the teacher would succeed he must **make himself thoroughly acquainted with the conditions upon which the success of the experiment depends**. This can only be done by continued practice until he can be confident of achieving that which he sets out to do. To perform an experiment with neatness, certainty, and despatch is not only necessary to its success as an illustration, but as a good example to the children. If it is performed in a clumsy bungling way, with repeated alterations and readjustments before any result can be obtained, time is wasted, and the attention of the children is frittered away, so that they fail to understand the meaning and bearing of what is done.

Everything which is needed in the way of apparatus or material should be so placed as to be just ready to hand when wanted, and as far as possible every source of difficulty should be provided for. What is to be noticed should be made clear before each point is brought forward, and the children thoroughly questioned upon the result until they are fully aware what has been established and what is thereby illustrated. A series of experiments also should be carefully connected one with another, so that each point may be made out in succession and its bearing upon the next distinctly recognised.

Few lessons are more interesting than those based on experiments if properly conducted, but they need a good deal of adroitness to bring them to a successful issue, and may easily fail, through bad management, to do anything towards the enlightenment of the child.

IV.—LECTURE, OR DIRECT ADDRESS.

Lecture is the term applied to that form of instruction in which the teacher imparts what he wishes to be learned by addressing the pupils directly and more or less continuously. From its similarity to ordinary **narrative** it is, as a method, sometimes known by that name.

Lecture is so called because in former times instruction was given, as the word indicates, by formal reading to those who were to be taught—a mode of communicating knowledge still employed at times with adults. The signification of the term, however, has been extended to cover any **direct extemporaneous address given for the purpose of teaching**. This is the form which the method most commonly takes nowadays, and it is the only one which should be employed in the case of children. The unsuitability of lecture as a mode of instruction to be at all generally used with the youngest pupils, and the defective and unintelligent manner in which it has been employed have brought the device into unmerited disrepute. Its true position in school work is even yet far from being generally recognised.

Direct address is often used in an unsatisfactory way, or where it should not be, because it is an easy matter to talk. To tell, however, is not necessarily to cause the child to know, and may fail altogether to be of any benefit to him. Everything depends upon what is said, and how it is said. Mere talk, no matter how simple, is very far from being **teaching lecture**, and should not be confounded with it. The one is aimless, discursive, disjointed, follows no definite line, and ends nowhere in particular; the other is purposive, methodical, connected, marked by distinct sequence, and leads up to a recognised conclusion.

Occasionally it seems as if vanity had something to do with the unsatisfactory use of direct address, the power to speak continuously upon a subject for a length of time being thought to shew a certain cleverness. In some cases the teacher comes to have a liking to hear himself talk, and harangues his class in melodramatic fashion. Need it be said that all this is not teaching, and shews ignorance of what true lecture should be?

Lecture is **by no means an easy device to adopt with success**; but the true teacher, who knows how to employ it, finds it frequently a method of much power. To some extent it is necessary in every lesson, and many lessons are mainly dependent upon it. It should not be employed without thought, and the teacher should always have distinctly in mind what he wishes to accomplish, so that what he says may bear as fully and forcibly on this as possible. Skill and judgment lecture demands; this however is not a ground for abandoning it, but for acquiring the power to use it aright—for learning its strength and its weakness, in order that the one may be utilised and the other avoided.

The proper employment of lecture is a matter deserving of careful attention; and the teacher should not rest content until he can not only keep children attentive by this means, but ensure that they will pick up at least all the more important elements of that which he brings before them. Many matters bearing directly upon this subject have already been treated of at greater or less length in the earlier parts of the book; and without repeating these more than is unavoidable, the chief points repecting the use of lecture will be considered in what follows.

(1) *As a general rule it may be said that the employment of lecture should be suited to, and in direct proportion to, the age, power, and advancement of the pupils.* The teacher has throughout to mould his work and adapt his language to the needs of those whom he has to teach. The important thing is to hit the happy mean between doing too much and too little to assist the child. The facts must be so stated as not to overtax his power, but in many cases it is well that he should experience a little difficulty. Very easy things are generally uninteresting, or at least soon become so. Children like to feel their own strength, and nothing gives them greater pleasure, or is more stimulating, than to have made out something for themselves. They will often warm up into a glow of enthusiasm

when they succeed in this way ; and in such a case very much may be done with them.

Lecture should rarely be employed, in any continuous form, with little children ; the exceptions being mostly confined to the occasional use of narratives, anecdotes, and the like. Still, lecture of one kind or another has to be employed again and again. There are many things to be fixed in the minds of the youngest children that no expenditure of time or trouble would suffice to question out of them, and these must be told. The telling, however, should be confined to short statements, each being thoroughly questioned upon from different points of view, and perhaps further explanation given, before the next point is introduced. Anything like a flood of words is to be carefully avoided. Tender plants need tender treatment ; they want water, but they will not bear drenching. So it is with young minds.

Little children have not the mental grasp needed in following the statement of a series of facts or ideas given continuously ; nor have they the power of concentrating or keeping up their attention for any length of time. If the lecture goes beyond a few simple points at most the pupils lose the connection and meaning of what the teacher is saying, and may easily fall into a half-dazed condition until some change brings them relief.

In the middle of the school lecture may be much more employed ; though not for long together without a change, and it still needs the greatest watchfulness on the part of the teacher to detect any signs of weariness. He has frequently to stop and have points repeated, to test how far what he has said has been grasped, to go back and run over again what has been gone through, and to bring out and emphasise just those parts which he wishes to be most accurately and certainly remembered.

Very much will depend upon the nature of the lecture given as to how far it should be used ; and the teacher who is cautious to note the effects of his teaching will soon learn where he may trust to lecture, and where he may not. Children, however, soon get bewildered at this stage by anything of the nature of a discourse, and especially if it is a little complex. They lack both the judgment and the experience necessary for seizing upon the main points of a subject without help when many things are presented in succession ; and for this reason, as well as others, the work should be varied by questions, and by opportunities for fixing what is presented

With advanced classes—where the pupils have become accustomed to listen attentively, and to note from the teacher's mode of dealing with his subject what are essential points and what are subsidiary matters—

lecture may be adopted as a method with much greater success than in the preceding stage; and properly employed in such a case it is often the most useful of all the devices. It cannot be too emphatically stated, however, that, even here, **in no lesson should it be used alone.** Change, reiteration, testing, summing up, are as important as ever; but they need not be so frequent, and more continuous attention may be demanded from the pupil. Considering what the future wants of the child will be, and how often he will need the power to follow continuous discourse or the steps of an argument, it is most important that he should be trained to do this in school. Lecture, judiciously employed, will be found of the greatest value in helping to serve this end.

It is the teacher's business to see that the pupil does not sit listlessly letting what is said go in at one ear and out at the other. **There must be no dozing; the child's mind must be active, and working with the teacher.** Anything which compels or incites to such activity is valuable, and the use of questions is as important as ever. With advanced children it is also a capital plan to let them take notes during the teaching. To do this at all well requires close attention, and the result shews how far such attention has been given successfully. The exercise too has other useful bearings. The writing of an abstract of a lesson after the teaching has been completed also tells in the direction required.

(2) *Lecture must be controlled by a definite purpose.* In any lesson where facts have to be taught, the line the teaching is intended to follow should, as already pointed out, be carefully settled beforehand, so that each fact may have a definite place in the scheme of exposition. The lecture of course will follow in this track. Each portion of the subject which has unity in itself will be gradually unfolded, until it becomes clear and the central truth of that section of the work stands out perfectly distinct with its illustrative and supporting truths in proper perspective. The difficulty is to accomplish this naturally and easily, so that, while each truth is mastered in order, there is an absence of stiffness and formality.

The lecture must be kept within clearly defined limits, and there must be no neglect of important parts of the lesson to talk of matters which have little or no connection with it; yet, at the same time, freedom must be left for play of mind on the part of both teacher and pupils. Aimless wandering off the path is always to be reprobated; but it is not every digression which is injudicious. **The teaching should be suggestive as well as definite;** and it is often worth while to stop and point out matters of interest on either hand, so long as this is done briefly. **Digressions** are harmful in proportion to the amount of time they take from the central subject, the extent to which they divert attention from the lesson, the remoteness of their connection, and the smallness of their importance.

Proper distribution of the work over the time of the lesson must not be neglected. There is always a tendency to say too much about the more interesting or better known parts of the subject, so that it often occurs that a teacher finds himself only part of the way through what he set himself to do when he ought to be nearing the end of his lesson.

(3) *The facts must be stated in a simple and direct way.* The teacher should speak clearly, and, with children, avoid the use of unfamiliar words or long and involved sentences. **That which underlies success here is for the most part thorough and complete understanding by the teacher himself of what he is unfolding.** Some teachers seem to find great difficulty in using simple and suitable language, and employ words which are not only hard to the children but which are not the best, apart from other considerations, to convey the ideas intended.

The mistake, however, must not be made of supposing that by simplicity is meant childishness. The language of teaching should, as to difficulty, always be a little in advance of the scholars; and it should be borne in mind that they learn to understand the teacher's language sooner than to speak it. Sometimes an idea can only be properly expressed by a word which is difficult to beginners. At first it may at times be well to express this by some periphrasis which can be more easily grasped, but it is foolish to go on doing so. Directly the idea is perfectly clear the word should be given. If the former was worth introducing, the latter is worth learning.

So long as the word used is the best possible to express what is meant there need be little fear but that the child will soon come to realise its meaning. As Richter says, "the teacher's mien, accent, and the forestalling effort to understand explain one-half, and this with the assistance of time explains the other."

(4) *The ideas must be connected.* Much lecture is of a very disjointed character, either from want of consideration, or from the teacher giving what he remembers at the moment, not what should have been given to carry on the children's thought. The facts must not be presented in any chance order, as circumstances suggest them

to the mind, or the lesson will degenerate into a mere patchwork and much of its value will be lost. **The points should follow each other logically and naturally,** so that their connection and mutual relationship may be apparent, and each may lead the mind on to the next. **There must be sequence in thought as well as sequence in statement.** The careful connection of the ideas is a vital matter if the lecture work is to be a success. When the facts are so developed as to have a combined meaning, and they are made to support each other, the comprehension of them is much more complete and recollection is materially aided.

An unskilful teacher, ill-informed about his lesson, sometimes bemuddles both himself and his children by stating his points out of their proper order and treating them as though they were isolated items of information. He brings forward some fact, but, having forgotten what he intended to say about it, he jumps to something else. Then, before he has finished with this, he possibly recollects what he intended to say about the previous point, and goes back to that without a word of warning. When he is again ready to move forward he has forgotten where he left off, and probably takes up some altogether new point. This dodging backwards and forwards often destroys the whole meaning of the teaching, and results in the children becoming completely confused.

(5) *The points must be presented with varying deliberation and emphasis.* The speed with which lecture should be given is a matter which will often call for good judgment on the part of the teacher. It should vary according to the difficulty likely to be experienced by the children in grasping what is said, and according to the importance of an exact remembrance of the facts stated. Not nearly enough attention is paid to this. **Many teachers lecture as though all the points were of equal value.** The lesson is like reading without emphasis; and the children are not helped, as they should be, in recognising what are the **fundamental facts** which they must hold securely. These should be given deliberately and forcibly, so that they may be fully realised; and they should contrast with the merely explanatory matters which the children are able to follow readily.

It is always well, where a point of any permanent importance has to be given, to approach it in such a way as to **arouse interest** in it, and give the children a glimpse of what is coming, before making the definite statement. "Whenever the teacher does not first excite inquiry, first prepare the mind by *waking it up* to a desire to know and if possible to find out by itself, but proceeds to think for the child, and to give him the results before they are desired, or before they have been sought for—he makes the mind of the child a two-gallon jug into which he may pour just two gallons but no more."—(*Page.*)

(6) *The lecture work must be vivid and interesting.* Children are good listeners when the subject is something which strikes their fancy, as a story or a narrative of adventure ; but they very soon tire of a plain statement of facts in which they take little or no interest. If therefore the teacher would succeed in his use of lecture he must call to his aid all the means at his disposal of making it attractive.

It seems sometimes to be thought that anything will do for children, so long as it is simple and is what has to be learned. This is very far from being so. It is just with children that the most consummate art is often necessary to present a subject successfully.

The teacher should present his facts in as attractive and striking a way as possible, and at the same time with that **persuasiveness** which is almost always a characteristic of good lecture. The value of **contrast** and **variety of light and shade** in this connection should also be kept in mind. The fresher the mode of statement the better ; and **in his attempts to put things in a new way the teacher need not cease to be simple.** Neither sententiousness nor indulgence in rhetorical flights is what is wanted, but the avoidance of that bald commonplace which has so little power to arouse the interest or quicken the intelligence.

Children, again, like movement, and are much influenced by a bright, sympathetic, earnest manner. An animated attractive style of address is a great gain in teaching, and tells more perhaps in lecturing than in any other direction. When lecture is given in a dull prosy manner, as though the teacher were retailing his lesson from a book, or when he talks in a drawling listless way, as if the whole thing were a bore to him, it is not to be expected that the children will be interested no matter what is said.

As long as the teacher succeeds in interesting the children "the eyes are bright and fixed on the common centre of attraction. So soon as teaching becomes slow, monotonous, and wanting in intellectual energy, the eyes lose their lustre and begin to wander off from the common centre. Thus it becomes obvious that **the teacher must himself be thoroughly interested in order to interest his children.**"—(*Calderwood.*)

No matter how presented, facts need to be fixed ; and this is perhaps more necessary with lecture than in some other cases. The teacher has not only to 'make his points,' but to test them in such a way as to insure that they have been properly apprehended ; and further to strengthen the impression by bringing them again before the mind. Unless this process of testing and fixing is thoroughly carried out, lecture will often count for but little in securing the permanence of knowledge.

EXPLANATION AND 'PICTURING OUT.'

These are not single devices marked by special and independent characteristics of their own, like those already dealt with, but composite processes, in which the teacher presses into his service any or every method that will assist him in making clear to the child what is indistinct or difficult of realisation.

Explanation consists in (1) simplifying the *words* in which knowledge is expressed, so that unfamiliar terms may be understood by means of familiar ones; (2) substituting known or easily appreciated *ideas* for others that are unknown or more difficult to realise—often by means of illustrations; and (3) giving additional related ideas shewing upon what that which is explained depends, and to what it leads, so as to secure *completeness of conception*. We may say that **to explain is to employ the right mental solvent of a difficulty** so that the underlying idea may combine with others of a like kind; or, to change the figure, it is to reduce a complex fraction of knowledge to its simplest form.

It is impossible to *explain* what one has only hazy or ill conceived notions of oneself. Hence the first requisite for success in explanation is a **thorough understanding** by the teacher himself of the subject he has to teach, so that he may be able to analyse any part of it on the instant, note its various bearings, and select the most likely point of attachment in what is known with which to connect it. In the next place he needs **quick perception and keen sympathy**, that he may realise at once the *nature* of the difficulty which bars the way to understanding, and determine precisely at what point the impediment occurs—that is, realise exactly what it is which needs explaining, and how assistance may best be given. And lastly, he must have **considerable facility of expression**, so that he may be able readily to state the new view in a simple straightforward way and there may be no hesitating or bungling to the manifest confusion of the child.

The mode of explanation will vary very much according to the nature of what is to be explained. In some cases the difficulty may be met directly, and a few simple words are all that is wanted; in other cases the teacher will have to proceed much more slowly and cautiously. When any serious difficulty presents itself in what is necessary for the child to understand, the teacher should **break up the subject by means of questions**, so that what has been already comprehended may be stripped away and the real matter needing elucidation laid bare. He will then proceed to direct attention to each point in turn, illustrating or simplifying as the case may require, until at length the whole is illuminated, and the child sees plainly what was previously dark or indistinct and consequently meaningless. When the explanation has been completed, further questioning should be given to insure that he has grasped the *ideas*, not merely taken hold of the teacher's *words*.

The pupil must be allowed time to realise what is presented to him by way of explanation; **everything may be spoiled by a little want of patience, or by incautious hurry.** Each step must be made clear before passing to the next, and anything of the nature of a pitfall must be guarded against. The teacher should be able to **estimate exactly how much is possible to children, and only just that amount of help should be given which is necessary.** Frequently too much is suggested, and the amount of self-effort reduced in consequence. Skill is often most conspicuously shown in directing the thought of the child, encouraging him, and preparing him for the central point of a difficulty, so that when it has to be met he is able to overcome it unaided. Nothing strengthens and stimulates a child more than this, or gives him greater confidence to attack future difficulties for himself. It is the very essence of training.

The following are some of the more **common errors into which the teacher is liable to fall in making use of explanation.**

(1) *Explaining at too great a length.* This is often due to want of definiteness and certainty of information on the part of the teacher. He feels that his first statement has not made the matter clear, and goes on talking in the hope that eventually the children will understand what he means. Time is wasted, the prolixity is wearying, and the point is often beclouded rather than illuminated.

Some teachers, again, possessed of a large fund of information, seem to have great difficulty in keeping it within bounds, and hence in explaining a point introduce matters which, while interesting in themselves, are not necessary for the elucidation of the subject in hand. Important parts of the lesson have consequently to be hurried over, or are thrust out altogether. The greater the teacher's knowledge is, the stronger is the temptation to fall into this error.

In any case where too much is said about what has to be explained the children are very apt to lose the point of the whole matter, and to fix their attention on what is said rather than on its bearing and purpose. As a rule, explanation should be as brief as is compatible with clearness and intelligent progress in the work.

"When a thing is clear," says Miss Edgeworth, "let the teacher never try to make it clearer; when a thing is understood not a word more of explanation should be added. To mark precisely the moment when the pupil understands what is said, the moment when he is master of the necessary ideas, is perhaps the most difficult thing in the art of teaching. The countenance, the eye, the voice, and manner of the pupil mark this instant to an observing preceptor."

(2) *Giving unnecessary explanations.* Some teachers appear to have little power of estimating correctly what are likely to be difficulties to a child, and consequently often waste time, as well as make the work tedious, by explaining things about which little or nothing need have been said. It may happen with any teacher, that an explanation which has been carefully prepared is not wanted when the point is reached in the lesson. What might have been a difficulty, standing by itself, has been cleared up sufficiently by the previous work.

Even of things which the pupil cannot understand it is not possible to explain everything; nor would it be well to do so if it were possible. **It is a mistake to suppose that children are benefited by having everything made easy for them**, or by seeing everything from the same point of view as the teacher.

For an explanation to be in place the difficulty should be one which it is necessary to remove if the purpose of the lesson is to be accomplished. Even here however a rigid adherence to rule will sometimes mislead the teacher. His good sense, based on knowledge of what is required, ought to tell him what it is well to say, and what should be left unsaid; and should also prevent him from supposing that what is clear to him is necessarily clear to his pupils.

(3) *Explaining in the wrong place.* Some care is necessary to secure that an explanation is brought in at the most suitable moment. It is not an infrequent experience for a teacher to **introduce prematurely what he has to say by way of elucidation**, so that the children are altogether uncertain as to what it is which is being explained. It is foolish to break into a chain of reasoning, or to stop a boy in the middle of a sentence in reading, in order to explain some word

or phrase which he does not understand. It may be wise to note the point and to seek a more favourable opportunity of speaking about it; but so long as the boy's mind ought to be occupied with other things the teacher should keep his explanations to himself.

Sometimes again an explanation is **omitted from forgetfulness** just when it should have been introduced, and then is given later on amidst quite other matters. It is better to leave it out altogether rather than bring it in at the wrong place, where it is a harmful distraction of the attention and does little or no good.

(4) *Giving sham explanations.* An explanation is unworthy of the name which does not assist the child to understand more clearly than before that which is explained. Such sham explanations are by no means infrequent. Commonly they take the form of a talk, in which other terms are introduced, but no simplification is effected, and no light is thrown upon the subject. Unless the elements of which the explanation is composed are easier to comprehend than the thing to be explained no help is given.

The attempts to explain a word by merely substituting for it a **synonymous word** quite as difficult and unfamiliar to the child is a case in point. The giving of a **dictionary definition** of a word, which is wide of the meaning in the actual passage before the child, is another instance.

Sometimes a teacher destroys the reality of an explanation by **thinking for the child.** He moves rapidly from point to point, and concludes that all is well because the child is able to give back the words used. There may be no real understanding at all in such a case, and both teacher and child may be deluded by the process.

The worst form of sham explanation is that in which the teacher, afraid to acknowledge his own ignorance, makes a **show of explaining** the matter and simply mystifies the child. No genuine teacher would descend to such a practice.

'Picturing out,' like explanation, is a compound process in which combined use is made of direct address, familiar oral illustrations, ellipses, and training questions. The purpose is to assist the child in forming a distinct mental picture of objects, scenes, etc., which are more or less difficult to realise, and which, from their nature or the circumstances attending the teaching, cannot be made clear by any appeal to the senses. 'Picturing out' differs from explanation in that **it aims at securing understanding by vividness of presentment**

L

rather than by simplification, though the latter is often included. It appeals to the imagination, and makes use of such concepts as are familiar. These it combines and presents to the child as a striking word-picture, in order that by this means he may be duly impressed and realise clearly what is required. While employing both description and illustration, 'picturing out' is more than either of these singly, and may often be used with advantage in place of, or as supplementary to, both these processes.

Like other composite methods used in teaching, from which it differs only in the way in which the expedients are combined, 'picturing out' is essentially a mode of securing, by means of the known, complete conception of what is previously unknown. It may often be employed with advantage in the case of younger children ; and in special cases is useful throughout a child's school career. Caution is necessary not to let it degenerate into a mere rambling description.

'Picturing out' was brought into prominent notice as a technical device by David Stow, who claimed for it great importance and made it the basis of his system of training. In a broader sense its use must have been not uncommon in all ages, inasmuch as all "teaching by means of parables" and attempts to reach the mind by word pictures through the action of the imagination are really but exemplifications of the principle of the method.

V.—FIXING DEVICES.

Every one recognises the importance in teaching of presenting knowledge to the child in an orderly systematic way, and in a form he can understand ; but the equal importance of **securing that the information given shall be fixed**, so that it may remain a permanent possession, is rarely attended to as it should be. It is impossible to secure that everything said in a lesson shall be remembered, nor is this at all necessary ; but **the child should have perfectly clear ideas of the salient points and main outlines of the subject**, and see how the facts are connected together. Of course every teacher will have numberless small devices of his own for securing the necessary depth of impression and consequent retention of facts ; but four expedients are of sufficient importance, and of sufficiently general application, to merit separate consideration. These are repetition, recapitulation, black-board heads, and review.

(1) *Repetition.* Every influence brought to bear upon the mind

leaves some impression behind it, and it is by means of this that the revival of the idea becomes possible. Sometimes the effect produced by a single presentation is sufficiently powerful to render retention certain; but in many cases it is of such an evanescent character that repetition again and again is necessary before the idea becomes fixed.

Jacotot's favourite maxim, "Repeat without ceasing," is only one of the many instances in which the **value of repetition in education** is insisted upon. The really important practical point is that the repetition should be accomplished without weariness to the pupil—that **the teacher should repeat without seeming to do so of set purpose**. Sometimes it is necessary to reiterate facts in the same words, so that the idea and the symbol may be permanently associated; in other cases it is better to repeat the points in a changed form, and this is generally best accomplished by means of questions.

(2) *Recapitulation.* This is going over the heads or important points of the lesson in order, not only to fix them, but to bring out the relative bearings and connection of the facts in such a way that they may appear in their proper perspective. Recapitulation may be employed at any point of the work, and is often useful for picking up the threads of a lesson; but there should also be **fixed places for the summing up of the teaching as far as it has gone**, and these will generally correspond to the ends of the divisions. Such systematic recapitulation gives a firm grasp of the lesson as a whole, and is also an important factor in securing correct recollection.

(3) *Black-board Heads or Summaries.* When properly used these are in accordance with the principle that **something should be learned thoroughly and exactly and the rest referred to that.** They are of the greatest service in facilitating and rendering certain the remembrance of the outline of the lesson. After each section has been recapitulated and summed up, the gist of this summing up—the key fact, or the fact which will serve to suggest the rest of that portion of the work—should be put upon the black-board, and read by the children until firmly fixed in their minds. If they can be induced by means of questions, to suggest the black-board head themselves—the teacher assisting only as far as is necessary to secure conciseness and correctness of expression—so much the better. It should be borne in mind that **the black-board heads are not fragments, and not merely suggestive words, but clear and pithy statements properly expressed in**

sentences; and that when the lesson is completed they should form a readable and intelligible abstract of all the more important features of the teaching. Though details are omitted there should be no break in thought.

The words should be well chosen, and the sentences simple and direct in construction. It is better to have two or even three short heads at the end of a division than one long one.

The reading is often of a very imperfect character. It should generally be simultaneous; and each head should be read first by itself, and then in connection with all those which have preceded it. In this way two senses are appealed to—hearing and sight. With younger children it is well to have each word read as the teacher writes it, so as to keep up attention, and then the statement given as a whole. In no case should the teacher turn his back on his class and leave them idle while he thinks out his sentence and writes it on the board.

The heads should be neatly and distinctly written; and **in the higher classes the treatment should form a preliminary training for the pupils in taking notes** on their own account. In the transition stage, the note or summary should first be brought out by the combined efforts of the class as a whole, and the sentence should be rapidly dictated by the teacher. As soon however as the children are able to manage for themselves this help should be withdrawn.

Black-board heads should be worked up to, not written down abruptly. An unskilled or forgetful teacher is very apt to neglect his black-board heads until too late, and consequently to bring them in at inopportune moments—sometimes as the result of chance, sometimes to fill up a gap when he is at a loss for something to say. In many cases they do not properly summarise the lesson at all, and are written down regardless of their connection with one another.

(4) *Review.* The periodical review of what has been taught, so as to prevent its becoming hazy and uncertain, or fading altogether, is a **matter of the greatest importance** in school-work; but it is also one which is often very much neglected. Few teachers seem to realise practically how rapidly information sinks beyond recovery, and how much is lost for want of being occasionally brought to the surface. It is a grievous mistake to allow matters to be forgotten which have cost both teacher and pupils a large expenditure of effort, when a small

amount of time devoted to them now and again would keep them fresh and ready for use.

Every running over of a subject, or of a course of lessons, not only **strengthens remembrance**, but **gives a broad view of the whole**, and thus **prevents the cramping and narrowing effect of continuous attention to details.** When review is properly cared for, knowledge no longer appears to the pupil as a series of isolated facts; and the form of the work can be so varied that the subject is looked at from a somewhat different point of view each time.

Regular lessons for the thorough review of what has been taught should be arranged for at stated intervals, or when a certain amount of work has been gone through; and no consideration of the apparent need for pressing on over new ground should be allowed to stand in the way.

Written test examinations, conducted by the teacher, and confined to matters which have been given in the lessons, are also a very useful means of review where the children are sufficiently advanced for this kind of work.

CHAPTER VII.

CLASS MANAGEMENT.

THE successful management of a class is conditioned by three sets of influences—(1) those dependent upon organisation, that is upon proper arrangements being made for conducting the work with the least loss of time and the maximum of comfort and efficiency; (2) those which are connected with the government of children, that is with the proper exercise of disciplinary power and control; (3) those arising from the way in which the teaching is given.

I. CLASS MANAGEMENT AS DETERMINED BY ORGANISATION.

Efficient organisation has a powerful influence upon the proper management of a class. With children working under unhealthy conditions, in physical discomfort, or with bad arrangements for carrying on the work, it is impossible for teaching to be as successful, or control as easy, as should be the case.

Every additional strain, whether physical or mental, to which either teacher or child is unnecessarily subjected, is so much energy running to waste. If the conditions by means of which this waste may be minimised were more carefully attended to, as they ought to be, the harmful effects attributed to overpressure would, at least in the case of healthy children, almost entirely disappear.

Although the full discussion of matters connected with organisation belongs properly to *School Management* in its narrower sense, yet, from their direct and indirect bearing upon teaching, the more important points are well worthy of careful consideration in connection with the present subject.

I. GENERAL CONDITIONS AS DIRECTLY AFFECTING THE HEALTH AND COMFORT OF THE SCHOLARS. Every school should be planned to suit the work to be done there. This is frequently neglected, and consequently many vexatious inconveniences arise from bad arrangements.

(1) *The Room*. The **most useful form of room**, where the school is of moderate size (say for from 50 to 150 children), and has to be under the direct control of the head teacher, is an oblong just sufficiently wide to allow of the class being brought out in front of the desks.

In large schools the **tendency of modern organisation is to break up the available floor space into separate rooms**, to contain from 40 to 80 children each according to needs. This is accomplished either by having the school built as a series of separate rooms, or by dividing up the large room by means of partitions.

These partitions may either slide, or fold, or be made like a Queen Anne blind and roll up towards the ceiling. There can be no doubt that for the ordinary purposes of teaching such a **separation of classes** is a great advantage where the teachers are sufficiently experienced to be left to themselves. The work is more directly under their control, and the disturbing influences arising from having classes alongside each other engaged in similar exercises are done away with.

It is difficult for a teacher to keep his class under proper control when a neighbouring class is noisy or disorderly, or an attractive lesson is going on near. If the main room is undivided, and several classes have to work side by side so as to be under the continuous supervision of the head teacher, the evils just referred to may be considerably lessened by separating the classes by means of curtains.

In the case of elementary schools the Education Department insists upon an average of 8 square feet of floor space and 80 cubic feet of air space for each child in average attendance. These however are the lowest allowances to escape a fine, and should certainly be exceeded wherever it is possible. In a school working up to its full complement of scholars the bodies of the children occupy a portion of the space ; and to this is to be added that taken up by furniture, etc. Even on days of maximum attendance the limits of air space per child should never fall below the 'Code' allowance ; and under ordinary working conditions **120 cubic feet per child** is much nearer what is required.

Even where the proper average amount of space is secured for each child certain classes may be very overcrowded ; and where this occurs the children are pretty certain to be restless. Some teachers do not even distribute the children in the best way over the space available for the class. All such little matters need to be looked to if the teaching is to be successful.

Cleanliness and pleasantness of the schoolroom are necessary conditions, not only of health but of that cheerfulness and brightness which should characterise children under instruction. **Dust is one of the teacher's enemies in school,** and should be scrupulously removed every day from the floor, furniture, and any crevices where it is likely to accumulate. Every one practically acquainted with schools must be aware how rarely this is done effectually. Dingy half-cleaned schoolrooms are only too common.

The lower part of the walls should be boarded or painted to a height of about five feet, and coloured some light tint of grey above. The ceilings should be whitewashed; but white is too glaring for the eye to rest upon with comfort when applied to the walls. **The general look of the room should be one of pleasant comfort;** and much may be done to add to its attractiveness by a judicious arrangement of pictures, diagrams, and maps. Pictures—such as large framed photographs of striking scenery, or of celebrated paintings within the comprehension of children, and many coloured prints now sold for school use—are not only useful for decorative purposes, but are a standing good influence upon children in other ways.

"Anything in the way of art that may hang on the walls should be thoroughly good of its kind. Cheapness nowadays luckily does not exclude the idea of beauty; where our forefathers were compelled to content themselves with worn-out impressions of inferior steel engravings, good etchings and admirable chromo-lithographs and examples of photogravure can now be had for very small prices. Even the Christmas numbers of the *Graphic* and *Illustrated News* will supply an effective and thoroughly wholesome sort of art at most trifling cost. I should be inclined to press this point of **effective decoration** with some persistence, as during the sympathetic period of youth impressions are readily taken in by the eye as well as by the other senses, and are so firmly retained as to leave their permanent stamp on the mind."—(*Dr. Farquharson.*)

The **floors of the room should be warm and dry, and as noiseless as possible.** Quarries or stone are unsuitable. Thin boards are noisy, and from their vibration send up a considerable amount of dust into the air during the movements of the children. The best floor is one made of wood blocks carefully laid in cement or asphalt to form a smooth surface; but thick, well-seasoned, and well-jointed boards make a satisfactory floor, and are, of course, much less expensive.

(2). *The Lighting.* **A room for teaching purposes should be well** lighted. If this is not secured it is often difficult for children to see in dull weather; and, apart from this, a half-lighted room has a gloomy look and exercises a depressing effect upon those immured in it day after day. The best light is one from the left, and well above the level of the children's heads. In no case should the windows be low down and directly in front of the children when in their usual working places. Nor should the children ever be allowed to sit with the sunshine either in their eyes or beating on their heads. In such circumstances proper attention is not to be expected. It is a mistake however to exclude sunlight altogether from a room. A judicious arrangement of blinds will easily secure all that is needed in this respect.

(3) *The Warming and Ventilation.* **The warming** is often a difficult problem to solve with complete success in the case of large schools. If a room is too hot the children become drowsy; and if too cold the discomfort distracts their attention from the teaching. With average children the temperature should not be allowed to fall so low as 55° F., nor rise above 65°.

<small>Even when a satisfactory temperature is secured, with many forms of apparatus the air is unpleasantly dry, and this is trying to those who have to talk Another common fault is the defective distribution of the heat, so that while one part of the room is comfortably warm, another is far too cold. Cold draughts to the feet are also frequently present. Where, too, the heating is badly managed, the room is generally much too cold in the early morning and too hot in the afternoon. All these things militate against the teaching; but with a little care and watchfulness on the part of the teacher they may almost always be considerably reduced, and in some cases removed altogether.</small>

The proper warming of a school is generally very closely connected with **efficient ventilation**. If school work is to be properly carried on, **a constant supply of fresh air is essential**; and this should be introduced without exposing the children to draughts. In many cases the air is warmed as it comes in; and such an arrangement where it does not unduly heat the air or rob it of its moisture is a great gain. It prevents injurious cold currents and economises the heat.

In all well-constructed schools the means and appliances for efficient ventilation are present; but the really important thing is that they should be regularly looked to and made use of. Theoretically these things are perfect enough; but practically they are often neglected to a deplorable extent. In a close stuffy atmosphere, much of which has been breathed over and over again, the children are certain to become dull and stupid; and the teacher, feeling his efforts meet with little response, is apt to grow irritable and cross. With conditions like these not only is damage being done to health, but the work suffers in many ways. Things, which in other circumstances would be easily learned, become matters of laborious effort, and weariness and overstrain soon follow.

Even with the best ventilation the **regular flushing of the room with fresh air is advisable.** It is never time wasted to send the children into the play-ground for a few minutes in the middle of an attendance, so that they may have a run in the fresh air; and while they are there doors and windows should be thrown open, if the weather will at all permit, in order that the air in the room may be thoroughly changed. It should be kept in mind that while the unwholesome state of the air in a room may strike any one very forcibly who comes into it from the outside, those working in it may be quite unconscious of its vitiated condition until the **physical consequences** force themselves upon the teacher's notice. Inattention, languor, headache, restlessness, giddiness, and nausea are all signs that the atmosphere has become thoroughly unfitted to support vital action properly. Relaxed or sore throat and dyspepsia on the part of the teacher are often also to be traced directly to working in a close room in bad air.

<blockquote>Currie justly says: "One day's work in a close room may not affect the teacher much; but no constitution can resist the effect of a continuance of this over several years. It is in the fact that such influences operate almost imperceptibly that his danger lies. Let the sanitary state of his schoolroom, then, be his first thought when he enters it in the morning; and let his thoughts recur to this at the end of every lesson."</blockquote>

(4) *Change of posture and of place.* Children get wearied by long continuance in the same posture, no matter how comfortable this may be for a certain time. It is a great mistake to allow them to remain sitting during the whole of the time they are in school, either from the point of view of health or that of work. **Arrangement should be made for alternating periods of sitting and standing,** and the change should, as a rule, be made at the end of a lesson. When, however, the children become restless and fidgety during the teaching, good may be done by a few moments **brisk physical exercise** and a change of posture. The relief afforded will, in many such cases, be evident

at once. Exercises of the nature of the 'extension movements,' well known to almost every teacher, are frequently beneficial in preventing children from becoming cramped and dull. They smarten up the attention and give a new impetus to effort, as well as do much to obviate those slouching, lounging, lolling, and crouching attitudes into which children so readily fall if left to themselves. Apart from the bad habits thus formed, such attitudes are often productive of disinclination to mental activity, and if persisted in may lead to physical mischief.

The commands necessary in the performance of the physical exercises referred to are, as a rule, best given by signals (such as movements of the hand, or the raising of the fingers), or by numbers. The signification of these the teacher can readily arrange for himself to suit his own ideas, but the same meanings should be used throughout the school.

Change of place is also a relief ; and where other arrangements will permit of it, it is certainly a gain to move children into another room for certain lessons, or to bring them from the desks on to the floor space in front. Some lessons, as reading, are very much better given with the children standing. Teachers are too apt to consider such things as of little or no importance ; whereas they frequently have very considerable influence on the teaching, and neglect of them increases the difficulties of control.

II. FURNITURE AS AFFECTING SCHOOL-WORK. All articles of furniture should be conveniently placed and kept in good order. Dirt should be carefully removed from time to time, and nothing of the nature of writing, scratching of names, or ill-usage should ever be allowed. Respect for the property of others cannot be too carefully instilled into children. In connection with class management only three items of furniture call more especially for consideration— galleries, desks, and seats.

(1) *The Galleries.* Galleries for oral teaching are best placed in rooms by themselves, so that the children may be more readily and completely under control, and the teacher may be free to adopt any device he pleases without the danger of interfering with other lessons going on near. In infants' schools, however, and in some schools organised on special systems, it is common to find the gallery at one end of the large room. It should not be placed where there is a large window at the back, or the light will be trying to the teacher, and

the children's faces being in shadow he will have some difficulty in seeing them as he should do. The best light is from the side or above.

Galleries are not uncommonly so crowded that the children cannot sit comfortably. In such circumstances restlessness and inattention are almost certain, and an undue proportion of the teacher's energy is spent in keeping order. In the case of galleries for infants, 14 or 15 inches *at least* should be allowed for each child; and with older scholars this should be extended to 16 or 18 inches. Many galleries are too deep from back to front for efficient teaching of all the scholars; five or six rows are as much as should be allowed, each platform being about two feet wide. The semicircular arrangement is a good one for little children. To allow of the children being moved readily in and out of the gallery, gangways about 16 inches in width up each side should be provided.

<small>In cases where economy is an important consideration, or where the semicircular form for infants is adopted, galleries are often so constructed that each step or platform serves as a seat for one row of children and a footboard for those in the row above. With this arrangement it is absolutely necessary to protect the children from the dirt of the boots and the accidental kicks and interference of those behind. This may be managed, and a back rest provided, by having a sloping board about 8 inches wide placed 9 or 10 inches from the front edge of the platform and running the whole length of the space occupied by the class. Neglect of this precaution is unfair to the children, and is pretty sure to be the source of many minor difficulties in the management of the class.

Even at the best, however, the plan is not a good one, and where possible it should be avoided. It necessitates the gallery as a whole being higher than is otherwise necessary or advisable, while effectual cleansing from dirt and dust is rendered more difficult, and any neglect in this respect is much more likely to escape detection.</small>

The best plan is to have movable seats, and these—of suitable heights for the children who are to occupy them—should be placed preferably at the *back* of each platform; though seats about four to six inches high placed on the *front* of each platform are sometimes used. In no case should the seats be fixed, inasmuch as the gallery cannot then be properly swept; and with the low forms just mentioned the spaces beneath simply become storehouses for dirt. Where separate seats are used at the back of the platforms the latter need not rise more than four or five inches above each other.

Gallery seats should always be provided with supports for the back, and these should not be too high; nine or ten inches for average children is ample. The common mistake is to support the shoulders instead of the middle of the back.

(2) *The Desks.* In schools for children above the infant stage no part of the furniture has such an important bearing upon the teaching or upon the health of the scholars as the desks. This is becoming generally recognised in theory, but very much remains yet to be done both in the way of proper provision and of careful adjustment to conditions before things can be said to be satisfactory from a practical point of view. To ill-devised desks with faulty seats have been attributed many of the evil effects of school work—notably curvature of the spine, contracted chests, and to a considerable extent the marked increase of short-sight.

School desks to be quite satisfactory should as far as possible fulfil the following conditions :—

(a) *They should be thoroughly serviceable for all uses to which they are liable to be put in teaching.*

This ought certainly to be the first consideration. It may be convenient in other ways to have desks which may be transformed into seats, tables, and so on; but usefulness for the ordinary purposes of teaching is the main thing, and against any serious defects in this respect no amount of usefulness in other directions ought to be allowed to weigh.

The desks should be rigid and not easily moved out of position by chance pressures. It is better to have them secured to each other by sleepers than screwed down to the floor. The **top of the desk should be continuous**—not broken by a flat portion at the upper side which adds to the width without being of any service. Every pupil should have an ink-well to himself, which should be placed to the right and sunk down to the level of the desk. A groove for pens should also be provided. **Desks for Infants** are not so much used for writing as for the performance of exercises like those of the Kindergarten, and hence they are generally made with flat tops and are much lower than ordinary desks.

From 18 to 22 inches should be allowed for each child in writing. If children are unduly crowded they are constantly interfering with each other and are much more difficult for the teacher to manage.

(b) *They should meet all necessary requirements for the maintenance of a proper position of body, and especially should be of suitable dimensions for the children who are to occupy them.*

Here we have to consider the desks more particularly from the hygienic point of view. The essential matters are (1) the height of the desk ; (2) the slope ; (3) the nature and height of the seat ; (4)

the distance between a perpendicular from the edge of the desk and the form.

Desks are frequently too high. When this is the case it is almost impossible for the child to sit comfortably while writing. He should be able to place the forearms on the desk without forcing up the shoulders or unduly raising the elbows. **For the ordinary range of children the desks should vary from about 25 to 30 inches in height** from the floor to the centre of the top of the desk.

As to the **nature of the slope** authorities are divided; the slope generally recommended varies between 1 in 10 and 1 in 5. Some teachers prefer desks in which the slope can be altered at will by a mechanical arrangement: there seems however to be no practical gain in this, for as a matter of fact the slope is very seldom altered in this way in school.

The seats again are almost always too narrow, and generally too high. The proper height is the distance from the knee to the bottom of the heel, so that the child may sit well on the form and yet have both feet upon the ground or the foot-board. Excluding desks for infants the height of the seats should be from $14\frac{1}{2}$ to $16\frac{1}{2}$ inches according to the size of the children. The best width is about 10 inches; though some authorities advocate a width of a foot. It is commonly held, at least by physicians, that the **seats should have backs.** The difficulties, however, of devising desks which shall meet all requirements—unless they are complex and expensive single desks that are out of the reach of ordinary schools—are so great that the problem cannot at present be said to have been satisfactorily solved. Desk seats with backs are still a rarity in elementary schools. It should be kept in mind that **it is the lower part of the back which needs support,** not the shoulders.

To prevent the child leaning forward in writing and indulging in the common but harmful practice of pressing the chest against the edge of the desk, the latter should slightly overhang, or at least be perpendicularly over, the edge of the form. If, however, the desks are permanently fixed in this way the child cannot properly stand up. Nevertheless the latter is the less evil of the two, and in no case should the desk be several inches removed as it generally is in the desks at present in use.

(c) *The design and arrangement of the desks should be such as to allow of the children being readily moved in and out, or of any child being easily reached by the teacher, and of the whole class being seen without effort from the teacher's position in front.*

In what may be called the **short length system of arrangement** single or more usually dual desks are used, and these are generally grouped in lines leading from the teacher with gangways between. Five or six or even more rows from back to front are common. The **advantages** are that any child can be readily reached from the side, or leave his place when called upon without in the least interfering with others; and, further, seats with backs may be used without any additional difficulty. The **disadvantages** are that the desks cover so great an area that the useful floor-space, which should be kept free in front of the class, is almost entirely taken up, and the children thus in many cases remain seated throughout an attendance, which is not well; or they have to stand between the desks for such lessons as reading, which is not a pleasing or convenient arrangement. The difficulties of controlling a large body of

CLASS MANAGEMENT 175

children, and of keeping them interested during oral teaching, are also increased from the want of that compactness in the class which every teacher knows is so helpful.

In the **long length system of arrangement** the desks are usually grouped in threes, each desk seating a number of children. This is the more common arrangement and seems to be the one generally preferred. So far as teaching is concerned there can be little doubt it is the more convenient, especially in small or narrow schools. Space should be kept between the desks for the teacher to move behind the children. The chief **advantages** are the compactness of grouping, and the ease with which change of posture and of place may be secured, by bringing the children out upon the floor space in front, when any lesson may be more suitably taught in this way. The **disadvantages** of the plan are that any particular child cannot be so easily reached by the teacher, or leave his place so readily, and that backed seats are at present almost a practical impossibility with this arrangement.

III. PROPER ARRANGEMENT OF SCHOLARS AND WORK. Under this head may be grouped all matters affecting class management which are dependent upon the right classification of the children, the adjustment of the work to the teacher's skill and knowledge, and the arrangement of times and subjects in such a way that the children may always be *suitably* employed and no part of their instruction may be neglected.

(1) *The classification of the children.* In order that the instruction given to a class may be so suited to every member of it that no one is unduly pressed and no one neglected, the level of attainment and of intellectual power must be fairly uniform throughout. It is not always possible to secure this, but if the classification is to be satisfactory it must always be aimed at. Where the children are faultily grouped, so that some are much more advanced than others, the difficulties of successful management, with respect to both teaching and discipline, are very much increased.

Children vary very much not only in knowledge but in their ability to master certain branches of learning. To adjust matters with theoretical exactness to the child's needs there should be a separate classification for every important subject of instruction within the school range. This, however, being practically impossible, teachers have been led to group the subjects in various ways.

The trouble and inconvenience as well as other disciplinary defects of even a **threefold classification**—namely, for (1) reading and literary subjects, (2) arithmetic and allied branches, and (3) mechanical subjects such as writing, drawing, etc.—are so great as to have prevented the adoption of this plan except in rare cases. At the present time it is probably entirely abandoned.

A **twofold classification**—founded on attainment in (1) arithmetic and other mathematical subjects, on the one side, and (2) literary work, including reading, writing, geography, and like subjects, on the other—is much less cumbrous, and satisfies all ordinary needs. There can be little doubt that for higher schools, at least, this is by far the best arrangement.

The conditions of the 'Code' examinations have led to the adoption everywhere in English elementary schools of a **single classification** based on average attainment in reading, writing, and arithmetic; and though the conditions are now somewhat altered, and greater freedom of classification is allowed, the single arrangement will probably still remain commonly in use. The *advantages* of this mode of classification are, that it simplifies arrangements and causes less difficulty from a disciplinary point of view; it secures attention being given to that grounding in elementary subjects which should form the basis of further studies; and consequently it promotes all-round development, and prevents specialisation of effort at too early an age. The chief *disadvantages* of the plan are, that it tends to reduce all the members of a class to the same dead level of acquirement, and the children, especially the brighter ones, are often hampered and discouraged by being kept marking time in certain subjects because they happen to be backward in some other, which may be of less importance. It is almost impossible to prevent this to some extent, where the child's position is determined by his ability to reach a certain fixed standard in *all* the essential subjects. There is also the evil that in elementary schools a child is often kept in the same class much longer than he ought to be, because he has not passed his examination.

It is to be hoped that the recent changes in the 'Code' requirements will lead to that **readjustment of classes at shorter intervals** and that **regular promotion** of the quicker scholars, which are so necessary if justice is to be done to all the children and the teaching is to have its full effect.

The defects of the single classification are much less felt, and are of much less importance, where young children have to be dealt with, than where older scholars have to be provided for, and it is essential for the future good of the latter that they should have every opportunity of making the most of any ability they may possess for work in some particular direction.

In **classifying children where considerable diversity of acquirement in the rudimentary subjects is shewn**, that subject should have most weight given to it which needs most careful teaching. In general this is arithmetic, but in the earliest stages progress in reading is of more importance and may well be taken as the main test.

(2) *The proper officering of the classes.* This is an important consideration. If the class is larger than the teacher can well manage, or if he is unable, without an undue tax upon his knowledge or skill, to handle effectively the subjects to be taught, difficulties as to management are sure to arise. A skilled adult teacher may, in favourable circumstances, be able to give a collective lesson to some 60 or 80 children ; but it is impossible for him with such a class to teach the ordinary subjects of instruction—such as reading, writing, and arithmetic—with that intimate knowledge of each child and that careful attention to the needs of individuals which are necessary if the children are to be properly educated. Nor is it possible in such a case, without unceasing watchfulness and a very severe strain upon his energies, for the teacher to keep every child in good order and constantly employed, so that, even from a mere knowledge point of view, the pupils may make all the progress of which they are capable.

The classes entrusted to young Pupil Teachers in elementary schools are often far too large for such a teacher to do justice either to himself or the children. As he is only learning his business, his teaching is apt to be formal and commonplace ; and the skill and judgment necessary to keep a large number of children steadily employed and interested in their work ought not to be expected of him. The difficulties of control, too, are increased by the want of that tact in dealing with idle or troublesome children which only comes from experience. His work is often so trying, and so many things seem to demand attention at the same time, that he is unable to think as calmly as he should do; and it is not to be wondered at if in such a case he grows irritable and snappish, and finally becomes disgusted both with himself and his work.

The teachers should be distributed to the classes according to their knowledge, teaching ability, and power of maintaining discipline. It is well, however, not to keep *young teachers* always at the same class, especially where they are employed to help an older assistant, inasmuch as a change now and again gives them increased experience and is a good thing in other ways, both for themselves and the children. Nevertheless they should remain at a class for a sufficiently long period to make their influence and teaching fully felt, and to obtain credit for such results as they are able to secure.

The circumstances of schools vary of course very much, and what is advisable on general grounds may be inexpedient for other reasons. As a rule, wherever it is feasible, it is well for pupil teachers in sole charge of a class to retain the same position for a year, and to change just after the examination. Anything which is likely to prevent them from viewing their work merely as a round of dull routine or from falling into a perfunctory performance of duty is worth attention.

In **apportioning the work** it should be remembered that the teaching in the middle of the school generally demands least skill. The top of the school—from the logical teaching and careful intellectual training necessary, the amount of knowledge required, and the very judicious disciplinary treatment which elder scholars demand—is of course the post of difficulty. Next to this in importance is the lowest section of the school, where the children are just commencing their studies in earnest, and the greatest care is needed to foster good habits and to instil into the pupils a love for the work. Here unwearying patience, gentleness and kindness of disposition, vivacity of manner, and the skill to present facts in a bright interesting way are all necessary. It is a great mistake to commit such work to the youngest or weakest teacher in the school, as is sometimes done.

That there are differences in the nature of the work to be performed in different parts of the school, and that the skill required is not always the same, goes without saying; but **any post is a post of honour**, and will afford the teacher plenty of opportunity for a faithful performance of duty and for putting out all the power of which he is possessed.

(3) *The arrangement of time and subjects.* No school should ever work without a Time-table. The careful preconsideration and arrangement of work, so that nothing may be left to chance or the hasty decision of the moment, is a part of his duty which no teacher can afford to neglect. Everything connected with the management of the class should be carried out with order and promptitude. Forethought in such matters saves a very great deal of trouble. **The proper arrangement of time and subjects is a most valuable aid both to teaching and disciplinary control**; and where such arrangement is made, every one knows what his work is, when it should begin, and when it should end. There is therefore no excuse on the part of the scholars for idleness with its accompanying temptations to mischief; and the consequent need for punishment of faults arising in this way is much reduced. The teacher is also saved much unnecessary worry and anxiety, and confusion and loss of time in beginning are prevented. There is, too, the further **moral value to the children** which arises from habits of punctuality, methodical application, obedience to law, and attention to each duty at the right time.

For details as to the method of constructing a Time-table, the values to be attached to the different subjects of instruction, and other matters which need to be taken into account, the reader must refer to books dealing specially with School Management.

The **more essential points to be kept in view in apportioning the time and subjects** are :—

(a) *The judicious distribution of the time at disposal for work among the various subjects.* This should be based upon their importance as instrumental to further acquisition, as affording a useful mental training, and as giving knowledge of permanent value in after life.

A definite plan insures that each subject within the curriculum shall receive the amount of time to which it is entitled ; and that no undue attention shall be given to those subjects which are pleasantest, or which cost least trouble, to the neglect of others, possibly of less interest but of equal or greater importance.

(b) *The regular recurrence of each subject at stated intervals.* This is necessary in order that steady progress may be made, and that attention to any subject may not be given by fits and starts.

There is always a temptation to desultory work where the hours of study are not fixed. The connection of the various parts is thus apt to be lost sight of. In no subject ought the interval between one lesson and another to be so great that the children cannot with ease remember what was last taught.

(c) *The relief afforded by distributing the difficult work.* The lessons should be arranged in such a succession, that with each change the mental working is as far as possible turned in a different direction from that in which is has just been employed—that is, that another set of faculties, as we commonly say, is more particularly called into exercise.

Thus, mechanical occupations, such as writing, are a rest after lessons demanding considerable mental effort ; lessons needing mostly an exercise of memory may well come after others in which the reasoning faculties have been largely employed ; literature is a relief after mathematics.

(d) *The disposition of the lessons in such a way that those demanding most strenuous effort shall come when the children are fresh to their work.* This is a matter very commonly neglected, yet there is no point bearing upon the distribution of the individual lessons which is of greater importance.

The best time for such lessons as arithmetic is as early in the morning attendance as can be arranged. Next to this are the times coming immediately after recreation.

Lessons which come late in the afternoon should be of an easy character; if merely mechanical so much the better.

(e) *The distribution of noisy lessons in such a way that as far as practicable they may not interfere with one another.* Thus, lessons necessitating much talking or simultaneous utterance should not be given to two adjoining classes at the same time, wherever any other disposition can be made.

Where the school has a large number of class-rooms the distribution of noisy work may usually be effected with ease. In many schools, however, most of the classes have to be taught near each other, and here the difficulty of adjusting the time-table, so as to minimise the interference of one class with another, has to be met. Lessons requiring unbroken attention should be free from external disturbance of any kind.

With talking going on in several directions at the same time it is far from easy to catch distinctly what is said. This leads both teachers and pupils to speak louder and louder, until sometimes the din is unbearable. Where the clash of lessons in this way is unavoidable, class management becomes increasingly difficult; and *each teacher should be on his guard not to speak himself, and not to allow his pupils to speak, in a louder tone than is absolutely necessary.*

(f) *The adjustment of the length of the lesson to the age and power of the pupils.* A lesson should be long enough to train the children to sustained application, but it should not be continued so long as to produce weariness. Beyond a certain limit, which is soon reached, we cannot teach a child twice as much in twice the time.

For the youngest children lessons of twenty minutes each are quite long enough. In the middle of the school the more suitable length is half an hour, with perhaps one longer lesson each day. In the higher classes the time may be extended to three-quarters of an hour, and with the oldest pupils in a large school hour lessons will generally be found advisable. In no case, however, should a regular lesson extend beyond this.

IV. THE BEARING OF APPARATUS AND BOOKS. Without proper materials for use the teacher is severely handicapped in his work. All sorts of makeshifts and expedients have to be adopted in order to reduce the resulting difficulties as much as possible; and this expenditure of energy is so much subtracted from that which should be given to informing and training the children; while, in many cases, decreased efficiency of such a nature as seriously to interfere with the progress of the pupils is scarcely to be avoided. Nor is it the teaching alone which suffers; for it is often not easy in such circumstances to keep children properly employed, and consequently more attention has to be given to matters of discipline.

(1) *Apparatus.* Many elementary schools it is to be feared are yet but badly equipped, in the way cf apparatus, with even the things necessary for the work to be carried on with ease and efficiency. It is a great mistake for managers to starve a school in this respect, even from the lowest consideration—that of grant.

It is the teacher's business to make himself thoroughly acquainted with all the most useful and effective kinds of apparatus in the market. Those who supply such things are now so well aware what is required, that there need be no difficulty on this account in securing what is wanted.

The apparatus should be exactly adapted to the purpose for which it is intended to be employed. It is often unnecessarily showy without essential features being properly cared for. Simplicity of construction, soundness of workmanship, and strength of materials arc all matters which should receive attention. With the more or less rough usage which is perhaps scarcely to be avoided in school, cheap things are very liable to come to pieces rapidly, and to prove anything but cheap in the long-run.

The more important things in the way of maps, pictures, diagrams, models, specimens, etc., have been briefly described in connection with illustrations. In addition to these may be noted a ball frame, 'number pictures,' a box of small cubes, sheets of tables, the commoner weights and measures, with diagrams (or better still models) of the others, for the teaching of **arithmetic**; a letter box (or a 'word maker') and some large lesson cards for the purposes of **reading**; together with apparatus and materials for performing simple experiments, or for the illustration of ordinary lessons in **elementary science**, reference to which will be made later on.

There should also be a plentiful supply of **slates, paper, pens, chalk**, and **dusters**. These may be thought small matters, but unless they are regularly attended to such things are very apt not to be forthcoming when wanted, and to cause the teacher no small amount of worry and embarrassment in consequence.

The **Black-board** is of such paramount importance in teaching that it ought not to be passed over in the present connection without a few words of consideration to itself. *Every class should be provided with a black-board*; and during lessons it should invariably be in its place before the children. In addition to the boards for regular use in this way there should be two or three for particular purposes; such as a large one for occasional maps, and another with horizontal and diagonal lines for the purpose of teaching writing. Some teachers also will prefer to have a board ruled on one side for music.

The commonest form of black-board is the one placed upon an easel. This is as a rule much the cheapest, and has the advantage that it may be readily set up anywhere, and stored away out of the road in some convenient place when not in use. More expensive boards made to swing like a looking-glass, or to slide up and down in a frame, are very useful, and in certain circumstances are much to be preferred. A wall conveniently situated may also in some cases be made a cheap and serviceable means of support. The following are the **principal varieties of black-boards** in common use :—

(*a*) **Ordinary boards for use with easels.** These should be well made, of good material, and the ends should be tongued with strips of iron. If light boards are required they should be framed. The best easel for general use is the square-topped reversible one with a map support. Lighter forms may be necessary in some cases; but the folding tripod one is unsteady and is best avoided.

(*b*) **Swing boards** are rather expensive, but are very valuable for use with higher classes where the nature of the work often demands a considerable amount of writing or drawing to be shown at once. When properly constructed they have the further advantage that the board can be *readily fixed at any angle* at which the work can best be seen by the children. If the frame is mounted on strong casters, such boards can be easily moved short distances so as to adjust them to the most convenient position; but they are too heavy to be frequently shifted from place to place, and hence are commonly used only where they can always remain before the class.

(*c*) **Sliding boards.** These, like swing-boards, are expensive, and are too heavy to be moved about much. If properly made they can be *easily adjusted to any height* suitable for writing. Several forms are in use. The best is probably one in which two boards are made to slide over each other in side grooves, and to balance one another as to weight by means of cords and small pulleys.

(*d*) **Boards attached to walls.** Where a class is so placed that a black-board supported against the wall in front is at a convenient distance, it is often advisable to adopt this plan, even if an ordinary board has to be employed for particular purposes. The board may be attached to the wall as a fixture, or, much better, one of the various sliding forms may be used. The best method is to have two boards balancing one another as described immediately above. The advantages of the wall arrangement are its cheapness, the fact that the board is *always there for use,* and *never in the way of any class movements.*

The teacher should not lose sight of the possibility that **there may be some members of the class who are short-sighted**, and consequently unable to see properly what is written on the black-board from their ordinary places in class. Such children are often too timid to speak of the defect, and may be blamed unjustly unless their condition is recognised. Directly it is known, they should be placed as near to the black-board as can be conveniently arranged for; and if then unable to see, they should be induced to procure spectacles wherever this is possible.

(2) *Books.* These are an important consideration in the teaching of some subjects. The number of kinds in the market is now so great that the teacher has himself to blame if those selected for use do not serve their purpose thoroughly in all essential respects. The higher we go in the school the greater is the number of subjects in which books may be used with advantage.

With children it is a great mistake to have books of too pretentious a kind. They should contain all the facts the pupils ought to learn, and no more. They are a **useful supplement to teaching but should not take its place**, whereas they are often overloaded with explanatory matters which it is the teacher's business to give in the lesson. If books are too large, not only are they needlessly expensive, but the children are very apt to be so confused with the number of details brought before them that they fail to get any real hold of the broad outlines which it is so essential for a child to master first. Children have neither judgment nor experience sufficient to know what to pass over lightly, or what to omit altogether as a matter to be learned, and frequently spend their strength on that which is least important. Progress is slow, and discouragement and dislike often follow. If children find no interest in what they have to do, the temptation is very great for them to find amusement in other ways, and increased vigilance—often backed up by artificial restraint and sometimes by punishment—is necessary to keep a class in proper order and steadily at work.

Books for children to learn from should be written in a simple direct way, and the statements should be as terse as is compatible with perfect clearness. Simplicity is not to be gained by leaving out everything which is likely to present any serious difficulty. Children are incited to effort by being shewn how to overcome obstacles for themselves, not by having everything removed which they may find trouble in surmounting.

Sometimes books written for children are excessively wordy and round-about from the attempt to make everything easy; and, even when they are clear, are so puerile as to be an insult to a child's intellect and common-sense. Twaddle, a child rightly detests. The opposite error, however, is not rare, the books being mere dry epitomes, often containing unsuitable facts, and, in some cases, so overloaded with unnecessary technical terms as to be a source of weariness and disgust to the pupil. The whole is strung together merely for purposes of cram, in complete ignorance of a child's capabilities, and without attention being paid to the more salient features of the subject or even to proper order and subordination.

Of books for use in schools those employed for the teaching of reading are, in elementary schools, much the most important, both from the fundamental importance of the subject, and from the fact that they are of course most extensively used.

The **books intended simply to teach reading** are commonly made up of miscellaneous extracts or specially written pieces; but, in addition to these, in the higher classes, standard works suited to the age of the children may be employed with great advantage, and every school containing older scholars should have such books in use. In the hands of a wise teacher they may be made to foster a love of reading and a taste for literature, as well as to furnish materials for exercise in reading aloud.

Of late years **reading books intended to give information upon some definite subject**—as geography or history—have been introduced into elementary schools. Properly used such books are in many ways a very great gain, and afford the child some training in acquiring knowledge from what he reads as well as some practice in correct utterance. They should not, however, be allowed to take the place of the ordinary books for the main purpose of teaching reading, and they should be written in a simpler style so as to present fewer difficulties.

The features which should characterise the reading books, and the essential qualities which should distinguish other books for class use —such as arithmetic books, copy books, grammars, geography books, atlases, etc.—will be referred to later on in connection with the teaching of the particular subjects.

All books intended for the use of children should be **well printed in sufficiently large type and strongly bound.** In many instances, too, **illustrations are a great advantage,** both in assisting the comprehension of the subject matter and in giving brightness and attractiveness of appearance. The illustrations should be good of their kind; not the wretchedly conceived and ill-drawn caricatures sometimes found, nor the blurred and otherwise faulty impressions, resulting from bad printing or from the use of worn-out 'electros' and defective 'process-blocks,' which are too frequently met with.

Some useful moral lessons may be enforced in connection with the treatment of books. The more children are taught to respect books and to treat them properly—especially if they are the property of others—the better. Of course in any case a book in constant use by children is certain to suffer a considerable amount of wear and tear; but cleanliness, careful handling, and the avoidance of needless destruction may be and should be insisted upon. If, however, a book is so badly bound as to come rapidly to pieces, a child should scarcely be expected to take much interest in its preservation.

II. CLASS MANAGEMENT FROM THE DISCIPLINARY SIDE.

All work has to be performed under conditions, and these have to be taken into account in the school-room as well as in the workshop or the home. The great thing is to make the conditions as pleasant and as conducive to success as possible, to reduce any deadening and obstructive effects, and where any influence exists, which in ordinary circumstances is opposed to our efforts (as the natural restlessness and volatility of children), so to mould our method of treatment as to turn this influence in a useful direction.

Perhaps no side of his work is so difficult for the teacher to learn, none so likely to try his skill and patience to the uttermost, as the **easy and efficient control of children while under instruction**, and the maintenance of such a **spirit of law and order** among them that they willingly and readily submit themselves to the teacher's guidance. In no part of his work, too, is failure so certain to be followed by disastrous consequences, both to himself and his pupils, as in this. Mere passive abstention from noise and riot on their part is not sufficient; there must be such steady and regular effort to do whatever is right that self-control becomes habitual, and they not only learn what is required of them, but are strengthened in all those qualities which go to make up true manliness. To secure this successfully it is not enough for the teacher to be well informed about what he has to teach, or even to be able to communicate knowledge skilfully; he must have the power to *influence* children, and this is rather a matter of character and of insight into child nature than of intellectual ability.

Much, of the greatest use, may of course be learned as to the requirements for success in this matter, and as to the expedients which are found useful in the disciplinary management of children; but it remains true that there are some otherwise very estimable men who find themselves incapable of controlling even a few pupils, and who rapidly get into difficulties with even a well disposed class.

I. GENERAL DISCIPLINARY QUALIFICATIONS IN THE TEACHER HIMSELF.—The following extract from the author's *School Management* gives, in a general way, the main characteristics which should distinguish the teacher from the point of view at present under consideration.

"He should be **an enthusiast** but no visionary, a **man of many devices**, yet fanatically attached to none; **hopeful**, and inclined to take a cheerful view of things, yet not easily deceived by appearances; **full of sympathy** for little children, and prepared to make all due allowances for natural waywardness; **having faith in himself** without arrogance or conceit, and, while fully recognising his own responsibility, ready to give a full share of credit to the efforts of those associated with him in the work. He must take care also to be at all times a **worthy example to his children**, bearing in mind the strength of the tendency in them to imitation. There is no calculating the mischief which an irritable gloomy temper may do.

"**His cheerfulness should keep his scholars on good terms with themselves**, and encourage them to face work and difficulty resolutely. He should be able to interpret the workings of any boy's mind in terms of that mind, and not heedlessly put a construction upon them in accordance with his own habits of thought and action. **He should be, as it were, in electric communication with every part of his school**, able on the instant to interpret action aright, and ready at once to remedy any derangement of the machinery, or make good any broken sympathetic connection. His influence should be felt at all points—'an influence unseen, perhaps, and unobtrusive but all pervading; free from the slightest taint of distrust or suspicion, but checking insubordination before the thought of it has taken form; exacting a faithful performance of duties, yet encouraging by its inspiration before despondency has attained a conscious existence; soft and gentle as a mother's hand on the brow of a sick child, yet holding the reins of authority, and controlling the very motives of action, like the hand of fate.'

"**Energy must not deteriorate into restlessness or noise, vigilance into espionage, confidence into neglect of precautions, or system into a mere mechanical routine.**"

That **the teacher should know his scholars** has been so frequently urged that the remark has become trite, and yet, in spite of its general theoretical acceptance, in practice its import is frequently attended to but little, or neglected altogether. The importance of such knowledge has been already pointed out in respect to its bearing on the work of teaching, but it applies with equal force to the management of children.

Unless the teacher knows those under his charge—knows them not only collectively or by name, but individually and intimately—it is impossible for him to gain that hold over them, which comes from loving respect and the feeling that he is their friend, and which stimulates them to act as he would have them, both as to conduct and work. Where this community of feeling and interest exists, disciplinary troubles are comparatively few, and such admonitions and corrections as are required make a far deeper impression than they otherwise would do.

It is the fact that the teacher and pupils are practically strangers to each other, which makes the work of management so trying and exacting when a teacher at first takes charge of a set of new boys. He cannot apply to the best advantage such skill in control and knowledge of government as he possesses, and hence, when any difficulty arises, he is often put to straits to discover exactly how it may best be met; for it is uncertain what effect his measures may have upon boys of whom he knows little or nothing. If he has not had a wide experience, he is almost certain to think the children worse than they really are; and, unless he is gifted with a large amount of tact and patience, he may easily be led into harshly repressive treatment and the employment of a much larger measure of punishment than is either wise or necessary. When he has become intimately acquainted with his pupils' peculiarities of intellect and character, he may without difficulty adjust his expedients to the necessities of the case; and things which before may have caused him serious embarrassment will probably lose their troublesome character almost entirely.

Now children cannot be known, in the way they should be, when they never come into contact with the teacher except during lessons. Many an opportunity will arise, which ought to be taken advantage of, for friendly and familiar chat about ordinary matters or things in which they take pleasure; and he should look upon it as a part of his duty to shew a real interest in their sports and pastimes, as well as in their work. A teacher who thinks it too much trouble or beneath his dignity to associate with his pupils in the playground, and, if he appears there at all, merely acts the part of a policeman to keep them out of mischief, has strange notions of his office and responsibilities. He is throwing away many valuable chances of getting that insight into the real characters of his children, and that power of exercising an increasing influence over them, which are necessary to effective discipline, and are such powerful elements in successful moral training. **Many a lesson in upright dealing and self-control may be taught in the playground by a wise teacher,** without the child being conscious of it at the time, which will strengthen the character in the present and may tell powerfully for good in the future.

If the teacher can play well, as every young teacher at least should be able to do, he will find it greatly to his advantage in many ways to take his part in the more athletic games, such as cricket, football, rounders, prisoner's base, and others of a like kind. Nay, more, in many instances he may do much good by organising games for the children and teaching them how to play, especially in town districts where they have few opportunities of playing except at school.

II. DISCIPLINARY TRAINING AND CLASS CONTROL.—By **disciplinary influence**, in a narrow school sense, is meant the combined agencies which the teacher brings to bear upon the child in order to make him amenable to law and order, and to arouse such energy as he possesses in a way to induce him voluntarily to put forth his efforts in the direction we wish; to train him to steady application and prompt and willing obedience, while at the same time we strengthen him to act more and more independently until he is able to become a law unto himself. In a word, we have so to stimulate and foster all right and noble instincts in him, that he may grow in strength, both morally and intellectually, and be ready and able to do his duty in any position in which he may be placed.

(1) *Order.* As a matter of fact it is not a difficult thing to control children, in ordinary circumstances, if the teacher has any natural

gift for government, and knows how to use it; but knowledge, patience, tact, and insight are all necessary to success. **If handled properly, children quickly come to like order, and are happiest when surrounded by it.** They respect power, and they respect law, when properly administered; but they soon learn to what lengths they can go. With a teacher who betrays his weakness and acts injudiciously and inconsistently—as a weak disciplinarian is pretty sure to do—they rapidly become so disorganised that they pay little or no heed to commands, or threats, or appeals for good behaviour, and lose no opportunity of talking, shifting their places, and amusing themselves by playing tricks on their neighbours, when such things can be done with a probable chance of escaping instant punishment. Even this they will often run the risk of, because, among so many engaged in the same way, they are aware that there is very considerable likelihood that they will escape.

Unfortunately in such a case **a weak teacher is frequently too irritated to be discreet,** and singles out some individual, to make an example of, who is by no means one of the greatest offenders. Nay, worse, a teacher of this kind will sometimes bully a timid and well-disposed child, who has been guilty of some small offence, when he has not the courage to take in hand one of the master spirits of mischief, because such a one may be troublesome to deal with, and it may be necessary to proceed to extremities with him. The teacher is perhaps unconscious of this at the time, but he should be on his guard, for it is a moral cowardice which sooner or later can only lead to disaster. **A peace at any price policy is pretty certain to end in war.**

[Without proper order it is useless to hope to carry on school work with any success. Neither teaching nor study can proceed with any useful effect amid a babel of sounds and continual interruptions, while the children rapidly fall into habits of carelessness, trifling, and inattention, if not into more positive forms of bad behaviour.] Mere silence or absolute passivity is not good order; a very silent class is in all probability not a working class. There is a noise of work as well as of disturbance, and the teacher should be able at once to recognise clearly the difference between the two. At the same time children should not be allowed to mutter or whisper their work to themselves—a bad habit more easily contracted than cured.

Bad order needs to be met firmly, calmly, and at once; the longer it is allowed to go on the more difficult it is to deal with. Disturbances may often be checked with ease at the beginning, by a little tact, and by firm but quiet and good-tempered insistence upon proper demeanour; if, however, they are allowed to proceed, the teacher may find that he has to tax his resources severely before he succeeds in restoring order. Neither coaxing, nor petting, nor begging, nor fierce scolding, nor any kind of violence will achieve what is wanted.

Compulsion has a distinct place in control, but **the use of force alone is utterly ineffective as a disciplinary influence.** It is of no use for a teacher to swoop down upon a noisy class and punish recklessly this and that offender. Even if he secures order for the moment by such means, the disorder will break out again worse than ever the moment his back is turned or some other opportunity occurs. Order which is obtained solely by compulsion is mere external compliance to avoid painful consequences. It is never to be trusted to, and so far from exerting any lasting influence for good upon the child, is very apt to be looked upon as the tyranny of a strong hand and to evoke a spirit of opposition. A few minutes rough handling of a child may undo all the good which months of careful training have accomplished.

The mistake is often made by inexperienced teachers of attributing to the whole class the faults of individuals. This is not only unjust, but an error in judgment in many ways. The troublesome few escape any special consequences to themselves, and are thus encouraged in what they consider the fun of annoying and irritating the teacher; while the better behaved children are discouraged, inasmuch as not only are their efforts unappreciated, but they are judged to be as bad as the rest.

Good order is necessary; but the term must not be misunderstood, and the teacher who acts without intelligence in this matter may be tempted to go too far. It is very far from wise to insist upon a rigid mechanical routine and the severity of demeanour of soldiers on parade. Children are certain not to be happy where this is attempted, and **happiness is of the first importance if wholesome discipline is to be secured.** Reasonable allowance must be made for their restlessness, playfulness, and the attempt to get some amount of amusement out of their school work. These are things to be kept under control, but they should not be magnified into serious breaches of law.

The conditions of work should be as natural and pleasant as possible so long as the work is not in any way interfered with. The child should feel quite at his ease; and while he should never be allowed to idle away his time, or to behave in a disorderly way, and no approach to rudeness or want of proper respect should be tolerated, a certain amount of freedom both of speech and action should certainly be permitted him. Without this, restraint becomes irksome, and the teacher and pupil are not likely to stand upon that quite friendly footing which is so important to the success of educational measures.

(2) *The Exercise of Authority.* The mode in which the teacher brings his personal influence and power of command to bear upon the children is one of the most important factors in disciplinary control. **Authority is not a matter to be talked about in school**; like instruments of punishment it is best kept entirely in the background till needed. When occasion arises for its exercise, it is not the substance of what the teacher says which affects the children, so much as the quiet confidence of his manner—the calm decision, the clear firm ring of the voice, the evident determination to have things done decently and in order. There is no stern magisterial demeanour, no parade of command, no attempt to enforce obedience by mere loudness of voice or angry assertion. On the contrary, there is an **undemonstrative consciousness of power**, which the children recognise instantly as arising from strength of character, fearlessness in the performance of duty, and perfect self-control—a power which is utterly distinct from any mere external exhibition of force, and which shews that while the teacher remembers the consideration and respect due to others, he is not likely to forget what is due to himself and the authority which he represents. Bluster is never mistaken by children for power, and is very apt to aggravate the mischief it is intended to cure.

In case of difficulty the young teacher should remember that **to have complete command of oneself is a first requisite for commanding others.** He must have faith in himself if others are to have faith in him. If he lacks confidence in his own resources, he is very apt to become fearful of consequences directly some little trouble arises, and often overacts his part. Being doubtful as to the success of any measures he may devise, he says and does far more than the circumstances call for. This is a serious mistake. To allow the children to see that he is at his wits' end what to do, and is too flurried to act discreetly, or possibly even justly, is to court defeat. Words must be used wisely; there must be no reckless scolding, no frequent haranguing of the pupils, no threatenings or grand talk about what the teacher intends to do. All these are signs of weakness not strength; and if he is continually crying "wolf! wolf!" he may know what to expect.

The teacher who is constantly saying "you *shall* do so and so," "I *will* be obeyed," "I will not be trifled with," and such like things, is just the one who is trifled with—even at the risk of ill-usage. The children seem as though they cannot resist the temptation mischievously to irritate the teacher, and will often act like wasps when they feel this.

The good disciplinarian does not use his strength to no purpose. He does his best to avoid giving the opportunity for any beginning of disorder; he looks to little things, and takes care that the children are not left unemployed. If anything wrong occurs, he notes instantly and exactly what is amiss, and applies the suitable remedy at once in a quiet easy matter-of-course way that shews he is fully conscious of what he is about and is perfectly master of the situation. **He speaks as one having authority, not as one wishing to gain it, and as though he did not in the least anticipate any opposition to his wishes.** He is charitable and considerate in his estimate of wrongdoing, but all the same he expects, and if necessary enforces, obedience to his commands. The children recognise clearly that he is patient with them, and inclined to overlook occasional lapses with a simple reminder, because they are weak, not because he has any fear for his own power.

In few ways can the teacher shew the weakness of his power to govern more than by **indecision**. Quick judgment and decided action are frequently necessary to the teacher, and the importance of these things must not be underrated, or lost sight of, because it is possible to confound them with rash haste, or with the following of some angry impulse of the moment. In the event of any difficulty turning up, such as determined unruliness, or an attempt to defy the authority of the teacher, dilatoriness in making up his mind—

whether proceeding from timorousness or any other cause—is sure to increase his troubles, and may lead to disastrous consequences to all concerned. **To apply a remedy quickly and steadily is half the cure.** The teacher should act calmly, and as considerately as the circumstances allow, but with promptness and if necessary with a strong hand. "There are moments," says an American writer, "in the course of education, and even of life, when the delay which reasoning demands would expose us to the danger which it is intended to avert." Occasions sometimes arise where any right course of action, though possibly far from the best, is better than none at all, and where the necessities of the case will not allow of any prolonged consideration.

When mischief is going on, is no time for nice weighing of all the reasons for and against a certain course of action. For the teacher to stand idly by vainly trying to decide what it were best to do, or to nerve himself to the requisite firmness to act, is simply to strengthen opposition to a serious extent. Where such hesitation and uncertainty do not proceed from sheer incapacity, they are probably as often as not but a disguised attempt to put off an unpleasant duty, in the hope that something may occur to render interference unnecessary.

(3) *The exercise of Tact.* This is a very important element in successful control, but its exemplifications are so varied, and shade into one another in such a subtle way, that it is by no means an easy thing to define with any exactness. Roughly it may be said, that by tact is here meant **an instinctive feeling, allied to common-sense on the one hand and considerateness on the other, as to what is suitable and judicious**—a nice discernment on the part of the teacher as to what will prove most felicitous in his treatment of children, so that he may put himself *in touch* with them, and consequently increase the effect of his influence by the wisdom of the mode in which it is applied. To put the matter in another way, tact may be viewed as **readiness of resource in appropriately adjusting means to ends**—skill in adapting words and actions to meet the needs of any difficulty in which the teacher may be placed, so that he may say the right word and do the right thing to stimulate the child to take the right course. Or, again, tact may be looked upon as quickness of perception in taking into account all the bearings of a case, and the ulterior consequences of any line of action, so as to come rapidly to a decision as to what is the most fitting course to be adopted, and discreetly and consistently to carry this out.

The exercise of tact requires that the teacher should have all his wits about him, and be ready to modify his method of treatment at any moment. It will assist him in discerning what should and what should not be done, and frequently save him from blundering in his dealing with children; while if he should fall into error, as every teacher is liable to do, it will help him to make the best of it and to reduce any evil effects as much as possible.

Some teachers are restless and fussy, and seem unable to refrain from meddling, in the hope of bettering some small matter, even when things are going well. To be continually interfering with a child in this way—giving needless cautions and multiplied instructions, or correcting over and over again some small fault, which he is quite conscious of, and probably doing his best to overcome—is to discourage him, and impede that wholesome growth which can only be vigorous when it is natural, and when no attempt is made to hasten it through impatience or over-zeal. It is like constantly changing the soil round a young plant and interfering with its roots, to have them grow in the direction we think best. **To be too officious in matters of discipline is often as indiscreet as to be lax.**

Other teachers again are continually coming across children, and needlessly irritating them or jarring their feelings, not purposely or even in many cases consciously, not from ill-temper or lack of kindness, but from **want of tact.** Such teachers often fail to understand why children do not take to them, and why, although they are earnest in their work and conscious of kindly intention, it is so difficult for them to get into touch with their pupils.

Tact must be founded on judgment and sympathy acting together; but it is not a matter for the acquirement of which we can lay down a series of rules. It is from its nature almost entirely the outcome of experience; and as much is frequently to be learned respecting it from the consideration of failures as of successes. A certain and varying pressure has to be put upon a tool, a certain speed of movement has to be given, and delicate and well-judged modifications of direction have to be made in order to smooth a cross-grained piece of wood; without these precautions it would simply be torn into holes. The good workman recognises instinctively what to do, he humours the wood in all sorts of ways, yet none the less certainly smooths his surface. So it is with tact in the treatment of children.

(4) *Obedience and uniformity of pressure in disciplinary measures.* Restraint is necessary if the performance of work in school is to be easy and exact ; but beyond what is necessary for the general comfort and convenience it is not wise to go. **Children should not be treated as machines, nor as evil-doers undergoing a term of punishment.** The love of liberty is natural to children, and, as far as is compatible with the discharge of duty, this is to be respected. Nevertheless, the teacher must not forget, in his endeavour to make things agreeable for children, that they have to be governed—that liberty is not "absence of necessity for obedience," and must never be allowed to degenerate into careless indolent habits, the following out of their own whims or likings when set work has to be done, disregard of authority or the rights of others, or lastly into opposition to just restrictions.

Steady application and ready obedience are essential, and a good deal of patience is necessary to secure these things. The children must distinctly understand what is required of them ; they must be guided into what is right, warned when on the point of going wrong, and incited to do their best by a generous appreciation of their efforts—poor as these may be when judged by any absolute standard.

There are many occasions, too, when higher motives fail ; and then compulsion must step in, and the child be unhesitatingly made to conform to the teacher's wishes. The more, however, children can be controlled by the teacher's influence, and the less by artificial restrictions and punishments, the more certainly will the discipline exercise a wholesome effect in the present, and the more lasting will be its results.

Mere external compliance is often all that can be secured at the moment, and this is something ; it is not, however, the kind of obedience calculated to train and benefit the child, and something higher must be aimed at. **True obedience is a rational obedience,** and is given cheerfully and at once, from a willingness to be led at any rate, if not from anxiety to do what the teacher wishes because it is felt to be right.

Anything like perfect disciplinary control is necessarily a matter of slow growth. The children have gradually to learn exactly what they may expect from the teacher, and how he is likely to view any shortcoming or misdemeanour. They have also to become convinced, from his habitual mode of dealing with them, that in his exactions and punishments he is anxious to be strictly just, and that any measures he may find it necessary to take, severe though they may seem, are dictated solely by consideration for the general good, and are not adopted merely to save himself trouble or annoyance.

The conditions of school life should be such that no well-disposed child finds difficulty in doing what is right, and no temptation is offered to naturally mischievous and troublesome children to do wrong. Good discipline is steady in its requirements and even in its pressure, so that children know exactly what they have to trust to. Its success is largely dependent upon the spirit in which it is administered. Children soon recognise a teacher for what he is, not what he may seem on the outside; and if he is really kindly disposed, and compassionate to their weakness, they will respect him all the more for being firm in his treatment of any deliberate or careless wrong-doing and resolute in being obeyed. He may even be exceedingly strict without losing their regard, so long as he is always just and considerate. It is not strictness, but ill-tempered harshness and indifference as to what they may feel, which alienates the sympathies of children.

Control which is severe and lax in turn is never strong, and is sure to fail to affect children as good discipline should do. A teacher who allows his pupils to be noisy and neglectful of work until the confusion can be borne no longer, and then suddenly rushes to the opposite extreme and exacts under pain of punishment a rigid obedience and unnatural quiet as a kind of penance, is certain to be continually in difficulties. The children are accustomed to this spasmodic kind of government; they know that before long the teacher's show of determination will moderate and his vigilance will relax, and hence they watch their opportunity to return again to their old state of doing pretty much as they please.

The circumstances of schools vary a good deal, both as to arrangements and the class of children in attendance. In some cases the maintenance of discipline is a comparatively easy matter, while in others it demands all the skill and resource which the teacher can bring to bear. Many children, especially in the poor and crowded districts of our large towns, come from homes where they can scarcely be said to be subjected to any kind of discipline whatever, and spend a large portion of their time in the streets under positively evil influences. Frequently, too, there is **an inherited bias against any kind of control or restraint**, and this should not be lost sight of.

All these things add to the teacher's difficulties, and necessitate on his part unwearying attention, much patient forbearance, and a decided, but at the same time kindly and uniform, administration of law. He has frequently to civilise as well as to train in other respects, and at first has to be content with moderate results. With steady insistence, however, and a slowly increasing pressure of requirements as the children are able to bear it and yield a voluntary obedience, all that is needed may certainly in the end be accomplished.

The direct disciplinary measures with which a child is brought into contact in school should exert a strong influence for good upon the development of character; but, **after all, the most powerful element is the moral atmosphere in which the child lives,** and, much as the school may do, there is also much which it cannot be expected to accomplish alone.

(5) *Class Movements, etc.*—The movements of a class in changing from one position to another should be conducted in an orderly, exact, and rapid way; but it is by no means necessary to insist on the stiffness and formality which distinguish military drill. The children should be taught to march, but in an easy, quiet, natural way. The arms should not be folded but hang at the side as in ordinary walking. No talking should be allowed, and still less anything like disorder resulting from scrambling haste or playful romping. **The teacher should control the movements from a distance** where he can be seen and heard, and avoid the common mistake of mixing himself up with the children, pulling this one and pushing that in order to get them into their places. No good disciplinarian does this. If any confusion begins a halt should at once be called, and the matter put right before the children are allowed to proceed.

A class should be **equally distributed over the space at command**, and every child should have room to sit or stand comfortably. Some teachers seem to have no eye for symmetrical arrangement, and allow the children to remain crowded in some places and scattered in others throughout a lesson.

The pupils should be taught to distribute themselves equally in the various rows, and at proper distances from each other, without the teacher having to interfere, though it may be necessary to put right here and there some little derangement.

In such lessons as writing, dictation, drawing, and arithmetic practice, the children can scarcely be too far apart; where oral teaching has to be given a more compact arrangement is to be preferred. The wider the class the further back the teacher should stand, so as to be able to see every child distinctly without being obliged to turn the head rapidly right and left.

Words of command should be short, smartly given, and in such a tone that every child can hear distinctly, though the teacher should refrain from anything like shouting. If a command has not been heard it should be given again, but when it has once been understood it should not be repeated without good reason. The teacher should wait a reasonable time and insist upon what he has said being attended to. It is a great mistake to rapidly reiterate orders again and again because they are not heeded at once ; when this is the case the children grow careless and rarely attend to what has been said until it has been repeated several times.

Some teachers employ a special signal (as the sound of a whistle or a small bell) to enjoin absolute silence and cessation of all movement. Such a signal has the advantage of being heard distinctly at any time, and in a large school there can be little doubt that something of this kind is often useful, though in the case of a single class it is not necessary.

Physical exercise for a minute or two at the close of a lesson is often a relief after the strain of mental work ; or may be used in special circumstances during the teaching to rouse the children from a state of apathy or inattention. As previously pointed out, the necessary orders are best given by signals or numbers.

Signals are generally better in school than words of command where they can be readily employed, as noise is thereby reduced, and the children are compelled to give their whole attention to the teacher if they are to perform what is required of them. They are often useful in class management in connection with other things besides physical exercises ; for instance, as a means of directing the children to stand or sit, of controlling such things as the simultaneous exhibition of exercises, and the movements into or out of desks, or, again, for the purpose of conveying a warning. In fact, **the less talking there is in connection with disciplinary measures of any kind, the better** for the teacher as well as for general comfort.

(6) *Reproof and Punishment.*—The mode in which **reproof** is given has very much to do with its power as a correctionary influence. It should be given earnestly, that the child may understand the importance of heeding what is said to him, but without any trace of petulance or irritability. These, however, must not be confused with **displeasure**, which is often a very useful disciplinary measure when the withdrawal of the teacher's good opinion is felt to be a loss, as

it ought to be. Even righteous anger is sometimes not only admissible, but natural and salutary, when some serious offence has been deliberately committed. The teacher must be on his guard, however, and be sure that his indignation is directed against the evil, and is not merely the outcome of aggravated personal annoyance or bad temper, as it is certain to be if it leads to hasty judgment, intemperate action, violence of language, or abuse. **Rightly employed, the teacher's anger will be felt by the child to be the strongest form of reproof.** To make use of it in the case of ordinary school faults or shortcomings is seriously to confuse a child's moral perceptions, and to destroy any good effect it may have when legitimately applied to more weighty matters.

A serious but not uncommon mistake in reproving children is for the teacher to allow himself to fall into the **habit of constant scolding or faultfinding**—the running fire of little rebukes, which goes by the name of 'nagging.' This keeps both the teacher and pupils continually in a state bordering on vexation and discontent, and such a frame of mind cannot but be productive of harmful results. The child soon becomes so accustomed to being rated in this way that he pays little or no attention to what is said, and grows callous to reproof even when justly deserved and rightly given.

As with incentives and stimulants of all kinds, **only the least amount of reproof or punishment that will accomplish the purpose should be employed**; and the means used should be as varied as the number at disposal or the circumstances will allow. If punishment is frequently appealed to in the same form a larger and larger amount becomes necessary to produce the desired effect. It has been rightly said that "the best remedy in the world may soon cease to be a remedy if it be too often applied."

The teacher should do his best to **enlist the sympathy of his class on the side of right**, to secure their confidence, and especially to get hold of the leaders among the children. The opinion of the general body acts powerfully here as elsewhere, and a pupil will feel correction with tenfold force if he knows that he stands equally condemned both by the teacher's judgment and by the right feeling of his fellows, although they may be truly and justly sorry for him.

The more delicate a reproof so long as it is effectual, the better; and as delicacy of feeling grows in the children, reproof should become correspondingly more and more gentle. A modern writer has said : "A man may easily produce such a state of feeling in his schoolroom that to address even the gentlest reproof to any individual in the hearing of others would be a most severe punishment; and, on the other hand, he may so destroy that sensitiveness that his vociferated reproaches will be as unheeded as the wind."

A child's feelings should never be wounded unnecessarily. Sneering or sarcastic remarks are utterly out of place with children, and are certain to be productive of much harm in administering discipline. Nothing scorches and shrivels up the good feelings of children sooner than a bitter mockery of them. They clearly understand the underlying unkindness of such remarks, even where they do not grasp their meaning; they feel that the teacher from his superior strength and position is taking advantage of their weakness, and, being outraged by such treatment of them, they rapidly lose all their affection for and desire to please the teacher.

Again, as the writer has said elsewhere, "**we should not apply unpleasant epithets to children or get into a habit of attributing vices to them**; we are very likely to complete thereby an only half-formed tendency, and to strengthen wrong-doing rather than to repress it. A child who is continually being called a liar is pretty certain to become confirmed in the vice. Unjust and unkind words often sting deeply, and rankle in the child's mind long after the cause which led to them is forgotten."

Good-tempered kindly ridicule is quite free from the malevolent feeling which accompanies a sneer or a sarcastic remark, and may occasionally prove an efficient means of rousing a boy to effort, enlisting his attention, checking foolish answering, and the like. It needs considerable tact, however, and a happy manner to employ it properly. Some teachers are certainly able to make use of it with good effect, and without the child feeling any bitterness or opposition; but it is not every one who can employ it in this way, and where such is the case it is much better left alone.

If the teacher has unintentionally or carelessly done a child an injustice, he should not be above acknowledging it. It is a mistake to suppose that to do this lowers his influence, or is destructive of his dignity, if it is done properly. The acknowledgment should shew the teacher's wish to be strictly just, and should not be put as an admission of want of self-restraint, or as the outcome of bewilderment. "None of us," as Mr. Calderwood remarks, "professes to be perfect; it would be the purest affectation to conduct a class on the assumption that we are."

It is perhaps scarcely necessary to remark, that, so long as correct discipline is secured **the less punishment of any sort is employed the more salutary will be the nature of the control exercised.** Punishment of some kind however will always be necessary in the management of either class or school; for there are certain to be frequent instances when the teacher's warnings and reproofs will remain unheeded, or regulations be set at defiance, and at times even serious moral offences will be committed, which will need to be dealt with. On such occasions it is not only necessary for the teacher, but entirely for the good of the children, that **punishment should step in to the support of law**; and the teacher must not shirk the weighty responsibility that devolves upon him in this matter.

The point to be insisted upon is not that the teacher should do without punishment, but that he should feel it his duty to do his utmost to manage with less and less of it as time goes on; and that the standard which he should set before him is the abandonment of the severer forms of penalty—such as corporal punishment—altogether. It may not be possible, even with the most earnest endeavour, to reach such a state of things—for some instance of gross misconduct may at any time turn up, which it would be no true kindness to the offender, and would be folly with respect to discipline, to pass over or treat inadequately; but it will have been a good thing for the teacher himself as well as for the children to have honestly made the attempt.

Moral suasion—by which is meant the teacher's exhortations and the influence of his personal character and authority—is admirable as far as it goes, and the more perfect the understanding between teacher and taught the greater will be its power. It is nevertheless quite inadequate to meet all cases, and has little or no effect upon children hardened by neglect, evil influences, or parental mismanagement, who are just those most likely to give trouble. Its effect, too, is very much strengthened by the fact that there is still punishment behind to enforce obedience if its behests are neglected or contemned. A grave practical difficulty also exists with respect to placing anything like sole reliance upon moral suasion, as usually understood. If expostulation is to be effective, a considerable time must be spent with each refractory pupil, to point out to him his position, and gain the necessary hold upon him to induce him to do right. This would be almost out of the question and make a heavy call upon the teacher's patience, time, and resources, even with a large class; while in dealing with a school of three or four hundred children, it would be absolutely impossible. Even if all that is sometimes claimed for it were *theoretically* true—which is very much to be doubted—some shorter and prompter method of dealing *practically* with delinquents would have to be adopted. It is to be doubted further whether children would not soon become insufferably bored by being frequently admonished in this way, in which case all good effect would certainly be lost.

In administering punishment, it is well as far as possible to **suit the penalty to the offence**; but this cannot always be done, and as a last resource, the teacher in many cases has to fall back upon the infliction of bodily pain. For any serious or determined misbehaviour corporal punishment has the advantage of being "short, sharp, and decisive"; and in some cases a brief but painful experience is just what is needed to arouse the child to a sense of his condition and stimulate his moral nature. If properly applied, it may be made quite sufficiently painful without endangering any part of the human frame. The head should always be held sacred; and under no circumstances should any teacher ever box a child's ears. Irremediable mischief of the gravest character may be easily done in this way in a thoughtless moment.

Care should be taken not to goad a child into obstinate disobedience or determined defiance. When the management is what it should be, instances of stubborn refusal to do what is required are rare. Such a case however may occur, and is often a difficult and delicate matter to deal with. *Unless the child is to be dismissed from the school, he must be compelled to obey*, but the mode in which this is to be done needs the greatest caution and circumspection. It is a matter which no subordinate teacher should ever attempt, and the only thing that remains for him to do, is to hand over the offender to the head teacher.

Punishment should be reasonable both in amount and kind, and on no account must it ever be allowed to pass into cruelty. All such old-fashioned punishments as beating with rulers, keeping for long periods without food, holding up weights, kneeling in uncomfortable positions, gagging, pinching, pulling of ears, and the like, are barbarous and strongly to be condemned.

The class teacher may find it necessary to send a child out for corporal punishment, but its actual infliction should always remain in the hands of the head teacher, who should also reserve the final right of judgment as to what is to be done with the offender. *The authority of the class teacher, however, must always be fully supported in some way or other*, or discipline will soon become an impossibility for him.

The mode in which punishment is inflicted has much to do with its effect. The teacher should listen to all that may be properly urged in extenuation of a fault, but he should not allow the child to *argue* with him in the hope of escaping, nor to cavil at his decision. His judgment should be final, and having been deliberately and justly arrived at nothing more should be said.

When decided upon, the **punishment should be administered soberly and earnestly**, and with sufficient severity for the child to wish to avoid it. *Sham punishments are a mischievous mockery and speedily bring the teacher's authority into contempt.* There must be no trace of personal animosity against the child, or of careless indifference; on the contrary, it should be evident that the teacher feels the infliction of punishment to be an unpleasant part of his duty, but one which he must not shrink from performing. That the **justice of the punishment should be recognised** is essential to its success, and this is not likely to be the case when it is either careless or capricious.

A great difficulty exists in **apportioning the same punishment to the same offence**, by whomsoever committed, as what is a severe punishment to one child may be a very moderate one to another. The teacher however can scarcely make distinctions of this kind without laying himself open to the charge of unfairness, and it is not always possible to estimate exactly how a punishment affects an offender. One thing is clear, **it is better to err on the side of mercy than of severity.**

Both in reproof and in awarding punishment, **the teacher must distinguish clearly between incapacity and absence of effort**, and the child should have the benefit of any doubt which exists in the teacher's mind with reference to the matter. It often needs the nicest judgment and a knowledge of the child's powers and character to estimate correctly the extent to which he has striven to do what is required of him. *Results are by no means a safe guide*; and if any minimum standard is laid down, so that all who do not reach it are deemed worthy of punishment, it should be within the reach of every member of the class with earnest application.

It must not be forgotten that **pain is the means, not the object of punishment.** Its object is to reform the offender, and to deter both him and others from a repetition of the transgression, to arouse him to a sense of his position, and so give better influences an opportunity of acting for his improvement. **Punishment alone can never effect what is required**; the wish voluntarily to do better and to rise to higher things must be given by other and gentler influences. Where there is no inward shame produced, the punishment does little good to the offender himself beyond securing an outward and unwilling compliance, and more than this is necessary for moral growth.

Where numbers have to be taught together, the regulations and disciplinary sanctions cannot fail to be to some extent artificial. **The heinousness of faults is not to be judged by the trouble or annoyance they cause**; and the teacher should keep clearly in mind the distinction between moral guilt (such as lying, dishonesty, or the use of obscene language) and a breach of school rules adopted for the furtherance of work and general convenience. It may be necessary to punish for such things as talking, inattention, carelessness, and the like—or better for the neglect of duty they involve —if the child is heedless of warning; but they are not morally wrong *in themselves*, and to regard them in the same way as iniquity is completely to confuse a child's moral notions.

A child should only be punished for doing things, either deliberately or carelessly, which he knows to be wrong; faults committed through ignorance or inexperience, accidental backslidings, momentary forgetfulness, are best treated by other means. It is impossible in school to lay down express regulations respecting everything, and there are weighty objections to increasing their number beyond a moderate limit. The cultivation of the child's moral intelligence becomes, therefore, a matter of great importance. Frequently a teacher has to be content for the time if a child keeps the letter of the law, and it is unsafe to punish beyond this; but *no opportunity should be lost of leading a child to see in what spirit he should act*, and it should be made a matter of honour with him not to do anything which he feels to be wrong whether forbidden or not.

Punishment in school should not be looked upon as vengeance of the law, and consequently a boy should never be allowed to feel that by suffering his punishment he has cleared off all scores with the teacher. *The pain is not administered to avenge the past, but to prevent, if possible, wrong-doing in the future*; and the withdrawal of the teacher's good opinion until the child shows anxiety to amend ought to be felt as a serious consequence of punishment. If we could insure that a child would never willingly or carelessly fall again in the same way, the best thing would be to forgive. But experience shews that in very many cases this is improbable, and that the child needs some painful association with wrong-doing to fix firmly in his mind the necessity for improvement.

Punishment and learning should be dissociated as much as possible. There is something wrong with the administration of discipline—

unless there is a very low moral tone in the class—when frequent punishments are necessary. Such a state cannot be one of happiness either to teacher or children. It is not likely that the schoolroom will ever be made as pleasant as the playground, but it may be made a very much pleasanter place than it frequently is. What the teacher has to aim at is to arouse such a sense of honour and spirit of zealous effort that punishment is required less and less, and the children perform what they have to do with cheerful alacrity. When this is the case most of the difficulties of class management disappear.

We may perhaps usefully conclude the consideration of this section of the work with the following **SUMMARY OF THE MORE IMPORTANT POINTS RESPECTING CLASS-DISCIPLINE.**

(1) Discipline is the **implanting and cultivation of a spirit of right conduct** — the **maintenance of law and order.** *Much beyond the exercise of force is needed as the means, and much more than merely passive obedience should be secured as the result.*

(2) In disciplining children, attention must be directed to inducing in them the **right frame of mind** to profit by whatever good may fall in their way, the **curbing of evil tendencies,** and the **correction of bad habits.**

(3) Every means should be taken to **cultivate a sense of honour and duty in children,** and as far as this is shewn to exist it should always be relied upon.

(4) **True discipline is a matter of slow growth,** the result of right government and the **steady action of good influences.** *It depends not upon what is said but upon what is done.*

(5) **The happiness of children is essential** to the successful administration of discipline. Sympathy, good temper, and an earnest desire for the welfare of the children lie at the foundation of all beneficent control.

(6) **The conditions of work should be made as pleasant as is consistent with strenuous application.** Restraint should not be carried beyond what is reasonably necessary. Care should be taken not to damp the natural ardour and gaiety of children.

(7) **Justice should be so administered that it is recognised as such** by the children, and their sympathies are secured on the side of right.

Incapacity must not be confused with absence of effort. It is never unwise for the teacher to acknowledge any mistake or misjudgment into which he may unwittingly have fallen.

(8) **Good order is absolutely necessary to progress.** It should be clearly expected and steadily insisted upon. *Children like order when surrounded by it.* They respect law when properly administered, and are the happier for being brought under its dominion.

(9) **The disciplinary requirements should be uniform in pressure.** The teacher should say what he means and mean what he says, that the children may know what to expect of him. Proper control is certain not to be secured if the teacher is severe and lax by turns. *Spasmodic government is weak government.*

(10) **Children should be made clearly aware what is required of them.** Ignorance *is* a plea in school law. The cultivation of the moral intelligence must not be neglected. *Inadvertence must not be treated as deliberate wrong-doing.*

(11) **The love of freedom in children is to be respected**; but liberty is not licence, nor is it the absence of necessity for prompt obedience when called upon.

(12) **Tact is necessary at almost every point in dealing with children.** They should never be needlessly irritated or goaded into opposition; nor should they be treated as though anxious to do wrong.

(13) **Authority should be felt as an invisible presence, not paraded or talked about.** Rashness, injustice, indecision, carelessness, and irritability all tell powerfully against good discipline.

(14) The teacher's **power is shewn by quiet confidence of manner**, calm decision, readiness of resource, and fearlessness in the performance of duty. *Complete self-control is necessary to the successful control of others.*

(15) **Commands should be given firmly and distinctly**; but a loud blustering tone is to be carefully avoided. *The teacher should speak as one having authority, not as one wishing to gain it*; and should never shew that he anticipates disorder or disobedience.

(16) **The fewer the orders given the better,** but they should be obeyed at once and properly when given. The teacher should **strive to control by the eye rather than the voice.** Every means should be

taken to reduce noise as much as possible. *A noisy teacher makes a noisy class.*

(17) **In controlling class movements the teacher should stand where he can be seen and heard distinctly.** The movements should be quiet, orderly, exact, rapid, and conducted in a natural way. Children should never be pushed or pulled into their places.

(18) **Disorder should be checked firmly, calmly, and at once;** neglect means trouble. The cause should be looked to and the remedy applied there. *It is of little use to doctor symptoms.* Good discipline is not to be expected with children unemployed.

(19) **Vigilance is necessary, but never espionage.** The teacher should be ever on the alert, and warn where necessary. *Little things should be looked to,* and mischievous children separated. It is often well to have dull, backward, and restless or troublesome children in front.

(20) **Reproof should be given quietly but earnestly,** and as delicately as is consistent with its being effective. *Threats, persistent scolding, violence of language, and abuse, are all out of place.* Sneering and sarcasm are cruel when applied to children; even good-natured ridicule is often a dangerous weapon.

(21) **The faults of individuals must not be attributed to a whole group.** Charity should be exercised in interpreting motives, and reasonable allowance made for backsliding. *The gravity of faults is not to be estimated by the annoyance they cause.*

(22) **Punishment should act as a deterrent to wrong-doing, and a stimulus to effort.** It should be given for the sake of the future, not to avenge the past. *Voluntary* right conduct must be secured by other influences.

(23) **The mode in which punishment is inflicted has much to do with its success.** It should be severe enough for the child to be anxious to avoid it, and carefully proportioned to the offence.

(24) **Punishment and learning should be dissociated as much as possible.** The least amount of punishment that will serve should always be used; and the nature of the punishment should be as varied as possible. " Familiarity breeds contempt."

(25) **A class needing much punishment is certainly not well governed**, and the teacher should look for the cause in his own administration.

III. CLASS MANAGEMENT FROM THE SIDE OF TEACHING.

So much has been said incidentally concerning this subject, in dealing with the general work of teaching, that it will only be necessary in this connection to mark more particularly a few points where the teacher is likely to go wrong, and to extend somewhat our consideration of one or two subjects of importance.

I. GENERAL TREATMENT OF CHILDREN DURING TEACHING.

(1) *Employment.*—Teaching one pupil is quite a different thing from teaching a class. In the former case everything can be exactly adjusted to the child's needs, both with respect to teaching and discipline ; whereas in a class there are sure to be considerable differences of ability, as well as much variation in the power to give anything like voluntary attention. The amount of interest which children take in any particular subject has also to be reckoned with. **Power gives pleasure**, and children, like adults, are generally most interested in things which they can do best. This alone causes very considerable difference to the way in which the various members of a class view any work in hand, and cannot but affect the earnestness of their efforts either consciously or unconsciously. In some cases positive dislike has to be overcome.

The general information and previous experience of the children, again, apart from the special subjects of school study, have a very important bearing upon the success of the teaching, and make certain things easy to some which are both difficult and tedious to others. Bad habits, also, whether arising from neglect or previous bad teaching, are often the source of considerable trouble in the management of a class.

The teacher has so to distribute the work and vary his method as to call upon each child for just that share which he is able to perform, and to induce him to use such power as he possesses without expecting from him more than he can give. **Nothing discourages a child more than continuous failure when he has tried his best**, and he should be saved from this as much as possible. Something useful must be found for every one to do, so that the brightest may find themselves fully occupied, and the dullest be encouraged by discovering that they can do something. The difficulty is to do this without sacrificing either ; and though it may not be possible to accomplish it at all perfectly with a large class, the necessity should always be present to the teacher's mind, and lead him to do his utmost in this direction.

Where only a few learn, and the rest, hopelessly perplexed, are allowed to remain idle so far as learning is concerned, difficulties are sure to arise as to order and attention. **Inactivity is repugnant to children**, and those who are left mentally inactive from being practically outside the teaching will naturally find some occupation for themselves of a nature troublesome to the teacher and obstructive to the lesson. Such children are scarcely to be blamed. What they need is to be saved from themselves ; and when properly treated, although they may not have learned all that could be wished, at least they will have picked up a little. What is of equal importance too, they will have had such faculties as they possess exercised, as well as have been prevented from falling into bad habits.

"The common maxim," says Pillans, "that idleness is the parent of mischief, is nowhere better exemplified than in a school ; and the best receipt for correcting evil habits where they exist, and still more for preventing the growth of them, is to keep the mind perpetually, agreeably, and usefully employed. This is the great secret of the art of teaching, and the object to which the efforts of the public instructor should be mainly directed."

Want of employment of children during a lesson is often due to defective judgment ; such as overlooking those who are least inclined to effort, or the over employment of any device where the bulk of the active work is done by the teacher, while the children remain merely listeners or onlookers—especially if what is being said or done has no particular interest for them. It is no bad rule, that the children should say as much as possible about a lesson, and the teacher only what is necessary. In this connection **questions frequently have a disciplinary value** in keeping up attention, and in preventing mischief, quite apart from their use in other ways. They are an easy and effective method of rousing a child when on the point of falling into a state of carelessness or mental torpor—the forerunner of weariness, and hence an incipient temptation to indulge in trifling or amusement. If the pupil feels that the moment he shews signs of listlessness or inattention, he will be called upon to answer a question upon what the teacher has just said, he has a strong motive for remaining on the alert, and anything short of deliberate idleness becomes almost impossible if the teaching is within his grasp.

(2) *Praise and encouragement.*—The feeling of gratification, which arises from finding their efforts are appreciated, acts powerfully upon children, and may be so employed as to become one of the most useful incentives to steady effort and orderly conduct. Hence the teacher should not be too sparing of **praise and encouragement** where they are deserved; and the **commendation should be given heartily**, not grudgingly. Much depends however upon the good judgment with which it is made use of. If given carelessly or indiscriminately, it soon ceases to have much value in the eyes of pupils.

It is a great mistake to withhold just approbation of earnest effort, or of the successful conquest of real difficulty; but in ordinary cases it is only seldom that it need be given directly in words. **A smile or look of pleasure from the teacher will often do as much to encourage a child as openly expressed commendation.** The latter may then be well reserved for cases of more distinguished merit, and will be much more highly esteemed on account of the value attached to it. A child who does not care for the good opinion of the teacher is to a large extent outside his influence; and where the majority of the members of a class care little or nothing for any expression of approval from him, he may be pretty sure that the fault rests with himself. In such a case he has thrown away one of his most powerful means of control.

In the employment of praise with individuals **the teacher must be guided a good deal by the character and temperament of the child.** The timid and hesitating need it to a larger extent than those who are more energetic and courageous; while with those inclined to be conceited, it should be used very sparingly, and may principally be directed towards the encouragement of a more modest bearing. Even in the latter case, however, *there must be no unjust depreciation of success,* and no pretence of failing to see the merit of what has been done. Such a course is sure to do harm; and **any kind of sham or deceit is bad with children.**

(3) *Treatment of forward children.*—Impetuous children are apt to

give trouble to an inexperienced teacher by their want of self-control, or by their attempts to attract attention to themselves. In their anxiety to gain the teacher's approbation, to display what they know, or to out-do others, they often forget that decorum of behaviour which is necessary to good order, and thrust themselves forward or volunteer information without being called upon.

Such children should not be punished or treated snappishly. What is needed is that they should be taught to restrain their impulsiveness within reasonable limits, and this may usually be managed with a little tact without resort to any severity. Their ardour is a good thing in itself, and simply needs to be brought under control. A restraining hand is constantly needed, repression rarely. **Allowance must be made for the natural characteristics of childhood.** It would be a grave error to try and make children as serious and reserved as adults.

A word or a look of warning should be given to children whenever their forwardness leads them to overstep just bounds, and in such a case they should be passed over in selecting those to answer; but **it is unwise as well as unjust to ignore them altogether,** as is sometimes done. Their rashness too will frequently lead them into mistakes which should be fully exposed in a kindly way, and the fact at the same time pointed out that a little care would have saved them from blundering.

(4) *Corrections during Teaching.*—**During teaching disciplinary corrections should be as few as possible.** Children cannot follow with any success the gradual unfolding and linking on of the various points brought before them, when they are continually distracted by the teacher breaking off in the middle of what he is saying to tell some boy to attend, or sit up, or fold his arms, or other things of a like kind. Such minor corrections, where at all frequent, are not only a harmful impediment to correct learning, but sometimes lead the teacher into difficulties by drawing off his attention from the lesson and making him forget the sequence of his work.

If a child needs a warning, all that is necessary will generally be afforded by a look, or a sign, or a question; and only where some serious lapse occurs should the teaching be interrupted to put matters straight before proceeding. Cases of this kind, however, ought to be rare.

It is astonishing how easily, in some instances, the bad habit is acquired of **filling in every pause that occurs in the teaching with** some **admonition or reproof,** even when there is nothing in the behaviour of the class which really calls for any interference whatever. It is well for the teacher to be on his guard in this matter, for the fault is by no means uncommon.

(5) *Some points concerning the teacher.*—The **proper management of the voice** in teaching has a distinct bearing upon the behaviour of the class. The teacher has to avoid the error, on the one hand, of speaking so softly or indistinctly that many of the children cannot hear at all, or only with the closest listening, in which case the attention is pretty sure to flag; and on the other, of setting a bad example by being over demonstrative and shouting—an example which the children are pretty sure to imitate and exaggerate.

The teacher's manner should be bright, easy, and natural. Any violence of gesture or theatrical showiness is to be avoided, though little dramatic touches (where the subject will admit of them) are sometimes not without their use. **Any manner is bad which attracts attention to itself rather than to the lesson.** Clearness and force of speech are essential. Emphasis and impressiveness should be employed in varying degrees, according to the nature of what is being dealt with. Where the teacher is timid, awkward, and hesitating, the children are apt to be troublesome. They should not be spoken to in a haughty domineering way; but it is absurd to beg of them, or to use a beseeching tone.

A word may here be said about the **teacher's position before his class** during teaching. He should stand sufficiently far away to see every child with ease. Directly a child is out of sight, or is only noticed by the teacher occasionally, there is a temptation for him to take advantage of the situation and amuse himself.

Usually, in speaking earnestly, a teacher approaches his class a little, but he should be careful not to fall into the **common error of advancing close up to the front row and addressing his lesson to some half-dozen children just in front of him.** Movement within reasonable limits is a gain. The teacher has to avoid the two extremes of remaining like a post in the same spot during the whole of the lesson, and of walking about in a fidgety restless way like a caged animal. If the black-board is properly placed, the teacher's general position will be near it, and at least it should serve as a reminder to him not to stand too close to the children.

II. THE SECURING OF INTEREST AND ATTENTION.

(1) *The nature of attention and its relation to interest.*—By attention is meant that controlling influence whereby other objects, ideas, or feelings, than the one selected, are excluded from the consciousness, at least to such a degree that opportunity is given for the full exercise of this or that phase of the mind's power upon the subject contemplated. Attention thus (1) **concentrates** the mental activity upon that which is brought before it by limiting the area of consciousness ; (2) **intensifies** the mind's action by stimulating it and directing its energy into a definite channel ; and (3) **controls** the mental working by keeping it continuously for a certain period of time within the narrow bounds assigned to it. This attentive condition of mind may be induced in two broadly distinct ways, and hence we come commonly to speak of attention as of two kinds—

(*a*) **Spontaneous, automatic, or instinctive attention,** which is directly the result of the inherent interest or attractiveness of that which is presented to the consciousness, and hence has to a considerable extent an emotional origin in some form of desire, pleasure, or pain.

(*b*) **Volitional or cultivated attention,** which is the result of a distinct determination or effort of the will, and thus is dependent for its successful action upon the growth of the will-power, and the consequent extent to which this can be brought to bear. We are conscious in such a case of a definite purposive effort accompanied by some feeling of muscular strain, and this seems to be one source of the fatigue experienced after attention has been given for a prolonged period.

As **the will is influenced by motives** which are for the most part essentially dependent upon some form or other of emotion, it would appear that spontaneous attention is the natural phase, or, as Ribot calls it, "the true primitive and fundamental form of attention," and that the volitional form is almost entirely the result of cultivation, brought about by repeated exercise of the spontaneous attention and the persistent effort to keep the mind fixed upon what it is about. Thus there gradually springs up the power to direct the mind steadily to an object as a matter of choice, and the connection with the will is strengthened by degrees until at last the attention is brought more or less completely under control.

Great power of voluntary attention has often been considered the most important element of genius; and in the case of many gifted children the tendency for the attention to develop readily and strongly seems certainly to be inherited. Although, however, the cultivation of the attention is a much easier matter with some than with others, in all instances is such cultivation necessary. Many persons whether from defective training or lack of natural capacity, never acquire at all any real power of directing the mind and keeping it concentrated upon a subject for any length of time, while the ability to do this with respect to more abstract matters—such as a long chain of reasoning—is a much rarer accomplishment than is commonly supposed.

As interest then is essentially bound up with the action of the attention (of the spontaneous form directly, and of the volitional form to a large degree indirectly), and as attention is an absolutely necessary condition of all success in teaching, it becomes of paramount importance for the teacher to see that the lessons are made interesting, and that school work generally is conducted in as pleasant and attractive a way as possible consistent with the real work of study being done. Interest, in fact, has in school a double value. In the first place it **is one of the most powerful agents which the teacher can employ to stimulate mental activity** and train the attention, thereby strengthening impressions and obtaining the first requisite of distinct remembrance. In the second place it **does much towards securing that inward satisfaction in the children which shews itself in good behaviour and steadiness of effort**, so that they have no inclination to seek amusement for themselves and consequently to fall into mischief and disorder. There is also the further fact, which should not be lost sight of, that apart from school work no more valuable intellectual habit can be formed.

To have a class gaping and staring about and shewing symptoms of being insufferably bored, even where other considerations keep them from being actively troublesome, is very trying to a teacher. In most cases however the fault will be found to rest with himself; and to become irritated and cross or to attempt to gain attention by threats of punishment is only to increase the real evil. Whatever the cause may be it should be looked to at once, and the first thing is to insure that the defect is not due to the teaching, whether arising from its being too difficult for the class to grasp, from the want of freshness and picturesqueness, or from the dull and monotonous manner in which the facts are presented.

Sir Arthur Helps, in *Realmah*, puts into the mouth of Ellesmere, a lawyer, an amusing story of a boy, who during a dull sermon had been deciding whether he would give £1. 17s. 6d. asked by a gypsy for a donkey, and having made up his mind left the church abruptly to complete the bargain. Ellesmere says, "Now the recollection of that transaction has stood me in good stead ever since. When I have been arguing before the House of Lords or the Privy Council, and have noticed that the attention of one of the Lords is wandering a little, I say to myself he is thinking whether he will give £1. 17s. 6d. for the donkey, so I must quit this branch of the subject, and rouse him up with a fresh argument. . . . . It is the most foolish thing in the world to go on, even with good argumentation, when you see that the audience is tired." It would be well if the teacher, when he sees the attention of his class is being given to other things than what he is saying, would remember the story and say to himself, "The boys are thinking whether they will give £1, 17s. 6d. for the donkey, I must rouse them up."

In early years the control of the attention by the will has not been established, and, though the child should always be expected to attend as far as the power to do so exists, it is not to be expected that he can give his attention in any satisfactory degree to that which has no interest for him, merely from being commanded to do so, willing as he may be to obey. Even where the child does his best to keep his mind fixed upon what is being said or done, if this has no attraction for him the attention flags almost at once. It is the wrong method in such a case to scold the child, and a still graver injustice to punish him for not doing what is beyond his strength. The power to control the attention at will is only to be expected after a long continued series of trials to keep the mind directed in the way required. Such efforts, too, must be made willingly, and this is scarcely likely to be the case unless the attendant conditions are pleasant.

How little real attention most young children are able to give is frequently shewn in teaching. After a teacher has been doing his best to teach something where a little more effort than usual is required, and comes to question them upon it directly afterwards, their minds will often be found to be an almost absolute blank with respect to what has been said, even when they have apparently been attending the whole time.

Attention, like other powers both of mind and body, grows in strength and vivacity by being frequently exercised. It is the teacher's business to supply suitable exercise under proper conditions, and to lend his aid with motives and influences of various kinds, until the child is able to give his attention without their assistance. As his power to attend grows, the pupil should be called upon for more and more persistent effort; but the teacher should be careful not to overdo the matter by exacting more than can be reasonably expected.

It must be remembered also that **what is interesting to one child may be far from being so to another**; that in one case attention is to be attracted in one way, in another case in another way, and so on. Provision should be made accordingly, so that the means employed may be sufficiently varied in character to stimulate all. It often needs very considerable skill, however, to hit upon devices which will keep the attention of a number of young children steadily active in one direction for long together, and the teacher will frequently be driven to many shifts and resources before it can be successfully accomplished.

(2) *Means of securing interest and attention.* In taking a preliminary view of the work of oral teaching, a few of the more general points connected with the present subject were referred to; and we have now only to extend the consideration somewhat, more particularly with reference to the influence of interest and attention in class management.

The following are some of the more important matters to be taken into account in order that the object in view may be secured :—

(a) **The work must be taken up in such a spirit and in such a manner as to be enjoyed both by the teacher and pupils.** If the teacher takes little interest in what he is doing, and allows it to be seen that he is himself bored by the work, the children are pretty sure to be bored also. It is essential, on the score both of attention and of good conduct, that children shall be *pleasantly* employed, and this is not likely to be the case unless trouble is taken to arouse in them a liking for their work. "What the teacher cares for," says Mr. Sidgwick, "the boys tend to care for too. Again, the mere fact that he is thorough, and takes trouble for them, and is thinking and doing his best, is borne in upon them sooner or later, and is sure to be a stimulus." The teacher should be careful to **keep children in good spirits.** Little good can be done if they are rendered dull, depressed, or miserable, either by treatment or surroundings.

It has been said that "the crying need of young minds is not so much knowledge as the love of knowledge." This, however, does not mean that the latter can be secured without the former, but that it is greatly more important to teach even a few things so as to arouse in the child a taste for learning, and to lead him to apply himself voluntarily, than to load the mind with many facts which he has been compelled to accept against his inclination, and it may be with disgust. Where the wish to learn has been engendered, the child gives his attention willingly as far as he is able, and hence has little time on his hands for mischief; but where learning is associated with dulness and unpleasantness his attention is with difficulty kept fixed, even for a few minutes, and he is very apt to be troublesome in the attempt to escape what he dislikes.

<small>The influence on the future of the child is also of great importance. In the one case he will continue to read and learn with increasing avidity and success after he leaves school, whereas in the other case, when the time comes that he is no longer compelled to learn, books are thrown aside, most of what has been learned under compulsion is forgotten, and in many cases he is brought to a state of intellectual ruin.</small>

(b) **Much may be done by a bright cheerful sympathetic manner on the part of the teacher.** The children recognise at once when a teacher is in touch with them. Being vivacious by nature, and delighting in activity, they are stimulated by the display of these qualities in those who have to deal with them, while few things have a deeper or more lasting effect upon them than a profound sympathy. On the other hand heaviness, carelessness, or listlessness of demeanour and a spiritless delivery affect the interest of a lesson in the most injurious way. Speaking generally, the younger the children the more powerfully is the influence felt of the various elements which go to make up a good teaching manner.

(c) **The information must be presented in as vivid and picturesque a way as possible.** A great deal may be done by skilful handling towards rendering even the most commonplace information interesting, the use of **fresh and striking illustrations** (especially pictures and well-devised experiments) being a very considerable aid to this. When the work is nothing but a wearisome reiteration of dead facts, without anything to give brightness or attract interest, the teacher will certainly not pre-dispose the children to view the information given as something which it is worth making an effort to acquire; and he will fail to secure that active mental attitude—that **alertness and glow of mind**—which is one of the most important elements of easy and thorough acquisition.

(d) **The teaching should be so conducted as to arouse in the child's mind the pleasure of conquest and possession.** Whatever he can do without the teacher's help he should be incited to do. It is a great mistake to attempt to remove all difficulties from the child's path under the idea that the work will be thereby made interesting to him. That which is very easy is rarely interesting; it is the sense of struggle and successful accomplishment which gives attractiveness, and the greater the difficulties overcome the greater the pleasure. Children like to feel that they have achieved something for themselves, and every conquest made is an inducement to still more sustained effort and closer attention.

(*e*) **The methods employed must be such as will lead to intelligent understanding, and they should be varied in character.** Constant appeal to the child's intelligence is necessary if he is to be interested, and where mechanical exercises are necessary they should be conducted in as varied a manner as possible, to prevent the irksomeness arising from constantly performing the same thing in the same way. Nor should any exercise, no matter what its character, be continued in the same form for very long together, as inattention and restlessness are often the result of too continuous a strain upon one set of faculties. In many cases much may be done to prevent work becoming wearisome by changing in some way the mode in which it is to be performed. The teacher's skill is frequently displayed by the way in which the various devices at his command are used so as to afford assistance and relief to one another. Much temptation to inattention and trifling arises either from want of proper occupation or from a desire for change.

All must share in the work, and the lesson must not be allowed to drag. It is quite possible, in the attempt to be thorough, to spend so much time on a single point that the children grow wearied before it is done with. It is better, in such a case, to pass on and return to the point again, than to allow the children to lose interest so that considerable pressure is necessary to keep even passable attention.

(*f*) **The facts should be so unfolded as to arouse curiosity as to what is to come next.** "Wonder," it has been remarked, "is the basis of knowledge, and intelligent interest and curiosity are but wonder in another form." Children are naturally inquisitive, and, properly employed, curiosity may be made a powerful means of stimulating interest and sustaining attention. It may thus be made an aid both to teaching and discipline.

"Every teacher knows, or should know," says Mr. Bain, "the little arts of giving a touch of wonder and mystery to a fact before giving the explanation." To arouse expectation it is necessary to attend carefully to the sequence of the various points so that one may develop out of another, and, where this is skilfully managed, the children soon become interested in finding out where the teacher is leading them. As this can only be done successfully by understanding clearly what is being taught at the moment, this is in itself a strong inducement to attend, and it is astonishing how acute children often become in discerning what the teacher is aiming at.

(*g*) **Emulation** is another means which, if judiciously employed, may be made of much service in securing interest and attention. Friendly competition is always a gain in class work, and may easily be so managed as not to involve the harmful results with which it has sometimes been credited.

CHAPTER VIII.

THE TEACHING OF THE PRIMARY, FUNDAMENTAL, OR INSTRUMENTAL SUBJECTS OF SCHOOL INSTRUCTION.

I. READING.

It is a commonly expressed opinion, and so far as the writer's experience goes certainly a correct one, that **of all the elementary subjects of school instruction reading is, as a whole, by far the worst taught.** No doubt the difficulties connected with the problem how to teach children to read easily, pleasantly, and well, are numerous and demand considerable judgment, patience, and skill on the part of the teacher; while, further, there are sure to be wide differences of opinion as to how this or that difficulty may best be met. So far as this means independence of judgment and the deliberate adoption of what appears to the teacher to be the best solution, such diversity of methods is a gain rather than otherwise; but it is somewhat humiliating to find that, in spite of knowledge of better things, some of the most wearisome and unintelligent of the old methods of teaching to read are still rife in very many of our schools.

The unsatisfactory nature of the teaching generally is to be traced to numerous sources, different in different cases. The following seem to be some of the most common causes of the defect complained of:—

(*a*) The force of old habits, and the tendency to rest content with methods sanctioned by custom.

(*b*) The fact that some of the worst plans are the easiest to adopt, and therefore the most acceptable to those who think more of their own trouble than of the good of the child.

(*c*) Want of understanding of the nature of the problem, and of how methods can best be brought into harmony with the nature of the child.

(*d*) Trusting too much to mere mechanical devices and exercises, and neglecting to train the intelligence properly.

(e) Lack of ingenuity in modifying and inventing exercises, so as to adapt them to the needs of the moment.

(f) The fact that many teachers seem to have little or no notion of reading *as an art*, and therefore take little or no pleasure in it; consequently the children are not stimulated by any enthusiasm or even interest on the part of those whose influence should be powerful in this direction.

(g) The absurd and mischievous feeling that it is beneath the dignity of a skilled teacher to go through the supposed drudgery of teaching early reading, which is therefore left to young assistants often ignorant of method. Bad habits are thus formed at starting, and continually stand in the way of the child's progress and success.

(h) Lastly, the sameness, deadness, and consequent wearisomeness of the work as frequently carried out.

Diderot, who held reading in the highest estimation, advocated a **special teacher for reading.** He says, "There are so few men, even the most enlightened, who know how to read well—a gift always so agreeable, and often so necessary." (See Compayré's *Hist. of Pedagogy*.)

The correct and successful teaching of reading is of the highest possible moment on many grounds. **In learning to read the child is first introduced to real study,** and the process may be made the most **powerful and effective means of training** brought to bear upon him in early years, not only in the way of developing his mental and moral nature, but in the formation of those valuable intellectual habits, which firmly and properly acquired are a possession for ever, and without which the greatest powers may prove of little service to their possessor. **The ability to read attentively and intelligently is by far the most widely useful and important of all the instruments put into the hands of a child.** The whole superstructure of education depends upon it. By its means he may, and if interest has been kindled in him he will, continue to gain knowledge his whole life long; it is the key which unlocks for him the stored-up wisdom of the race, and makes possible for him a progress which would otherwise be utterly out of the question. To implant in the mind of the child a love of reading is really to do more for him than to fix in the memory any number of mere facts; it is to set him seeking for himself, to refine his pleasures and increase very largely his sources of enjoyment, as well as to do much towards putting to flight those powers of ignorance and dulness which are the ultimate sources of so much sin and misery.

The full realisation of the fact that the reading of the school should be the basis of all that is most valuable in the education given is a crying want at the present time. By this is not meant that reading should trespass upon the provinces of other departments of teaching, very far from it, but that for children there is no subject which may have such important issues, or which may be made so far-reaching and stimulating in its effects. Properly taught there is no section of school work that is not influenced by it, no faculty which either directly or indirectly it may not be made to touch and vivify, no aspect of culture for which it may not prepare the way, no healthy side of human nature either intellectual or moral that is beyond its reach and may not be invigorated by it.

So long as the teaching of reading is looked upon merely as a piece of unpleasant drudgery to be got over somehow or other, so long will the subject occupy its present debased position and its methods be unsatisfactory. It is the lack of any adequate recognition of the position reading ought to occupy, and of the nature and importance of the training it should give, which keeps the work of teaching it, as ordinarily carried out, so dull, lifeless, and mechanical. When we wake up to the importance of these things, we may hope to see systematic observations made, careful experiments carried out, and the principles which should govern the work accepted and placed upon a satisfactory foundation. Then it will be possible to map out with a clearness and certainty not now attainable the easiest and pleasantest paths to be followed.

So far from having discovered all that ought to be known respecting the best ways of teaching the subject, we have done little more than make out a few possible routes; and we are still largely dependent upon certain merely empirical processes which have been found to produce the partial results which have been aimed at. There is as yet scarcely any consensus of opinion concerning many matters which would appear obvious; while few of our methods have any foundation in established principles, and many differ so widely as to be entirely opposed in all essential particulars.

If what has been said as to the importance of reading be true, and what respecting the defective instruction in this subject be just, certainly **no part of our school work is more urgently in need of reform**; and it is high time that the methods commonly employed were carefully scrutinised, so that, where found to be defective, they may be abandoned in favour of processes more intelligent and less exacting, and more in accordance with the supreme importance of the work to be done.

I. SOME GENERAL PRINCIPLES AND CONSIDERATIONS.

(1) *The nature of the problem.* In teaching reading we have three things to consider and deal with—(a) the **idea** in the mind ; (b) the articulate sound or **spoken word** whereby this is through the medium of the voice represented to the *ear* ; (c) the graphic symbol constituting the **printed or written word** by means of which the idea is represented to the *eye.*

These three things may be associated in pairs in three ways—idea with sound, sound with sign, sign with idea.

The association of ideas with word sounds constitutes the learning of **spoken language**, and this power to express his wants and thoughts orally the child gradually gains by experience and by imitation of the speech of those around him. It is, properly speaking, no part of the work of the school to teach a child to talk, though the teaching given may in some degree assist in rendering speech more easy and exact by proper exercise of the vocal organs and the correction of faults. **The school, however, is directly and vitally concerned with the development and permanent fixing of the association between the word signs and the corresponding word sounds, and between the word signs and the corresponding ideas.** The process of effecting these associations with certainty and completeness—so that the child is able to translate on the instant signs into sounds, and to recognise with facility the ideas for which the written or printed words are the symbols—constitutes what is known as learning to read ; while the opposite transition, from sound or idea to the corresponding written sign, is that which essentially underlies all that is useful and intellectual in writing, as applied either in the form of transcription and writing from dictation, or in the higher form of composition.

We see, therefore, that in considering reading in its broad sense we have to take into account **two phases**, which, though they are closely allied and mutually support and assist each other in practice, are yet fundamentally distinguishable — (1) the translation of signs into sounds, that is, reading aloud in such a way that a hearer may readily and clearly gather the meaning of what is read, which leads us to **reading as an art**; and (2) the translation of signs into ideas, that is silent reading for the sake of gathering the knowledge that the symbols convey, which leads us to **reading as an instrument of acquisition.**

Now as it is of the highest importance to the welfare of the child that he should be taught to read well from both these points of view, the distinction between them should not be lost sight of, and the value of each should be much more clearly recognised than seems to be at all commonly the case.

Again, a little consideration will shew us that in the earliest stages of reading, where the fresh forms brought before the eye are so numerous, and recognition is in many cases so imperfect and uncertain, the child's attention will be almost entirely absorbed in the effort to name the words correctly, and will only in a slight degree be given to the truths the words express. As, however, his knowledge of the forms of words increases, attention to these becomes less and less exacting, and his mind should be more and more directed to the clear grasp of the information intended to be conveyed in what is read. There is thus in the teaching of reading a **formal and more or less mechanical stage**, where training to exact and ready recognition of the signs and accurate utterance of the sounds is much the most weighty matter; and an **intellectual stage**, where the essential thing is that the child shall be led to master the sense, and be able to set forth this in such a way that it may be at once intelligible to others. It is true that in practice these stages overlap and interlace in a very complex way, but nevertheless they are in themselves quite distinct considerations, and this should be clearly kept in mind, for by them the character of the work put before the child in reading and the methods of conducting it will be very largely governed. As the importance of one decreases that of the other increases, until eventually the formal difficulties almost or quite disappear, and leave room for the full cultivation of those higher graces of reading which alone make it worthy of being called an art.

(2) *Known to unknown.*—This elementary principle, which we have already met with in other connections, is as valuable and trustworthy in the teaching of reading as elsewhere, and leads us to several important considerations.

The ground from which we have to start in teaching a child to read is spoken language, with which he should be familiar to such an extent as to be already possessed of a considerable vocabulary of simple words with their associated ideas, and to have sufficient command over the vocal organs to form with ease and correctness all the ordinary sounds required.

In speaking he makes use of words, but knows nothing of their elements, either as letter-names or letter-sounds ; hence **his first introduction to reading should be through words and not through the alphabet,** while, further ... the words used should be such as are already familiar to him in spe ..., and thus have fairly definite ideas attached to them. Moreover, since he will know most thoroughly those words that stand for things, the ideas corresponding to which have been gained through the senses, the words selected for use in the first reading lessons should be of this character. There is also the advantage in this that they can be readily illustrated by objects or pictures, and the association of sound, sign, and idea be thus more completely made.

As will be shewn hereafter, **the learning of the alphabet as a preliminary to the teaching of reading is by no means necessary,** and is much better postponed till the printed words have lost something of their strangeness for the child, and he is able to give his attention to the parts because the whole is known to him. The analysis of words into their elementary sounds, and the learning of the letter names, will then find a place naturally enough.

The reading lesson is sometimes viewed as an important means of teaching words which are absolutely unknown to the child from all sides. This is opposed to what is stated above, and to the principles of correct method. The teaching of such words should be accomplished, in the first instance, by quite other means. **In the earliest stage the reading lesson should not be looked upon as a means of extending the child's vocabulary at all,** and even later on only in a minor degree. To introduce a number of strange words into a lesson merely as an exercise in pronunciation, would be to make the lesson unintelligent ; while to attempt to explain and illustrate them properly, would subtract time from the lesson which ought not to be so utilised, and possibly to teach words which would be of no further use to the child, even when learned.

Again, in spoken language the child employs words in connection with each other—that is, in sentences—and he understands clearly enough the force of the connecting words he uses. **Everything has a meaning for him ; and so it should be in reading.** In this way we employ from the first the stimulus and interest arising from the recognition that reading has as much sense in it as speech, and that

P

he is only learning a way of gathering by the *eye* what is meant instead of by the *ear*.

This does not preclude the use of parallel lessons or interpolated exercises in such things as phonic analysis, comparison of words, word building, and articulation drill. These are **tributary methods**, and properly used may be made of much service, but they must not be viewed as the real reading lesson. The principle does oppose itself, however, directly to such senseless schemes of teaching reading as begin with alphabet drill and pass on to meaningless combinations of the ab, eb, ib, ob, ub type.

<small>The points contended for above have been recognised by many of the ablest writers on Education, and here and there have been put into practice. They formed an important feature of Jacotot's method, for which it has been claimed that by its means children mastered the elementary portion of reading *in a fortnight*. Making allowance for some exaggeration, and for the enthusiasm of the teacher, there is here at least food for thought—and ground for experiment. At the present time it is to be feared that the very general if not almost universal practice in schools is to make children plod wearisomely along the old lines, involving manifest detriment to their education and the waste of time and opportunity, as well as loss to the community at large.</small>

(3) *Simple to complex—law to exception.*—The words familiar to the child by sound and meaning will be found to be represented by signs of very variable degrees of complexity and irregularity of formation. Were we therefore to choose the words for his first reading lessons simply on the basis of their familiarity, or the frequency of their employment, the moment we attempted any analysis of the words into their elements, whether letter-sounds or letter-names, we should bring him face to face with so many difficulties and anomalies at once as to utterly confuse him, and destroy his faith in the application to new cases of anything he has learned. One experience would repeatedly contradict another, until he would be able "to trust neither his eyes nor his ears." This loss of confidence would be a very serious matter in itself, but its ulterior consequences would be graver still, and tend to destroy that **habit of expecting things that have happened once to happen again with the same consequences** which plays so remarkable a part in a child's education.

In a very able little book called *The Problem of Teaching to Read*, Professor Meiklejohn brings the following *Bill of Indictment* against our English Notation :—

(1) An Alphabet of 26 letters is set to do the work of 45 sounds.

(2) In this Alphabet of 26 letters, there are now only eight true and fixed quantities.

(3) The remaining 18 have different values at different times and in different positions; and sometimes they have no value at all. In other words they have a topographical value.

(4) Some of these 18 letters do—in addition to their own ordinary work—the work of three or four others.

(5) A Vowel may have from 20 to 30 functions in our English Notation; a Consonant may have two or three.

(6) There are 104 ways of representing to the eye 13 vowel sounds.

(7) Six of these vowel sounds appropriate to themselves 75 ways of getting printed.

(8) In the most purely English part of the language, the letters are more often misleading than not. In the word cow or they, for example, there is no single letter that gives any true knowledge or guidance to the child. That is, the letters in the purely English part of our composite speech have an historical, but no present, value.

(9) The monosyllables of the language contain all its different notations, and these with the maximum of inconsistency.

"The problem is not to make the child acquainted with 26 letters; it is really to make him acquainted with and thoroughly practised in 158 eccentric and self-inconsistent habits, which the English have acquired, in the course of time, of writing down the sounds of their mother-tongue. . . . Of these 158 habits, some are inconsistent with and destructive of each other; and the *experience* of the child is not a regular process of addition and cumulation, but sometimes of subtraction and loss."

The following are among the illustrations given by Professor Meiklejohn of the way in which our notation breaks faith with the child. In the *experience of his eye*. In the words boat, toe, yeoman, soul, sow, sew, note, beau, hautboy, owe, floor, oh, O, we have thirteen different ways in which long ō is represented; and in the words wise, boys, pies, eyes, size, guise, sighs, we have i+s represented in seven ways.

Nor is the *experience of his ear* to be depended upon any more satisfactorily. Thus, in the words seam, steak, earth, hearth, bread, yea, we have one symbol standing for six different sounds; and in conceive, height, vein, heifer, we have one symbol representing four sounds.

Now in all matters of education it is **most important to fix in the mind of the learner the idea of law and regularity first**, in order that he may have firm footing on starting. He will then feel that at least he knows something to which he can trust, so that when exceptions are brought in little by little their proper nature will be apparent to him, and even if numerous will not destroy his faith in the usefulness of what he has just learned. He will realise that although this is not the whole truth, yet it is truth as far as it goes, and is *generally* to be relied upon in interpreting new cases.

Of the words therefore which are familiar to the child, we have to select for first use such groups as present the sounds in a regular way. **The main difficulty is with the vowels**, and these should be introduced power by power, the simplest first. The less usual and less regular sounds will succeed, while complexities, such as diphthongs and silent letters, will be postponed until the simpler forms have been fully mastered.

The exact **order in which the sounds shall be presented** we need not trouble ourselves about, beyond the first steps, as if we select well-written reading books this will have been determined for us by the writers; it is their business rather than the teacher's to look to this. There is no generally accepted view as to any one exact order being pre-eminently best, but most are agreed that words in which the *short* powers of the vowels occur should be employed first.

It should be noted that the **length of words has little to do with the difficulty of learning them**. Many of the long words, especially those derived from Latin, are, from their regularity of notation, amongst the easiest of all to master, directly some power has been gained of breaking words into their syllables. With a little experience of this kind a child who could read all the monosyllables of the language would be able to read anything which might be put before him. It is, therefore, a mistake to arrange a child's reading book according to the number of syllables the words contain, many dissyllables being far easier than quite common monosyllables.

(4) *The reading lesson must be made interesting.*—Few things probably point more distinctly to the faultiness of the methods commonly employed for teaching reading in the earlier stages, than the fact that learning to read is, in schools, usually viewed by teacher and pupils as the most dreary of task-work, and that many of the most unpleasant of the child's experiences—the recollection of which will remain with him his life through—are connected with this side of school work. **Without interest there is no real attention**, and consequently the same thing has to be gone over again and again until its very repetition becomes nauseous.

The subjects introduced to the child's notice must be suited to his years and experience, and they must be treated in a way calculated to excite his interest. All proper means, too, must be taken to secure additional attractiveness; such as good woodcuts in the books, pleasant mode of conducting the work, variety of occupation, illustrations on the black-board, and so on. **Manner will often accomplish more than method**; and without cheerfulness, sympathy, and zeal, on the part of the teacher, the best plans may be rendered ineffective.

At all hazards the reading lesson must be prevented from becoming

mere lifeless drudgery; and the work throughout must be made intelligent. Meaningless work is not likely to be interesting. It should be held to be one of the first and most essential requisites in any method employed for teaching reading, that it should be **sufficiently attractive to arouse in the child a desire to master what is put before him.** There is a great deal more in any satisfactory teaching of the subject than merely 'hearing' reading and correcting mistakes, and unless this is clearly realised any improvement in method is scarcely to be hoped for. -

It is sometimes urged that children have not the same dislike for merely mechanical exercises as adults. This is true, and such exercises may easily be made interesting to them, but this is no reason for the adoption of bad methods, or for the employment of non-intelligent processes when better are to be had. It is not creditable to us as teachers that "reading without tears" should be spoken of as a rarity, or that the subject should be referred to as the child's "bridge of sighs"; and there is absolutely no excuse for the sameness, dulness, and artificiality which characterise so many reading lessons.

(5) *Principle of Comparison and Contrast.*—The value of the comparative method, that is, of placing things side by side and drawing the child's attention to points of likeness and of unlikeness, has been already pointed out. This training to recognise similarities and detect differences is specially advantageous where forms (as those of letters and words) have to be studied, both in the **phonic analysis of similar words,** which is so useful, and in the **discrimination of signs likely to be confused with each other.**

Hence in teaching reading, more particularly in the earlier stages, **comparison and contrast should be frequently employed,** the words or letters being placed alongside each other on the black-board. In this way the salient features are brought out, the impression is rendered more definite, and the signs are recognised with greater ease and certainty when they are again met with.

(6) *One thing at a time.*—The object of the lesson is to teach *reading,* both as an art and as a means of instruction; but it should *not* be made the vehicle of all sorts of information, nor should it furnish opportunity for a variety of exercises having really nothing whatever to do with the actual work to be accomplished. **The attempt to cram a number of things into the time spoils many a reading lesson, and ends in nothing being done satisfactorily.** In many cases the actual practice in reading, which should be the main

thing, is reduced to a wretched minimum altogether insufficient for the purpose in hand.

In view of the future wants of the child it is important, and very important, that he shall be **trained to grasp and retain the sense of what he reads**; but this is no excuse for turning the reading lesson into a kind of object lesson, or for giving all the various grammatical, geographical, and historical information with which the teaching is not unfrequently overloaded. It should be noted also that **the real point of the matter is, that the child shall here gather his information from the book as he reads, not learn additional truths given by the teacher.** These, if necessary, should be taught at another time and in another way.

The fact must never be lost sight of that the one thing to which effort is to be directed is to teach the child to read intelligently and well, and anything which does not bear directly upon this in a helpful way should be rigorously excluded.

(7) *Reading and writing to be taught in connection.*—If we view writing as the expression of words or thoughts by certain symbols composed of more or less complex lines, which symbols thus have a distinct meaning, then **reading and writing are the natural complements the one of the other.** In writing we translate speech into symbols; in reading we reproduce the sounds from a recognition of the signs. It is evident therefore that there is a natural connection between the two, and this connection should be maintained in the teaching.

In any study of form, such as is necessary in writing and drawing, the **eye and the hand should be associated,** the one observing the forms and the other reproducing them. The process of writing **compels attention to the forms of words,** and in this way the knowledge of them is rendered more certain and exact. Writing is thus a great aid to reading in the earliest stages, where instant recognition of the signs is the main thing.

The mere **mechanical imitation of the letter-forms** in writing is a much less exacting process, and properly taught a much more interesting one to the child, than learning to read as commonly managed. This mechanical reproduction therefore **may well begin some time before reading** is commenced, and there need not be any direct or manifest attempt to teach the names of the symbols until reading is begun, though in practice it will be found that the child will generally be anxious to know the names of the signs he makes, and will, without any serious effort, learn most of the script letters in this way.

When reading is begun writing should be closely associated with it, the child being called upon to draw or write the letters (according as he is able) from the forms put upon the black-board, and, as soon as he can do this fairly, to connect them into words. This gives variety to the work, and is also a gain in finding employment for the child's fingers. As the reading progresses the associated writing will not form part of the same lesson, but will be taken later, the connection between the two being kept up by selecting portions for **transcription** from the passage previously read. When transcription becomes less important the association will be made through the **dictation** lesson ; and, finally, when the child can express his thoughts in writing, through **composition** in the form of outlines of the story, or of an abstract of the subject-matter contained in the reading lessons.

As a **means of teaching spelling**—which is mainly a matter of the eye and an indirect help to reading—writing, especially in the forms just mentioned, is invaluable.

<small>The close connection of reading and writing in teaching is very strongly insisted upon by many continental writers ; and this 'read-write' method, as it is sometimes called, is much more commonly employed in the schools abroad than with us.</small>

II. METHODS OF ASSOCIATING SOUND AND SYMBOL. (THE SO-CALLED READING METHODS.)

The methods which have been adopted for enabling the child to give the right sound of the word when the symbol is placed before him are essentially of two types, one synthetic the other analytic.

(A.) **SYNTHETIC PLANS.** In these the child's attention is first directed to the *elements* of words—either as letter-names or letter-sounds—and through them to the sounds of the words themselves. It may be urged against any such plans that they are **opposed to the ordinary mode in which the child becomes acquainted with objects** ; the natural process being, first the learning to recognise the thing as a whole from its general look, and then the consideration of each of the various parts separately. Letters are in themselves meaningless, and to fix the child's mind upon these, before he learns the word, certainly tends to make him overlook the cardinal fact that **words represent ideas** and in all cases have a meaning to be mastered.

<small>Calkins justly says, " The natural way for a child to learn language is to begin with the units of language, which are *words*. Language deals with thoughts ; words are symbols of thought. Letters are elements of the *forms* of words ; simple sounds are</small>

the elements of the sounds of words; but in neither case are these elements units of language. The true starting-point for reading must be with the thought and its sign as a whole. Subsequently the sign may be analysed, and the elements of both its sounds and forms learned."

Even the best of the synthetic plans, though they may commend themselves to enthusiastic advocates, or to those who have fallen into "the superstition of method," are **marked by too much intricacy and elaboration of system** to commend themselves for general adoption; and, unless very skilfully managed, **may easily become utterly dreary and meaningless.** After all, too, the means proposed **meet but very inadequately the difficulties** the child has to encounter.

"Mechanical and artificial methods of teaching may be employed with apparent success, as systems of mnemonics are sometimes made to appear valuable as aids to memory, but careful observation and experience will prove that they possess little or no genuine merit."— (*Calkins*).

(1) *The Alphabetic or Name Method.*—The plan is so called because the child is made to give in succession the **alphabetic names** of the letters composing a word before pronouncing it; and this is done, at least in most cases, on the assumption that such a proceeding assists him in arriving at the sound. In so far as spelling compels a child to examine the word, it no doubt helps to fix the *form* in his mind; but this will not lead him to the sound, and to make him name the elements *first* is to misdirect his attention, and to confuse him by calling upon him to do something else than what is actually the work of the moment. It makes a pretence of helping him without in the vast majority of cases giving him the slightest clew.

The **method is indefensible**; but although almost universally condemned it is nevertheless still lamentably prevalent in our schools, even where no attempt at defending it would be made beyond the fact that children do learn to read by it, and that it is an easy plan for a young teacher to adopt. **Children will, in the end, pick up by experience the sounds of the letters, and the power to combine them, whatever method is adopted,** if only sufficient patience is exercised. This, however, is not the point; but that they shall learn pleasantly, quickly, and intelligently.

The plan has the sanction of long custom, but is **roundabout, tedious, and illogical.** Where a child has been habituated to preliminary spelling he rarely attempts to discover the sound of any unfamiliar word until he has droned through the letters.

Much of the mechanical, monotonous, and unintelligent reading so often complained of in schools is doubtless due to the use of the Alphabetic method in the early stages. It combines spelling and reading unnaturally. **Spelling is largely learned through reading, but the converse is not true.**

The spelling and saying of each word from four to six times over in succession by all the children simultaneously, and often in the most objectionable sing-song way, is by no means uncommon in our class-rooms; but it is a plan to be strongly condemned, and one which no teacher worthy of the name ought for one moment to tolerate.

The condemnation of the Alphabetic plan is by no means confined to teachers and writers on education. Lord Lytton makes Dr. Herman say in *The Caxtons*—" A more lying, roundabout, puzzle-headed delusion than that by which we *confuse* the clear instincts of truth in our accursed systems of spelling, was never concocted by the father of falsehood. For instance, take the monosyllable *cat*. What a brazen forehead you must have, when you say to an infant *c, a, t,*—spell *cat* : that is, three sounds forming a totally opposite compound—opposite in every detail, opposite in the whole —compose a poor little monosyllable, which, if you would but say the simple truth, the child will learn to spell merely by looking at it ! How can three sounds which run thus to the ear, *see-eh-tee* compose *cat*? Don't they rather compose the sound *see-eh-té* or *ceaty*? How can a system of education flourish that begins by so monstrous a falsehood, which the sense of hearing suffices to contradict? No wonder that the hornbook is the despair of mothers ! "

(2) *The Phonic Method.*—As the *names* of the letters cannot possibly lead to the *sound* of the word, the idea seems reasonable at first sight to teach their powers instead. The phonic plan thus attempts to lead the child to master the *sound* of a word by giving in succession the **sounds of the various letters**, at first separately, and then with more rapid utterance, until they blend into what is required.

The method is by no means new, having been known at least a century and a half in France, though but little employed. Of late years it has been tried in England in several forms that vary only in detail, mainly in the way of overcoming the **inherent difficulty of giving the sounds of the consonants by themselves**, which only in a few cases can be accomplished with any degree of satisfactoriness. All the help is made use of also which is to be obtained from classifying words and sounds, presenting them in order of difficulty, and omitting as many anomalous forms as possible until the child has made some progress.

Apart from the **fundamental defect that any synthetic process is contrary to the child's habits in learning forms**, the practical difficulties met with in carrying out the method are so numerous and important, and the skill and resource needed in the teaching are so considerable, that the plan (so far as the writer's experience goes) has not met with much favour in England.

The **vowels** being simply **musical tones of different quality**, offer little or no difficulty as to their being sounded alone, but very great difficulty from their being represented in such very various ways, so that, as previously noted, the child's experiences are being constantly contradicted.[1]

"Our language is said to possess **13 different vowel sounds**, but there are **104 ways of representing these vowel sounds to the eye**. ... Now it is practically impossible for the young learner to get up these 104 ways of writing down our vowel sounds; what he does, and what he must do, is to learn each word as a separate and individual entity, to remember the *look* of it, and to reproduce that look when he writes it down."— (*Meiklejohn.*)

With respect to the **consonants**, the powers of *s*, *z*, and *h* may be given by themselves; and the sounds of the liquids, *l, m, n, r,* may also be taught without much trouble. But as the consonants are mostly but different ways (depending upon the use of lips, teeth, tongue, and throat) of allowing the breath to burst forth in commencing a vowel tone, or of cutting off the flow of such tone, it is clear from the very nature of the case that they cannot be properly sounded alone.

Knowledge of the powers of the letters alone is utterly inadequate to meet the difficulties with which the child is brought face to face. Whatever devices we have recourse to, there are very many words in our language which defy any effort to construct their sounds out of the sounds of their component letters. To confine ourselves to two illustrations only, we may take (1) the words ending in *ough*, and (2) words containing *silent letters*—as neigh, light, psalm, knot, feign, indict, corps, yacht, doubt, calm, etc. Perhaps the most anomalous word in the English language is the word *quay*, the sound of which is a complete contradiction of the child's ordinary experience.

"The language contains more than **1300 words the notation of which is not in harmony with the pronunciation**; and these 1300 words are the commonest—the most in daily use. Of these **800 are monosyllables**—and these too in most common use."— (*Meiklejohn.*)

With languages of almost entirely regular notation like Spanish, or German, where in the vast majority of cases, at least, the signs have fixed sounds, the difficulties to be overcome are far less serious; and, with some admixture of analytical teaching at first, the plan may no doubt in such cases be carried through with much greater success than the old alphabetic mode of teaching. It does not follow, however, that this is a reason for its introduction into an anomalous language like English.

It has been pointed out by more than one writer, that the frequent attempts on the part of the child to give the power of such letters as *d, b, p, t, m,* without any accompanying vowel sound, has a **tendency to produce stammering**.

(3) *The Phonetic or Phonotypic Method.*—This is really but a **modification of the Phonic method**, with special features of its own intended to meet some of the objections urged against the older plan.

---

[1] For a complete classification of the vowel powers, see Marcel's *Language as a Means of Culture.* Vol. ii., appendix.

In order to overcome the difficulty arising from the want of correspondence between the number of letter signs and of letter sounds in English, various ways have been proposed of modifying the existing characters, where necessary, by certain added marks or changes of form, so that each elementary sound may be uniformly represented by a single sign. One scheme has 65 characters, and it would seem that at least 45 are necessary in order to represent the elementary sounds of the language with even approximate completeness.

The powers of this **extended alphabet** having been learned, the child would proceed as in the Phonic method. The first books put into his hands would be printed in the new characters, and when these were mastered he would be put back to the same lessons printed in the ordinary way. Thenceforward the modified letters would be abandoned.

The difficulties of our notation are not surmounted by the plan, but only postponed. The additional signs greatly increase the **weariness of learning the alphabet**, and with so many groups of letters of similar form it is difficult to believe but that confusion must result. By those who advocate the plan, however, the practical difficulties are said to be not so great as they appear.

Perhaps the best arranged of the books specially prepared for carrying out the method are *Dr. Edwin Leigh's Readers*, drawn up on what the author calls the system of "pronouncing orthography." In these the general shape of the letters is kept throughout, so that the look of the word is but little altered, and the child recognises a letter-symbol at once as some form of *o* or *a*, etc. The added marks are in some cases so minute that much care would be necessary to distinguish them with certainty.

The necessity for using peculiarly printed books is certainly against the plan, inasmuch as **the child has, in many cases, to learn two forms for the same word** before he can read ordinary type; and it seems far preferable to fix the right form in the mind at once by presenting that alone to the eye.

(B.) **ANALYTIC PLANS.**—In these the natural method whereby the child becomes acquainted with objects is followed, and **the words are taught, with respect to both form and sound, as wholes first.** It is not until the child has had an opportunity of fixing in his mind the general look of the word and its associated sound that he is led to examine its parts. And this is done, not as an essential to reading, but to compel close attention to the *form*, in order that future recognition may be assisted, and the pupil may be able to spell the word correctly when called upon to *write* it.

The child cannot be said to read until he does so without any conscious direction of the mind to the elementary sounds which go to make up a word, and he is able to name it at sight from its appearance as a whole. To this the analytic plan habituates him from the first.

Analysis naturally precedes synthesis; and, as a matter of fact, however much it may be disguised, **the analytic process really enters into all methods of associating sound and sign in reading.** The induction leading to the mastery of the letter powers is carried on for the most part unconsciously, and is gradually perfected as the child gains experience of the sounds by practice in reading, and **comes to recognise their force from the effects they produce** in the different words brought under his notice.

It is this realisation of the force of letters *in different combinations* which gives the child the power to master new words; and, whatever method is employed, he is certain to gain this power in the end. The practical question for decision by the teacher is as to which method puts the child in the best position for gaining the necessary experience of words, and lends its aid to the inductive process in the most rational and effective way.

(1) '*Look and Say*,' or '*Word and Name*,' *Method.*—The words 'look and say' indicate the fundamental feature of the plan. In dealing with a word new to the child, which he is unable to pronounce, he is first told to look at it carefully while the teacher sounds it clearly and deliberately, then, still attending to the symbol, he imitates the sound as given until he can reproduce it easily and perfectly. To ensure intelligence and assist remembrance, **the idea underlying the word is closely associated with it**; and finally, the child is led to analyse the word into its parts, and to spell it so as to fix the exact image in his mind.

As the child progresses, various modifications and additions—such as the **syllabling of words** and the **comparison of words of similar sound or form**—may be introduced, in order to assist him in seizing upon just those things which it is important for him to notice.

The method associates sound, sign, and idea in a natural way. It presents no difficulty to the child which is not inherent in our system of notation, and is **analogous to the way in which he learns spoken language**; while, further, it is so simple and direct in application that it may be readily carried out even by the youngest teacher.

Even those who advocate some other plan admit, for the most part, that the first irregular monosyllables have to be mastered on the 'look and say' principle; and as all words have in the end to be recognised from the picture they present to the eye as a whole, it seems reasonable, on this ground alone, to accustom the child from the beginning to that mode of recognition which he must eventually employ, so as to preserve for him a uniformity of experience and method of attack.

It is sometimes urged against the method that it proceeds upon the Chinese principle of learning each word-symbol independently. There is however this vital difference; in Chinese no analysis of the symbol is possible, but in the 'look and say' plan analysis of the word into its elements, *after it is known as a whole*, is insisted upon. The objection assumes that the method gives a child no power to master new words, whereas it not only does this but does it most effectively.

The fact that a child is not allowed to spell a word until he has learned to sound it has led to the method being sometimes called "reading without spelling."

The learning of the alphabet is no integral part of the plan, though it may easily be associated with it if the names of the letters have not been previously acquired.

The method has grown greatly in favour of late years, and is very generally recommended by those who should know most concerning the difficulties of teaching and the best methods of overcoming them. The uncertainty, guessing, and miscalling of words sometimes said to arise from the method are, where they exist, almost entirely due to defective teaching.

(2) *The Syllabic Method.*—This is only a variety of the 'look and say' method, the principle being practically the same in both and the first steps almost identical. **Great importance is attached to the classification of syllables**, and these are so arranged as to bring strongly before the child those most used in the composition of words. Directly he passes to words of more than one syllable he is taught to break up such words into parts, each of which he can sound with one effort of the voice, and to note these in turn before attempting to give the sound of the word as a whole. Supposing a word to occur which the child cannot sound unaided, it is written on the blackboard with the syllables distinctly marked, and each of these is taught as in the 'look and say' plan. The sound of the complete word can then be given with ease. **This is a most valuable exercise, and a great aid to the mastery of new words of more than one syllable**, whatever plan is used in the early stages. Properly taught, a child soon learns to read readily even the longest words of regular notation.

(C.) **MIXED PLANS.**—Instead of making use of either of the analytic or synthetic plans alone, some teachers prefer to employ a method in which are united certain features drawn from both groups. The following are the only plans of this kind calling for special notice.

(1) *Phono-Analytic Method.*—This is an attempt to combine the 'look and say' and phonic principles in natural order,—analysis coming first and synthesis after. The '**look and say**' plan is used for the mastery of the first elements of reading, and as a means of teaching words of irregular notation; then **phonic drill** and the **comparison of words** of similar sound are brought in to secure the rapid learning of the powers of the letters, and thus to enable the child to arrive at the sounds of words of regular formation by the constructive process. As a further aid to this the **words are very carefully classified** according to their sounds, the more irregular forms being introduced gradually as the child gains experience.

The first lessons proceed upon the 'look and say' plan until the child has accumulated a sufficient number of easy monosyllables for analysis. From these a suitable word—say *man*—is selected, and the sound of the word is given slowly and deliberately while the child attends to the way in which the sound is produced. The syllable *an* is then put upon the black-board alongside the original word, and the two are sounded in succession, by both teacher and pupil, until the latter realises the power of the letter *m*, and learns the way in which the organs have to be disposed and the breath managed to produce the effect. Other letters are then inserted in front of the syllable taken, each being treated as before; and the exercises are further extended by keeping the first part of the word constant and changing the final letter in a similar way.

The child's knowledge is tested from step to step by calling upon him to read in easy sentences the words acquired; and when he has mastered the powers of the consonants both in commencing and concluding a syllable, all words of fairly regular form are taught as in the phonic method pure and simple.

<small>Different teachers carry out the details of the plan in somewhat different ways. There is generally a tendency to overdo the more mechanical parts of the process. The *Globe Readers*, edited by Mr. A. F. Murison, are specially prepared with a view to the teaching of reading by this method.</small>

(2) *Word-building Plans.*—Several have been suggested, which are in many respects similar to the Phono-analytic. The excellent *English Method* of Messrs. Sonnenschein & Meiklejohn is the most successful attempt yet made to analyse and classify the fundamental combinations of the language.

METHODS OF ASSOCIATING SOUND AND SYMBOL IN READING.

I. SYNTHETIC.
Elements (*letters*) taken first; compounds (*words*) second.

1. Name Methods.
(*Spelling before Reading.*)
Names of the letters uttered first.

PRINCIPLE.—*Naming the letters compels attention to form of word, hence recognition.*

(a) Alphabetic Method.
Names of the letters composing a word named in order first, then the sound of the whole word given.

2. Sound Methods.
(*Letter-sounding before Reading.*)
Sounds or powers of the letters uttered first.

PRINCIPLE.—*Sounds of the letters of a word uttered rapidly give the sound of the word.*

(a) Phonic Method.
The *sounds* or *powers* of the ordinary letters supposed to be uttered first, then by rapid utterance and blending the sound of the word results.

(b) Phonetic Method.
A single sound fixed to each of ordinary letters; variations of the letters used for all the powers not then provided for. Sounds of this *extended alphabet* uttered first, word-sound supposed to follow.

II. ANALYTIC.
Compounds (*words*) taken first; elements (*letters*) second.

1. 'Look and Say' Method.
(*Word-reading before Spelling.*)

PRINCIPLE.—*Words are recognised by their look as a whole, and not by noting every letter.*

Sound of the whole word taught directly first; spelling (or naming of the letters) not taken until sound of word is known.

2. Syllabic Method.
(*Syllable-reading before Spelling.*)

PRINCIPLE.—*Words are recognised by recognition of their syllables.*

Syllables classified; words of regular sound taken first, and all of more than one syllable broken up. Attention directed to sound and form of syllables first.

Method of Phonic Comparison, or Phono-Analytic Method.
Combination of Phonic and Analytic Methods.

Association in first lessons made by 'Look and Say'; then syllables admitting of it have main part uttered by 'Look and Say,' and the completing sound (initial or final) by Phonic method. Much stress laid on *comparison of words*, e.g. (b)an, (c)an, (f)an, (m)an, (r)an, etc.

III. Nature and Elements of Good Reading.

A person, in speaking, not only employs words but makes use of certain peculiarities of intonation and modulation, with the addition in many cases of certain minor devices. These are intended to assist the communication of the exact sense which it is wished to convey, and also, it may be, to arouse in the hearer a certain amount of accompanying emotion. In written and printed language these personal elements are lost; and therefore, when the symbols are translated again into speech by reading, it is the province of the reader to supply the missing aids in such a degree as is necessary to produce the desired effect.

Jacotot's chief maxim for the acquisition of a proper style in reading was—"**Read as you would speak.**" This was a revolt against the artificial delivery, unnatural or sing-song tones, false emphasis, and affectation which must always have been common; and as **a first rough canon** for the correction of such faults the dictum is of much use. It has however been very frequently repeated as though it summed up the whole matter, which it does not, and has been indiscreetly urged to such lengths as to mislead with respect to the higher qualities of good reading, and at least partially to obscure its real nature.

Just as there is great difference between the liveliness, broken phrases, quick transitions, and even the modes of expression, used in conversation, and the more staid, formal, exact, and deliberate style of a set composition; so, in reading, while the delivery should never be artificial or affected, there should be a more sober manner, greater reserve, and less sudden changes of intonation than in speaking. This is seen in the fact that in ordinary circumstances we rarely or never have any difficulty in deciding whether a person is reading or speaking, even when the reading is the best of its kind. To read a piece of ordinary prose in exactly the same way as we should converse would be to make our reading appear flippant and wanting in the dignity we expect. Even in the necessarily more impassioned utterance of lyric and dramatic poetry there is the same clear distinction. **Reading and theatrical declamation have not the same objects, and should not be confounded.** It is the business of the actor so to simulate the personality of the character he presents to us as to sink his own individuality entirely, and to make us lose consciousness that he is other than he pretends to be. This is never the object of the reader; and hence many things are rightly allowed in stage declamation which would be entirely out of place in reading. In the latter, while we may be affected even with deep emotion, and everything may be done to make us realise fully all that the passage is intended to convey, yet **the manner and delivery of the reader are marked by a studied moderation, and we never think of him as other than he is.** Good reading, says a writer quoted by Stow, should "be distinct and yet not dramatic, varied and yet not affected. The reading itself should be like a clear transparent medium; the reader should be lost sight of, whilst the author himself appears."

The character of the composition and how it is intended to affect us—whether to give us a clear insight into truth, convince us by argument, stimulate the imagination, rouse in us a feeling for what is beautiful, or move us to pity and the like—will almost entirely determine how a piece should be read; and **the good taste of the reader will be shewn in adapting his style of reading to the nature and style of the language** with which he is dealing.

The main things to guard against in the case of children are artificiality of tone and a laboured drawling delivery, indistinctness of utterance, careless blundering or miscalling of words from randomness or want of proper attention, and lack of intelligence leading to the false use of emphasis or its absence altogether.

The chief matters to which attention has to be given in teaching reading, so as to secure correctness both of utterance and style will now be considered in order:—

(1) *Pronunciation, Enunciation, and Articulation.*—These words are often used in a vague general way to denote pretty much the same thing—the correct production of the sounds of words—though they are sometimes employed in different senses. The three things indicated are of course closely connected, and shade into each other, but wherever the terms are to be used side by side in connection with technical matters they should certainly be differentiated.

In a restricted sense then it will be found convenient to use the term **pronunciation** for the correct production of the *vowels*; and careful consideration will shew that it is upon giving the right power and quantity to these that *purity* of utterance is very largely dependent.

The pronunciation of the long *u* as in *Tuesday*, of *ew* as in *dew*, and of *ue* as in *due*, as though the sound in all these cases were represented by *oo* is a common error; while the converse mistake of pronouncing *too* as if it were *tew* obtains in some districts. It is worth noting that most of the provincialisms which give trouble in school are due to variation from the acknowledged standard in the sounding of the vowels. Such pronunciations as *maën* (man), *waërm* (warm), *Jarge* (George), *noight* (night), *moine* (mine), *clim* (climb), *nayther* (neither), *watter* (water), *coom* and *kem* (come), *waërds* (words), and a hundred others, are examples.

Enunciation should stand for the proper sounding of the *consonants*; and it is to this that *distinctness* of utterance, so that the ear may readily distinguish the sounds of words, is due. Lips, tongue, teeth, and throat, all need to be properly used. A word may be sounded loudly and yet be difficult to catch, for if the consonants are not clearly given the distinctive character of the word will be more or less blurred.

Faulty enunciation shews itself perhaps most commonly in the sounding of groups of consonants at the end of a word or syllable. Thus the dentals (*d* and *t*) are frequently omitted in words ending in *nds*, *nts*, *sts*, *cts*, etc. (as in commands, instruments, posts, acts, etc.). The letter *g* is often dropped at the end of words like telling, standing, speaking; while *g* and *r* are sometimes inserted, as in *kitching*, *garding*, *strawr*, *drawr* (for kitchen, garden, straw, draw). A sharp consonant is also sometimes changed into a corresponding flat one, as *s* into *z*. The letter *h* is a constant source of trouble in elementary schools. Frequent correction is necessary, but the teacher may easily be tempted to spend much more time over it than is wise.

Very occasionally bad enunciation may be due to some defect of the vocal organs, but much more frequently it arises from defective perception of the sounds, and very commonly from carelessness which easily becomes confirmed into a habit.

Articulation is the proper jointing on of the *syllables* of a word and the correct separation of the words in a sentence, so that none of the parts are slurred over, dropped out altogether, or run one into another. "In just articulation," says a writer quoted by Mr. Gill, "the words are not hurried over, nor melted together; they are neither abridged nor prolonged; they are not swallowed, nor are they shot from the mouth; neither are they trailed and then suffered to drop unfinished."

Articulation is a matter needing much attention in schools, not only in reading but in repetition. Sometimes the most grotesque mistakes arise, from allowing words to be articulated in such a slipshod way that they are run together into a compound and all meaning is lost. It is said that once, a little girl, on being taken to the sea-side, asked where the '*dindimies*' were, her question arising from the fact that she had been allowed to say 'the sea and all the dindimies' for 'the sea and all that in them is'; and Stow tells of a gentleman who, after he had left school, was astonished to find that his earliest reading-book was 'Reading made easy,' not '*Readie-me-deezy*' as he had been accustomed to call it.

Much bad articulation has its source in bad enunciation, but many defects are also due to a **slovenly slurring over of certain sounds of a word**, arising chiefly from carelessness or hurry, and sometimes from imperfect listening or faulty imitation—as for instance *behol'n, partic'larly, extr'or'nary, ridic'lous, pecul'arly, libr'ry, Febr'ary, man'n th'orse* (man and the horse), etc. This is especially the case when the final letter of a word is the same as the initial letter of a word following—as in *righ'time, lai'down, boy'sake, blow'inds*, etc. Sometimes a syllable is inserted as in 'tremenduous,' 'umberella,' etc.

Another rather common result of defective articulation is the transfer of a final consonant to the next word if this begins with a vowel; thus, 'he saw an ostrich' becomes 'he saw a nostrich,' 'so sure an aim' sounds like 'so sure a name,' and so on.

(2) *Accent, Emphasis, and Stress.*—This is another instance of three terms which have been loosely used, sometimes in the same sense, sometimes to denote distinct things It will be useful as well as conducive to clearness to limit their meaning and assign to each its own province.

Accent is the additional force of voice laid upon a certain *syllable* of a word in accordance with established usage, or upon certain syllables at regularly recurring intervals in poetry to mark the rhythmical flow necessary to metrical composition.

Accent is important not only because it is a necessary element of correct utterance, but also because in some cases a change of accent in a word gives it a different meaning and makes it another part of speech—as *súbject, subjéct; cónduct, condúct; présent, presént; cóntent, contént; prógress, progréss; désert, desért; réfuse, refúse*, etc.

Emphasis is the means employed to direct special attention to or bring into prominence some individual *word* in a phrase or sentence, in order to make clear and give point to the particular shade of meaning intended to be conveyed. The more natural and typical mode of securing emphasis is by giving additional force to the word in saying it, but it is also marked by sudden change of voice or pitch, a pause before or after the word, greater deliberation in utterance, and sometimes even by lowering the voice almost to a whisper. Occasionally also, in speaking, emphasis is aided by gesture.

Of all matters to be attended to in reading of the higher kind none is more important than emphasis. It is of the greatest assistance to the hearer in grasping the meaning of what is read, and its just use is one of the best tests of intelligent understanding on the part of the reader.

False emphasis is a very common fault in reading, and the most careful attention needs to be given to it in teaching the subject. **Clear understanding of the passage is essential to correct emphasis**, for, unless this has been gained, it is impossible for the reader (except as a matter of accident, or of parrot-like imitation) so to place the emphasis as to render evident the exact sense of what is read. Frequently a sentence will bear several shades of meaning according as this or that word is brought out.[1] As a rule, however, it is not difficult to determine exactly what is intended, and insight into the passage is shewn by selection of the particular word for emphasis which gives the most evident and reasonable signification to the whole.

The word **stress** is commonly used in a very general sense for additional force of any kind given in reading or speaking. It would be convenient if the word, so far as technical use is concerned, could be reserved for the increased intensity or distinct marking given to a *group of words*.

In this sense stress is to the logically distinct portions (whether phrases or sentences) which go to make up discourse what emphasis is to individual words.

Stress, like emphasis, is a very necessary element of good reading, and becomes of the greatest importance if a passage is at all lengthy or involved. Without it the hearer would often have much difficulty in making out the interdependence or logical relationship of the various parts ; but, by laying stress upon some portions and sinking others into a secondary place, the structure of the whole is made clear, and the meaning consequently rendered much more easy to grasp.

(3) *Tone, Pitch, and Intensity.*—The **tone** should be pleasant, distinct, and full without being noisy. The sound should come clear away, not strike the back of the throat, nor become muffled in the mouth and wanting in proper resonance from imperfect adjustment or from the lips and teeth not being properly opened.

The character of the tone depends largely upon the way in which it is produced, and the **proper use of the voice** in speaking and reading is a matter which does not receive the attention it deserves.

Improper production of the voice leads to the harshness and unpleasantness of tone so frequently heard in reading ; much greater effort is used than ought to be the case, the throat suffers, and fatigue soon follows. This should be looked to.

---

[1] Thus in the old example—"*Shall you ride to London to-day?*" a different meaning would be expressed in the answer as each word is emphasised in turn.

The **proper management of the breath**, the least amount necessary being used, and inspirations taken at convenient places, is another matter which is important. Much may be done by a little judicious instruction.

The **pitch** of the note most frequently used, and to which the voice continually returns, should be that which is the most natural and costs the least effort for the reader to employ. Where this is the case, it is easy to pass above or below for purposes of modulation as the nature of the reading requires.

Generally speaking the pitch of school reading is too high; and not unfrequently, when a boy is corrected because he cannot be heard, he is allowed to raise the *pitch* of his voice, instead of being made to produce the tone properly or to increase its force and to speak more distinctly.

The **intensity or force** of the sound should be such that it may be heard with ease. There should be no strain or shouting on the one hand, nor "mumbling inaudibility" on the other.

In some schools children develop a **loud, artificial, screaming tone in reading**, quite unlike their natural voice, and pitched very much higher. This is a very objectionable mannerism, which the teacher should never allow to be formed, or, if he finds it, should do his best to completely eradicate. It is unpleasant to listen to, prevents anything like proper modulation, adds greatly to the noise in school, and not unfrequently is a source of annoyance to neighbouring classes.

(4) *Pace and Fluency.*—The **pace** of reading will depend upon the nature of what is read, and will frequently need to be varied even in the same piece. It should be sufficiently slow for every word to be heard distinctly, but must be neither drawling nor heavy. In the presentation of abstract matters, or of weighty truths which are difficult to realise, increased deliberation is necessary; while, as a rule, merely illustrative matter, easy description, and in fact any simple and direct statement, may be taken more quickly.

Some sentences, especially impassioned utterances, need to be read rapidly to produce their proper effect, others lingered over that their full force may be appreciated. The more intricate and involved the statement the slower and more emphatic the reading should be, so that each point may be followed, its relationship grasped, and the meaning of the whole made clear by the time the final conclusion is reached. This is notably the case in argument.

By **fluency** is meant the readiness with which the words are uttered in succession, and the grace and *ease* which should characterise the delivery of the sentences. Fluent reading is marked by a sense of rhythm, and is neither laboured nor stilted—the words flow naturally, and without any obtrusive effort, awkward breaks, or stumbling over difficult words.

Fluency depends upon instantaneous recognition of the forms, the power to look ahead of the words actually being sounded and take in the structure of the sentence, quick interpretation of the sense, and complete command of the vocal organs.

(5) *Pauses and Phrasing.*—The function of **pauses** is to enable the hearer to distinguish and grasp the relationship of the various parts of a more or less complete passage. They mark out for him the limits of parenthetical clauses, attributive phrases, etc., and assist him in piecing together parts of the main statement which, owing to exigences of composition, may have been separated. To guide the reader somewhat in making these pauses printed stops are inserted at the more important points; such stops are general indications by the author as to how he wishes the passage taken. Frequently, however, in reading, something more than recognition of the *structure* of the sentence is necessary in order to bring out the full *sense*, and pauses are required where no stops occur. These the good judgment of the reader must supply.

The right use of pauses must be taught through the understanding. It is very easy for the teacher to be too rigid in enforcing attention to the *printed* stops. Mechanical rules are useless. The common instruction to count one for a comma, two for a semicolon, and so on, except as intended to give the most general notion of *relative* length, is absurd.

Phrasing in reading is the grouping together of words according to their logical connection and interdependence. A good reader will associate closely those words which go to make up each part of a complete thought, pretty much as a good musical performer brings out the various musical phrases of which a movement is composed. This natural collocation of words according to notions and relationships is a very important element in good reading, but it is a matter which is rarely attended to as it ought to be. It depends mainly upon the correct use of pauses, aided frequently by change of intonation and variation of stress.

Even in the lowest classes something may be done towards securing correct phrasing; and directly a child can say the words properly he should be taught by the teacher's example to group them in sets. Mere attention to the stops is not sufficient; the pupil has to be trained to recognise at once which are the main ideas and which are merely supplementary and shewn how to make this clear in his reading.

(6) *Modulation, Intelligence,* and *Expression.*—**Modulation** is the employment of certain variations of pitch, inflexions of voice, or changes of intonation, which are natural to speech and should be to reading. It gives brightness and variety to reading, assists in making clear the ideas, and is an important means of securing emotional expression. It is opposed to a droning dead level of utterance, 'sing-song,' or a 'lesson saying' character; and should banish the wearisomeness and dulness which can scarcely fail to arise from a mechanical and monotonous flow of words.

In modulation the voice usually glides from one point to another, and as the intervals are not distinctly marked, nor limited to certain fixed and determinable values, as in music, they are generally difficult to catch. Musical intervals may, however, frequently be recognised in the inflexions, and especially in the cadences, where intervals of a fourth or fifth are commonly employed.

Ordinary modulation makes use of a range of four or five notes, both above and below the middle or common pitch of the voice, and even a wider range is not rare, especially in declamatory passages, where "the alterations of pitch are numerous and complicated." The octave, however, seems as a rule the greatest single interval used.

Helmholtz says: "Attentive observation on ordinary conversation shews us that regular musical intervals involuntarily recur, although the singing tone of the voice is concealed under the noises which characterise the individual letters, and the pitch is not held firmly, but is frequently allowed to glide up and down. . . . The end of an affirmative sentence followed by a pause is usually marked by the voice falling a fourth from the middle pitch. An interrogative ending rises, often as much as a fifth above the middle pitch." Of course the habits of different nations, as well as of individuals, vary greatly in these respects.

That the use of modulation plays a very important part in conveying shades of meaning and feeling will be at once apparent if we consider a few cases—for example, the varieties of meaning which may be given to the words 'yes' or 'no' by differences of inflexion. The first alone may in this way be made to express certainty, doubt, hesitation, agreement, satisfaction, displeasure, a question, or even the opposite of its usual meaning.

Intelligence in reading is that quality which is concerned with the correct presentation of the thoughts or *truths* of the passage being read, and by means of which the *sense* is brought out so fully and distinctly that the hearer is able at once to grasp what is being conveyed. The reader makes his points, and wherever anything of the nature of a climax occurs he prepares the way for it by a judicious use of the devices at his command, so that it strikes the listener with full force.

Unless the child clearly understands what he is reading, intelligence is impossible, and hence from the very beginning this matter should receive constant care, apart from the further consideration that, as reading is the great means whereby knowledge is to be gained, the formation of a *habit* of attending closely to the sense of what is read is of the greatest importance. Where the reader has a quick perception of the meaning of a passage himself, he will, as a rule, have little difficulty in making this clear to others.

Intelligence is opposed to artificiality, eccentricities of manner, over employment of gesture, and in fact any kind of mannerism, as these things distract the attention from the subject-matter.

In reading ordinary narrative, description, or scientific discourse, the essential thing is to make perfectly clear the sense to be conveyed. In much poetry, however, and in many higher passages of prose, there is over and above the truths which the words involve, an implied *emotional element* or accompaniment of feeling—as joy, grief, fear, humour, and the like—as well as, in many cases, a *beauty of form*, both of which should be made evident.

Expression gives a fitting presentment of these things in the reading; it realises the *associated emotion* or personal feeling, brings out the *rhythmical beauties* of the language without obtruding them, and interprets the *spirit of the passage* in such a way that it becomes manifest to the hearer and arouses in him the effect intended.

Just expression is the highest quality of reading, and the one most difficult to secure. It is one of the chief sources of the pleasure derived from listening to good reading, and is that which more than anything else raises it to the dignity of an art. An impassioned and beautiful passage will tax a reader's powers to the utmost, and before he can hope to do anything like full justice to it he must put himself into entire sympathy with its spirit and purpose. Sensitiveness of feeling, rapid insight, sound judgment, imaginative power, refined taste, and full command of the voice and the various devices employed in reading, are all more or less necessary to complete success.

Perfect expression is scarcely to be looked for in schools, and any pretentious affectation of graces, or fine reading as it is sometimes called, is strongly to be deprecated. Still a good deal may be done by a wise and skilful teacher in the higher stages; and it is something gained to realise what true perfection in this matter means, and to know in what direction it is to be sought. When other difficulties have been overcome, attention should be directed to correct expression whenever the passage needs it, and the children are capable of appreciating it. They may then be gradually trained by the teacher's example to give, in their reading, something at least of what is required. Mere parrot-like imitation, however, is worthless, and may easily become a delusion and a snare.

THE TEACHING OF READING 249

IV. LESSON METHODS OF TEACHING READING.

To teach reading well is not easy, and it should not be left entirely in the hands of unskilled teachers. The work should be supervised and frequently tested by the master. Abundant and carefully corrected practice must be secured, as well as intelligent application of the instructions given and of what may be learned from the teacher's model reading.

The **more essential features of any reading method** are that it should be—

(a) Natural, and appeal throughout to intelligence.
(b) Simple and direct as possible.
(c) Conducted in an interesting way.
(d) Suited to the particular stage at which the learner has arrived.
(e) So arranged as to lend assistance by judicious repetition of impressions, comparison of like things, and association of ideas.

The **spirit of the work** has very great influence upon success in teaching reading. Full sympathy with children, a bright and lively manner, and a large stock of patience are necessary. It is the possession of these qualities which makes women generally the best teachers of reading in its early stages.

(1) *Position of Class and Teacher.*—Reading is best taught with **children standing.** The position should be easy, with the head well up, and shoulders back. The book should be held at the correct angle and distance from the eye, and clear of the mouth.

The **semi-circular or horse-shoe arrangement** of the class is the most convenient, though some teachers prefer the hollow square, or the phalanx. For a number of small drafts reading together a circular grouping is useful.

The position of the teacher during the teaching should be in front of the class, and sufficiently far back for him to see every pupil without turning round. Occasionally, however, as in superintending the reading of a number of drafts, and so long as pointing to the words read is advisable during simultaneous reading in the early stages, it is better for the teacher to move behind the children. A little common sense will soon tell him what position it is best for him to take up during any particular part of the work.

Reading should be taught where there are no distractions, and it is best managed in a room by itself. It should not be taken where there is noisy work going on near, nor where it will interfere with the teaching of another class.

(2) *Explanations in the Reading Lesson.*—It cannot be too strongly insisted upon that in teaching reading **a distinct sense must always be associated with what is read**; without this anything like intelligence in reading is not to be hoped for. Very frequently the words are allowed to remain mere empty forms symbolising nothing—a paper currency without any specie basis. Hence the necessity for explaining any word or phrase which would otherwise have no meaning for the child.

It is very easy however to fall into the opposite error and say too much, or to indulge in talk respecting matters not actually needed for the comprehension of the subject in hand. **The reading lesson must not be overloaded with explanation**, nor must it be made a vehicle for all sorts of miscellaneous information. What is called 'incidental teaching' in a reading lesson is nine times out of ten only another name for wandering.

The **amount of explanation** to be given will depend upon the nature of the lesson, the stage of progress reached, and the general knowledge and intelligence of the children. No hard and fast rule can be laid down. The teacher must use his judgment, and keep clearly in mind that he is teaching *reading*; he will not then be likely to go far wrong. What is to be chiefly aimed at is the **elucidation of obscurities**, not the giving of the meaning of a term in a definition or set form of words for the child to learn. He may be taken to understand a word when he can use it correctly, although he is unable to give any formal definition of it. It is impossible to explain everything, and only such words and phrases as are important, and to which the context or the child's past experience will afford him no clew, should be dealt with.

In order that explanations in a reading lesson may serve their purpose properly they should be :—

    (a) **Always given in connection with the context**—the children having their books open, and their attention being directed to the word as part of the sentence first.

    (b) **Brief**—sufficient to ensure understanding and no more.

    (c) **To the point**—so that the children may have something definite to remember. It is a mistake to give the various shades of meaning a word may have in different connections.

(d) **Simple**—so as to be easily intelligible ; not dictionary definitions, nor mere synonyms as difficult to comprehend as the thing to be explained. Children will often quote these glibly enough while the real meaning is as dark to them as ever.

(e) **Suitable**—both with respect to the lesson and the exact nature of the help required.

(f) **Needed.**—It is a common error to take up time in talking about obvious matters, or things the wise teacher would leave to the pupils' general intelligence.

(g) **Made interesting**—so as to give brightness and variety to the lesson.

The **means to be employed** will vary with the nature of the case. Often what is wanted is an illustration, and if this can be given through the senses so much the better ; sketches on the black-board are particularly useful. In some instances an example or an anecdote will best serve, and in others the child's experience may be profitably appealed to. A question or two should always be asked before an explanation is offered that the teacher may see exactly how far the children may be made to help themselves, and what he has to supply. Logical analysis of the subject-matter, so as to bring out the relationship of the various parts, is frequently helpful ; and occasionally a rapid oral paraphrase by the teacher, the children filling in omitted words, may be effectively employed.

After all has been done that ought to be attempted in a reading lesson, there are certain to be some words which, from their nature and the limitations imposed upon the teacher, are imperfectly understood, and a few beyond the comprehension of the child at the stage reached. It is of no use to enter into a long digression respecting these, and the teacher must rest content with the hazy notion imparted by the general sense of the passage until the child's ideas are sufficiently expanded to allow of full comprehension.

Difficulties of words or subject-matter, involved constructions, idioms, figurative language, allusions, the form of the piece, or the style in which it is written, will all at one time or another need to be dealt with ; and to do this effectively, in the higher classes at least, it is **necessary for the teacher to look over the lesson carefully beforehand** that he may be prepared with what is wanted.

Word-building exercises are frequently useful if kept in their proper place, even from the reading point of view. For instance a few minutes now and again may advantageously be spent in referring to the formation of a word, and shewing how derivative words have been formed from it. Care, however, should be exercised in giving **derivations from foreign languages**, the learning of these being for the most part a waste of time with children. When a word occurs which forms one of a group from the same root, it is better, if time can be spared, to direct attention to the common element in the words as we know them, to give its primary meaning, and to show how this meaning underlies the force of each word of the group. As instances of what is meant we may take the words *compel, dispel, expel, impel, propel, repel* ; or again, *exceed, precede, proceed, recede, succeed*. It is a considerable help for the child to know the common prefixes and affixes, and these should be learned outside the reading lesson.

Places mentioned in the lesson should be pointed out on the map, but beyond this only a brief reference to other matters relating to them should be made at most. This is *not* an opportunity for giving a short geography lesson as some teachers seem to think.

As to the exact **place in the lesson where the explanations may best be introduced** there is considerable difference of practice. As soon as the child has begun to read they should be taken after the difficulties of utterance have been mastered, and before any attempt is made to teach correct emphasis, modulation, phrasing, and the other matters connected with intelligence and expression. Briefly we may say that the most suitable place is *after word-saying* and *before style*.

Some teachers prefer to give explanations before any reading is commenced, but this is not to be recommended, inasmuch as it is more clearly evident when the children have read a passage what points they do not understand, and how far they need help; while, further, the meaning is more easily made clear when they know what has gone before.

(3) *Correction of Errors in Reading.*—Children are naturally imitative, and bad habits seem to be contagious with them; hence it is important they should hear as little blundering as possible. Constant correction is necessary, but some discrimination must be used. Too frequently this part of the work is conducted without order or system, and with little or no realisation of the conditions and limitations under which it should be carried out. Perfection cannot be secured at once, and the teacher may easily be so exacting over little things as to destroy the effect of corrections respecting weightier matters. When too many improvements are pressed upon the child at the same time, none of them make any adequate impression, and he is pretty certain to be so bewildered as to remember nothing clearly; while the further mischief results that the same corrections have to be made over and over again.

The following are a few **practical suggestions** :—

(a) Those who are not reading should be expected to note, and, as far as they are able, to correct the mistakes made ; but the hands should not be held out until the reader has finished. This **mutual correction** encourages attention, and gives all a share in the work. The teacher can easily add anything further which is necessary.

(b) In the earliest lessons a child may be stopped at the point where he makes the mistake ; but as soon as sentences can be read with fair fluency **all corrections should be deferred until the reader has completed the portion** he is called upon to give.

(c) **One thing at a time** ; until errors connected with the saying of the words have been dealt with, corrections respecting style should be postponed, or at most receive but a passing reference.

(d) **Detection is not correction.** Telling children their faults is not sufficient, they must be shown how to amend them, and encouraged to make the necessary effort.

(e) **Common faults should be specially noticed,** and some means devised to effect their cure. The formation of bad habits in the earlier stages is to be particularly guarded against.

(f) **Corrections must not be made in a way to worry and discourage children.** Some teachers seem to delight in 'lying in wait' for errors and pouncing upon them.

(g) It is **sometimes necessary for the teacher to exaggerate a fault,** that the children may clearly perceive its nature.

(h) **An undue proportion of time must not be spent over backward children** ; it is common for corrections to be reiterated again and again to these while the rest of the class is idle.

(4) *The Teacher's Model Reading.*—It is of the very greatest service to the learner to hear good reading, and to note exactly how the words are said and what changes of tone and emphasis are made use of to bring out the full force of the meaning or to produce some particular effect. Hence **pattern reading by the teacher should form a recognised and systematic part of the method of every reading lesson.** Properly given, it not only sets a standard of good reading for the children to

aim at, but is an incentive to effort, and helpful in many ways, especially if it is evident that the teacher is thoroughly interested himself in the matter.

The passage selected for the model reading should be typical and not too long. The teacher must read *for* the children, not *with* them; and in some instances it will be found advantageous to point out before the reading is begun what things should be noticed. The children must be taught to listen attentively and to imitate exactly, that they may learn to produce the effects readily themselves, as well as to recognise the purpose each is intended to serve, and thus may be able to apply what they have learned to other parts of the lesson.

The amount to be read before the children are called upon to imitate will vary from a word to a short paragraph; and will depend upon the number of things to be attended to, the difficulty of what is to be imitated, and the children's power of remembering and reproducing effects.

In the lower and middle stages the imitation of the teacher's reading should be mostly simultaneous, inasmuch as the matters to be attended to are for the most part general, and lend themselves readily to treatment by combined utterance. The work is also an agreeable change to the children, and much more actual practice is secured. Later, when higher qualities have to be brought in, and the reading becomes more intellectual, the case is reversed. The objects to be secured are different, and the requisite delicacies of modulation and graces of style would for the most part be slurred over, if not entirely lost, by employing simultaneous utterance. The children also are better able to learn by hearing others read, while thorough appreciation of the effectiveness of the teacher's reading is now more important than exactness of imitation, and more room has to be left for individual interpretation. **The imitation in the higher stages should therefore be individual.**

(5) *The use of Simultaneous Utterance in teaching reading.*—Much that has already been said respecting simultaneous answering (see p. 128) applies also to simultaneous reading. In the lower stages it **supplies a large amount of practice**, which is the thing chiefly required, and judiciously used it may be made to save both time and labour. Wrongly or carelessly employed it may easily become worthless and even injurious. It should **never be used alone**, but always in connection with a large amount of individual practice, that things may receive consideration which it is not calculated to secure, and individual faults may be thoroughly corrected.

Almost all matters connected with mechanical utterance may be improved by simultaneous reading; but as these gradually become perfected, and attention has to be given to intellectual qualities, it should be employed less and less.

In addition to the increased practice it gives, it is chiefly useful as a means of—

(a) Correcting common faults of intonation.
(b) Modifying individual mannerisms.
(c) Securing distinct enunciation and proper pitch.
(d) Giving confidence and firmness to the reading.
(e) Regulating the speed of reading by stimulating drawlers and restraining the hasty and careless.

The teacher must be specially careful not to allow shouting, or reading in a coarse, unnatural, or sing-song tone, as these things soon become habitual. He must also be on the alert to detect idlers who are not reading at all, and those who are simply 'chiming-in' without attending to their books.

The plan of conducting the reading should occasionally be varied. For instance, instead of the whole of the boys reading at once, the two halves of the class may sometimes read alternately, or a few boys only may be called upon.

(6) *Spelling in the Reading Lesson.* Both for its own sake, and for the assistance it gives in fixing the forms of words in the mind, spelling should not be neglected in connection with the reading lesson. Its natural place, as already pointed out, is after the learning of the sound of the word. Exact observation is more important than the naming of the letters in order—**the use of the eye first and of the ear afterwards is the correct plan.** The child should be trained to give careful heed to the spelling of any word not known to him which he meets with in the lesson. He should feel that this is distinctly expected of him, and, as a spur to attention and a further means of securing the remembrance of the forms learned, a few minutes' test spelling should be given at the end of the reading lesson.

When a word of difficult form occurs in the reading lesson it should be **put on the black-board**, and if of more than one syllable it should be **separated into its parts by hyphens.** The child should be made to look at it carefully, then to sound it deliberately with the syllables clearly marked, and finally to spell it with a **slight but distinct pause after each syllable.** This pause between the syllables is important for several reasons, among other things it prevents the child falling into the error, so common with some, of naming two letters of the same kind together when they ought to be separated; for instance, spelling such a word as 'occurrence'—o, double c, u, double r, etc.

The old fashioned '**house-that-Jack-built**' **style of spelling,** as it has been called, of spelling the first syllable, then sounding it, then spelling the second syllable, sounding it, then sounding the two syllables together, and so on, should be abandoned.

(7) *Relative amount of attention to be given to matters of word-saying and of style in the teaching of reading in the different stages.* In the early stages of learning to read a large amount of attention must be given to the mere **mechanical matters** connected with utterance or correct *word-saying*; later, the teaching has to be chiefly directed to **intellectual matters** so as to secure the correct reading of the sentences, with attention to such things as emphasis, intelligence, modulation, and so on, which we may conveniently group under the head of *style*.

The relative importance of these at different stages of the child's progress, and the proportionate amount of time to be given to each, may be roughly indicated by the following diagram.

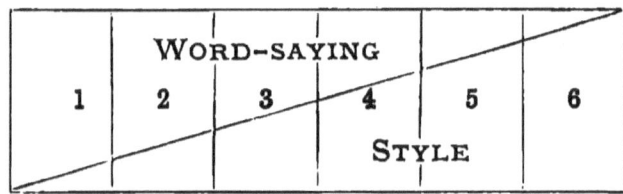

The figures represent the ordinary standards of the elementary school, the portion of each rectangle above the oblique line showing the amount of attention to be given to word-saying, and the portion below the line the amount to be given to style.

So long as the child has difficulty in recognising the symbols, and has to give *conscious* attention to them, so long will the more intellectual rendering, depending upon the rapid appreciation of the sense and of the interdependence of the various parts, be interfered with. By the time he has reached the end of the sixth standard the reading of the words should give him no further trouble, except in very occasional instances; the teacher's efforts therefore should now be wholly directed to securing the higher qualities of good reading.

(8) *Miscellaneous Suggestions.*

(a) **The child should not be helped more than is necessary**, but trained rather to help himself. The further he progresses the more self-reliance is to be expected of him.

(b) Simply hearing reading and correcting mistakes is not teaching it; eye, ear, voice, judgment, and taste, have all to be trained. **The child must be aided by both precept and example.** Word drill is useful as far as it goes, but it must not usurp the place of true reading.

(c) **Care must be taken not to disgust the child with the work.** Some means must be found of banishing tedium, and with it listlessness and inattention. Intellectual activity must be aroused, and there must be life, interest, and 'go' in the lesson.

(d) **The lessons should be taken in the order in which they occur in the book**, not at hap-hazard as is often done. If the book is properly constructed the lessons will be graduated, and this help must not be thrown away.

(e) **Each lesson should be mastered before it is left,** so far as this can be done reasonably ; but time must not be wasted in stickling for perfection. A little well read is better than much merely scampered over.

(f) Endeavour should be made at all times to **prevent the formation of bad habits.** Much time has often to be spent in curing faults which ought never to have been allowed to form.

(g) **The pupils should rarely read in turn.** Inattentive ones should be challenged, and plenty of practice secured to those who are backward. Every child must share in the reading.

(h) The teacher should be familiar with the lesson, and in hearing reading should as a rule **attend to the reader not to the book.**

As an occasional treat it will be found of advantage for the teacher to read some attractive narrative or poem to the children ; or they may be allowed to read from some interesting story book in turn, the rest of the class listening.

The Alphabet.

The learning of the alphabet is necessary on many accounts ; and eventually it has to be learned so thoroughly that the child is able on the instant to recognise the **form** of each letter, to give its **sound** or power correctly in combination, and to state its **name.** The three things in fact have to be closely associated together. Further, for purposes of general convenience the order of the letters must also be perfectly known.

The great mistake, however, which has been made in the past, and which is still almost universally prevalent, is assuming that the mastery of the alphabet is necessary *as a preliminary to reading,* in-

R

stead of leaving it to be taught incidentally and gradually as the reading of words progresses.

Horace Mann says, "I am satisfied that our greatest error in teaching children lies in beginning with the alphabet... How can one, who as yet is utterly incapable of appreciating the remote benefits which in after life reward the acquisition of knowledge, derive any pleasure from an exercise which *presents neither beauty to his eye, nor music to his ear, nor sense to his understanding.*"

As usually taught, it still remains true that "a more difficult or tiresome lesson than the alphabet a child is never doomed to meet with in his whole future course;"[1] and there can scarcely be a doubt, that the want of interest in books and the dislike of reading which many children display is in part to be traced to the weariness and unpleasantness of their first experiences. Unfortunately, too, many teachers have come to regard the dull mechanical grind which the child is made to go through day by day in learning his letters as a necessity, and naturally find the task as repulsive to themselves as it is dreary to their pupils.

A large number of devices have been proposed for getting rid as far as possible of the tedium and irksomeness attendant upon learning the alphabet. Many of these answer well enough in the teaching of individuals, but fail to meet the school difficulty of teaching a large number of children together.

The following are the principal plans which have been made use of, or suggested, for teaching the alphabet by itself. Some, it will be found, turn the process of learning into a game or amusement; some depend mainly upon utilising the child's love of activity; others again appeal to the power of association; and still others rely upon mechanical repetition more or less systematised.

(1) *Alphabet blocks.*

Locke suggests pasting letters on the sides of large dice, or on blocks with many faces, and allowing children to use these to play games with. He would have the small letters taught first. Various modifications of the plan have been used for home teaching.

(2) *Solid Letter-forms.*

Quintilian would have children familiarised with the shapes of letters before their names or order are learned, and suggests the use of ivory letters "which the children take pleasure in handling, seeing, and naming." St. Jerome also advises ivory or wooden letters that the names may be learned in play. "The ancients moulded toothsome dainties into the form of letters, and thus, as it were, made children swallow the alphabet."[2] Basedow in his school bakery did the same thing.

(3) *Graved or printed letter-forms.*

Letters printed on separate cards or tablets have almost entirely superseded solid letters. Such letter tablets may be used in many ways, both as materials for games between parent and child, and as a part of the more formal class teaching. Exercises analogous to type-setting have been frequently suggested from Rollin downwards.

---

[1] Dunn. [2] Erasmus—quoted from Compayre's *History of Pedagogy.*

(4) *Association of pictures with the letters.*
This association has been made in two principal ways :—
(a) By putting alongside the letter a picture of some familiar animal or object whose name is easy and begins with this letter—as *a* with apple, *b* with bag, *c* with cart, etc. The association is sometimes strengthened by rhymes, of which the well-known one beginning "A was an *Archer* and shot at a frog," etc., is an example. Such rhymes help to fix the order of the letters.
(b) By placing with the letters the picture of some animal or object supposed to produce a sound suggestive of, if not actually like, the *sound* of the letter. Thus a sheep may be associated with *a*, a cow lowing with *m*, the winding of a clock with *r*, and so on. Such "**interjectional imitative**" **methods**, as Mr. Hall calls them, have found considerable favour in Germany, and much ingenuity has been exercised in framing them. They point to the phonic method.

(5) *Constructive exercises of the Kindergarten type.*
The capital letters may be constructed by the children with short wooden rods, or card strips; or better still with straight and curved pieces of stout wire of suitable shapes and sizes. Jointed laths, formed of a number of pieces connected together so as to move readily in one plane, may also be used.

(6) *Alphabet sheet and pointer.*
The teacher points to a letter and the children are made to repeat the letters indicated again and again till known. Of all ways of teaching the alphabet this is probably the dullest and the worst. The weary reiteration is often carried on for many months, if not longer, before the child becomes even tolerably acquainted with the letters.

(7) *Letters printed one at a time on the black-board.*
This concentrates attention and avoids the confusion arising from seeing many forms at once. Generally the help of classification is brought in, and the letters are taught in groups according to similarity of form, comparison and contrast being also made use of. Pillans suggested teaching the letters in 'brotherhoods' according to similarity in the way they are sounded—as labials, dentals, etc.

(8) *Drawing of the letters.*
This was suggested by Dr. Bell, and in the hands of a good teacher may be made an effective method. It trains both the eye and the hand, and strengthens the recollection by compelling close attention to the form. The simplest letters are taken first, each being imitated in turn from the teacher's drawing on the black-board and learned at the same time. The device is often useful in connection with others, and may readily be made to pass into writing. The marking over of letters printed in red on black-board or slates has also been advised.

(9) *Object-and-Word Method.*
The alphabet may be pleasantly and intelligently taught with the help of a series of objects (or pictures of them), each having a name of not more than three, or at most four, letters; and in this connection it may be helpful to remember nine short words, each the name of an object, which have been pointed out by Mr. Livesey as containing the whole alphabet—*can, box, jug, fez, vest, drum, quill, whip, key.* Many other suitable words may of course easily be found.

The object would be shewn and briefly talked about, its name would then be printed on the black-board, and the two associated pretty much as in the preliminary lessons described below. The word would next be separated into its letters, and each of these taught with the help of any device for making the work interesting. The forms might be *fixed* by a constructive or a drawing exercise, and the child's knowledge *tested* by appeal to the letter box. The necessity for frequent review must of course not be forgotten.

To any teacher who feels bound to teach the alphabet first this plan is recommended. He may, however, if he be so disposed, with a little ingenuity readily combine some of the devices given above in various ways to suit his own views or predilections.

First Steps.

As already pointed out the **child should not begin with the alphabet,** nor should his first lessons consist of unnatural combinations of words of two letters. He must be taught to realise the meaning and use of printed or written language and its relationship to speech. What he *reads* should be as natural as what he *says*. From the first he should feel that he is learning something which has a meaning and is worth learning.

In framing his method, the teacher must **take into account the natural characteristics of the child**, and not confront him with too many difficulties at once. The work must be made stimulating by arousing his curiosity and utilising his love of doing something; while, at the same time, his sympathies should be aroused, his efforts appreciated, and his liking for change and novelty humoured so far as not to allow the sameness of the exercises to become wearisome.

(1) *Lessons introductory to Reading.*—Before the actual work of reading is commenced a short series of introductory lessons should be given, to make clear to the child the nature and function of printed or written words and the relationship between sense, sound, and symbol.

The words employed in these lessons should be simple in form and sound, and be the names of *things* with which the child is well acquainted. If suitable words can be found from the first printed lessons the child will have to use, so much the better.

The **steps of the teaching** in these earliest lessons[1] will be somewhat as follows :—

(a) The teacher exhibits some object well known to the children, and calls upon

---

[1] The teaching of the first lessons in reading pretty much on the lines here laid down has been advocated by several educational writers; but no one has indicated the nature of these early processes more clearly than Mr. N. A. Calkins. In his *New Primary Object Lessons* will be found several lessons worked out more or less in detail.

them to name it. He questions them briefly respecting it, and brings out clearly that the **name** and **object** are different, but that when we hear the one it makes us think of the other.

(b) The object is next sketched rapidly on black-board, or a picture of it is shewn, and the object and the representation are placed side by side. By simple questioning the children are led to distinguish clearly between the two, and to perceive that while the **picture** suggests the **object** to the mind its nature is different.

(c) The **word** standing for the object is now printed on the black-board alongside the drawing, and it is explained that this is a **mark** for the **spoken name**, and that when we know what name the mark stands for it brings this into our minds, just as the picture makes us think of the thing itself.

(d) Simple exercises and questions are then given to fix in the children's minds the differences in nature and use of the **object**, the **picture**, the **spoken name**, and the **printed or written name**.

After a few words have been taken in this way the process may be shortened by leaving out the picture, or by substituting it in some cases for the object. Attention should be directed to the fact that when we know the word-sign well we are able to give the corresponding spoken word at once.

A few lessons of this kind properly handled should make the nature of word symbols sufficiently clear to the children, and impress upon them that **every such symbol should have a meaning for us.** Reading lessons properly so called may now be begun forthwith.

(2) *First Series of Reading Lessons—Simple Word Reading.*—The first lessons in actual reading are best **taught from the black-board**, the teacher printing each word in good bold letters. The chief things to be looked to are correct utterance, thorough learning of the word forms so that they may be recognised at once wherever met with, and clear appreciation of the sense.

The sentences should be taken in order from the first lesson on the reading sheets selected for use, and when a dozen or twenty such sentences have been mastered on the black-board the children may be introduced to the sheets themselves. From these the sentences already taught should first be read for the purpose of review and to accustom the children to the actual point. When what has been previously learned has been gone through the method will be somewhat modified in details, the **sentence being read from the sheet and only entirely new words taught on the black-board.** The steps of the plan, however, and the general mode of treatment will remain the same.

SKETCH PLAN OF FIRST BLACK-BOARD LESSON.

(a) **Word exhibited.** The teacher prints on the black-board the principal noun of the sentence selected.

(b) **Association of sound and symbol.** The children are made to look at the word carefully, and to read it simultaneously after the teacher until it is said perfectly.

(c) **Association of symbol and idea.** In order to fix the meaning of the word clearly in the minds of the children the teacher illustrates the object on the black-board, or shews a picture of it, says a few interesting words respecting it, and asks a few simple questions about it.

(d) **Addition of other words.** The remaining words of the sentence are added one at a time, each being taught by itself first, and its force made clear as far as possible, and then taken in connection with the other words which have been learned.

(e) **Reading of the sentence.** When the sentence has been completed the whole is read through simultaneously a time or two after the teacher, who points to each word as it is said.

(f) **Test Exercises.** Lastly the children are called upon to read the words without help, both simultaneously and individually, forwards, backwards, or in any order indicated by the teacher.

In succeeding lessons only words new to the children will be taught separately in the way suggested before being taken in connection with those that are known. When the sentences on some five or six sheets—according to the nature of the lessons—have been well mastered, the children will be ready for the introduction of new elements.

(3) *Second Series of Lessons—The Teaching of the Alphabet.*—In the second series of lessons the **reading will be conducted from the sheets**, the black-board being used for the teaching or illustration of any difficult word, and for the **gradual teaching of the letters by the dissection of known words**, which will be the special feature of this part of the work. The small letters will be taught first.

With an ordinary class of young children the best plan is probably to go back and revise the lessons already taught, and to make use of words selected from these for teaching the letters. **The children thus have only one difficulty to face at once,** and before the whole of the lessons previously read have been revised, most of the small letters will, with the additional teaching given, have been learned. With quick children however it may be advisable to go straight on, and to select for analysis from each lesson some word after it has been taught as a whole.

To teach the letters, a **typical word** selected from the sentences read should be taken each lesson time. This should be **put on the black-board, analysed into its parts, and the name of each letter well learned.** The knowledge thus gained should be fixed by some appeal to hand and eye, and finally tested by suitable exercises.

Not more than three, or at most four, new letters should be introduced to the children in any one lesson, and plenty of drill should be given in naming and combining the letters which have been previously mastered. It is a great mistake to hurry the process. The **teacher should proceed slowly at first,** and be careful to keep the children thoroughly interested. Then, as their knowledge extends, and the forms of the letters become for the most part familiar to them, the work may be carried on more rapidly. **The order of the alphabet may easily be taught after the forms and names are known**—for instance by an 'alphabet song.'

Children are often very curious about things which they see we are keeping back from them; and if no anxiety is shewn to get on quickly, and the letters are not thrust upon them in such a way as to make the learning a task to them, a little trouble will prevent the work from becoming wearisome.

As to the principle which should govern the selection of the words for analysis, opinions may differ. The best plan seems to be to **take a word having for final sound the one which occurs most frequently in the lesson**—as for instance the sound *at* or *an*. Some, however, may prefer to take the most difficult word of the lesson; or the one which promises to be most attractive to the child from being the name of some interesting animal or object; or, again, one containing letters which occur most commonly. If thought advisable the letter learning may be confined to alternate lessons.

SKETCH PLAN OF THE LESSON.

First part of the lesson.

(a) Until the sentences which have been previously taught have been gone through, the first part of the lesson will be little more than a revision exercise, the children **reading the sentences simultaneously** and individually without help, except in the **grouping of the words,** which the teacher will indicate by means of the pointer.

(b) When the pupils arrive at the new lesson they will **imitate the teacher's reading** word by word, and sentence by sentence, while carefully observing the words as pointed to, and then **read by themselves** as before.

(c) Such teaching as is necessary for purposes of **explanation,** or correction, and any supplementary exercises, will then be given. If any word presents difficulty, or from its strangeness is liable to be forgotten, it should be taught on the black-board.

(d) **Individual test exercises** in reading will follow, and no analysis will be attempted until the reading is mastered.

Second part of the lesson—Letter learning.

(*a*) Attention directed to sentence containing word chosen for analysis—**word put on black-board**—letters printed below in order with spaces between. Children observe each letter as pointed to—**letters named deliberately and clearly by teacher and repeated by children till known.**

(*b*) **Test Exercises.** Individuals called upon to name any of the letters indicated without help, to find similar letters on the sheet, sort them from the letter-box, etc.

(*c*) Teacher draws first letter on black-board, the children observing the process. Individuals called up to imitate teacher's copy, and then the **children draw the letter** as well as they are able on their slates. Remaining letters of the word are treated similarly, and lastly the word is read and spelled from the slates.

(*d*) **Revision Exercises.** Children select from the letter-box, as called for, any letter learned, name letters at sight as exhibited by teacher, etc. Word built up by individuals, with the tablet letters, from dictation, and from memory, then said and finally spelled.

In a few weeks, with anything like skilful teaching, all the small letters, with the exception perhaps of a few which occur but rarely, will have been mastered, and the children will have been progressing in reading at the same time. Any **unknown letters may be taken as they occur.** The capitals also may be taught in a similar manner, as they turn up in the lessons; or by printing a known word on the black-board in small letters and in capitals, one below the other, and calling to our aid the principle of comparison and contrast.

When some progress has been made, occasional **drill with some form of Word-maker** will be found very useful, and might with advantage be much more frequently employed than is the case in English schools.[1]

Unless writing is begun before reading, as it very well may be, the drawing at first will, in most cases, be little more than a rough approximation to the form; but the exercise is useful, and an interesting one to the child. As the lessons progress the hand gains power and the imitation becomes more exact; so that, by the time the print letters have been well learned and the script forms come to be introduced, the child is ready to begin writing.

Jacotot's Reading Method.

This proceeded on the same main principle as the rest of his system—"Learn something thoroughly and refer everything to it."[2] Incessant repetition was insisted on

[1] For description with a diagram of a useful disc form of word-maker, see Professor Meiklejohn's *Problem of teaching to read.* For a slip form with classification of the letters, see Marcel's *Language as a means of Culture*, vol. ii. p. 391.

[2] See the late Professor Payne's essay on *The Principles and Practice of Jacotot's system of Education* where numerous illustrations of the method of teaching will be found.

in practice. Jacotot used no alphabet sheet, primer, or specially prepared reader, the child being put at once to an ordinary book—Fénelon's *Télémaque*.

The **method in outline** was as follows:—

(a) Teacher read first word clearly, the pupil imitating and pointing. First two words read in the same way, then the first three, and so on, *always beginning at the beginning*.

(b) At the end of some four words or so a short pause was made. The pupil was questioned, exercised in pointing out each word named, and made to note any similarities of form or sound, till the words were thoroughly learned. To test this he was made to find the same words elsewhere in the book.

(c) The remaining words of the sentence were then added, one at a time, the reading being conducted exactly as before, and the questioning and recognition exercises being repeated.

(d) The words were now analysed, first into syllables, and then into letters, comparison and contrast being used wherever available. Both syllables and letters were repeated till well known.

(e) A few succeeding sentences were treated in exactly the same way, and the pupil was then called upon to go on by himself, *always reading from the first word as before*. Help was given by the teacher only in the case of new words, syllables, or letters.

The plan was pursued till some sixty lines or so had been gone over, and the child had become intimately acquainted with all the words, syllables, and letters of the piece. Nearly the whole of the alphabet and many combinations were thus learned ; and it was held that when this had been done the early difficulties of reading had been overcome, so that the child could now read.

In case of further difficulty the teacher at once referred back to what had been learned, and this was made the stepping-stone to any new letter or combination.

After two lessons in reading the child began to write, a *sentence in small hand* being put for him to imitate; and thenceforward reading and writing were made to assist each other.

The Primer Stage.

(1) *The Books.*—The first lessons should be simply those of the reading sheets printed in smaller type. The whole of the lessons have to be specially written and arranged to ensure their suitability, proper sequence in the introduction of new words, and consistency of plan. They must be graduated as to difficulty both of thought and language ; the words employed should be of regular notation, and those of similar sound should be associated together. New words should be introduced in such order and variety as to afford the necessary practice, without overburdening the child, or making the lesson unduly difficult by their number.

The matters treated of should be such as can be readily understood, and the statements such as an intelligent child can take interest in. **The sentences should be as perfectly natural as possible,** and should carry on the thought so as to give continuous sense to the lesson, not be a series of disconnected statements or fragments of speech.

Something no doubt has to be sacrificed in the language to the exigencies of the teaching, but this is no excuse for the commonplace inanities so often found. The sooner, too, we get rid of the idea that a word is difficult in proportion to its length the better.

The lessons should be short, printed in bold type, and copiously illustrated with pictures—for the most part of the objects named. Silent letters should be printed in *hair-line* type, and any dissyllables should be divided by a hyphen. Only a few new forms or typical words should be introduced in the same lesson, and to prevent these being forgotten care must be taken to give a sufficiently frequent repetition of them in after lessons. A list of the new words introduced should be printed either at the beginning or at the end of the lesson, both in script and in ordinary type, that they may be readily reviewed and copied by the children.

(2) *General character of the work.*—This stage marks an important step in the child's reading—the introduction to the book. The lessons which have been previously learned on the cards should be rapidly read through again, varied by any additional exercises the teacher may find it advisable to introduce in order to prevent the work becoming monotonous. To keep the lesson bright and interesting is to do much towards making it successful.

The real work of the stage begins when the new lessons are reached. The **main points to which the teacher's attention should be directed,** are—

(a) The **thorough learning of the words,** so that they may be instantly recognised in future.

(b) The perfecting of the **knowledge of the letters,** both print and script, and the learning of the **spelling of the words.**

(c) The training of the child to perceive **similarities of form and sound,** and the mastery of a large number of regular combinations, so that the inductions he arrives at may be applied with confidence to further cases, and irregular forms may strike him as exceptions.

(d) Accustoming the child to **break up the longer words into syllables,** and to look to these in attempting to give the sound of a word at sight.

(e) The gradual giving of an insight into the **powers of the letters** chiefly by exercises in phonic analysis.

(f) Incessant **correction of errors** and faults of utterance, and the banishment of unnatural tones.

At this stage the children should **point to each word** with the finger as they read it. This directs and assists the eye, keeps the attention fixed, and helps to secure that the child does not merely catch the sound of the word from others without observing it.

Some teachers advise the teaching on the black-board of all strange or difficult words before the reading commences ; but it is not always easy to know exactly what words will prove difficulties, and when the children come to read individually it is easy to deal with any word which is found to give trouble.

SKETCH PLAN OF NEW LESSON.

(a) **Teacher read the sentence word by word** distinctly and deliberately, the **class imitating simultaneously,** and pointing to each word as read. Whole sentence read by teacher and then by children.

(b) **Individuals called upon to read** the sentence directly or in any order, the teacher looking carefully to matters of utterance, and correcting mistakes.

Any word which gives trouble should be put on the black-board, and read and spelled by class or by individuals. For occasional variety the 'word-about' plan— each child reading a word in turn—may be used. Remaining sentences treated in a similar way.

(c) A few minutes' **easy conversation with simple questioning to ensure understanding** and make reading intelligent—reference made to pictures—children allowed to tell what they see.

No formal definitions of meaning should be given. In illustrating the force of words which are not names, it is often useful to employ them in a variety of simple phrases.

(d) **Whole lesson read through in sentences** by class and by individuals **without help,** attention being giving to grouping of words and easy and intelligent rendering.

Occasionally the teacher should read the lesson through as a model; or, as a reward, one of the best readers may do this, the rest of the class looking out for any mistakes.

(e) Teacher writes a few of the more **difficult words on the black-board,** and children **transcribe** these on their slates ; or they may write certain of the letters or words from dictation.

(f) **Selected words written on black-board and spelled** by class, then individuals called upon to spell these and other words from memory.

At suitable opportunities the teacher may usefully introduce **phonic exercises**, either in the way of analysis or drill, founded on the lesson just read. These may take the place occasionally of the transcription exercise, in which case not more than one should be given at once, or special times may be set apart for them. The exercises may be varied in almost endless ways to suit the needs of the moment. The following examples will illustrate the kind of exercise intended :—

A word selected from the lesson may be written on the black-board, for instance, *cat*, and the children may then be called upon to dictate to the teacher any words they can supply of similar sound—as *bat, fat, hat, mat, pat, rat, sat*, etc. These should be written down in a column under the first word, and read and spelled.

Again, a suitable syllable may be written on the board, like *an*, and the children required to make other words by putting a letter in front—as *ban, can, fan, man, pan, ran*, etc. Attention may be directed to the **powers of the initial letters** by giving them with increased and prolonged effect, as m..an. The position of the lips, teeth, tongue, etc., may also be pointed out.

As a further example, we may take the lengthening of the vowel sound when a word is changed into another by adding *e*, as *man, mane ; fat, fate ; pin, pine*, etc. The words selected as types should be written on the black-board and read, the effect of the change in spelling being clearly pointed out and illustrated. Other similar pairs of words should then be used as tests.

Easy Narrative Stage—Standards I. and II.

(1) *The Books.*—There are certain general purposes which the books should serve, not only in the present stage but throughout the school course. In constructing or selecting the lessons there must be kept in mind, the chief things to be aimed at being—

(*a*) To **provide suitable materials for the teaching** of just those points in the reading to which attention has to be directed at this particular stage.

(*b*) To **give children a liking for reading**, by the selection of interesting topics and the treatment of these in a vivid and attractive way.

(*c*) To **cultivate the taste**, so as to lead to the appreciation of what is true, and beautiful, and good, by providing pieces which, while they are within the child's comprehension, are well written and varied both in matter and style.

A common defect in the lessons of the early books is the **goody-goody tone**, and the strained and artificial moral lessons deduced. Another is the **general baldness and** poorness of the language, often without any approach to either force or beauty. There is also in many cases a too great anxiety to thrust forward what is called useful information, which is here of little importance.

In the stage at present under consideration most of the lessons will need to be specially written, so as to secure **proper sequence in the introduction of new words**, and **careful graduation** as to difficulty, though many simple and suitable lessons may be selected from children's literature, especially pretty and bright little poems with well-marked rhythm and rhyming lines.

After they have been read such poems should be learned. Children have a natural liking for jingling sounds, and the poems may be made a most useful means of training both the ear and the taste if judiciously handled, and the teacher does not blur their beauty by talking too much about them.

The **lessons should appeal to the pupil's experience and feelings**, and consist of short stories, fables, and descriptions of well-known animals or of any matter generally attractive to a child. As far as possible **the narratives should have a personal element running through them**, as this is an additional source of interest. **Short dialogues** are very useful in aiding the naturalness of reading, but they must be bright, and if amusing or humorous so much the better. The **imagination too must not be neglected**, and the occasional introduction of simple tales of the 'fairy' type is a gain in many ways.

Children delight in the wonderful, and even the extravagant if properly managed need not detract from their appreciation of the true.

Some of the lessons should be directed to **stir the affections gently and pleasantly**, and enlist the child's sympathy on the side of right conduct; but painful subjects should be excluded. The moral of the stories should be natural and obvious, but should not be explained, and all moralising of the commonplace kinds should be carefully eschewed.

The sentences should be short but not jerky. **Simplicity of style need not mean absence of any literary quality.** The anxiety to give a great variety of word forms often leads to absurdities of statement, or the straining of the sense, in order to introduce them. **New words should not be too numerous**, and it is a good plan to have them printed in bolder type when first brought in. Longer words should be divided into syllables.

Woodcuts should still be introduced to illustrate the principal points of the lesson. They need not give any large amount of detail—even simple outlines serve—but they must be well drawn. Bad illustrations are worse than none; they have a mischievous effect upon the perception of form, and prevent the growth of any right appreciation in matters of art.

(2) *General character of the work.*—In this stage the teaching should be directed chiefly to the **prompt recognition of the words** and the **perfecting of mechanical facility in uttering them.** The mastery of the powers of the letters should be completed—including double vowels, and such groups of consonants as are of common occurrence—so that the children are able to give at sight the sound of new combinations of ordinary form. A considerable number of the monosyllables of anomalous spelling, which occur at all frequently in the language, should also have been taught by the end of the course.

The after progress of the children will depend very largely upon the processes they are accustomed to, and the consequent habits they form, at this stage. At no point in the child's progress is good teaching more important. The following are some of the chief matters which should be looked to :—

(*a*) **Thorough correction** as well as detection of mistakes.

(*b*) **Distinct articulation** and **correct pitch.**

(*c*) **Intelligent understanding** of what is read.

(*d*) Sufficient repetition to secure the **fixing of the forms** without allowing the work to become wearisome.

(*e*) The **gradual training of the ear** to appreciate sounds and rhythm.

(*f*) **Attention to the forms of unknown words** as they are read, and the learning of the spelling of them.

(*g*) The **syllabling of longer words.**

(*h*) The training of the children to **reading of the words in natural groups.**

(*i*) The gradual perception of the **meaning and use of such matters** as emphasis and modulation from the endeavour to express the sense from the illustration afforded by the teacher's model reading, not by being told directly.

(*j*) Exercises in **phonic analysis** and **word comparison.**

(*k*) **Practice** in reading at sight.

SKETCH PLAN OF LESSON.

(*a*) **Imitation of teacher's reading.** Teacher reads slowly a few words or phrase at a time until end of sentence is reached. Sentence read as whole in similar manner. Length of portion read before children imitate gradually increased as progress is made.

The children should point with the finger so long as they have any difficulty in following the words with the eye as they are read. When attention can be given to a whole phrase at a time pointing should be discontinued, as it would now interfere with the work and make the reading stiff and laboured.

(b) **Reading without help.** Sentence read simultaneously by the children without assistance. Individuals called upon to read it. Knowledge tested by having sentence read backwards, or a word each in turn, etc.

Any word which presents special difficulty should be put upon the black-board and analysed.

(c) **Brief explanations and illustrations of subject-matter.** In explanations the words are always to be taken in connection with the context. Exercises given in framing sentences containing the more difficult words.

The children should be questioned in a brisk, simple manner. Exercises to secure intelligent understanding may be varied in many ways.

(d) **Practice and additional exercises.** Each sentence treated in a similar way to that just described—backward children should receive a good deal of individual practice.

At suitable opportunities the teacher should use supplementary exercises in comparison of words, articulation drill, etc.

(e) **Model sentence-reading.** When whole passages have been gone through as above, and the words are well known, teacher should read certain portions as models, and call upon individuals to imitate his rendering. At first the portions should be sentences; later on they may be longer. Children selected to apply what they have learned by reading intelligently other passages not read by the teacher.

The portions read by the child in this part of the work should always be complete statements, not lines or scraps.

The teacher should beware of false reading, the child inserting words or substituting others for those in the book in such a way as still to make sense. Badly trained children are often given to this.

Some educators insist that the lesson should be finally read through as a whole either by the teacher or by one of the best readers in the class.

(f) **Oral spelling of the more difficult words, etc.** This should occupy the last few minutes of the lesson. Each word as spelled should be put upon the black-board, and the list finally read and spelled simultaneously.

A few easy questions or a series of ellipses to draw attention to the outline of the story will also be found useful.

In the succeeding transcription or dictation lesson the passages used should be taken from the reading lesson just mastered. Various other interesting exercises in connection with the reading lessons may be given, as writing lists of words with some common characteristic, etc.

Teachers sometimes waste time and weaken interest in the reading by introductory talks about the lesson. **It is a mistake to tell the story beforehand.** Some again prefer to teach all new words with the help of the black-board before the actual reading begins. This is not advisable, as the children learn the fresh forms more readily in connection with known words when they have the sense of the passage to assist them.

The teacher should be on the look-out for, and do his best to prevent, **merely repeating from memory** instead of reading, the child allowing his eye to run over the words without taking in the meaning of what is read.

It is easy for the teacher to damage his work by going too fast, anxiety to get over a great deal of ground leading to hurry and consequent superficial learning.

Lower Intellectual Stage—Standards III. and IV.

(1) *The Books.*—By the time the child reaches this stage the more elementary difficulties of reading will have been mastered, and a much larger number of suitable extracts may be found. The lessons should include such matters as simple accounts of natural objects, explanations of common phenomena, descriptions of manners and customs, and narratives of adventure; nor must the imagination, and the moral and emotional side of the mind, be neglected. Stories of deeds of heroism and moral tales are most useful, but if the child is to be benefited the moral must not be obtruded or artificial. Simple poems, mostly of the ballad type, and passages of descriptive poetry are also of much value, if judiciously selected and properly used. Too often, those selected are either so poor or commonplace from a literary point of view as to afford no training to the taste, or are above the child's comprehension, and hence do not appeal to his sympathy or imagination.

Lessons directly intended to give useful information, and interest the child in natural things, should be more frequently introduced than heretofore. They should be varied in character, but should be **arranged on some definite plan** to harmonise with one another, so that the child's ideas may be broadened and extended naturally, and some general line of relationship may run through the whole. **Scrappiness is a common fault.** The statements should be simple and lucid, and technicalities should be avoided. Most of these lessons will have to be specially written, and in writing or selecting any new lessons of this kind it should be borne in mind what facts bearing on the subject, or leading up to it, have been previously given.

It is better to spread a story or longer narrative over several lessons than to spoil it by condensing and excising to such an extent that all fulness of meaning and beauty are lost.

Style should receive greater attention than in the preceding course, and the lessons should be carefully graduated both as to word difficulties and as to the intellectual demands made upon the child. Not unfrequently the subject-matter is too abstruse for the child to grasp properly, or is stated in too pretentious a way. In such a case intelligence is sure to suffer. The ideas introduced should neither be too difficult nor too many. An intelligent child should be able with ordinary attention to catch the sense of what is given.

The function of **illustrative woodcuts** is now chiefly to add brightness and attractiveness to the book, and occasionally to assist the imagination in realising what is stated. They must be good of their kind if introduced at all.

(2) *General Character of the Work.*—As the difficulties of word recognition pass away, the child comes to have the power of taking in a phrase or short sentence at a glance, without special attention to each individual word, and until he can do this he cannot be said to read in the full sense.

He ought now to be able to read easy prose with fair facility. **Strange forms of words**, beyond his power to master unaided, will of course occur, and these will have to be carefully taught; but they ought not to be so numerous as to interfere with the general grasp of the sense, and though stumbles will be made they should not be frequent. **Articulation difficulties**, from peculiar collocations of syllables or words, will also be occasionally met with, necessitating in some cases an appeal to the black-board, careful drill, and deliberate utterance until the difficulties disappear.

Good habits with respect to natural pitch of voice, smoothness of tone, clear enunciation, and other matters connected with **correct utterance**, should be strengthened until the right way becomes the easiest one for the child; in fact, while the teaching is directed more and more to intellectual qualities, mechanical matters must not be neglected.

The teacher needs to be constantly on the watch to correct the **affected modulations** or 'sing-song' so common in school reading. Caesar is reported to have reproved this fault in these words: "If you are singing you sing poorly, if you are reading why do you sing?"—(*Compayre.*)

The chief thing to be insisted upon at this stage is **intelligence**, more being demanded from the child in the matter of style so that the sense is made fully evident in a natural way by suitable emphasis and modulation.

The lessons of an emotional character will afford a means of training in the more elementary matters connected with **expression**. The first things to secure in this respect are the proper production of sounds of different pitch and character, and a manner and tone of voice in accord with the nature or sentiment of the piece read.

<small>The **easy and natural production of the voice**, so as to avoid the harsh or strident and artificial tones so often heard, as well as the fatigue and irritation of the throat arising from wrong vocalisation, is a matter of great importance both to the reader and the speaker, and should receive much more attention in schools than is usually accorded to it.

The **general sequence of the teaching**, namely recognition and utterance, explanation, style, cannot be violated if the method is to be satisfactory; but so long as this order is maintained, the details of the work may be varied in almost endless ways, according to the skill and invention of the teacher. Very many lessons are spoiled by the teacher having no fixed principle of order in the work, matters of style being dealt with before the children can read the words properly, and explanations being given last.</small>

SKETCH PLAN OF LESSON.

(*a*) **The Mastery of the Words.** Teaching directed in this part of lesson to the elimination of errors of utterance Individual reading, mostly by backward children, until the whole piece has been gone through. Mistakes and faults thoroughly corrected with help of the black-board as they occur.

<small>Words which give difficulty should be said slowly and distinctly by the class and then by the individual concerned. Mutual correction should be encouraged, but hands should not be held up until the reader has finished.

The *eye* should be trained to break up words at once into their syllables, the *ear* to distinguish readily differences of sound, the *voice* to produce smooth clear tones with the least amount of effort.

Exercises in articulation, phonic analysis, comparison of words, and word-building may often be introduced with good effect.</small>

(*b*) **Explanations.** Given to secure intelligent understanding and to arouse interest, so that the pupil may enter into the spirit of the piece and be better able to make clear the meaning to others. The children should be briskly questioned, and what is necessary added by the teacher. What is said should be direct, couched in simple language, and as brief as the needs of the case will admit of. There must be no discursive talk; and more attention must not be paid to individual words than their value in the lesson warrants.

The teacher must use his own judgment, according to the circumstances, as to whether it is better to take the explanations paragraph by paragraph, as each is read, or to run through the lesson again after the first reading is completed.

(c) **Reading with Intelligence and Expression.** Means to be employed are the teacher's model reading and corrected practice, the foundation being the child's understanding of the piece. Selected passages read by teacher—children imitate until they can read the passage correctly alone. This should be followed by individual test reading. This section of the work should occupy the larger portion of the lesson time.

At first the imitation may be simultaneous. When the more elementary matters of style have been fairly mastered, it is better for the children to listen attentively to the teacher and imitate individually.

The children may be assisted in understanding any particular mode of modulation, by writing the sentence on the black-board with the words at different heights according as the voice should naturally rise or fall.

(d) **Questions on Subject-matter and Spelling.** From the beginning children should be trained to the habit of attending to the information contained in what they read, and of noticing the spelling of any unfamiliar word they may come across. Hence the last few minutes of the lesson should be spent in testing both these things.

It is valuable to have the best pieces of poetry learned by heart, but this should not be done until the children have learned to read them correctly in class, or faults may only become the more firmly established.

The association with writing will be made chiefly through the dictation lesson; and, whenever opportunity offers, the children should be practised in reading script.

Higher Intellectual or Literary Stage— Standards V., VI., and VII.

(1) *The Books.*—The books of this stage should form the child's introduction to literature, and should above all things stimulate a love for reading and foster good taste in the choice of what is read. The extracts selected should be of increasing length, of standard excellence, interesting in themselves, and within the pupil's comprehension, at least with a little assistance. They should also be sufficiently varied both in style and subject-matter to call into exercise all the higher qualities of good reading and to appeal to the imagination and stir the emotions as well as provide food for the intellect. There should be no evident design to thrust information upon the child.

Style is here even more important than subject-matter. Sameness and scrappiness are both to be avoided. The poetry, especially, will need to be very judiciously chosen, so as to afford the necessary training without being of so difficult a character as to be beyond the pupil's appreciation.

"Till children take pleasure in the silent, passive, cursory reading of good literature, touching but not pressing the keys, learning the great task of catching the meaning of others' minds undistorted, the responsibility of the school does not entirely cease."—(*Hall.*)

To teach a child to like books, and to treat them with respect as friends, is to do much towards securing his future development, and to add an additional pleasure to life.

Care should be taken at all times to prevent, as far as possible, corruption of the child's taste by poor literature. The badly-written, low-toned, and often pernicious rubbish which so frequently forms a boy's home reading, when he reads at all, is only to be banished by introducing him to something higher, and teaching him to appreciate it.

It should be a recognised part of the work of this stage to read through suitable standard works in addition to the ordinary readers, certain lessons being set apart for this purpose. This reading should be as little as possible broken by corrections and comments, only such as are absolutely necessary being given, and these in the briefest way. Numerous cheap editions of good books of thoroughly interesting character are published, with which children ought to be acquainted, and from which the necessary works may be selected.

(2) *General Character of the Work.*—Matters of **elocution** will now occupy an increasing proportion of the time. The **teacher must be a good reader himself** if success is to be achieved, and the teaching must be thorough and earnest. The pupils have to be taught not only to grasp the facts conveyed, but to appreciate such characteristics and beauties of style as are within their comprehension, as well as the way in which these may be rendered evident in their reading. They must *feel* what good style is, not merely be able to quote the teacher's phrases about it. Simply telling what is to be done respecting emphasis, modulation, and so on, is quite inadequate, and only leads to artificial imitation, not to natural expression. Elocution rules are of little value, except occasionally as reminders. The points must be mastered a few at a time; and it should be kept in mind that interest in reading is the key to the solution of many difficulties.

SKETCH PLAN OF LESSON.

(*a*) **Preliminary Reading.** Piece read rapidly through to catch any word difficulties, and to give the pupils an insight into the general drift of the lesson. Attention must also be given to the true subordination and interdependence of the sentences and their various parts.

<small>The corrections needed ought not to be numerous, and should for the most part be made by the pupils themselves.</small>

(b) **Explanations.** Only difficulties in the way of understanding should, as a rule, be treated. Such matters as involved constructions, allusions, figures of speech, and so on, will all at times need attention ; but the mistake must not be made of endeavouring to explain everything which may possibly give difficulty to any particular pupil.

<small>Shades of meaning may often usefully be pointed out, and the teaching should strengthen the pupils in the exact use of words.</small>

<small>In certain cases a few words should be said about the form of the piece, or about the author, but any lengthy talk is here out of place.</small>

<small>In the highest section the pupils should be taught how to use a dictionary, and occasionally they may be set to prepare the meanings of difficult words before the reading begins. The teacher's questions will soon shew when the judgment of the pupil has been at fault.</small>

(c) **Teacher's Model Reading.** This is at this stage of great importance, both as setting before the pupils a standard to aim at, and as pointing out how certain graces of rendering are to be secured and the sense and spirit of the passage conveyed in the most effective and felicitous way. Judgment will be shewn in selecting passages which best illustrate what is required.

<small>The imitation of the teacher's reading should be individual, though the class may occasionally with beneficial results be called upon to give a passage simultaneously to impress some special point of teaching.</small>

<small>The teacher must not insist too rigidly on exact imitation of his own reading, and hence longer passages may be read by him without a break than in the previous stages. His object should be to enlighten the child and assist him in understanding the means employed in good reading, not to fetter him. In emotional passages especially, what is needed is to put the child into entire sympathy with the author, and then to lead him to express what he feels naturally, without defect on the one side, or exaggeration on the other.</small>

(d) **Test and Practice Reading.** A large portion of the time of the lesson should be taken up with practice reading of passages which have not been presented as models by the teacher. The work will need to be treated with care and skill, and frequent help and correction will be needed in many directions. Ease and grace of delivery are to be looked to. The children should also have room left them for individual interpretation wherever any emotional element enters into the lesson.

The importance of taking breath at the proper places, and of managing the voice in such a way as to produce clear and resonant tones with the least expenditure of effort, must not be forgotten. Reading ought not to be more fatiguing than speaking, but frequently from its artificiality it is much more so.

The teacher will often find it of advantage to listen to the reading with closed book.

(*e*) **Examination, etc.** Where the facts of the piece read are of importance in themselves, the pupils should be questioned before the close of the lesson upon the main points of the subject-matter; and the spelling of any strange or difficult words should be fixed in a similar way. The teacher's judgment will be the best guide as to how far these matters should be carried.

> Professor Laurie wisely says: "The teacher must beware of tarnishing the beauty of a lesson addressed to the imagination or feelings by examination of the kind applied to the ordinary subject-matter." The reading may sometimes be usefully connected with the composition lesson, the facts learned in the former lesson being made the basis of an abstract, or short thesis, or paraphrase.

(3) *Recitation.*—The learning of passages of approved excellence, especially of poetry, is a valuable exercise in several ways. Properly employed it may be made to strengthen the memory, to train the ear to appreciate delicacies of sound and rhythm, and to store the mind with many beauties of thought and language. The passages selected for learning should have been previously read in class and any necessary explanations given; then, after they have been learned, the pupil should be called upon to recite them aloud. As he is not hampered by having to attend to the book, and the conditions are much more like those of ordinary speech, the delivery should be freer and more spirited, and more latitude should be allowed in the devices used to impress the hearer than in reading. The danger to guard against is allowing the pupil to overdo gesture, emphasis, and modulation, so that the recitation becomes inflated, unnatural, and pretentious.

II.—SPELLING AND DICTATION.

The very great importance attached to good spelling—the writing or naming of the component letters of words according to established custom—is a matter of quite modern growth. It is probably to be traced more to the fact that good dictionaries have been prepared, and have come into common use as authorities for the forms of words, than to any other influence. Systematic attention to uniformity of spelling scarcely dates further back in England than the publication of Johnson's Dictionary (1755).

To spell correctly in accordance with a fixed standard is now an essential feature of ordinary education, but for centuries in England spelling was pretty much a matter of "the taste and fancy of the speller." It was once even looked upon as something of an accomplishment to spell words in as many different ways as ingenuity suggested. Any one may see illustrations of this in the *Paston Letters* written during the reigns of Henry vi. and Edward iv. ; and Dr. Angus points out that William Tyndale (1485-1536) spells so simple and commonly used a word as '*it*' in eight different ways—*it, itt, yt, ytt, hit, hitt, hyt, hytt*.

That much yet remains to be done in the way of improving the teaching of spelling is abundantly evident. Dr. J. H. Gladstone has calculated that "an average English child, spending eight years in school, and making the not unusual number of 400 attendances per annum, will have spent on an average 2320 hours in spelling, reading, and dictation." Yet with all this expenditure of time the results are declared to be unsatisfactory in our Elementary Schools; and matters are clearly not better in the Higher Schools, for it is said that the Civil Service Examinations shew "how lamentably imperfect is the acquirement of spelling even among those who have received a liberal education."

Important, however, as correct spelling is, it should be remembered that it is only a means to an end—correct writing—and that the time taken up in learning to spell difficult words, with which the pupil is not likely to meet, might be much more profitably spent.

I. PRINCIPLES AND CONSIDERATIONS.

(1) *Appeal to the eye.*—In learning to spell, the association of the letters through the eye gives rise to a much stronger impression than when the association is made through the ear. The image of the word as a whole is received by the eye, and the parts are remembered not because they have been enumerated, but because they occupy a fixed and natural position, just as do the parts of an object or picture.

A **wrongly spelled word will catch the eye at once**, though we have often to look again to see where or how it is misspelled. In cases of doubt, too, about the spelling of a word we have once learned, writing it will generally enable us to settle which is the correct form. The **training of the eye** by careful observation of the forms of words is essential to the learning of spelling, and should be insisted upon and encouraged in every way possible.

Mr. Fitch says: "The person who spells well is simply he who carries in his memory a good visional impression of the picture of the word as it appears in a written or printed book." That **the eye plays the most important part in learning to spell** seems to be almost universally recognised as a matter of fact; it is strange, therefore, that in our methods of teaching spelling this should be so often practically forgotten.

Mr. Robinson points out that the deaf and dumb almost invariably spell correctly;

and that those who have learned a language like Latin or Greek rarely blunder in writing the words, although there has been no formal learning of the spelling.

(2) *Appeal to the ear.*—In order to strengthen and fix impressions it is always well to **make use of a second sense** where this is possible, while the **frequent repetition of the letters of a word in invariable sequence** also brings to our aid one of the principles of association. Appeal to the ear by oral spelling, although of secondary importance, is thus distinctly helpful, and should not be neglected.

Oral spelling undoubtedly has its value, and may frequently be adopted where other means would be inadvisable. Many opportunities will occur of fixing the spelling of words in this way which the wise teacher will not allow to slip.

Bad spelling when words are dictated is occasionally due to defective training of the ear; the sounds of the words are not properly distinguished, and consequently the forms are incorrectly written. Children taught spelling mainly by oral repetition will frequently fail to detect blunders in the writing of words, although they are able to give the letters correctly when challenged.

(3) *Meaning an aid to spelling.*—The **association of the sense and use of a word with its form** is always an assistance in the recollection of its spelling. It is thus of some importance, as is often strongly urged, that when the spelling of a word is to be learned **it should be presented in its natural place in a sentence**, and if necessary explained.

This is entirely opposed to the old-fashioned plan of setting children to learn columns of strange words, arranged regardless of any useful principle or natural connection. The practice was necessarily as laborious as it was distasteful to the child.

(4) *The right form first.*—The **pupil should have nothing to unlearn.** Until the correct spelling of a word is at least fairly fixed in the mind any misspelt form should be carefully kept from the child. He should always, therefore, have an opportunity of learning the spelling of a word before he is called upon to give it unaided, either in writing or orally. One of the secrets of success in teaching spelling is to let **the pupil make as few mistakes as possible.**

There can be no doubt that the less a child is subjected to the disturbing influence of bad spelling the better. The importance of this does not seem to be appreciated by many teachers. The plan, once common and not yet altogether abandoned, of **giving pupils wrongly spelled passages to correct** from memory is highly mischievous as well as absurd.

Some teachers object to children marking the mistakes in dictation on the same ground. The cases are, however, not parallel, as in examining dictation the child should always have the correct form in front of him to mark from, the persistence of the wrong impression being thereby neutralised.

(5) *Good spelling eventually a matter of habit.*—In learning to spell we have at first to give special attention to the form of each word, both in observing it, and in reproducing it, until by frequent repetition in the same way the work in the end becomes automatic or mechanical. Spelling cannot be said to have been properly learned until by constant practice it has thus become a fixed habit. The formation of this habit by the provision of a regular and systematic course of suitable exercises it is the teacher's business to secure.

In ordinary writing we concern ourselves only with the sequence of the words, or the thought, and until some word arises about the form of which we are doubtful, give little or no *conscious* heed to the spelling, any more than we do to the individual letters of words in reading, or to the movements of the fingers in playing a musical instrument.

(6) *Interest and Graduation.*—As in other departments of school work, the teacher should endeavour to stimulate the child's efforts by making the exercises as bright and as interesting as possible. The work must be carefully graduated according to the pupil's power and progress, and at no point must he be discouraged by being brought face to face with too many difficulties at a time.

The learning of the spelling of such an irregular language as English is at best a difficult and tiresome task, and the child needs every encouragement. Any device which will lighten his labour or reduce its tediousness is worthy of attention.

(7) *Comparison and Contrast.*—The grouping of words having some common characteristic of form, and their examination side by side so as to bring out the nature of this common element, is often a considerable aid to teaching spelling. The result of such examination may in some cases be usefully stated and learned as a 'spelling rule.'

Contrast may also occasionally be effectively employed—as in words having similar sounds but different forms, in allied words which have come to us directly from Latin or indirectly through French, and in numerous other cases.

The principle of comparison is but the application of the wider **associative law of similarity**. The analogies pointed out must be real not fanciful, and be such as the pupils with a little help can readily discover for themselves.

II. THE LEARNING OF SPELLING THROUGH READING.

In all cases spelling is learned by directing attention to words a sufficient number of times for the mind to retain a knowledge of the forms, so that when needed the component letters rise **into consciousness in correct order, and finally without effort.** Now as the correct forms of words are being **constantly** brought before the eye in reading, this becomes **one of the most valuable of all means of learning to spell.**

<small>This is true not only of the set lessons but also of the private reading of the pupil, which, for this reason as well as others, should be encouraged at all points. The knowledge of word-forms gained in this way may be supplemented, and the fixing of the results facilitated, by various other exercises; but it still remains true, in the main, as insisted upon by Mr. Spedding, that "it is by reading we all learn to spell." It has, indeed, been pretty generally recognised that those who read much usually spell well, and, if the reader is intelligent and observant, this can scarcely fail to be the case.</small>

Not only is the recollection of the spelling rendered more certain and easy by the **frequent repetition of the impression** involved in reading, but there is the additional advantage that the **words are presented to the child in their natural places in sentences,** and he has the association of the sense to assist his remembrance. Hence from the very first it is of the greatest consequence that **the pupil should form the habit of noting carefully the spelling of words he meets with,** especially of such as are new to him. He should distinctly understand that he will be expected to reproduce the spelling of the words he has thus had an opportunity of observing; and the extent to which he is able to do this should be systematically tested, in order to keep the necessity of attention before him as well as still further to fix what he has learned.

<small>The oral spelling tests at the end of the reading lesson have been already referred to. Teachers differ much as to the amount of time they give to this exercise, but that the test should be sufficient to secure the points mentioned above there can be little question.</small>

At first the child will need to be specially aided in observing the spelling during his reading lessons. The ordinary means of doing this is to draw attention to any difficult forms met with by writing them upon the blackboard and having them spelled orally. As, however, the pupil rises in the school the unfamiliar forms he comes across should be fewer and fewer, and thus less time need be occupied in teaching the spelling of new words.

In connection with the learning of spelling through reading may be mentioned the exercise commonly known as '**conning**'—the silent reading of a lesson or passage by the pupil with the attention directed to the spelling alone so that any unknown words may not only be discovered but their forms learned.

This is a very useful device for employment with the middle and upper classes, if it is judiciously applied, and if the work is afterwards thoroughly tested by dictation or some similar means. Sometimes it is advisable to have the words copied out for future reference.

III. TRANSCRIPTION.

Although transcription is often viewed simply as a writing exercise, it is a most useful means of teaching spelling. It trains the eye to note the forms of words, and fixes the parts in the mind, just as drawing impresses the forms of objects and leads to the perception of many details which would otherwise have escaped attention. Before a child can write a word accurately he must observe it carefully. The eye, during the writing, is fixed continuously on the letters and this tends strongly to render the impression permanent.

The trouble which the pupil at first experiences in forming the letters is from the side of spelling not a disadvantage, as it compels him to proceed slowly, and not only concentrates attention, but prolongs it.

Transcription bridges the gap between copy-writing and dictation, and forms a capital introduction to the latter. When, however, dictation is begun, transcription should not be abandoned, as is often the case, for it is of quite sufficient value to justify its employment throughout the school. Nor is it so easy an exercise, properly performed, as it seems. A child needs considerable practice before he can copy a fairly long piece without error.

Accuracy of spelling, good writing, and neatness must be insisted upon throughout; nor must the lesser matters of capitals, stops, paragraphs, and arrangement be neglected. It is evident, therefore, that if the exercise is to serve its purpose in the best way, it must be thoroughly supervised, and any mistakes corrected. Without this the work may soon become mischievous instead of beneficial, and bad habits will be contracted, the correction of which will be a tedious matter to both teacher and child.

The transcription of a passage compels attention to *all* the words, and hence prevents the pupil from giving no heed to the familiar words which he can read, but which he may be unable to spell correctly when called upon to write them from dictation.

In the early stages transcription should be largely employed; and, as it appeals to the child's love of doing something with his fingers, it is generally an interesting as well as a beneficial exercise. He should always understand what he copies, and hence the passages for transcription are best selected from the previous reading lesson. The work may be varied in endless ways by an ingenious teacher—as writing words beginning with a certain letter, words of two syllables, all the names of objects in the lesson, etc.

As soon as the child can form the letters fairly slates should be abandoned, if it can be managed, and paper and lead-pencil or pen substituted for them. The amount of trouble and expense is by no means great, while the change is a distinct gain to the child in all ways.

In the upper classes, transcription may with advantage be substituted for copy-book writing, when the pupils can write a pretty good hand. The passages to be transcribed should not be too long, and should be selected either for the value of their subject-matter, or for the beauty of their style. Poetical extracts and short poems of standard excellence will of course not be forgotten.

IV. DICTATION.

The word dictation is used to indicate, (1) a **method of teaching** spelling, in which the characteristic feature is the dictating or reading out of words to be written, and (2) merely the **test** portion of this, including the writing of the words, and the detection of the mistakes made. The confusion arising from the use of the word in these two senses, and the consequent employment in practice of the test portion only as if it were the whole method, has had a most harmful effect upon school work.

That **dictation as a method of teaching** is of the greatest value, if properly carried out, every one is agreed ; but to employ it without any previous preparation of the words, and to merely mark and count up the mistakes without doing anything further to ensure their correction, as is commonly the case, is baneful. Teachers cannot be too emphatically cautioned not to allow such a practice to prevail in their schools.

Carried out in this way, dictation is utterly ineffectual as a method, and an injustice to the children. If they learn to spell at all, it is in some other way, and often, it is to be feared, in order to avoid the punishment involved. It is not to be wondered at in such a case that they dislike spelling, and make slow progress.

There are, then, **two essential processes in teaching spelling by means of dictation**, the learning of the word-forms by the child before he is called upon to write them, and the thorough mastery before he leaves them of the correct spelling of all the words which he writes incorrectly. The chief uses of the dictation paper or test portion of the method are as follows :—

(a) It **exercises both eye and ear**, and impresses the spelling in the best way, by calling upon the pupil to write the words from recollection.

(b) It is **a suitable and effectual test**, enabling the teacher to judge what progress the class is making, and affording him an opportunity of strengthening any weak points.

(c) It **strengthens habits of attention, accuracy, and neatness.**

(d) It is an **excellent practice in writing** as rapidly as is consistent with forming the letters properly; it gives ease and freedom to the writing, and helps to form a good 'current hand.'

(e) It **makes children ready and expert in putting down what they hear**, and is a good introduction to 'note-taking.'

(f) It **directs attention to the parts of sentences**, and "accustoms the ear to those of good form."

It is sometimes objected against dictation that it produces bad writing, and puts before the eye blurred impressions, as well as numerous wrong forms. Where such is the case, the fault is due, not to the method, but to the defective way in which it is carried out.

(1) *The passage and its preparation.*—It should never be the teacher's object to find some passage containing unknown words, unless these are to be specially prepared as a preliminary to dictation. As a rule it is best for many reasons to select the piece to be dictated from the reading-book, and not at hap-hazard from any page, as is often done, but from the lesson just previously read. When the first difficulties have been overcome, occasional passages of poetry, as well as of prose, should be given. At times it is useful to repeat a passage which has been indifferently done.

It is not well to dictate only the hard words, though when the spelling of a whole lesson has been mastered a few of these may be given in addition to the portion selected. Where the teacher's object is to test the children's knowledge of a certain group of words previously taught as a spelling-lesson, he will find it a good plan to write a passage himself containing these words employed in their usual sense. The same may also be done with a list of words it is necessary to review.

The passage for dictation should always be such as the children can understand, and should contain no difficulties but those of spelling. Further, it must not be too long. It is a mistake very frequently made to occupy most of the time of the lesson with the 'giving out.'

Generally speaking the main part at least of the **preparation of the spelling should be done before the time of the actual dictation lesson.** This is generally best managed in connection with the reading lesson, which should serve as the usual mode of preparation. Some opportunity of previously learning the spelling there should always be, and the following will all be found useful in their way, either singly or combined—transcription of the whole passage or of special words, the writing of difficult words on the black-board, oral spelling, conning, and the learning of spelling as home lessons. The teacher must use his own judgment as to which will be the best means to employ in given circumstances.

With the upper classes preparation during the reading lesson ought to be sufficient; but with the lower ones it is advisable to refresh the children's memories as to the words most likely to be misspelled by writing them on the black-board, or by a few minutes' oral spelling, or by both combined.

With the younger pupils transcription is very useful in addition to reading; and in the case of beginners it is a good plan to let them copy out the difficult words and have these before them during the dictation proper, so that they may refer to them for the spelling of any word they are uncertain about. Or, if the words have been written on the black-board, they may be allowed to remain in sight of the children for a similar purpose.

If the passage is not taken from the reading book, it should, except with the more advanced children, be written out on the black-board, and then treated by any of the devices mentioned above.

(2) *The delivery, giving out, or dictation proper.*—In the middle of the school **writing of the piece should occupy about a third of the time allotted to the lesson,** and in any case it should be finished by the end of half the time.

The passage should be read through slowly with clearly marked pauses, and then given out distinctly, and in a sufficiently loud tone for the pupils to hear without effort. The speed and the amount to be given out at one time will depend upon the proficiency of the class. Many teachers dictate too slowly. **The word should be given out once only,** so as to avoid interrupting the children while writing, and to train them to listen attentively in the first instance. If a child misses any words he should omit them; any accident or fault due to the teacher may easily be allowed for afterwards.

At first only single words will be given out, the number being gradually increased as progress is made. No hard-and-fast rule of so many words should be adhered to, the teacher being guided by the sense and the nature of the sentences.

Each word should have its accustomed sound, not be altered to suggest the spelling. The enunciation, however, should be distinct, so as to enable the child to distinguish such words as *patients* and *patience, axe* and *acts, except* and *accept*, etc.

In giving out poetry to the upper classes, wherever the rhyme is a sufficient guide, or the children have been told the endings of the lines in a complete stanza, they should be left to determine where to begin a fresh line for themselves. Such matters are a good training, and soon become easy when the pupils are made to attempt them.

Punctuation should receive increasing attention. The younger children should be told the stops; the more advanced ones should punctuate for themselves. Any reasonable punctuation, however, should be passed.

The best place for the teacher to stand during the giving out is undoubtedly in front of his class, so that he may exercise the most careful supervision to prevent the children copying from one another, and note instantly anything amiss. If, however, he adopts the plan of marking mistakes during the dictation, he is compelled to move round the class; but it is often well in such a case to let a monitor call out the words.

Some teachers mark alternate pupils *A* and *B*, and give out two passages at the same time. This is not advisable, as it is very confusing, especially to young children.

Directly a child has completed the portion dictated he should look at the teacher. This is a mark of good discipline; it prevents staring about and the temptation to see what others are doing, and is at the same time a means of letting the teacher know when all have finished.

The **spacing and posture of the children should be looked to**, and the position of the book or paper, the quality of the writing, the proper use of capitals, the spacing of the words, the evenness of the margin, and the general neatness and arrangement of the work, should also receive careful attention. At first the child should not be allowed to divide a word at the end of a line; later on, when he has learned to syllable words, he should be taught to do so, and any absurd division should to counted as a mistake.

(3) *The detection of mistakes.*—The looking over of the exercises for the purpose of testing their correctness may be managed in various ways, according to circumstances :—

(*a*) **Detection by the teacher.** This is no doubt the best plan theoretically, and wherever it is practicable, as with a small class of a dozen children or so, it may with advantage be adopted. The detection is thorough, and there is no room for quibbling about the accuracy of the marking; while at the same time the teacher becomes personally acquainted with the nature of the errors made and the acquirement and progress of each child. He is thus better able to judge as to what measures should be taken to secure further improvement. With beginners this plan should always be employed, the examination being made after the writing of every few words.

The method may be carried out in several ways.

(i) Each exercise may be marked by the teacher **directly the writing of the whole piece has been completed**, the children meanwhile being set to learn something so as to keep them employed. The teacher should face those whose exercises he has not yet examined.

(ii) The teacher may move round behind the pupils and mark the errors **while he is dictating**. A vigilant outlook must be kept to prevent copying, and care must be taken to interfere with the child as little as possible.

(iii) The exercises may be collected, looked over **at some convenient time**, and the correction taken at the beginning of the next dictation lesson. This is not as a rule advisable.

(*b*) **Detection by a monitor or by the most advanced pupils.** This should secure that the marking is well done, but it is not a good method to adopt where any more satisfactory one can be found. It entails the postponement of the correction of errors, which is better taken immediately after their detection, while the words are fresh in the children's minds. Further, it affords those who examine the exercise no return for their irksome labour and profitless expenditure of time ; and, may, if they are frequently called upon for such work, unsettle their own spelling.

It is urged too, by many teachers, that the temptation to unfaithfulness is very great and that lapses are common. This will depend upon the character of those selected, and the nature and amount of the supervision exercised by the teacher In a well-disciplined school this ought not to be an insuperable objection.

(*c*) **Detection by fellow-pupils—exchange of exercises.**—For the teacher to attempt to mark every child's dictation exercise, with a class of forty or fifty, would render it impossible to confine an exercise of any length within the limits of a single lesson, and would involve an expenditure of time and energy on his own part which might be employed to greater advantage. He is therefore driven to adopt some other plan.

With a large class there can be little doubt that, if properly carried out, the most effective and satisfactory method for general adoption is for the pupils to examine each other's exercises. This, however, should be done under the careful supervision of the teacher, who should see every paper to ensure neatness and good writing, as well as to acquaint himself with the progress each child is making. A few selected exercises should also be looked carefully through by him in order to test the accuracy and honesty of the marking.

The **method of exchanging exercises should be simple**, but it is not advisable to effect it always in the same manner. The teacher will easily be able to vary it in many ways without either confusion or loss of time.

If the children are to mark the mistakes properly some means must be found of placing before them the correct spelling; and in order to neutralise the harmful effect of having misspelled words brought under their notice, **they should, in examining, always have something to see.** The best plan after the first stage is for them to mark from their reading books. In the lowest classes and where the passage is not taken from the reading books the whole of the portion dictated should be written on the black-board. **It is a very common method for the teacher to call out the spelling** of the whole passage, or of the more difficult words. "This system," says Mr. Robinson, "has the greatest sanction of any, but in practice I have always found it fail." Of all means of making known the correct spelling this seems to be the worst. If the spelling is given out with sufficient slowness for all to follow, the quicker children will not wait, and often guess at the spelling of the few words about which they are doubtful; while if the teacher moves at an average rate the slow and backward pupils are either left behind and have to do the best they can, or are prevented by hurry from giving sufficient care to be certain of the correctness of the words. In both cases the result is bad. In the earlier stages, especially, the child is very apt to be confused by having to attend at the same time to the form of word before him and to the letters called out by the teacher. It is also to be objected further that the plan adds to the teacher's talking and the general noise of the school, and it prevents him from going round and supervising the work while the marking is going on. It is true that the objections are much less weighty in the case of advanced pupils, but even here the plan is not a good one.

(*d*) **Detection by the pupils themselves.**—Some teachers urge that the children should examine their own work, inasmuch as exchange of exercises shews doubt of their honesty and "degrades the mind by the distrust it implies." Such an objection to the plan of mutual correction is entirely sentimental, and it is the teacher's fault if the children look upon the examination of their work by their neighbours as a reflection upon their uprightness. It certainly seems better in ordinary circumstances to remove temptation entirely out of the child's way. There is further the very weighty objection that **with the best intentions it is exceedingly easy to pass over one's own errors** without detecting them.

If the method is tried, and the results looked into carefully, the teacher will soon discover that it is not the best one for general use. Where, however, he knows his children, the marking may occasionally be conducted in this way as a test of accuracy; but if this be done, he should look over a good number of the exercise himself afterwards.

Mode of noting the mistakes.—The best plan for marking misspellings is to put a perpendicular or oblique line through the place

T

of error, and another line under the whole word to direct attention to it, thus—certa|nly, fr|endly. A simple cross will serve for a word omitted. The mistakes should be counted up, and the number entered at the foot of the exercise.

Another plan recommended by some, is to write a good-sized figure over each error according to its number, thus—c⁴rtion. re²tition. sep³rate.

Scoring a number of lines over a word so as partially or wholly to obliterate it should never be allowed; and neatness of marking should always be insisted upon. There seems little or no gain in the elaborate schemes of marks occasionally found in use, and on the whole they are best avoided. The simpler the mode of noting errors, so long as it is effectual, the better.

> It is sometimes objected to the plan advised above that it makes the mistakes obtrusive; but that they should catch the eye readily is in itself a gain, and it need scarcely be said that the plan does not involve the careless disfigurement of the exercise books, not unfrequently met with, which seems to be the real source of the objection.

(4) *The correction of errors.*—Much of the value and efficiency of the dictation lesson depends upon the effectual correction of the mistakes made. Unless this part of the work is thoroughly performed, the exercise may easily do more harm than good. **The permanent removal of blunders is always to be aimed at**; if they are merely indicated without the correct forms being learned, they are certain to be repeated. To secure this necessary learning, the plan very generally adopted is to **have all words in which mistakes have been made written out correctly** a sufficient number of times to efface the false impressions, and, as far as possible, to fix the right spelling in the mind. No fixed rule should be laid down as to the actual number of repetitions in writing; this will depend upon the nature of the class, and must be left to the judgment of the teacher.

In many cases the mere writing out of the mistakes will not be sufficient to secure all that is needed, and the teacher should **further test the words by oral spelling**, and aid remembrance by any useful hint, device, comparison, or short rule, which may prove of service. The children should constantly be called upon to apply what they have learned in the spelling-lessons, and any unusual forms or exceptions to rules should be specially noted with the help of the black-board.

The corrections are best made as a part of the lesson in which the blunders occurred. During the writing out of the corrected forms those who have made no mistakes, or who have finished earlier than the others, must be found something else to do, either of the nature of transcription or learning. This, however, must not be viewed as a task. As soon as a child can write a fairly long passage it is much better to have the dictation done in books than on scraps of paper. Slates should be employed as little as possible. The words to be written out should be copied below the passage; the child may then be called upon to revise them every now and again, the corrections being tested until they are completely mastered. If a piece of dictation is badly done, it should be repeated shortly afterwards. Mistakes made by a number of the children should be dealt with on the black-board; and the teacher should register such common blunders in a note-book, so that they may be dictated again at some future opportunity.

The **blunders made in dictation exercises** are not all equally reprehensible. They may arise from a variety of causes, *e.g.* :—

(*a*) From **ignorance or forgetfulness**, the words being such as a child could not spell if challenged.

(*b*) From **carelessness or hurry**, the words being written incorrectly where the child is able to spell them if called upon.

(*c*) From **defective hearing**, due either to want of appreciation of sounds, or to indistinct enunciation on the part of the teacher; *e.g.*—writing *patience* for *patients*, *axe* for *acts*, etc.

(*d*) From **mechanical awkwardness in writing**, the want of facility compelling conscious attention to the formation of the letters as well as to the spelling.

(*e*) From **confusion**, due to hesitation, nervousness, and other causes.

To inflict punishment of any kind justly for errors in the dictation exercise needs very careful discrimination of the cause which led to them. Except for neglect of opportunities, or deliberate carelessness, it should not be employed at all.

V. SET OR FORMAL LESSONS IN SPELLING.

(1) *Necessity and purpose of such lessons.*—Valuable as reading, transcription, and dictation are as means of acquainting the child with the forms of words, there are **many matters connected with spelling which are best taught by special lessons** arranged for the purpose. In addition therefore to any incidental teaching, set lessons in spelling should be given throughout the school, with the exception perhaps of the highest class. Such lessons may be made very beneficial, but they are very generally neglected, and beyond occasional passages of teaching suggested by some chance circumstance, any definite instruction in spelling seems to be rarely attempted.

It is not necessary that these instructive lessons should be frequent —once a week would suffice—but they should be regular, and arranged in a progressive and systematic course. They must be planned with an eye to the wants of the children for whom they are intended, and, generally speaking, should serve one or more of such purposes as the following :—

(a) The **review and extension** of what has been learned in other ways, so as to systematise the work, and add anything which may be helpful.

(b) The **exemplification and illustration** of such principles of word formation and derivation as throw light upon the spelling.

(c). The teaching of some at least of the **commoner "spelling rules,"** with such exceptions as are of frequent occurrence.

(d) The **grouping of words** wherever the child may be thereby assisted in overcoming the difficulties connected with them.

(e) The encouragement of attention to such matters as the **structure of words** analogous in form, the powers of the more frequent combinations of letters, and the syllabling of the longer words.

(f) The **fixing of anomalous forms,** and of any words which experience shews that the children are particularly liable to misspell, by contrast or any other method which the teacher can devise.

(g) The occasional explanation and illustration (with advanced pupils) of the **reason for certain forms** by appeal to the history of the words.

(2) *The nature of the lessons.*—Too often the spelling lesson is little more than the mere repetition of the spelling of a list of words selected without regard to any useful principle of classification or structure. The work is dull and mechanical, and soon becomes distasteful. Nothing is done to assist the child in his efforts to master the forms, and naturally the results are, for the most part, of an evanescent character. Properly conducted, **the teaching given should render the process of learning to spell as intelligent as the difficulties connected with the subject will allow**; it should stimulate attention and arouse interest, train the pupil to observe carefully, and reduce as far as possible the amount of mechanical reiteration necessary.

The following will indicate in a general way the **nature of the teaching to be given.**

(a) **Careful observation** lies at the foundation of all success in learning to spell; hence in teaching a new word the first step is to present it in an attractive way, to direct attention to its parts, and thoroughly to familiarise the child with its sign, sound, and sense.

The word should be distinctly written on the black-board, examined and if necessary analysed, the letters named in order simultaneously, and finally the spelling should be given by individuals.

(*b*) To strengthen the impression made, and fix the form more firmly in the mind, the child should be called upon to **write the word** from the black-board, or compose a sentence containing it. When **comparison with similar forms** can be usefully introduced this should be done, or appeal made to any spelling rule under which the word happens to be included.

Any peculiarity of form or unusual combination of letters should be noticed; and, with an advanced class, if the source of the word, or the way in which it has been introduced into the language, throws any light upon the form, a brief reference will add to the interest of the lesson as well as assist remembrance.

(*c*) To facilitate recollection, and render permanent what has been taught, the pupils should be **tested in various ways**, and called upon to reproduce the words, both at the end of the lesson and from time to time afterwards, until both eye and ear have become thoroughly accustomed to the correct spelling, and it gradually passes into a habit.

In learning to spell the child must not be hurried; work which is scampered over is sure to be disappointing. Thoroughness and steady intelligent effort are the great elements of success. The formal spelling lessons should be arranged according to a definite scheme, so that the teaching may not only be progressive and suited to the child's needs, but may be associated with and assist that given in the reading and dictation lessons.

"It would seem," says a writer in Sonnenschein's *Cyclopædia of Education*, "that the right way to master spelling would be to familiarise the pupil with the typical modes of representing the sounds in English successively, and then to proceed to the subordinate or exceptional modes in detail, taking the unique or very rare cases as may be found convenient."

(3) *Spelling Rules.*—Our language is too irregular in notation for spelling rules to be of much value as a means of teaching spelling in the first instance. There are, however, a few fairly uniform sequences of letters and modes of change in forming inflexions and derivations, which when known undoubtedly assist the recollection of the forms and give greater certainty in spelling words belonging to these groups. With these the pupil should be made familiar.

The chief use of such rules is to sum up for him in brief form the result of a number of individual experiences, and to furnish him with general tests of correctness in certain cases, to which he can appeal when in doubt. Even where the rules formulated have many exceptions, they are not without value if properly employed. They show what the tendency of the language is in such cases, and that there are certain general laws of structure, however much they may be departed from ; while at the same time they stimulate observation, and keep the attention awake to similarities of form. The child is thus led to discover for himself many analogies, which without such suggestion would probably go unnoticed.

The rules should be learned inductively. A number of words analogous in form should be introduced gradually upon the black-board and examined side by side, until, by a little guidance as to what to observe, the pupils are able to discover the rule for themselves. This should then be put into the best form by the teacher, and finally learned. Where there are few exceptions these may be learned with the rules, but in other cases they are best mastered as they occur and noted for future reference.

When once a spelling rule has been learned the children should be frequently called upon to quote and apply it until this can be done with ease and certainty.

A few of the commoner spelling rules are given below ; for others the teacher may refer to Professor Meiklejohn's *New Spelling Book*, Dr. Abbott's *How to Parse*, or any good manual of spelling.

(a) *When the vowels* ei *and* ie *have the sound of* ee, ei *follows* c *but* ie *all other consonants.* Or if the teacher prefers the rule in rhyme the following may serve :—

When <i>e</i> and <i>i</i> or <i>i</i> and <i>e</i>
Are sounded like the <i>e</i> in me
After all consonants but <i>c</i>
The <i>i</i> must go before the <i>e</i>.

Exceptions.—Financier, plebeian, seize, weird. The words leisure, either, and neither are pronounced in two ways ; if one of these modes be adopted these words will also be exceptions.

If the diphthong has any other sound than ee *the order of the letters is always* ei.

The spelling -ceive "represents the Latin *cap-*, French *cev-*; whereas *ie* is the non-Latin termination."—(*Abbott.*)

(b) *A final* y *is changed into* i *when a syllable is added, unless*—

    (i) *The affix begins with* i *as*—ing, ish, ist.

    (ii) *The* y *is preceded by a vowel.*

Exceptions.—Dryness, shyness, and a few others ending in -*ness*; shyly, daily, gaiety, gaily, laid, paid, said, slain.

Chimneys, journeys, and moneys are very frequently misspelled.
Note plenteous and piteous.
A verb ending in **ie** usually changes this into **y** in forming its present participle. Thus dying, lying, tying, vying; but hieing.

(c) *The final* e *of a word is retained when a syllable beginning with a consonant is added, but dropped if the affix begins with a vowel.*

Exceptions.—Abridgment, acknowledgment, argument, awful, duly, judgment, lodgment, truly, wholly, woful, and some others.

Words ending in **ce** or **ge** retain the **e** before an affix beginning with **a**, **o**, or **u**, to prevent the hardening of the consonant, as: chargeable, manageable, noticeable, peaceable, serviceable, etc.

When **e** is preceded by **e**, **o**, or **y**, it is generally retained before -**ing** and -**able**, as: agreeable, hoeing, dyeing, etc.

Note gluey, singeing, swingeing, tingeing, and unsaleable.

(d) *When a monosyllable, or a word accented on the last syllable, ends in a single consonant and a vowel affix is added:—*

(i) *If the final consonant is preceded by a single vowel then the consonant is doubled to keep the vowel sound unaltered*, as :—fitting, manumitted, occurring, remitted, etc.

(ii) *If the final consonant is preceded by a diphthong, or double vowel, the consonant is not doubled.*

Exceptions.—gases, woollen.

(e) *When a syllable is added to a word ending in a single consonant which is not accented on the last syllable the final consonant is not doubled*—as benefited, annalist, centralise, vassalage, etc.

Exceptions.—Biassed, worshipped, worshipper, worshipping, crystallise, tranquillise, medallion, and some others.

Words ending in a single 1 do double the consonant before -**er**, -**or**, -**ed**, and -**ing**—as apparelled, cavilling, counselling, councillor, quarrelled, traveller, etc.

Paralleled follows the original rule.

(4) *Some miscellaneous spelling difficulties.*—The following are offered as hints. The teacher may readily fill up the lists from a good spelling book, or with a little trouble from a dictionary.

(a) **Words with silent letters**—as gnat, gnarled, campaign; knight, knack, knapsack; wreak, wrought, wheelwright; psalm, psychology;

coign, condign, debt, indict, malign, neighbour, ought, phthisis, trait, yacht, etc.

(*b*) **Words sounded alike but spelled differently**—as aisle, isle; cereal, serial; faint, feint; nay, neigh; right, write, wright, etc.[1]

There is a large number of such words the clew to the spelling of which is the meaning. This therefore should receive careful attention in the teaching.

A few words should be taken at a time; each pair should be put upon the blackboard, carefully contrasted as to form and meaning, and the children called upon to suggest sentences in which they are correctly used.

The teacher should also frame a series of sentences, containing the words taught, for use as dictation lists, something after the following examples:—

The *dyer* is constantly *dyeing* and yet *dies* but once.
I doubt *whether* this *weather* is good for *wethers*.
The horse's *mane* is in the *main* black.
The girl was set to *pare* a *pair* of *pears*.
The *hale* old man trudged on in spite of the *hail*.
You can see the *yew* tree under which the old *ewe* is lying.
He *threw* a stone *through* the window.
That is not the *way* to *weigh* the potatoes.
In *vain* the wind tried to turn the *vane*.
Jane *sewed* her frock while Tom *sowed* the seeds.

(*c*) **Words with letters and compounds having more than one sound.**—The vowels and their compounds present an almost hopeless array of irregularities, and are the greatest of all difficulties to the child in learning both to read and spell. These cannot be dealt with here. They are best taught as they turn up in connection with the reading lesson, advantage being taken of any opportunities for grouping and comparing them. The consonants are more amenable to treatment.

Attention may usefully be directed to the following:—

C (=k before a, o, u; =s before e, i, y)—as in calcareous, cocoon, courteous, cue, cuirass; centrifugal, cipher, cymbals, lettuce, cyclopædia; eccentric, succeed.

G (hard and soft)—as in gauge, gazetteer, gearing, geyser, gibbous, goal, gained; gaol, gesture, gimbals, gipsy, gyrate, tragedy.

Ch (=sh, tch, k, kw)—as in chaise, chagrin, champagne; chalice, chanticleer; ache, chaos, chimera, chalybeate; choir.

S (sharp and flat)—as in nauseous, mystical, sacrilege, sagacious; organise, premise, preserve, presidency.

Sch (=sh, sk, s)—as in schist, scheme, schooner, schism.

[1] See a list of nearly 800 such words in Professor Meiklejohn's *New Spelling Book*.

SPELLING AND DICTATION 297

Qu (=k, kw)—as in antique, conquer, mosquito, picturesque, piquant, quoit; conquest, query, quarantine, soliloquy, tranquil.

Th (=th, dh, t)—as in thistle, thermometer; themselves, thither; thyme.

(*d*) **Words liable to be confounded from similarity of sound**—as words ending in -ants and -ance, -ents and -ence, -al and -le, -ar and -er, etc; for example, assistants and assistance, concert and consort, principal and principle, altar and alter, council and counsel, profit and prophet, except and accept, fisher and fissure, illicit and elicit, and a large number of others.

Enunciation should be looked to, and the ear trained to appreciate the differences of sound, these being somewhat exaggerated at first to mark the contrast.

(*e*) **Words ending in *ll* when either augmented or prefixed to others** —*e.g.*, albeit, already, altogether, befall, bulrush, dulness, forestall, foretell, fulfil, fulness, instalment, recall, skilful, wilful, withal, etc.

Note that *fill* and *full* always lose one *l* in combination.

(*f*) **Words ending in *-cede* and *-ceed*—**as accede, concede, intercede, precede, recede, secede; exceed, proceed, succeed.

Both forms come from the same Latin root. Those early introduced into the language received the English spelling *-ceed*. "These words are very common in Shakespeare's plays. Other compounds were not introduced till afterwards, when it was no longer the custom to Anglicise the spelling of foreign words. Hence the Latin or French spelling *-cede* is retained."—(*Abbott.*)

(*g*) **Words ending in *-able* and *-ible*—**as delectable, disposable, indispensable, indomitable, unsuitable, etc.; audible, contemptible, discernible, feasible, incorruptible, incompatible, indigestible, indestructible, reprehensible, incompressible, etc.

(*h*) **Words ending in *-ough*—**as borough, bough, chough, clough, cough, dough, enough, furlough, hiccough, hough, lough, plough, rough, sough, slough, thorough, though, through, trough, tough.

(*i*) **Confusion of *i* and *e*—**in such words as arboreal, censorial, competitive, equatorial, repetition, rarefied, privilege, etc.

(*j*) **Miscellaneous list of a few difficult words and words frequently misspelled.**—Abscess, accommodation, adolescence, apophthegm, apparelled, asinine, assassination, assessment, asthma; balance, banisters, battalion, bayoneted, beleaguer, broccoli, buccaneer, buoyancy, camelopard, caoutchouc, caravansary, castellated, catarrh, chiffonier, colloquy, colonel, colonnade, committee, connoisseur; dahlia, demesne, dentifrice, desiccated, dessert, diaphragm, diarrhœa, dilettante, diphthong, disembogue, dishabille, dysentery; ecstasy, effloresce, eleemosynary, embarrass, ennui, epigrammatic, equanimity, erysipelas, eschalots, excrescence, exorbitant; filibuster, fuchsia, fusilier, fustian; galleon, gauge, gherkin, guarantee, guerilla; habiliment, hackneyed, hæmorrhage, harangue, harass; illicit, immigrant, indictment, inflammation, inveigh, inveigle, ipecacuanha; jeopardy; kaleidoscope; lachrymose, lieutenant, litigious, luscious; manœuvre, meerschaum, mignonette, mistletoe, mnemonic, mortgagee, myrrh; naphtha, narrative, necessary, nonpareil; obeisance, obloquy, occurrence, oscillate; pachydermatous, paletot, palisade, palliasse, paroxysm, pelisse, periphery, phaeton, phlegm, phœnix, pirouette, plaguy, pneumatic, poignant, promissory, propagate, pseudonym, ptarmigan, pumice, pursuivant, pusillanimous; quaternary, quay, queue, quintessence; reconnoitre, reminiscence, remissness, rendezvous, resurrection, rodomontade; saccharine, sausage, schedule, scissors, scythe, separate, sergeant, sleight, soliloquy, steadfast, strychnine, superintendent, supersede, surreptitious, surveillance, sycophant, symmetry, synecdoche, synonym; tasselled, tattooing, tesselated, trousseau, tyranny; unparalleled; vacillate, vermilion, victuals, viscount; yeoman, yacht.

The Spelling Book.—Although the child's first spelling manual should no doubt be the reading book, and throughout the school the reading books will be found of very great use in this connection, yet in the middle and upper classes a well-arranged spelling book will also prove of considerable service in many ways.

The unintelligent manner in which such books have been commonly employed, and the faulty way in which many of them are arranged—the words being grouped according to the number of syllables, and easy and difficult forms mixed up together—have brought the spelling book into undeserved disrepute. In many instances the valuable help of analogy is almost or entirely ignored.

A good spelling manual should be a handy book of reference for the pupil, and a storehouse of materials for the formal lessons. It should illustrate the more general principles of word formation, and give (1) such rules as will assist the pupil in certain cases of difficulty, (2) groups of words having some common characteristic, and (3) lists of any special irregularities and words which experience has shewn are generally stumbling-blocks to the pupil.

VI. INCIDENTAL AIDS TO SPELLING.

(1) *Writing from memory passages learned.*—The child is thrown upon his recollection of the spelling here pretty much as he is in

dictation. All such work should be carefully marked, and any mistakes in spelling should be corrected.

(2) *Composition.*—The composition exercise, like the one just mentioned, may be made to give effective help to the learning of spelling. In the later stages it may sometimes take the place of the dictation lesson. Correct spelling must be insisted upon as in all other written exercises.

(3) *Individual oral spelling.*—Any new and difficult words which turn up in the ordinary lessons should be taught on the black-board, and spelled orally to fix the forms.

(4) *Lessons in word building.*—These are especially helpful in teaching the spelling of derivative forms, and in suggesting analogies.

(5) *Phrase spelling.*—This is an oral exercise advocated by some to accustom children to rapid spelling. A phrase is given out as in dictation, and the child spells the words with a pause after each instead of writing them, the exercise being continued till a paragraph, or even a whole lesson, has been gone through.

(6) *Spelling contests.*—These are useful as an occasional change. They usually excite a good deal of interest, and stimulate attention to spelling. One boy spells all the words propounded to him until he fails, when the propounder, after having spelled the word correctly, takes his place.

III. WRITING.

Writing is of all subjects the easiest to teach, if the nature of what is to be accomplished is rightly understood, and the conditions of success are carefully attended to. **The aim should be to enable the child to write, with ease and rapidity, a bold, graceful, and clearly legible hand, without eccentricities, and without ornament.** The requirements of modern education are such that there is no time for the acquirement of a merely elegant accomplishment; and the teaching of *caligraphy*, or writing as a fine art, with its elaborate finish, flourishes and embellishments, has rightly all but disappeared from our common schools.

In the teaching of writing there are two phases—(1) a mechanical, or copy-book phase, and (2) a higher, applied, or instrumental phase. From the **first point of view** writing is treated more or less as an end in itself. The object here is to train the child to the skilful use of the pen, by calling upon him to reproduce, as exactly as may be, certain letters or words placed before him in script characters as models. The exercises are for the most part merely imitative, but the teaching given should render the imitation intelligent.

From the **second point of view** writing is regarded simply as an **instrument for higher ends**—as a means of translating thought into symbols, of registering ideas and communicating them to others. The object is to train the child so to use his skill in writing as to apply it with the greatest readiness and success in any direction required, whether for the furtherance of his own education, or in the ordinary affairs of life.

The two phases are of course closely allied. In practice they should mutually support each other, and both should receive attention in school work.

In many cases the school is judged by the quality of the writing turned out, the parents being able to see and appreciate progress in this respect. The popularity of the old schoolmasters was often largely due to the success with which they taught the subject.

I. General Considerations.

(1) *Writing should be begun early.*—The exercise, being very largely mechanical, **makes little demand upon the brain**, and may with good effect be begun early—before reading is attempted. There are many advantages in following this course. It is a good early training in attention, it employs the fingers, and finds an outlet for the child's natural activity and love of doing something; while, as the imitative impulse is strong in children, the exercise may be made interesting and even amusing in the early stages without much difficulty. Very considerable progress may be made in a few months, and this is of much assistance when the child comes to learn to read, and indeed in all succeeding subjects.

This early work must not be viewed merely as a means of keeping children employed. The fact that they are often left almost entirely to themselves in writing seems largely answerable for the bad writing frequently observed in schools. **The greatest care is necessary to prevent the child from falling into bad habits** as these will be exceedingly difficult to eradicate. There must be no practising of defects.

Locke, Le Salle, Jacotot, and others of the older educationists would make writing *follow* reading; but the present generally received opinion is the reverse of this, and in many of the continental schools, notably in some of the German States and in Switzerland, the elements of writing are taught before reading is begun. Any one who has tried this plan can scarcely fail to have been impressed with the advantage of the course.

(2) *Hand and eye must both be disciplined.*—Writing is frequently taught as though the power to guide the hand were the only thing needed ; but in all training in the reproduction of forms **the culture of the eye to distinguish delicacies of outline, relative distances, symmetry, and so on, is of equal importance with the culture of the hand.** A child's difficulties in learning to write are probably due quite as much to defective appreciation of the forms by the eye as to want of control over the hand. **He must perceive before he can imitate** ; he cannot reproduce correctly that which he observes very imperfectly, or does not see at all. And yet this training of the perception is often almost entirely neglected, so far as any direct teaching is concerned, and the pupil is left to bungle time after time, when what is wanted is to direct his attention to the exact nature of the outline he has to reproduce.

In writing, too, in addition to **correct motions of the hand** as in drawing, the **proper manipulation of the pen** is also necessary, so as to give clearness of line, freedom of movement, and a certain delicacy of varying pressure.

This training of hand and eye together is a slow process in the early stages, and one needing much attention. After the first freshness has worn off, the work is apt to become tedious to the child from the continuous care and exactness required. Encouragement, appreciation of the pupil's efforts, and the adoption of any means that may suggest themselves of adding interest and reducing the sameness of the exercises, are necessary to anything like rapid success.

The movement of the hand in writing is at first no more under the dominion of the will than that of the fingers in playing a musical instrument. **The nervous mechanism can only be brought into perfect play by frequent practice at regularly recurring intervals,** carried on for a considerable period, and performed in the same way. At first, each movement is the result of conscious effort, but, as control over the muscles is gained, the motions of the hand become more and more automatic ; and the child cannot be said *to write* until he ceases to give conscious heed to these, and concentrates his attention on the forms.

(3) *The size of the writing should be within the power of the child's hand.*—In commencing the teaching of writing it has been a common practice to begin with 'text,' or 'large hand,' under the idea that it enabled the pupil to gain command of the pen more rapidly than writing of a smaller size. The assumption that it is necessary to begin in this way is not borne out by facts, and it is now generally regarded as a mistake.

A hand in which the small letters are half an inch or so high is much too large for a little child to write with any success. So far from strengthening the fingers rapidly, it quickly produces fatigue, and is apt to make the movements stiff and cramped, while the inability to make the long strokes required, without their being shaky and uneven, discourages the pupil, and in many cases leads to the very objectionable practice of drawing the hand as a whole down the paper.

To begin with small letters, as Jacotot did, is a mistake in the opposite direction. **The writing should be of sufficient size for the correct shape of the letters to be distinctly recognised, and for mistakes of formation to be clearly evident.** In the earliest stages the small letters should be about a quarter of an inch high, that is, about the size once commonly known as 'round-hand' or 'half-text.'

'**Text-hand**' has come to be a very vague term, meaning in most cases nothing more than a large hand. It is a relic of the time when writing a copy was viewed as an artistic performance. The French teachers seem to have been the first to specially disapprove of it. It should not, however, be neglected, or abandoned altogether, as some would have it. It has a use, and a place; but its place is not at the beginning.

In Mulhaüser's system the 'text-hand' is $\frac{1}{8}$ inch between the lines for the smaller letters, the tall letters, like l, b, etc., being double this; in 'round hand' or 'half text' the small letters are $\frac{1}{12}$ inch high. In the *Instructions to Inspectors*, the **Education Department defines the 'large hand' of the Code as not less than $\frac{3}{4}$ inch for the small letters**; no distinction being made apparently between 'large' and 'text' hand.

(4) *The character of the writing to be aimed at.*—Writing for practical purposes should be **easy to read and easy to produce**. It should be bold, simple in formation, regular in size and spacing, uniform in shape and curve, and free from stiffness, angularity, and ornament. **Legibility** is the first essential, but **beauty of form** is not to be neglected. **The curves should be founded upon the ellipse, not upon the circle**, and should flow gracefully into each other; they should neither be ugly nor broken. The letters should be completely formed, not merely suggested, and neither too contracted nor too round and sprawling. In many engraved copies the contrast in height between the small and the long letters in 'small-hand' is unnecessarily great. The strokes should be firm and clear, and the thickness of the down lines proportional to the size of the writing; though less attention is paid now than formerly to difference in thickness of up and down strokes in ordinary current-hand. Sudden

changes and strongly marked variations in this respect are objectionable.

To be able to write a neat compact hand expeditiously is a valuable acquisition ; and when a child has learned to write well with care and deliberation, **rapidity** should be attended to. Speed, however, is not to be secured at the expense of correct formation, and it must not be allowed to lead to slovenliness or scribbling.

Good models are a necessity, and the child should not depart from these until he can imitate them satisfactorily. A good school hand is the foundation of a good ordinary hand, in which individual peculiarities are pretty sure to make their appearance. These give character to the writing, but would be entirely out of place in the writing of a beginner. Many children write too small; they should be disabused of the idea that it is a clever thing to write a very small hand.

Lord Palmerston, in a letter from the Education Department, dated 24th May 1854, which has attracted a good deal of attention, says—"One great fault in the system of instruction in the schools of the country lies in the want of proper teaching in the art of writing. The great bulk of the lower and middle orders write hands too small and indistinct, and do not form their letters; or they sometimes form them by alternate broad and fine strokes which make the words difficult to read. The handwriting which was practised in the early part and middle of the last century was far better than that now in common use."

The best general standard of the modes of forming the letters is certainly that of Mülhaüser, and the slope of 60° recommended by him is that by far most commonly adopted. Tastes differ somewhat, however, and some prefer writing less inclined and rather more open than that of Mulhaüser; while a few even advocate quite upright writing. The angular hand which used to be taught to girls had nothing to recommend it, and, fortunately, since women have found such useful employment as clerks, it has rapidly fallen into disrepute.

(5) *Writing must be taught.*—Too often writing is treated in school as if it would teach itself—as though to provide the child with the necessary materials and to set him to work were all that is required. Without careful teaching, the more mechanical side of the work must remain mere blind imitation, uninteresting and unintelligent. Nor is examination and the marking of errors enough; the child must be encouraged, and shown as often as need be how to produce the forms and to make the corrections required. **There must be no uncertainty as to what is to be done, and as to how it is to be accomplished.**

The lessons must be given according to a definite and carefully pre-arranged scheme, developed according to progress, and carried through with a settled purpose. Writing must not be left to chance any more than any other subject, for scarcely any part of school work demands more conscientious and painstaking attention, especially in the earlier stages.

As already noted the teaching is not difficult. Success depends more upon the moral qualities involved in a resolute adherence to a consistent line of action, than upon intellectual power. "Almost any system," says Mr. Robinson, "will produce good penmanship if carried out zealously and efficiently, while on the other hand even the best systems will be practically worthless if joined with unfaithfulness and negligence."

One test of good writing is uniformity in the work. Where writing is badly taught many different styles exist, even with the same copies; the children have clearly not been trained to observe properly, and the execution is extremely varied and unequal.

(6) *The position of the body in writing.*—The posture in writing must be **comfortable and natural**, and this is impossible unless both desk and seat are of proper height and suitably adjusted. Twisting or contortion of any kind, tilting the body forwards against the edge of the desk, and the hanging down of the head are not only physically injurious, but bad from the point of view of writing. Curvature of the spine, malformation of the chest, and short sight are some of the evil results complained of.

The **body should be erect**, the head well up, and the **feet placed firmly on the floor** or foot-rest in front, not drawn in under the body. The **left arm should lie easily on the desk**, with the hand upon the paper to secure it in its place. The **right arm should be at right angles to the front of the desk**, which must be about level with the elbow so as not to force up the right shoulder and destroy the balance of the body. **The teacher must see that the right position is not only assumed at starting but that it is maintained.**

There must be no sprawling or lolling, and the pupils must not be allowed to lay the head upon the left arm, as they frequently do if not checked. Unless vigilance is exercised, bad habits will soon become common in spite of preliminary warning.

(7) *The management of the pen.*—The proper management of the pen does not come by nature but must be *taught*; nothing but imitation and corrected practice will enable the child to use it with success. It should be **held lightly**, so that the fingers may be as flexible as possible, but with sufficient firmness to obtain complete control over it. If grasped tightly the fingers are stiffened, freedom of motion is interfered with, and elasticity of touch is lost, while the pressure is apt to be too great. The pupil must be shown how to

take hold of it between the thumb and second finger, sufficiently far from the point to allow of the necessary sweep, and with the forefinger resting upon the top and slightly curved upwards, not bent into an angle with the middle joint some distance from the holder. **The hand should be supported by and move over the paper upon the little finger,** and this with the third finger should be curved inwards easily, not bent suddenly. The elbow should be near the side of the body.

The pen should lie in the direction of the fore arm. The essential thing is that the points of the nib shall press equally upon the paper, or jagged and uneven strokes will result. The holder should not be too upright nor on the other hand should it lie in the hollow of the thumb. The wrist should not move in forming any single letter and never in a direction from front to back until a new line is begun.

It used to be insisted upon that the holder should point towards the shoulder, but much less importance is attached to this now. At the same time, the holder should not be turned outwards to the right, or the bottom curves of the letters will almost certainly be wrongly made.

To make children hold the pen correctly at first is half the battle, but it needs constant care and a good share of patience. Want of sympathy with them in the difficulties of their early attempts may easily prevent progress by making them feel that success is hopeless. They should learn to manage a pencil properly first, and should not be burdened with a number of verbal directions or rules. The device of indicating the places for the fingers by marks or notches on the holder is a very old one; but with good teaching it is unnecessary, and except in rare cases of confirmed bad habit is not to be recommended.

(8) *Correction must be thorough and systematic.*—All who have had much experience in the teaching of writing would probably agree that **the great secret of success is constant and vigilant supervision and correction during the exercise**; and this is generally the weakest side of the work. Children very easily go wrong, and if unchecked soon fall into habits of careless haste, inattention, slovenly imitation, and general untidiness.

Mistakes should be noted almost as soon as made, and at least there should be no repetition of them. **Continued blunders or carelessness are a reflection upon the teacher.** In no part of his work is it more important to 'make haste slowly' than in writing. Quality not quantity is wanted; and until good habits are confirmed and the child can write fairly well, he can scarcely write too deliberately. The teacher should see that no instruction is neglected, and **every**

U

line should be examined before the next one is attempted. Slow and accurate work in the beginning is the sure way to secure rapid progress in the end.

Some children require much more attention than others, and in spite of their efforts make but indifferent progress; so long as the writing is the best they can produce, such pupils should receive equal encouragement.

(9) *Children should not write too much at a time.*—In teaching writing, long-continued exercises, especially in the early stages, are a great mistake. The movements required in writing are trying to a young child and should **never be carried to the limit of fatigue**; yet this is a matter very frequently neglected. The judicious teacher will so vary the work of instruction, practice, and correction that the necessary relief may be afforded.

The fact that writing often grows worse towards the end of an exercise is not always due to carelessness. There is no doubt that in not a few of such cases the defect is to be attributed to the fingers becoming cramped and fatigued by too prolonged effort.

II. THE SO-CALLED WRITING METHODS.

(1) *Copying Plans.*—The imitation of script forms from a model by means of style, or pencil, or pen, has been the common mode of learning to write in all ages; and though certain plans are sufficiently marked by some characteristic device to merit separate consideration, yet beyond the earlier stages, copying necessarily enters largely into all such methods.

In the practical application of the copying method, pure and simple, teachers differ in their estimate of the value of models of a certain kind, and as to the mode in which these should be presented to the child.

(*a*) **Copies written by the teacher for each child.** This is the old method, and is still strongly advocated by some. Much of the success of the old teachers seems to have been due to it, and for individual pupils or a few children it is doubtless the best plan: with the larger classes common at the present day it is impracticable.

One great advantage of the plan is that perfect graduation is secured, as the copy can be exactly suited to the needs of the child. Further, the child's work is regularly brought under the notice of the teacher and he can adopt special remedies for particular defects. The pupil also sees a copy which has actually been written, and is by this stimulated and encouraged much more than by an engraved line, the perfection of which he looks upon as unattainable.

(b) **Copies set upon the black-board.** In the early stages of teaching writing to a large class this is an excellent plan. It can be adopted in almost all circumstances, and it is to be regretted that it is not more practised in the present day. The teacher can choose his own style, the work can be easily graduated as required, and the nature of errors can be readily demonstrated by contrasting faulty forms with the correct ones of the copy.

The copy should be set in the presence of the children, and they should be made to observe the mode of forming and joining the letters, the correct spacing, etc. All the members of the class should write the same copy at the same time, which until the children can write fairly well is an advantage in many ways.

(c) **Engraved head-lines printed in the books.** Few, probably, who have thought much about the teaching of writing would be inclined to defend this as the best plan, at least until the child has mastered the ordinary difficulties. The method owes its very common adoption to the fact that it is an easy plan and economises the teacher's time. There can be little doubt that it is answerable to a great extent for the very defective nature of the teaching given, and sometimes for its almost entire neglect. Too often the teacher seems to think that when he has placed in the hands of the child a suitably engraved copy-book there is nothing more necessary beyond an occasional correction of errors. The injurious effect of this course is especially felt in the lower stages.

Great care is needed in the selection of the books to see that the models are good, the style uniform throughout the series, the graduation reasonable and according to a definite scheme, and that wrong modes of forming the letters—very frequently met with in printed books—are avoided. In the copies there should be no eccentricities, such as half a dozen different ways of forming the same capital letter. Several short words are better than one very long and unfamiliar one. The use of long and out of the way words merely because they begin with a certain letter and will fill up a line is absurd. Mr. Brodie notes *sumiologist, opinionist, inodochium, ichneumon, etc.* Moral truisms and doubtful maxims are also much best abandoned.

Various devices have been adopted to prevent the child from copying his own writing after the first line or two, instead of imitating the model; but, after all, this is mainly a matter of good training and discipline. In one set of books the copy is printed separately and fastened round a thread, so that it can be moved down the page as required.

An oblong form of book opening lengthways is best, as the number of lines is then not so great as to make it troublesome to turn the eye constantly to the copy. In the early books the copy should be repeated half way down the page.

(*d*) **Written or engraved copies printed on slips of card-board.** The advantages claimed for this plan are, that the copy can be exactly suited to the child's need, that he may be made to repeat a copy as often as necessary if the imitation is faulty, or any unusual difficulty occurs, and that the model can be moved down so as to be always just above the line the pupil is writing.

The disadvantages are, that without the greatest care the slips soon become disfigured, bent, torn, and dirty, so that they cease to be models of neatness and cleanliness. More attention is also necessary to provide each child with just the kind of copy he needs than can often be given with a large class.

That good writing may be secured in this way by a careful teacher is unquestionable, but without vigilant supervision the pupils readily fall into the bad habit of writing the first line from the model and then putting it on one side altogether.

The teacher who cares to try this plan may readily write a series of copies to suit himself; or he may cut off the head lines from a set or two of good copy books and paste them upon the prepared slips.

Jacotot's Method.

In this method reading and writing were closely associated, the one being made to assist the other. The powers of observation and comparison were carefully trained, the script letters were soon learned, and the child is said to have progressed rapidly.

1. After two lessons in reading, a sentence the pupil had read was put before him *in small hand* (either written by the master or engraved), and this he was required to copy as best he could.

2. The first word having been completed, he was made to compare his writing with the original by numerous questions, so as to direct his attention to the discovery and correction of faults and defects in his work. "The principle must never be lost sight of," says Jacotot, "that **the pupil always corrects himself.**"

3. Each word was gone over in a similar way, and the sentence worked out until the child could transcribe the whole tolerably well.

4. When a sentence had been thus mastered he was called upon to write it from memory, and again to note his faults by comparison with the copy.

5. After "considerable practice in small hand he was carried forward to exercises in bolder styles of writing," in other words, he moved from small hand to large hand.[1]

A *Sentence Method*, clearly but a modification of Jacotot's plan, was recommended by Mr. Moseley, one of H. M. Inspectors, in 1846.[2]

Instead of beginning with parts of letters and then proceeding to words, the child was set to write a short sentence at once. When he could do this fairly the sentence was gradually varied and extended, and finally written from memory. The method is

[1] See Prof. Payne's Lecture on *Jacotot.*
[2] Report of Committee of Council on Education, vol. i. 1846.

said to have incited the children to diligence, and the result to have been remarkable. Mr. Moseley stated: "I found infants writing the sentence well who had only been learning to write a fortnight." The novelty of the plan and the teacher's enthusiasm were no doubt largely answerable for this. The method had grave defects: it reversed the principle "*from simple to complex,*" it put too many difficulties at once before the child, and failed to give the necessary training in the intelligent and exact appreciation of form.

(2) *The Tracing Plan.*—In order to aid the child in overcoming the difficulty of imitating unaided the forms required in writing, the tracing plan puts these before him at first in faint or differently coloured ink, and he is required to go over them with a pen and black ink until he has gained sufficient mastery over the movements and the necessary power of observation to proceed alone.

The method is usually associated with the name of John Locke, who describes it in his *Thoughts concerning Education* (section 160). He had already tried it with the children of a Quaker family in Rotterdam. In France the plan seems to have been brought into notice by Taupier.

The idea is an old one. Quintilian suggested that to accustom the child's hand to the movements required he "should practise on wooden tablets on which letters have been traced by cutting."[1] St. Jerome afterwards recommended the same thing.

Locke says: "The first thing should be taught him is to hold his pen right; and this he should be perfect in before he should be suffered to put it on paper: for not only children but anybody else that would do anything well should never be put upon too much of it at once, or be set to perfect themselves in two parts of an action at the same time, if they can possibly be separated. . . . When he has learned to hold his pen right, in the next place he should learn how to lay his paper, and place his arm and body to it. These practices being got over, the way to teach him to write without much trouble is to get a plate graved with the characters of such a hand as you like best; but you must remember to have them a pretty deal bigger than he should ordinarily write; for every one naturally comes by degrees to write a less hand than he at first was taught, but never a bigger. Such a plate being graved, let several sheets of good writing paper be printed off with red ink, which he has nothing to do but go over with a good pen filled with black ink, which will quickly bring his hand to the formation of those characters, being at first shown where to begin, and how to form every letter. And when he can do that well, he must then exercise on fair paper; and so may easily be brought to write the hand you desire."

The principle of attending to one thing at a time and mastering one difficulty before another is attempted is a valuable one. The

[1] Compayré's *History of Pedagogy.*

tracing plan is in accordance with this; it gives just the assistance the child needs in the early training of the hand, and may be used with much profit in the case of beginners. It teaches but little however in the way of imitation, and hence should be gradually abandoned as the child comes to trace over the characters with some amount of freedom and certainty. In the transition stage the child should trace a line or two and then attempt the imitation of the copy without this aid. Even later on, when the child experiences difficulty with any letter or combination, the teacher will do well to write the word in pencil a time or two for him to mark over.

As an introductory method the tracing plan is in its right place; but it must not be continued too long, or the child ceases to progress as he should do, and the after writing is apt to be cramped and stiff. The chief defect of the method lies in the fact that a child may trace over certain characters many times and fail to notice with any care the forms with which he is dealing. It is a training for the hand rather than the eye.

Many modern series of copy-books rightly make use of the tracing plan in the early stages, though in some the graduation is excessive.

(3) *Constructive Plans.*—In any constructive plan of teaching writing there are three things to be considered: the **analysis of the letters into the elementary forms** of which they are composed; the **classification of the letters according to difficulty**, so that those made up of the simplest elements shall be taught first; and lastly the **synthesis of the elements to form the letters**, and the combination of these into words. The analysis and classification are the work of the teacher, the practice of the elements and their synthesis into the letters is the means by which the child learns to write.

Pestalozzi's Plan.

The first to suggest the teaching of writing by the constructive method seems to have been Pestalozzi about the year 1790. This was afterwards more fully worked out by himself and his disciples.

He based his writing lessons on drawing, and had a set of graduated copies engraved which followed the successive steps of his method. In speaking of the advantages of his plan he says: "The child is kept a sufficient time to the drawing of the elementary or fundamental lines of which the different letters are composed. These elementary lines are put together according to a gradual progress, in which the most difficult letters are placed at the end and their formation is moreover facilitated by the previous practice of less difficult combinations, to which even the most complicated characters contain only slight additions."[1]

[1] See Biber's *Pestalozzi and his Plan of Education.*

The Mulhaüser Writing Method.

In 1829 M. Mulhaüser was appointed by the Genevese Commission of Primary Schools to inspect the writing classes under their superintendence. Finding the writing bad, and the teaching unmethodical and capricious, he brought out his famous 'method' in which, beginning with the elementary forms arrived at by analysis, and adopting the easiest constructions, he systematised the modes of forming the letters and reduced each to a definite standard. The child was thus enabled "to determine with ease, the height, breadth, and inclination of every part of every letter," and this not by abstract rules, but by practical expedients.

The method was put to the test and rapidly came into favour, not only in Switzerland but elsewhere. It was brought into notice in England by a *Minute on Methods of Teaching* in the Report of the Committee of Education for 1844, and still more by the publication soon afterwards of a manual of the method under the sanction of the same body.[1]

The chief merits claimed for the Mulhaüser style of writing were :—

(a) The exact and well-defined nature of all its parts.
(b) The harmonious proportions existing between them.
(c) Its consequent beauty and legibility.
(d) The absence of ornament.

The paper is divided into rhomboids by means of two sets of equidistant parallel lines crossing each other. One series is horizontal and determines the length of the various letters, the distance between alternate lines being called a '*height*.' The other series of lines is inclined at an angle of 60°. These serve as guides to the proper inclination and width of the letters and the mode of combining them. The distance between two oblique lines is called a '*space*,' which is thus equal to the 'half height.'

There are **four elementary parts of letters** :—

(a) The *right or straight line*, made by either upward or downward motion, and of different but determined heights.

(b) The *curve line*, either single, as in the letter *c*, or double, as in the letter *o*.

[1] *Manual of Writing founded on Mulhaüser's Method*, London 1849.

(c) The *loop*, turned upwards, as in the letters *e, f,* and downwards, as in *g, j,* etc.

(d) The *crotchet*, as in the last part of the letters *i, b, w, v.*

In describing the letters for writing, two other terms are used—'*link*' and '*hook.*' The '*link*' is a fine curve descending from the right line and continued upwards to the half height, as in the curved portions of the letter *u.* The '*hook*' commences at the half height and ascending curves round into a descending right-line, as in the commencement of the letter *n* or *m.*

"The letters are arranged according to their construction, beginning with the simplest and proceeding in regular series to the most complex." The following is the **classification and order :—**

(a) Right-line and link letters—*i, u, t, l.*

(b) Hook, right-line, and link letters—*n, m, h, p.*

(c) Curve letters—*c, o, e.*

(d) Double curve and right-line letters—*a, d, q.*

(e) Loop letters—*j, g, y.*

(f) Crotchet letters—*b, f, v, i, w.*

(g) Complex letters—*k, s, x, z.*

Until the children had mastered the writing of all the letters **each lesson consisted of two parts,** called "study at the circles" and "study at the desks." In the former, or theoretical work, the pupils learned the terms used in describing the letters, and the instructions respecting heights, spaces, etc., from "Tablets of Rules," the mode of forming the parts being explained and illustrated. In the desks the children were called upon to write the letters from dictation of their elements, and finally to write words from the models.[1]

As an analysis of forms, and as a definite standard of style and of the mode of making, spacing, and joining the letters, Mulhaüser's system leaves little to be desired. It should be thoroughly known by every teacher, and the knowledge practically applied in his own way to the teaching of writing.

For detailed descriptions of the letters, illustrative copies, and the mode of forming the capitals, see the excellent *Mulhaüser Manual* of Mr. Cowham, who has done useful service in recalling the attention of teachers to the valuable points of the system.

The detailed mode of carrying out the work as originally intended, however, is not to be recommended in the case of children. The elaboration is far too great for beginners, and the preliminary theoretical work of learning the technical terms and the various rules, as well as the writing of the letters from dictation of their parts, is best abandoned. Such theoretical matters as are of importance—*e.g.* the relative proportions of the various parts of the letters—the pupils will best learn gradually by observation, and by imitation of the teacher's work upon the black-board, not by abstract rules. The mode of ruling the books is a considerable assistance in the early teaching of writing.

III. THE TEACHING OF WRITING.

Most modern schemes for teaching writing combine in a greater or less degree various features from almost all the so-called methods just described. Simple drawing exercises usually precede writing, and the use of the pencil is taught before the pen is introduced. The letters are presented to the child in the order of their simplicity of formation; and the tracing plan and the Mulhaüser lines are frequently brought in as mechanical aids in the early stages.

All children may, with reasonable care, be taught to write passably, though some learn much more easily than others even when the latter are anxious and painstaking. In a few cases excellence is very difficult to secure, and there can be little doubt that inherited capability has something to do with the matter. It is said that English boys taught to write in France rarely write in the French style.

(1) *Introductory Lessons.*—The teaching of writing should be based upon easy exercises in drawing of the Kindergarten type, together with lessons on 'form' such as are commonly given in infant schools. The two should be so arranged as to illustrate and assist each other.

The book or paper for the drawing should be faintly ruled into squares of about a quarter of an inch. Various graduated exercises should be given in drawing lines of definite length from point to point in any required direction; at first along the ruled lines, and later from any one point to any other. The lines may soon be combined into easy patterns, including the simple forms of the straight-line print capitals.

In this way the child may be gradually familiarised with the use of the pencil, and will gain the power of making a fairly firm and even stroke of definite length. At the same time he is taught to observe and obtain some notion of relative distances.

Books with the copies printed in addition to the ruling may be bought, but the best plan is to have a black-board ruled in squares, and for the teacher to illustrate the drawing of each line, and build up the copy part by part, the child imitating each in turn as the teacher draws it. Each line should be examined and corrected before the next is proceeded with.

Where paper cannot be afforded, slates ruled in the way required may be used; but all exercises connected with writing are best performed on paper, and this is now so cheap that there is little excuse for not employing it. The difficulty about pencils may easily be overcome, as has been proved in the case of ordinary drawing.

(2) *Pencil Writing.*—**It is a mistake for children in learning to write to begin with the pen**, as may be proved by making the experiment. The pencil is much easier to manipulate, and to use it in this stage is in accordance with the principle of distributing difficulties and learning one thing at a time.

The child will already have learned to hold the pencil properly, and he should now be put to write, not draw, the simpler elements of the letters, beginning with straight strokes of settled length and slope, and passing to such letters as *i, u, m, n.* Combinations of these into words should next be taken, and then the other letters in a similar way according to their difficulty. Lines to guide the pupil as to the size of the letters should always be used in these lessons; but as the chief thing now is to teach him to *write* the various forms required, **the way in which the movements are made must be specially attended to**, and he must not be distracted or burdened by too minute criticism as to spacing, uniformity of slope, and similar matters. The curves particularly need looking to, the hand being kept in the same direction and no twisting of the direction of the pencil being allowed.

It is best not to employ printed copies, and the writing of each letter should be continued until it can be made correctly and with some amount of ease. The black-board must be freely used for instruction in the mode of making the letters, as well as for the illustration of special points.

Too much is sometimes made of **the value of drawing as an assistance to writing**, as though the two things were practically pretty much the same. As a training of the eye, drawing is of course an aid to the appreciation of the exact shapes of the letters, especially in the early stages; but it may be doubted whether, beyond teaching the proper holding of the pencil and giving some command over it, drawing is any considerable help in training the *hand* for writing. In the case of drawing the touch is firm, the pressure uniform, and the movements comparatively slow: in writing the touch is elastic, the pressure variable, and the movements rapid. That the skill required differs in the two cases is shewn by the fact that many accomplished draughtsmen are bad writers, while good writers are by no means necessarily good draughtsmen. A boy who had only learned to draw well, would still find it a troublesome matter to learn to write.

(3) *Early lessons in writing with the pen.*—The first lessons should be similar to those gone over with the pencil, attention being at first specially directed to the **proper management of the pen and ink** and the formation of the letters. All the class should write the same copy at the same time, and the letters should be taught in groups, so that the mastery of one will prepare the way for the next. As soon as a few letters have been learned they should be linked into words, and such matters as spacing, joinings, and slope carefully looked to. Repetition should be secured by new combinations. The following classification of the letters serves very well—

(i.) i, u, n, m. (iv.) j, y, g.
(ii.) t, l, p, h. (v.) v, w, b, r.
(iii.) o, a, d, q, c, e. (vi.) s, k, f, x, z.

Many teachers will prefer to use the engraved headlines, in which case such books should be chosen as introduce the letters in a reasonable order and give sufficient well arranged practice. In any case thorough demonstration and illustration on the black-board must not be forgotten. The want of such teaching, where a class has to be dealt with, is a common defect.

The first two or three lines after the copy should have the letters or words printed in faint ink for tracing on Locke's plan, the rest of the page being left for practice without this aid. Guide lines, after the manner of the Mulhaüser rhomboids, to assist in the acquirement of proper spacing and slope, will also certainly facilitate progress at this stage.

If the teacher doubts this, he should test the matter practically for himself. Were this done more frequently, a juster estimate would be formed than is often the case respecting many of the so-called improvements upon the older methods.

The teacher should do his best to train the child to a **thorough knowledge of the forms of the letters**, so that he may have a fixed standard in his mind, and be able to produce any form correctly from memory. He should be encouraged to write boldly and firmly: much weak writing results from timidity. Children again vary considerably in their power of appreciating form, and some appear guilty of carelessness who simply have not learned to observe.

SKETCH PLAN OF EARLY LESSONS.

(a) *Observation and Instruction.* First letter of copy (whether engraved or not) written on black-board by teacher, while children observe carefully. Each part illustrated separately to impress mode of formation. Brief and explicit directions given together with any necessary cautions.

(b) *Imitation.* Pupils write letter in their books, teacher superintending and giving attention chiefly to those who find most difficulty. Care taken to secure correct holding of pen and natural position of body.

(c) *Examination and Correction.* Pupils stop writing, work examined and all individual mistakes marked. Any common errors illustrated and corrected on black-board, the children being thoroughly questioned as to the nature of the mistake. Faulty forms contrasted with the teacher's copy.

(d) *Practice.* Remaining letters treated in the same way. The whole word then written before being examined; and finally a line in a similar manner.

It is sometimes advisable to devote a portion of a lesson to the comparison and contrast of forms likely to be confounded with one another from their similarity. Young teachers should note and classify faults as an aid to their teaching. A coloured pencil is useful for the purpose of marking mistakes.

Children must be taught to *observe* the copy, not merely glance at it to obtain the sequence of the letters. Frequent and thorough correction is certain to pay in the end, although the work may appear to progress slowly at first in consequence. It should be impressed upon the pupil that he should write first well, then quickly.

Whatever style of writing the teacher adopts the black-board should always be ruled with two sets of parallel lines, the one horizontal the other inclined at the angle settled upon for the slope of the letters. The lines greatly facilitate the setting of a good copy, and are of much assistance in demonstrating the proper formation, proportions, and spacing of the letters. In dealing with faulty forms on the black-board it is often advisable to exaggerate the errors somewhat, that their nature may be clearly apprehended. After a mistake has been explained and illustrated, the teacher should again show how to make the letter correctly, and he may sometimes with advantage have it made upon the black-board by the children themselves.

The following are a few mistakes commonly met with:—

(a) Unequal size of curves at top and bottom—hooks begun too low.

(b) Axis of ellipse in such letters as o, a, d, g, of different inclination from that of the associated right line letters.

(c) The ellipse or o portion of the letter commenced in the wrong place.

(d) Crotchet wrongly made in the letters r, b, v, w.

(e) Letters not of uniform heights, widths, and slope—*t* and *p* frequently too tall.
(f) Bad spacing—letters crowded in some places and too much spread in others.
(g) Faulty junctions; a meaningless stroke prefixed to letters like *o, a, d,* when these commence a word.
(h) Straight-line elements crooked, patched, or broken.
(i) Ragged scratchy lines from faulty holding of the pen—downstrokes of varying thickness.

(4) *The withdrawal of mechanical aids.*—When the children can form the letters correctly without difficulty and combine them into words with proper junctions and spacing of the parts, mechanical aids should be gradually withdrawn. Tracing should be first given up, and then the oblique lines serving as guides to the slope and width of the letters. Simple horizontal lines to indicate the height of the long letters, and vertical ones to show the spacing of the words should be retained somewhat longer.

The same copy should still be written by the whole class, even where engraved headlines are used. It should also be put upon the black-board by the teacher, and any difficulties connected with it explained; but much less time should be taken up with this explanatory teaching than previously, as the **main thing at this stage is carefully supervised practice.**

Exercises on all the letters should be given, the more difficult combinations being gradually introduced. Each copy should consist of a short sentence, as being more interesting; or of two or three words introducing the particular association of letters to be practised. The copy should be repeated at least once down the page. The writing should not be all of one size, 'text-hand' being introduced now and again to accustom the fingers to a larger sweep and firmer stroke.

It will be found that one of the chief difficulties the teacher has to cope with at this stage is getting the child to attend closely to the model. The supervision will need to be as thorough as before, each line being examined as it is written, and all the pupils for the present being made to write at the same speed. In particular cases the teacher will often find it useful to pencil in a few letters for the child until the difficulty with which he is contending is overcome.

(5) *The Introduction of the Capital Letters.*—The previous practice of the small letters in 'text-hand' will have prepared the child to some extent for the **greater certainty and freedom of movement**

required in forming the capitals ; but the step at best is by no means easy. The curve of double flexure which enters into many of the capitals, as *J, F, T, S,* etc., is a new and difficult element to make with the necessary grace and flow of line ; while the adjustment of the various curves, so as to keep the letters properly balanced, and the determination of the right slope without any straight line portion to serve as a guide, necessitate a considerable amount of judgment and knowledge of form.

The pupils will need to be gradually trained to the recognition of the nature and relationship of the different parts by being frequently shewn on the blackboard how to form the letters, by having their attention drawn to the characteristic features of each, by class criticisms of faulty forms, and by correction of the errors of individuals.

The capital letters of similar formation should be taught in succession, and when one group has been mastered the next least complex one should be taken. Each curve must be formed continuously and smoothly; there must be no stiffness or irregularity, no breaks, and no patching of the lines. The size at first should be that required in 'round-hand,' and from this the pupil should pass to larger letters when he has gained sufficient power. The writing of capital letters alone is not an interesting exercise, and as soon as some practice has been obtained to ensure general correctness they should be taken in connection with words.

(6) '*Small-Hand.*'—In beginning 'small-hand' the best plan, where it can be managed, is to have a sentence set in 'round-hand,' and then the same sentence in small hand. In any case the **writing should be bold and clear**, and the upstrokes not too fine. The pens used are often unsuitable, and make the writing look weak and finical. Careful formation of the letters is of more importance than the finish of the strokes. Exact imitation of the model is still to be insisted upon, and neither the size of the writing nor the spacing of the words must be less than the copy.

Vigilant supervision is as necessary as ever. The teacher should move round the class continually to encourage effort, check any hasty or slovenly work, and correct any faults which may make their appearance. Incomplete formation of the letters, want of evenness, and irregularity of height are not uncommon defects.

The alternative forms of the letters *r* and *t*, commonly used in 'small-hand,' should be illustrated on the black-board. The looping of the letters *b, h, k,* and *l,* should also receive attention ; and the pupils should be cautioned against the frequent mistake of bending what should be the straight line portions of these letters.

(7) *The passage from exact imitation to freedom.*—As soon as some practice has been gained in 'small-hand,' the child should not be confined solely to this. Occasional copies of the larger kinds should be interspersed, for the purpose of continuing the training of the hand to increased certainty and skill in the management of the pen.

When by such exercises a firm regular hand in the style of the models has been secured, **copy-book practice should be reduced**, and its place gradually taken by other writing exercises. Greater freedom in the formation of the letters may now be allowed, and **rapidity of execution should be fostered** until a good current hand can be written. Carelessness, or scribbling, however, must never be permitted; and though continuous supervision will not be so necessary as heretofore, all exercises should be carefully examined and the defects corrected.

Few things will do more for the pupil at this stage than having constantly before him **examples of a good current hand** such as it is desired he shall write; and for this purpose some of the published specimens of the style of writing favoured by the Civil Service Commissioners may be used with great advantage as standards, apart from any exact imitation of them as copies.

The transcription, without blunders of any kind, of passages of prose and poetry is a good training in exactness as well as in writing; and the work may be varied by the writing of such things as letters, bills, composition exercises, and passages committed to memory. **Italic printing** is also useful, and the occasional introduction of exercises in this will be found a gain to the pupils.

SUPPLEMENTARY HINTS.

(a) **The head-teacher should periodically see all copy-books.**

(b) In the earlier stages, the children that need most attention should be placed in front. **Short-sighted children are often neglected**; they should be always placed where they can see what is written on the black-board.

(c) The teacher's marking of errors should be neat, so that the books may not be disfigured.

(d) Care should be taken that the books are moved further away from the pupils in writing the lower lines of a page, so that the hand and wrist may be properly supported on the desk.

(e) The children should be **shown how to use blotting-paper**, passing the hand over it with a gentle pressure first, then more firmly.

(f) Blots and smears should not pass unnoticed, and **no scribbling on the covers** of the books or on the desks should ever be allowed.

(g) The teacher should vigorously insist upon the **avoidance of uncleanly habits**, such as spattering the ink about the desk or floor, inking the fingers, putting the pen in the mouth and spitting out the ink, and wiping the pen on the hair or clothes.

(h) **Copy-books should not be taken home** until they are finished, as, if this be allowed, they will scarcely escape being soiled, crumpled, and torn, and perhaps written in by others. Those belonging to each class should be collected at the end of every writing lesson by a monitor and neatly fastened between two thin boards to preserve them from damage.

(i) **The pens should be properly cleaned** when collected, and any damaged ones replaced, not merely thrown into a box with the ink left to dry on them and clog up the points.

(j) Good ink is also essential, and the **ink-wells should be periodically washed out** and refilled that there may be no deposit of mud from accumulated dust. A copper can with a fine spout should be used for filling; tinned iron rapidly corrodes.

IV. ARITHMETIC.

There is perhaps more general agreement theoretically as to the broader principles which should govern the teaching of Arithmetic, and as to the main lines of the methods by which the various parts should be presented, than is the case in any other of the common subjects of school instruction.[1] Practically, however, some of the more important objects which ought to be aimed at are frequently lost sight of, or remain unheeded; while others are pushed more prominently forward than their real value is warrant for. Nor are the true claims of Arithmetic to its place in school studies always so clearly understood as they should be.

I. SCOPE AND OBJECT OF ARITHMETICAL TEACHING.

(1) *Position of arithmetic in the school course.*—Viewed from the side of its practical utility—that is, merely as a matter of knowledge, and of power to make such calculations as are commonly required by the great majority of mankind—arithmetic is not entitled to the high place assigned to it in the school curriculum; and still less is this the case if it is looked upon almost exclusively as a business art to be applied mainly in the shop or the counting-house. When, however, it is taught in such a way as not only to give skill in computation, but to become one of the most effective means of mental training—especially in the way of developing the reasoning power, and of teaching the child to think clearly and connectedly—it gains immensely in importance, and is then, next to reading and writing, the most profitable subject which the pupil is called upon to learn.[2] It affects directly or indirectly almost every branch of

[1] See Bain's *Education as a Science*.   [2] See Fitch's *Lectures on Teaching*.

school work, and the qualities it develops are of the greatest service to the possessor in meeting the needs of daily experience. The value of arithmetic thus depends very largely upon the way in which it is taught.

(2) *Arithmetic viewed as a science and as an art.*—As an art arithmetic is concerned with certain elementary processes and rules of calculation which can be carried out by figures alone. **From this point of view arithmetic aims at making good computers**, and affords the necessary instructions and exercises for the pupils to become expert in the various methods by which such calculations as are necessary in the ordinary affairs of life, or in business, can be made in the shortest and best way.

The processes are of two kinds, pure and applied. The former are of fundamental importance and deal with abstract numbers only —as the first four rules, the pure portions of vulgar and decimal fractions, the theory of proportion, and evolution ; the latter are essentially but extensions of the processes of pure arithmetic to the solution of questions relating to money, weights, measures, etc.—as the compound rules, reduction, practice, interest, discount, and various other more or less direct applications.

As a *science* arithmetic takes into account more particularly **the properties of numbers and the principles which underlie the methods of dealing with them.** It shows how, from known facts, we may proceed to others by applying certain modes of reasoning and calculation, and makes evident *why* these must lead to correct results if accurately carried out. **It appeals to the understanding at every step** ; and one of its most valuable features is that it does not require anything to be accepted on trust or authority, but leads the pupil to see that there are branches of knowledge where he may rightly expect demonstration at every point. It does not view the subject as something to be *learned by rote* ; but as a series of truths and processes to be *thought out.* The interdependence of the various parts is brought clearly into view, and each is treated as a logical development of what has gone before.

The scientific view of arithmetic does not in the least disregard the need of numerous exercises in computation ; but it endeavours to secure that they shall be such as to give an insight into the real nature of the subject, and that they shall be performed intelligently.

It emphasises the importance of the fundamental processes, and leads to the expansion of the work in such a way that, while a solid foundation is laid for the further prosecution of mathematical studies, the pupil gains power in many directions besides those concerned merely with calculation.

Where the two views are properly combined, **the memorising of rules is subordinated to the clear grasp of principles and of the relation of these to practical applications**, so that the pupil is able to make many of these applications for himself without any set rule respecting them. Every new process or development is so treated as to throw further light on the meaning and scope of what has gone before, as well as give a glimpse of what has to come after. Where the pupil is able to proceed so far, there will be no break in the training given, from the inculcation of the first notions of number up to the use of letter symbols and the more general reasoning which algebra supplies.

It would be a great mistake to suppose that arithmetic can be in any degree adequately treated from the scientific side in a first course: such treatment can only come gradually as the child's understanding is strengthened and he gains power to reason. But it is an equal mistake to keep the pupil at a constant drill in merely manipulating figures, when he ought to be learning to think and to realise the principles which underlie his work. The only thing to be insisted upon is, that, **so far as the child's power and understanding will serve without forcing him, the work ought to be made intelligent**, and that, as he develops, the logical side of the subject should be brought more and more into view. Something indeed may be done from the first if due care and patience be exercised.

The limits of arithmetic, as found in our text-books, are not natural ones, but are simply those which have been sanctioned by common usage, or such as are supposed to include a suitable elementary course. The rules given have varied according to what were thought to be the needs of the time; and some once common—as 'tare and tret,' 'alligation,' 'partnership,' of various kinds, etc.—have practically disappeared from our books. Ordinary commercial requirements, however, still receive almost exclusive consideration in the way of applied rules, some of which are likely to prove of little, if of any, use to the common run of pupils, and others are certainly not of such pre-eminent value as the time and attention devoted to them would seem to indicate. The great extension of science and of science teaching of late has brought into importance many matters, especially relating to physics, which, as knowledge, have a distinct value to the ordinary student, and are interesting and useful for purposes of training and of practice in calculation. From the standpoint of a general education these deserve to be treated as parts of applied arithmetic as much as many of the things still set forth at length in our books.

(3) *General objects of teaching arithmetic.*—The two main objects

to be kept in view by the teacher in his treatment of arithmetic in school are—

(*a*) **To familiarise the pupil with the ordinary processes and rules of arithmetic**, and to render him expert in computation by the best methods, so that he may be able, with readiness and reasonable certainty, to make such practical calculations as are likely to fall in his way within the common limits of the subject.

(*b*) **To secure to the child the benefits of the mental training which the right teaching of the subject is calculated to afford**, so that, while practical needs are as fully satisfied as circumstances will allow, his understanding generally is developed, and some power is given to reason correctly from such data as are put before him.

Though closely associated in practice, and mutually helpful, the means to be adopted to accomplish these objects are by no means the same; and much care and judgment are often necessary to adjust properly their relative claims, and to combine them in the most effective way. When this is done, "the path along which the pupil is led may be longer than the usual route; but then it is in broad daylight, he is more independent of his guide, and derives more health and vigour from the exercise."

What we have to aim at is **drill without weariness**, and the **training of the intelligence without forcing or hurry**. Both things are necessary; the child has to learn both to *do* and to *think*. He may have been practised until he has gained considerable facility in mechanical computation, and yet have little or no real understanding of his work; and, on the other hand, he may have been intelligently taught, and yet, from want of necessary practice, be able to make the calculations required only slowly and inaccurately.

The purpose of the school is to give a broad general training, not to make business specialists. Those matters, which are valuable to all alike, and which all need, should receive attention first, then rules of more restricted usefulness. If the pupil has been properly taught, he will be able to acquire readily anything further desirable in the way of technical applications as they are wanted.

<small>Each business (whether banking, merchant's work, or what not) has its own needs, and to some extent its own methods, often widely different from those given in our books; and what business men complain of is not that the boys from our schools do not know these special applications, but that they often lack a thorough grounding</small>

in the ordinary arithmetical processes, and consequently show little aptness in learning what is required, or skill in using it when learned.

The exact view to be taken by the teacher respecting the nature and scope of what should be taught will depend largely upon the status and prospects of the pupils themselves—how far it is possible to carry them in the time they will probably remain at school, and what use they are likely to be called upon to make of their arithmetic in the future ; for, clearly, a class of pupils, most of whom will carry on their studies to a much higher point, should not be treated in the same way as those intended for business or the workshop at an earlier stage. No matter where the pupil stops, or what he may be destined for, he ought at least to gain something of the training which the study of arithmetic properly conducted is calculated to give, apart from mere smartness in mechanical computation ; and to girls, especially, this more intellectual side is much the more valuable.

(4) *Value of arithmetic as a general means of training.*—The training to be obtained from the proper study of arithmetic is valuable and varied. There is scarcely any intellectual faculty that it may not be made to strengthen. Processes and rules may be forgotten, from want of opportunities to apply them, but the beneficial effects of having been put through the mental gymnastic training which the work should afford are lasting, and extend far beyond the limits of the subject itself. We may briefly sum up some of the more marked of the **benefits to be derived from an intelligent study of arithmetic** as follows :—

(*a*) **It gives vigour, freedom, and flexibility to the mind** ; it helps to bring the faculties under control, and **affords a most valuable logical training** in continuous thinking and the drawing of correct inferences.

(*b*) **It promotes quickness of apprehension** and of mental movement ; it puts the pupil habitually on the alert, and makes him ready in resource and prompt in seizing upon the essential points of any matter presented to him.

(*c*) **It strengthens the power of attention,** and cultivates the habit of applying the mind closely and steadily to one thing at a time.

(*d*) **It brings strongly into view the importance of a clear grasp of ideas, exactness of statement, and systematic arrangement** ; and impresses the pupil with the necessity of caution in dealing with and interpreting facts.

(*e*) **It encourages the habit of looking into things,** and exercises ingenuity in unravelling any complex relation or involved statement.

(*f*) **It fosters self-reliance**, stimulates the pupil to face difficulties courageously, and shows something of what may be done by patient investigation.

(*g*) **It develops the power of abstraction**, and leads to the comprehension of the nature of abstract quantities and the appreciation of abstract reasoning.

(*h*) **It aids the training of the memory**, by accustoming the pupil to the association of ideas in natural sequences and to the recognition of the importance of their connection and true subordination.

<small>The committing of a rule to memory and the working of a multitude of examples to give the requisite facility in dealing with the figures is a very different thing from the understanding of a method, so as to be able to apply it readily to cases of very varied character. **Merely imitative arithmetic is valueless for the purpose of intellectual growth.** The reasoning must be done *by the child*; but to quote simply the teacher's explanation, and to go through the mere word-repetition of the logical forms, is not to think, and must not be mistaken for training.

When arithmetic is taught in the imitative non-intelligent way, the pupils are quite unable to proceed with any problem or unusual form of exercise until they have been put upon the track of the rule; and though they may be able to work sums exactly after the teacher's model, they do this without any clear understanding of what they are about. In such a case, as Dr. Lieber points out, the subject comes to be looked upon as "something not much better than a play with certain signs according to conventional rules; a discrepancy which is pregnant with the worst consequences, the more apparent the more the scholar advances in mathematics, or the more he is called upon to apply them."</small>

II. General Considerations respecting the Conduct of the Work.

(1) *The relation of mental to written arithmetic.*—What is called **mental arithmetic**, that is, the solution of exercises without any written aid, is of frequent service in daily life, and properly taught is of the greatest utility in the ordinary processes of calculation. It **should supply the gymnastic training whereby computation is rendered more rapid and certain, and the work to be written down is in many cases shortened and simplified.** The great mistake which is made is to teach mental and written arithmetic as though they were distinct matters, with different aims and methods, instead of closely associated parts of the same work. There should be the most intimate connection between the two, and the essential nature of the work should be viewed as the same in both, the pen being used to record the partial results arrived at mentally, where the numbers

are too great, and the manipulation of them too complicated, for the mind to carry forward the working without such aid.

The dissociation of mental and written arithmetic has many evil results; and in part, at least, accounts for the common neglect of systematic training in dealing with numbers mentally, as well as for the want of accuracy and facility so often noticeable in written exercises.

Mental work naturally precedes and leads up to written solution; and as far as possible the methods employed should be assimilated. Mere tricks, dodges, and short cuts, which may be used for the solution of some particular kind of example, but which have no place in ordinary work, are of little moment compared with the power to perform easy calculations by methods which can be employed in all cases. The value of the latter is not likely to be over-estimated. Facility in adding and multiplying numbers is of special importance and should be carefully provided for.

It is not wise to attempt a complete course of mental work before beginning written exercises. The two should proceed side by side; and when a child can employ a process with success mentally, he should be taught to apply it in the harder cases where he will need the assistance of the pen. The distinctly gymnastic exercises are best given at the beginning of the lesson; but they should not be continued too long, and certainly not to the point of fatigue. It is the regularity of mental exercises, not the mere length of time devoted to them, which does good.

Good questioning has much to do with successful progress in mental arithmetic, and the teacher must not shirk the trouble and activity necessary for performing this part of the work well. The exercises should be interesting and varied, and given with sufficient smartness to keep every one on the alert. Place-taking, and class matches in which one half of the pupils is pitted against the other, are occasionally useful.

In giving harder exercises to be worked mentally, any difficulty beyond that of calculation should be avoided, and hence it will be well to let the children have the data written on paper or the black-board, so that they may keep these clearly before them.

(2) *Explanatory work—General method of procedure in teaching a rule.*—The rule should be gradually **arrived at by the pupils inductively**, that is, through their own observations and conclusions, its full force and meaning being grasped practically, as far as possible, by the examination of a number of examples, before any attempt is

made to express it in a formal statement. Taught in this way the principles are clearly understood, and the words have a meaning for the pupils which they have seen to be true ; their intelligence is exercised throughout, and as the rule simply embodies the result of their own experience, it is more easily remembered, and is a more useful possession to them than if merely accepted on the authority of the teacher. It is almost always well to gratify the child's love of discovery ; the consciousness of power when he has made out a thing for himself is a strong incentive to further effort.

"Whenever," says a writer in Knight's *Quarterly Journal of Education*, "a child can be led to form, to think out, as it were, a rule for himself, it is most desirable that he should ; but it does not, therefore, follow that, in cases where he is unable to do so, the rule should be suppressed or omitted; nor does the mere fact that he may be taught, without the rule, to perform the same operations, prove that the rule is superfluous, or ought not to be communicated, when the operations without it are much more laborious and circuitous than when it is applied. Where, indeed, the principle of the rule is unintelligible, even when communicated, it may generally be desirable to suppress it: there may be more harm in accustoming the mind to take things upon trust than in leaving it without the practical assistance to be derived from the rule itself. But the more common case will be that of a rule not within the compass of the learner to discover, but admitting of full explanation and proof, such as he can comprehend, when it is once announced to him. And these rules it appears to us desirable to communicate ; not in the first instance, indeed, before the want of them has been found, and their value consequently appreciated, by examples of the same operations performed without them ; but as soon as these preliminary steps have been gone through, and without waiting till the same cautious process has been carried into other departments of the subject."

The **steps of the teaching in introducing a new rule** will be somewhat as follows :—

(*a*) **Explanation of the process in its simplest form,** with any concrete illustrations necessary to secure full understanding and the working of easy examples mentally.

(*b*) **Thorough questioning** as to the meaning of each step, so as to **lay bare the principle** on which the rule is to be based.

(*c*) The **working and dissection on the black-board of more difficult examples** in accordance with the rule to be afterwards given, so that the nature and order of the steps may be clearly apparent.

(*d*) **Questioning to bring out exactly what has been done;** and, where any gain will result from so doing, to express this in a neat and perspicuous form of words for use as a practical rule.

(e) **The working of test examples by the pupils themselves** so as to ensure that the whole has been understood, and the method at least clearly grasped.

In many cases it will be advisable to **analyse the process ultimately to be adopted**, and to consider each step separately, until the exact nature of what is to be done is clearly comprehended by the children. The work may then be shortened and condensed, and the most suitable form given for expeditious solution.

<small>Although frequently too much is *said* in describing the mode of working, the teaching is often defective from not being properly thought out. The teacher is content if the children merely follow certain routine instructions without obtaining any real insight into what they are doing. Little actual power is gained, and progress is not likely to be rapid or substantial when this is the case.</small>

The teacher should lay stress upon the principles underlying a process, and as far as possible the rule to be memorised should be deduced from these; he should also keep the pupil's mind clear as to what is assumed and what is proved, and point out distinctly the difference between particular instances and general conclusions. The recognition of the general as distinct from the particular is a very important part of the training to be gained from arithmetic, and the confusion of the two is a frequent source of error. **Where the work is to be based upon reasoning, each conclusion should be evident to the pupils**; and when these conclusions have been combined, and the general result grasped, exercises should be given in applying the same mode of reasoning to various problems in many different directions.

<small>The teaching may easily be spoiled by going faster than the pupils are able to follow surely; and it is important at first to make them state clearly what they have done at each step of the work, until they are able to give an intelligible account of every part of an example—what each line of figures represents, and so on. **Changes of unit should be specially noted**; if the value of the unit in each case were kept clearly in mind, many exercises would be easy which too often prove stumbling-blocks in the way of progress.</small>

In many instances we cannot hope to make a child fully comprehend a rule until he has frequently applied it; but we may lead him to feel its need and make clear to him how it is to be used.

Complete understanding is rarely to be secured at first; and the wise teacher will patiently go back again and again to an obscurity until it gradually clears away and full light breaks through.

Children differ much in the quickness with which they pick up a new process; what is looked upon as dulness and slowness is often merely the result of imperfect development. It is to be remembered, also, that **strangeness is itself a difficulty**, and that to scold children as stupid when they are doing their best is to put them on the high road to failure.

The language employed must give no trouble, and hence the terms to be used should be mastered independently before any reasoning in which they occur is given.

After explanation of a new process of working the first sums set should be exactly similar to those gone through during the teaching, and sufficiently easy to be readily solved if this has been understood.

(3) *The general conduct of practice work—Nature of the examples, disciplinary measures, etc.*—Directly the children are able to work easy examples with success, the arithmetic lessons will be almost entirely a matter of well-ordered practice until a new rule has to be introduced; though occasionally passages of class teaching will be given when any pretty general failure shews that a difficulty has been encountered, or when it is desirable to include any matter of more advanced character.

The **main things to be looked to** will be :—

(a) The suitability of the examples.

(b) Neatness of figures, good form, and logical arrangements.

(c) The thoroughness of the disciplinary measures to ensure regular and vigorous effort and perfect honesty of performance.

(d) Careful correction of the exercises.

(e) Judicious individual help given to duller or more backward pupils.

The **examples must be progressively arranged**, so as not only gradually to increase in difficulty as exercises in computation, but, when the necessary mechanical skill has been attained, to demand more and more that the child shall exercise his wits. Before a rule is left, his experiences in applying it to different types of sums should have been of a very varied character, one set preparing the way for, and leading up to, others of a more advanced character.

Many of the exercises should be given in words, either dictated or written on the black-board, so that the pupils may be accustomed to different forms of statement, and exercised in making the necessary translation into figures.

Problems should be introduced early, as they are most valuable for the purpose of training the intelligence, and may easily be made in a high degree interesting and stimulating. They should be **fairly deducible from the principles previously learned**; and the gradual passage from easy exercises of thought to more difficult and complex questions should be specially attended to, as at every point the pupil is to be encouraged to think, and shewn how much he can really do by making the essay in earnest. The difficulties which present themselves are usually of two kinds; first, that of disentangling the various points, so as to make out the conditions given, and find the mode of discovering the relation sought; and, secondly, that of stating the whole in logical order and the best form, so that it may be clear that the pupil realises the force of each step in the reasoning.

Examples of the fanciful and artificial kind so frequently met with should be avoided. In many such cases the statements are of the most improbable and absurd character; while the conditions are such as would never be met with in actual experience, and are often glaringly at variance with common sense.

It is most unwise to keep pupils plodding wearily through pages of exercises of exactly the same kind with the idea of securing perfect accuracy; as it is also to set long and tedious 'grinds,' the very magnitude of which is a source of alarm and confusion, and not unfrequently arouses disgust for the whole subject. As an *occasional* test of strength in later practice such examples may perhaps serve a useful purpose; but for ordinary exercise, like dumb-bells that are too heavy, they do much more harm than good. Too often it is the teacher's ease, not the child's advantage, which is considered. "In arithmetic, throughout," says Mr. Safford, "time must be taken away from riddles, puzzles, operations with enormous numbers, long sums on the slate or black-board, and given to solid work in the elements of numbers, especially mental work, to extemporised examples, to practical applications of arithmetic which really mean something."

Frequently in the exercises of beginners there is an **absence of any definite arrangement**: the figures are crowded together and badly spaced, and the various parts of the solution are scattered over the paper in patches. It should be made perfectly clear that **much is required beyond merely getting the correct answer**. Where the steps have to be stated in logical form, these should be distinctly marked, and not confused by the insertion of small subsidiary calculations which should be jotted down at the side or performed mentally. Badly made figures are often mistaken, and irregularity in the columns from the figures not being properly placed under one another is also a common source of error.

In some cases it is very useful to **teach the pupils to prove their results**; the exercise is good practice, it is generally interesting to children, and adds to their appreciation of the value of accuracy.

Neatness is of course to be insisted upon, but the elaborate red ink ruling sometimes indulged in is little more than a waste of time.

The **disciplinary measures**, especially those taken to secure that the exercises are honestly and independently performed, **are a matter of the gravest concern in the class practice of arithmetic.** In no part of the teacher's work is neglect followed by more disastrous consequences than in this. So adroit are children in copying from one another, where the inclination to do so exists, that unless it is rendered practically impossible by mechanical arrangements, or the greatest vigilance is exercised, it is very likely to elude the teacher's notice, and may go on to a lamentable extent. **Both morally and intellectually copying has the worst results**; and, if not vigorously checked, it will rapidly spread, like a disease, and soon sap all self-reliance and honest independent effort, as well as destroy all real pleasure in success on the part of a large proportion of the class. Where the habit exists to any great extent, the teacher should look upon himself as almost entirely to blame, and he should never rest until it is completely eradicated.

Copying should always be treated as a grave offence. It is of no use merely to appeal to a child's honour, for the sense of duty is but imperfectly developed in him; but the dishonesty and evil results of the vice should be clearly pointed out, and some punishment will often be necessary to enforce the teacher's injunctions. **Severe punishments alone, however, are by no means a sufficient remedy,** and in many cases not a proper one.

With regard to arrangements for the prevention of copying, if the pupils are in the desks, as they will be generally for arithmetic practice, they should be separated as far as possible, and two sets of similar sums given out so that **adjacent children have different work.** If the class is on the floor in a semicircle, alternate pupils may be made to advance one step to the front, and those which remain in their places to turn right about face, or every succeeding pair may be made to stand back to back. Each child should be taught to attend absolutely to his own business, and to turn over his paper or slate directly his work is completed.

There must be no loitering, for **rapidity is an important element** in good working; and it will generally be found, where the pupil has been properly trained, that **speed and accuracy go together.** In the higher classes, when a rule has been fairly mastered, the pupils may be allowed to work independently from books. They should not have access to the answers, however, nor should these be given until the work is completed. The correction of the exercises should be thorough, not merely the perfunctory marking of a sum as wrong. As a rule, the **pupil should discover his error for himself,** and obtain the correct result before the example is left.

To encourage rapidity, when all the members of a class are working the same examples, some teachers let the **pupils call out the order in which they complete their work,** and enter the corresponding number upon their slates. In many cases, also, it will be found to repay the small amount of time and trouble needed to **record the number of sums worked correctly** by each pupil. It is a **stimulus to effort,** while at the same time it **enables the teacher to see exactly what progress is being made by individuals,** and consequently what special attention is needed. **A time limit is also occasionally useful.**

It will often be necessary during early practice work to **help individuals who have not fully grasped the teaching** in order to prevent their remaining idle. The best way is to lead them to recognise what is needed by means of questions.

A child's difficulties are often very real, and may easily be missed by a careless or inexperienced teacher. This leads him to go into further explanation, or over the whole work again, when what is wanted is to **find out the exact point at which the pupil's endeavour to understand breaks down,** and give just the help needed and no more.

(4) *Good habits of calculation.*—Unless carefully looked after, children readily adopt roundabout and clumsy ways of procedure, or continue to use the detailed modes of statement employed in learning a process, long after these should have given way to more abbreviated forms which allow the mind to pass rapidly from one partial result to another. **Bad habits of calculation once contracted are difficult to get rid of,** and often stick to a person through life. In employing the ordinary processes—especially of addition, subtraction, multiplication, and division—the pupils should be accustomed from the first to good methods of performing the individual steps, and to the **use of as few words as possible in working,** whether spoken aloud or gone over mentally.

In addition for instance, children should be taught to **add by naming the successive sums without mentioning the individual numbers.** Thus, in adding 9, 8, 4, and 6, they would say 9, 17, 21, 27. So in subtraction, directly the pupils can explain the subtracting of a digit from a smaller one above, they should abandon the practice of stating each step in detail. Thus in subtracting 28 from 56, they would say 8 from 16 at once ; and a little later on they should be taught to give the results merely, without mentioning how each is obtained.

Beyond the most elementary stage **counting on the fingers should not be allowed** ; and even there it should be limited, for the most part, to purposes of demonstration and illustration until the sums of any two digits have been fixed in the mind. **Carrying figures should not be written down,** and when the child has made some progress should not be mentioned in passing from one step to another.

There should be **no mumbling or whispering of the figures during work** ; and the small subordinate calculations, often required before a certain step can be stated, should be performed as far as possible mentally.

(5) *The learning of Tables.*—There is no royal road to learning arithmetical tables, but one method of doing this may be much more intelligent and satisfactory than another. **Tables should not be brought before children too soon,** nor should they be given them to be learned by heart without preparation. They should rather sum up and systematise previous work, so that the pupils may both understand and appreciate the value of the orderly arrangement and the grouping of similar results. Where the children are led to **construct the tables for themselves,** after having investigated beforehand the individual truths, such tables will be much more real and intelligible, as well as more attractive, than when simply presented without explanation as a piece of task-work, to be learned by ceaseless repetition only, and without any idea of their usefulness or the mode of their application.

When the nature of a table is clearly understood, the results should be gone over continually in the same order, so long as the repetition, whether simultaneous or otherwise, is not allowed to become wearisome by being carried too far at one time. **Drill of this kind brings in the aid of association, gives a certainty which is rarely secured in any other way, and fixes in the mind a standard form, as it were, to which appeal can be made in case of difficulty.** The associations in the end tend to become completely automatic, so that the results come instantly and spontaneously into the mind ; and so long as there is any hesitation, or any effort is required, the tables cannot be said to be known as they should be.

Facility of application is to be gained by numerous and varied miscellaneous exercises, performed mentally, and embodying the truths which have been learned.

In the case of **addition and subtraction tables** the results should be arrived at by **actual objective demonstrations**, and, as far as possible, they should be taught at the time ; the formal drill will then come in to fix the facts which have been gone over, and to give readiness in reproducing them.

The multiplication table should be the outcome of continued additions of the same numbers, each column being built up and learned before the next is proceeded with. The pupil will thus realise the relationship between addition and multiplication, as well as the saving of time and labour effected by remembering the results once for all, instead of having to stop and calculate each afresh every time it is wanted.

Opinions differ much as to the **advisability of learning the extended multiplication table from 13 to 20 times.** It is a heavy business, and for ordinary pupils who will be but little concerned with calculation afterwards it certainly seems that the time required may be much better employed. For those, however, who are going on to higher mathematical studies, the knowledge of these extended results is useful, and in the end would no doubt save considerable time, especially if such pupils were taught to apply them in the many different ways possible. Still, the application of the method of multiplying such numbers mentally seems to serve almost as well.

For the full illustration of the **tables of weights and measures** the school should possess a pair of scales with a series of ordinary weights, a two-foot rule, a yard measure, a pole, and a 22-yard tape or chain. It is something for the children to know these objects, but it will add greatly to the reality and value as well as to the interest of the teaching if they are allowed to use them, as is so often recommended and so rarely done. In this respect the continental schools are distinctly ahead of us.

(6) *Shortened processes, contracted methods, and approximations.* That mode of working and of stating a sum should be taught first which enables the pupil to apprehend most clearly the principle of the process, and leads him to see throughout exactly what he is doing, and why he does it ; but, when this has been accomplished, the work should be abbreviated to the best form for ordinary practice, and any time-saving device should be adopted which is within the child's power.

Thus, the pupil will soon learn to dispense with unnecessary ciphers in multiplication, and to use the ordinary form of short division, multiplication, and division by factors, the compact mode of working G.C.M. in place of that which takes the form of long division, cancelling, etc. The abbreviated method of performing long division, recommended by De Morgan, will be mentioned hereafter.

If intelligently taught, **children soon learn to recognise when a process is round-about and cumbersome**; and if skilfully questioned will often be able to suggest how the work may be curtailed. **When the time comes for introducing an abbreviated process, the two modes of working should be exhibited on the black-board side by side,** any improvement which the children can devise being made use of and supplemented by the teacher until what is wanted is arrived at. The two processes should then be carefully compared, and the saving effected made clear by questioning, counting the number of figures in each, noting the increased clearness and compactness of the work, and so on.

The **contracted methods** of multiplication and division of decimals, and of finding square and cube roots, are of much value in solving those harder examples which the pupils will meet with when they have mastered the ordinary modes of working and come to the review and completion of these subjects. The saving of time will then be appreciated, and the working will afford excellent practice in accurate calculation as well as encourage the pupils to attack courageously examples which, without such aid, would often be extremely tedious and troublesome. The methods should be thoroughly taught, and when once learned should not be allowed to be forgotten.

The methods of obtaining approximate results, accurate as far as is of any practical value or as the data upon which they are founded will allow, should also receive much more attention than they usually do, especially in the case of advanced pupils who are continuing their mathematical work. In higher applied arithmetic, particularly where decimals are employed, such methods are a great saving of labour, and impress upon the pupils the importance of exercising their common sense, and of examining how far the particulars given will warrant the accuracy of the result.[1]

It does not follow that a decimal is always the more accurate the further it is carried; and to continue the working beyond the point at which the result ceases to be trustworthy, or of the slightest importance, is absurd. Frequently, from the very nature of the data given, they cannot be depended upon beyond about two places, and hence to calculate the answer in such cases to seven or eight places is not only a waste of time, but gives the pupils a wrong notion of what should be aimed at, namely, rational results.

The **use of logarithms should be taught as an extension of higher arithmetic**, and not postponed until the theory of them comes to be considered in algebra and trigonometry. The solution of many of the more difficult examples in such rules as interest and annuities will thus be brought within the pupil's power at an earlier date than is commonly the case.

(7) *Books, etc.*—Arithmetic books should not be put into the hands of the pupils too soon, and it is a mistake to begin with a large and complete treatise at first. **At no stage should books take the place of teaching.** The accounts of the various processes should be given rather in the concise form suited to review than in the full and

---

[1] Many of our best arithmetics give some examples of the modes of arriving at approximate results of necessary degrees of accuracy, and the teacher may obtain much assistance from a little book by Mr. H. St. John Hunter, called *Decimal Approximations*. See also two papers on *The Art of Computation for the purposes of Science*, by Mr. Sydney Lupton, in *Nature*, January 1888.

detailed way necessary for a first explanation. Model solutions should also be inserted, in order that the pupils may have constantly before them good patterns of arrangement. The main use, however, of the books is to **supply well-devised and carefully graduated collections of examples for practice.** They are, in fact, to a large extent, a part of the time-saving machinery of teaching.

There is no lack of excellent **advanced treatises on arithmetic**, those of Brook-Smith, Pendlebury, Lock, Barnard Smith, Marshall and Welsford, and Elsee being among the best. Small and cheap books of examples, covering the ground usually gone over in a year, are also numerous, and will be found very useful for *Standard* work. The defect of many such books is that the examples are not nearly sufficiently varied in form, and the collections of simple and interesting problems are far too meagre.

Arithmetic cards are very useful in preparing for examinations within defined limits, like those of the 'Code.' If properly constructed, they should afford a large amount of diversified and profitable practice of the kind needed; and they may also be often usefully employed as *time-tests*.

III. The Nature of the Teaching to be given in the Early Stages.

The nature of the teaching to be given will depend upon the mental development of the child; and, unless this is attended to, it is impossible that he should perform intelligently what is required of him, or realise in any adequate degree the notions with which he is to be made familiar.

The general order of procedure, according to the nature of that which has to be taught, may be stated in various ways, as **from things to ideas, from concrete to abstract, from intuition to the employment of the reasoning power, from illustrations to principles, from examples to rules, from particular truths to general ones.** In all the earlier teaching of arithmetic, at least, the work is necessarily to a considerable extent empirical and analytical; and it is only when clear ideas and some grasp of principles have been gained that the more scientific and synthetic side of the work can be successfully treated. This however is no argument for its neglect when the right time arrives.

It was Pestalozzi's idea that in learning arithmetic children should follow a similar course to that whereby mankind gradually developed the power to calculate and reason respecting numbers.

(1) *First ideas of number as associated with actual things.*—In the first stage the **senses of the child are active**, and it is to these the

teacher must appeal if he would succeed. Touch and sight must be made to assist each other. By seeing and handling objects the child comes to recognise them as independent things, and to realise the difference between one and more than one. By and by he comes to perceive something of the nature of a unit, and of a group as made up of a number of single things. He thus gradually learns to count, and eventually gains more or less clear ideas of the simpler numbers as representing groups of actual things. **The teaching must be systematic but not formal**; and while real training is being given, the whole must wear to the pupils the aspect of a pleasant pastime.

Objects of various kinds which the children can handle and group for themselves—as toy bricks, counters, beads, marbles, short laths, strips of card, small tiles, tin soldiers, etc.—as well as number pictures and black-board drawings, may all be made of the greatest use. The exercises may be varied in almost endless ways. Much patience and brightness of manner are necessary. The teacher must enter into the spirit of the work himself in such a way as to make it interesting, and while the pupils are guided by suggestions, questioning, and so on, care must be taken not to subject them to undue constraint. They must not be driven, but *led* to exercise their own ingenuity, and to tell all they can find out. Their curiosity will thus be aroused, they will be anxious to know more, and will listen with pleasure and even avidity to what the teacher has to say.

(2) *Realisation of simple abstract numbers.*—The next step is to get the child to pass from the realisation of numbers, as representing groups of things present to sense, to the abstract notions of these numbers stripped of all associations with actual objects. **The passage is a critical one**, and needs to be very carefully made. It has often been pointed out that the best way of accomplishing it is through the use of concrete numbers, as representing groups of things familiar to the children but no longer before them. This recollection of a group of objects helps the conception of the number of them, until eventually the pupils come to realise clearly what is meant by three apples, or five books, in their absence, and are able to represent by a series of strokes or marks upon the black-board the number of things named. By long continued and diversified exercises of this kind the pupils gradually recognise that the numbers are really independent of the things themselves, and may be thought of apart from them.

Any power on the part of the children to realise abstract notions is at first non-existent; but by the presentation of suitable ideas and exercises it will develop gradually and naturally, if no attempt be made to unduly hasten its growth. It is the teacher's business to recognise at every point exactly how far this development has taken place and to arrange his exercises and method accordingly.

(3) *First notions of the addition and subtraction of numbers.*— When the children have obtained tolerably clear ideas of the value of the numbers up to ten, and can count to some distance beyond that point, it is time for them to be made acquainted with the processes of addition and subtraction. **The numbers to be added must be represented concretely, and the results reached at first by counting the actual objects.** By frequent and regular oral practice, not too long continued at one time, the totals of any two numbers less than ten must be gradually fixed in the mind until they can be given at once as a single act of memory. **Subtraction is best introduced, perhaps, by adding two groups of objects and then taking each in turn from the total**; and when once the pupils have clearly grasped the notions of addition and subtraction, the two kinds of exercise may proceed side by side.

The common practice is for the teacher to move too rapidly to more difficult exercises, instead of constantly and thoroughly practising the children in the manipulation of easy numbers well within their power. Some skill is needed to prevent the exercises becoming tedious from continued iteration of the same results, but to an ingenious teacher the frequent change of form necessary will not present any great difficulty.

In the hands of a skilful teacher the ball frame is a very useful piece of apparatus for these early exercises. By its means all the ordinary simple facts to be dealt with may easily be demonstrated. Many different forms of the apparatus are in use, one of the best being that figured by Mr. Fitch,[1] in which the wires after proceeding some distance vertically are bent round horizontally, and the size of the balls is increased from right to left. There is also a ledge at the bottom for the exhibition of small cards on which the figures are printed in bold type.

"The numerical frame has been in use since 1812. It is said that it came from Russia, and that Russia herself borrowed it from China."—(*Compayre.*)

(4) *The representation of numbers by written symbols.*—The pupils will now be prepared for learning how to express easy numbers by written symbols, and will doubtless in many cases have felt the want of some means of doing this when called upon to represent a number by a series of strokes. They should, without any reference to the decimal notation, be taught to write the numbers from 1 to 20; so as to be able to give at once the number corresponding to any

[1] *Lectures on Teaching*, p. 314 (1881).

symbol, or *vice versa*, and also to represent by written figures little sums in addition and subtraction after these have been worked mentally.

The teaching of the symbols, or figures representing numbers, is a much easier matter than training the pupils to conceive the numbers themselves as objects of thought. The oral work will gradually be systematised in the form of tables, the results being in the first instance discovered by the pupils themselves and put upon the black-board. These will be gone over time after time in this and succeeding stages until they are known with certainty and exactness, and instantly come up into the consciousness without effort when wanted.

(5) *Introduction to the principle of the decimal notation.*—When the earlier portion of the work has been properly taught, the principle of the decimal notation may readily be explained, the changes from one denomination to another being fully illustrated objectively in a way shortly to be described. At the hundreds a pause should be made, and the working extended to simple examples in addition and subtraction, the latter, however, being still confined to cases in which each figure in the subtrahend is less than the corresponding figure in the minuend.

In the examples concrete numbers should be used, and the results may be tested as often as is thought desirable by appeal to actual objects. Oral work will be regularly continued, a portion of each lesson being allotted to this, as will also easy exercises in the analysis of simple numbers, so that the children may be led to recognise the various ways in which each may be made up.

(6) *The gradual withdrawal of objective demonstrations.*—As soon as the children have become familiar with the use of concrete numbers, and have progressed sufficiently to be able to grasp in some degree the meaning of abstract numbers and to employ them in their exercises, objective demonstrations and illustrations should gradually be withdrawn as a basis of the teaching, and only used in cases of difficulty, or to make clear some new principle. **The intuitional stage of arithmetic is a very important one, as upon the way in which this is mastered will depend very largely the future success of the pupils in understanding the fundamental processes of the subject, and their power to apply them intelligently.** But, while the children must not be pressed unduly, it is a mistake to keep them confined to such exercises when they become capable of being led step by step to perform easy exercises of thought, and to draw

simple conclusions without any association with actual things to assist them.

The gradual passage from teaching based upon appeals to the senses to that of a more abstract and logical kind needs to be very carefully made, and to connect the two satisfactorily demands a good deal of insight into the way in which the child's mind is expanding, as well as judgment in devising suitable and varied exercises.

Grube's Method.

This is a carefully developed attempt to give the child **full and accurate notions of the nature, properties, and combinations of all numbers up to 100,** by means of thorough analysis and comparison based on well-selected and systematically arranged illustrations. The order of the work is perfectly clear and regular throughout. Each number is in turn made the subject of special teaching of the object-lesson kind, and all the elementary operations of addition, subtraction, multiplication, and division, within the limits of the number, are performed in connection with it before the next number is considered.

"The four processes," says Mr. Soldan,[1] to whom the present writer is very largely indebted for the account of the method here given, "are the direct result of **comparing,** or '**measuring**' as Grube calls it, two numbers with each other. Only when the child can perform all these operations, for instance, within the limits of 2, can it be supposed really to have a perfect knowledge of this number. So Grube takes up one number after the other, and compares it with the preceding ones in all imaginable ways." This systematic 'measuring' and the presentment of it to the eye by arrangements of large dots is characteristic of the whole plan; the leading principle of the work, however, is **full objective illustration.**

The *First Stage* includes the numbers from one to ten, and with this work Grube would occupy a year, about two hours a week being probably the time he intends to be devoted to this subject. Whatever may be thought of the further extension of the method, there can be no doubt that for this early teaching the plan is an admirable one; and that a pupil who had gone through the whole method would be thoroughly equipped for after work, and find many of his difficulties lightened.

[1] See *Grube's Method of Teaching Arithmetic explained,* by Mr. F. Louis Soldan, where the teacher will find a full account of the details, and very numerous illustrations of the mode of applying the method.

The steps of the work with each number are as follows, the first three being exercises in what is called the *pure number* :—

(a) **'Measuring'** (i.e. comparing) the number with each of the preceding numbers, commencing with 1, by means of addition, multiplication, subtraction, and division ; comparison by all these processes being gone through with one pair of numbers before the next is taken up. "In the process of measuring, pupils must acquire the utmost mechanical skill."

> "Since this measuring," says Grube, "can take place either in relation to difference (arithmetical ratio), or in relation to quotient (geometrical ratio), it will be found to comprise the first four rules. A comparison of two numbers can only take place by means of one of the four processes.
>
> The comparison is always to be made by means of objects (as fingers, beads, members of the class, lines, etc.), which represent the numbers dealt with, so that at every step the children reach by actual experience the truth they have to learn.

(b) **Practice in solving rapidly exercises similar to those which have been gone through**, so that the children may acquire readiness, and the knowledge acquired by observation may be thoroughly committed to memory.

> The four elementary processes are combined in various ways, so as to afford extensive and diversified exercise, until the pupils can give at once the final result of several steps taken quickly in succession.

(c) **Finding and solving combinations of the numbers being treated**, in order to bring out more particularly their numerical relations.

> These relations are dealt with by brisk questioning of a very simple kind, the same fact being asked for in a variety of ways.

(d) **Exercises in examples with applied numbers.** These are really little problems involving only the numbers and relationships already known. They are "given to show that applied numbers hold the same relation to each other that pure numbers do." "Copious examples, clothed in the most varied forms, should be solved," and illustrated by means of drawings, strokes, etc.

> Grube lays stress on these exercises, as offering "a good test as to whether the results of the examination of the arithmetical relations of the number treated have been converted into ideas by a process of mental assimilation."

ILLUSTRATION—THE NUMBER FIVE.

i. The Pure Number.

(a) MEASURING.

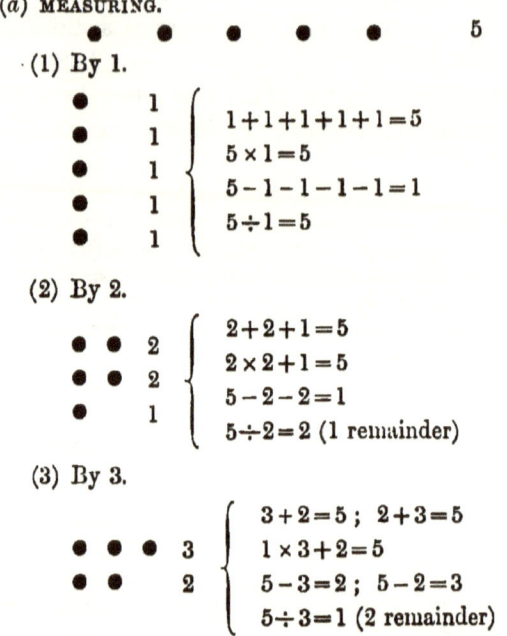

(1) By 1.

$1+1+1+1+1=5$
$5 \times 1 = 5$
$5-1-1-1-1=1$
$5 \div 1 = 5$

(2) By 2.

$2+2+1=5$
$2 \times 2 + 1 = 5$
$5-2-2=1$
$5 \div 2 = 2$ (1 remainder)

(3) By 3.

$3+2=5$; $2+3=5$
$1 \times 3 + 2 = 5$
$5-3=2$; $5-2=3$
$5 \div 3 = 1$ (2 remainder)

(4) By 4.

$4+1=5$; $1+4=5$
$1 \times 4 + 1 = 5$
$5-4=1$; $5-1=4$
$5 \div 4 = 1$ (1 remainder)

"All the solutions of these examples are the result of observation from illustrations placed before the eyes of the class; without them this kind of instruction is worthless."

(b) PRACTICE IN THE RAPID SOLUTION OF MISCELLANEOUS EXAMPLES.

The exercises are made as varied as possible, and the steps are given out as rapidly as the children are able to follow. Thus—

$3 + 1 - 2 \times 2 + 1 - 3 = ?$;
$3 + 2 - 4 \times 4$, take one half of it, $+ 3 = ?$; etc.

The operations are performed in the order indicated, the bracketing power of the multiplication sign being here disregarded.

"It would be a great mistake to drill on the same example until the pupils can remember it. . . . Every example should be a new one to the pupil, and judgment should be appealed to as well as memory."

(c) COMBINATIONS.

The questions and exercises are here directed chiefly to test understanding, and to bring out the relationships of the numbers in different ways.

How many times must I take 1 to get 5? What number is one-fifth of 5? How many must I take from 5 to leave 3? How many must I add to 3 to get 5? I take away 1 from 5, what is half the number? etc.

ii. **Applied Examples.**

These are small problems of a very easy character which the pupil is called upon to solve mentally. For instance: A man has three cows in one field and two in another, how many cows has he in the two fields? Robert is five years old and Willie is three, how much older is Robert than Willie? Five apples were given to three boys, the youngest received one, how many did each of the others get? A boy has three marbles, he loses two, has three given to him, and gives two away, how many has he in the end? etc.

Grube insists upon **frequent and regular review**, upon the lesson being a **training in the correct use of language**, and upon the teacher laying special **stress on the process of solving each example**. *No new number is to be dealt with until the previous one is perfectly mastered.* The children should be encouraged to draw little pictures for themselves in illustration of their work.

Sufficient time must be spent by the pupils in **writing the figures** for them to do this with neatness and despatch. **Each number has an invariable diagram associated with it**, and as this always follows the same order and mode of construction as the preceding ones, the pupils "soon become able to prepare the work for each coming number by writing its diagram on their slates."

In the *Second Stage* we pass to the numbers from 10 to 100, which are to be studied during the second year, as the lessons are now supposed to be longer. The work is substantially of the same kind as for the smaller numbers, objective illustrations (fingers and lines more particularly) being still considered a most important element in the exercises. "**Each new number is not compared with all the numbers below itself, but with the numbers from 1 to 10 only**

Oral comparison by addition and subtraction usually takes the form of counting upwards or downwards by twos, threes, fours, etc." This is continued until the greatest facility is gained. Practice in the rapid solution of miscellaneous examples is to be particularly attended to.

"Comparison by means of addition and subtraction forms, as a rule, the subject of oral work only: comparison by multiplication and division is practised both orally and in writing."

"More time is to be given to the lower numbers, from 1 to 24, and especially to numbers that are of importance in applied examples as representing some division in compound numbers, such as 12, 14, 15, 16, 18, 20, 21, 24, 25, 28, 30, 36, 48, 56, 64, 72, etc."

"**Greatest diversity of expression** and sufficient variety are aimed at in the selection of examples, in pure as well as in applied numbers, so that the pupil may free himself gradually from the uniformity of the elementary diagram and schedule. Applied **examples should not go beyond the limit of qualitative relations taken from daily life with which the pupil is familiar.** This will give him an opportunity of inventing examples himself, and the permission to give an example to the class may be made a reward for that pupil who succeeds in finding the solution of some examples first."

IV. SUGGESTIONS RESPECTING THE TEACHING OF THE RULES.

Where the early stages of arithmetic have been properly dealt with, the more formal teaching of the subject, as far as rules and processes are concerned, will follow naturally. The necessity for **intelligent understanding at every stage** must be kept clearly in view, so that, as far as the development of the child will allow, he may get firm hold of the principles involved, learn to reason for himself, and eventually acquire the power to follow a complex chain of reasoning presented to him. The **teaching will gradually grow more and more methodical** as the pupil becomes disciplined to follow the instruction; and much varied practice, both in oral and written work, will need to be given throughout to ensure the requisite speed and accuracy in calculation.

At certain intervals in the teaching of the rules the **previous work should be thoroughly revised,** and increased attention given on each occasion to the more distinctly scientific side of the subject. Such revision should not only freshen up what has already been learned, and extend the pupil's practice to more difficult examples and problems, but should broaden and deepen his views of the subject and make clear the relationship of the various processes.

The explanation of the rules themselves, and of the ordinary forms in which the calculations should be made, will not here be given; as the teacher should already be acquainted with them, and if not, they may be found in any good arithmetic book.

(1) *Notation and Numeration.*—The kind of preliminary teaching which should be given has already been described. The children will have been taught how to write down the figure corresponding to any number of objects within the limits of the ordinary digits. The main point of the difficulty to be overcome is to give them a clear idea of the principle of the local value of the figures in a number.

In order to illustrate this the teacher may make use of three cardboard trays (one for individual objects, another for groups of ten, and a third for hundreds) and thin strips of wood or card which can be tied together. If preferred, large beads, some loose and others strung on threads in tens, may be used; or the subject may be illustrated in scores of other ways which the teacher may devise for himself.

The trays should be represented on the black-board by means of three rectangular compartments—labelled, as the points are reached in the teaching, ones place, tens place, hundreds place. In these compartments the corresponding figures should be written as the objects or groups are exhibited. The mode of combining things into tens, and the writing of the figure representing them in a special place, should be fully illustrated, and the children should be called upon to write in the proper compartment on the blackboard the figures corresponding to the number of individual objects (less than 10), or of groups of ten, which are shown, each set of things being at the same time placed in its proper tray.

The use of the cipher to show where there are no objects of that kind to be represented should be made clear, as well as the reason for not putting it in front of a number, and the pupils should then be exercised in writing down numbers as the teacher names them, without illustration. At first the numbers should be given out as 1 ten and 3 ones, 5 tens and 4 ones, and so on; but very soon the meaning of the suffixes *'teen* and *'ty* in such words as thirteen, twenty, etc., should be explained, and the mode of giving out changed to the ordinary one. The introduction of the word *units* will give no trouble.

The **passage to numbers of three figures** will be explained in a similar way to that described above for the change at 10, the columns now being separated by lines. The whole should be illustrated objectively, and the pupils thoroughly practised, first on the black-board and then on their slates, in writing down in the proper spaces any numbers up to 999.

When this can be managed readily, the lines may be abandoned, and the three initial letters H, T, U introduced, both on the blackboard and on the slates, to mark the heads of the columns in which the figures are to be written. Beyond this point the teacher should not proceed until the children can write down quickly and correctly any number within the limits, whether containing ciphers or not.

The principle should now be fully understood, and in the succeeding work the teacher should not proceed to thousands, then to tens-of-thousands, and so on, in separate steps, but **introduce the three columns for the thousands at the same time.** These should be considered a group, and it should be made perfectly clear to the children that the numbers are to be written down exactly as before, except that those called thousands will be entered in three places specially set apart for that purpose. These should at first be separated off by a vertical line thus—

Thousands.			Units.		
H	T	U	H	T	U
3	0	4	3	0	4
5	2	1	7	4	3 .

The presentation of millions and thousands of millions should be made in exactly the same way; and the children should be taught not only to write down the numbers but to read them when written. In case of any difficulty, the pupil should be called upon to write down the group of three figures as he has been accustomed to do, and then to transfer it to its proper place.

Suppose, for instance, he has to write 304 millions, and writes 34 millions instead, he should be made to write 304 by itself, and then shown that this number will always be written down in the same way, but if millions, it will be written in the millions places, and so on.

It is astonishing how quickly most children pick up notation and numeration in this way. The introduction of ciphers soon ceases to present any difficulty, and often the greatest interest is evinced in the exercise from the pleasure of being able to perform it with certainty and success.

When the pupils have learned well the relative position of the groups, and can write down readily any reasonable numbers with the aid of the headings, these should gradually be withdrawn, an intermediate step being the substitution of three dots for the initial letters to mark the columns in each group, thus—

| •   •   • | •   •   • | •   •   • |
| 5   6   0 | 3   0   2 | 7   4   5 |

The dots and divisional lines may be retained for some time, until eventually the whole are abandoned, and the vertical lines are broken up into commas, which should continue to be used throughout.

In view of assisting the decomposition of numbers, it is useful to practise the pupils in writing down the parts of a number first, and then to combine them, thus—

$$\left.\begin{array}{r}30{,}000\\5{,}000\\600\\70\\3\end{array}\right\} = 35{,}673.$$

A number may also be written on the blackboard and the class called upon to name the parts separately in order, or to give the denomination of any figure pointed out, as 5 thousands, 7 tens, and so on. The effect of 0 placed to the right of a number as amounting to a multiplication by 10, should be clearly apprehended.

The teaching of notation and numeration will not be carried through all at once, but gradually extended and combined with the working of easy examples in the elementary rules. There is not the slightest reason, however, for taking so long a time over it as is usually taken.

The fundamental idea of our decimal notation seems to have been derived from the primitive habit of counting on the fingers, and the figures are still called *digits*. The device of giving the figures a local value, increasing tenfold to the left, was a very great advance; and towards this the invention of the cipher must have been a most important step. The date of the introduction of the decimal system of notation into Europe is not clear. "Certain it is that the system was in the hands of the Persians and the Arabs before the twelfth century, and that they ascribe it to the Hindoos. **There seems to have been no general use of Arabic numerals in Europe before the invention of printing,** and the works of Caxton do not contain them except in woodcuts. Merchants continued to keep their accounts in Roman numerals till the sixteenth century."—(Sonnenschein's *Cyc. of Education*.)

(2) *Addition.*—To give children the training required at this stage, there must be a judicious admixture of oral and written work. Unless the pupil learns to add rapidly and accurately his whole after work will be hampered; but this is to be secured far more by **systematic practice in adding aloud** than by grinding at long written examples.

One capital means of oral exercise is to put upon the blackboard all the **combinations of a single number with the numbers under a hundred, which produce a certain figure in** the units place.[1] For instance, the following will be the first two series of the combinations producing 5.

1	1	1	1	1	1	1	1	1	1
4	14	24	34	44	54	64	74	84	94

2	2	2	2	2	2	2	2	1	2
3	13	23	33	43	53	63	73	83	93

Each set should be taken in order and gone over again and again by the class simultaneously until the results are known.

Taking each of the digits in turn, and adding the same number continually until a hundred is reached is another useful oral exercise which has already been referred to, and which affords the most ample and varied practice. Thus if we select the number 3 as the one to be added we have

1, 4, 7, 10, 13, 16, 19, 22, etc.,
2, 5, 8, 11, 14, 17, 20, 23, etc.,

and so on, commencing with each digit up to 9.

Ordinary **miscellaneous mental exercises**, mostly of an applied kind, should not be forgotten. The children should also be trained to **add together mentally any two numbers, each of which is less than 100,** until they can give the sum at once. "The shortest method of doing this is not by adding the units, carrying if necessary to the tens, and then adding the tens, but by adding the tens of the one number to the whole of the other, and afterwards adding the units." With advanced pupils it is quite possible to extend this to the adding of two columns at once, which saves half the carrying, but is difficult to manage without considerable practice.

The mode of performing written exercises in addition is quite simple, and needs the careful working of a few examples on the blackboard rather than any elaborate explanation. The **chief point of difficulty is the principle of carrying**, the change of unit being at first a troublesome step for the child. This may, perhaps, best be taught in connection with the analysis of numbers, the child being called upon to go through the work in detail until it is clearly understood.

For purposes of verification the pupil should be taught to add in the opposite direction to that which he at first adopted.

(3) *Subtraction.*—In the earliest exercises each figure of the subtrahend should be less than the corresponding one of the minuend. Beyond this point one or other of the following methods is in use.

(*a*) '**Borrowing and carrying**' plan. Suppose we have to subtract 259 from 345 ; the child in going through the process in detail, would

[1] The teacher may see the combinations for the whole of the digits worked out in Mr. Calkins' *New Primary Object Lessons.*

say—"9 from 5 I cannot, borrow 10, 9 from 15 leaves 6 and carry one to 5, 5 and 1 are 6," etc. The method is completely worthless as an exercise of intelligence, and is now being generally abandoned.

<small>Mr. Fitch says : " Language like this, which simulates explanation and is yet utterly unintelligible, is an insult to the understanding of a child."</small>

(*b*) **Plan of 'equal additions.'** This is based upon the principle that *the difference of two numbers is not altered if the same number be added to each.* Ten is chosen for convenience. Taking the example given above, the child would say—"9 from 5 I cannot, add 10, 9 from 15 leaves 6, add 1 to the next figure in the bottom line, that is 5 and 1 are 6," etc. This is a great improvement on the 'borrowing and carrying' plan in language, and, although artificial, it is intelligible, and not difficult to explain.

<small>Many teachers favour this plan, especially those who have been taught the 'borrowing and carrying' plan themselves in childhood. Mr. Fitch says : " By the 'equal additions' method we do not solve the problem proposed but another giving the same result."

In a **variety of the plan**, the figure to be subtracted is taken from 10, and the result added to the digit in the top line, thus—"9 from 10 leaves 1 ; 5 and 1 are 6, put down 6," etc.</small>

(*c*) **'Decomposition,' 'changing,' or 'natural' plan.** This has grown rapidly in favour of late years, and there can be little doubt that, all things considered, it is much the most satisfactory method to adopt. Taking the same example as before, the detailed working would be— "9 from 5 I cannot, take 1 ten from the 4, change it into ones, and add it to the 5 making 15, 9 from 15 leaves 6 ; there is now 3 in the tens place, 5 from 3 I cannot, take 1 from the hundreds," etc.

The analysis of the numbers is of much importance in explaining the principle. For the first few sums the steps may be separated thus :—

$$345 = 200 + 130 + 15$$
$$259 = 200 + 50 + 9$$
$$\overline{86 = 80 + 6}$$

The first explanations should be gone over slowly. The principle may easily be illustrated objectively by some strings of large beads ; and as an aid to correct working, until the method is completely grasped, the pupils may also be allowed to cross off the figures changed, as in (i) below, or dots may be placed over them as in (ii).

```
      (i)              (ii)
   2  3             .  .  .
   3̶  4̶  5          3  4  5
   2  5  9          2  5  9
   ─────            ─────
      8  6             8  6
```

The great source of trouble is supposed to be changing across a series of ciphers as in the following example:—

$$5,000,004$$
$$3,125,985$$

No doubt this needs careful teaching, but when once the children have been made to comprehend the case with one 0, the rest is rapidly understood; and it is astonishing how soon the children come to grasp the idea, which should be impressed upon them, that when we change across any number of 0's they all become 9's.

A trial of the plan will soon convince the teacher that the difficulties are often much over-estimated, and that when children have been thoroughly taught the principle of notation, the understanding of the mode of working demands no more from them than with any other plan, while it is at least equally rapid in practice. The method, also, is **perfectly in accord with the needs and experiences of the pupils in other parts of arithmetic**—*e.g.* the changing of money, etc., in compound subtraction exactly as in ordinary life, and the analysis of numbers in explanation all through. This preservation of the uniformity and continuity of the child's experiences is of more importance than may at first sight appear.

(*d*) **Plan of so-called 'complementary addition.'** In this the child has to find in each case some number which, added to the bottom figure, will give the corresponding figure in the top line. Thus, with the previous example, in going fully through the work, he would say—"9 and 6 are 15, put down 6 and carry 1 ; 5 and 1 are 6, 6 and 8 are 14 ; " and so on.

This plan was suggested by De Morgan as rendering easier the shortened form of long division. It has recently been brought under the notice of teachers as though it were a new discovery. As a general method of teaching *subtraction* it is certainly not advisable.

Whatever plan of subtraction is adopted, that alone should be taught, not only to the same children, but throughout the school. To change from one to another would utterly confuse the pupil ; and to be expert he needs to **perform the work always in the same way until it grows into a habit.**

THE TEACHING OF ARITHMETIC 351

All methods of subtraction in the end become mechanical in practice, and must do so if the work is to be rapid; but this is no reason why the child should not clearly understand the process he uses, and be able to give a reasonable explanation of it when questioned. The detailed modes of statement given above would not of course be adopted in ordinary working.

Oral exercises should form part of the regular class work. These may readily be given by subtracting each of the digits continuously from all the numbers in turn from 10 to 100. Thus, suppose 4 to be the digit chosen, and 37 the number at which the subtraction is to begin, the class would say 33, 29, 25, 21, etc. Practice should also be given in **subtracting at once numbers of two figures**; the tens of the subtrahend should be subtracted first and then the units from the result.

(4) *Multiplication.*—The children should be made to realise that multiplication is but a **short mode of arriving at the result of a series of repeated additions of the same number**; and that it is made possible only by remembering the series of sums of each digit taken up to a certain number of times. A simple example or two worked out by actual addition, and then by multiplication, will make evident how much time and trouble is saved by fixing these individual results in the mind instead of having to recalculate them every time we need to employ them.

The best way of stating the results having been illustrated, the pupils should construct the tables for themselves as previously mentioned. Each column should be taken up in turn, carefully learned, and practice given in the application of it to the working of examples before the next is proceeded with.

Multiplication by one figure offers no difficulty directly the tables are known, and if notation has been properly taught the pupil will already understand that multiplying by 10, 100, etc., is at once performed by adding the required numbers of ciphers.

In explaining the process of **long multiplication**, it is useful to analyse the first example or two as in (i) below; then to show how the work may be best arranged, as in (ii), and finally to point out the uselessness of the ciphers struck off:—

(i)

$$9764 \times 4258$$
$$= 9764 \times (4000 + 200 + 50 + 8)$$

$$\begin{cases} 9764 \times 8 = 78112 \\ 9764 \times 50 = 488200 \\ 9764 \times 200 = 1952800 \\ 9764 \times 4000 = 39056000 \end{cases}$$

$$9764 \times 4258 = 41575112$$

(ii)
$$\begin{array}{r}9764\\4258\\\hline 78112\\48820\text{Q}\\195280\text{Q}\\390560\text{QQ}\\\hline 41575112\end{array}$$

The children should be questioned so as to find out for themselves the rule for writing down the partial products in their proper places, viz.—*the first figure of each line must be written under the figure used as a multiplier for that line.*

Children frequently find difficulty with **examples where ciphers occur in the middle of the multiplier**, as 5432 × 2007. In any error arising from misplacing a partial product, they should at once be made to give the rule, and then to point out where in their working it has not been followed.

Some teachers advocate, as following the natural order of thought and language, **beginning to multiply with the figure on the left**, so that each partial product commences one place farther to the right than the preceding one. This is consistent with the order in which the partial products are usually obtained in compound multiplication, and it is claimed that the plan has further advantages when the pupil comes to deal with decimal approximations. The rule given above as to the place of the right-hand figure of each partial product must of course be adhered to.

When the ordinary modes of working have been mastered, the children should be taught how to multiply together mentally numbers of two figures, as well as the more useful devices for **multiplying by special numbers** which may be found in books on mental arithmetic. Many numbers may be treated in some particular way, and the pupils should be encouraged to discover easy methods and short cuts for themselves.

The fact should be pointed out that multiplication by several numbers in succession gives the same result as multiplying by the product of the numbers; and this should lead up to multiplication by factors, which is often useful in the compound rules.

For the purpose of testing the accuracy of their work, advanced pupils should learn and practise the process of '**casting out the nines.**' "It is not a complete check, since if one figure were made too small, and another as much too great, it would not detect this double error; but as it is very unlikely that such a double error should take place, **the check furnishes a strong presumption of accuracy.**"[1]

[1] For a complete explanation of the principle upon which the test of 'casting out the nines' is based, as well as of the mode of applying it, see De Morgan's *Arithmetic*, App. II. The student may also consult, with advantage C. Smith's *Treatise on Algebra*, sec. 235.

THE TEACHING OF ARITHMETIC

(5) *Division.*—It may readily be explained to children, with the aid of the black-board, that division really enables us to find out how many times we can *subtract* one number from another. The relation of division to multiplication should also be made clear, and the teacher should explain how the results contained in the multiplication-table may be made use of to assist us in solving examples in division.

It will be found advisable in introducing the actual process to begin with simple cases *worked in the 'long division' form.* The adoption at first of this way of working enables the children to grasp more easily the actual mode of dealing with each step ; and the procedure is in accordance with the principle that a shortened form should not be introduced until the more detailed one has been mastered. The nature of the process may be still further illustrated by **dissecting a few examples on the black-board** and placing the analysis alongside the form of working the child is being taught, as in (i) and (ii) below.

$$
\begin{array}{r}
\text{(i)} \\
7\,)\,45682\,(\,6526 \\
42 \\
\hline
36 \\
35 \\
\hline
18 \\
14 \\
\hline
42 \\
42 \\
\hline
\end{array}
\qquad
\begin{array}{l}
\text{(ii)} \\
\left\{
\begin{array}{r}
42000 \div 7 = 6000 \\
3500 \div 7 = 500 \\
140 \div 7 = 20 \\
42 \div 7 = 6 \\
\hline
45682 \div 7 = 6526
\end{array}
\right.
\end{array}
$$

When the children can work simple sums in the way described, they may be introduced to the ordinary 'short division' form, and shown the saving of time and labour effected by its use.

The **nature of the remainder** should be explained, and at first the figure should be written down slightly to the right of the quotient, with the word *remainder* after it ; later on, the remainder should be written as a fraction, and the meaning of this as expressing *parts of a time* should be explained.

The teacher ought not to find much trouble in extending the mode of working first explained to ordinary cases of **long division.** The analysis of a few examples, as before, will make clear that we really arrive at a final solution by taking the work in parts, dealing with each of these in turn, and combining the individual quotients; though in practice we connect the steps with one another in the most convenient form, and use as few figures as possible to obtain the required result.

The **chief difficulties children encounter in long division** are (1) finding correctly and readily the partial quotients when these are not obvious, and (2) the manipulation of so large a number of figures. The mastery of both these matters is mainly the result of the experience derived from carefully graduated practice. The pupils may be aided, however, in overcoming the difficulty with the partial quotients by being shown how to use the first two figures of the divisor as a trial divisor, and to test the possibility of the division mentally before setting any figure down. Practice will soon make them expert when once the method of procedure is understood.

Some teachers adopt the plan of letting the child construct at the side of the slate or paper a table of all the products that can be required in the example by multiplying the divisor by each of the digits in order. It can then be seen at a glance how many times the divisor is to be taken at each step. This may be useful in the case of long exercises; but, as an ordinary means of working, it increases the number of figures to be written, and does not enable the child any more successfully to overcome the real difficulty.

De Morgan recommended an **abbreviated method of working long division**, in which the multiplication and subtraction are performed together, figure by figure, and the remainders alone written down as each digit is obtained. The process, however, is difficult for beginners, as the performance of the two steps at once confuses them. A large amount of practice is necessary to secure accuracy, and it is doubtful whether, with any but very expert computers, the much increased liability to error does not counterbalance any saving in the way of time and statement.

Division by factors is often useful, and should be well mastered. The change of denomination after each step of the division should be carefully noted, and what each line represents, as well as the nature of each remainder, should at first be written down as below.

```
4 | 67435
7 | 16858  fours  . . . .  3 units remainder
    2408   twenty-eights .  2 fours remainder
```

Complete remainder $= (2 \times 4) + 3 = 11$

This will render easier the explanation how to determine the complete remainder, a point which needs to be thoroughly understood.

THE TEACHING OF ARITHMETIC 355

The pupils should be practised in breaking up numbers into factors, and the difference between *prime* and *composite* numbers should be fully explained. The factors of all composite numbers up to 100 should be well learned, and the children called upon occasionally to write the whole series of primes and factors on their slates. The following few numbers will illustrate how this should be done :—

$$20 = 2 \times 2 \times 5$$
$$21 = 3 \times 7$$
$$22 = 2 \times 11$$
$$23 = \text{prime}$$
$$24 = 2 \times 2 \times 2 \times 3.$$

(6.) *The Compound Rules.*—These are generally interesting to children, and with suitable examples afford good practice ; but more time is often spent over them than is necessary or politic. The teaching will, as a rule, give little trouble, if it be made clear to the pupils that they have only to make use of what they already know in a somewhat different way from that to which they have hitherto been accustomed, and if stress is laid upon the change of denomination. The most difficult points are the multiplication and division by $5\frac{1}{2}$ and $30\frac{1}{4}$ in long and square measure respectively ; and these will need very careful teaching, unless they are deferred, as they well might be, until the pupils have mastered the elementary work of fractions.

A distinct warning should be given that we can add and subtract *like* quantities only ; and that in multiplication and division we cannot multiply and divide by *things*, but only by the *abstract numbers* representing them, and then apply the proper denomination to the result obtained. Thus we cannot divide ten shillings by fifteen pence, but must reduce both to the same kind, deal with them *simply as numbers*, and then interpret the nature of the answer, which is neither shillings nor pence, but so many *times*.

In compound multiplication by several figures it is useful at first to make the class write opposite each partial result what it is they have obtained, as 'ten times the top line,' and so on.

The teacher will need to be cautious in setting subtraction sums in long and square measure. The following is a very much more difficult example for children than may at first sight appear : Subtract 5 sq. poles 30 sq. yds. 8 sq. feet from 6 sq. poles 7 sq. ft. It is not unknown also for a careless teacher to set such a sum as the following: Take 5 yds. 2 ft. 11 in. from 1 pole 1 ft. 3 in., which is arithmetically impossible.

The difference between **ascending and descending reduction** sometimes gives trouble, the children being uncertain whether to multiply or divide. This arises from lack of understanding of the relation of the units employed. The point should be illustrated objectively, and the principle fixed by questioning.

<small>The importance of directing the pupil's attention strongly to the nature of the units he is dealing with, and to the *correct interpretation of the results at every step*, has been several times noted. This is particularly necessary in reduction. Thus, if we multiply 3 tons by 20 we obtain 60 *tons*; but in reducing 3 tons to hundredweights, while we again multiply by 20, the result is 60 *hundredweights*. In both cases the process is the same, but the answers are quite different in kind, and should be arrived at by a different line of thought. In the latter case we ought to reason thus—1 ton contains 20 hundredweights, therefore 3 tons will contain 3 times as many; and to be strictly consistent we ought to multiply the number of hundredweights in a ton by the number of tons; but as the result is the same whichever number we take as multiplier, and it is far more convenient in reduction to multiply by the 20, this order is always adopted. The pupils ought, however, to understand exactly what they are doing.</small>

(7.) *Vulgar Fractions.*—It is not well before commencing fractions to delay the children by teaching the common book rule for finding the G.C.M. of two or more numbers. This is rarely required in ordinary practice, and may with advantage be postponed until the class have mastered the elementary work of fractions and come to the solution of the more difficult examples which will naturally find a place when the subject is reviewed.

All that is really needed at first is to make the pupils familiar with the meaning of the terms *measure, common measure, greatest common measure*, and to explain, and give practice in, the very useful method of **finding the G.C.M. of a series of numbers by decomposing them into their factors.**

<small>Any fractions that the children meet with, which have denominators too large to be readily dealt with in this way, may easily be left until the ordinary rule falls to be taught. These, however, will be but few. The factors of all composite numbers up to 100 will be already known, and these the pupils should by no means be allowed to forget. The ' **criteria of divisibility** ' should also now be taught, and practice given in their application.</small>

Elementary notions of fractions should be imparted before the children come to take up the subject as a special part of their course. Their nature should be thoroughly illustrated objectively by means of rods of wood differently divided by lines, strips of paper with the parts differently coloured, lines on the blackboard, coins, or any other means which an ingenious teacher will readily devise for himself. When the subject is explained in this way, children usually take to the more formal work with interest, and rarely find much difficulty, either in understanding or in applying the processes, until they come to the inversion of the divisor in division.

In this early part of the work the attention of the pupils should be drawn to the following points among others which are perhaps more obvious.

(a) The thorough understanding of the terms *numerator* and *denominator*.

(b) The illustration, by measuring, of the order of magnitude, in such a series as $\frac{1}{2}, \frac{1}{3}, \frac{1}{4}, \frac{1}{5}$, etc.

(c) The equivalence of such fractions as $\frac{1}{2}, \frac{2}{4}, \frac{3}{6}, \frac{4}{8}$, etc.

(d) That with the *same denominator*, that fraction is greatest which has the greatest numerator; and that with the *same numerator*, that fraction is least which has the greatest denominator.

(e) The change from *proper* to *improper* fractions as the values with any denominator pass through *unity*, thus—

Proper Fractions.					Improper Fractions.		
$\frac{1}{4}$,	$\frac{2}{4}$,	$\frac{3}{4}$,	$\frac{4}{4}$,	$\frac{4}{4}$ or 1 ,	$\frac{5}{4}$,	$\frac{6}{4}$,	$\frac{7}{4}$, etc.

(f) That multiplying or dividing both the numerator and denominator by the same number does not alter the value of a fraction.

(g) The value and employment of cancelling.

(h) The fact that we can add or subtract like quantities only, and hence that it is necessary to prepare the fractions where the denominators are not alike, so that they may be so, before the addition or subtraction is performed.

The children must not be pressed on too fast; many easy examples should be solved mentally, and the written work should deal only with simple cases until these can be managed with complete success. Much more real progress will be made in this way than by puzzling over more complicated exercises before the principles have been thoroughly mastered.

The extension of the meaning of the terms multiplication and division, when we come to fractions, must be carefully noted. Thus the pupil has always found hitherto that multiplication means *increase*, and division *decrease*, in the numbers dealt with; but in *multiplying* by a proper fraction the product is numerically *less* than the multiplicand; and in *dividing* by a proper fraction the quotient is always numerically *greater* than the dividend.

This arises, of course, from the nature of fractions. The points should be carefully explained and illustrated by diagrams on the blackboard. The importance of interpreting the results arrived at will also again be apparent. Thus, in multiplying 5 by $\frac{2}{5}$, we have to take 5 two-fifths of a time which is necessarily *less* than taking it once, and the answer is 2 of the *same kind of unit*. Again, in dividing 3 by $\frac{2}{7}$, 3 contains 21 sevenths, and therefore contains 2 sevenths $10\frac{1}{2}$ times, where the quotient is numerically *greater* than 3, but refers to a *quite different unit*; and if we take this new unit (*i.e.* the divisor) into account, it still remains true that divisor×quotient= dividend. Until he reaches fractions the pupil is accustomed to say that a greater number into a less number will not go.; he has now to discover that such a case as $\frac{3}{4} \div \frac{12}{5}$, where the divisor is the larger, is quite a possible operation, and that the result in such a case expresses what *part of a time* the divisor will go into the dividend.

The inversion of the divisor in division is usually the first serious obstacle in the way of understanding which the pupil meets with in his study of fractions ; and many children who work the rule have not the faintest notion of the reason for it. The following notes will perhaps be helpful as showing how the subject may be dealt with, and will still further illustrate some of the points referred to above.

NOTES OF LESSON—DIVISION OF VULGAR FRACTIONS.

I. Change of Unit or denomination.

1. Take a few simple cases, illustrate on blackboard, and question children respecting them until they are able to arrive at the fact, that when we divide one number by another the quotient tells us how many groups, each like the divisor, are contained in the dividend.

The results may be put upon the black-board thus—

Pence ÷12=groups of 12 pence, or *shillings*.
Ounces÷16=groups of 16 ounces, or *pounds*.
Feet ÷ 3=groups of 3 feet, or *yards*.
Units ÷ 7=*groups of seven*.

2. When the general principle has been grasped, fractions should be introduced, and if necessary the points may be demonstrated by means of objects (such as apples, or paper circles, etc.) which can be cut up as required, or by diagrams on the black-board. The fact that division here means separating into parts, each like the divisor, must be made clear.

$1 \div \frac{1}{2} = 2$, each being a *half*.
$2 \div \frac{1}{5} = 10$, each being a *fifth*.
$4 \div \frac{2}{3} = 6$, each being *two-thirds*.
$\frac{6}{7} \div \frac{2}{7} = 3$, each being *two-sevenths*.

A fraction÷a fraction=so many times, or *parts of a time*, the divisor.
Direct attention to change of denomination and sum up.

B. B. Hd. *When we divide a number (fractional or integral) by a fraction, the quotient tells us how many times, or <u>parts of a time</u>, this fraction is contained in the dividend.*

II. **Quotient less or greater than dividend as divisor is greater or less than unity.**

By means of division, in various ways, of some concrete unit known to the pupils (as a shilling), lead them to see the following points :—

1. If we divide a number by another *greater than unity* the quotient will be *less* than the dividend.

2. If the divisor is the same as the dividend, the quotient is unity.

3. If the divisor is *less than unity*, the quotient will be *greater* than the dividend.

The following will illustrate the kind of examples to be used :—
1 shilling $\div 3 = \frac{1}{3}$ shilling (quotient *less*).
1 shilling $\div 2 = \frac{1}{2}$ shilling (quotient *less*).
1 shilling $\div 1 = 1$ shilling (quotient *unity*).
1 shilling $\div \frac{1}{2} = 2$ halves of a shilling (quotient *greater*).
1 shilling $\div \frac{1}{12} = 12$ twelfths of a shilling (quotient *greater*).
Compare the results carefully with one another and deduce B. B. Hd.

B. B. Hd. *If we divide by a fraction, the quotient will be less or greater than the dividend according as the divisor is greater or less than unity.*

III. **How we get the quotient when we divide by a fraction.**

1. If we divide a shilling into twelfths or pence, we get 12 such parts ; that is, $1 \div \frac{1}{12} = 12$, where we have really *multiplied the dividend by the denominator of the divisor*.

2. We multiply the dividend, whatever it may be, by the denominator of the divisor in order to bring the former to the same kind or denomination as the latter.

3. As the dividend now represents the same kind of parts as the divisor, we have only to divide by the number of such parts in the divisor, that is, by its numerator.

Illustrate by a few easy examples. For instance $2 \div \frac{3}{4} = (2 \times 4) \div 3$, *i.e.*, bringing the 2 to fourths by multiplying by 4, we have then 8 fourths to be divided by 3, which $= \frac{8}{3} = 2\frac{2}{3}$. Demonstrate this to sight on the black-board by means of two circles (or squares) divided into quarters, three being marked off in each case by a thicker line. It will be seen that there are 2 three-quarter-pieces, and 2 quarters over, each of which is $\frac{1}{3}$ of a three-quarter-piece. Hence the result of the division is $2\frac{2}{3}$ as before.

When by such work the children have been made thoroughly to understand the point, question so as to arrive at the statement of it.

B. B. Hd. *In dividing any number by a fraction, we multiply by the denominator of the divisor to bring the dividend to parts of the same kind, and then divide by the numerator of the divisor to get the number of groups required.*

IV. Discovery of the Rule.

1. By means of an example draw children's attention to what is actually done, and question from them that this is equivalent to multiplying by the divisor turned upside down.

Thus $2 \div \frac{5}{6} = (2 \times 6) \div 5$ which is equivalent to $2 \times \frac{6}{5}$, where the divisor is simply inverted, and the multiplication sign takes the place of the sign of division.

2. Work an example directly by inverting the divisor, the children dictating what is to be done. Test the accuracy of the work by putting the division in the form of a fraction and multiplying the numerator and denominator of this complex fraction by the same number, namely, the *reciprocal of the divisor.*

Thus, $\frac{5}{6} \div \frac{2}{3} = \frac{5}{6} \times \frac{3}{2} = \frac{10}{8} = 1\frac{1}{4}$.

$\frac{\frac{5}{6}}{\frac{2}{3}} = \frac{\frac{5}{6} \times \frac{3}{2}}{\frac{2}{3} \times \frac{3}{2}} = \frac{\frac{10}{8}}{1} = 1\frac{1}{4}$ as before.

Question for a brief and convenient way of expressing what has to be done until the children arrive at the rule.

B. B. Hd. *Hence the rule—Invert the divisor and multiply.*

(8.) *Decimals.*[1]—The thorough mastery of vulgar and decimal fractions is one of the most important matters in the whole range of arithmetic, and will well repay the time and trouble necessary for its accomplishment. Decimal fractions especially have many most useful applications, and it is in this part of their work that those who have been through their arithmetic will generally be found to be weakest.

It would be unwise, of course, to attempt anything like complete treatment of the subject on going through it the first time; but when the more difficult points fall naturally to be taught, they should not be left until the pupils are thoroughly familiar with them.

In teaching the extension of the common notation downwards to include decimal fractions, this may be dealt with much in the same way as from units upwards, and at first the columns may be marked in a similar manner. It should be pointed out that **if the units place**

---

[1] The introduction of decimal fractions, like that of compound proportion, does not date back further than the sixteenth century.—*Cyc. of Education.*

be regarded as a kind of central position, the places equidistant from it to right and left will have similar names, -*ths* being added to the denomination on the left to form the corresponding fractional denomination on the right. For instance, the third place to the *left* of the units is the thousands place, the third place to the *right* is the thousandths place.

As soon as the places are understood, the fractions should be given out as in the ordinary way: that is, ·0013546 would be called 13546 ten-millionths, and so on.

After the principle of the notation and the meaning of the decimal point have been learned, the effect of moving the point so many places right or left should be explained. The rule as to pointing in multiplication may easily be led up to by the analysis of a few easy illustrative cases.

Considerable practice should be given in reducing decimals to corresponding vulgar fractions, until the relationship of the two is well understood; and before division is attacked the method of reducing a vulgar fraction to a decimal should be taught. The **pointing in division** generally gives trouble. The principle should be mastered before any rule is given. The best plan, perhaps, at first, is to equalise the number of places in the two decimals, and then to view them as the numerator and denominator of a vulgar fraction to be reduced to a decimal. As multiplying the numerator and denominator by the same number does not alter the value of the fraction, both the decimals (the number of places having been equalised) may now be looked upon as whole numbers, and proceeded with accordingly. The pupil will soon learn from experience of this kind to judge pretty correctly where the decimal point will come: the rule may then be explained and formulated.

The great practical value of contracted methods and modes of obtaining approximate results, especially in decimals, has been already referred to.

In dealing with **concrete quantities** of various denominations it is generally advisable to **reduce them to the decimal of the unit of highest denomination.** For instance, in the case of money, it will be found best to convert the sum given into the decimal of £1.

It is not difficult, with a little practice, to *express a sum of money as the decimal of £1* at once with sufficient accuracy for common purposes; and when the pupils have become familiar with the ordinary methods, they should be taught how to manage the reduction. It will be seen that 2s.=£·1, 1s.=£·05, 6d.=£·025, 3d.= £·0125, ¼d.=£·001 (very nearly). Thus £31, 17s. 1½d.=£31·856; for £31, 17s. 0d.= £31·85, and 1½d.=£·006. The most the pupil has to do is to add two or three easy decimals, and very soon the values of many common amounts become known at sight. A sum of money expressed as a decimal of £1 may also be easily reconverted into the ordinary denominations. Thus £19·792=£19, 15s. 10¼d.; for £·775=15s. 6d., and we have £·017 left, which=4¼d.

Similarly, if it is thought worth while, weights may be expressed approximately in decimals of a ton, by noting that 2 cwts.=·1, 1 cwt.=·05, 1 qr.=·0125, 7 lbs.=·0031 (nearly), 2¼ lbs.=·001 (nearly).

Those, at least, who are proceeding further in their studies than the elements of arithmetic, should certainly be made familiar with the **Metric System of weights and measures**, more especially those employed in physical calculations.

With respect to *circulating, repeating,* or *recurring* decimals, little more should be attempted, at first, than an explanation of their nature and the way in which the period is marked. The modes of treating them present a good many difficulties, are of little practical use, and may well be postponed for a considerable time. Even the rule for converting a repeating decimal into a vulgar fraction is often taught without any attempt to show the reason for it; and although it is possible to put the proof in a form which may be understood, the whole subject can be much more efficiently treated when the pupil comes to Geometrical Progression in Algebra.

(9) *Practice.*—This is an easy rule in itself, but is often made unnecessarily tedious and troublesome by being broken up into a series of sub-rules treated independently, and by the nature of the examples set, or the degree of accuracy insisted upon. The general principle may readily be explained by reference to a series of partial payments, each being some definite fraction of the whole amount owing, as 10s. in the £, then 4s. in the £, etc. When the general principle is understood, the pupils may be shewn, by a number of illustrative examples of different kinds, how to apply it to various typical cases, in each of which they should be practised until the mode of working has been mastered.

The exercises will be more intelligently performed if the pupils are at first made to write opposite each line of the working exactly what it represents. Occasionally, too, an example may with advantage be worked a second time by a different series of aliquot parts.

Use should be made of the subtraction as well as the addition of partial amounts in solving examples, where this will result in any gain, as is often the case. For instance in the example, 256 articles at £5 17s. 6d., it is easier to take the cost at £6 and subtract $\frac{1}{8}$ of the cost at £1, than to proceed in the ordinary way.

(10) *The 'Unity Method' and Proportion.*—The so-called 'unity method' of working sums which usually fall under 'rule of three' is very **valuable as a means of teaching children to reason**, and to analyse their work so as to proceed step by step with certainty; but it is **cumbrous in application**, and may easily be carried too far. It should be taught before proportion, but not to the disparagement of the latter, nor as a substitute for it. As a means of quick calculation proportion is by far the more valuable process of the two. It will often be found advantageous to make the children work the same examples both by the 'unity method' and by proportion.

Although frequently neglected, **the nature of a ratio should be thoroughly taught** before anything is said of proportion. The child must clearly grasp the idea that we here compare one quantity with

THE TEACHING OF ARITHMETIC 363

another, not to discover how much greater one is than the other, but to see how they are related as to magnitude by noting how many times, or parts of a time, the one will go into the other. This must be fully illustrated objectively until the nature of the relationship is understood. The mode of expressing the ratio, both by placing two dots between the quantities, and by writing them as a vulgar fraction — which is only another way of exhibiting the same thing in a different form — must be carefully explained.

Throughout, the pupil should look upon the two dots as a division sign, and hence should be in no doubt as to which term of the ratio is to be the denominator in the fractional form.

The terms *antecedent* and *consequent* must be fixed, and the teacher should insist strongly on the fact that **we compare like quantities only**, and that when the two numbers which constitute a ratio refer to things, they must be of the same kind. Attention should also be drawn to the expression of the same relationship by different figures as $\frac{1}{2}$, $\frac{2}{4}$, $\frac{5}{10}$, etc.

The meaning of **proportion as the equality of two relationships expressed by ratios**, the use of the four dots and the corresponding sign of equality, and the terms *means* and *extremes*, will be explained and illustrated. The pupils should then be taught that *the product of the means always equals the product of the extremes*, and shown how to find *any* one of the numbers which constitute a proportion by means of the other three. Sufficient practice to ensure that this is mastered should be given before further progress is made.

The application of the rule to ordinary problems, and the mode of procedure necessary to determine the proper places of the given quantities in the proportional statement, should be abundantly illustrated by examples on the black-board, the pupils being questioned again and again, until they are able to follow the reasoning intelligently and to apply the same method to other cases for themselves.

It should be pointed out that it is **convenient to consider the letter symbol for the required quantity as the fourth term**. The nature of this should be settled, and the term of like kind found and put in the third place. The conditions of the example should then be examined carefully to determine whether the fourth term will be greater or less than the third, and the other two placed in the corresponding order. With beginners it is useful to emphasise the relationship of the quantities when found thus :—

less : greater :: less : greater
5 : 9 :: 13 : x

As we cannot multiply or divide by things, in continuing the work, after having completed the statement, we must treat the terms as abstract numbers, and interpret the nature of the result when it is found. Furthermore, if the terms of any ratio are compound, as sums of money, they must be reduced to the same denomination before we proceed. **The working should not be mixed up with the statement,** but be given below and disconnected from it.

Compound Proportion necessitates the investigation of an increased number of relationships, but the extension is not very difficult if simple proportion is well understood ; for, after the settlement of the third term, each pair of quantities has to be considered in connection with the required result in the way mentioned above, and quite independently of the other ratios. Compound proportion is thus merely the combination in one statement of several sums in simple proportion, the third term being the same throughout.

(11) *Higher Rules.* The higher commercial rules are frequently made to depend, in the first instance, too much upon formal methods, instead of being presented to the pupils as particular applications of principles and rules already known to them—more especially of proportion. An amount of time, too, is often spent over difficult or troublesome examples in compound interest, discount, and the like, which might much more profitably be given to other things.

Whether the pupils are going on with algebra as a subject or not, they should at this stage be taught at least sufficient to make use of letters for numbers intelligible and to give them some glimpse of general reasoning ; as well as enough of the processes to enable them to employ the **methods of simple equations** effectively. These not only furnish an elegant and **powerful instrument for solving problems,** many of which would otherwise be out of reach, but they also afford an **admirable training in analysing conditions and in reasoning upon the facts given.**

Indeed, **a little knowledge of algebra on the part of the pupils is a very great help in many ways,** and will enable the teacher to treat as much of interest and discount as falls within the range of arithmetic, as well the methods of finding square and cube roots, in a much more effective and easily remembered way than without such aid.

Square Root.

The determination in parts of a square root of more than one figure, and the relation of these to the whole square, may easily be illustrated by a diagram on the blackboard, or by a large square card, marked as below. If the letters are beyond the pupils, the figures alone may be used.

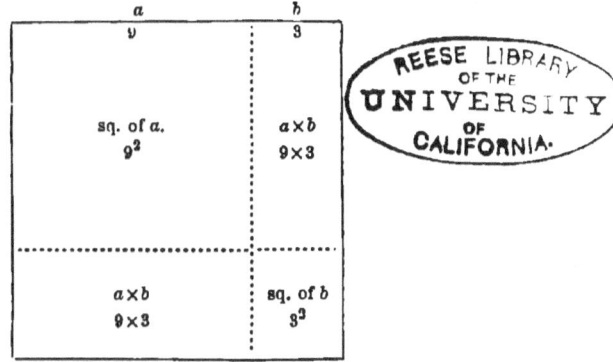

The method of finding the square root of a number may be approached as follows. Take an easy number of two figures and multiply it by itself, as $24 \times 24 = 576$. We know this now to be an exact square, and we have to try and find its root, supposing this to be unknown, bearing in mind what the diagram has taught us. Show that 576 is greater than the square of 20 and less than the square of 30; therefore the first figure of the root will be 2, in the tens place. The square of 20 is 400 and subtracting this from 576 we have 176 left, which will be seen from the diagram to equal $2(20 \times$ second part of the root$)+$the square of the second part of root. Dividing, therefore, by (2×20) we get 4, and subtracting $(2 \times 20 \times 4)$, that is, 160 from 176 we have 16 left, which is clearly the square of the second part of the root. Hence $576 =$ the square of $(20+4)$, that is, 24 is the square root. The process should now be abbreviated, put in correct form, and the rule derived.

Cube Root.

The method of finding the cube root may be illustrated in a similar manner to the above, only in this case a good sized cube of wood should be used. One face should be divided as in the diagram, and the lines should be carried round so that every face is marked in the same way. The cube should then be cut through by a saw along all the lines, so that it may be dissected or put together again at will. If each edge is divided properly into the same two parts it will be found that we have the cube of a, the cube of b, 3 pieces with dimensions $a \times a \times b$, and 3 pieces $a \times b \times b$. That is, we can show objectively that

$$(a + b)^3 = a^3 + b^3 + 3a^2b + 3ab^2.$$

Fixing of the rules for square and cube root.

Pupils who can understand the formulæ for the square and cube of a simple binomial may readily be taught from these to remember the rules for extracting the square and cube roots, and how to recover them at once if forgotten. Thus

$$(a + b)^2 = a^2 + 2ab + b^2$$
$$= a^2 + (2a + b)b,$$

where a is the part of root first found, the expression inside the bracket is the complete divisor, and the first term of this the trial divisor. We must remember, however, that the first figure of the root really stands in the tens place so far as the second is concerned, and hence in taking twice the part of the root already found we must attach a cipher to it.

Similarly, for cube root,

$$(a + b)^3 = a^3 + 3a^2b + 3ab^2 + b^3$$
$$= a^3 + (3a^2 + 3ab + b^2)b,$$

where the expression inside the bracket gives the form of the complete divisor, the first term of this being the trial divisor. This interpreted into words gives the rule. A caution, however, is necessary, as in the case of square root, respecting the local value of the first figure of the root; so that supposing this to be 2, the trial divisor will be 3×20^2, or 3 times the square of the figure itself followed by two ciphers.

For advanced pupils the contracted methods of finding the roots in the case of long examples must not be forgotten.

V. DRAWING.

With the teaching of drawing as a branch of art we are not here concerned, but a few words fall to be said respecting its position as an ordinary subject in the school curriculum. In this connection it is to be regarded as **an instrument or means of education**, and it should be taught for the sake of the assistance it gives in acquiring or setting forth knowledge, not as an end in itself.

From this point of view, drawing is **closely allied to writing**. Both are means of conveying information through the eye, but in a different way, the one being imitative, the other merely symbolic; and though writing has of course the wider range of usefulness, yet drawing is such a serviceable auxiliary that its neglect is a distinct educational loss.

The value of drawing is now almost universally recognised, and for some years past the teaching of it has been made compulsory in the elementary schools of nearly every European nation.

The **object of teaching drawing** in the common school is not to give children a preliminary artistic training, but to equip them for ordinary every-day needs, which are simpler and altogether less technical. The merely ornamental and artistic side of drawing will remain the accomplishment of the few; but **every child should learn to sketch rapidly**, both from sight and from mental realisation of the form, any common object or section which he desires to represent.

Now it is just this very useful power of rapid sketching which children so rarely acquire in the schools. The defect is to be cnarged almost entirely to the **view taken of the subject**, and **to the methods** employed in teaching it; for there can be little doubt that, properly managed, it is possible to train the great majority of children to the amount of acquirement here indicated, as easily as it is to teach them to write.

<small>The lines of the drawing may be faulty in many ways, and as an artistic performance it may be worthless, yet, so long as it expresses what is intended, it is as useful as if it were technically much more perfect. "All attempts," says Professor Laurie, "to introduce drawing into elementary schools, on the æsthetic footing, have been and will be futile, except under peculiarly favourable circumstances."</small>

The great value of drawing to the common run of pupils lies in the fact that it gives them **an exceedingly useful means of embodying ideas or of recording facts of a certain kind**, which words would in many cases very inadequately express, even with a much greater amount of trouble.

The practical usefulness of drawing, however, is by no means the only advantage to be derived from the study; **indirectly it has a very important bearing on the general education of the child.** Drawing a thing brings out many points which would otherwise be overlooked; and, in addition to the knowledge gained, the exercise gradually **accustoms the child to observe carefully** what is brought before him, to note the relative importance of the various parts, to compare one thing with another, to estimate distances and proportions, and to recognise how known elements may be combined into new forms. All this is valuable, and to some extent at least assists in the training of the perceptive faculty, attention, judgment, imagination, and memory. Nor, if the subject is taught as it should be, will the cultivation of the æsthetic and emotional side be wanting, although attended to only in a secondary degree. The **sense of beauty will be aroused**, and the pupil will be led, little by little, to appreciate the pleasure to be derived from the recognition of symmetry, harmony of colour, and orderly arrangement.

Drawing, as it is usually taught in our elementary schools, seems to be a compromise between the art view and the practical view. The exercises are commonly performed in far too slow and laborious a way, details are made too much of, and more stress is laid upon fineness and finish of line than the matter deserves, if we consider the use which the great majority of the pupils will need to make of their attainments.

From the practical side the key to the whole problem is rapid and varied practice, and from this point of view it would certainly be well if much more expeditious performance were insisted upon, and the pupils were taught to draw with much less frequent patching and alteration. They should be led to **keep in mind the design or object as a whole**, to note carefully the relative proportions, to put in the main lines quickly first, and to 'block-in' details before attempting to draw them exactly. No over-elaboration should be allowed, and in this way several exercises might be completed in the time now devoted to one. Finish would suffer to some extent, no doubt, but progress in really essential particulars would be much more rapid.

The **use of the brush**, as well as of the pencil, might be introduced with considerable advantage to a much greater extent than it is at present in schools. The ability to put in an even wash of colour to indicate tint, difference of parts, or variety of material, is often practically useful, and, as children delight in colour, the exercise would be both interesting and recreative in itself, and give an impetus to effort in other directions.

The value, too, of **drawing with the pen point** is not sufficiently appreciated; and advanced pupils should by all means be encouraged to sketch at once in ink in their note-books any diagram or arrangement of apparatus it may be desirable to record.

(1) *Training of hand and eye are both necessary.*—In drawing the child has to *see* and to *produce*. **Eye and hand are equally concerned**, and both need to be specially trained before the required skill can be attained. The *eye* has to be exercised in observing accurately the nature of the lines to be imitated and the angles they make with one another, as well as in estimating their relative lengths and positions. The *hand* has to be disciplined, until it acquires the power to guide the pencil with certainty in any direction, and gains the delicacy of touch necessary to produce uniformly even lines of different degrees of strength.

The systematic training of the hand is generally attended to, but the equally important training of the eye is frequently left almost entirely to chance.

It is impossible for a child to draw what he does not see; and it is true in this connection, as in others, that "the eye sees only that which it brings the power of seeing"—that is, the particulars it has been trained to perceive. Very many of the faults which occur in the drawings of beginners arise simply from **defective observation**; and frequently a pupil, who has considerable skill in the mere drawing of lines, fails from this cause to produce even a passable representation of a copy or an object.

(2) *General nature of the work—Drawing from objects.*—Some educationists advocate that the child should draw exclusively from objects. This is probably an over-statement of the case; but there can scarcely be a doubt that as soon as the pupil can draw straight and curved lines with fair facility, whatever other exercises may be thought desirable it would be of the greatest advantage to him to **draw repeatedly from actual objects.** Nothing will make up for lack of training of this kind.

> Thus Rousseau would always have Emile draw from the object, and keep him "clear of the ordinary drawing-master who would put him to imitate imitations."[1]
>
> Sir Philip Magnus says, in his work on *Industrial Education*, "The pupil must be brought face to face with natural objects. It helps him little or nothing that he can copy *copies*. He must depict *things*. He must look at things till he knows them, and must acquire the ability to represent them on paper. . . The prevailing practice of the best foreign schools is found to fully support the views of educationists as to the importance of accustoming the child as soon as he can use a pencil or a brush to draw from real objects."

Imitation is a natural instinct with children, and in most cases at a quite early age they delight in the free use of the pencil. Even their first crude attempts at depicting objects in which they take interest are a great source of pleasure to them. This pleasure the teacher should do his best to retain; and though systematic instruction and exercises designed for the special purpose of training will be necessary, yet the recreative character of drawing should not be lost sight of. In any case, the **pupils should not be too much hampered by restrictions** and adherence to a routine course.

The drawing of simple and interesting objects of clearly defined and symmetrical form—of which many leaves and flowers are good examples—might be made to alternate with the more formal work of copying designs from the flat. As soon, too, as the mechanical difficulties have been fairly overcome, the children may be set to design simple arrangements, as floral patterns, for themselves. A suitable subject should be exhibited, and each pupil be left free to develop his own ideas, not those of the teacher.

> This is a good discipline, it excites much interest, and many children soon come to display very considerable taste and invention in the exercise. The danger is of making this and other parts of drawing too formal, and too much of the nature of task-work.

[1] See Quick's *Educational Reformers*.

Sufficient of the **principles of perspective** to ensure fairly accurate representation of straight lines and curves in different positions may be taught with the help of the black-board in a few lessons; judicious correction of errors as they occur will do the rest. It must, however, be repeatedly impressed upon the pupil that he has to draw an object *as he sees it*, not as he knows it to be; and this should be illustrated until he realises that the representation will vary with every different position of the observer and aspect of the object. In no part of the work does the eye need more careful training than here; and the child must be taught how to estimate *apparent* distances, and to distinguish these from real dimensions.

(3) *Early Exercises.*—In the earliest stage the exercises should be **preparatory to both writing and drawing.** They should be of the Kindergarten type, so as to afford pleasant and suitable occupation and at the same time to train the hand and eye in the manner required. An ingenious teacher will be able to vary the exercises in numberless ways. The lessons should not be more than about twenty minutes long.

Some teachers set the children to place dots on their slates at equal distances in rows, triangles, squares, crosses, or any easy pattern, and then pass to similar figures bounded by straight lines. Others prefer exercises more distinctly like those of Froebel, and make use of slates or paper ruled in quarter-inch squares. The crossings of the lines form definite points which can be referred to and counted in any direction; and by means of these the pupils learn to draw perpendicular, horizontal, and oblique lines, and to combine these into interesting designs—mostly of a geometrical character—including the straight line print-capitals made in the simplest way.

If books with printed copies were used, the *tracing plan* might be employed with as much advantage in the first stage of drawing as of writing. The same caution would be necessary, however, not to carry the plan too far.

As the children come to use the pencil pretty freely, and some power of estimating distances and direction is gained, mechanical aids, of whatever kind, should be gradually withdrawn. The exercises, whether in imitating copies or sketching objects, will now be of the ordinary kind. After general directions have been given how to proceed in any case, much individual guidance and instruction will be necessary.

The **drawings should be of good size** so that errors may be distinctly evident and suggestions for amendment more readily understood. The **pupil should as far as possible be led to discover for himself what is wrong**, and then shewn how to correct it.

The black-board should throughout be freely used for purposes of illustration, analysis of examples, etc. Many teachers build up a copy a little at a time on the black-board, so that the children can follow what is done step by step. In certain stages of the work the plan has many advantages.

CHAPTER IX.

THE TEACHING OF THE SECONDARY OR SO-CALLED CLASS SUBJECTS OF SCHOOL INSTRUCTION.

I.—GEOGRAPHY.

GEOGRAPHY is a subject which has attracted a good deal of attention of late years, and various efforts have been made, both in this country and abroad, to improve the methods of teaching it, and to present a juster estimate of its real nature and usefulness. As to the main lines upon which the teaching should proceed there is pretty general agreement; but a very wide discrepancy still exists in very many cases between the views of educationists and the common practice of the schools. Old non-intelligent methods of cramming facts —often merely by the reiteration of names in catalogue style from a map—are still rife, and, so long as storing the memory with items of information which the examiner is likely to ask for is looked upon as the chief, if not the sole, end in teaching, they will probably to remain so.

The teaching of geography in Schools has suffered from—

(a) Mistaken views as to the real nature and value of the subject, and the fictitious importance given in the books to matters of little real moment.

(b) The tyranny of examinations, which has in many instances driven teachers to adopt methods which they know to be radically defective as educative influences.

(c) The overloading of both text-books and teaching with uninteresting details, tiresome to learn, and of no possible value as part of a child's mental equipment.

(d) The disparagement and neglect of the subject in favour of others which are supposed to *pay* better, or which tradition has prescribed.

(e) The over-earnest and ill-advised advocacy of some enthusiasts, who would force it into a position of predominance in school to which it has no rightful claim.

I. THE NATURE AND ORDER OF THE INSTRUCTION.

Geography deals with the present state of the earth's surface, and its relation to man as affording him the means of subsistence and in many ways conditioning his daily life.

Properly taught the subject should **expand the child's ideas, and widen his sympathies.** It should enable him to realise in some degree what the earth—with its varied features of sea and land, mountain and plain, river and lake, of forest, desert, and cultivated ground—is like ; and especially the characteristics of those portions with which as a nation we are most immediately concerned. It should give him some conception of what has been done by man to improve or make use of natural conditions for his own benefit, and how the great human family is divided into nations, each with its own government, modes of living, and centres of industry. Further, the study of geography should add to the pleasure of life by arousing an **intelligent interest in natural scenery and phenomena,** and lead to a closer observation of the action of those forces which are at work producing the varied changes of climatic condition and slowly but surely modifying the whole external aspect of the globe.

The kind of geography which should receive most attention in schools, is such as could be learned by intelligent observation in travelling over a district, or still better by residing in it. It should interpret as well as present. The facts should be treated in such a way as to fall naturally into some rational scheme of classification ; and, wherever possible, to exemplify natural laws or form the groundwork of those broader generalisations which give coherence and deeper meaning to what would otherwise be simply a collection of unrelated truths.

The subject may easily be so treated as to be one of the most entertaining and attractive in the whole school course ; and, without going beyond what may reasonably be taught to children, it may be made to yield a **valuable disciplinary training** of the observing powers, the conceptive faculty, and the imagination, as well as afford some exercise in the ordinary processes of reasoning.

<small>The geography taught should not be mere topography ; and still less should the teaching be confined to simply loading the memory with lists of capes, bays, mountains, rivers, etc., and their position on the map, as is often the case. Many details of this kind it will of course be necessary for the pupils to learn ; but this need not, and should not, prevent the subject being taught intelligently, and with clear recognition of what will be most valuable for the children to acquire in the time at disposal. Judgment should be exercised, in selecting the facts, as to which are really useful as information, or necessary to the understanding of some more valuable principle. Not only is the learning of names without ideas corresponding to them</small>

useless both as knowledge and training, but it is apt to delude all concerned into the belief that the child knows what he does not.

The essentials of the physical geography of a district or country must be fairly grasped before the political, industrial, and historical aspects can be properly appreciated. Physical conditions—as natural position and means of communication, climate, the nature of the soil, water supply, and the occurrence of valuable minerals—have always exerted a powerful influence upon the distribution, character, pursuits, and prosperity of a nation. Such connections should always be clear to the teacher's mind, and frequently it will be advisable to point them out to the pupils, or to lead them to discover them for themselves.

The essential unity of nature and consequently of the natural sciences should not be lost sight of by the teacher. No one subject can be properly presented without including much that finds also a fitting place in other related branches of the great whole. Thus, **geography draws material and help from many sources**, and the true understanding of the facts and relationships of which it is made up involves some knowledge of geology, physics, chemistry, natural history, and the like. It is impossible, of course, to teach children even the barest elements of all these sciences, nor is this contemplated, but they may all be usefully laid under contribution to **raise geography above the level of a mere collection of dry bones**; and in many ways the subject may be made to serve as an introduction to the more formal study of science.

Geography also has a distinct use as the **handmaid to history**; and though both subjects have now assumed an importance which prevents our combining them, as recommended by many of the older educationists, yet their many points of contact should be kept in mind.

Two opposite views have been put forward as to the order in which the various topics should be presented.

According to the one plan the **pupil commences with the district in which he lives**, and then passes outwards in an ever increasing circle to the consideration of the county or division, the mother country, the neighbouring countries in order of their proximity, the continent of Europe, the other continents, and finally the earth as a globe.

The other plan begins with the **consideration of the earth as a whole**, then proceeds to a general view of the continents, the fuller geography of Europe, and so on downwards to the mother country and the home district.

As usually stated the question as to which of these sequences should be adopted in teaching geography resolves itself for the most part into whether we should proceed from the parts to the whole or from the whole to the parts. In actual work the order from the district outwards has generally been followed This is looked upon as proceeding from the parts to the whole ; and, as on psychological grounds the opposite sequence seems to be the natural one in mental acquisition, the commonly received order is judged to be at variance with theoretical conclusions. This is not really so ; the confusion arises from the assumption as to what is to be considered the *whole* in such a case.

Thus Professor W. H. Payne says :—" If the consensus of philosophic opinion is trustworthy, there is no basis whatever for this sequence. On the almost uniform testimony of psychologists the organic mental sequence is from aggregates to parts ; so that if the method of presentation is to be in harmony with the organic mode of the mind's activities, the sequence should be as follows: the globe, the eastern continent, Europe;" and so on downwards. The principle doubtless is true enough when properly applied, but the conclusion by no means follows. If by 'whole' is meant the largest aggregate, then according to this one ought to begin with the universe, or at least the solar system of which the earth is but a part. This is clearly out of the question. If, however, by 'whole' is meant *one* of the various aggregates between two extremes, we have to select one which the child is able to realise. This is certainly not the earth, for he has at first not the slightest conception of it. In all cases the principle must be so applied that the *whole* from which the child is to proceed is something which he can at once grasp mentally—and usually through the senses—before troubling himself about the details.

The practical conclusion is that neither sequence should be followed in the way commonly stated. The first whole to the child is the district in which he lives, and which he knows from having seen it repeatedly. From this he must be led to examine the elements of which it is made up, as mountain, river, valley, etc., and through his clear perception of these he must be trained to conceive the general character of a larger whole which can then be studied in its parts.

To proceed from that which is near to that which is farther off is a right principle in teaching geography, so long as that which is near is *known*. The order in which things farther off are to be taken up does not depend upon mere proximity, but upon quite other considerations. The child will pass as readily from the study of the home country to that of a country a thousand miles off, as of one which is only a tenth of the distance ; and before taking up the detailed geography of particular countries he should know something of their relative position and general relationship to one another as parts of a greater whole.

Probably all who have given any serious attention to the subject would agree that **the elementary notions which form the basis of all true geographical teaching must be gained through the senses.** The child must be taught to observe and tell what he has seen, until clear and exact ideas are implanted in the mind, and the terms to be made use of are definitely associated with vivid and accurate conceptions. Unless this is the case the realisation of what is afterwards brought before him in words will be hazy and uncertain; and the learning of geography will be to him rather the memorising of certain statements than the acquisition of any actual knowledge of things. **Both the interest and the value of geography thus depend very largely upon its being made real to the pupil,** especially in the early stages.

Two things are to be kept in view in any method of arranging and teaching the facts; (1) the disciplining and strengthening of the mind, so that the child may the more easily gain further knowledge, for himself, and make ready use of what he has learned; and (2) the intelligent acquisition of such definite information as will be of real service to him in after life. The subject must be so taught as to be stimulating. Much of the teaching given has reference simply to the surface of the map, instead of that of the country; or at most seeks to fix in the mind what is contained in the text-book, and is much too sketchy and mechanical to leave any vivid impression or true understanding.

The **Comparative Method** may be frequently employed with much advantage. The examination side by side of two parts of the globe, where the resemblance is sufficiently striking to engage the attention, and is not merely fanciful or accidental, tends to emphasise the characteristics of both, and to give the mind a clearer grasp of them. In many cases the same general causes have led to similarity of feature or condition, while other more local agents or influences have modified them in different directions. The **points of likeness should be considered before points of difference.**

At first the teaching should be entirely oral, and this should be continued until the elementary notions of geography have been fully realised, and the pupil has gained the power of forming the concepts necessary to render the study of the book intelligent. The temptation to lecture too much must be withstood. Questioning should be much employed throughout, the questions being directed to test the child's grasp of the facts and set him thinking, not merely to secure the repetition of names and fragments of information. Illustrations will also need to be largely used—the modelling of surface features, pictures, diagrams, maps, black-board sketches, and objects, all being frequently employed, and in such a way as to render the teaching as real as possible.

The teaching must not be confined merely to **descriptive lessons**, valuable as these are in their place and when properly managed. The tendency is for them to become loose and rambling, and for the teacher to say too much in his endeavour to 'picture out' vividly. He must know a good deal more than the contents of an ordinary text-book, and must clearly realise what a country is like himself, if he is to succeed in raising any adequate conception in the mind of the child. **Mere empty talk has done much to bring descriptive lessons into disrepute.** If description is to serve its purpose in the best way, it must be **associated with a clearly defined outline of the most essential facts and important conclusions.** A good deal of reiteration will be necessary to fix these in the mind; and it is in this connection that map-drill will find a fitting place.

Modelling is a most valuable aid in the early teaching of geography, and is not nearly so much employed in this country as it should be. Every school should possess a wooden tray of convenient size, with a supply of potter's or modelling clay, and the teacher should not rest until he has become expert in their employment. Experience will soon teach him at what consistency the clay can best be used, how to keep it moist by means of a damp cloth, and so on; and a few wooden tools he can easily make for himself. For some rough purposes slightly damp moulder's sand is preferable to clay, as it can be more speedily manipulated before the class.

Models in which a number of details have to be shewn are best prepared prior to the lesson, unless the teacher is very skilful. **A carefully finished model of the district with the surface coloured to represent the different parts should be made and preserved.**

A collection of **pictures and large photographs of natural scenery** is a very important means of giving interest and reality to the lesson, as well as of getting rid of the conventional and inaccurate notions which children frequently pick up; for instance, of a mountain as a cone, and of a range as a line of distinct peaks. **Children cannot examine good pictures too much.**

The qualities which should characterise **printed maps for use in teaching** have been previously referred to in considering illustrations (see p. 140); and other points of importance in this connection are also there mentioned.

In no subjects perhaps is **rapid black-board drawing** so essential as in teaching geography. In addition to the maps constructed either in front of the class or prepared beforehand, the black-board should be used for outline sketches of scenery or of particular forms, vertical sections, and other diagrams, the enlargement of any special part of the general map, etc. Even poor drawing is better than none.

II. SUGGESTIONS RESPECTING THE METHOD OF TEACHING GEOGRAPHY.

(1) *Early teaching—the elements of geographical description.*—The earliest teaching should be directed to implanting in the child's mind

clear and accurate notions of the various physical features which go to make up the general aspect and configuration of a country, and to acquaint him with the terms used in referring to them.

In connection, too, with these elementary ideas, without attempting anything like formal teaching or complete explanation, many simple ideas may be gradually instilled respecting the conditions upon which these surface characters depend and the forces which are at work in producing them.

The essential feature of the method at this stage is the employment as far as possible of the actual observation of the pupils themselves. The teacher has to arouse their curiosity in the things around them, to open their eyes, to guide them as to what to look for, and to assist them in making out something of the phenomena which lie open to their gaze. **They must be led, not driven to observe.** It has been said that the child learns more real geography in his rambles than from his text-book ; and if he has been taught to use his eyes, this is no doubt to a large extent true.

By far the best plan would be to take the children out of doors and **bring them face to face with nature**, as Pestalozzi did, and as so many since his day have recommended. Unfortunately, however, the present conditions of school work in most cases give but little chance of this, even in favoured districts, and in many town schools it would be impracticable on other grounds. The children too in such schools are at the further great disadvantage that they have few chances even of getting into the country ; and the teacher has to do the best he can for them in the circumstances.

Not only is the **knowledge gained by the pupil's own observation** valuable both for its own sake and in view of after studies, but, what is of still more importance, he is being trained to the habit of noticing carefully the various objects which he meets with, and of trying to make out the dependence of one thing upon another, more especially in the way of cause and effect.

Such opportunities as occur to the teacher of pointing out to the children the actual facts in the field should be made the most of. Any information, too, which they are able to glean for themselves, from observation of the surrounding district, should be allowed to be given in class, and should be worked into the plan of the lesson.

Half-holiday walks under the guidance of the teacher may be made a source of the greatest pleasure to the pupils, and of profit to them in many ways, if the teacher is sympathetic, and will take the trouble to point out to them the numberless objects of interest which may be found if they only use their eyes.

The teaching at this stage should be largely of the conversational kind, and the endeavour should be made to secure clearness and accuracy of impression by a plentiful use of all the available modes of illustrating the subject concretely. A general model of the district should be shewn and the parts named. Each of the more important elements should then be moulded separately by the teacher in front of the class. Such things as a mountain range, a river basin, a lake, and so on, should follow, use being made of such objects as the district affords, to give clearness of conception to these more extended notions.

As far as possible the **forms exhibited should be characteristic ones** so as to serve as types; and if they are taken from examples near at hand, or from actual instances of which pictures can be shewn, so much the better. At first the models should be quite simple, the general character only of that which is represented being given, and details and subordinate features added later on.

Definitions should be the outcome of such teaching as is described above, not precede it; and they should not be given until the pupils have been made clearly acquainted with the things themselves. The statements will then focus what has been learned in the way of information, and help to fix it.

(2) *Relative position—the meaning of a map—representation of the district.*—After pretty correct notions of the district as a whole and of its more marked features have been gained, and these ideas have been extended until the children are able to form some general conception of the geographical elements which go to make up a country, their attention should be called to the **direction, relative size,** and **position** of the objects with which they are familiar.

They should be taught to know the **cardinal points** with reference to the school, to note the place of the sun in the heavens at different hours of the day, and by means of its position at noon to find the south, and hence the other points. After a little experience they should be able to estimate roughly the direction of any distant object, and to realise that the direction will vary with the point of observation. They should also be led to notice the diminution in the apparent size of objects as they are farther and farther removed, as well as their position with reference to one another.

In school the teacher will be assisted by having a **meridian line laid down permanently on the school floor**. A simple descriptive lesson should also be given on the **mariner's compass** and its use in determining directions. A rough **sun-dial** too may easily be set up in the playground, and will prove a source of both interest and instruction.

As a preliminary to the introduction of the map, some notion should be given of what a **ground plan** is, and of how we represent objects and their relative position on it by means of lines and marks. The teacher may begin by drawing on the black-board a plan of a table-top which is within sight of the class, with a few objects upon it; and this may be followed by a plan of the school-room and of the principal articles of furniture it contains, as commonly recommended.

In constructing this plan, the measurements should actually be made, and the results noted down for after use, by the members of the class, under the teacher's guidance. This should be done at some convenient time when class-work is not going on. No great accuracy need be aimed at. All will now take the greatest interest in seeing the plan drawn during the ordinary lesson time, and in contributing their share of the work.

In proceeding to explain the **meaning of a map** the general order of the steps should be as follows :—

(a) The teacher should place before the class **a model of the district** with the vertical relief somewhat exaggerated, and the streams and pools marked by blue colour. The nature of the model as affording a bird's-eye view of the surrounding country should be made clear, and the various objects named by the pupils.

(b) The direction of the **cardinal points on the model** should be indicated, and the fact that we always place the north at the top of any representation should be explained.

(c) A **map of what is shewn on the model** should be carefully drawn bit by bit on the black-board. The pupils should have their attention directed to each part as it is arrived at, and the conventional mode of representing the different features should be explained and illustrated. Frequent questions should be put, and the class should be allowed to offer any suggestions.

(d) When the map is finished it should be **carefully compared with the model** point by point, the names added, and the two then placed side by side horizontally in their proper direction. The essential difference between a map and a picture should also be made clear.

(e) **A map of the district,** either printed or carefully drawn on paper, should now be introduced, and the correspondences between the facts represented on this and on the black-board map and the model should be gone over in order.

(f) Finally, the children should copy the main features of the black-board map as well as they are able on paper or their slates.

It is not intended that the whole of the above should be taken in a single lesson. How much may be dealt with at once will depend upon circumstances. The work may easily be rendered comparatively useless by being hurried. Many teachers, in their anxiety to move forward, abandon the home district long before it has been made to teach anything like all it should.

In case the school is unfavourably situated—as in the centre of a large town—so that the surrounding district affords little of use for purposes of illustration, a model of an imaginary district may be employed and the map drawn from this.

Where no good printed map of the parish is available, the teacher may readily base his map for permanent use on the six-inch map of the ordnance survey; and in any case the school should possess the sheets covering the immediate district, mounted to form a single map, for reference.

When the map of the district has been fairly mastered as a whole, portions of it should be drawn on the black-board on an enlarged scale and in rather fuller detail. As each is gone over, the pupils may be set to imitate it, and the fact that such imitation will often be exceedingly crude need not in the least induce the teacher to give it up. The importance of map-drawing is very great, and skill has to be reached gradually by practice in this as in any other case.

As soon as some facility has been gained, the children may be allowed to attempt the sketching of a map from the model; and later on, when they clearly understand how to represent the facts, they should be **encouraged to attempt the representation of little pieces of the district for themselves from actual observation** out of school hours. This need not startle the teacher; let him try the plan, and he will be astonished at the result.

At first the efforts of the pupils should be confined to filling in a few further details on a very simple outline map they have drawn under the teacher's guidance in class; afterwards the work may be extended to such things as a plan of their own house and garden, the roads leading to their home, a stream course and a few meadows, and so on. They should be shewn how to begin, and how to settle in a rough way the relative position of objects to be represented. Imperfect as the representations may be, the value of the exercise will soon be discovered. The child's love of doing something is called into play, his faculties are being trained, and he is stimulated in such a way that the things he learns are not readily forgotten.

The importance of practising the children in the **estimation of distances, areas, and angles** has several times been mentioned. In this connection many opportunities for exercise will occur, and the pupils may be shewn how distances may be stepped, or roughly estimated by the time taken to walk them, etc. The foot, yard, and mile especially should be made as real as possible. Figures alone have little or no meaning for the child, and, whether they express heights or distances, should rarely be given without some attempt being made to enable the pupil to form some notion at least of what they stand for.

At this stage **frequent practice in the interpretation of a map** is the most important object to be kept in view; and for this purpose, as soon as the map of the district has been fairly exhausted, a good printed map of the county, or of England, with the physical features very distinctly marked, should be made use of, the child being called upon to point out mountains, hills, rivers, coast-lines, and so on. Such terms as island, peninsula, bay, gulf, cape, headland, and other features connected with sea and shore, may now also receive more particular attention. It is the *nature* of the various features and the corresponding *descriptive terms* which have to be taught, not the individual names. The last will find a fitting place later on.

The **power to interpret and make skilful use of the map** is among the most valuable things a child can learn in connection with geography, and one which will prove of frequent use to him in daily life, yet not nearly so much attention is given to it as its importance would warrant. There are comparatively few persons of ordinary education who can read a map well; who, for instance, can find their way readily about it, estimate distances on it from the scale, make out the general 'lie' of the country, and determine something of the nature of the coasts; or, who can tell from the nature of the shading much of the character and shape of a mountain, and from the river lines and their surroundings can form some general notion of the relative velocity of the current in different parts. These, however, and other similar matters may be gleaned from a thoroughly good map.

(3) *The Mother Country.*—Some writers urge that in passing outwards from the district the river-basin should next be taken up; but if the previous work has been properly comprehended, the child will experience no difficulty in passing at once to the consideration of the mother country. This seems on many grounds the most natural and expedient course to pursue.

England then being decided upon, the first thing will be to give the pupils **some idea of the country as a whole**; for instance, the fact that it forms part of a large island, its surroundings, its form and dimensions, the direction of its main slopes, the general character of its surface, the chief regions of elevation, and the great drainage areas with the most important rivers. What is to be aimed at is a **clear realisation of the nature and relation of the broad physical features**, and an accurate and firmly grasped knowledge of their names and positions. The fuller information and details to follow will then find a natural place, and may easily be associated with what has already been learned. If the work is properly carried out, the facts will be presented in a connected, orderly, and rational way, and in proper subordination and perspective.

The essential feature of the teaching is the way in which the facts are presented, so that the children may, as far as possible, see what the country is like, and gain adequate conceptions of the truths to be learned. The best means of illustration, upon which the first teaching should be based, is a model of the country with all minor details omitted, and those points made prominent which are to form the groundwork of the child's knowledge. All that can be learned by observation should be brought out by skilful questioning, and this should be supplemented by so much lecture and explanation only as is necessary to enable the pupils to grasp the broad facts mentioned above. Any lengthy description would here be entirely out of place.

A **clay model**, sufficiently accurate to serve the purpose, is not difficult to mould, if the teacher possesses any skill at all and will take a little trouble; but in default of this, a relief map will answer reasonably well if not too full of detail. If neither be forthcoming, the teacher must fall back upon a map giving a bird's-eye view of the country.[1] An ordinary political map is a very poor and inadequate substitute, and is by far the least helpful mode of illustration. A good black-board map, especially if drawn in coloured chalks, is much to be preferred to this.

When all that the model has to teach has been mastered, a simple physical map with the features distinctly marked, should be placed alongside the model and the two compared. The facts should be revised in connection with the map, and for further teaching the use of the model may be discontinued.

The **physical features** should now be considered in detail **group by group**; and, after these have been well learned, the **political divisions** and other related matters should follow in order. A connecting line of thought should run through each part of the work, and as soon as the lessons dealing with any group of facts have been completed the whole should be carefully reviewed.

[1] Maps in actual relief, and photo-relief maps giving approximately a general bird's-eye view of the country are to be bought, and should be possessed by the school.

The teaching of the details may generally best be given from a black-board map, which should be boldly drawn and display just the information needed at the time. This prevents the distraction arising from having in view a number of things of different kinds at once, and promotes clearness and interest. In some instances the most effective plan is to build up the map bit by bit in front of the class as the various matters fall to be taught; in other cases it should be prepared either in full or in part beforehand. A second black-board should be used for special points and illustrations—as outline sketches or the enlargement of any portion of particular interest—and for summaries of the information given.

The teacher should certainly make use of **coloured chalks**. They add to the attractiveness of the map in the case of children, and are often of much use in assisting them to distinguish clearly the representation of features of different character.

A map with the surface 'slated' so as to take chalk, and with the outlines permanently drawn in white, will often save both time and trouble. The additional information may easily be entered during the teaching, and varied as required.

A simple series of printed maps of England—each illustrating some particular phase of the geography—may also be purchased, and should be at the disposal of the teacher. Where these are not employed for teaching from, they will be found very useful for purposes of comparison, examination, and review.

Map-drawing is an indispensable aid to the learning of geography. It compels attention again and again to the character and relative position of the various objects, and as it appeals to the eye it is **one of the best fixing devices** the teacher can employ. Systematic practice in it should be given, and such matters as the various modes of representing the facts, the use of guides lines, and the value of accurate proportions should be carefully explained and illustrated.

The work should be done under the teacher's supervision, and at this stage entirely from the black-board map. Only such features and names should be inserted as have been previously taught.

Mountain chains should be represented by dark lines of different thickness, according to height, and important peaks by small circles. Hâchures are far too difficult for children to draw satisfactorily, and are useless for rapid sketching. To depict a range like an elongated centipede, as though it were of the same character and height throughout, tends to give a completely wrong impression. The fact also that a river-line should thicken as it proceeds towards the mouth should also be pointed out, and this will still further help to distinguish it from a coast-line.

When the pupils can draw maps with some success they should be **taught to reproduce them from memory.** The exercise is both a capital test of knowledge and a useful means of training

The **use of colours** will give additional zest to map-drawing, and should be allowed as a reward for the acquirement of a certain amount of skill. The children should also be shewn how to make the Italic letters and simple block capitals.

Alongside the more formal teaching of the geography of England, both physical and political, there should be given a series of simple lessons dealing with physiographical relations, more particularly such as are necessary if the nature of the geographical facts is to be at all clearly comprehended. **Field observations should by all means be continued**, and as many of the things as possible shewn on the ground. "One of the commonest and decidedly one of the greatest faults in all teaching," says Colonel Parker, "is the fruitless attempt to force the pupils to think of concepts, that are not in their minds."

Nothing like exhaustive treatment is of course to be attempted, especially at first ; but much of an entertaining and valuable character may be brought within the comprehension of the children by a teacher who knows his business. The **lessons should be progressive**, the subjects being gradually presented in greater fulness as the children become able to understand them ; and the truths brought forward should, as far as possible, lead one into another. Many useful generalisations will be reached in this way.

The following will serve to indicate the **kind of subjects contemplated** :—

(*a*) How **a river** is formed—tributaries—a river basin. The character of a typical river in (1) its upper or *mountain track*, with its torrential flow and fairly straight course ; (2) its middle or *valley track*, its growth in size, and the cause of its meandering, its rapids, its waterfalls, etc. ; (3) its lower or *plain track*, and the formation of a delta. The way in which a stream erodes its channel, and transports the material to a lower level, or to the sea. The formation of gorges, terraces, and valleys. The use of rivers as waterways—importance of good outlets.

(*b*) The nature of a **mountain**—plateau regions with peaks rising from them—true mountain chains—high moorlands and craggy summits—pictures of typical forms.

(*c*) The way in which **lakes** are formed ; how they gradually silt up where rivers or streams flow in. The character of the stream flowing out, its clearness, etc.—how it gradually deepens its channel, and at last drains the lake. Hence Mr. G. K. Gilbert's saying that "rivers are the mortal enemies of lakes."

(*d*) The **sea-coast** and its teaching—wearing away of coasts by the waves—formation of cliffs and caves. The gradual deposit of the material elsewhere, so as to add to the land.

(*e*) **Evaporation and condensation**—formation of **clouds, rain, snow, and ice**—local nature of showers—what becomes of the rain—rise of **springs**.

(*f*) The accumulation of snow on high mountains—the **snow-line**—first notions of the formation and nature of a **glacier**.

(*g*) Different **kinds of soil**, as sand, clay, loam, gravel ; how pebbles are formed.

(*h*) The **rocks** beneath us ; a quarry ; character of granite, sandstone, mudstone, slate · minerals and metals—iron—coal.

(4) *The earth as a whole—distribution of land and water—the continents—simple astronomical relations.* There is a good deal of diversity of opinion as to the order in which the succeeding instruction in geography should be given. Many of the points raised are not at all essential, and may be left entirely to the judgment of the teacher. In order that the child may get a larger view of things, and understand more clearly what is afterwards brought before him, it certainly seems best at this stage to give him some notion of the **earth as a sphere floating in space**, with its surface made up of land and water distributed into large masses, each with its own strongly marked characteristics.

After the first introductory ideas have been given, a **globe should be exhibited**, the position of England pointed out, and the relation of the continents and great oceans made clear. The mode of representing such a globe on a map should then be carefully explained, and the globe itself compared part by part with a map of the world in hemispheres placed alongside it.

The **nature of a profile section** should be explained; and by numerous drawings of this kind on the black-board taken in connection with the map, the general disposition of the highlands and mountain chains of the continents, the great slopes and the chief rivers draining them, should be thoroughly taught. In a similar way the names, positions, and characteristics of the great oceans, the nature of their coast lines, their varying depths, the distribution of the great islands, and the more marked phenomena of polar seas, should be carefully gone over. **The more important facts must be kept well to the front**; and the work must not be hampered by too much detail, or the pupils will fail to grasp the broader truths and generalisations which it is so important they should realise.

In addition to the learning of the more important physical features, attention should be called to such points as the following :—

(*a*) The relative proportion of **land and water** surface, and the massing of the land in one hemisphere—of which England is about the centre—and of the water in the other.

(*b*) The **typical build of a continent**—generally speaking bordered by great mountain ranges running more or less near the coast, higher on one side of the continent than the other, and separated by a great central plain.

(c) The fact that the **steep slope of a coast-range is towards the sea**, and that roughly the higher the range the deeper is the neighbouring ocean.
(d) The **tendency of the great land masses and of peninsulas to run north or south**.
(e) The **height of the land** compared with the **depth of the ocean**.
(f) The dependence of the **size of rivers** on the area of their drainage basins and the amount of rainfall.

As soon as the general nature of the continents has been apprehended, and some notion gained of their comparative sizes, they should be considered singly in greater detail, beginning with Europe. The teaching however should still be confined to the more marked characteristics. The points previously learned should be reviewed, and these as well as the new facts should be distinctly associated with the continent to which they belong. In addition, also, to the broader physical features, the position of the chief countries may be taught with advantage.

The lessons should be conducted with a good map of the continent, and at first this should be carefully compared with the smaller representation on the map of the world. The black-board should also be freely used. A good deal of 'drill,' too, will be necessary, and the importance of map-drawing in this connection should not be forgotten.

Some of the more easily grasped facts relating to the **earth as a planet** may here find a fitting place. Thus, the teacher should explain the rotation of the earth round an axis, what is meant by the poles and equator, the cause of day and night, lines of latitude and longitude and their use in determining the position of places on the surface, the zones of temperature, the revolution of the earth round the sun in the course of the year, and the cause of the seasons. Other more difficult matters should be reserved for a later stage.

All these points will require to be skilfully presented and abundantly illustrated, the explanation of **the diurnal and annual motions of the earth**—about which children have often only the vaguest notions—especially needing much care. **The globe should be in constant use.** For lesson purposes, one which can be readily removed from its stand, and with the surface blackened or 'slated,' so that the teacher can represent on it just the facts he wishes to illustrate, will be found exceedingly useful.

The series of **supplementary lessons on natural phenomena and allied physical facts** should be continued. As far as possible the actual observation of the children should be utilised, and many simple experiments may be brought in to render the teaching more real and interesting.

As examples of the kind of lessons which will be useful at this stage, the following may be indicated :—

(a) **Heat and cold**; the sun as the great source of natural heat; radiation and absorption; the decrease of temperature as we ascend above the surface. The construction of the thermometer and its use in measuring temperatures. Distribution of heat over the earth's surface.

(b) **The atmosphere**—its constituents, pressure, etc. The barometer and its use to measure air pressures; the moisture of the atmosphere; dew, fog, and mist.

(c) The action of the sun on the atmosphere; the **origin of winds**; land and sea breezes; prevalent winds of the British Islands. The winds as distributers of moisture; **rainfall** and how measured; the circumstances on which rainfall depends; what is meant by **weather**.

(d) Rainless regions; the **nature of a desert**; the great deserts of the earth.

(e) **The ocean**; nature and cause of waves; ocean depths; the saltness of the sea.

(f) The nature of **ocean currents**; action of prevalent winds in causing ocean currents; oceanic circulation.

(5.) *The British Empire.*—The geography of the British Empire should be taken up in detail before the geography of particular countries with which England is less intimately concerned. The geography of England already taught should be reviewed, and numerous opportunities will occur, in dealing with other parts of the Empire, of giving many additional facts, and of emphasising others respecting the mother country, more especially facts of political and commercial significance.

The geography of **Scotland and Ireland** should receive full and careful treatment; too often these are very much neglected. The physical facts should be taught first, as a basis, and in other respects the method should follow pretty much the lines already laid down. The work, however, may proceed more rapidly, as the pupils will now be better prepared to realise what is said.

Before dealing with the remaining portions of the Empire, the nature of a colony and of a dependency should be explained; and a general view of the whole should be given, so that the pupils may have a **clear conception of the extent and distribution over the globe of the various parts**, as well as of their names and positions. The influence of the position of England—near the centre of the land hemisphere—and the importance of its oceanic communications should also be pointed out. These points may best be taught by means of a large map of the world on which the portions of the Empire are distinctly marked.

In dealing with the various divisions in order, the map of the world should be kept in front of the class for reference, and all that may be inferred from an inspection of it should first be elicited from the pupils by questioning. The physical and political features should then be taught in connection with a map drawn on the blackboard part by part as required. In addition to the general geography many useful points may be dealt with, and some of them—as the character of the country from an emigrant's point of view, the natural productions, and the interchange of commodities with the home country—should be specially noted.

A **certain amount of drill will be necessary** to ensure the learning of the names and positions. This should come after the teaching, which in no case must be allowed to degenerate into mere 'cram.' The work may be still further fixed by means of **map-drawing**, in which the pupils should be practised until they are able to produce a fairly accurate representation from memory.

As the child has to study for himself, and is liable to forget many of the more or less disconnected statements he hears, a **simple text-book** may be introduced at this stage with advantage. This should not be a mere dry epitome, but it should be concise, and the facts should be associated together in the best way for learning. It should summarise and to some extent supplement the teaching. The more important points should be stated with sufficient fulness for the child to get a clear grasp of them, and they should stand out distinctly from less essential matter.

The book should be studied—not learned by heart for repetition—in connection with a small atlas, which if judiciously chosen will also serve for the pupils to draw their maps from.

The series of **supplementary lessons** should still further extend the children's ideas respecting some of the subjects which have been brought before them, and others of similar character may be added.

The following are instances of the kind of lessons contemplated:—

(*a*) The **crust of the earth**; the nature of a section; disposition of rocks; igneous and sedimentary rocks; suitability of soils for certain crops.

(*b*) The **great races of mankind**. Savage tribes met with in our colonies, and their modes of life.

(*c*) The **food supplies** we get from different parts of the empire; the raw material they send us for manufacture; comparison of the chief productions of the different colonies.

(*d*) Causes which have conduced to **England's greatness**.

(*e*) **Ocean routes** to distant parts of the Empire, and the time taken to reach them. Our ocean-going steamers and sailing ships. Ocean telegraphs. Foreign postage.

(*f*) **Emigration**; the difficulties an emigrant is likely to meet with in the different colonies; struggles of early colonists.

(g) The kind of food used in various parts of the world; the different nature of the dress worn according to climate.

(6) *The detailed geography of particular countries. Astronomical relations of the earth.*—Europe will naturally fall to be taken first. The broad physical features should be reviewed, and the relative position of the different countries with their capitals should be thoroughly learned before they are dealt with separately.

The order of study of particular countries will be that of important relations with our own land, France and Germany occupying the foremost places. The teaching should be such as to arouse interest and induce the children to read for themselves. It should be mainly a vivid presentment of the more essential matters concerning the surface and productions, and the manners, customs, and dress, of the people. It should also emphasise such features as affect the climate of the country, the distribution of its population and industries, its commerce, etc.

The basis of the teaching should be the black-board map drawn in the presence of the children. The map of Europe however should always be at hand for purposes of reference or comparison—for instance the correction of the false impression that Belgium and Russia are about the same size because the teacher's maps of these countries happen to be so.

Intelligence and the connection of the information should be cared for at every step; and vigorous questioning should play an important part in the work. The lesson should be developed as naturally and freshly as possible; it must not be a mere spiritless recitation by the teacher of a catalogue of facts interspersed with passages of map drill.

Many of the details should be left to be got up from the text-book and the atlas, with which every member of the class should now be provided. If the teaching has been well managed, the pupils should have little difficulty in interpreting for themselves the statements of the book.

Useful **comparative lessons** may frequently be given; and any means which the teacher can devise of imparting a personal interest to the work is worth considering. Imaginary journeys are an old device in teaching.

The **countries of the other continents** will be dealt with in pretty much the same way as those of Europe, though events of public interest occurring at the time will often influence the order in which the countries should be treated, as well as the fulness of information given respecting them.

At this stage the **connection of geography with history** should not be lost sight of. Opportunities will frequently occur of giving additional interest to the work, and of teaching many useful points, by reference to the scenes of great events, battle-fields, the birthplaces of remarkable men, and similar matters.

Regular practice in **map-drawing** will now form an essential feature of the work. For 'memory' purposes only a single line of longitude and one of latitude, to fix the general position, should be exacted. When sufficient progress has been made, the general nature of the **common projections** of the globe, and the mode in which maps are constructed, may be explained to the pupils, and they may be shewn how to lay down the lines of latitude and longitude for a map on the 'conical' projection—say of Europe—for themselves.

More **advanced work** should also be given respecting the earth as a planet; and with this may be combined a large number of very useful lessons dealing with the more scientific or physiographical side of geography. The supplementary lessons previously given will have prepared the way for the fuller teaching here contemplated; and by means of experiments and diagrams much of it may be made thoroughly interesting.

Throughout, stress should be laid upon facts which aid in the comprehension of other points, and upon the more important principles and generalisations with which individual facts should as far as possible be associated.

The following will serve to give the teacher some notion of the subjects which may usefully be taken up:—

(a) The **position of the earth with reference to the sun**, the nature of its orbit, and the velocity of its orbital motion; gravitation; the planets; the **relation of the moon to the earth**; the phases of the moon; the tides. The pupils should also be taught to recognise the 'Great Bear,' and shewn how to find the pole star by means of the 'pointers.'

(b) The **refraction of the atmosphere**; twilight; the mirage; the rainbow.

(c) What is meant by the **climate** of a country, and the conditions upon which it depends. The use of the barometer to foretell the weather; isobars, and the nature of a weather chart. **Atmospheric circulation**; trade winds; calm belts; monsoons; the nature of a cyclone; storm warnings. Thunderstorms.

(d) **Action of mountain ranges** in deflecting air currents upwards, and hence causing them to deposit their moisture; snowfields; avalanches; **formation of a glacier**, its surface features, movement, and moraines; signs of ancient ice action. **Polar ice**; icebergs.

(c) **Movements of the earth's crust**; the folding of rocks; the formation of a mountain range; the carving of the range by the action of frost, rain, torrents, ice, etc. Gradual lowering of the surface of a country by **denudation**; amount of material carried down by rivers. Relation of scenery to geological structure.

(f) **Volcanoes**—the crater, ashes and lava, the nature of an eruption, the building of a cone, distribution of volcanoes over the globe. Dead volcanoes, and how they became so. **Geysers** and hot springs. **Earthquakes**.

(g) The form of the floor of the **great oceans**; the Gulf Stream and its influences; other great ocean currents; ocean temperatures. Shore and deep-sea deposits; the building of coral reefs.

The **selection of a suitable text-book** is a matter to which the teacher should give careful heed; and when it is chosen, the pupil will need a good deal of guidance and help if he is to make intelligent use of it. Perhaps the most marked defect of the common run of geography books for children is their scrappiness. Far too much is often included in the way of names and details, and consequently the more important matters are inadequately presented. The style is too much that of a classified catalogue; there is no stimulating element of thought, and no development. The subject is not treated in a way to arouse the child's interest or curiosity; and rarely is any aid afforded him in forming the valuable habit of seeking some logical connection between the points or other helpful mode of association. What is wanted, in short, is not a book of reference, but a book to *learn* from.

In a similar way many of the **atlases** for class use contain far more than the child needs in *learning* the subject; and consequently the main features do not produce that clear and decided impression upon the eye which they should do. The child, too, cannot readily find what he wants, or confine his attention to it, because he is bothered by the presence of things for which he has not the slightest use. The maps should be clearly defined, and well drawn; and the physical features especially should stand out with sufficient boldness to be recognised at once.

(7) *Geography through Reading Books.*—A good deal of useful information may be given and interest infused into the subject by the employment of a series of well written and carefully illustrated geographical reading books. These should be used as supplementary to the oral lessons where the subject is systemically taught. In any case, an important object to be kept in view in the reading is to **train**

the children to acquire information for themselves, by putting them through the process repeatedly in the form they will hereafter have most occasion to use. The formation of good habits of attending to what they read, and of discriminating between truths of primary consequence and merely subordinate matter is necessarily an important consideration. Any needful explanations and illustrations should be given, but these must not be allowed to interfere unduly with the main purpose of the lesson.

The map should always be displayed, and the places mentioned in the book should be pointed out as they are referred to. At certain points in the lesson the pupils should also be thoroughly questioned upon what they have read. Names and a few essential points may also with advantage be put upon the black-board. There is room for a considerable amount of discretion in managing these points well. Properly conducted, the work should stimulate the pupils to read for themselves, and help should be given in the selection of books of travel which may be within their reach in the school collection or in public lending libraries to which they have access.

II. HISTORY.

History is a difficult subject to teach, if anything beyond the memorising of certain groups of facts is aimed at and it is to benefit the pupil as it ought to do. The difficulties do not arise from uncertainty as to how the truths should be presented, or from the complexity of the method to be employed, but are mainly due to the nature of the subject itself, which appeals largely to the imagination and necessitates a vividness and realism of treatment that are not easy to secure. The temptation is great, also, for the teacher to lay stress on the individual facts rather than on their connection and general bearing; and a good deal of judgment is required in settling how far to go, what to emphasise strongly, what to glance over, and what to leave out altogether.

The circumstances of the children, their age and power of comprehension, and the nature of the training the subject may be made to afford at each stage of progress, will all need to be taken into account.

I.—GENERAL CONSIDERATIONS.

(1.) *What history should do for the child.*—Intelligently taught, history should make the child acquainted with the great events which have moulded the lives and circumstances of the people, and made the nation what it is. It should give him information which may be made to serve valuable ends hereafter, strengthen his judgment, and train him to the recognition of cause and effect. Properly managed it will also have a moral effect; it will widen the pupil's view of the conditions of life, "correct the narrowness incident to personal experiences," and shew him that every citizen has a duty as a member of the general body.

The teaching of history, more than of almost any other subject, is apt to be shorn of all its higher and better results by the necessity of keeping examination requirements constantly in view. To secure the mere cram of book facts, for reproduction in the same form at a given time, is not a difficult matter, but it should not be called teaching history.

(2.) *The influence of the teacher's qualifications.*—The effective teaching of history, due regard being had to the needs of the particular pupils under instruction, depends largely upon the personal characteristics of the teacher, and demands, in addition to skill in presenting facts clearly and logically, a considerable amount of knowledge, quick sympathy, and the power of graphic description. There is probably no subject commonly taught in schools on the treatment of which the teacher's views of life, political bias, intellectual habits, and the extent of his reading exercise so powerful an influence as on the teaching of history. Unless he is interested in his subject, and is gifted with the power of picturing out scenes and events, there will be an absence of that picturesqueness and power of vivifying the truths brought forward, which are so necessary to anything like an adequate presentment of history to children, even in its simplest aspect.

It is not knowledge of a text-book merely that will equip a teacher for dealing satisfactorily with history. Without an acquaintance with much beyond the information the pupils are to learn, his teaching will lack its proper background, the facts will be seen out of their true perspective, and he will scarcely be likely to group them in the most effective way for them to produce a clear and lasting impression on the mind.

The teaching of history should not be intrusted to a young teacher. His experience of life, and his grasp of the relationship and importance of the various points, are necessarily insufficient to enable him to do justice either to his subject or to himself, and the result is pretty sure to be a distinct loss to the pupils.

(3) *Guiding Principles.*—In selecting nis material for teaching, and in determining his methods, the teacher will often find it of service to take as his guide certain simple general principles as applied to history, the truth of which is generally acknowledged. These will help to render his work consistent, as well as give definiteness and certainty to his views as to what should be done; while, at the same time, they will prevent him from going astray, and in not a few instances will throw light upon doubtful points of procedure.

The following are some of the most useful of these principles :—

(*a*) **The child should be called upon to learn only that which he can understand.** What is called the philosophy of history, the broad generalisations, critical views, and many of the truths connected with the sociological side of the subject, are almost entirely beyond the grasp of pupils in schools, and should be reserved for a later stage.

(*b*) **The teaching should be such as to exercise the pupil's judgment and reason as far as they are developed.** Nothing is gained, however, by attempting to force these faculties, but rather the reverse; and to make him quote parrot-like the results of judgment in others is a very different thing from leading him to exercise his own.

(*c*) **It is characteristic of a healthy child's nature to delight in action.** Stirring events, such as battles by sea and land, and adventures of all kinds, have a strong attraction for boys. Nor need we hesitate to indulge this natural taste, so long as we keep within reasonable bounds. Whatever may be thought of the value of the 'drum and trumpet' history, as it has been termed, its influence in giving a liking for the subject generally is important, and should be kept in view in school teaching.

'*d*) **The child is far more interested in persons than in things and abstractions.** He is fond of stories, and will listen with avidity to narratives of heroic deeds or personal experience, while he cares little or nothing for discussions about political liberty, the growth of knowledge and opinion, the progress of education, and the like, however valuable we may consider them to be. Surely it is unwise in the teaching of such a subject as history to ignore these natural predilections. Children do not learn readily things which they do not care for—which have no points of contact with their own consequence occurred, should be passed over rapidly, sufficient only being given to bridge the gaps between the parts which need to be more fully treated. Many of the details which often find a place in our text-books, but which are neither interesting nor useful, may without loss be ignored altogether. The **art of leaving out** is especially useful here.

A **knowledge of the dates of accession** will prove of such frequent service to the pupil as a means of localising events in time, not only while at school, but in after years, that they should be thoroughly fixed in the mind. In addition to these, the dates only of really important events should be learned, and that at the time the lesson is given. They should not, however, be allowed to be forgotten, and to prevent this they should be grouped into a scheme and carefully revised from time to time. Any further dates afterwards needed should be associated with these, and the whole kept fresh and ready for use.

A brief and judiciously-selected chronology is indeed most valuable, if intelligently learned; but the matter may easily be overdone; and the memorising of long lists of dates, dissociated altogether from the teaching, is to be strongly deprecated. They are mastered laboriously, many of the dates are never wanted, and the effort to retain so many weakens the impression of the more important ones.

The **treatment of history at this stage should be realistic**, and some points will need to be presented "with almost dramatic force." The **pupils must be put into sympathy with the past**, and the events called up before their minds in such a way that the actors have a living reality, and are not allowed to remain, as is frequently the case, the merest shadows, or nothing more than names. **Vividness of impression is necessary throughout**, but it is not by itself sufficient here. The **teaching must be definite and coherent**, and the facts must be associated in such a manner that they may be most readily and certainly remembered. Too often the information is given in a fragmentary way without connecting links or unity of plan, and there is no proper realisation of the relationship of each individual truth to the rest of the group or to the general subject.

Children tend to care for what they see the teacher cares for, for what he is enthusiastic about; and this is especially so in the case of history. If he is dull and careless, and the teaching pointless and commonplace, even a naturally interesting subject like history may soon be rendered dead, tedious, and distasteful.

(3) *Epoch teaching—the more distinctly intellectual stage.*—In this stage the history should be studied in periods or epochs ; and, as the general sequence of the more important facts will now be known, there is no reason why the teacher should not take the most recent period first, or in fact any period he pleases. Whichever is taken, it should be worked through in order. That which has been previously learned should be thoroughly reviewed, and made the basis of the new work. The extent to which the teaching should be carried will of course depend upon the time at disposal, the power of the pupils to think, and the particular object in view ; but, wherever possible, sufficient information should be given, in addition to what is already known, to secure the mastery of a fairly complete view of the period selected.

Care is as necessary as ever not to bewilder the pupils by presenting more details than they can properly grasp, and not to destroy the prominence of the more essential truths by dwelling on incidental occurrences and unimportant matters.

Each teacher will probably prefer his own mode of treatment ; but whatever plan is adopted, **the guiding principle of the teaching should be to cement the facts into a clear and consistent whole,** so that each new acquisition may be related to the rest and find a natural place in the scheme.

Clear and accurate knowledge of the events as they occurred is important, but this is not all which should be acquired at this stage. The influence of the events upon the people, upon the growth of our institutions, and upon the welfare of the nation as a whole should be pointed out ; and the pupils should also learn something of the use to which the facts may be put—how they may be made to throw light upon the present order of things, to assist in the understanding of the grounds upon which political opinions and practice should be based, and to afford guidance for the future. In a word, **history properly taught should do something towards preparing the pupil for the duties he will hereafter be called upon to discharge as a citizen.**

The work should be more intellectual and have a more distinctly disciplinary value than heretofore. **The pupils should be called upon for frequent exercises of judgment within their power, and be gradually trained to reason upon the facts given.** The strengthening of the judgment, indeed, is one of the most important educative

(b) **Attempting too much in the way of detail,** so that the pupils are confused by the number of points brought before them, and get no clear grasp of the central truths.

(c) **Laying too much stress upon chronology,** as though this by itself were history—the cram of long lists of dates, many of which the pupil will never want, and which he will rapidly forget when learned.

(d) **Giving too elaborate an account of ancient times,** so that the more useful recent history is either never reached, or is hurried over in a quite inadequate way.

(e) **Introducing critical doubts to children**—telling the story and then destroying the effect by shewing that probably this or that part of the narrative is false. This is altogether unsuited to the young, and can scarcely fail to prove injurious.

(f) **Teaching as though impressions alone were needed,** and forgetting to give the solid substratum of facts without which history is practically valueless.

(g) **Presenting matters which the pupil is unfitted to receive intelligently,** neither his previous instruction and experience of life nor his power of judgment being sufficient for the purpose.

(h) **Arousing sham sentiment in the minds of the pupils,** and attributing to the personages of history thoughts and feelings, "which are untrue, and which would be unimportant if true."[1]

The complaint is often made, and in many instances not without reason, that a number of things in history of little use are taught to children, while other things which should be of service to them are omitted; that they learn, for instance, a great deal about the Ancient Britons and the earlier and less important periods, and leave school before they come to the valuable history of the times which more immediately preceded our own.

II. THE THREE STAGES OF HISTORICAL TEACHING.

So far as the school is concerned, the teaching of history appears to fall naturally into three stages, that aspect of the subject being presented in each which most nearly accords with the character and wants of the pupils at the time.

(1) *Earliest teaching—the picture and story stage.*—Anything like formal teaching of history with young children would be entirely out

[1] Mr. Wells in his lecture on *The Teaching of History in Schools* points out that the verse-writers are the great sinners in this respect.

of place ; but it is quite possible, even at an early age, to do much to prepare the way for later instruction of a more systematic kind.

The child's love of stories and pictures should be utilised, his interest and curiosity aroused, and his imagination appealed to. The lessons should deal with what may be called the romantic side of English history, more especially such matters as narratives of personal adventure, accounts of what men did in past times—how they lived, and dressed, and travelled, and fought—deeds of heroism, picturesque descriptions of striking events within the children's comprehension, and the like. There is no reason whatever why these subjects should not be taken in chronological order.

The art of telling a story well is one to be specially cultivated by the teacher if he would succeed in interesting children in history. The teaching should be characterised by vividness of presentment and vivacity of manner. 'Picturing out' should be largely employed, and the lessons made as pleasant as possible. The learning of facts is at this stage of quite secondary importance ; and, though many useful points will be remembered, if the teaching is what it should be, no attempt should be made to thrust upon the pupils either lists of dates or abstracts of the teaching.

Coloured historical prints, several series of which may now be purchased, will be found of considerable use, and in many instances may with advantage be made the basis of the teaching.

Some writers, especially on the continent, would have the teacher begin with stories such as those about the old Greek heroes, or even with fairy tales ; others, as Professor Braun, would begin with "certain preliminary talks" about the family and the surrounding district; then proceed to lessons intended to give children some notion of the lapse of time ; and lastly carry him back rapidly from the present to early times.[1]

(2) *Outline teaching—the information stage.*—The pupil has now to begin the study of history in earnest, the object at this stage being the acquisition of a clear and well arranged outline of the more important facts. This will form a foundation for further study, and at least be useful, as far as it goes, if the pupils end here. The information should be grouped under leading events rather than under monarchs ; and it should be given with increasing fulness as we come down to recent times. Minor points, which have little or no bearing on the general story, and portions of the narrative when nothing of much

[1] Wells—*op. cit.*, p. 26.

consequence occurred, should be passed over rapidly, sufficient only being given to bridge the gaps between the parts which need to be more fully treated. Many of the details which often find a place in our text-books, but which are neither interesting nor useful, may without loss be ignored altogether. The **art of leaving out** is especially useful here.

A **knowledge of the dates of accession** will prove of such frequent service to the pupil as a means of localising events in time, not only while at school, but in after years, that they should be thoroughly fixed in the mind. In addition to these, the dates only of really important events should be learned, and that at the time the lesson is given. They should not, however, be allowed to be forgotten, and to prevent this they should be grouped into a scheme and carefully revised from time to time. Any further dates afterwards needed should be associated with these, and the whole kept fresh and ready for use.

<small>A brief and judiciously-selected chronology is indeed most valuable, if intelligently learned; but the matter may easily be overdone; and the memorising of long lists of dates, dissociated altogether from the teaching, is to be strongly deprecated. They are mastered laboriously, many of the dates are never wanted, and the effort to retain so many weakens the impression of the more important ones.</small>

The treatment of history at this stage should be realistic, and some points will need to be presented "with almost dramatic force." The **pupils must be put into sympathy with the past**, and the events called up before their minds in such a way that the actors have a living reality, and are not allowed to remain, as is frequently the case, the merest shadows, or nothing more than names. **Vividness of impression is necessary throughout**, but it is not by itself sufficient here. The **teaching must be definite and coherent**, and the facts must be associated in such a manner that they may be most readily and certainly remembered. Too often the information is given in a fragmentary way without connecting links or unity of plan, and there is no proper realisation of the relationship of each individual truth to the rest of the group or to the general subject.

<small>**Children tend to care for what they see the teacher cares for**, for what he is enthusiastic about; and this is especially so in the case of history. If he is dull and careless, and the teaching pointless and commonplace, even a naturally interesting subject like history may soon be rendered dead, tedious, and distasteful.</small>

(3) *Epoch teaching—the more distinctly intellectual stage.*—In this stage the history should be studied in periods or epochs ; and, as the general sequence of the more important facts will now be known, there is no reason why the teacher should not take the most recent period first, or in fact any period he pleases. Whichever is taken, it should be worked through in order. That which has been previously learned should be thoroughly reviewed, and made the basis of the new work. The extent to which the teaching should be carried will of course depend upon the time at disposal, the power of the pupils to think, and the particular object in view ; but, wherever possible, sufficient information should be given, in addition to what is already known, to secure the mastery of a fairly complete view of the period selected.

Care is as necessary as ever not to bewilder the pupils by presenting more details than they can properly grasp, and not to destroy the prominence of the more essential truths by dwelling on incidental occurrences and unimportant matters.

Each teacher will probably prefer his own mode of treatment ; but whatever plan is adopted, **the guiding principle of the teaching should be to cement the facts into a clear and consistent whole,** so that each new acquisition may be related to the rest and find a natural place in the scheme.

Clear and accurate knowledge of the events as they occurred is important, but this is not all which should be acquired at this stage. The influence of the events upon the people, upon the growth of our institutions, and upon the welfare of the nation as a whole should be pointed out ; and the pupils should also learn something of the use to which the facts may be put—how they may be made to throw light upon the present order of things, to assist in the understanding of the grounds upon which political opinions and practice should be based, and to afford guidance for the future. In a word, **history properly taught should do something towards preparing the pupil for the duties he will hereafter be called upon to discharge as a citizen.**

The work should be more intellectual and have a more distinctly disciplinary value than heretofore. **The pupils should be called upon for frequent exercises of judgment within their power, and be gradually trained to reason upon the facts given.** The strengthening of the judgment, indeed, is one of the most important educative

2 c

results which the study of history should secure; but, as already pointed out, the faculty must not be forced.

Direction, interpretation, and help in many ways the teacher will need to give: but if the pupils are to be benefited beyond merely acquiring information they must be **made to think for themselves.** To simply import into their minds the judgments of others, as so many additional facts, is, as Mr. Currie calls it, "mechanical instruction of the worst sort," and fosters the mischievous habit of quoting phrases and opinions without any real understanding of them.

Alongside the more specific teaching of history, there should also be given a **supplementary series of lessons** upon such subjects as the nature of the constitution; how laws are made; how taxes are levied; how justice is administered; the advance of civilisation; the growth of individual liberty; the duties, rights, and privileges of citizens; the progress of industries and manufactures; etc. Other matters, as the story of inventions and discoveries, the development of our navy, and the growth of large towns, may also be made of much interest; and Mr. Fitch makes the capital suggestion of lessons on **great books**—"their influence on history, and their value as indicative of the thought and intellectual movement which produced them, and as helping to shape the thought or the policy of the age which succeeded."

The **higher aspects of historical study** need a trained and acute intellect, and are clearly quite outside the province of the common school. To attempt to teach philosophic views, or what may be called the science of history, in any real way, is **altogether impracticable in the case of children,** and can only lead to failure, if not to something worse. To expect the pupil, for instance, to generalise in the way required is to expect an impossibility; he has neither the mental grasp necessary to marshal the array of facts, nor the insight and logical power needed to make the induction. We cannot force him beyond his power, but we may arouse in him the desire to know, give him much of the material necessary, and at least secure that he shall have nothing to unlearn if ever he is able to proceed further.

III. SUGGESTIONS RESPECTING THE METHOD OF TEACHING THE SUBJECT.

(1) *The ordinary course of lesson procedure.*—The general method of teaching history will be that of an ordinary oral lesson. The **basis of the method should be vivid lecture,** but this must by no means be exclusively employed. The facts selected for treatment should be dwelt upon with sufficient fulness for the pupil to get clear and accurate notions of them, and the more important should be emphasised and reiterated as often as is necessary to secure their being firmly retained. The teacher must tell the story as if he had been an eye-

witness; it must be to him a living reality, not a mere recitation of dead facts. There must be no perfunctoriness, no rambling hither and thither in an aimless sort of way, and no vagueness. It must be remembered also that the connection of the details is a vital point.

The minds of the pupils must be kept active, and throughout comprehension should be tested by rapid and searching questioning. At convenient points in the lesson, what has been gone over should be recapitulated, all misconceptions put right, and a concise and well-ordered **summary of the more essential truths put upon the black-board.** This digest of the teaching should be copied by the class and thoroughly learned—whether as home lessons, or in any other way, the teacher will best be able to decide.

Any mode of illustration—as pictures, diagrams, coins, etc.—which is available, and which will assist in giving reality to the child's conceptions, should not be disregarded. The **map should always be kept in view** during the lesson, and the positions of all places mentioned should be pointed out. Important battles should be illustrated by sketch-plans on the black-board; almost any good text-book will now supply the materials.

It is not a waste of time to make a **clay model of an important battle-field**, with strips of differently coloured paper to represent the disposition of the troops of the contending armies. Teaching by illustrations of this kind is always attractive and leaves a lasting impression upon the mind of the child.

(2) *The use of the comparative method.*—The tracing of analogies is not only a useful exercise in itself, but in the teaching of history it may be made especially advantageous, and should form an integral part of the method from the time the study of the subject is seriously taken up. **One series of events often supplies a commentary on another**, and to compare the two is a very considerable aid to the understanding of both. In this way the present may often be called upon to assist in the explanation and interpretation of the past, and one period may be made to throw light upon a second. The causes, also, which led to some great change, and the conditions which governed its development, will be more clearly comprehended if they are compared with the action of similar influences in another age. "Without the ever active spirit of comparison," says Mr. Currie, "the past is separated from us by an impassable gulf; it has little reality and interest for us."

The employment of the method should of course be progressive, the points compared being at first few and simple, and gradually increasing in number and difficulty as the child becomes able to apprehend more complex relationships. Success depends upon the skill with which the teacher arranges the facts, the suggestiveness of the teaching, and the clearness and certainty with which the pupils can be made to grasp the points of similarity and contrast brought forward. As far as possible they should be led by adroit questioning to discover these points for themselves.

(3) *The emotional element—moral teaching.*—There is a human and emotional element in history which can scarcely fail, if the subject is properly presented, to have considerable influence, quite apart from the mere acquisition of information; and if this is absent, the teaching loses no inconsiderable share of its ultimate usefulness.

The subject should be so handled as to have a moral as well as an intellectual value for the pupil. It should arouse enthusiasm for what is good and noble, inculcate respect for what is great, and lead to the recognition of our duty and responsibility in social and political matters. Many opportunities will occur of instilling incidentally valuable practical lessons bearing on conduct or belief; of illustrating and enforcing the importance of law and order; and of stimulating the growth of such moral qualities as generosity, endurance, magnanimity, faith, and the like. "History," says M. Compayré, "teaches patience to those who lack it, and hope to those who grow discouraged."

There must, however, be no dry moralising. The subject should be so treated that the moral influence is felt, not merely talked about. Only occasionally will it be necessary to formulate distinctly the lesson to be learned, or to draw out any direct application of it.

In this connection **biography has an important bearing**, beyond the fact that the history of the nation is inseparably bound up with the lives of its great men. The attraction of the personal element for children has already been pointed out; it is something they can understand, and does much to prevent the teaching of history becoming a series of cold abstractions. Children are great hero-worshippers; and it is well they should be so, for the contemplation of noble deeds —of what men did and suffered in old times to uphold the right and advance a higher ideal of life—is one of the most potent influences in the formation of character. "There is no kind of sermon," says Professor Blackie, "so effective as the example of a great man." It is the teacher's business to see that this valuable means of moral training is not neglected.

Nor must the **cultivation of patriotism** be overlooked. The teaching of history fails in an important respect if it is not given in such a way as to foster in the child a love of his native country. He ought to feel elation at its progress, its greatness, and its victories; and the more he knows of its story, and realises what a glorious inheritance it is which has been handed down to us from our forefathers, the more firmly rooted will become the determination to defend its liberties and keep its honour untarnished.

An important aid towards implanting this patriotic feeling is the **learning and singing of national songs and songs of home life.** " The songs of a country are the truly national part of its poetry, and really the only poetry of the great body of the people." It is impossible, perhaps, to estimate the effect upon the people of England of such songs as *Rule Britannia, Home Sweet Home,* and many another similar ballad; but it is equally impossible not to believe that it has been great. "I knew a very wise man," said Andrew Fletcher a couple of centuries ago, "that believed that if a man were permitted to make all the ballads, he need not care who should make the laws of a nation." Lord Wharton boasted that by *Liliburlero* he had "rhymed King James out of his kingdom."

(4) *The use of a text-book.*—In spite of the division of opinion among teachers respecting the advisability of using a text-book in teaching history, there seems no good reason against its proper employment in all stages except the introductory one, while there are some distinct advantages. Very much, however, will depend upon the nature of the book selected, and upon the way in which it is treated by the teacher.

Wherever oral teaching is given, the book should play a secondary part, its main use being to give definiteness to the pupil's impressions, and to enable him to revise his work as often as necessary. The previous teaching will thus guide him as to what to spend his strength upon, and give any necessary explanations and illustrations. As a further aid, Mr. H. C. Bowen would have the books carefully marked.

The **bad mode of using the book** is to have so much learned by heart, or got up by the pupils, without any help being given towards its comprehension, and then for the teacher merely to test this knowledge by a few questions. All that should be gained by contact with the teacher's mind and by his influence is thus lost.

(5) *Supplementary reading, etc.*—**Any teaching of history is defective which does not induce the children to read for themselves;**

and no amount of exact knowledge of facts, got up at the teacher's dictation, will make up for the lack of any liking for the reading of history apart from school work.

The sooner the pupils can be brought to the point of reading intelligently for themselves such histories as that of Macaulay the better. Broader reading later on will correct the defects and mistakes of any particular book, but at least **the first histories read should be interesting ones.** Nor should the reading be confined to histories properly so called; and, in addition to the national ballads already referred to, **historical plays and poems** and **historical novels** may all be laid under contribution. The more important of the shorter poems should be learned, and to these might be added a few selected historical scenes from Shakespeare. To know by heart such poems as *Chevy Chase*, Campbell's *Battle of the Baltic*, Macaulay's *Armada*, Ayton's *Edinburgh after Flodden*, Tennyson's *The Revenge* and *The Charge of the Light Brigade*, is a gain from the point of view of literature as well as of history and of patriotism.

> It has been objected to the reading of historical novels, that in many the history contained is only of the slightest value, and that the boy "reads the tale and skips the history." But after all the aim is not so much to instruct as to interest him; and, if the tale is well told, it will appeal to him "in a way which no mere historian can," and give a picture of the times that will not soon be forgotten. The pupils should be aided in the selection of books, and induced to read a few of the best thoroughly rather than to scamper over many.[1]

(6) *The teaching of History through Reading Books.*—Historical reading books should be well within the child's power so far as language is concerned, conceived in a congenial spirit, and brightly and pleasantly written—in fact quite unlike either a summary or a manual. Of late years a number of carefully graduated and attractively illustrated series have been published, many of which have at least the merit of being readable as well as instructive.

When history is not taken up as a distinct subject of study, such a series should by all means be employed. It must be remembered, however, that while the practice will have a beneficial effect upon the reading, the main object is to give the pupils some acquaintance with the outlines of *English history*, and to introduce them to books

---

[1] Mr. H. C. Bowen has published a classified and descriptive catalogue of some five hundred *Historical Novels and Tales*, which the teacher will find of much service in selecting books for reading or for a school library.

as a means of acquiring information. Hence the language of the lessons should be somewhat easier than that of the ordinary reading books, and, in order not to distract attention from the sense, **only absolutely necessary corrections should be given.**

The reading should be accompanied by any really helpful comments, explanations, and illustrations; but **any lengthy digression is to be avoided.** The pupils should also be thoroughly questioned at definite stages, and the chief points put upon the black-board. Properly carried out, the work should give the children the power and the will to continue their reading further with intelligence and profit.

III. ENGLISH.

One of the most astonishing things in connection with the education of our own country is the neglect which the study of English has suffered in the past—a neglect that still obtains to a considerable extent, especially in our secondary schools.

Few perhaps would now deny the importance of a correct knowledge of the mother tongue; but we are not yet quite rid of the **idea that English is unworthy of serious study** for purposes of training and discipline compared with such a language as Latin, and that as a matter of knowledge all that is practically useful may readily be picked up incidentally.

"That a language should be, as English is," says Mr. Woodward, "so apt and clear in expression as to commend itself to almost universal use, so wide and full in its capacity to voice high thought and deep feeling as to win universal acclaim, and yet should be comparatively worthless for the training of its own children, is a paradox that falls below the dignity of a tolerable joke."

So long as the teaching was confined to formal grammar, introduced often at far too early an age, and the child was set merely to memorise definitions, minute classifications, rules, and lists of exceptions from a book, much might justly be urged against the subject. Taught, however, in a more liberal spirit and by better methods, English is surely deserving of full recognition, and no child ought to pass through our schools without having received such training in the subject as his years will allow. Unfortunately we teach nothing now-a-days that is not to be examined upon; and liberal teaching demands liberal examination.

I. GENERAL CONSIDERATIONS.

(1) *The general scope and object of the teaching.*—**Knowledge of language is one of the conditioning elements of the growth of mind**; and

the more specific teaching connected with the subject may be made to contribute to the education of the child much that is of peculiar value, if the various parts of the work are introduced at the right time and in the right way. In any adequate treatment of language in schools, the **nature of the work to be done** is for the most part as follows :—

(*a*) **To provide suitable material for the mind to work upon,** and make the pupil acquainted with something of what has been thought by the great writers, and of what has been done to develop clear, forcible, and beautiful forms of expression.

(*b*) **To train the understanding** of the pupil, so that he may not only grasp readily the thought underlying language, but gain such a knowledge of words and literary forms as will enable him to employ them with accuracy and facility.

(*c*) **To discipline the intellectual powers**—more particularly of conception, judgment, and reasoning—so that they may be strengthened and rendered more acute by exercises in abstract thought which the formal study of grammar should give.

(*d*) **To extend the pupil's vocabulary and attach precise meanings to words,** so that vagueness of idea and uncertainty and looseness of thought and expression may, as far as possible, be prevented. This is especially necessary in the case of children who come from uneducated homes.

(*e*) **To cultivate the taste, and develop in the pupil some appreciation of what is highest and best in literature,** so that enjoyment may at least be within his reach, and he may recognise what a pleasant world here lies open to him.

Almost every subject taught in school may be made to contribute something towards the ends aimed at, especially in the way of **incidental training** and corrected practice in the use of words. Such opportunities as occur should be used, but not abused so as to interfere injuriously with the subject in hand.

The more specific teaching of English, however, falls to be given as instruction in *grammar, composition,* and *literature* ; and the gain to the pupils will depend very largely upon what is selected to be taught under these heads, and upon the way in which the subjects are handled. The practical everyday needs of correct speaking and writing are to be cared for at all points.

THE TEACHING OF ENGLISH 409

Some linguistic training is certainly necessary, and for the great majority of pupils, especially those attending our elementary schools, the benefits to be derived from such training are only available through the systematic study of English. In any case, a thorough grounding in the understanding and use of the mother tongue, and some knowledge of its grammatical technicalities, should certainly precede the learning of any other language; though it is not necessary that the latter should be postponed until the former is completed. No other language has the same fulness of meaning for us, or the same power of evoking feeling as our own, and none is of such importance as a subject of school study.

If the pupil is to use his native language with grace, force, and facility, he must be taught. Without the power to use it correctly, and to understand readily the literary forms of it employed in books, he is hampered in all his studies, as well as in the expression of his thoughts. "Great command over the resources of language," says Mr. Fitch, "is only another name for great command over the ideas and conceptions which make up the wealth of our intellectual life."

(2) *The relation of grammar to language.*—Much confusion has arisen as to what should be taught, and as to the method of teaching it, from viewing grammar as though it were a body of laws imposed upon language from without, to which it must necessarily conform.

The principles of grammar, in so far as they are true and helpful, have been arrived at from a study of the language; and in the case of a living language they express what the usage is, not what it necessarily must be. The language grows, and consequently changes from age to age, and, where needful, the grammar has to be modified in accordance with these changes. Thus the language of Chaucer is no longer the language of to-day, nor will the same grammar apply to both.

No doubt the introduction of printing and the spread of literature minimised these changes, while the general uniformity of spelling and usage which resulted tended to stereotype our grammar to a considerable extent; but the changes still go on, though at a less rapid rate. Grammar conditions the usages of the time, and though its tendency is "to freeze the current of natural speech" it never succeeds in doing this.

Thus, Professor Max Müller says: "The grammarian must beware of attempting to exercise summary jurisdiction over speech. His function is to register the usages of the present, not to legislate for the future."

We are sadly impeded in the teaching of our own language by two circumstances: first, that our early grammars were fashioned on Latin models, and that to a large extent later ones have had to follow suit; second, that when the teaching of English came to be recognised it was naturally taught on the same lines that Latin had been.

In a dead language, like Latin, both the language and its grammar have become fixed; and the language may properly be taught through its grammar. But in a living language like English, which is the child's mother tongue, he has learned to speak it—and if he comes from an educated home, to speak it with fair correctness—without any help from an explicit knowledge of grammar.

The order of the teaching, therefore, is language first and grammar second; and the grammatical rules should be arrived at by an examination of a large number of words and sentences with which the pupil is already familiar.

It should be recognised, also, that much besides grammatical knowledge is needed to secure the correct use of English. As Mr. Fitch remarks, "the faults which occur in speech, the confusions, the clumsy constructions, the misuse of words, and their mispronunciation, are not, as a rule, sins against grammar, properly so called; and are not to be set right by learning English accidence or syntax."

(3) *The grammatical element in English.*—**Modern English is a highly composite and analytic language**; that is, only in comparatively few cases does it express shades of meaning or relationship by inflexions. In this respect it differs greatly from Latin, which is one of the most completely synthetic or inflected languages. Hence the misfortune of having had English grammars framed as though the language were a highly inflected one.

Such inflections as exist in our language—except in the case of a few words not yet completely naturalised—have come down to us from old English, and are simply relics which have escaped the analytic tendency. Hence some, who view grammar merely as an account of inflections or syntactical forms, would have us believe that English is almost without grammar.

Grammar has to do with the forms of the language, whatever those forms may be. "To deny that English has a grammar is to deny it law and order." There may be poverty of inflectional changes, but there is no poverty of means to express every needed variation of thought. The relations exist, although in a form which is more subtle and less visible to the eye than in the case of a synthetic language; and surely grammar has as much right to deal with these substituted modes of expression as with the original modification of words for the same purpose.

"Inflections," says Professor J. W. Hales, "are not the soul of grammar. A language does not become ungrammatical when it passes out of that stage. The main function of grammar is concerned with more perpetual and imperishable matters. That function ceases only when a language loses its articulateness—ceases to serve for the expression of thought—ceases to be language. However deficient the English language may be in case-endings and such grammatical landmarks, in power of expression, in delicacy, in elasticity, in versatility, it is not deficient. So that it presents endless varieties of that grammatical culminating subject of inquiry and interest—the sentence."

(4) *The value and use of Grammar as a subject of school study.*— **The clear and connected thinking necessary to grasp the formal or abstract notions of grammar is a most important discipline of one side of the mind,** and the most essential thing in the teaching of English grammar is sacrificed, if the subject is not so handled that this discipline may be secured. **Grammar is usually the child's first introduction to abstract thinking**; the process is difficult, and needs the most careful graduation and adjustment to the pupil's powers. It is clear the effort must not be demanded of him before the development of his faculties is sufficient to enable him to perform with some measure of success what is required of him. It cannot be too strongly insisted upon that **the child's mind must grow naturally**, and that forcing it by methods which strain but do not strengthen the faculties cannot but prove injurious.

The book study of merely technical grammar has often been regarded as though it were everything in the teaching of language; and the importance of a full vocabulary, of an exact knowledge of literary forms and the meanings of words, as well as of literature itself, has been very largely overlooked.

Grammar systematises the pupil's knowledge of the forms of language, gives point and force to corrections, and guides his judgment though it does not limit it. It puts what he knows into a convenient form for remembering; and renders truths respecting language explicit and definite, which without its aid would remain implicit and indistinct.

"The laws," observes Professor Seeley, "may be new in form to him, but their substance he is familiar with already; he recognises their truth as soon as they are stated, his memory furnishes him with illustrations of them."

The study of grammar brings into relief and fixes in the pupil's mind a standard of accurate usage, fortifies him against the influence of bad examples by making clear the nature of wrong forms and faulty constructions, and thus renders his imitation of what is correct more certain, rapid, and intelligent. Properly taught, the subject should deepen his observation and insight, induce him to examine language forms closely, and lead him to discover for himself something not only of the relationships of words, but also of the niceties and refinements of speech.

It is often said that the importance of the study of English grammar is very much overestimated. It is not the importance of grammar properly taught which is exaggerated, but of an unintelligent knowledge of *the grammar book*, acquired by a wrong method simply for examination purposes, and of the practical value of mere grammar rules as a means of securing correct speaking and writing. "The direct operation and use of grammar rules," says Mr. Fitch, "in improving our speech and making it correct can hardly be said to exist at all."

This old Lindley Murray notion about grammar being "the art of speaking and writing the English language with propriety" still vitiates much of our teaching. It is true, as shewn above, that English grammar has indirectly a distinct practical use, but this is quite secondary to the main disciplinary purpose of the teaching. **Grammar gives us certain criteria whereby we may test the correctness of language**, just as logic gives us criteria for testing the soundness of reasoning: but we do not learn to speak and write correctly by acquiring a knowledge of grammar, any more than we learn to reason consistently by studying logic. In both cases accuracy is far more due to the daily influence of good example and to frequent correction than to formal rules.

(5) *The age at which formal grammar should be begun.*—**Most authorities are opposed to beginning the study of formal grammar early.** Thus Professor Bain would not have it begun before the completion of the tenth year, and Professor Laurie not until a year later. To some extent the time will depend upon the development of the child and the way in which the subject is taught; but, as a general rule, there can be no doubt that the view given above is the correct one, and that at least technical grammar should certainly not be commenced before the necessary power has been gained to grasp the subject intelligently.

II. THE TEACHING OF ENGLISH GRAMMAR.

(1) *General principles and outline of the method.*—Many of our errors in the teaching of English are due to the fact, already pointed out, that **we have confused the method of learning the living mother tongue with the means to be adopted for securing the mastery of a**

dead language. Grammar, especially, is taught far too much as a series of dogmatic statements about language presented in book form; and the information required is too often poured into the child's mind in a way which renders it distasteful and prevents its being properly understood. It is this vicious system of teaching English grammar, as though it were a set of forms, rules, and lists of exceptions to be memorised, which has been mainly instrumental in bringing the subject into disrepute.

There is, again, **too much grammar for grammar's sake,** rules being multiplied and elaborate classifications given which have no practical value, either as a means of education or as useful knowledge; while, as to method, we are still not clear of what has been called "the old senseless routine of nomenclature learning and the droning march of the parsing class."

It has often been correctly pointed out that children are easily interested in realities of almost any kind, and that **words properly treated are real**; but the matters with which grammar is more directly concerned are abstract and difficult to grasp, and consequently are very apt to be dry and tedious.

In order then that the work may be rendered intelligible and agreeable, it must be based upon a study of words and usages; and in order that the more formal grammatical truths may be comprehended they must be introduced gradually. If the facts are made clear, and firmly grasped, the **principles will unveil themselves all in good time,** and the pupil will come to realise that language is not a mere capricious arrangement of words, but is "law-directed and law-abiding." He must be made to understand why a usage is correct, and taught to apply again and again what he learns, so that it may be fixed and he may recognise that it has a use.

"The desire,' says Professor Laurie, "to attain to a measurable result in acquisition is ruinous. What we should aim at is a natural and pleasing activity of intelligence in the direction and on the lines of the various subjects we teach. Let us have quality, and quantity will take care of itself."

The common principles of method have a distinct application in the teaching of grammar. The following are some of the more important points which should guide the teacher in this part of his work:—

(*a*) **Both method and material must be adapted to the needs and stage of development of the pupil.** What he is called upon to do must be kept well within his power, or his intelligence will suffer. It has been rightly said that the more formal matters of grammar should be taught "with a strong leaning to mercy." Full comprehension of the subject is a work of time; but **such teaching as is given should have a meaning for the pupil throughout.**

The teacher must beware of introducing to the child matters which may be important from a philological point of view, but which are altogether beyond his power to comprehend. It is not to be expected that what he is unable to understand, at least in some degree, will have the slightest attraction for him, and "he cannot stretch a hand through time to catch the far-off interest of years."

(*b*) **The grammar of the mother tongue should be learned inductively and applied deductively.** The formal definitions, rules, and abstract principles should be the natural outcome of the pupil's examination of language as commonly employed; they should not be given directly and then explained and illustrated. We must proceed from such facts as can be *observed* to simple generalisations; and from these gradually to others of a more difficult character. When a definition or rule has been thus learned, it should be abundantly employed as a test in deciding the character of further examples. Frequent and intelligent application of rules is the only means by which their bearing can be fully comprehended and their usefulness made clear.

(*c*) **The pupil must be led from the consideration of the whole to that of the parts.** Sentences are the units of language; they have a meaning for the child and are constantly being used by him. The first formal teaching should therefore be directed to the recognition of the two essential parts of the sentence—the words used to express what is spoken of, and those used to assert something respecting it. When these parts are clearly understood, the words 'subject' and 'predicate' may be made known. As the pupil's power grows, he may be taught to separate the simple subject from words which modify it; and similarly with the predicate. In this way he should proceed step by step to the ultimate examination of each individual word and its relationships—that is, to detailed parsing.

(*d*) **Regular forms and correct expressions must be permanently fixed in the mind before exceptions and incorrect usages are brought forward.** Until considerable progress has been made, and the rules have been thoroughly mastered, exceptions—as Fénelon advocated three hundred years ago—should only be noted as they crop up in the pupil's reading. Later on it may be useful to collect and systematise them for reference, and to have them learned in connection; but in no case should a rule be given and followed immediately by a list of exceptions. Confusion is pretty sure to result, and the child loses faith in a rule which seems to him "more honoured in the breach than in the observance."

The once common plan of setting bad examples of English before children for correction is wrong in theory and mischievous in practice. The less they see and hear wrong usages the better.

> The story is told of a boy who was set to justify or correct the sentence—"He is taller than me." This he did as follows—"This is wrong; it should be 'I am taller than him,' because the first person is more worthy than the third."

(*e*) **The difference between terms and things must not be lost sight of.** In teaching grammar far too little attention is often given to keeping a clear distinction between abstract and concrete, and between the ideas underlying grammatical terms and those conveyed by the words which express the corresponding qualities or existences in things. Hence arises no little confusion in the mind of the learner—a confusion which is slowly, if ever, got rid of.

> Thus the pupil must be made to understand that a noun is not a *thing* but a word or symbol standing for it; that gender is a grammatical distinction in *words*, and must not be confounded with sex, nor must masculine and feminine be confounded with male and female. Verbs again are not *actions*; nor is tense *time*, but a grammatical form of the verb, or distinction attributed to it, which corresponds to the time of the action. Adjectives, again, do not express the qualities of nouns but are the symbols of attributes belonging to *things*; and similarly an adverb expresses an attribute of the *action*, not of the verb. Even grammatical number is not number in the ordinary sense, but a form of the *word* corresponding to number in the things signified.

Much of the successful mastery of English grammar depends upon the ready recognition of analogies, hence the **comparative method** will be frequently employed. **The teaching will be almost entirely oral;** and, as it is necessary to appeal to the eye as well as to the mind, constant use will be made of the black-board. The work must be kept from being slow and dull, and the method modified or varied at any point where the pupils fail to grasp what is being taught. **Principles must not be introduced prematurely,** and the teacher should keep in mind whither the instruction is tending, so that the present may prepare the way for that which is to follow. **Frequent review will also be necessary.**

The exercises and illustrative examples should be judiciously selected and systematically arranged to suit the development of the subject. Want of care in this respect is a common defect. No preparation is made, and the exercises are consequently left to the chance of the moment. In such a case it is not to be wondered at that they are often unsatisfactory.

(2) *Earliest teaching—introductory work.*—Before anything of the nature of formal grammar is attempted, a good deal may be done which will have a useful bearing on the after instruction. Young children have generally only a very limited number of words at command; and the first business of the teacher is to extend their vocabulary, and make clear the meanings of such words as are brought within their view in the ordinary teaching. **The reading lessons and the object lessons, more particularly, may be made to have a powerful effect upon progress in the knowledge of language.** It is important also from the first to accustom the pupil to express himself simply, naturally, and correctly in words which are known to him; and, in this connection, ellipses and easy questions are of the greatest use as a means of securing the necessary practice. Frequent corrections will be necessary; and in teaching new words full use should be made of the black-board.

The teacher should refer to Abbott and Seeley's *English Lessons for English People* for an explanation of the way in which the greater number of our words are learned, and their meanings gradually narrowed down by use and experience until they become exact. Children will frequently grasp approximately the sense of a strange word if they hear it used in connection with others all of which are clearly understood.

(3) *The Sentence—Subject and Predicate.*—It has already been pointed out that **the child's introduction to actual grammar should be through the sentence.** He should be led to the recognition of the two main parts and a knowledge of their nature by the examination of a large number of examples put upon the black-board. **The determination should be made to depend upon a clear apprehension of the sense,** and questions will necessarily play an important part in the teaching.

The practice in the simplest analysis should throughout be **to a large extent oral;** and the reading book may be made to afford abundance of suitable examples if a little care is exercised in their selection.

Alongside this work a series of **simple constructive exercises** should also be given, so that the pupils may not only know a sentence when they see it, but be able to shape easy sentences correctly for themselves. Beyond this point they should not proceed for some time.

(4) *Easy Analysis of Sentences—The Parts of Speech.*—This stage marks what may be regarded as the **real beginning of formal grammar**. The introductory work described above will have taught the child to distinguish between subject and predicate, and the teaching may now be extended to **more detailed analysis**, the words belonging to the subject being considered apart from the subject itself, and those which modify or complete the predicate being detached from the predicate proper. The separation of these adjuncts should be led up to by the teacher taking to pieces a variety of simple sentences on the black-board and pointing out the *use* of each part. The way in which the parts are named should then be explained; and when they can be determined with fair certainty in easy cases, the reading book may be introduced and oral exercises given systematically.

The **grammatical analysis of the sentence should be largely based on the logical analysis of the meaning**; and, at this stage, the teaching should be free from all technicalities not really needed as a matter of convenience.

From this general analysis the teacher may easily pass to the parts of speech, taking the noun first, then the verb, adjective, and pronoun in order. The function of conjunctions and prepositions, as connectives and relational words, is more difficult to grasp; hence they should not be taught until the other parts of speech have been well learned.

In dealing with any part of speech it should be kept in mind that the pupil should pass from recognition of the function of the word to its classification, from use to definition. The **order of the steps of the teaching** will be as follows:—

(*a*) The examination of a number of sentences on the black-board in such a way as to lead the pupils to note the **office or use of the particular word** (or instance of the part of speech to be taught) in each, and hence to recognise its general or characteristic quality.

2 D

The importance of directing attention to the function of a word first, in connection with the context, cannot be too strongly emphasised. We cannot settle correctly till we see how a word is used, and realise its force in the sentence, what part of speech it is: for its classification is not fixed, but, as Dr. Abbott has pointed out, "the genius of the English language is that *any word may be any part of speech*." "In English," remarks Mr. Woodward, "the power of any word and its influence in the sentence are rarely dependent on its form or discoverable by formal tests, but rely almost entirely upon its logical relation to the context. The part-of-speech designation cannot be determined at sight, but only by its connection and dependency."

(*b*) **The explanation of how the mode in which a word is used enables us to place it in a class** with other words which are employed in a similar manner, and the **framing of a suitable definition** to serve as a classification test to be applied in future determinations.

The ideas to be contained in the definition, and as far as possible the wording, should be questioned from the pupils: the whole may then be moulded into shape by the teacher so as to give the greatest attainable clearness, directness, and simplicity.

The teacher must not be in too great a hurry to pack everything into a cut-and-dried formula. The clear grasp of the meaning and application of the definition is absolutely necessary if the after work is to be intelligently performed: and not until this has been secured should the definition be committed to memory.

(*c*) **The consideration of the name to be given to the class**, that is, how we are to designate the part of speech; and, as far as it is useful and practicable, the **explanation of the grammatical term used** and how it came to be employed instead of some word more easily understood.

The **technical names** of the parts of speech are a difficulty to children, but the terms are too deeply rooted in the language to be given up. Many teachers advocate the employment at first of such terms as 'name-words,' 'say-words,' 'sort-words,' 'relation-words,' and so on. The children soon feel we are keeping back other names and want to know them. When this curiosity is aroused, the grammatical terms may be given. These should be introduced one at a time as the children are prepared for their reception. A few suggestive words of explanation about the new term will be useful, but the teacher must exercise his judgment, and give only what will be really helpful.

The instruction at this stage should be entirely oral, and at first the sentences presented for observation should be mainly, if not altogether, furnished by the teacher or the scholars, as the illustrations will in this way be far more likely to be suitable and interesting than if they are merely taken from books. Later on, however, the reading books will be found very useful as storehouses of examples. In the exercises it will be useful to give some instances in which the same word is employed in different ways.

The **preposition and the conjunction** are the most difficult parts of speech to explain intelligently. It will be found that children are considerably helped in grasping the first general notions of these words if they are led to look upon the use of the preposition as similar to that of a nail or glue, and the office of the conjunction as that of a hinge.[1] In dealing with the preposition it has been thought advisable by some to teach prepositional phrases as 'relation-phrases' first, and to lead the pupils to see that such phrases are generally employed to modify the meaning of the verb, and sometimes to stand in place of an adjective. The force of the 'relation-words' or prepositions would then be brought out, and finally the definition given.

When all the parts of speech have been dealt with, they should be **grouped so as to show their relationships** and to make clear that they include all the uses to which words can be put in a sentence. In this way the pupils should be led to see **why there are eight parts of speech and no more**: or, since the interjection is simply an emotional outburst quite unrelated to the sentence, we may say that there are only seven fundamentally distinct kinds of words used in the expression of our thoughts. The purpose each part of speech serves in relation to the rest will thus gradually be made clear and some further insight gained into the necessary features of sentence structure.

(5) *Detailed Grammar—formal analysis and parsing.*—So far as the facts of grammar are concerned, the work at this stage should be chiefly devoted to the **teaching of the inflections**. Such forms as are in common use should be well learned, but they should be fully explained and illustrated before being committed to memory.

If properly used, as a summary of the teaching, a suitable **textbook** will now be of considerable service. Essential matters, like the use of the apostrophe in connection with possessives, the forms of the pronouns, the difference between transitive and intransitive verbs, tense, and the correct use and force of the auxiliary verbs *shall* and *will*, *may* and *can*, etc., should be carefully taught; but the elaborate classifications sometimes found in grammar books serve no useful purpose, and only tend to make the subject repulsive.

[1] See Professor Meiklejohn's admirable *Short English Grammar.*

The pupil's knowledge of the **terms necessary for general analysis** may be gradually extended by his study of sentences, alongside the teaching of other particulars respecting the words; and **syntactical relations** may be explained little by little in a similar way. The mode in which these relations should not be taught is by having them committed to memory merely as a series of rules to be afterwards applied.

Time must be given for the pupil to realise one thing thoroughly before another is presented. Too often the child is hurried from point to point without any clear understanding what he is about, and ends by becoming hopelessly bemuddled.

A good deal of difference of opinion exists as to the **value of analysis** and the place it should occupy in the teaching of English grammar. Reasonably and intelligently taught, it may certainly be rendered a valuable exercise. The more common faults are making the analysis too intricate in form, insisting upon minute distinctions of little moment, and allowing the work to degenerate into a mere 'pigeon-holing' of parts.

As previously noted the **grammatical analysis should be arrived at through the logical analysis of the sense.** Attention is thus compelled to the underlying thought, and the exercise is prevented from becoming a "study of mere empty forms." For teaching purposes the black-board should be in constant use, and **the sentences should be 'mapped out'** in such a way that the relation of the parts may strike the eye. The common book arrangement in rectangles is inelastic and uninteresting.

As disciplinary exercises, analysis and parsing should proceed side by side, and the one be made to assist the other. The examples should be carefully graduated, and for a long time they should be of a fairly easy character. The unravelling of mere structural puzzles only obscures the teaching of ordinary constructions.

The work for the most part should be conducted orally, as in this way a much larger amount of practice is secured and the corrections are thoroughly made. Further, the great tendency in children is to guess and not think; and in written exercises it is almost impossible to get them to consider the points in the way they can be led to do by skilful questioning. The *habit* of thoughtful consideration, therefore, should be established before written exercises are employed to any great extent; and, when they are made use of, they must be very carefully corrected.

The power to parse, viewed as a mere accomplishment, is almost, if not quite, useless. The value of the exercise depends entirely upon its being conducted in such a way as to discipline the faculties. The practice as usually carried out might with much advantage be considerably simplified, and confined, at least with younger pupils, to such particulars as can be clearly made out and have a regular application in English.

(6) *Auxiliary Exercises—Derivation, Word-building, etc.*—Derivation taught in a reasonable way, and within clearly defined limits, may be made a very useful auxiliary exercise to the ordinary teaching of English. It is a gain to the pupil to know that there are other languages besides our own, that to some of them we are indebted for many of the words which now form part of our speech, and that in the transfer they have been modified in form and further altered, by the addition of suitable syllables either before or after the fundamental forms, to express various changes of meaning.

The subject is one which demands judicious management, and that the teacher shall constantly bear in mind the needs of the child and the strengthening of other parts of the work. **The teaching may easily be overdone,** especially where the pupils have no knowledge of any language but their own. The mere giving of the root as part of the explanation of every word is a quite useless proceeding.

Only the more important roots, from which groups of words have been derived, should be taught; and, as a preliminary, the **common prefixes should be carefully explained and fully illustrated** by numerous examples upon the black-board, until their force in combination is thoroughly understood. When the prefixes have been mastered, the lessons should take something of the following form :—

(*a*) **A number of words from the same root should be written under one another on the black-board**; as, for instance, *compel*, *dispel*, *expel*, *impel*, *propel*, *repel* ; or, *adduce*, *conduce*, *deduce*, *educe*, *induce*, *introduce*, *produce*, *reduce*, etc. The children will often be able to supply many of the words themselves.

(*b*) **The forms of the words composing the group should be compared,** so as to bring out the element common to the whole; the meaning of this part should be explained, and the Latin root given from which it has been derived.

(*c*) **To the meaning of the stem or root portion should then be added the signification of each of the prefixes** attached to the words taken, and the children should be questioned until they can give the fundamental idea of each word in turn.

(d) As a last step, **constructive exercises** should be given, the pupils being called upon to frame, either orally or in writing, a number of sentences in which each word dealt with is made use of in its proper sense.

A series of lessons taught in this way, together with the incidental references which may often be made in the teaching of other subjects, will help to make the child's knowledge of meanings accurate, and will enable him to appreciate the fundamental relationship of the various words of each particular group. The work will also illustrate the composite nature of our own language and the way in which it has grown to be what it is.

Instruction in **word-building** should be associated with the lessons described above, and should direct attention to the consideration of other forms derived from the original English words, especially from such as "have a progeny." The grouping of words will thus be continued, and the **various processes illustrated by which words have been formed from one another** by means of affixes and prefixes.

For instance, *nouns* from verbs, adjectives, and other nouns; *adjectives* from nouns, verbs, and other adjectives; *verbs* from nouns, adjectives, and other verbs; and so on. Almost any good manual on language will furnish all that the teacher needs in the way of information: and the examples he can easily supplement and arrange to suit his own purposes. The work must not be made a matter of cram.

The **force of the affixes** which are of frequent occurrence should be rendered clear by the examination of a number of instances, supplied as far as possible by the pupils themselves; and the forms and meanings should be fixed by further exercise in classifying examples drawn from recollection or the examination of the reading book.

The **changes in signification and use, as well as in form, which words have undergone** in the past, and the mode in which these changes came about—their life-history so to speak—may be made a most attractive study to advanced pupils, if the teacher is well informed and handles the material at all skilfully; and something of the romance attaching to the story of particular words may often be brought within the comprehension of even young pupils.

Archbishop Trench in his *Study of Words* has shewn us how many interesting truths, records of human experience, relics of customs, and phases of old-world thought lie hidden in words; and how their meanings have gradually changed with time, until the thought or feeling the word originally symbolised has become blurred almost past recognition in the present usage. The teacher should also read Max Müller's *Science of Language* and make use of a really good dictionary in which the history of the words is traced.

Systematic treatment of the history of words may be possible only in very few cases, but occasional lessons may be given to the higher classes in almost any school; and many opportunities will arise, especially in connection with the explanation of the reading lesson, where a few minutes may well be spent in directing attention to the more prominent points in the history of some word which lends itself to such treatment. Properly managed, teaching of this kind is stimulating in a high degree; the imagination is exercised, interest is excited, and the full force and meaning of the words dealt with is made clear and impressive in a way which the most careful learning of definitions can never secure.

The importance of attaching exact and correct ideas to words is not appreciated in schools as it should be; and far too little help and encouragement is given towards securing the intelligent and habitual use of a dictionary. Advanced pupils should be provided with a serviceable book, like *Chambers's Dictionary*, and trained to refer to it regularly when a word occurs with the meaning of which they are not familiar.

(7) *The place of historical grammar.*—Historical grammar often throws considerable light on current usages, by shewing how they grew up and what the forms were originally. It thus **tends to intelligence, where suitably employed,** but it has no power to determine what should be in the present. There are reasons " for most of the apparent absurdities and anomalies of modern English," and the discovery of these is interesting to the student who has thoroughly mastered the elements of ordinary grammar and is capable of appreciating the explanations. To introduce them, however, in the early stages is, in nine cases out of ten, simply to perplex the pupil, because he has not yet got firm hold of the present forms which the historical references are to account for. Even in the higher stages historical grammar needs to be appealed to with discretion, and should be taught as an aid, not as an end in itself. The great thing is to guide the pupils into the correct use of the language as it exists to-day.

In elementary schools, except for very occasional illustration, historical grammar is best left alone; for here there is neither time nor reason for dealing with "curiosities of the ancient tongue which would involve both teacher and pupils in learned researches which are beyond their sphere." Too often, so much is said about the old forms that the real point of the explanation, namely, making clear the present use, is missed.

(8) *The use of a text-book.*—A suitable grammar book is a very

useful help to the teaching, if properly employed, as it **enables the pupil to revise and fix what he has been taught, and to realise the relationship of the various parts.** Such a book should be simple and compendious in form, and present the various facts and principles which make up the substance of the instruction in their proper perspective. **The information should not be set to be learned until it has been taught orally** and fully illustrated on the black-board. Any minor matters which are inserted in the book should be omitted by the pupil until the essentials have been mastered.

Many of our elementary grammar books are too technical, and repel the pupil by the form in which the facts are stated; the definitions are not unfrequently loose and unsatisfactory, and the classifications in many cases far more minute than is necessary for any practical purpose. As Professor Laurie observes: "However accurate the distinctions may be if they are too numerous they defeat their own ends."

It is a common mistake to make use of too advanced a book. The statements which the pupil has to learn are not easily grasped, and the presence of much that he has nothing to do with prevents the rest from being seen in its true connection and importance.

III. ENGLISH COMPOSITION.

The **practical study of composition** of an easy kind may be begun earlier than the study of formal grammar; but when the latter is taken up the two subjects should be taught side by side. Such truths respecting word-forms and syntactical relations as the pupil learns in the one he should be called upon to apply in the other; and his knowledge of these, if properly appealed to, should put him on the alert against inaccuracies and give fuller meaning and force to the teacher's criticisms.

The great importance of training children to express their thoughts readily and correctly is probably recognised theoretically by every teacher; but the instruction is too often desultory and unsatisfactory. The work is too much of the nature of hap-hazard experimenting, regular and suitable practice is not properly provided for, and the graduation of the exercises is far too little attended to.

(1.) *Qualities to be aimed at in composition.*—The teaching of composition in schools should be directed to secure the writing of plain straightforward English prose, free from error and obscurity. The following are the more important qualities which the teacher should dwell upon and illustrate again and again in his correction of the composition exercises.

(a) **Naturalness and simplicity.** The statements should be expressed in an easy natural way and be the real outcome of having something to say. The words should be such as the pupil is familiar with, and the simplest which will serve the purpose exactly. Long high-sounding words, fine writing, pretentiousness, sham sentiment, and moralising are to be distinctly discouraged. We should be careful not to damp out individuality by insisting upon the language being of the kind we ourselves should make use of. Honest failure is better than a mere patchwork of set phrases and platitudes adopted second-hand.

Composition is too much dissociated from speech, as though the mode of expression in writing and speaking were different. A boy who talks fluently enough often becomes awkward and artificial when set to write, because he thinks he has to express himself in a *book* way.

(b) **Correctness.** The language employed, both as to words and sentence structure, should be in accordance with commonly accepted standards of accuracy. A knowledge of grammatical forms and rules will here be of use to the pupil, and to these he should be constantly referred when he falls into error.

Blunders in the use of inflexions, bad spelling, and wrong punctuation will all need to be carefully dealt with. Slang, although frequently tolerated in common conversation, should find no place in composition; nor should vulgarisms and provincial words be allowed to pass.

(c) **Clearness.** This is one of the most essential things to which attention should be directed, and one which may be taught with success. What the sentence is intended to mean should be evident at once; there must be no ambiguity, no vagueness. Want of clearness arises chiefly from imperfect realisation of the thought to be expressed, from the muddling up in the same sentence of matters which should be distinct, and from clumsy construction due more especially to the faulty arrangement of the words.

"Clearness," says Dr. Abbott, "is simply an intellectual quality, not depending like strength and elegance upon emotional or æsthetic gifts. Clearness may therefore be easily taught in the preparatory schools, and the principles and rules upon which it rests may be made a part of the intellectual equipment of the pupil."

(d) **Directness and force.** To be effective ordinary prose should be concise and vigorous without being abrupt or wanting in smoothness.

The sentences should be well balanced, and so arranged that the form may strike the eye readily. There must be no wordiness, no rambling, no unwieldy or involved constructions; and such words should be chosen as will appeal to the mind most powerfully in the way intended. Expenditure of effort to make out the structure means so much loss of attention to the sense.

Feebleness of thought and poorness of expression generally go together. A sentence may be clear and free from positive error, and yet may be the baldest commonplace. The use of hackneyed words and phrases often gives an impression of weakness.

The gradual training of the child to recognise what really good English is has an important bearing in the teaching of composition. It gives him some sort of standard whereby to judge, and should at least make clear to him the necessity for avoiding the commoner and grosser faults in his own efforts.

Much may also be done with advanced pupils to lead them to appreciate the beauties of style; but, *so far as practice is concerned*, the higher qualities of prose—depending very largely, as they do upon emotional sensibility, the cultivation of the taste, an extensive vocabulary, and a delicately trained ear—lie almost entirely outside the scope of school work.

The qualities of artistic prose are well set forth in the following passage from Sir Arthur Helps' *Realmah*, describing the characteristics of a sentence of the highest kind. "It should be powerful in its substantives, choice and discreet in its adjectives, nicely correct in its verbs: not a word that could be added, nor one which the most fastidious would venture to suppress: in order lucid, in sequence logical, in method perspicuous; and yet with a pleasant and inviting intricacy which disappears as you advance in the sentence: the language throughout not quaint, not obsolete, not common, and not new: its several clauses justly proportioned and carefully balanced, so that it moves like a well-disciplined army organised for conquest: the rhythm not that of music, but of a higher and more fantastic melodiousness, submitting to no rule, incapable of being taught: the substance and the form alike disclosing a happy union of the soul of the author to the subject of his thought, having, therefore, individuality without personal predominance: and withal, there must be a sense of felicity about it, declaring it to be the product of a happy moment, so that you feel that it will not happen again to that man who writes the sentence, or to any other of the sons of men, to say the like thing so choicely, tersely, mellifluously, and completely."

(2) *The means to be employed in teaching composition.*—These are chiefly as follows:—

(a) **Direct instruction as to what is required.** Before the pupil is set to write, the teacher should explain clearly what is to be done, and how it may be accomplished. A few simple rules respecting such things as the arrangement of words, the sequence of ideas, and the avoidance of common faults, will be found useful; but any lengthy theoretical statements are not needed. The composition manual should be known by the teacher, but will be of little assistance to young pupils.

"Half-a-dozen rules," remarks De Quincey, "for evading the most frequently recurring forms of *awkwardness*, of *obscurity*, of *misproportion*, and of *double meaning*, would do more to assist a writer in practice, laid under some necessity of hurry, than volumes of general disquisition."

(*b*) **The imitation of a good model.** Consciously or unconsciously the pupil will be pretty certain to imitate the forms he is accustomed to see and hear. His everyday experiences will have more influence upon his practice than rules and theoretical explanations. Hence arises the importance of familiarising him with good models, and of ensuring that the language employed both in the teaching and in the reading books is good of its kind.

After the composition exercises on any subject have been criticised, the teacher should give a 'fair copy' himself on the blackboard, and discuss the reasons for the placing of particular words, the arrangement of the parts, etc. "A grain of showing," as Mr. E. E. Bowen observes, "is worth a bushel of telling."

(*c*) **Graduated and regular practice with careful correction of errors.** The framing of sentences as answers to questions in the ordinary lessons will afford much useful practice in oral composition, especially if the teacher is careful to correct any clumsy constructions or mistakes in grammar which occur. As the pupil's power of expression grows, longer statements should be required of him, until at length he is able to give a straightforward account of any simple occurrence. **Systematic written exercises,** however, are by far the most important means of training in the skilful use of language. They must be arranged to suit the progress of the pupils, and thoroughly corrected and criticised; in fact, their efficiency depends almost entirely upon the care with which the errors are pointed out and the defects discussed. It is useless to try to correct all faults at once. Those which are most serious at the time should be dealt with first; and when these have been got rid of, others should be attacked in order.

The tendency is for the pupils to give insufficient heed to what is said by way of correction. The exercises should be read out before the whole class, and any one allowed to offer suggestions for improvement. The black-board should be in constant use; and, after the corrections have been made, it is often well to have the exercise re-written in the light of the criticisms which have been offered. In the higher stages, the faultiness of any particular construction may in many cases be brought home more strongly by calling upon the pupils to analyse the defective sentences.

Smaller matters, such as the statement of the title, the division into paragraphs, the punctuation, neatness of arrangement, good writing, the leaving of a margin of the same width for corrections, and so on, should not be disregarded.

(*d*) **The training of the ear.** What is called a 'good ear' is a useful auxiliary in the writing of English, when the more essential qualities of correctness and clearness have been acquired, and some amount of facility and grace may be looked for. The pupils should gradually be trained to perceive that certain arrangements of words are more easily uttered and pleasanter in sound than others; and that in good writing the sentences do not proceed by jerks, or end abruptly, but flow smoothly, and leave both mind and ear satisfied at the close.

The recognition of the metrical flow of poetry, reading aloud, and recitation, are important aids to this cultivation of the ear; but in actual composition the provinces of poetry and prose must be kept quite distinct. With advanced pupils, the avoidance of harsh combinations, jingling words, and rugged constructions, may fairly be looked for; and eventually something even may be done towards leading them to appreciate the subtle and almost infinitely varied rhythm of the highest prose, so different from the regular fall of the words in poetry, but producing an effect not less pleasing to an ear trained to detect it.

(3) *The nature of the exercises.*—The power to write really good composition is only to be gained by practice. To teach the subject well, the exercises need to be carefully graduated and arranged, so as to stimulate thought, and cultivate observation, judgment, and good taste, in a manner suited to the pupil's development at each stage of the work.

The **subjects** set to be written about should be definite, capable of simple treatment, and sufficiently limited in scope to allow of their being satisfactorily handled in the space and time allowed. They must also be within the pupil's understanding and knowledge, and such as will be likely to prove interesting enough to engage attention. **The first condition of success is that the pupil shall have adequate information** for the purpose; if he has nothing to say, and is required to invent, he is pretty certain to write rubbish, and to write it badly.

The choice of subjects should receive much more careful attention than is commonly given to it. Many of those recommended in books are far too ambitious, and demand greater breadth of view and grasp of detail than can reasonably be expected from youthful writers. **Matters of an abstract nature should, as a rule, be avoided.** The virtues were once favourite subjects; but it is to be hoped that common sense has banished dissertations upon them from most of our schools.

(a) **Reproduction of a simple narrative or story.** The matter must be communicated, or got up, before the children are set to write. The common plan is for a short story, as one of Æsop's Fables, or any amusing incident, to be narrated by the teacher so as to bring out into relief the more important points. These are still further impressed by questioning; and any necessary instructions are given. The pupils are then called upon to give an account in writing of what they have heard, and the exercises are criticised and corrected as already described.

In the earliest exercises it is well to have the story written out first as a series of short answers to questions which are given one at a time, so as to compel attention to each point in order. The whole may then be re-written in the usual way.

(b) **Easy description.** This exercise demands more judgment than the last, and for some time more help will be needed in the way of suggestion as to treatment. The objects to be described should be such as are known to the pupils first hand. Any interesting thing with which they are acquainted, or which can be placed before them, together with such subjects as a country walk, a cricket or football match, and so on, may be made use of.

The importance of seizing upon the salient features first and omitting unimportant details, as well as of taking the points in some natural order, must be made clear by the teacher; and in the early exercises it will be well to put upon the black-board a rough outline of the facts which the pupils may fill in for themselves.

A good exercise by way of variety is to place a picture in front of the class, or to select a suitable one that the children have in their reading books, and to let them tell in words what the picture shews. In this some latitude should be allowed to the imagination.

(c) **Abstracts of Reading Lessons, etc.** The story or information given in the reading lesson will often form an admirable subject for a succeeding composition exercise, and might with advantage be much more frequently made use of than it is. The plan of calling upon the pupils in this way to give an outline of what they have read encourages them to give attention to the subject-matter during reading, helps to perfect their knowledge of the words, and saves the time otherwise required in many cases for giving the necessary information.

The exercise may be varied in many ways. In some instances a brief abstract of the important points of the whole lesson may be required, with or without the books open. This will form a useful introduction to what is known as *précis* writing.

(*d*) **Letter writing.** This is an exceedingly useful form of exercise, and one which should always form part of the composition work. No child should leave school without being able to write a passable letter.

In the **early stages** the letter should be of the simplest kind, to a schoolfellow or relative. The mode of beginning and ending such a letter should be explained, and attention drawn to the little courtesies and inquiries which are usual beyond the information to be conveyed. The teacher should then point out how to proceed with the body of the letter, and give some examples himself upon the black-board by way of illustration. The mode of folding the letter properly, and of directing the envelope should also be exhibited.

In the **higher stages** more conventional modes of address and subscription should be explained. The pupil should be shewn how to apply for a situation, what points respecting his qualifications, etc., should be given, and the order in which these should be stated. Business forms should also be discussed, and the necessity for brevity and clearness insisted upon. The conditions should be varied from time to time, and the teacher should put a few notes upon the blackboard as to what is to be communicated in each case.

When these matters have been fairly mastered, information may be given as to how to address persons of different ranks in society, and how to refer to them in the body of a letter. These forms should be entered in the pupil's note-book for future use.

(*e*) **Reports of oral lessons.** In the upper classes the pupils should be taught how to take notes in a short suggestive way, so as to enable them to write out afterwards a much longer and connected account of the lesson. The preparation in this way of reports of the more important lessons, especially those in science, has many points of usefulness, and may easily be made to serve all the purposes of a composition exercise.

When the pupils begin to use note-books, the teacher should give some examples on the black-board of the kind of notes he wishes taken. Only when the *form* of the statement is important should the teacher's actual words be taken down in full, and for this time should be allowed.

(*f*) **Themes, etc.** The word 'essay' is a pretentious term as applied to school exercises, and is best abandoned. Many suitable subjects— historical, geographical, scientific, and general—may easily be found ; but, as mentioned above, subjects of an abstract nature, especially such as need wide knowledge and experience of life to handle at all successfully, should be avoided. There is nothing gained, but much lost, by calling upon the child to attempt things beyond his power.

The pupil should be perfectly clear as to what is required of him. The directions should be few, and as definite as possible. The teacher should explain the manner in which the material should be selected, and shew how it may be arranged in the most suitable order for one point to lead on naturally to the next. The importance of an attractive beginning in order to secure attention, and of an effective ending so as to leave the mind impressed, should also be pointed out and illustrated.

In connection with this part of the work, attention should be drawn to synonymous terms, niceties of meaning, the right use of the relatives and connectives, the avoidance of exaggeration and of the frequent use of superlatives, and to the influence of different arrangements of the words in a sentence. The so-called '**figures of speech**'—especially the use of metaphors and similes—should be explained and illustrated by numerous carefully selected examples. The not uncommon fault of mixing up metaphorical expressions—as in the case of the gentleman who said, "I will not allow this to go on, and when I put my foot down, I put it down with a firm hand"—should be very carefully pointed out.

The pupil must be made to feel that to write **continuous composition** at all well, it is necessary to take pains ; and that he cannot hope to succeed unless he first decides upon what he is going to say, and arranges the points in a natural order.

All the members of the class should write upon the same subject, and all should benefit by the criticisms given of each exercise in turn.

(*g*) **The answering of an examination paper.**—In these days, when so much is made to depend upon examinations, it is astonishing that definite instruction is not more often given as to the mode of setting about the answering of an examination paper. Many an examinee, who is well informed, fails to put down what he knows in the best way, or in the most expeditious manner, because he has never been shewn how.

The **commoner faults found in written answers** are want of logical coherence, rambling pointless statements, faulty subordination of parts, wordiness, writing what is not asked for, and bad arrangement. The careful criticism and teaching necessary to correct these should be a distinct gain from the point of view of composition; as should also the accompanying training to select what is important out of what is known, and to state this with just the necessary amount of detail and no more.

To answer an examination paper well requires, in addition to knowledge, a certain amount of skill, which is only to be gained by **properly supervised practice**. If the exercise is to be of much benefit, a good deal more must be done besides merely correcting mistakes in matters of fact, which is often all that is attempted. One important help is for the teacher occasionally to give a series of answers himself upon the black-board as models.

(*h*) **Paraphrasing.**—Teachers and writers are by no means agreed as to the usefulness of paraphrasing as a school exercise. Many condemn it in no measured terms. Professor Laurie says: "A more detestable exercise I do not know. It is an impious and unholy use of pen and ink." Very much depends, however, upon the way in which it is carried out.

In many instances the same structure is kept, and all that is attempted is the mere substitution of less suitable words for those which have been deliberately chosen by the author to convey his meaning. It is impossible to find proper equivalents for many of the terms, and delicate shades of meaning are not unfrequently quite lost. Sometimes even the general sense is very badly expressed, and in any case whatever force and beauty the original may possess is pretty sure to be destroyed.

It may be urged, however, that paraphrasing properly conducted compels attention to the sense, enlightens the pupil as to the resources of language, and leads to the recognition of the skill with which the original is put together. It is a test of understanding, and affords a good practical training in the use of words, a training of much the same character as that derived from translation. It may be doubted, also, whether, after all, the appreciation of the passage as literature really suffers to any great extent.

A very useful preliminary exercise is to have passages of verse written out in direct prose order. The sentences should be put in the simplest form, and any omitted words supplied ; but the original language should be kept as far as possible, so as not to weaken down the sense or interfere with the aptness of the phrases and the beauty of the images employed.

Paraphrasing proper, if used at all, should come late, inasmuch as it demands a knowledge of words and a skill in composition which can only reasonably be expected from advanced pupils. The sense of the passage should be thoroughly mastered with the help of the teacher first, and the mode of dealing with any specially difficult phrase indicated. The pupil should then be called upon to express the whole, without any undue lengthening out, in such a way as to maintain the spirit or general character of the composition and the same relative prominence of the ideas to be conveyed.

The pieces set for paraphrasing should be carefully graduated, and such as the pupil can clearly understand with a little help and trouble. In many cases those selected are far too difficult, and the exercises correspondingly unsatisfactory and useless.

IV. ENGLISH LITERATURE.

Literature may be made one of the most **educative and humanising** of all school studies. It is more than knowledge, and **appeals to the imagination and the æsthetic emotions**, as well as to the understanding. Taught in a liberal spirit, it should not only give information and store the mind with valuable ideas and beautiful images, but conduce to the elevation of thought and character, and add to the happiness of life by opening up new sources of pleasure. If this is lost sight of the mere instruction in facts will count for little.

The first object of the teaching should be to enable the pupil to *enjoy* what he reads, and to guide and enlighten him so that he may come to appreciate something of the power of the author as a thinker, and of the value and beauty of the work as art. He has to learn gradually what is meant by **style** in literature, and to realise the elevation of tone, breadth of view, and perfection of thought and expression, which characterise its highest form.

In the early stages appreciation is the most important thing ; but eventually more critical matters will be introduced and the pupil will be led to discern the difference between the clothing of a thought in an exquisite garment of language exactly appropriate to it, and a florid style adopted merely for display regardless of its suitability to the ideas to be expressed.

The nature of the work has been felicitously expressed by Mr. H. C. Bowen : " By the study of literature as *literature*, I mean the study of a poem or prose work for the sake of its substance, its form, and its style ; for the sake of the thought and the imagination it contains, and the methods used to express these ; for the sake of its lofty, large, or acute perception of things ; its power of exposition, the beauty, force, and meaning of its metaphors, its similes, its epithets, the strength and music of its language."

Interest in literature may be fostered almost from the first by the **learning and repetition of simple poems.** These should be good of their kind, natural in expression, and level with the child's understanding. The subjects must be such as are within the range of his experience and sympathies and appeal more to the emotions than to the intellect. Some suitable pieces the reading books will supply; and others may easily be found. Throughout, also, the **reading by the teacher** of entire pieces, whether poems or stories, will do much towards inducing in the pupil a liking for books.

With reference to the **early teaching of literature**, no direct instruction, beyond that which the reading lesson supplies, should be given until the pupil can read fluently. **Short poems or selections** may then be taken, and examined with closer attention than the time which can be spared from the reading lesson allows. The characteristics of the piece, both as to form and substance, should be pointed out, and any difficulty in the way of understanding should be removed ; but the discussion of all critical matters should be reserved for a later stage. The work must be attractive, and carried on largely by means of questions. The important thing is not how much the pupil can be made to remember of what the teacher has said about this or that passage, but how much he can be made to see in it for himself.

The **more advanced teaching** of literature should deal with pieces sufficiently complete in themselves to allow of the design of the whole and the relationship of the various parts being made out. A book of extracts is altogether too scrappy to afford the training required. For his own pleasure the pupil can scarcely read too widely; but, for purposes of study, it is far better to **master one or two typical works**, than to scamper over a great many and get no adequate notion of any one of them.

The **work chosen** should be treated from the literary standpoint, and, as far as possible, it should be made to illustrate the characteristic features of its class. It should be read through carefully so that a general view of the whole may be obtained, before the different topics to be considered are dealt with in detail. Unusual or obsolete words, allusions, and any difficulty of construction or meaning, should then be explained. The **artistic qualities of the style**—its appropriateness, grace, happy choice of words, beautiful imagery, picturesque epithets, skilful arrangement of the parts, and so on—should be pointed out as opportunities occur; and when the whole has been gone through, it will often be useful to group the more marked instances of each for further consideration. The story or plot and the characters portrayed should be considered separately. The attempt to deal with all the various points in a single reading only distracts the pupil and leaves no clear impression of anything. The more striking and typical passages should also be learned by heart; and if properly mastered in other ways these will serve as standards of reference as well as store the mind with beautiful thoughts and felicitous expressions.

The instruction should be earnest, but neither dry nor formal; and it must not be overloaded with a multitude of references, grammatical exercises, derivations, antiquarian notes, and unnecessary details which obscure that with which the pupil is chiefly concerned. To treat a work of art merely as a *corpus vile*, to be made use of only as material for dissection and the study of tissues, is to degrade it, as well as to disgust the pupil and miss all the higher and better things which the study should give. **Above all we must not make the subject repulsive.**

It has often been urged that the main consideration is to make the pupil acquainted with books, not with what has been said of them, and this so far is no doubt true; but **criticism**, so long as it is suggestive and stimulating, has a rightful place in teaching, and, judiciously employed, is distinctly helpful. Critical insight is a matter of slow growth, but it can be cultivated; and a wise teacher may do much by his remarks to open the pupil's eyes to beauties which he would not discover for himself, and to enable him to realise far more completely than he could unaided the spirit, meaning, and purpose of that which he reads. The thing to guard against is allowing him to quote parrot-like a series of critical phrases without any adequate comprehension of what they mean. **Sham admiration and pretence are always to be discouraged.**

The spirit in which the teacher conducts the work has much to do with his success. He should be well read, apt in the use of parallel passages and illustrations, and in full sympathy with his class and his subject. He is not likely to induce boys to take interest in that in which he takes no delight himself.

IV. ELEMENTARY SCIENCE.

The training to be derived from the right study of science is different from that to be obtained from the learning of mathematics or of languages. No one of these is sufficient in itself to form a complete means of mental development; and each should form part of any scheme intended to afford the child the all-round education which it is so desirable should be provided for him.

The facts of science, it is true, have in themselves a practical value merely as knowledge; but, apart from the training of which they may be made the vehicle, this value would not *in itself* be sufficient warrant for the systematic introduction of science into our schools. When properly dealt with, however, **science has a just claim to an important place in education, and supplies a training which nothing else can give in so satisfactory and easily attainable a way.**

Science, like other things, has suffered from the over-zeal of some of its advocates. To vaunt its claims as paramount to those of everything else, and almost as though it were the only thing necessary, is to defeat the object, desirable as it is in itself, with which those claims are put forward.

(1) *The aim and purpose of the work.*—The aim of the early instruction in science should be to afford a useful training to the faculties, and prepare the pupil for the more formal and systematic treatment of the subject later on, and serve as a guide to his future studies. It should give him some idea of what is meant by the term Science, and make him acquainted with such of the more simple principles and fundamental truths as are within his grasp; as well as

enable him to gain some insight into the way in which these truths have been arrived at—that is, into the *scientific method*.

The child's curiosity is being continually aroused in the things by which he is surrounded, and many are the questions he asks concerning them. The teacher should keep in mind this natural tendency, and so stimulate the pupil's interest by means of it, as to make him anxious to know more. "How much better and more intelligent would early training be," observes Archdeacon Wilson, "if curiosity were looked on as the store of force, the possible love of knowledge in embryo in the child's mind, which in its later transformations is so highly valued."

One great object in teaching elementary science should be to bring the child into actual contact with the realities of nature, and this in such a way as to **train the observation, the judgment, and the reasoning**. The teaching will also afford frequent opportunities for cultivating the conceptive power, and the simpler phases of imagination which are concerned in the mental realisation of things that are beyond the sphere of the action of the senses.

The pupil must be trained to use his eyes, hands, and ears as instruments for gaining knowledge ; and especially must he be taught how to direct his attention to one thing at a time so that he may take in rapidly what it is necessary for him to *see*. He must further be led to weigh evidence carefully, to connect one fact with another so as to determine the natural sequence of events in any given phenomenon, and finally, to make easy deductions from the observed facts or established conclusions.

"The spirit of observation," says Compayré, "is the best of professors." The importance of training the senses to greater acuteness, rapidity, and certainty of action, inasmuch as the perceptions gained through their agency form the foundation of all real knowledge and are a necessary condition of the correct interpretation of what is conveyed in words, has been already pointed out. No subject offers better opportunities for such training, and for impressing upon the pupil how much he can discover for himself with a little effort, than elementary science. To teach it, however, as a number of independent items of information to be merely fixed in the memory is to lose sight entirely of its educational value.

Another important object of the teaching should be the **formation of good intellectual habits** ; especially those concerned with connected and direct thought, steady and vigorous attention, careful investigation before arriving at a decision, cautious generalisation, and exactness both of idea and statement. The study of science should also have a **moral value**, and cultivate the spirit of thoroughness, of perseverance, of self-reliance, of patience in the presence of difficulty, and of absolute loyalty to truth. "Science," says Archdeacon Wilson, "encourages the habit of mind which will rest in nothing but what is true; truth is the ultimate and only object, and there is the ever-recurring appeal to facts as the test of truth."

The pupil has to learn to judge justly for himself, and in doing this he should as far as possible be saved from error. Anything which adds to his power of distinguishing that which is true from that which is false is not without its importance in education.

The value, also, of **scientific knowledge** in making us acquainted with many facts which have a useful bearing on everyday life, and in widening the horizon of our ideas should not be lost sight of. It has been said that "ignorance produces as many disasters as malevolence." "It is something to know that there are scientific problems; to know enough to know that others know more, to be able to say this must be referred to a chemist and this to a geologist."

(2) *The general nature of the teaching.*—In no section of his work does the teacher need to be more fully and accurately acquainted with his subject, or to take more pains to present it in a suitable form, than in elementary science. "The power of teaching a little," says Professor Huxley, "depends on knowing a great deal, and that thoroughly." Ready recognition of the difficulties which stand in the way of understanding, lucid explanation, simple and exact statement, logical development of the subject matter, adroit handling of the illustrations, careful connection of the ideas, and skilful summing up are all necessary.

Book knowledge alone is insufficient. The teacher must know his facts from all sides, and as far as possible at first hand; he must realise their interdependence and relative importance, and make up his mind how they can best be brought before the pupil so as to educate as well as inform him. His teaching must be controlled by a definite plan; he must be perfectly clear as to what is and what is not to be taught, and be cautious not to do himself what ought to be done by his class.

The work should be so arranged that not only do the points follow each other in natural sequence, but the lessons themselves are clearly related, and one prepares the way for the next.. In fact, **the steady development of ideas in a connected series is the foundation of all real work in the subject.** The teacher must realise the extent to which the faculties of the pupils have been developed, and keep in view that as the child's mind expands he passes from the mere perception of an object as a whole to the recognition of particular characteristics, then to the discovery of similarities and relationships, until eventually he comes to generalise consciously, and gains the power to follow the steps of simple reasoning and to appreciate its force.

As far as they will admit of it, without undue expenditure of time, **the lessons should be made objective, experimental, practical.** Things should come before words ; and, whenever feasible, the more important truths, at least, should be demonstrated in the simplest and most striking way which can be devised. **The general method of procedure should be one of joint investigation by teacher and pupils ;** but of course it must be carried out with common sense, and with the necessary modifications to suit the nature of the lessons and the conditions under which they are given.

It must be remembered that connected thought is difficult to children, and when the passage from particulars to a general truth has to be made the teacher should proceed more cautiously and deliberately, so as to give time for the new idea to be fully apprehended. Like a train passing over the points at a junction, the teaching should 'slow down' to avoid running off the line. Each fact should be emphasised as gained, and, if necessary, instance after instance should be adduced until the pupils see their way. To become impatient and tell them the conclusion we wish them to arrive at for themselves is to destroy the value of the exercise.

The transition from facts to law, from experiments to the truth demonstrated, is a critical one. Too often the connection is only partially brought out, and in some cases so imperfectly that the two things remain separate in the pupil's mind, each being viewed as a piece of information to be learned independently.

It is often useful when a difficulty occurs to investigate its nature by means of a series of questions, so as to discover exactly what it is which needs to be further illustrated or explained. If this is not done, a good deal of time may be wasted by going over the whole matter again ; and after all the real point may be missed.

The objects introduced should be thoroughly examined by the pupils, not merely glanced at and the teacher's statements taken on trust. The only sure course is to test by means of questions how far the observations have been made. Where no other available means of illustration exists, pictures will be found of considerable use, and certainly far better than description alone.

In the case of experiments, the apparatus should be exhibited first so as not to distract attention from what is to be observed, the conditions should be made clear, and the pupils told exactly what to look for. The demonstration should then be gone through, thoroughly questioned upon so as to bring out the point, and the result put upon the black-board.

<small>Selected members of the class may often profitably be allowed to assist in the demonstrations. The children should also be encouraged to repeat at home any experiments which can be managed with a little exercise of care and skill, and to construct simple pieces of apparatus for themselves.</small>

As far as it can be done conveniently, the early teaching of science in schools should be divested of **technical terms**; but where clearness and exactness of statement cannot be as well secured without them, it is unwise to go a long way round in order to avoid their use. In such a case they should be led up to gradually, and when the want of them is felt they should be given and their application illustrated.

Perhaps the commonest fault in the teaching of elementary science is the **overloading of the child with too many facts at once**, and requiring him to learn a number of unimportant or irrelevant matters that weaken the impression made by the more essential truths. The teaching, again, is often too ambitious, too formal and bookish. There is too much anxiety to cover a great deal of ground, the facts are stated in too advanced a way, and words are attended to while ideas are neglected. Memory is substituted for reason, and the ready reproduction of statements and phrases picked up from the teacher or the book is mistaken for real understanding.

<small>This is to degrade the teaching of science to the level of the 'Gradgrind' system satirised by Charles Dickens years ago in *Hard Times*; to present a totally wrong view of what is useful knowledge; to foster that spirit of conceit which only too often accompanies superficiality; and to delude the pupil into the belief that he knows what he does not.</small>

(3) *Early Instruction.*—The object lessons, which should form part of the work in every school, will have prepared the way, to some extent at least, for the more systematic and connected teaching which should be given under the head of science even when the lessons are of the simplest kind. The teacher should have no difficulty in arranging for himself a series of related lessons of a scientific character which will be attractive and intelligible to an average child, and afford the means for the kind of training required at the time. Nothing like a complete view of any subject is possible, and much

will depend upon the "wise selection of things to be taught." In many cases the illustration and application of a few simple scientific principles may be made a fruitful source of pleasure and profit.

Everyday needs and the practical usefulness of the information should not be neglected; but it should be remembered that the way in which a child learns a thing often makes all the difference whether it is to be considered valuable or not. A series of physiographical lessons to be taught in connection with geography has been already sketched out.

(4) *The teaching of individual subjects.*—From an educational point of view the most important groups of the experimental and observational sciences are **Physics, Chemistry,** and **Biology**; and this seems to be the best order in which they should be taken up when they come to be seriously studied as subjects. Here, however, we are only concerned with the elementary teaching which should precede such study, and which will form a useful training as far as it goes for those who will proceed no further. At whatever point it may be cut short, such training will not be lost time. For the more advanced work of such a school course, probably most teachers would agree that Botany and Elementary Physics are best suited, and, further, they are to some extent representative.

(*a*) **Botany.** This may be made a most attractive subject, if the teaching is simple, the work largely of a practical kind, and the pupils are kept free from the ordinary text-books. The examination of plants is always interesting to children if properly introduced, the observations required at this stage are easily made, and the lessons should prove an agreeable change from other work.

The flower should be dealt with first. All the pupils should have specimens served out to them; and they should be taught to make such simple dissections as are necessary for the demonstration of the various parts and for learning their disposition with reference to each other. Constant use should be made of the black-board for large sketches of what is observed, as well as for terms, and a large diagram of a typical flower with the parts named should be drawn by the teacher and copied by the pupils into their note-books for reference.

When, by the examination of a large number of specimens, the commoner types of floral structure have been made out, and the pupils can determine pretty readily the number and arrangement of the essential parts, the other portions of the plant should be taken up in a similar way. The examples dealt with should be grouped, and the work continued until a fairly correct statement of the more important characteristics can be given. From this the pupils should gradually be taught how plants are classified according to the natural system, and at length they should learn how to use a simple 'flora' intelligently.

<small>Good use should be made of the summer months, and every opportunity should be seized for promoting a **habit of outdoor observation**, and an interest in the plant life of the roadsides, fields, and woodlands. Excursions conducted by the teacher are productive of much good in many ways; and the pupils should be encouraged to make a **collection of wild flowers**, and shewn how to press and mount them. The collecting spirit is strong in almost all boys, and, if turned in a useful direction, may do much to further their real education.</small>

(*b*) **Elementary Physics.** A knowledge of the commoner principles and truths included under the head of physics is so important in many ways, that it deserves to take a foremost place wherever science is systematically taught in school.

In teaching the subject, a selection will necessarily have to be made, and it seems best on the whole to make the pupil acquainted with the **elementary principles and conceptions of mechanics** before proceeding to any one of the divisions which deal with the manifestations of energy. Of these divisions, **Heat** is probably the most suitable to take up first, inasmuch as many of the facts are fairly easy to understand, and may be demonstrated, as a rule, without much trouble; while, further, the subject has an important bearing on many other branches of science.

Whichever subject is selected, the work should be to a large extent experimental. **Delicate instruments and elaborate apparatus are not necessary**, and moreover are not the best for school purposes. Almost all the larger truths which should be presented at this stage may be illustrated by means of simple appliances, and in many instances the teacher may make these for himself at a comparatively small cost. The construction of his own apparatus out of common materials, and the adaptation of what he already possesses to other uses, is a valuable experience in itself, and one which will conduce in no small degree to the improvement of the teaching.

<small>A good elementary **text-book** may be made of considerable service, if employed as a summary of the teaching and it is not set to be got up until all explanations and</small>

demonstrations have been given. It should follow the lines the teaching would naturally take, and state concisely and pointedly only what the pupil ought to know.

The **study of science**, carried out as it should be, vivifies the intelligence, strengthens the mental grasp, and gives an impetus to the pursuit of knowledge; it enables us to harmonise and understand the nature of the phenomena by which we are surrounded, makes us conscious of great and important truths which would otherwise remain unnoticed, and furnishes us with a fuller conception of the variety, extent, and grandeur of the universe; it opens the way to wonder and delight by giving us glimpses of the underlying order, beauty, and obedience to law, which characterise the works of creation; and it increases our sense of responsibility to and reverence for the Maker and Father of all, "in whom we live and move and have our being."

"To convince boys," says Mr. E. E. Bowen, "that intellectual growth is noble, and intellectual labour happy, that they are travelling on no purposeless errand, mounting higher every step of the way, and may as truly enjoy the toil that lifts them above their former selves, as they enjoy a race or a climb; to help the culture of their minds by every faculty of moral force, of physical vigour, of memory, of fancy, of humour, of pathos, of banter, that we have ourselves, and to lead them to trust in knowledge, to hope for it, to cherish it; this, succeed as it may here and fail there, quickened as it may be by health and sympathy, or deadened by fatigue or disappointment, is a work which has in it most of the elements which life needs to give it zest."

INDEX

INDEX

A

ABBOTT, Dr., on what we know as children, 148; on spelling, 294; on English, 416, 418, 425.
Abstraction, 136, 325, 411.
Abstract, ideas, 136; numbers, realisation of, 337-338, 355.
Abstracts of lessons as composition exercises, 429.
Accent, in reading, 243.
Accuracy, of idea, 16; of knowledge, 93, 102.
Acquisition, of information for lessons, 58; reading as an instrument of, 224.
Action, child's love of, 157, 258, 260, 395.
Activity, in children, 8, 209, 258, 381.
Addition, 338, 347-348; complementary, in subtraction, 350-351.
Admiration, sham, in literature, 436.
Æsthetic emotions, 433.
Affixes, 422.
Aim, in teaching, 60, 81; of critic, 84.
Air, necessity for change of in rooms, 169, 170; effects of breathing bad, 170.
Alphabet, learning of not necessary as a preliminary to reading, 225, 237, 257-258; nature of, 227, 234, 235; extended, in phonetic method, 235; modes of teaching, 257-260, 262-263; by letter blocks, 258; by solid letter forms, 258; by letter tablets, 258; by association with pictures, 259; by "interjectional imitative" methods, 259; by constructive exercises, 259; by sheet and pointer, 259; on black-board, 259; by drawing, 259; by object-and-word method, 259-260, 262-264; order of, 263.
Alphabetic method, in reading, 232-233.
Amateur, so-called clever, 86.
Analysis, topical, 17; method of, 49-51; in extension and intension, 49; by questions, 100; phonic, 229, 238, 266, 268, 270, 274; in reading, 235, 236, 251, 262; of words into letters, 262 of examples in multiplication, 351; of examples in division, 353; of numbers, 353; of sentences, 416-421.
Anecdotes, as illustrations, 145.
Anger, in discipline, 199.
Answers, qualities and treatment of, 118-131; good, 119-122, 126; bad, 122-125; speculative, 125; ridiculous, 125; mode of dealing with, 125-128; simultaneous, 128-129; mistakes by teacher in treating, 129-131.
A posteriori method, 49, 50.
Apparatus, the school should possess, 138, 139, 141; for experimental lessons, 141, 142, 442; construction of by teacher, 141, 412; placed ready, 150; kinds of, 181-182;

in arithmetic, 337, 338; in geography, 377, 381, 383; in history, 399, 403; in science, 442.
Application, habit of, 13.
Apprehension, difference of in children, 79; consideration of in questioning, 113; difficulty of, 136; incomplete, 144; quickness of, 324.
Approximation, in arithmetic, 335.
A priori method, 49, 50.
Arithmetic, position of in school course, 320-321; as a science and as an art, 321-322; limits of in text-books, 322; general objects of the teaching of, 322-324; value of as a means of training, 324-325; general method of teaching a new rule, 326-329; conduct of practice work in, 329-330; disciplinary measures in, 331-332; good habits of calculation in, 332-333; learning of tables, 333, 334; shortened processes and approximate methods in, 334-335; books on, 335-336; cards for testing, 336; first notions of number in, 336-337; abstract numbers in, 337-338; earliest addition and subtraction, 338; teaching of the figures, 338-339; principle of the decimal notation, 339, 345; Grube's method, 340-344; notation and numeration, 345-347; addition, 347-348; subtraction, 348-351; multiplication, 351-352; division, 353-355; compound rules, 355-356; vulgar fractions, 356-360; decimals, 360-362; practice, 362; 'unity method' and proportion, 362-364; higher rules, 364-366; square and cube root, 364-366.
Arrangement, of information in teaching, 39, 61; of desks, 174-175; of class in reading, 249; of information in reading books, 268, 269, 272-273, 275-276; in arithmetical exercises, 330.
Art, of education, 2, 3; characteristics of a work of, 36-38; of leaving out, 60, 400; criticism of, 84; of reading, 224; of arithmetic, 320, 321; of drawing, 366.
Articulation, in reading, 242-243; difficulties of, 273.
Assimilation of ideas, 22.
Association, of ideas, 17, 97, 281, 325; of sound and symbol in reading, 224, 227, 231-239, 250, 261; of symbol and idea, 223, 262; of reading with writing, 231, 275; of form and sense in spelling, 280, 281; of geography and history, 374, 391, 396.
Atlases, 392.
Atmosphere, effects of bad, 170; moral, 197.
Attention, importance of, 3, 19-20, 28, 32, 81; to small things, 77; focussed by questions, 103; influence of illustrations on, 136, 217;

means of securing, 136, 216-219; nature of, 213-216; spontaneous or automatic, 213; volitional, 213, 214; effect of interest on, 214-215; troublesomeness of defective, 214; in early years, 215; growth of by exercise, 215; influence of pleasantness on, 216, 217; influence of on the future of the child, 217; effect of methods on, 218; stimulus to of emulation, 219; to information in reading, 275; training of from arithmetic, 324.
Authority, exercise of by the teacher, 191-193; not paraded, 206.

B

Bacon, on conversation, 44.
Background, in teaching, 38.
Bain, Prof., on the terms analysis and synthesis, 49; on contrast, 147; on wonder and mystery, 218; on the value of arithmetic, 320; on the age for beginning grammar, 412.
Ballads, national, influence of, 405, 406; learning of historical, 406.
Ball frame, 338.
Basedow, school bakery, 258.
Beauty, of literary form, 248; sense of, 367.
Bell, Dr., on teaching the alphabet by drawing, 259.
Bias, in favour of special methods, 30.
Biber, Dr., on Pestalozzi's method of teaching writing, 310.
Bill of indictment against our English notation, 226-227.
Biography, bearing of in teaching history, 404.
Black-board, summaries on, 62, 64, 163, 403; sketches on, 141, 142, 327, 380, 381, 386, 387, 402, 441; importance of, 181; kinds of black-boards, 181-182; use of in reading, 255, 259, 261-262, 264, 267, 271, 272; in spelling, 282; in writing, 307, 316; in arithmetic, 327, 337, 345, 351-353; in drawing, 371; in geography, 377, 380, 381, 383, 384, 386, 393; in grammar, 416, 420, 421; in composition, 427, 428; in elementary science, 440, 441.
Black-board heads, 62, 64, 163, 403.
Blackie, Professor, on example of great men, 404.
Blunders, remarkable, 82; in answering, 123, 126; in spelling, 280, 287-291; in writing, 305; in composition, 425.
Bluster, 191.
Body, posture of in school work, 170, 174; position of in writing, 304.
Books, for study, 20-21; error of trying many, 21; information from, 26; general qualties of for school use, 183-185; treatment of, 183; for use in teaching reading, 184, 265-266, 268-269, 272-273, 275-276; for spelling, 298; for writing, 306-308; in arithmetic, 332, 335-336; for drawing, 370; on geography, 392-393; on history, 400, 405, 406; lessons on great, 402; on grammar, 409, 419, 423-424; for literature, 434, 435; for science, 442.
Botany, teaching of, 441-442.
'Borrowing and carrying' plan in subtraction, 348.
Bowen, E. E., on the value of showing over telling, 427; on the work of education, 443.
Bowen, H. C., on the marking of history

books, 405; list of historical novels, 406; on the study of literature, 434.
Braun, Prof., on lessons preliminary to history, 399.
Breath, proper management of in reading, 245, 278.
'Brimstone and treacle' method, 28.
British Empire, geography of, 388-389.
Brodie, E. H., absurd words as copies in writing, 307.

C

Cæsar, Julius, reproof of sing-song, 273.
Calculation, good habits of, 326, 332-333, 348, 350-351; shortened methods of, 334-335.
Calderwood, Prof., on interesting children, 157; on perfection, 200.
Calkins, N. A., on teaching the elements of reading, 231, 232, 260; addition exercises, 348.
Capacity for taking pains, 41.
Capitals, teaching of, in reading, 204; in writing, 317-318.
Cardinal points, 379.
Cards, arithmetic, 336.
Carlyle, on books, 20.
Carping, not criticism, 85.
Casting out the nines, 352.
Censure, 85.
Chance, methods, 5; words, effect of, 38.
Change, necessity for, 8; child's love of, 81; in lecture, 154; value of, 170-171.
Chalks, coloured, use of, 142; in teaching geography, 384.
Cheerfulness, of teacher, 4, 27, 30, 186; of children, 30, 182.
Chemistry, 374, 441.
Children, attention and interest of, 8, 27, 28, 29, 103, 107, 122, 136, 156, 157, 213-219; curiosity of, 8, 53, 103, 136, 218, 260, 263, 337, 378, 437; knowledge of by teacher, 25, 26, 94, 145, 187-188; order of development of faculties of, 26; peculiarities of moral character of, 27; happiness of, 27, 190, 205, 216; acuteness of in reading character, 29, 196; allowed to think for themselves, 32, 122, 129, 161; treatment of dull, 32, 80, 117; help given to, 80, 159; brilliant things said by, 82; questioning of one another, 118; difficulties of, 119, 148, 332; faults of in answering, 122-128; forwardness in, 124-125, 127, 211; training of observation of, 137, 139, 148, 368, 373, 385, 437; good listeners if interested, 157; delight in action, 157, 381, 395; influenced by manner, 157; effects of bad air upon, 170; relief to by change of posture and place, 170, 171; influence of bad desks on health of, 173; classification of, 175-177; short-sighted, 182, 319; training of in playground, 188; management of, 189-190, 208-212; not treated as machines, 195; obedience of, 195, 202; inherited bias of against restraint, 196; influence of moral atmosphere on, 197; punishment of, 198-208; feelings of should not be wounded unnecessarily, 200; love of freedom in, 206; employment of, 208-210; commendation of, 210; treated according to character and temperament, 210; position of for teaching,

INDEX 449

249, 287, 304; liking for jingling sounds, 269; allowance for natural characteristics of, 211; interest of in persons, 269, 395, 404; should be taught to like books, 268, 276; corruption of taste of, 276; appreciation of style by, 276; strangeness a difficulty to, 329; influence of history upon, 393-395, 404; love of for stories, 397, 399; overloading of with too many facts, 401, 440.
Chinese principle of word learning, 237.
Chronology, 398, 400.
Cicero, remark on teaching, 12.
Class, control of, 188-205; movements of, 197-198, 207; officering of, 177-178; position of for reading, 249; separation of from others, 167, 180.
Classification, of children, 175-176; readjustment of, 176; of syllables in reading, 237; of words in phono-analytic method, 238; of methods of associating sound and symbol in teaching reading, 239; of letters in writing, 312, 315; of plants, 412.
Class Management, influence of organisation on, 166-185; from the disciplinary side, 185-208; order in, 188-191; authority in, 191-193; tact in, 193-194; obedience in, 195-197; movements in, 197-198, 207; bearing of reproof and punishment on, 198-208; general treatment of children in, 208-212; means of securing interest and attention in, 213-219.
Class matches, 118.
Cleanliness of school-room, 168.
Clearness, of answers, 120; in reading, 242; in composition, 425.
Collection of objects, for teaching, 138; encouraged in boys, 442.
Colours, use of in map-drawing, 385.
Comenius, on repetition, 8.
Commands, 171, 192, 198, 206.
Commonplace book, 82.
Common things, value of, 138.
Comparative Method, described, 45; specimen lesson on, 73-76; list of lessons on, 76; in geography, 376, 390; in history, 403-404; in grammar, 415.
Comparison, as a mode of illustration, 135, 143, 144, 146, 149; of sounds in reading, 229, 236, 237, 238; in spelling, 281, 293; in writing, 316; of numbers, 340, 341, 344. (See COMPARATIVE METHOD.)
Compass, mariner's, 380.
Compayré, Prof., history of education, 221, 273, 309, 338; on the moral influence of history, 404; on observation, 437.
Complementary addition, plan of in subtraction, 350-351.
Composition, as an aid to spelling, 299; importance of, 424; qualities to be aimed at in, 424-426; direct instruction in, 426-427; the use of a good model in, 427; graduated and regular practice in, 427-428; training of the ear in, 428; subjects to be written about, 428-429, 431; simple narrative, 429; easy description, 429; abstracts, 429-430; letter writing, 430; reports of lessons, 430; themes, etc., 431; answering of an examination paper, 431-432; paraphrasing, 432-433.
Compound rules, 355-356.
Compulsion, 190.

Conceptive faculty, trained by geography, 372.
Concrete to abstract, 336, 339.
Conditions, physical, 23, 87, 166-171; of work, 191.
Confidence, 8, 187.
Confusion, from want of discrimination, 144.
Conjunction, teaching of, 419.
Connection, of ideas, 6, 37, 39, 61, 81, 87, 114, 115, 438; of lessons in series, 67.
Conning, 282-283, 286.
Consonants, powers of, 233, 234; enunciation of, 242; in spelling, 296-297.
Continents, teaching the geography of, 387.
Contracted methods, in arithmetic, 334-335.
Contrast, in illustrations, 143, 147; in lecture, 157; value of in learning to read, 229; in spelling, 281; in writing, 316.
Control, of children in class, 188-208.
Conversational Method, described, 42; instance of, 48; advantages of, 44; use of in geography, 379.
Copies, nature of in writing, 307.
Copy-books, 307-308, 319, 320.
Copying plans, in writing, 306-309.
Copying, prevention of, in dictation, 287; in arithmetic, 331.
Correction, during teaching, 211-212; of errors in reading, 252-253, 267; of errors in spelling, 290-291; in writing, 305-306, 316; in arithmetic, 329, 332; in composition, 427-428.
Counting, 333, 338, 347.
Cram, 16, 372.
Critic, nature of the work of, 83, 84; weak, 83; shallow, 86; unobservant, 86.
Criticism, of lessons, 82-89; nature of general, 84; aim of, 84; defective, 85; in literature, 84, 435-436; of faults in written answers, 432.
Criticism lessons, 82.
Cube root, 365-366.
Culture, 23.
Curiosity, in children, 8, 53, 103, 136, 218, 260, 263, 337, 378, 437.
Current hand in writing, 319.
Currie, on the sanitary state of the school-room, 170; on merely importing into the minds of children the judgments of others, 402; on comparison in history, 403.
Cyclopædia of Education, on the mastery of spelling, 298; on the introduction of the decimal system of notation, 347.

D.

DATES, 398, 400.
Decimal notation, introduction to principle of, 339; teaching of, 345, 347; historical note on, 347.
Decimals, teaching of, 360-362; mode of expressing a sum of money as the decimal of £1, 361.
Declamation, not reading, 240, 241.
Decomposition plan of teaching subtraction, 349-350.
Decoration of schools, 168.
Deduction, 47; in science, 437.
Deductive method, 47-51.
Definitions, should be the outcome of teaching, 47, 48; difficulty of, 110, 111; made

2 F

clear by illustrations, 144; dictionary, 161; in geography, 379; in grammar, 418.
De Morgan, on abbreviated method of long division, 334, 354; plan of complementary addition, 350; process of 'casting out the nines' described by, 352.
De Quincey, on rules for composition, 427.
Derivation, 252, 421.
Descartes, on method, 10.
Description, lessons of in geography, 377; in composition, 429.
Desks, qualities of, 173-175; effect of bad on health, 173; for infants, 173; space for children in, 173; dimensions of, 173-174; slope of, 174; seats for, 174; arrangement of, 174-175.
Desultoriness in study, 18, 19.
Detection of errors in dictation, 287-290.
Developing method, 45; of Socrates, 101.
Development, logical, of method, 61; of faculties, 4, 26; of lessons, 36-37, 102; of ideas, 438.
Devices, in teaching, original, 9; different estimates of, 91; experience in use of, 94; questions, 92-131; lecture, 89, 151-162; ellipses, 131-134; illustrations, 135-151; repetition, 162-163; recapitulation, 163; black-board summaries, 163-164; review, 164, 165.
Diagrams, 139-140, 150, 340, 342, 343, 365, 377, 403, 441.
Dialogue, instance of from Thring, 43-44; in reading lessons, 269.
Dickens, on attention, 19; the 'Gradgrind' system, 440.
Dictation, as a method of teaching spelling, 284; essential conditions of success, 284; uses of the exercise, 285; preparation of the passage, 285-286; the 'giving out,' 286-287; modes of detecting mistakes, 287-289; methods of marking, 289-290; correction of errors, 290-291; causes of blunders in, 291.
Dictionary, use of, 16, 277, 423.
Diderot, advocated a special teacher for reading, 221; on the order of teaching in history, 397.
Difficulties, of children in grasping ideas, 20, 33, 60, 329, 332; of subject, 59, 60; not conquered by omitting, 60; prepared for, 64; faced courageously, 78; of questions, 113-114; in answering, 119, 133; of ellipses, 134; of providing illustrations, 145-146; of lecture, 152; of certain terms, 155; of keeping information within bounds, 150; stimulus from conquest of, 159, 217, 218; of teacher, 197, 201; of notation of words, 227, 234, 235; of language in reading books, 251, 260, 273; of articulation, 273; of spelling, 294, 298.
Digits, 338-339, 347.
Digressions, 78, 79, 88, 145, 155, 407.
Discipline, artificial, 89; in class management, 185-208; difficulties of, 185; nature of, 185, 188, 205; qualifications of teacher for, 186-188; order as a part of, 188-191, 206; compulsion in, 190; conditions of work as affecting, 191, 205; authority in, 191; obedience in, 195; uniform pressure of, 195-196, 206; in class movements, 197; reproof and punishment as a part of, 198-

205, 207, 208,; summary of important points respecting, 203-208; corrections during teaching, 211; importance of, in teaching arithmetic, 331.
Discovery, 39; method of, 48, 50; child's love of gratified, 327.
Discrimination, 13.
Disheartenment from failure, 10.
Disobedience, 192, 202.
Disorder, 189, 207.
Displeasure in discipline, 198-199.
Distances, estimation of, 367, 370, 382.
Division, abbreviated method of, 334, 354; teaching of, 353-355.
Divisions of lessons, 62.
Drafts, in teaching reading, 249.
Draughts, in school-room, 169.
Drawing, on black-board, 141, 142, 150; relation of to writing, 314-315, 366; instrumental value of, 366-367; objects to be aimed at in, 366-367; nature of practice in, 368; use of the brush and of the pen in, 368; training of hand and eye in, 368; from objects 369; early exercises in, 370; use of black-board in, 371.
Drill, too much, 11, 88; lessons, 54; in geography, 54, 387, 389; in reading, 256, 264; in arithmetic, 323, 333.
Dulness, in teaching, 8, 27, 80, 81, 157; in children, 32, 80.
Dunn, on remembrance by the eye, 148; on tiresomeness of learning the alphabet, 258.
Dust, necessity for removal in school-rooms, 168.

E.

Ear, in reading, 226, 227, 255, 270, 274; in spelling, 255, 280; training of to recognise rhythm, 270, 428; use of in science, 437.
Earnestness, of teacher, 31, 40.
Earth, as a planet, 391.
Echo questions, 89, 106.
Edgeworth, Miss, on over-explanation, 160.
Education, definition of, 1; science and art of, 2, 44; general laws of method in, 6-8; imparted by ideas, 7; treadmill theory of, 11; value of repetition in, 163; the teaching of the instrumental subjects of, 220-371; importance of reading in, 221; place of writing in, 299-300; value of arithmetic in, 320-321, 323-324; value of geography in, 373; work of history in, 393-394; neglect of English in, 407; value of English in, 408-409; importance of composition in, 424; value of literature in, 433-434; place of science in, 436-437; work of, 443.
Effort, spasmodic, 10, 80; systematic, 18; of teacher, 31, 40; self, 15, 35, 159; in recollecting facts of lesson, 80; relaxation of from failure, 110; indisposition to, 115; secured by encouragement, 126; absence of, 203; steadiness of, 214.
Ellipses, definition and function of, 131; advantages of, 132; suggestions as to use of, 133, 134; testing and training, 133; faulty forms of, 134; cautions respecting the use of, 134.
Elocution, 240-248, 273-274, 276.
Emotional element, in reading, 248; in history, 404; in literature, 433.

INDEX 451

Emphasis, in teaching, 99, 106, 156, 212; in reading, 243-244, 270.
Empirical methods, 44.
Employment, of questions, 93-94; of children during teaching, 208-210.
Emulation, 219.
Encouragement, 210.
Energy, 11, 22, 103, 166, 187.
English, anomalous words in, 227, 234; neglect of the study of, 407; nature and objects of the teaching of, 407-409; necessity for some linguistic training, 409; relation of grammar to language, 409; modern English an analytic language, 410; grammatical inflections in, 410-411, 419; discipline derived from the study of grammar, 411; age at which grammar should be begun, 412; the teaching of English grammar, 412-424; the teaching of English composition, 424-433; the teaching of English literature, 433-436.
Enunciation, in reading, 242, 243, 255; in giving out dictation, 287.
Enthusiasm, contagious, 27; of teacher, 186, 400; for what is good, 404.
Epithets, unpleasant, not to be applied to children, 200.
Equal additions, method of in subtraction, 349.
Erasmus, on an ancient mode of teaching the alphabet, 258.
Errors, investigation of in criticism, 82; in answers, 127; in dealing with answers, 129-131; in explanation, 159-161; in reading, 252-253, 267; in dictation, 290-291; in writing, 316-317; in arithmetic, 329, 332; in teaching history, 397-398; in English, 415, 425, 437.
Espionage, bad in discipline, 207.
Exactness, in study, 12, 13, 16; secured by review, 22; of questions, 103; of answers, 119; of statement in science, 440.
Examination, value of, 23; bad effects of too close attention to requirements of, 34, 53, 394; by questions, 97, 113, 114; on a prepared passage, 112; by ellipses, 131, 133; of subject-matter in reading lessons, 275, 278; of writing, 305-306; influence of in geography, 372; answering of on paper, 431-432.
Example, of teacher, 186.
Examples, of conversational method, 42; in arithmetic, nature of, 48, 322, 329, 330; fanciful, 330; tedious, 330; use of concrete, 339; setting of bad in English for correction, 415.
Exercises, physical, 170-171, 198; effect of on attention, 215, 218; too long continued, 218; constructive for teaching alphabet, 259; revision in early reading, 264; phonic, 268, 270; early in writing, 300, 313, 315; mental and written in arithmetic, 325-326, 329-330, 350; in drawing, 367, 368, 369, 370; in map-drawing, 381, 384, 391; constructive in grammar, 417; auxiliary to grammar, 421-423; in composition, 427, 428-433.
Expectation, that things will happen again, 226.
Experience, value of, 3, 26; difference of, 41; in the use of questioning, 94; in performing experiments, 48, 141, 150-151; de-

pendence of tact upon, 194; of children, 208; of eye and ear in reading, 227.
Experiments, in science, 18, 48, 89, 141, 145, 150, 439, 440-442; conditions of success must be earned, 150-151.
Explanation, led up to, 99; nature of, 158; mode of, 158-159; common errors in the use of, 159-161; at too great length, 159-160; unnecessary, 160; sham, 161; in reading lessons, 250-252, 263, 267, 271, 274, 277; of the rules in arithmetic, 326-329; of the principle of the decimal notation, 339, 345-347; of meaning of a map, 379-381; of how words are classified, 418.
Exposition, method of scientific, 49, 50.
Expostulation, 201.
Expression, of face, 106; facility of, 158; in reading, 248, 274.
Extension movements, 171.
Euclid, as an instance of the synthetic process, 49-50.
Eye, an aid to memory, 148; sees only what it brings the power of seeing, 148; use of in reading, 224, 227, 230, 255, 274; part played by in learning to spell, 255, 279; in writing, 230, 301; in drawing, 367, 368; appeal to in geography, 384; training of in teaching science, 437.

F.

FACILITY of expression, 158.
Facts, to laws, 7, 439; distinct from theories, 16; relative importance of, 16, 17, 34, 81, 156, 162; key, 16; selection of, 17; perspective of, 17, 34, 61, 103, 156; interdependence of, 17, 34, 39, 61, 81, 87, 103, 108, 115, 155, 438; grouping of, 62, 81; questioning for, 97, 99, 102; statement of, 155; fixing of, 157, 162; presented so as to arouse curiosity, 218; in geography, 373; in history, 394, 397, 399-400, 401; in composition, 428-431; connection of in science, 437; overloading of children with, 440.
Faculties, order of development of, 26; variation in power of, 82.
Failures, caused by want of method, 10, 11; in teaching, 59.
Fairy tales, 269.
Farquharson, Dr., on school decoration, 168.
Farrar, Archdeacon, story from the Talmud, 30.
Fashion in teaching, 91.
Fatigue, from overwork, 19; of class to be considered, 34; bodily, from too long continuance in one posture, 170; from length of lesson, 180; in writing, 306.
Fault-finding, 85, 199.
Faults, common in teaching, 87-89; heinousness of not judged by teacher's annoyance, 204; of lessons in reading books, 268, 269, 272; common, in written answers, 432.
Field, observations in, 378, 385, 442.
Figures, carrying, 333; teaching of, 338-339; origin of, 347; of speech, 431.
Fingers, counting on, 333, 347.
Fitch, on spelling, 279; on arithmetic, 320, 338, 349; on language, 409, 410, 412.
Fixing, of information by questions, 103; devices, 162-165; by repetition, 162, 163; by recapitulation, 163; by black-board sum-

maries, 163-164; by review, 164-165; by map-drawing, 384.
Fletcher, Andrew, on the songs of a nation, 405.
Fluency, in reading, 245-246.
Force, of impression, 31, 113; ineffective alone in discipline, 190, 205.
Formalism in teaching, 27, 28, 41.
Form, in a lesson, 36-37, 38, 58; of subject-matter on notes, 62; study of, 230, 368, 369; beauty of, 248.
Forms, of questions, 103-114; of the letters, 230, 257-260; of words, 230-281, 234, 235-236, 270, 273, 279, 280, 282, 283, 292, 293, 422; in writing, 301, 302, 306, 311-312, 316, 318; in drawing, 368, 369; of language, 410, 411, 412, 414.
Forwardness in children, 127, 211.
Fractions, teaching of vulgar, 356-360; decimal, 360-362.
Furniture, of schoolroom, 171-175.

G.

Galleries, 171-172.
Genetic method, 45.
Genius, 10, 41, 84, 214.
Geography, causes of defective teaching of, 372; nature and order of the instruction in, 372-377; relation of to history, 374, 391, 396; two views as to order of topics in, 374-375; comparative method in, 376, 390; modelling as an aid to the teaching of, 377, 383; early teaching in, 377-379; meaning of a map in, 379-382; of the mother country, 382-385; map-drawing in, 384, 385, 389, 391; physiographical lessons in connection with, 385, 387-388, 391-392; the globe in, 386-387; of the continents, 387; of the British Empire, 388-389; of particular countries, 390-391; of the earth as a planet, 391; text-books and atlases in, 392; through reading books, 392-393.
Gesture, 30, 106, 243.
Gladstone, Dr. J. H., on time spent in learning to read, etc., 279.
Globe, use of in geography, 386, 387; geography of, 386-387; projections of, 391.
Goody-goody tone in reading-books, 268.
Good taste, in reading, 241.
'Gradgrind' system, 440.
Graduation in teaching, 34, 35, 439; in reading books, 265, 269.
Grammar, relation of to language, 409; analytic nature of in English, 410; inflections of, 410-411, 419; discipline derived from, 411; age at which study of should be begun, 412; outline of method of teaching, 412-416; work introductory to, 416; subject and predicate in, 416-417; constructive exercises in, 417, 422; easy analysis in, 417; teaching of parts of speech in, 47-48, 417-419; teaching details of, 419; use of a text-book in, 419, 423-424; formal analysis and parsing, 420-421; derivation, 421-422; word-building, 422; history of words, 422-423; place of historical grammar, 423.
Grouping, of facts in teaching, 62; of words in reading, 246, 263.
Growth, of mind, 26, 45; physical, 26; of lessons, 45; of discipline, 195, 205; of attention, 215.
Grube, method of teaching early arithmetic, 340-344.
Guessing, 106, 108, 122, 123, 237.

H.

Habit, of desultory reading, 18; of scolding, 199; of expecting experiences again, 226; influence of in spelling, 281; in writing, 300; of mumbling in working arithmetic, 383; scientific, 438.
Habits, good intellectual, 12, 13, 19, 35, 137, 393, 437; effect of bad intellectual, 13; correction of bad, 205; prevention of the formation of bad, 257, 300, 304, 332, 333; avoidance of uncleanly, 319; good in calculation, 332; of out-door observation, 373, 375, 376, 378, 385, 442.
Hales, Prof., on inflections, 411.
Half-holiday walks, 378.
Hall, on "interjectional imitative" methods, 259; on pleasure in reading, 276.
Hand, in writing, 230, 301; in drawing, 230, 368; in science, 437.
Happiness of children, 27, 190, 205, 216.
Happy inspirations, 64.
Harmony of effect in a lesson, 37.
Harrison, Prof., on examinations, 34.
Hart, Prof., on value of teaching to the teacher, 12.
Headings in notes of lessons, 62.
Heating of school-room, 169.
Helmholtz, on musical intervals used in reading, 247.
Help, estimation of amount to be given, 159.
Helps, Sir A., on attention, 214-215; on a good sentence, 426.
Herbart, introduction of developing method, 45.
Hints, respecting the teaching of a lesson, 81, 87-89.
History, a difficult subject to teach well, 393; what it should do for the pupil, 393-394; influence of teachers' predilections on teaching of, 394; moral effect of, 394, 404; guiding principles in the teaching of, 395-396; associated with geography, 374, 391, 396; of other countries, 396; scope of the teaching in, 396; order of presenting the facts of, 397; common mistakes in the teaching of, 397-398; picture and story stage in the teaching of, 398-399; information stage in the teaching of, 399-400; place of chronology in the teaching of, 400; epoch teaching in, 401-402; lessons supplementary to, 402; higher aspects of, 402; ordinary method of teaching, 402-403; use of map in, 403; comparative method in, 403; emotional element in, 404; bearing of biography on, 404; cultivation of patriotism in the teaching of, 405; use of a text-book in, 405; reading supplementary to, 405-406; ballads in, 405, 406; the teaching of through reading books, 406-407.
Honour, sense of, 205.
House-that-Jack-built style of spelling, 255.
How to study, 12-24.
Humour, in teaching, 28.

INDEX 453

Hunter, H. St. John, book on *Decimal Approximations*, 335.
Hurry, in study, 15; in teaching, 34, 81, 87, 121, 122, 159, 272.
Huxley, Prof., on being completely wrong, 16; on thoroughness of knowledge, 438.

I.

Ideas, gained through the senses, 7, 26, 135, 336, 376; rendered exact by teaching, 12; importance of in study, 15-16; association of, 17, 97, 325; sequence and connection of, 37, 39, 61, 81, 87, 108, 115, 155, 438; subordination of, 34, 35, 61, 103, 156; fixing of, 103; difficult to grasp, 119, 155; new, how acquired, 135; bearing of illustrations upon, 136; association of with sounds and signs, 223, 231, 236, 247, 250-252, 260, 261, 268, 280, 408, 421, 423; of number, 336-337; expansion of through geography, 373, 385; elementary in geography, 378; exactness of in grammar, 408, 411, 415.
Idleness, 8, 209.
Ignorance, produces as many disasters as malevolence, 438.
Illustrations, nature of, 135, 136; advantages of, 136, 137; kinds of, 137-144, 148; objects as, 137-139, 140, 337, 339, 377, 383, 439, 441, 442; pictures and diagrams as, 139, 140, 150, 340, 342, 377, 399, 403, 439, 441; maps as, 140, 150, 377, 380, 382, 383, 384, 387, 390, 393, 396, 403; models as, 148, 365, 377, 380, 383, 403; experiments as, 48, 141, 145, 150, 439-440, 442; on blackboard, 141, 142, 150, 377, 380, 381, 383, 386, 387, 403; by comparison, 135, 143, 144, 146, 376, 403-404; by example, 142-144; by parallels, 144; suggestions as to use of, 144-151; faults in the use of, 144, 145; element of surprise in, 147; influence of in securing attention, 217; in reading books, 266, 269, 273; in arithmetic, 337, 339, 340, 342, 365; in geography, 377, 380, 383, 384, 385, 387, 390, 393; in history, 396, 399, 403; in elementary science, 429-440, 442.
Imagination, development of, 26; cultivation of in reading, 269, 272, 278; in drawing, 367; in geography, 373; in history, 398, 399, 400; in literature, 433, 434; in science, 437.
Imitation, in teaching, 9, 31, 38, 57; a natural instinct with children, 186, 369; in writing, 230, 301, 302, 306-310, 316; in expression, 248; of the teachers' reading, 248, 254, 263, 267, 270, 271, 275, 277; in arithmetic, 325; in drawing, 369; of a good model in composition, 427.
Impressions, first, most powerful, 7; force of, 31, 113; by chance words, 33.
Inactivity, repugnant to children, 209.
Inattention, 29, 214, 218.
Incapacity, not to be confused with want of effort, 203, 205.
Indecision, in the teacher, 192-193.
Index, of what has been read, a key to knowledge, 21.
Indifference, in the teacher, 31.
Individuality, of children, 7, 11; of teacher, 30, 35.
Indolence, 103.

Induction, 47, 49.
Inductive method, 47-51; in arithmetic, 48, 326-329, 336-340, 356; in science, 48, 437, 439, 441, 442; in spelling, 294; in geography, 375, 377, 378; in grammar, 410, 413, 414.
Infants, galleries for, 171; desks for, 173.
Inflections, 410-411, 419.
Influence, of manner, 28, 29, 30, 31, 94, 115, 157, 212, 217, 228; of personal element, 29, 30, 42, 191-192, 304, 400; of small things, 30, 77; of chance words, 33; of preparation on teaching, 55, 57, 64; of criticism on teaching, 83, 85; of organisation, 166; of pleasant surroundings, 168; of bad desks, 173; of teachers' character, 186-187; of discipline, 188; of moral atmosphere, 197; of commendation and encouragement, 210; on the child's future, 217; of teacher's characteristics on the teaching of history, 393-395; of examinations on history, 394; of patriotic songs, 405.
Information, new, 20, 21; index to, 21; book form of, 39-40; teaching form of, 40; should be real, 52, 53; lessons of, 52, 53, 58; kept fresh, 54; amount of, 59; development of by questions, 102; gathered through reading, 230; thrust forward in reading lesson, 269; in history, 400.
Injustice, 200.
Inspirations, in teaching, 11, 64.
Instruction, method of, 48, 50.
Intellectual habits, good, 12, 13, 19, 35, 137, 393, 437; bad, 13, 332.
Intellectual sauntering, 124.
Intelligence, general, 2, 7, 27, 53, 79; in mode of study, 14-16; in teaching, 27, 54, 300; in reading, 247-248, 273-274; in arithmetic, 323, 344; in geography, 373, 390.
Intensity, in reading, 245.
Interest, general, 8, 27, 28, 29, 60, 103, 117, 122; in study, 20; from illustrations, 136; aroused by lecture, 156; affected by manner, 157; relation of to attention, 213-216; means of securing in teaching, 216-219; in reading, 228-229; value of in teaching spelling, 281; of teacher, 304; of children in persons and stories, 395, 399, 404; of subjects in composition, 428; in literature, 434.
Intervals, musical, range of in reading, 247.
Introductions, to lessons, 79, 88, 89.
Irony, use of by Socrates, 101.
Irritation, of teacher, 180.
It, various modes of spelling by Tyndale, 279.

J

JACOTOT, on repetition, 8, 103; on learning, 16; reading method of, 226, 240, 264-265; writing method of, 302, 308.
Jerome, St., on learning the alphabet, 258; on learning to write by tracing, 309.
Jevons, Prof., on analysis and synthesis, 49, 50.
Johnson, Dr., English Dictionary, 279.
Jokes, in teaching, 28.
Judgment, in teaching, 9, 40, 94, 113, 194, 203; development of, 26; in criticism, 83; in reading, 248, 277; in drawing, 367; in selecting facts in geography, 373; exercise

of, in history, 395, 401-402; cultivation of in composition, 428, 429; training of from science, 437, 438.
Julius Cæsar, reproof of sing-song, 273.
Justice, 203, 205.

K

Key facts, in study, 16.
Kindergarten, exercises, 173; mode of learning the alphabet, 259; exercises in writing, 313; exercises in drawing, 370.
Knight's *Quarterly Journal of Education*, on the teaching of arithmetic, 327.
Knowledge, mode of presenting, 8, 11, 28, 39; of method, 10; sham, 14; teacher must know limits of his own, 14; elementary, 14; superficiality of, 14; at first hand, 18; of science, 18, 438; index a key to, 21; fixed by application, 22; of teacher respecting children, 25, 26, 94, 145, 187-188; possessed by children, 27, 61, 80; connected, 39; right view of, 39; defective, 59, 80, 68, 93, 159; control of, 59; of teacher gained by observation, 378; in history, 394; of book not sufficient, 394, 438; of dates, 400; of the forms of language, 411.
Known to unknown, 7, 51, 135, 162; in teaching reading, 224-226; in history, 396.

L

Language, of questions, 104-106; training in from ellipses, 132; in teaching, 155-156, 217; spoken, 223, 231; of reading books, 223, 265-266, 268-269, 272-273, 275-276; relation of spoken to reading, 225, 236; English, anomalous words in, 227, 234; in history, 400; English, 407-433; nature of teaching of in schools, 408-409; relation of grammar to, 409-410; teaching of, 412-424; qualities to be aimed at in writing English, 424-426.
Latin, influence of, on English grammar, 409; grammar of fixed, 410.
Laurie, Prof., on examination in reading, 278; on teaching of drawing, 367; on age at which grammar should be begun, 412; on the desire to obtain a measurable result in teaching, 413; on too numerous distinctions, 424; on paraphrasing, 432.
Law, spirit of, 185, 205; maintenance of, 201, 205; punishment in school not to be viewed as vengeance of, 204; of similarity, 281; from facts to, in science, 439; natural, 443.
Laws, scientific, 2, 439; general method of, 6-8; of association, 17, 281; of mental and physical growth, 26; of word structure, 294.
Leading questions, 106.
Learning, made pleasant, 8; by heart, 15; relation of, to teaching, 25; of letters, 257-260, 262-263; of tables, 333-334; of dates in history, 400.
Lecture, abuse of, 89, 151, 155, 159; nature of as a teaching device, 151; not mere talk, 151; difficulty of, 152; with little children, 153; in middle of school, 153; with advanced classes, 153-154; not to be used alone, 154; controlled by a definite purpose,
154-155; simplicity in, 155; connection of ideas in, 155-156; deliberation and emphasis in, 156; must be vivid and interesting, 157; influence of manner in, 157; in geography, 376, 377; in history, 393, 395-396, 399, 400, 402; in grammar, 415; in literature, 435; in science, 438.
Legibility in writing, 302.
Lessons, general characteristics of, 36-40; arrangement and connection of facts in, 39, 61; common defects of, 39; notes of, 52-76; of information, 52, 58; training, 52-54; object, 53, 66-76, 416, 439, 440; drill, 54; review, 54; need for preparation of, 54, 55, 56; two types of, 58; subject-matter of, 58-62; acquisition of facts for, 58; selection of facts for, 59; commencement of, 61; grouping of information in, 62; preparation of method of, 62-64; overcoming difficulties in, 64; specimen notes of, 66 67, 70-76, 260-261, 261-262, 263-264, 267, 270-271, 274-275, 277-278, 315, 358-360; series of, 67; lists of, 68, 69, 76; long introductions to, 70, 88; practical hints respecting teaching of, 81-82; criticism of, 82-90; obscure defects in, 87; common faults in, 87-89; types of faulty, 89-90; experimental, 150-151, 442; distribution of, 179-180; noisy, 180; length of, 180; reading, 260-278; transcription, 283-284; dictation, 284-291; in spelling, 291-293; in word-building, 299, 422; in writing, 313-320; in arithmetic, 336-366; in drawing, 369-371; in geography, 377-393; descriptive, 377; in history, 398-407; in grammar, 412-424; in composition, 424-435; in English literature, 435-436; in science, 438-442.
Leigh, Dr., reading books, 235.
Le Salle, on the order of teaching reading and writing, 300.
Letter-box, 260, 264.
Letters, vowels, 227, 234; consonants, 254; powers of, 232, 233, 234, 235, 236, 238, 266, 268, 270; silent, 266, 295; small, in writing, 302; size of, in writing, 302; analysis of script, 311-312; order in which writing of should be taught, 312, 315; capital, in writing, 317-318.
Letter writing, 430.
Lieber, Dr., on imitative arithmetic, 325.
Lighting of school-rooms, 168-169.
'Lilli-burlero,' 405.
Literature, English, reading books an introduction to, 275, 276; bad, 276; value of in education, 433; nature and purpose of the work in, 433-434; appreciation of style in, 433, 435; interest in, 434; the early teaching of, 434; more advanced teaching of, 434, 435; criticism of, 435, 436; sham admiration of, 436.
Little things, influence of, 77, 207.
Livesey, list of words containing the alphabet, 259.
Locke, on cramming, 15; on learning the alphabet by tablets, 258; on the order of teaching reading and writing, 300; tracing system of learning to write, 309.
Logarithms, use of, 335.
Logical methods, 46-51; tabular view of, 50; in arithmetic, 324; in grammar, 414, 417.
'Look and Say' method in reading, 236-237.

INDEX 455

Looseness in teaching, 89.
Lupton, S., on art of computation, 335.
Lytton, Lord, on the alphabetic method of teaching to read, 233.

M

MACHINERY of lesson, kept out of sight, 82.
Magnus, Sir Philip, on drawing from objects, 369.
Manner, of teacher, 3, 4, 28, 29, 30, 31, 94, 115, 157, 212, 217, 228; of critic, 85; of putting questions, 115, 116; forwardness of, in children, 127, 211; influence of, in teaching reading, 249; in teaching history, 390.
Mann, Horace, on beginning reading with the alphabet, 258.
Mannerisms, of teacher copied, 31; in reading, 255.
Map-drawing, 381, 384-385, 389, 391.
Maps, drill in connection with, 54; as illustrations, 140, 150, 377, 383, 387, 393; meaning of, 379-382; interpretation of, 382; on black-board, 380, 381, 384, 390; of district, 381; relief, 383; in teaching history, 396, 403.
Marcel, on self-effort, 8; on the powers of the letters, 234; on a slip form of word-maker, 264.
Mariners' compass, 380.
Mechanical, exercises, 7, 229; methods, 53; corrections, 89.
Meiklejohn, Prof., instance of comparative method, 46; on our English notation, 226-227; on words of anomalous pronunciation, 234; English method of, 238; on a disc form of word-maker, 264; spelling book, 294; short English Grammar, 419.
Memorising, 16, 272, 322, 325, 440.
Memory, vagueness an enemy to, 16; aided by association of ideas, 17, 97, 325; writing an aid to, 23; development of, 26; aided by illustrations, 136; repetition of words from, 272; training of from arithmetic, 325; substituted for reason in learning history, 440.
Meridian line, 380.
Metaphors, 144.
Method, definition and character of, 5, 6; importance of, 5, 9-11; Carlyle's notion of, 6; general laws of, 6-8 special, 8-9; originality of, 9, 30; necessity for, 10, 11; advantages of, 10; teacher's employment of, 11, 12; in study, 15; formalism in, 41; conversational, 42, 379; developing, 45; genetic, 45; comparative, 45-46, 73-76, 376, 390, 403, 415; of discovery, 48, 50; of instruction, 48, 50; of scientific exposition, 49, 50; *a priori*, 49, 50; *a posteriori*, 49, 50; preparation of in notes of lessons, 58-76; change of, 81; Socratic, 101; influence of on attention, 218; alphabetic, 232-233; phonic, 233-234; phonetic, 234-235 'look and say,' 236-237; syllabic, 237; phono-analytic, 238; Jacotot's reading, 264; Jacotot's writing, 308; sentence, in writing, 308; Locke's tracing, in writing, 309; Pestalozzi's writing, 310; Mulhäuser's writing, 311-312; Grube's, of teaching the elements of arithmetic, 340-344; the scientific, 430-437.

Methods, discovery of new, 9; typical, 40-51; empirical, 44; inductive and deductive, 47-51; logical, tabular view of, 50; mixed, 51; of associating sound and symbol in reading, 231-239; of teaching the alphabet, 258-260; approximate and contracted in arithmetic, 334-336.
Metric system, 361.
Mind, clearness of, 22; growth of, 26; method of stupefying, 107; alertness of, 217.
Misapprehension, 144.
Misconceptions, put right by questioning, 98.
Mistakes, in answering, 123, 126; made by teacher in treating answers, 129-131; correction of in reading, 252-253, 270; as few as possible in spelling, 280; detection and correction of in dictation, 287-291; in writing, 316-317; in teaching history, 397-398.
Modelling, as an aid in teaching geography, 377, 383.
Model reading, 253-254, 271, 275, 277.
Models, for purposes of illustration, 140; in arithmetic, 365; in geography, 377, 380, 383; in history, 403.
Modulation, in reading, 247, 270.
Monosyllables, difficulty of in English, 227, 234, 237.
Monotony, in teaching, 27, 38; in reading, 247, 255, 273.
Moral atmosphere, 197.
Moral influence, 87.
Moralising, 404.
Moral, teaching in history, 404; value of science, 437.
Moral suasion, 87, 201.
Moseley, Canon, on a sentence method of teaching writing, 308, 309.
Mountains, representation of on maps, 384.
Movements, of children, 197-198, 207.
Müller, Prof. Max, on the function of the grammarian, 409; *Science of Language*, 422.
Mulhäuser, writing method of, 302, 303, 311-313.
Multiplication, teaching of, 351-352.
Mumbling, in arithmetic, 333.
Murison, A. F., *Globe Readers*, 238.
Murray, Lindley, notion of grammar, 412.
Museums, school, 138.
Music, a relief from study, 23.
Musical intervals in reading, 247.

N

NAGGING, 199.
Nature, teacher's knowledge of, 18; child brought face to face with, 139, 141, 373, 376, 378, 439, 442; unity of, 374.
Newton, Sir Isaac, on attention, 19.
"No answer plague," 123.
Noise, from use of ellipses, 184.
Notes of Lessons, need for preparation of, 54-55; what is meant by, 56; conditions of preparation of, 56-57, 59; use of examples of, 57; two types of, 58; acquisition of information for, 58-59; selection of facts for, 59-61; arrangement and connection of facts in, 61; grouping of facts in, 62; preparation of the method of, 62-65; outline notes, 65; specimen notes of object lessons, 66, 67, 70-76; sketch plans of reading lessons, 261-263, 263-264, 267, 270-271, 274-275, 277-278; sketch

of writing lesson, 316; on division of vulgar fractions, 358-360.
Notation, of words in English, 227, 234, 235, 294-297; teaching of in arithmetic, 339, 345-347.
Novels, historical, 406.
Numbers, mode of adding, 332, 348; realisation of abstract, 336-338, 355; use of concrete, 337, 339; representation of by written symbols, 338-339; Grube's analysis of, 340-344; notation of, 345-347; multiplying by special, 352; divisibility of, 356; fractional, 356-357.
Numeration, teaching of, 345-347.

O

OAKELEY, H. E., on types of faulty lessons, 89-90.
Obedience, of children, 195-197, 202.
Object of teaching kept in view, 32-33.
Object Lessons, nature and use of, 53; specimens of, 66-76; in teaching reading, 260; in arithmetic, 337; influence of on language, 416; in science, 439, 440.
Objects, use of in teaching, 16, 137, 149; kinds of as illustrations, 138-139; collecting of by children, 138, 139, 442; comparative size of, 149; use of in beginning reading, 259, 260, 261; use of in arithmetic, 337, 338, 339; drawing from, 369; in teaching science, 439, 441, 442.
Observation, of teacher, 9; development of, 26; cultivation of, 113, 137, 139, 148, 149; want of in adults, 139; nature of, 148, 149; in spelling, 282, 292-293; in drawing, 368; in connection with geography, 373, 385; training of in science, 437, 441.
Officiousness in discipline, 194.
Once saying not sufficient in teaching, 79.
One thing at a time, in teaching, 7, 32, 139; in learning to read, 229, 253, 260, 262; in arithmetic, 324.
Oral, teaching, general view of, 25-35; illustrations, 142-143.
Order, in study, 15; of ideas in teaching, 50-51, 61-62; spirit of, 185; maintenance of as a part of discipline, 185, 188-193, 205, 206; necessary to progress, 206; of sounds in reading, 228; of the alphabet, 263; of presenting the subject-matter in geography, 374-376.
Organisation, influence of, 166; the room, 167-168; the lighting, 168-169; warming and ventilation, 169-170; change of posture and place, 170-171; furniture as affecting school work, 171; galleries, 171-173; classification of children, 175-177; distribution of teachers, 177-178; time-tables, 178-179; apparatus, 180-183; books, 183-185.
Originality, in teaching, 9, 30, 38, 63.
Outlines, of lessons, 65-67; of history, 399-400.
Overcrowding of lesson with information, 59, 88.
Overloading of children with facts, 401, 440.
Over-pressure, 11.
Over-questioning, 95.
Over-strain, 10, 32.
Over-teaching, 80, 159, 160.

P.

PACE, in reading, 245.
Page, D. P., on stupefying mind, 107; on thinking for the child, 156.
Pain, as a means of punishment, 202, 203.
Palmerston, Lord, on good writing, 303.
Paraphrasing, 432-433.
Parents, duty of teacher to, 11.
Parker, Colonel, faults in teaching, 385.
Parsing, 420-421.
Partitions, in school-room, 167.
Parts of speech, 417-419.
Paston Letters, variety of spelling in, 279.
Path of least resistance, 27, 35.
Patience, need of, 159, 249.
Patriotism, cultivation of, 403, 406.
Pauses, in reading, 247.
Payne, Prof. J., on Jacotot's method, 264, 308.
Payne, Prof. W. H., on the order of presentation in geography, 375.
Peace at any price, 189.
Penalties, suited to offence, 202.
Pen, management of, 301, 304-305, 315; children should not begin with, 314; cleaned, 320.
Perception, 7, 26, 89, 135, 148; in reading, 227, 230, 237; of similarities of sound and form, 266; in arithmetic, 336-337; training of by drawing, 367; in geography, 376; in science, 437.
Perfection of workmanship, 38.
Perfunctoriness, 31.
Personal element, in teaching, 29, 30, 42, 191-192, 394, 400; attraction of, for children, 395, 404.
Perspective, of facts in study, 17; in teaching, 34, 61, 103, 156; in drawing, 370.
Persuasiveness, in lecture, 157.
Pestalozzi, reaction started by, 45, 93; writing method of, 310; on the teaching of arithmetic, 336.
Phonetic method, 234-235.
Phonic analysis, in reading, 229, 238, 266, 268, 270, 274.
Phonic method, 233-234.
Phono-analytic method, 238-239.
Phonotypic method, 234-235.
Photography, illustration from, 77.
Photographs, in teaching, 140, 377.
Phrases, introductory to questions, 104, 105.
Phrase spelling, 299.
Phrasing, in reading, 247.
Physical, conditions, 7, 23-24, 87, 166-171; exercises, 198.
Physics, 441; teaching of elementary, 442.
Physiography, lessons in connection with geography, 385, 387-388, 389, 391-392.
Pictures, use of in teaching, 139, 140, 150, 261, 267, 340, 342, 377, 399, 403, 439, 441.
'Picturing out,' 161, 162, 399.
Pillans, Prof., on idleness, 209; on teaching of letters in 'brotherhoods,' 259.
Pitch, of voice in reading, 245, 247; range of in reading, 247.
Place, change of, 170-171.
Plan, of work in study, 18; absence of in teaching, 87; introductory to map, 380.
Plants, as illustrations, 138, 441-442; collecting of, 442.

INDEX 457

Playground, value of, 188.
Pleasantness of schoolwork, 27, 42, 115, 146, 191, 216.
Pleasure, from power, 208; of teacher, 210; from conquest, 217; from reading, 268, 276.
Poetry, liking of children for, 269; use of in reading books, 269, 272, 276; learning of 275, 278, 405, 406, 434; recognition of the rhythm of, 428.
Pointing, with the finger in reading, 237; in division of decimals, 361.
Porter, Noah, on remembrance, 15.
Posture, change of, 170-171; during writing, 304.
Position, of teacher before class, 212, 249, 287; of children in reading, 249; in dictation, 287; in writing, 174, 304.
Power of the teacher, 191.
Powers of the letters, 232, 233, 234, 235, 236, 238, 266, 268, 270.
Practice, crystallisation of, 9; needed by the teacher, 55; in reading, 270, 271, 275, 277; in writing, 301, 305, 317; conduct of in arithmetic, 329, 331; teaching of the rule of, 362; in the interpretation of a map, 382; in map-drawing, 384, 391; in composition, 426, 427-428, 432.
Precision, 12, 13, 16, 35, 103.
Prefixes, teaching of, 421.
Preparation, of notes of lessons, need for, 54-55; amount of, 55, 64; must leave teacher free, 56-57; of subject-matter of lesson, 58-62; of method of lesson, 62-65; wrong use of, 80; of reading lesson, 251; of spelling for dictation, 285-286.
Preposition, teaching of, 419.
Principles, of teaching, 6-8, 36, 44, 135; scientific, 60, 436-437; of arithmetic, 332, 336; of grammar, 409, 412; of mechanics, 442.
Prints, as illustrations, 139, 140, 399.
Problems, in arithmetic, 329.
Processes, of arithmetic of two kinds, 321.
Programme of work in study, 18.
Progress, step by step, 7; stimulus from, 20.
Projections of the sphere, 391.
Prolixity, in explanations, 159-160.
Promotion, 176
Prompting, in answering, 130.
Pronunciation, in reading, 241-242.
Proportion, in a lesson, 37; teaching of the rule in arithmetic, 362-364.
Prose, qualities of artistic, 426, 428, 433, 435; rhythm of, 428.
Provincialisms, 242, 425.
Punctuation, in reading, 246; in dictation, 287; in composition, 425.
Punishments, 198-208; reproof, 198-202; ridicule, 200; injustice in, 200; sham, 203.
Pupil, should have nothing to unlearn, 280; should make as few mistakes as possible, 280.
Pupil teachers, 177.
Purpose, in study, 18; in teaching, 35, 39, 60; of formal spelling lessons, 292.

Q.

Questions, preparation of, 63; use of, an old device, 92; a test of the teacher's power, 93; conditions of successful use of, 93-94; value of, 95, 96, 98, 99-100; relation of, to other devices, 95; indiscreet use of, 95; objections sometimes urged against, 95; not a quick method, 96; kinds of, 97; testing, 97-99, 102; leading up to explanation, 99; training, 99-101, 102; analysis by, 100; Socratic, 101; comparison of testing and training, 102; purposes for which employed, 102-103; forms, qualities, and use of, 103-118; direct, 103-104; irrelevant, 104; want of order in employment of, 104; proper choice of words in, 104-105; verbiage in employment of, 104-105; difficulty of, 106, 113; echo, 89, 106; leading, 106; clew given to answers by mode of putting, 106; stupefying mind by bad use of, 107; 'yes' and 'no' questions, 107-108; containing their own answers, 108-109; demanding long answers, 109; beyond children's knowledge, 109-110; requiring definitions, 110; necessitating reasoning, 111; variety in the use of, 112-113, 117; on a prepared passage, 112; use of to secure repetition, 112, 113; considerations respecting difficulty of, 113; should be connected in series, 114-115; mode of putting, 115-117; distribution of over subject and class, 116-117; put to teacher by children, 117; put by children to one another, 118; attention to answering of, 118; qualities of good answering, 119-122; partial answers, 120; full statement of answers, 120; effects of hurry on answering, 121; qualities of bad answering, 122-125; guessing, 122-123; reckless answering, 123; "no answer plague," 123; speculative answers, 125; ridiculous answers, 125; mode of receiving and dealing with answers, 125-128; simultaneous answering, 128, 129; mistakes respecting the treatment of answers, 129, 131; difficulties broken up by questions, 159; disciplinary value of, 209; use of to test grasp of subject-matter in reading lessons, 275, 278; use of in arithmetic, 326; use of in history, 403.
Quintilian, on the use of ivory letters, 258; on tracing plan of teaching to write, 308.

R.

RAPIDITY in teaching, 34-35; in reading, 245, 246; in writing, 255, 303; in working arithmetic, 331-332.
Ratio, teaching of, 362-363.
Reading, interest in wholesome, 13; desultory, 18; recreative, 23; teaching of, 220-278; need of reform in the teaching of, 220, 222; causes of unsatisfactory teaching of, 220-221; importance of, 221, 224; principles and considerations in the teaching of, 223-231; nature of the problem of, 223; association of signs and sounds in, 223, 231-239; as an art and as an instrument, 223-224; mechanical and intellectual stages in, 224; spoken language the starting-point in, 225; learning of alphabet not necessary as a preliminary to, 225, 237, 257, 258, 260; how far a means of teaching new words, 225; tributary methods, 226; simple to complex in, 226-228; difficulties of our

English notation in teaching, 226-227; order in which the sounds should be presented in, 228; necessity for interest in, 228-229; comparison and contrast in, 229; limitation of the lesson to the teaching of, 229-230; association of reading and writing, 230-231, 275; nature of synthetic plans in, 231-232, 233; the alphabetic or name method in, 232-233; relation of spelling to, 232-233, 237, 255, 266, 270-271, 275; the phonic method in, 233-234; powers of the letters in, 234; phonetic or phonotypic method in, 234-235; nature of analytic plans in, 235-236; 'look and say' method in, 236-237; syllabic method in, 237; phono-analytic method in, 238; English method of teaching, 238; tabular view of the methods of associating sound and sign in, 239; nature of, 240; differs from declamation, 240; pronunciation in, 241-242; enunciation in, 242, 243, 255; articulation in, 242-243; accent in, 243; emphasis in, 243-244; stress in, 244; tone, pitch, and intensity in, 244-245, 247; pace and fluency in, 245-246; function of pauses in, 246; phrasing in, 246; modulation in, 247; intelligence in, 247-248, 273-274; expression in, 248, 274; essential features of any method of, 249; position of class and teacher in, 249; explanation in, 250-252, 263, 267, 271, 274-275, 277; relation of word-saying and style in, 252, 256; correction of errors in, 252-253, 267; teacher's model in, 253-254, 271, 275, 277; simultaneous utterance in, 254-255, 262, 263, 267, 270, 271, 275; miscellaneous suggestions respecting the teaching of, 256-257; tiresomeness of learning the alphabet in, 258; modes of teaching the alphabet in, 258-260, 262-263; lessons introductory to, 260-261; of simple words, 261-264; Jacotot's method of teaching, 264-265; the primer stage of, 266-268; easy narrative stage of, 270-272; lower intellectual stage of, 273-275; higher intellectual stage in, 276-278; recitation in connection with, 278; influence of on spelling, 281-282; of poems, etc., by the teacher, 434.
Reading-books, general qualities of, 183-185; for primer stage, 265-266; introduction of new words in, 265-267; for easy narrative stage, 268-270; style in, 268, 269, 273, 275-276; dialogues in, 269; illustrations in, 269, 273; for lower intellectual stage, 272-273; for higher intellectual stage, 275-276; the child's introduction to literature, 275; standard works as, 276; in geography, 392-393; in history, 406.
Realism, in teaching history, 400.
Reason, development of, 26; exercise of in arithmetic, 321, 322, 323, 324, 325, 327; exercise of in history, 395, 401; exercise of in science, 437.
Reasoning, should be direct for children, 8; ideas before, 35; demanded by questions, 99-100, 111, 113; in arithmetic, 328.
Recapitulation, of work, 81, 128; defective, 88; use of ellipses in, 132; as a fixing device, 163.
Recitation, 278.
Recollection, 15, 22, 113, 136, 255.
Recreation, 8, 23.
Reduction, in arithmetic, 355-356.

Relief maps, 383.
Remembrance, 15, 113, 136, 255.
Repetition, necessity for, 8, 79; by questioning, 103; by simultaneous utterance, 128; of questions, 130; of answers by teacher, 130-131; as a fixing device, 163; in learning the alphabet, 250, 259; of words, 270, 272; of poetry, 275, 278, 405, 406, 434; in teaching spelling, 282.
Reproof, as a disciplinary measure, 198-201; not to be confused with displeasure, 198; the use of anger in, 199: habit of scolding in, 199; least amount employed which will serve the purpose, 199, 211; sympathy of class on side of right in, 199; sensitiveness to, 199-200; child's feelings not wounded unnecessarily in, 200; unpleasant epithets not to be applied to children, 200; use of good-tempered ridicule in, 200; injustice in, 200; given quietly but earnestly, 207; unnecessary, 211, 212.
Resource, readiness of, 193.
Result-grinding, 34, 413.
Results, secured by method, 10; to be aimed at in teaching, 40; not a safe guide as to amount of effort, 208; approximate in arithmetic, 325; evil effects of confining attention to, 413.
Review, necessity for, 8; value of, 22, 54, 81; lessons of, 54, 165; by means of ellipses, 132; as a fixing device, 164; in reading, 260; in arithmetic, 343, 344; in English, 416.
Reynolds, Sir Joshua, story of, 87.
Richter, Jean Paul, on the attempt to compound what should be developed, 61; on questions, 96; on difficult words, 155.
Ridicule, 101, 200.
Room, Government requirements respecting, 167-168; shape of, 167; partitions in; 167; cleanliness and pleasantness of, 168, floor of, 168; lighting of, 168-169; warming and ventilation of, 169-170.
Robinson, on the spelling of the deaf and dumb, 279-280; on calling out the spelling of words in dictation, 289; on the teaching of writing, 304.
Rote learning, 15.
Round-hand in writing, 302.
Rousseau, on drawing from objects, 369.
Routine, relief from, 118; of school work, 178-180.
Rules, for spelling, 293-297; memorising of in arithmetic, 322; teaching of in arithmetic, 326-329, 345-366; in grammar, 414.
Ruskin, criticism of Turner, 84.

S

Safford, on unsuitable arithmetical examples, 330.
Sarcasm, 200, 207.
School, museums, 138; apparatus for, 138, 139, 141; organisation of, 166-185; rooms, 167-171; furniture of, 171-175.
Science, of education, 2, 18, 44; teaching of elementary, 48, 141, 436-443; of arithmetic, 331-332; calculations in, 322, 335; training derived from the right study of, 436-438, 443; place of in education, 436;

aim and purpose of instruction in, 436-438; moral value of the study of, 437-438; book knowledge of not sufficient, 438; general mode of lesson procedure in, 439; too many facts given, 440; teaching of often too ambitious, 440; early instruction in, 440-441; botany, 441-442; elementary physics, 442; value of the study of, 443.
Scolding, 192, 199.
Scribbling, 319.
Section, profile, nature of, 386.
Seeley, Prof., on laws of language, 411; on learning of words, 416.
Selection, in preparation of lessons, 59, 441; of historical facts, 396-397.
Self-effort, 15, 35, 159.
Senses, should be largely exercised in the case of little children, 7, 26, 45, 89, 148, 336-337, 339, 378, 437; ideas gained through, 7, 26, 135, 336, 376.
Sentences, as answers, how far insisted upon, 120; pace and fluency in the reading of, 245; recognition of the structure of in reading, 246; intellectual qualities in the reading of, 246-248, 256; method of in writing, 308-309; the units of language, 414; introduction to grammar through, 416; analysis of, 417-421.
Sentiment, in history, 398.
Sequence, of ideas in teaching, 37, 39, 61, 81, 87; use of notes in securing, 56; of questions, 114, 115, 155, 156; in the introduction of new words, 269; of the teaching in reading, 274.
Shakespeare, genius of, 84.
Sham, knowledge, 14; conversational method, 42; explanations, 161; punishments, 203; evil effect of on children, 210: sentiment, 398; admiration in literature, 436.
Short-sighted children, 182, 319.
Sidgwick, A., on thoroughness in the teacher, 216.
Signals, 198.
Similes, 144.
Simple to complex, 7; in reading, 226.
Simplicity, in teaching, 23, 155.
Simultaneous utterance, in answering, 128-129; in reading, 254-255, 262, 263, 267, 270, 271, 275.
Sing-song, in reading, 233, 247, 255, 273.
Size, comparative, 149.
Sketches, on blackboard, 141, 142, 327, 380, 381, 386, 387, 402, 441.
Slang, in composition, 425.
Slope of writing, 303, 311.
Small things, influence of, 30, 77.
Smartness, 134.
Smattering of knowledge, 12.
Sneering, 200, 207.
Socrates, on ignorance, 14; method of, 92, 101.
Soldan, F. L., on Grube's method, 340-344.
Songs and ballads, influence of national, 405-406.
Sonnenschein, English method of teaching reading, 238.
Sounds, liking of children for jingling, 269.
Spedding, on learning to spell by reading, 282.
Speech, readiness of, 94; parts of, 417-419; figures of, 431.
Speed, in teaching, 34-35, 272, 439; of reading, 245, 255; in writing, 303; in working arithmetic, 331-332.
Spelling, irregularity of, 227, 234; taught by writing, 231; in connection with reading, 232-233, 237, 255, 266, 267, 270, 271, 275; house-that-Jack-built style of, 255; uniformity of, a recent matter, 278-279; only a means to an end, 279; learnt largely through the eye, 279; appeal to the ear in teaching of, 280; aid to from the meaning of words, 280; the right form to be presented first in, 280; giving wrongly spelled passages to correct in the teaching of, 280; force of habit in, 281, 282; interest and graduation in teaching of, 281; comparison and contrast in, 281; learning of through reading, 281-283; transcription as a means of teaching, 283-284; teaching of by means of dictation, 284-291; formal lessons in, 291-293; rules for, 293-297; miscellaneous list of words difficult to spell, 297-298; spelling book, 298; incidental aids to spelling, 298, 299.
Square root, 364-365.
Stammering, 234.
Standard works, reading of, 276.
Stimulus, absence of in teaching, 11; from teacher's qualities, 29; from questioning, 98, 103; from illustrations, 136; from punishment, 207; from reading, 225, 893; from curiosity, 260; from recording work, 332; of moral qualities from the teaching of history, 404; from the study of science, 443.
Stops, use of in reading, 246; in dictation, 287; in composition, 425.
Stories, use of in reading books, 269, 292; child's love of, 397, 399; art of telling, 399; introductory to history, 390.
Stow, D., on training, 133; on good reading, 241.
Strangeness, of ideas a difficulty, 20, 59, 113, 329; of words, 273.
Stress, in reading, 244.
Study, stratification plan of, 7, 18; suggestions respecting, 12-24; influence of on teaching, 12-13; effect of on the teacher, 13; bad intellectual habits in, 13; not too wide a range of subjects in, 13, 14; error of beginning too many things in, 14; superficiality in, 14; value of exactness in, 14; intelligence in, 14-16; place of rote learning in, 15; effort needed in, 15, 18; not hurried, 15; no one method of, 15; cram in place of, 16; relative importance of facts in, 16-17; selection in, 17; connection of facts in, 17; of things rather than words, 17-18; simultaneous plan of, 18; aimless, 18; a too elaborate plan in, 18; effect of desultory reading on, 18; spasmodic work in, 19; concentrated attention in, 19; effect of interest on, 20; importance of suitable books in, 20-22; value of review in, 22; relaxation from, 23; recreative reading in. 23; importance of physical exercise and change in, 23, 24; child introduced to by reading, 221-222; of form, 230, 368, 369; of history in epochs, 401; of English, neglect of, 407; of literature, 433.
Stupefying mind, 107.
Style, relation of to word-saying in reading, 224, 256; in reading, 240, 247-248, 268, 269,

270, 273, 275-276; in composition, 426; in literature, 426, 433, 435.
Subject-matter, conditions of selection for lessons, 59; arrangement of on notes, 58, 62; general treatment of, 63; of reading books, 265-266, 269, 272-273, 275-276; questions on in reading lessons, 275, 278.
Subjects, choosing of difficult for lessons by teachers, 59; for comparative lessons, 76; arrangements of on time-table, 178-179; of historical ballads for children, 406; for composition, 428, 429, 431.
Subordination of ideas in teaching, 34, 61, 103, 156.
Subtraction, teaching of, 333, 338, 339, 348-351; 'borrowing and carrying' plan in, 348-349; plan of 'equal additions' in, 349; decomposition plan in, 349-350; 'complementary addition' plan in, 350-351; oral exercises in, 351.
Success, in teaching, 25-28.
Suggestions, brief, respecting teaching, 35, 81. 87-90; respecting discipline, 205-208.
Summaries, on blackboard, 62, 64, 163, 403.
Sun-dial, 380.
Superficiality, 14,
Supervision, of reading by the master, 249; in writing, 305-306, 314-319; in arithmetic, 331-332; of map-drawing, 384; of practice in answering an examination paper, 432.
Surprise, in illustrations, 147.
Syllabic method in reading, 237-238.
Syllabling of words, 236.
Symbols, association of with sounds in reading, 223, 227, 231-239, 250, 261; association of with ideas, 223, 261, 262.
Symmetry in a lesson, 37.
Sympathy, between teacher and taught, 4, 8, 13, 29, 30, 42, 80. 81, 94, 145, 157, 158, 186, 194, 217, 249, 305; necessary in order to judge correctly of the need of illustration, 145; in lecture, 157; in explanation, 158; tact founded on, 194; of class on the side of right, 199, 269; importance of, 217; in teaching reading, 249; with the author, in reading, 277; in the early teaching of writing, 305; with the past in history, 400.
Synonyms, in place of explanations, 161.
Syntactical relations, 420.
Synthesis, method of, 49-51; Euclid an example of, 50, 51; in reading, 231-232; in science, 437.

T

TABLES, arithmetical, 333-334.
Tact, 193, 194.
Taking pains, capacity for, 41.
Talk not teaching, 33, 89, 151-152, 377.
Talmud, story from, 30.
Taste, cultivation of by reading, 23, 248, 268, 269, 275; corruption of by poor literature, 276; cultivation of by literature, 408, 426.
Taupier, tracing plan of teaching writing, 309.
Teacher, knowledge and experience of, 2, 3, 4, 11, 25-27, 58, 59, 88; neglect of the art of education by, 3, 11; qualities needed in, 3, 4, 31, 32, 41, 94, 186-188; manner of, 3, 4, 27, 28, 29, 35, 94, 115, 157, 212, 217, 399; threefold character of the work of, 4; low estimate of the work of, 11; must employ the best methods, 11; value of teaching to, 12; should never cease to be a student, 13; must know his children, 25-27, 94, 145, 186-188; need not fear to be amusing, 28; must be sympathetic, 29, 30, 42, 80, 81, 94, 145, 157, 158, 186, 194, 217, 249, 305; may be childlike without being childish, 30; originality of in teaching, 30, 38, 63; not a mere imitator, 31, 38, 57; indifference in, 31; often too much done by, 31; must keep touch with class, 32; mind of ever on the alert, 32; must speak simply, 33; preparation of his work by, 33, 55-57; must vary speed of his teaching, 34, 439; must learn to look at knowledge in the right way, 39; judgment of, 40, 94, 113, 194, 203; capacity of for taking pains, 41; part played by in conversational method, 42; much of the work of runs to waste, 55; effect of imperfect knowledge of, 59; facing of difficulties by, 78; self-criticism by, 85; difference between clumsiness and ignorance of, 86, 156; common defects in the work of, 87-89; skill of in questioning, 100-101; questioning of by children, 117; defective dealing with answers by, 129-131; impatience of, 130, 159; difficulty, of in providing illustrations, 145, 146; facility of expression by, 158; must keep his information within bounds, 159; common errors of in explaining, 159-162; must estimate the child's difficulties,.160; must not think for the child, 161; number of children taught at once by, 177; personal characteristics of, 186-188; example of, 186; should be able to play, 188; weak discipline of, 189-190, 192; authority of, 191 193; consciousness of power in, 191; indecision in, 192; tact of, 193-194; control of class movements by, 197; use of anger by, 199; proper management of voice by, 212; position of before class, 212, 249, 287; model reading of, 253-254, 271, 277; must be a good reader, 276; influence of personal qualities on teaching of history, 394.
Teachers, distribution of, 177-178; qualifications of, 185-188; pupil, 177.
Teaching, method in, 5-12; rational, 7; simplicity in, 23, 155; general nature of, 25, 81, 86; pleasantness in, 27, 42, 146; manner in, 28, 29, 30, 31, 94, 115, 157, 212, 217, 228; formalism in, 28, 41; variety in, 29, 37, 81, 157; influence of personal element in, 29, 30, 42, 191-192, 394, 400; sympathy in, 30, 42, 80, 81, 94, 145, 157, 158, 186, 217, 249, 305; individuality in, 30, 35; originality in, 30, 38, 63; wordiness in, 33, 104; not mere talk, 33, 151-152, 377; back ground in, 33; subordination of ideas in, 34, 61, 103, 156; speed in, 34, 272, 439; summary of more important characteristics of, 35; governed by general principles, 36; art of must be learned, 26; sequence and connection of ideas in, 37, 39, 61, 81, 87; common defects of, 39, 87-90; purpose in, 39, 60; relation of training and instruction in, 40; general methods in, 40-51; preparation of lessons for, 54-76; waste of, 55; overcoming of difficulties in, 64, 78; illus-

tration of the process of from landscape photography, 77; attention to details in, 77; digressions in, 78, 79, 88, 145, 155, 407; repetition in, 79, 163; attention to individuals in, 80, 81; over-teaching, 80, 159, 160; practical hints respecting, 81; criticism of, 82-87; distinction between ignorant and clumsy teaching, 86; obscure defects in, 87; fashion in, 91; devices of, 92-165; time allowed for children to think in, 122; keeping knowledge within bounds in, 159; general treatment of children during, 208-212; means of securing interest and attention in, 213-219; employment during, 211-212; position of teacher during, 212; nature of in English, 408.
Technical terms, 415, 418, 440.
Temperature of room, 169.
Terms, applied to questions, 97; not generally current, 110; in grammar, 415, 418, 420; distinction between terms and things, 415; technical in science, 440.
Test exercises in reading, 263, 264, 277.
Testing of teaching, 23, 62, 165.
Text-books, general nature of, for study, 20-22; qualities of, for children, 183-185; in arithmetic, 322, 335-336; in geography, 389, 392; knowledge of, not alone sufficient for teacher, 394, 438; in history, 405.
Text-hand in writing, 302.
Themes, 431.
Theories, nature of, 16.
Things, not mere words, 26, 89, 148, 336, 337, 378, 437.
Thought, 40.
Thring, Rev. E., dialogue from, 43; on mistakes, 123; on the value of common things, 138.
Time-tables, 178-180.
Time-tests in arithmetic, 336.
Time, economy of, 10; waste of, from beginning many things, 14; in study, 19, 24; waste of in questioning, 95; waste of over answers, 131; taken up in explaining at too great a length, 159; distribution of, 129; misused by introductory talks in reading lessons, 272; occupied in learning, reading, spelling, and dictation, 279.
Tone, in reading, 244-245, 255, 274; goody-goody in reading books, 268.
Tracing plan, in writing, 309-310; in drawing, 390.
Training, of senses, 7, 26, 45, 89, 148, 336-337, 339, 378, 437; relation of, to instruction, 40, 44, 45, 52, 99; intellectual, 44; from induction, 48; lessons, 52-53; from object lessons, 53; by questions, 96, 99-103; of observation, 113, 137, 139, 148, 149, 373; by ellipses, 132; of eye, 148, 224, 227, 230, 255, 274, 279, 301, 367, 368, 384, 437; disciplinary, 168-208; in playground, 168; of attention, 214-219; from reading, 221, 230; of ear, 226, 255, 270, 274, 280, 428, 437; from arithmetic, 321, 322, 323-326; of memory, 325; from drawing, 366, 367, 368; from geography, 373; from history, 333-334, 401, 404; from English, 406, 409; in expression, 424; from science, 436.
Transcription, in connection with reading, 264, 267; in teaching spelling, 283-284, 286.

Treadmill theory of education, 11.
Trench, Archbishop, on *Study of Words*, 422.
Trial and error, process of, 44.
Tyndale, William, varieties of spelling from, 279.
Types, of methods, 41-51; of lessons, 52-54, 58; of faulty treatment, 89-90.

U

Understanding, of teacher, 55, 158; methods should be such as to train, 80, 218; removal of obstacles to by questioning, 99; re-expression of ideas by children in their own words a test of, 121; essential to correct emphasis in reading, 244; necessary to intelligence in reading, 247, 248; of what is read, 270, 273, 276; appealed to in arithmetic, 321, 322, 323, 324, 327, 328, 339, 344; in geography, 373, 385; in history, 395, 400, 401; training of, by English, 408, 411, 412, 415; training of from science, 437, 439.
Unity of idea, in a lesson, 37.
Unity of nature, 374.
Unity method, in arithmetic, 362.
University, a collection of books the true, 20.
Utterance, simultaneous in answering, 128-129; impassioned, 240; of words in reading, 241-245, 254-255, 273; correction of faults of in reading, 267.

V.

VAGUENESS, an enemy to memory, 16; in questions, 103; in ellipses, 134.
Variety, in teaching, 29, 37, 81, 103, 157; in details of lessons, 37-38; of method, 103, 218; of questions, 112; of difficulty in questions, 113; of objects as illustrations, 138.
Ventilation, 169-170.
Verbiage, 33, 104.
Verbs, auxiliary, 419.
Vigilance, 187, 207, 304.
Vivacity, 27, 94, 115, 157, 212, 217, 229.
Voice, inflection of a clew to answers, 106; tone of, 116, 245; proper management of in teaching, 212; proper production and use of in reading, 244, 245, 247, 248, 255, 274, 278; pitch of, 245; modulation of, 247.
Vowels, difficulties respecting, 227, 228; nature of, 234; in pronunciation, 241, 242; in spelling, 294-295.
Vulgar fractions, teaching of, 356-360; notes of a lesson on division of, 358-360.

W.

WALKS, half-holiday, 378.
Warning, of school-room, 169.
Waste of teaching, 55.
Waste of time, from beginning many things, 14; in study, 19; over questions, 95; over answers, 131; from explaining at too great a length, 159; by introductory talks in reading lessons, 272.
Weariness, prevented by method, 10, 81; from mechanical nature of work, 11, 229; bodily, 24; of children taken into account

in teaching, 85; from bad conditions, 170; relieved by physical exercises, 170; from sameness of exercises, 260.
Wells, on ignorance of historical geography, 396; on sham sentiment, 398.
Wharton, Lord, boast of that he had "rhymed King James out of his kingdom" by Lilliburlero, 405.
Whole to parts, in reading, 231-232, 236; in geography, 374-375.
Why? the use of the question, 111.
Will, influenced by motives, 213-215.
Wilson, Archdeacon, on curiosity, 487; on the scientific habit of mind, 438.
Wonder, the basis of knowledge, 218; use of by teacher, 218; delight of children in, 269.
Woodcuts in reading-books, 266, 269, 273.
Woodward, on the neglect of English, 407; influence of a word in a sentence not discoverable by formal tests, 418.
Word about-plan in reading, 267.
Word-building, in teaching reading, 238, 251; in teaching spelling, 299; in teaching English, 422.
Word-maker, 264.
Words, simplicity of in teaching, 33, 121; chance effect of, 33; choice of in questioning, 105; ideas associated with, 142, 236; how far taught by reading, 225, 229; length of, 228; phonic analysis of, 229, 268; of anomalous form, 234; monosyllabic, 234; syllabling of, 236, 274; comparison of, 236; learning of, 261-272; introduction of new in reading books, 265, 269; grouping of in spelling, 292; sounded alike but spelled differently, 296; with letters and compounds having more than one sound, 296, 297; miscellaneous list of difficult to spell, 297-298; history of, 422-423; in composition, 425.
Word-saying, in reading, 252, 256.
Work, threefold character of in school, 4; systematic, in study, 18; desultory, 19; review of, 22, 54, 81, 132, 164, 165, 260, 343, 344, 416; of art, 36; critic's estimate of, 84;

proper distribution of, 155, 178, 179; conditions of, 191, 205; mental in arithmetic, 326; object of in drawing, 366, 367; nature of in geography, 373-379.
Works, choice of in literature, 435.
Workmanship, perfection of, 38.
Worry, minimised by method, 10, 11.
Writing, an aid to memory, 23; taught before reading, 230, 300; as a means of teaching spelling, 231, 283-284; the teaching of, 299-320; aim of in schools, 299; mechanical and applied phases of, 299, 300; instrumental value of, 300; should be begun early, 300; bad habits in prevented, 300; order of with respect to reading, 300-301; discipline of hand and eye in, 301; proper manipulation of the pen in, 301, 304-305, 315; size of for children, 301-302; text-hand, 302; roundhand or half-text, 302; character of to be aimed at, 302-303; legibility in, 302; beauty of form in, 302; rapidity in, 285, 803; Lord Palmerston's letter on, 303; slope of, 303; needs careful teaching, 803; uniformity of a test of good teaching, 304; position of the body in, 304; thorough and systematic correction in, 305-306; not too much at one time, 306; copying plans of teaching, 306-309; copies written by teacher in books, 306; copies set on black-board, 307; engraved head-lines, 307; nature of copies, 307; best form of book, 307; copies written or engraved on slips, 308; Jacotot's method of teaching, 808; sentence method of teaching, 308-309; the tracing plan in, 309-310; Pestalozzi's plan of teaching, 310; the Mulhaüser writing method, 311-312; introductory lessons in, 313-314; with pencil, 314, relation of drawing to, 314-315; with pen, 315; order and forms of letters in, 315; sketch plan of early lesson in, 316; mistakes commonly met with in, 316-317; the withdrawal of mechanical aids to, 317; teaching of the capital letters, 317-318; small-hand in, 318; the passage from exact imitation to freedom in, 319; supplementary hints respecting teaching of, 819.

THE END.

Printed by T. and A. CONSTABLE, Printers to Her Majesty,
at the Edinburgh University Press.

www.ingramcontent.com/pod-product-compliance
Lightning Source LLC
Chambersburg PA
CBHW051858300426
44117CB00006B/446